# Russia and Eastern Europe

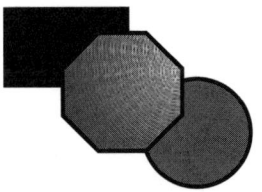

Russia and Eastern Europe
A Bibliographic Guide to English-Language Publications 1992-1999

Helen F. Sullivan

Robert H. Burger

―――――――――

Slavic and East European Library
University of Illinois at Urbana-Champaign

2001
LIBRARIES UNLIMITED
A Division of Greenwood Publishing Group, Inc.
Englewood, Colorado

To Anna, Sarah, Meg, and Nell

Copyright © 2001 Libraries Unlimited
All Rights Reserved
Printed in the United States of America

No part of this publication may be reproduced, stored in a retrieval system, or transmitted, in any form or by any means, electronic, mechanical, photocopying, recording, or otherwise, without the prior written permission of the publisher.

Libraries Unlimited
A Division of Greenwood Publishing Group, Inc.
P.O. Box 6633
Englewood, CO 80155-6633
1-800-237-6124
www.lu.com

Library of Congress Cataloging-in-Publication Data

Sullivan, Helen F.
　Russia and Eastern Europe : a bibliographic guide to English-language publications, 1992-1999 / Helen F. Sullivan, Robert H. Burger.
　　p. cm.
　ISBN 1-56308-736-7
　1. Europe, Eastern--Bibliography. 2. Russia--Bibliography. 3. Soviet Union--Bibliography. 4. Russia (Federation)--Bibliography. 5. Former Soviet republics--Bibliography. I. Burger, Robert H. (Robert Harold), 1947- II. Title.

Z2483 .S86 2001
[DJK9]
016.94'009717--dc21   2001038273

Contents

Introduction xi

1—General and Interrelated Themes 1

General Reference Works 1
History 2
Economics 3
Government and Law 11
International Relations, Foreign Trade 13
Political Theories, Nationalism, Communism, Religion 15
Language and Literature. 21
Military Affairs 23
The Arts 24
Society, Social Issues, Sociology 24

2—Russia, the Soviet Union, and the Russian Federation 27

General Reference Works 27
    Bibliographies. 27
    Biographies 29
    Handbooks and Encyclopedias 32
    Libraries, Archives, and Museums 33
    Description and Travel 33
Anthropology and Folklore 35
The Arts 37
    General Studies 37
    Architecture 41
    Fine Arts 42
    Music 44
    Dance 47
    Film 49
    Theater 51

2—Russia, the Soviet Union, and the Russian Federation (*continued*)

- The Economy ... 53
    - General Studies ... 53
    - Statistics ... 55
    - Economic History ... 56
    - Economic Theory and Planning ... 59
    - Perestroika ... 60
    - Agriculture ... 61
    - Industry, Management, and Manufacturing ... 62
    - Labor and Trade Unions ... 63
    - Unemployment ... 65
    - Resources and Their Utilization ... 66
    - Business and Entrepreneurial Activity ... 66
    - Finance and Credit ... 68
    - Dismantling of the Command Economy ... 68
    - Foreign Economic Relations ... 70
    - Privatization ... 71
- Education and Culture ... 73
    - General Studies ... 74
    - Mass Communications ... 76
- Geography and Demography ... 78
- Government and State ... 80
    - Bibliographies ... 80
    - General Studies ... 81
    - Law ... 82
    - Politics and Government, Special Studies ... 84
    - Political Parties ... 100
    - Communism, Communist Party ... 100
    - Perestroika, Glasnost ... 104
    - Police Terror, Espionage, Propaganda ... 106
- Diplomacy and Foreign Relations ... 108
    - General Studies ... 108
    - To 1917 ... 109
    - 1917 to Present ... 110
    - With the United States ... 115
    - With Western and Third World Countries ... 119
    - With Communist Countries ... 124
    - Breakup of East European Satellites ... 127
- History ... 128
    - Bibliographies, Encyclopedias, Source Materials ... 128
    - General Studies, Readers ... 131
    - Historiography and Archaeology ... 133
    - Pre-Petrine Muscovy/Russia ... 135
    - Imperial Russia ... 138
    - Revolution and Civil War ... 150
    - RSFSR and USSR ... 156

Contents ● vii

Military Affairs 165
   General Studies 165
   To 1917 166
   1917 to Present 167
   Navy 169
   Special Studies 170
   Nuclear Arms 172
Russian Language 173
   General Studies 173
   Dictionaries and Glossaries 173
   Textbooks and Grammars 174
Russian Literature 174
   Bibliographies, Biographies, Encyclopedias 174
   General Studies and Histories 176
   Anthologies 184
   Critical Studies 188
   Individual Authors 207
   Special Studies, Censorship 234
   Émigré Literature 234
Philosophy and Political Theory 235
   Marxism in Russia and in the USSR 236
   Intellectual and Cultural Histories 237
Psychology 238
Religion 238
   General Studies 239
   History 239
   Special Studies 242
Science, Technology, and Research 243
   General Studies 243
   Telecommunications 245
   Environmental Protection 246
Social Conditions and Sociology 248
   General Studies 249
   Alcoholism and Drug Abuse 251
   Social Problems and Social Change 251
   Women 255
   Special Studies 259
   Handicrafts 261

3—Commonwealth of Independent States, Other Former Soviet Republics, Jews, and Other Minorities 263

   General Studies 263
   Baltic Republics 265
      Estonia 269
      Latvia 269
      Lithuania 270

Ukraine 273
    Bibliographies, Encyclopedias 273
    General Studies 273
    Sociology 274
    History 275
    Government and Politics 280
    Economics and Business 285
    Religion 286
    Music, Architecture, and Art 288
    Language, Literature, and Folklore 288
    Dissident Movement 292
    Émigrés 292
Central Asian Republics and Peoples 293
Other Republics 301
    Armenia 304
    Azerbaijan 304
    Georgia 305
    Belarus 306
Siberian Peoples and Cultures 307
Jews 309
    General Studies 309
    Emigration 309
    History 311
    Special Studies 314

4—Eastern Europe 317

General Reference Works 317
Bibliography 319
History 319
Government, Politics, and Law 325
Foreign Relations 332
Communism 333
Economics, Trade, and Business 333
Language and Literature 341
National Minorities 344
Holocaust 345
The Society, Sociology 351
The Arts and Culture 354
Science and Technology 355
The Downfall of Communism 356

5—Albania 359

6—Bulgaria 365

History 365
Economics, Trade, and Business 368
Language and Literature 368
Government, Politics, and Law 368
The Society, Sociology 369

7—Czech and Slovak Republics 371

General Reference Works 371
History 372
Economics, Trade, and Business 378
Government, Politics, and Law 379
Language and Literature 381
Individual Authors 386
National Minorities 388
Arts and Culture 388
Velvet Revolution 389

8—Hungary 391

General Reference Works 391
History 392
Economics, Trade, and Business 398
Government, Politics, and Law 400
Foreign Relations 401
Language and Literature 401
Individual Authors 402
The Society, Sociology 403
National Minorities 404
Arts and Culture 406

9—Poland 409

General Reference Works 409
History 411
Economics, Trade, and Business 416
Government, Politics, and Law 421
Foreign Relations 425
Communism 426
Language and Literature 426
Individual Authors 428
The Society, Sociology 431
Religion 433

9—Poland (continued)

Dissident Movements 434
National Minorities 434
Arts and Culture 436

10—Romania 439

General Reference Works 439
History 439
Economics, Trade, and Business. 443
Government, Politics, and Law 444
Foreign Relations 446
Communism 446
Language and Literature 447
Individual Authors 447
The Society, Sociology 448
National Minorities 448

11—Former Yugoslavia 451

General Reference Works 451
History 453
Economics, Trade, and Business. 459
Government, Politics, and Law 459
Foreign Relations 462
Language and Literature 463
Individual Authors 464
The Society, Sociology 464
Religion 465
National Minorities 465
Arts and Culture 467
Civil War. 468

Name Index 483

Subject Index 505

Introduction

This volume continues earlier works by Stephan Horak and by the present authors. Horak's base volume, covering items in English from 1900 to 1975, was expanded by two five-year supplements, the last one appearing just before his death in 1986. Sullivan and Burger, authors of the present volume, jointly produced two works, *Russia and the Former Soviet Union: A Bibliographic Guide to English Language Publications, 1986–1991* and *Eastern Europe: A Bibliographic Guide to English Language Publications, 1986–1993*.

The present volume covers Russia, Albania, Bulgaria, Czech Republic, Slovak Republic, Hungary, Poland, Romania, and states of the former Yugoslavia. Because of the reassimilation of East Germany into Germany, we have omitted Germany in the coverage of the present volume. The years covered by this volume have been witness to rapid change in the Slavic and East European world. It is no accident that much scholarly attention has been focused on these current events and many books deal with effects of the transition from socialism to market economies, and the social, political, and cultural effects of this transformation. Another area of tumult was the Yugoslav peninsula. The civil war that occurred there has also been the occasion for much writing. Also, the reader will find an increasing amount of attention devoted to the Holocaust, reflecting the wider attention that this historical event has attracted in the past decade. Finally, of major importance were the changes that took place in Ukraine. Because of the voluminous amount of material that was published on this particular area during the last decade, the authors were not able to do the topic justice. However, the reader interested in such matters should consult *Independent Ukraine: A Bibliographic Guide to English-Language Publications, 1989–1999* by Bohdan S. Wynar (Englewood, CO: Ukrainian Academic Press, 2000) for a more comprehensive annotated bibliography of citations dealing with Ukraine. Dr. Wynar's reputation as a scholar and bibliographer is enhanced by this latest work.

As with our other bibliographies, this one is a representative selection of titles as opposed to a comprehensive listing. The titles were selected from books reviewed in the *Slavic Review* and the OCLC WorldCat database. The pool of titles from which we selected included English-language titles on Russia from 1992 to 1999 and those dealing with Eastern Europe from 1994 to 1999. This then brings our coverage through the end of the 20th century complete for both Russia and East Europe.

Certain categories of materials were excluded from this bibliography: items under 50 pages, most governmental publications (hearings, reports), occasional papers, serials, juvenile literature, locally published genealogies, gallery guides, reprints, émigré settlement publications, music scores, most multilingual publications, guidebooks published prior to 1998, dissertations and theses, general business guides, nonbook media, and volumes not available to the compilers. The test for this last category of materials was the availability of the book in the Illinois academic library network of 45 libraries served by the DRA computer system.

As with all bibliographies attempting a representative selection rather than comprehensive coverage, some titles were not selected that technically fell within our scope. The compilers believed their first responsibility was to include all major works on the area. The importance of the works was determined either by critical acclaim and coverage, uniqueness of subject matter or perspective, or significance of the author. There will, no doubt, be some omissions because of oversight and lack of time; we apologize for these omissions.

As with our previous volumes we have tried to maintain an arrangement similar to the original Horak volumes. Titles are arranged in sections by country, and further subdivided by subject area. The titles are consecutively numbered throughout. Within each section entries are arranged alphabetically by author, or lacking an author, by editor, or, lacking both of these, by title. Each entry includes complete bibliographic information and a descriptive annotation. In this volume we have omitted any indication of where the book was reviewed. The bibliographic description of each title includes full author, title, date, place of publication, publisher, extent, ISBN, and series information. Volumes published as part of a series are accessible through the individual volume title. There is no series index.

The annotations included here are descriptive rather than critical. They are intended to assist the student and researcher in choosing individual works on a topic of interest by describing the topic, arrangement, bias, intended audience, and special features of each book. Because both compilers contributed annotations on an equal basis, and we each have different areas of expertise, the annotations necessarily vary in emphasis and detail. Further, some works did not readily lend themselves to such straightforward description (for example, novels). In some cases, the best descriptions of the book were found in the introduction and conclusion. Those quotations are included in the annotations with appropriate attribution.

Access is provided through the general subject arrangement and the author and subject indexes. While the author index is self-explanatory, a word on the compilation of the subject index might be helpful. The subject headings are based on the Library of Congress usage, with some additions for more specific access. The numbers after each heading refer to individual citations in the main bibliography. Although we tried to make the headings as specific as we deemed useful, certain headings still had an extremely large number of entries.

Procite, the bibliographic reference database software, was used to organize all the data for this bibliography and to generate the indexes, with further modification of the manuscript using Microsoft Word.

As with our other volumes, this one could not have been completed without the assistance or forbearance of many people. We wish to gratefully acknowledge the excellent editorial support of Bohdan Wynar of Libraries Unlimited and the monetary support provided by the University of Illinois Library Research and Publication Committee and the University of Illinois Research Board for student assistants.

Jan Adamczyk and Julia Gauchman of the Slavic Reference Service have been very generous with their time and assistance, as well as their good humor and moral support. Bill Dickey, Marlen Vavrikova, Kris Peters, Janna Valente, and Chris Scarboro tolerated a host of impediments such as harried supervisors, poor handwriting, and unclear directions in order to search, retrieve, organize, and manipulate data for this volume. Our respective spouses, Chuck Mode and Ann Burger, have again valiantly suffered our panic attacks, frustration, and boredom that a project like this inevitably produces. As always, the staff of the Slavic and East European Library have made this burden easier by virtue of their support and good cheer.

As indicated earlier, this book is dedicated to our beloved daughters, Anna [Helen], and Sarah, Meg, and Nell [Bob], who at their best were completely unaware of this project, and at their worst occasionally wondered how many more books did we have to cart home before it was all done. We are grateful to them because only our presence mattered.

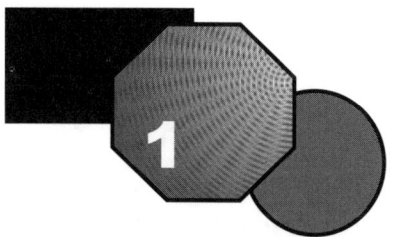

General and Interrelated Themes

General Reference Works

1. Open Media Research Institute. **The OMRI Annual Survey of Eastern Europe and the Former Soviet Union, 1996: Forging Ahead, Falling Behind**. xvii, 428p. Armonk, N.Y.: M. E. Sharpe, 1996. Includes list of contributors and index.

This second annual survey of the 27 countries of the former Soviet bloc is divided into nine parts. Each part contains essays, sidebars, profiles of key personalities, and documents relevant to a specific country or topic for 1996. Part 1 is an introduction by J. F. Brown that succinctly summarizes the import of that year's events. Parts 2-6 cover, respectively, Central Europe, Eastern Europe, Southeastern Europe, Russia, and Transcaucasia and Central Asia. Parts 7-9 cover broad topical issues: regional economic developments, building democratic institutions, and issues in foreign policy. The more than 40 contributors are either OMRI (Open Media Research Institute) employees or those in academia, government, and the private sector that have knowledge of the area. The maps, summary statistics, and well-written and informative essays provide a comprehensive and authoritative view of developments in Eastern Europe and the former Soviet Union for 1996.

2. **The Modern Encyclopedia of East Slavic, Baltic, and Eurasian Literatures**. Vol. 10: Holub, Yurka—Ivanov-Paimen, Vlas Sakharovich. Edited by Peter Rollberg. 246p. Gulf Breeze, Fla.: Academic International Press, 1996.

This volume continues the previous nine volumes of *The Modern Encyclopedia of Russian and Soviet Literatures* that was issued by the same publisher from 1978 to 1989. Since the Soviet cultural and political reality officially ceased to exist in August 1991, the changed title is a reflection of the solution to a problem faced by all East European, Baltic, and Eurasian scholarship: viz. what do we call this new entity in the wake of such a tremendous upheaval? By using linguistic and geographic terms, the publisher has provided a respectable solution to this problem. In this new incarnation after its seven-year hiatus, heavier emphasis than before is now placed on the literature of the newly independent nations. The major literatures covered are Armenian, Azerbaijani, Belorussian, Estonian, Georgian, Latvian, Russian, Udmurt, and Ukrainian. In total, about 80 literatures are eventually supposed to be represented.

In contrast to other encyclopedias issued by Academic International Press, where many articles are translated by American and European scholars from the original sources, this present endeavor only includes original articles by qualified scholars. Most articles are given attribution to the person writing them; those not so attributed are composed by the editorial staff. Each entry consists of a brief one- or two-sentence identifier and then goes on to include a more extensive essay, followed by bibliographic references to other English and vernacular sources.

The articles in this volume were well written and highly informative. Users could not ask for more in a reference work of this type. Articles on specific persons, for example, include prominent biographical details in addition to a critical appraisal and discussion of the authors' work. Entries also exist for literary artifacts, literary schools, and other relevant material. Relevant and useful bibliographies are included for most entries. What is not clear from the introduction by the editor, Peter Rollberg, is whether this and subsequent volumes will also cover émigré literatures (as the title page of previous volumes indicated), or whether coverage will be confined to literature only produced within the new national boundaries.

The only drawback to the use of these volumes is the decision of the editor not to use the Library of Congress (or other consistent and widely used) transliteration scheme. Because of this names beginning with IA and IU will be spelled as YA and YU, "occasionally" (p. vii) the initial letter E will be rendered Ye, terminal yi and ii will be rendered as y, terminal oi as oy, terminal soft signs dropped, and medial soft signs rendered as i. This inconsistency is likely to confuse and frustrate any user (especially since no cross-references are provided from variant names). In spite of this minor stylistic flaw, this and subsequent volumes should prove to be useful and relevant to the needs of students and scholars alike.

History

3. Byrnes, Robert Francis. **A History of Russian and East European Studies in the United States: Selected Essays**. xv, 271p. Lanham, Md.: University Press of America, 1994.

Robert Byrnes, former professor of history at Indiana University, has collected 15 of his essays that elucidate the formation and development of Russian and East European studies in the United States. They are not meant to present a coherent account, but instead to provide the raw material for a future history. Even so, these essays will give the reader a real sense of the development of Slavic studies in the United States and those responsible for it.

4. MacKenzie, David. **Serbs and Russians**. xxvii, 435p. *East European Monographs*, 459. Boulder, Colo.: East European Monographs; New York: Distributed by Columbia University Press, 1997. Includes bibliographical references and index.

The author has been investigating Serbian and Russian relations for over 40 years. This collection of selected articles on this topic is arranged in four parts. Part 1 includes general articles on the Serbian relationship in history and the historical roots of the Bosnian crisis. Part 2 focuses on important Serbian national leaders. Part 3 is devoted to Russian relations with Serbia and Part 4 to Serbian conspiracies, conspirators, and trials. The volume also includes a bibliography of MacKenzie's publications and his written impressions of a visit to Serbia made in 1995.

Economics

5. **Adam Smith Goes to Moscow: A Dialogue on Radical Reform**. Edited by Walter Adams and James W. Brock. xxiii, 156p. Princeton, N.J.: Princeton University Press, 1993. Includes index.

The policy making involved in choosing between economic progress and anarchy and exhaustion is the subject of this unusual book. The problems inherent in such choices are embedded in a drama, whose main characters are the prime minister and the advisor. Although the drama is a creation of the imagination, the issues discussed are palpably real. Topics included are the agenda for reform, marketization, the monopoly dilemma, privatization, stabilization, government and the market, and inherent tensions.

6. **Foreign Investment in Russia and Other Soviet Successor States**. Edited by Artisien-Maksimenko and Yuri Adjubei. xxi, 277p. New York: St. Martin's Press, 1996. Includes bibliographical references and index.

This volume assembles and interprets data on foreign direct investment in some of the successor states to the USSR, namely Russia, Ukraine, Kazakhstan, and the Baltic states. The individual articles by various authors are arranged in three parts: contextual and thematic aspects, individual country studies, and summary and conclusion.

7. Blanchard, Olivier. **Post-Communist Reform: Pain and Progress**. viii, 183p.: illus. Cambridge, Mass.: MIT Press, 1993. Includes bibliographical references (pp. [175]-180) and index.

This volume, produced by the World Economy Group, who had published a previous study on reform in Eastern Europe, emphasizes three main steps in the reform process: macrostabilization and price liberalization, privatization, and restructuring. By 1993 in Central Europe stabilization was thought to be a thing of the past. Major steps in privatization had taken place and restructuring was at the top of the agenda. These essays, therefore, focus on what the writers then thought to be the two most urgent problems: faster privatization and reform of the banking system. The essays collected here present an excellent analysis of the problems as seen from a 1993 perspective.

8. Blejer, Mario I., and Fabrizio Coricelli. **The Making of Economic Reform in Eastern Europe: Conversations with Leading Reformers in Poland, Hungary and the Czech Republic**. 156p. *Studies of Communism in Transition*. Brookfield, Vt.: Edward Elgar, 1995. Includes index.

In order to understand the "human dimension" of events occurring in Eastern Europe regarding political and economic reform, the authors interviewed three of the main actors in the reform process. The issues covered touched on six interrelated themes: (1) personal and intellectual formation; (2) process of thinking about the reforms; (3) the design of the reform package; (4) expectations; (5) the actual working of the reforms and the issue of productive support; and (6) the proposals.

9. Buchanan, James M. **Post-Socialist Political Economy: Selected Essays**. ix, 285p.: illus. Cheltenham, Eng.: Edward Elgar, 1997. Includes bibliographical references.

This is a collection of essays by James Buchanan addressing the problems faced by the post-socialist countries as they attempt to reform their economic systems. The essays are divided into four sections on science, post-revolutionary economic theory, the government and the economy, and federalism. The essays in the volume were originally delivered as lectures or seminars.

10. Centre for Co-operation with European Economies in Transition, and Organization for Economic Co-operation and Development. **Methodes de Privatisation des Grandes Entreprises: Methods of Privatizing Large Enterprises**. 178p.: illus. Paris: OECD, 1993. Includes bibliographical references.

The content of this volume is based on a seminar held in 1991 in Pultusk, Poland, on the subject of designing and implementing policies for privatizing large enterprises. The major practical aspects covered are the scope of privatization, steps taken prior to privatization, accounting and valuation issues, modalities of privatization, financial market aspects, the legal and institutional framework, the influence of the macroeconomic situation, and the political and social dimensions.

11. **Labour Statistics for a Market Economy: Challenges and Solutions in the Transition Countries of Central and Eastern Europe and the Former Soviet Union**. Edited by Igor Chernyshev. xii, 339p. Budapest, Hungary; New York: Central European University Press, 1994. "Prepared for the International Labour Office." Includes bibliographical references.

The articles in this volume describe some of the major issues in statistical transition in the field of labor in Central and Eastern Europe. The essays are presented in four parts: (1) major challenges in labor statistics; (2) labor force, employment and unemployment; (3) wage and labor cost; and (4) classification of occupations.

12. Clark, Ed, and Anna Soulsby. **Organizational Change in Post-Communist Europe: Management and Transformation in the Czech Republic**. xv, 249p. *Routledge Studies of Societies in Transition*, 11. London: Routledge, 1999. Includes bibliography (pp. 234-45) and index.

The authors summarize their work by stating that "our intention is to contribute to the understanding of important empirical and theoretical themes. On the first front, we aim to describe and analyze the specific conditions of the economic transition of post-communist society in the early 1990s, and the resultant changes in enterprise and management patterns. Second, the book confronts two fundamental theoretical questions, using these changes in the Czech Republic as the empirical location: these are the relationship between institutional stability and change, and the social and institutional (re-) construction of socio-economic reality" (p. xi).

13. **Trade Growth in Transition Economies: Export Impediments for Central and Eastern Europe**. Edited by Richard N. Cooper and Janos Gacs. xiii, 363p.: illus. Cheltenham, Eng.: Edward Elgar [and] IIASA, 1997. Includes bibliographies and index.

As Cooper points out in his introductory essay, the need to sell a country's products abroad forces domestic producers to find the right combination of price, quantity, and quality that is necessary to compete in the world market. For transition economies this problem is of particular importance. The essays in this volume explore the various impediments to exports that transition economies face. Individual essays cover Bulgaria, Estonia, Hungary, Latvia, Romania, Slovakia, and Slovenia. The three final essays cover topic areas such as government export policies, foreign direct investment, and recovery of Russia's trade with East European small economies.

14. Crawford, Beverly. **Markets, States, and Democracy: The Political Economy of Post-Communist Transformation**. ix, 278p.: illus. Boulder, Colo.: Westview Press, 1995. Includes bibliographical references and index.

This series of essays examines the post-communist transformation of East European economies and the effect of Western aid programs on this process. The essays are arranged in four parts: overview and historical legacies, the liberal ideal, the international context, and economic policy choices. One writer admits that the term "transformation" is almost a euphemism because of the magnitude of the task with which the new post-communist governments had to deal.

15. **Transformation Management in Post-Communist Countries: Organizational Requirements for a Market Economy**. Edited by Refik Culpan and Brij Nino Kumar. xvii, 250p. Westport, Conn.: Quorum Books, 1995. Includes index.

Transformation management is "about re-naturalizing and revitalizing enterprises in former socialist societies" (p. xi). The individual essays exploring this topic are grouped in five parts: (1) environment and strategy for transformation; (2) structure for transformation; (3) behavior and personal development for transformation; (4) processes for transformation; and (5) illustrative cases.

16. **Going Global: Transition from Plan to Market in the World Economy.** Edited by Padma Desai. xii, 507p. Cambridge, Mass.: MIT Press, 1997. Includes bibliographical references and index.

This volume of essays is the first of two to deal with global economic change. The present volume "focuses on the international implications of domestic changes in the former socialist countries. Issues such as exchange rate management and policies concerning foreign trade and capital flows, insofar as they affect integration into the world economy, are analyzed at length" (p. xii). The countries specifically covered here are the Czech Republic, Hungary, East Germany, Poland, the Baltic states, Finland, Russia, Kazakhstan, Uzbekistan, China, Vietnam, and India.

17. Dobek, Mariusz Mark. **The Political Logic of Privatization: Lessons from Great Britain and Poland.** xiii, 162p.: illus. Westport, Conn.: Praeger, 1993. Includes bibliographical references (pp. [149]-157) and index.

By analyzing the two cases of privatization—Great Britain and Poland—Dobek creates a framework by which to analyze and to provide guidance for other privatizations elsewhere, especially in Central and Eastern Europe. In constructing his framework he focuses on four groups of political issues: "the tension between the political and economic aspects of privatization and possible outcomes; the political and economic goals that privatization seeks to achieve; the political logic that any privatization program should follow to be successfully implemented; and finally, the different modes of privatization and the political ramifications of each" (p. 2).

18. Ernst, Maurice. **Transforming the Core: Restructuring Industrial Enterprises in Russia and Central Europe.** xx, 315p.: illus. Boulder, Colo.: Westview Press, 1996. Includes bibliographical references and index.

"The objective of this study is to assess the effectiveness of policies designed to transform large state industrial enterprises in Poland, Hungary, the Czech Republic, and Russia and to draw lessons from this experience that could inform policy makers in these and other transition countries as well as in the West" (p. 2). The first three chapters establish the context for the study, discussing the conditions during the economic transition generally and government policies that affected state enterprises. There follows a series of chapters, each focused on a particular country. Because the governments in each of these countries have historically had sweeping control not only over the economy but other aspects of society, their role is treated differently than in other economic studies. The author believes because of the unique situation in Eastern Europe the enterprises of the region do not respond to macroeconomic incentives as they would in a market economy.

19. **Restructuring and Privatization in Central Eastern Europe: Case Studies of Firms in Transition**. Edited by Saul Estrin, Josef C. Brada, and Alan Singh Inderjit Gelb. xxxiv, 400p. *The Microeconomics of Transition Economies.* Armonk, N.Y.: M. E. Sharpe, 1995. Includes index.

These 36 case studies are arranged in three parts, depending on their country of residence. The three parts are Czech and Slovak firms, Hungarian firms, and Polish firms. Within each part individual firms are identified by their product focus, e.g., defense, heavy chemicals, textiles, glass, food processing, etc. In an overview essay the editors state that in all three countries many firms have managed to transform themselves. More important, however, is the privatization program itself. While most ownership changes have taken place with firms that are in sound financial condition, the authorities have not been able to deal with firms "whose economic situation is not sustainable" (p. xxv). Some lessons from Poland, they speculate, may have relevance to the same process in Russia.

20. Frydman, Roman. **Privatization in Eastern Europe: Is the State Withering Away?** xv, 221p. Budapest, Hungary; New York: Central European University Press, 1994. "A Central European University Privatization Project Book"—p. [2] of cover. Includes bibliographical references (pp. [211]-216) and index.

The individual chapters of this volume describe and analyze the attempts to build capitalism on the ruins of communism. The authors are themselves major actors in these attempts and therefore their accounts can also be read as policy proposals that they may have to implement and evaluate. Finally, their work represents an analysis of the problems to achieve capitalism and the strategies that may overcome those problems.

21. **Restructuring Networks in Post-Socialism: Legacies, Linkages, and Localities**. Edited by Gernot Grabher and David Stark. viii, 349p. Oxford, Eng.: Oxford University Press, 1997. Includes bibliography and index.

These 13 essays, which focus on Eastern Germany, the Czech Republic, Hungary, Poland, and Russia, are arranged in three sections: (1) Recombinant Networks: property transformation and restructuring of large firms; (2) Entrepreneurial Networks: new firm formation; and (3) Policy Networks: restructuring institutions. The main argument of the book is that networks that link firms and not the firms themselves are the proper analytic unit in the new Eastern Europe, and not only are those units to be restructured, but also they do the restructuring.

22. **Institutional Frameworks of Market Economies: Scandinavian and Eastern European Perspectives**. Edited by Jerzy Hausner, Bob Jessop, and Klaus Nielsen. x, 301p.: illus. Aldershot, Eng.: Avebury, 1993. Papers presented at a conference in Cracow, Dec. 6-8, 1990.

Most of the 15 papers in this volume were originally presented at a conference in Cracow in 1990. They explore "some of the general features which are important in the process of formation and change of the institutional frameworks of market economies" (p. vii). The emphasis is on Poland and the Scandinavian countries.

23. Herbert, Ulrich. **Hitler's Foreign Workers: Enforced Foreign Labor in Germany Under the Third Reich**. xxi, 510p. Cambridge, Eng.: Cambridge University Press, 1997. "Originally published in German as: Fremdarbeiter: Politik und Praxis des 'Ausländer-Einsatzes' in der Kriegswirtschaft des Dritten Reiches . . . 1985"—t.p. verso.

This is an account of a massive forced labor instance in the 20th century. More than 12 million workers were forced into labor for the Third Reich. The phenomenon is examined from the viewpoint of the Nazi leadership, the entrepreneurs and the authorities, and also through the eyes of the workers themselves. After an introduction laying out the history of forced labor, the author proceeds chronologically from 1939 through the end of the war.

24. Kaple, Deborah A. **Dream of a Red Factory: The Legacy of High Stalinism in China**. xvi, 163p. New York: Oxford University Press, 1994. Includes bibliographical references (pp. 149-60) and index.

Kaple's intent is to "capture the essence of a larger society through the prism of a smaller world, in this case, through the eyes of factory managers and workers. It is the story of the Chinese Communist Party's (CCP) 'dream' of transforming China into a modern, socialist, industrialized country and, in particular, the way in which the Party went about changing the structure of factory administration. This book is also a reinterpretation of the Sino-Soviet relationship . . . this book chronicles the CCP's reliance on an idealized version of the Soviet 'model' and how Stalinism ultimately became an integral part of Chinese communism" (p. vii).

25. **Economic Transition in Eastern Europe and Russia: Realities of Reform**. Edited by Edward P. Lazear. vi, 447p.: illus. Stanford, Calif.: Hoover Institution Press, 1995. Includes bibliographical references and index.

This volume, written to be accessible to the interested layperson, is arranged in four parts. Part 1, containing the key paper by Lazear, deals with the appropriate steps and actual policies of economic reform. Part 2, "Fundamental Components of Economic Reform," contains six papers dealing with macroeconomics in Russia, democracy and economic reform, privatization, revenue assignment, credibility, and gradual versus rapid liberalization in foreign trade. Part 3, "Specific Problems in Reform," has four papers concerned with such topics as contract enforcement institutions, publicly provided private goods and services in a transition economy, the red mafia, and defense conversion. Part 4, containing two papers, focuses on comparisons and evaluations.

26. Myant, Martin R. **Transforming Socialist Economies: The Case of Poland and Czechoslovakia**. xii, 297p. Aldershot, Eng.: Edward Elgar, 1993. Includes bibliographical references (pp. 277-88) and index.

This volume examines the difficulties of transforming the centrally planned economies of Poland and Czechoslovakia into modern market systems. Part 1 (Chapters 1-2) discusses the failure of planning and the limits of reform. Part 2 (Chapters 3-6) and Part 3 (Chapters 7-11) cover the economic transformation of Poland and Czechoslovakia, respectively. Part 4 (Chapter 12) analyzes successes and disappointments in both countries.

27. **Transforming Post-Communist Political Economies**. Edited by Joan M. Nelson, Charles Tilly, and Lee Walker. xi, 513p. Washington, D.C.: National Academy Press, 1997. Includes index and bibliography (pp. 493-96).

The papers in this volume were originally presented at workshops sponsored by the National Research Council. An overview essay by Douglas North on "Understanding Economic Change" is followed by five sections that deal with the following broad areas: (1) institutional change, property rights, and corruption; (2) transforming management, labor, and production; (3) social trends, household behavior, and social-sector policies; (4) transforming the role of the state; and (5) research priorities for post-communist economies.

28. Porket, J. L. **Unemployment in Capitalist, Communist, and Post-Communist Economies**. xix, 230p.: illus. *St Antony's/Macmillan series*. New York: St. Martin's Press in association with St. Antony's College, Oxford, 1995. Includes bibliographical references (pp. 216-27) and index.

Porket argues that "unemployment assumes two forms, that of open unemployment and that of hidden unemployment, and that the form unemployment assumes has an impact on the utilization of the employed labor force, and vice versa. It maintains that while market capitalism has an inherent tendency toward open unemployment and an economical use of the employed labor force, command socialism has an inherent tendency toward labor shortage and overmanning (also known as overstaffing), the objective dimension of hidden unemployment" (p. xv).

29. Poznanski, Kazimierz Z. **Constructing Capitalism: The Reemergence of Civil Society and Liberal Economy in the Post-Communist World**. vii, 230p. Boulder, Colo.: Westview Press, 1992. Includes index.

This book, like its sequel *The Evolutionary Transition to Capitalism*, is a compendium of articles about the road to capitalism in Eastern Europe. The articles are arranged in three parts: (1) Regional Political Economy; (2) Reconstruction of Markets; and (3) Dilemmas of Democratization. It also includes an epilogue by the editor on "Markets and States in the Transformation of Post-Communist Europe." The purpose of the book is "to provide an analytical framework to better understand why the 'real' socialist systems disintegrated in the way they did, and also what patterns of change have already begun to emerge in the recent period of transition to more market-oriented, pluralistic structures" (p. 3).

30. **The Evolutionary Transition to Capitalism**. Edited by Kazimierz Z. Poznanski. Boulder, Colo.: Westview Press, 1995. Sequel to: *Constructing Capitalism* (1992). Includes bibliographical references and index.

This volume is the product of two U.S.-Polish Economic Roundtables and is a sequel to *Constructing Capitalism* (Westview Press, 1992). All the studies here, according to the editor, are placed within the framework of evolutionary theory and focus on post-communist reforms. The editor contends that this volume "should be considered the first coherent statement of the evolutionary perspective on the current process of transition in post-communist economies (and possibly on the more general issue of comparative economic systems as well)" (p. lx). The nine papers are arranged in three parts: (1) Paradoxes of transition: Eastern Europe; (2) Radicalism versus gradualism: the Asian experience; and (3) the Evolutionary paradigm: theoretical debate.

31. **Enterprise and Social Benefits After Communism**. Edited by Martin Rein, Barry L. Friedman, and Adreas Worgotter. xxiii, 315p.: illus. Cambridge, Eng.: Cambridge University Press, 1997. Includes index and bibliographic references.

The contributors investigate the scope, magnitude, and determinants of enterprise social benefits in Eastern Europe several years after the transition from command economies occurred. The papers are in two sections: (1) distinctive analytic frameworks, where the determinants of enterprise benefits are explored; and (2) institutional analyses, which are more distinctive in the degree of institutional information provided. One paper on China provides an interesting contrast to the other studies. The main conclusion is that "enterprise benefits may play a significant role in determining the efficiency of enterprises and may also serve social functions" (p. 20).

32. **Privatisation and Economic Development in Eastern Europe and the CIS: Investment, Acquisition and Managerial Issues**. Edited by Haydn Shaughenessy. xvi, 186p. New York: John Wiley, 1994. Includes bibliographic references.

This volume contains 11 essays by consultants and legal and business experts in the field of privatization and economic developments in Eastern Europe. Topics included are European privatization in perspective, foreign investment, reform processes, privatization in individual countries, insuring against risks of doing business, and planning and financing infrastructure projects. An appendix includes selected IFC- and EBRD-supported investment funds.

33. Tiusanen, Tauno. **Post Communist Capitalism and Capital: Foreign Investors in Transitional Economies**. 137p. Commack, N.Y.: Nova Science Publishers, 1993. Includes index.

This study focuses on the role that foreign direct investments play in transitional economies. Its four chapters deal with the legacy of communism, the key issues of macroeconomic stability and investments for restructuring, the global economy and post-communism, and the future of foreign direct investment in transitional economies.

34. Turnock, David. **The East European Economy in Context: Communism and Transition**. x, 425p.: maps. London: Routledge, 1997. Includes bibliography (pp. 361-89) and index.

Turnock deals with the history and current situation of former communist economies of Eastern Europe apart from the former states of the Soviet Union. Initial chapters provide background of the economic situation in Eastern Europe to 1945 and under communism. He then examines relevant political and social issues and the transition to a market economy. This is followed by individual chapters on the northern countries and the Balkan countries and the problems of restructuring in agriculture and industry. A concluding chapter presents the prospects for the regions of Eastern Europe.

35. **The Political Economy of Property Rights: Institutional Change and Credibility in the Reform of Centrally Planned Economies**. Edited by David Leo Weimer. xvii, 363p.: illus., map. *Political Economy of Institutions and Decisions*. Cambridge, Eng.: Cambridge University Press, 1997. Includes bibliographical references and indexes.

The contributors to this volume address two important theoretical questions about the transformation of property rights in post-communist countries and China. These questions are: "What aspects of political systems give credibility to systems of property rights, and what can be learned about large-scale change of economic institutions from the transformation of property rights in post-communist countries? . . . [The contributors] argue that the credibility of property rights arises from the strategic interaction of political and economic actors, and they apply this perspective and test its implications, using a variety of qualitative and quantitative methods" (frontispiece).

36. Adam, Jan. **Why Did the Socialist System Collapse in Central and Eastern European Countries? The Case of Poland, the Former Czechoslovakia and Hungary**. xiii, 244p. London: Macmillan, 1996. Includes bibliographical references and index.

Adam approaches this topic in an unconventional way. In the first of four parts Adam provides an introduction to the entire topic, providing general reasons for socialism's collapse. In Part 2 (Chapters 2-6) Adam looks at the traditional, unreformed system focusing on Poland, Hungary, and the Soviet Union. In Part 3 (Chapters 7-10) he examines economic reforms that began as early as the 1960s in their relation to the collapse. In Part 4, he provides conclusions.

Government and Law

37. Askin, Kelly D. **War Crimes Against Women: Prosecution in International War Crimes Tribunals**. xviii, 455p. The Hague: Martinus Nijhoff, 1997. Includes bibliographical references.

Although much of this book covers the development and prosecution of war crimes against women all over the world, there are several central chapters dealing with war crimes against women in Yugoslavia. The types of crimes covered include ethnic cleansing, rapes, and forced prostitution. One major chapter, covering almost 20 percent of the volume covers the prosecution of gender crimes in the International Criminal Tribunal for the former Yugoslavia.

38. **New States, New Politics: Building the Post-Soviet Nations.** Edited by Ian Bremmer and Ray Taras. xxi, 743p. Cambridge, Eng.: Cambridge University Press, 1997. Includes index, list for further reading, and one appendix.

The intent of this volume is to understand "the state-building process underway in the Soviet successors. Recognizing national development and, where applicable, early trappings of statehood from the Soviet period and earlier, it sets out to explain the important political events that have marked the successor states in their first five years of existence" (p. xviii). The book is arranged in seven parts. Part 1 is an introduction to post-Soviet nationalities theory. Part 2 covers Russia and its nations (North Caucasus, Middle Volga, and Siberia). Part 3 is devoted to the "new" Eastern Europe (Ukraine, Belarus, and Moldova). The Baltics, the Transcaucasus, and Central Asia comprise Parts 4-6. Part 7 is a concluding essay on nationalism and national interests.

39. **Politics, Power, and the Struggle for Democracy in South-East Europe.** Edited by Karen Dawisha and Bruce Parrott. xx, 472p. *Democratization and Authoritarianism in Post-Communist Societies*, 2. Cambridge, Eng.: Cambridge University Press, 1997. Includes index.

"This book brings together distinguished specialists on Albania, Bosnia and Herzegovina, Bulgaria, Croatia, Macedonia, Romania, Serbia/Montenegro, and Slovenia. The authors analyze the challenge of building democracy in the conflict driven lands of the former Yugoslavia and in neighboring states. They focus on oppositional activity, political cultures that often favor strong presidentialism, the role of nationalism, and basic socioeconomic trends" (frontispiece).

40. **Stalinism and Nazism: Dictatorships in Comparison.** Edited by Ian Kershaw and Moshe Lewin. xii, 369p. Cambridge, Eng.: Cambridge University Press, 1997. Includes index.

The 13 essays collected here were selected from papers presented at a conference in 1991. The purpose of the conference was to explore the similarities and differences in the development of Russia during the 20th century. These essays have a narrower chronological focus. The introductory essay by the editors puts the problem in perspective and summarizes the contents of the papers included here. The editors' "Afterthoughts" essay places a conceptual cap on the exercise by pointing out, among other things, the differing role and scale of terror in the two regimes and the commonality of their self-destructive tendencies.

41. Lukic, Reneo, and Allen C. Lynch. **Europe from the Balkans to the Urals: The Disintegration of Yugoslavia and the Soviet Union.** xvii, 436p.: maps. New York: Oxford University Press, 1996. Includes bibliographical references (pp. [403]-419) and index.

The authors admit that the present volume is an attempt to explain a transformation of East Central Europe and the former Soviet Union that is far from complete. In 18 chapters the authors explore the implosion of the Yugoslav state and the Soviet Union between the years 1989 and 1995. In Part 1 (Chapters 1-2) the authors provide an introduction, the conceptual premises of their study, and an overview of the disintegration of the communist federations of East Central Europe and the Soviet Union. In Part 2 (Chapters 3-6) they describe ethnofederalism and its manifestation in both Yugoslavia and the Soviet Union. In Part 3 (Chapters 7-10) they focus on Gorbachev and the disintegration of the USSR and then the disintegration of the Yugoslav state, the wars of Yugoslav succession, and the debacle of Bosnia and Herzegovina. In Part 4 (Chapters 11-17) they trace the international consequences of the breakup of Yugoslavia and the USSR. Part 5 (Chapter 18) is a conclusion.

42. **Political Culture and Civil Society in Russia and the New States of Eurasia.** Edited by Vladimir Tismaneanu. xiii, 384p.: maps. *International Politics of Eurasia*, vol. 7. Armonk, N.Y.: M. E. Sharpe, 1995. Papers presented at a workshop sponsored jointly by the University of Maryland at College Park and the Paul H. Nitze School of Advanced International Studies of Johns Hopkins University. Includes bibliographical references and index.

"This volume analyzes the nature of the emerging political cultures and their impact on the processes of democratization in these new states. In this search for a new organizing principle, two potential sources of guidance are the idea of civil society and an intensified sense of national identity. The book points to the relative weakness of civil society and the persistent quest for national identity, its varieties, and its various political consequences" (p. xi).

International Relations, Foreign Trade

43. **Finland and Poland in the Russian Empire: A Comparative Study.** Edited by Michael Branch, Janet M. Hartley, and Antoni Maczak. xi, 311p. London: School of Slavonic and East European Studies, University of London, 1995. "This book brings together a selection of papers presented at a conference held at the School of Slavonic and East European Studies in December 1989"—p. [vii].

The papers in this volume were originally presented at a conference in London in 1989. The aims of the conference were: "to establish the extent of interdependence between the border countries of the Empire and Russia itself; and to consider how mutual perceptions of each other engendered first suspicion and the hostility" (p. vii). The papers themselves are arranged in broad subject categories: incorporation, government, economy, culture, and identity.

44. Burg, Steven L. **War or Peace: Nationalism, Democracy, and American Foreign Policy in Post-Communist Europe**. xiii, 258p. New York: New York University Press, c1996. "A Twentieth Century Fund book." Includes bibliographical references (pp. 227-48) and index.

"In this book, Burg traces the development of the newly non-communist states of Central and Eastern Europe. He stresses a 'need for a stable framework for international peace,' including the creation of an institutionalized capacity to deal with challenges in both domestic and international affairs. He offers practical advice about how to support democratization within these new states and appropriate outside response mechanisms for multilateral crises" (p. xiii).

45. **Beyond Confrontation: International Law for the Post-Cold War Era**. Edited by Lori Fisler Damrosch and Rein Mullerson. xxvi, 345p. Boulder, Colo.: Westview Press, 1995. Includes bibliographical references and index. "Published under the auspices of the American Society of International Law."

This joint Russian-American publication on international law juxtaposes differing views of issues in international law with the aim of understanding the law better and working toward mutually acceptable solutions. In addition to several chapters covering the role of international law in the contemporary world and related issues, there are individual articles on legal regulation and the use of force, international cooperation against terrorism, stability in the law of the sea, environmental law, the law of outer space, international law, and the peaceful settlement of disputes through the rule of law.

46. Gardner, Hall. **Dangerous Crossroads: Europe, Russia, and the Future of NATO**. xii, 279p. Westport, Conn.: Praeger, 1997.

The primary question raised in this book is whether the United States, Europe, and Russia will ultimately be able to forge a comprehensive system of European security. The author argues that "once NATO enlarges to include Poland, the Czech Republic, and Hungary, it will soon find itself torn between two conflicting imperatives. NATO will need to work with Russia, Ukraine (and other non-NATO states) to forge a comprehensive system of regional security on the one hand, but concurrently integrate its new members into its exclusive military command on the other with a predilection to invest far greater resources into the latter" (p. ix). This is the dangerous crossroads to which the book's title alludes.

47. Gleason, Abbott. **Totalitarianism: The Inner History of the Cold War**. 307p. New York: Oxford University Press, 1995. Includes bibliographical references and index.

Recognizing that "Totalitarianism was the great mobilizing and unifying concept of the Cold War" (p. 3), Gleason proceeds to explore this concept by analyzing its origins prior to the Second World War and continuing through the 1980s. In turn he examines the fascist origins, a new kind of state (Italy, Germany, and the Soviet Union in the 1930s), wartime in the English-speaking world, the cold war, brainwashing (communist

China as a totalitarian state), the origins of totalitarianism, totalitarianism among the Sovietologists, the cold war in postwar Europe, the cold war in Eastern Europe, and the evil empire.

48. **Origins of the Cold War: An International History**. Edited by Melvyn P. Leffler and David S. Painter. xiii, 322p.: maps. *Rewriting Histories*. London: Routledge, 1994. Includes bibliographical references.

This unusual collection of essays of the cold war does not limit its focus to Russia and the United States. It is, rather, a revelation of the sources of the international tensions that so molded foreign relations in the second half of the 20th century. "This volume explains how and why the Cold War spread from the industrialized core of Europe and Japan to the Third World periphery, eventually engulfing the whole world. It also shows how groups, classes and elites used the Cold War to further their own interests" (frontispiece). The essays are divided into four sections: "Soviet and American Strategy and Diplomacy"; "Europe and the Cold War"; "Linking Center and Periphery"; "The Cold War and the Third World."

49. Mayhew, Alan. **Recreating Europe: The European Union's Policy Towards Central and Eastern Europe**. xxi, 403p.: 2 maps. New York: Cambridge University Press, 1998. Includes bibliographical references (pp. 394-400) and index.

"In this book an academic with wide experience in policy-making in the European Union and Central Europe investigates the relationship between the European Union and countries of Central Europe as it is today. He examines the detail of the Association Agreements, and provides the first analysis of their operation in key areas like trade and competition policy. Part III of the book considers the costs and benefits of enlargement and investigates the key problems in both East and West, including the CAP, EU Structural Funds, budgetary policy and migration. Finally, the book investigates alternative strategies for enlargement" (frontispiece).

50. **International Relations Theory and the End of the Cold War**. Edited by Thomas Risse-Kappen and Richard N. Lebow. xv, 292p.: illus. New York: Columbia University Press, 1995. Includes bibliographical references.

These essays, initially presented at a conference at Cornell University in 1991, seek to explore the implications of the end of the cold war for international relations theory.

Political Theories, Nationalism, Communism, Religion

51. **Adaptation and Transformation in Communist and Post-Communist Systems**. ix, 326p. Boulder, Colo.: Westview Press, 1992. Includes bibliographical references and index.

"With the Communist and post-Communist world continuing to undergo momentous change, this volume provides thoughtful analysis of the often difficult and unstable political evolution facing the countries in transition. Drawing on various theoretical perspectives, the contributors consider the key issues of legitimization, cultural change, religious policy, the role of the media, and economic reconstruction as well as the processes and prerequisites of pluralization" (back cover). Contributors include Sabrina Petra Ramet, Daniel N. Nelson, Patricia J. Smith, Valerie Bunce, Marc J. Blecher, Dougals Durasoff, and Owen V. Johnson.

52. Bell, Andrew. **Ethnic Cleansing**. 1st. ed. 346p.: illus., maps. New York: St. Martin's Press, 1996. Includes bibliographical references (pp. [322]-332) and index.

The author defines ethnic cleansing as "a planned, deliberate removal from a certain territory of an undesirable population distinguished by one or more characteristics such as ethnicity, religion, race, class, or sexual preference. These characteristics must serve as the basis for removal for it to qualify as cleansing" (pp. 3-4). His book is in three parts. In Part 1 he gives a historical overview of cleansing, a typology of cleansing, and cleansing as a metonym of collective identity. In Part 2 he examines specific areas where it has occurred, not only in the Slavic and East European world, but also in Palestine, Rwanda and Burundi, Sri Lanka, and Ulster. In Part 3 he presents suggestions for solving irreconcilable ethnic conflicts.

53. Berend, Ivan T. **Central and Eastern Europe: 1944-1993: Detour from the Periphery to the Periphery**. xviii, 414p. *Cambridge Studies in Modern Economic History*, 1. Cambridge, Eng.: Cambridge University Press, 1996. Includes bibliography (pp. 382-400) and indexes.

This work, written by a person who lived in Hungary during the period covered, intends to present "a complex analysis of post-World War II Central and East European history integrated into a broader framework; to connect history with the transformation of the present and the perspective of the future" (p. xvii). It is arranged in three parts: "Out from Europe: the introduction of state socialism, the Stalinist decades, and revolts against them," "Temporary success and terminal failure: the post-Stalinist decades—modernization, erosion, and collapse," and "Back to Europe? Post-1989 transformation and pathways to the future."

54. Brubaker, Rogers. **Nationalism Reframed: Nationhood and the Nation Question in the New Europe**. xi, 202p. Cambridge, Eng.: Cambridge University Press, 1996. Includes bibliographical references.

Brubaker uses both theoretical considerations and concrete examples to show how nationalism can be understood and "the practical uses of the category 'nation,' the ways it can come to structure perception, to inform thought and experience, to organize discourse and political action" (p. 7). Countries covered here in some detail include the Soviet Union and its successor states, the Balkan states, Hungary, and Germany.

55. Chavance, Bernard. **The Transformation of Communist Systems: Economic Reform Since the 1950s**. xi, 225p.: tables. Boulder, Colo.: Westview Press, 1994. Includes bibliographical references (pp. 213-14) and index.

Chavance's book, translated from French, presents a history of economic reform in communist systems. The author first presents an analysis of the traditional system, including nationalization, state control, and central planning. He then moves on to describe adjusting of the traditional system, then radical reform, and finally a final dismantling of the entire system. Case studies used in the presentation of his typology are Poland, the Soviet Union, East Germany, Yugoslavia, Czechoslovakia, Hungary, and China.

56. Dawson, Jane I. **Eco-Nationalism: Anti-Nuclear Activism and National Identity in Russia, Lithuania, and Ukraine**. xii, 221p., [4] p. of plates: illus., maps. Durham, N.C.: Duke University Press, 1996. Includes bibliographical references (pp. [199]-208) and index.

In the first years of Russia's democratic movement, beginning in 1989, the author began an investigation of one aspect of the emerging civil society: the ability and willingness of citizens to speak out against nuclear power. However, the tenor and content of the public discussion was not as Dawson expected. Rather than well-crafted arguments around the scientific and environmental aspects of the issue, Dawson found that most of the arguments evolved from a concern with nationalism. That is, "the movements against nuclear power were in fact often more indicative of popular demands for national sovereignty and regional self-determination. The shoddily constructed and carelessly operated nuclear power stations that littered the countryside were much more than environmental threats; they were in fact symbols of Moscow's indifference to the welfare and very survival of the non-Russian nations of the Soviet Union" (pp. ix-x). Specific geographic areas from where she drew her conclusions include Lithuania, Ukraine, Russia, Tatarstan, and Crimea.

57. Djilas, Milovan. **The Fall of the New Class: A History of Communism's Self-Destruction**. xiv, 432p. New York: Alfred A. Knopf, 1998. Includes index.

In the last work published before his death Djilas incorporates excerpts from previously published works in order to provide the reader with a guide to his intellectual and spiritual journey. Djilas' message, in essence, was "We cannot eradicate evil, evil is real, a palpable presence. Man and society are unperfectible. But love your struggle, your conscious, despairing struggle."

58. Hoberman, J. **The Red Atlantis: Communist Culture in the Absence of Communism**. 315p.: illus. *Culture and the Moving Image*. Philadelphia: Temple University Press, 1998. Includes bibliographical references and index.

J. Hoberman examines the role communism played in the 20th century in this broad study of a lost utopian vision. "In the spirit of those de-territorialized dogs and their implanted ideological memory, this book—itself a collection of exhumed and annotated fossils—acknowledges the loss of that Communist utopia which, in fact never existed" (p. 10).

59. Holmes, Leslie. **Post-Communism: An Introduction**. xiv, 384p.: illus., map. Durham, N.C.: Duke University Press, 1997. Includes bibliographical references and index.

This introduction to post-communism in Eastern Europe and the USSR offers a good topical survey. The structure of the book lends itself to classroom teaching. Part 1 covers theoretical approaches; Part 2 focuses on the transition to post-communism; Part 3 examines early post-communism from the point of view of institutional politics, economies, social policies and problems, civil vs. uncivil societies, and changing allegiances. A final, fourth part offers concluding remarks.

60. **Russian Nationalism, Past and Present**. Edited by Geoffrey A. Hosking and Robert Service. viii, 217p. *Studies in Russia and East Europe*. London: Macmillan in association with the School of Slavonic and East European Studies, 1998. Conference proceedings from the School of Slavonic and East European Studies of London University, March 1995.

This is a collection of essays on the development and future of nationalism in Russia. Contributors include Phillip Boobbyer, Simon Dixon, Peter J. S. Duncan, Geoffrey Hosking, John Kiler, Maureen Perrie, E. A. Rees, A. N. Sakharov, and Robert Service. They were all present at a conference in March 1995 held at the School of Slavonic and East European Studies in London.

61. Linden, Carl, and Jan S. Prybyla. **Russia and China on the Eve of a New Millennium**. x, 341p. New Brunswick, N.J.: Transaction Publishers, 1997. Contains bibliography and index.

This volume contains 10 essays that describe communism's erosion and 1989 collapse and related developments through the mid-1990s. The essays are presented in two parts. Part 1, Europe and Russia: Totalitarian Collapse and Transition, focuses almost entirely on Russian and related theoretical issues. Part 2, China: Totalitarian Retreat and Reformation, deals with primarily economic issues and the market economy. Prybyla provides a summary chapter that ties the East European and Chinese experience together.

62. Luther, Sara F., John J. Neumaier, and Howard Lee Parsons. **Diverse Perspectives on Marxist Philosophy: East and West**. vi, 158p. *Contributions in Philosophy*, 0084-926X; No. 53, 11.623. Westport, Conn.: Greenwood Press, 1995. Includes bibliographical references (pp. [147]-148) and index.

The essays contained in this collection essentially represent a dialogue of different perspectives on Marxist philosophy. From it we are introduced to "new ways of revising Marxism; new interpretations of humanism; greater utilization of the resources of Western and Eastern philosophies; various comprehensive world views; . . . 'cosmosism,' taking its inspiration from the Russian founder of astronautics, Kostantinn E. Tsiolkovskii, from Nicholas Roerich, and others; searches in Western thought for a model of 'civic society'; and a re-examination of the history of Russian philosophy, with attempts to construct a distinctively Russian world view out of Russia's pre-socialist economic and cultural history" (p. 16).

63. Milojkovic-Djuric, Jelena. **Panslavism and National Identity in Russia and in the Balkans, 1830-1880: Images of the Self and Others**. v, 177p. *East European Monographs*, 394. Boulder, Colo.: East European Monographs; New York: Distributed by Columbia University Press, 1994. Includes bibliographical references and index.

In his introduction, the author sums up the topic of his work in the following manner: "My inquiry aims to examine the emergence of Panslavic postulates manifested in the course of three major events: The Slav Congress in Prague 1848, the Ethnographic Exhibition in conjunction with the Slav Congress in Moscow 1867, and the resurgence of Panslav solidarity during the uprising in Bosnia-Hercegovina 1875-1878. As an aspect of the Slav national revival, Panslavism evolved as a unifying relational event, stressing the historical and cultural continuum of the whole of Slavdom" (p. 1).

64. **Legacies of the Collapse of Marxism**. Edited by John H. Moore. xix, 255p.: illus. Fairfax, Va.: George Mason University Press, 1994. Includes bibliographical references.

These essays were originally presented as conference papers in 1992 in Washington, D.C. It is worth remembering that the perspectives of the authors are tightly constrained by their writing only two years after the 1989 revolutions and as a result, the outline of things to come had hardly begun to emerge. Several papers focus on the collapse itself, while others explore the themes of nationalism, civil society, geopolitics of ethnic mobilization, minority rights, market exchange, and conservative political philosophy.

65. Pei, Minxin. **From Reform to Revolution: The Demise of Communism in China and the Soviet Union**. 253p.: illus. Cambridge, Mass.: Harvard University Press, 1994. Includes bibliographical references (pp. [213]-243) and index.

In trying to understand the processes involved in the transition from communism, the author compares the processes in China and the Soviet Union. In Chapters 1-2, he explores the general problem of regime transition in communist states and develops two analytical frameworks to support further arguments. In Chapters 3-4 he presents two detailed case studies that compare the emergence of the private sector in Russia and China. In Chapters 5-6 he focuses on the process of democratization as it played itself out in the mass media in China and Russia.

66. Prokurat, Michael, Alexander Golitzin, and Michael D. Peterson. **Historical Dictionary of the Orthodox Church**. 440p. *European Historical Dictionaries*, no. 9. Lanham, Md.: Scarecrow Press, 1996. Includes bibliography and appendix.

The editors of this ambitious volume have focused on the last 150 years. The dictionary's approximately 700 articles include material on major features of Orthodoxy from the second century A.D. This work is not intended as a comprehensive resource. "Our goal in writing may be described as a dictionary insofar as that format might include a one-volume desk encyclopedia or a reference work sometimes called a handbook."

As with other volumes in this series, the volume includes a chronology, an overview article summarizing the main features of Orthodoxy's development, and a general profile of its theology and the geographic area in which it is prominent. This is followed by a map, the dictionary entries, an appendix of the Orthodox Churches of the world, and a bibliography.

The dictionary entries include many general headings such as "anthropology" along with entries specific to Orthodoxy such as "Lausaic History." The general terminology allows the reader unfamiliar with Orthodoxy to learn many aspects of its traditions. There is extensive cross-referencing between the texts.

The bibliography is organized by subject. It includes bibliographies, periodicals, newspapers, works on art, aestheticism, canon law, cultural studies, and many other topics. The volume does not include an index.

67. **Nation and Politics in the Soviet Successor States**. Edited by Ray Taras and Ian A. Bremmer. xxvii, 577p.: illus. Cambridge, Eng.: Cambridge University Press, 1993. Title on cover: *Nations and Politics in the Soviet Successor States*. Notes: Includes bibliographical references (pp. 561-65) and index.

This collection of essays examines nationalities and nationalism in the immediate wake of the collapse of the Soviet state in 1991. The essays are arranged in nine parts. These include an introduction, the center (Russia), the "new" Eastern Europe (Ukraine, Belarus, Moldova), the Baltics, the Transcaucasus, Central Asia, nations without states (Middle Volga, North Caucasus, Siberia), and a conclusion. The volume also contains a chronology of ethnic unrest in the USSR, 1985-1991, and Soviet census data for 1989.

68. **Ideology and System Change in the USSR and East Europe: Selected Papers from the Fourth World Congress for Soviet and East European Studies, Harrogate, 1990**. Edited by Michael E. Urban. xxvii, 271p. New York: St. Martin's Press, 1992. Includes bibliographical references.

The papers contained in this volume were originally presented at the Fourth World Congress for Soviet and East European Studies in 1990. The 14 papers have been arranged in three thematic groups: (1) ideology, conflict, and change in the USSR; (2) nationalism, socialism, and crisis in East Europe; and (3) perestroika and the humanities in the USSR.

69. Walicki, Andrzej. **Marxism and the Leap to the Kingdom of Freedom: The Rise and Fall of the Communist Utopia**. xii, 641p. Stanford, Calif.: Stanford University Press, 1995. Includes bibliographical references (pp. [619]-635) and index.

"The aim of this book is to carefully reconstruct Marx and Engels' theory of freedom, to highlight its centrality for their vision of the communist society of the future, to trace its development in the history of Marxist thought, including Marxism-Leninism, and to explain how it was possible for it to be transformed at the height of its influence into a legitimization of totalitarian practices" (p. 1).

70. Wood, Ellen Meiksins. **Democracy Against Capitalism: Renewing Historical Materialism**. xii, 300p. Cambridge, Eng.: Cambridge University Press, 1995. Includes bibliographical references and index.

Ellen Meiksins Wood defends the role of Marxism as a critique of capitalism. "In this book she sets out to renew the critical program of historical materialism by redefining its basic concepts and its theory of history in original and imaginative ways, using them to identify the specificity of capitalism as a system of social relations and political power" (p. i). The first part of the book is devoted to a discussion of historical materialism and the specificity of capitalism. Part 2 explores the struggle of democracy against capitalism.

Language and Literature

71. Bethin, Christina Y. **Slavic Prosody: Language Change and Phonological Theory**. xv, 349p.: illus., map. *Cambridge Studies in Linguistics*, 86. New York: Cambridge University Press, 1998. Includes bibliographical references (pp. 302-46) and index.

Bethin "gives a coherent account of the Slavic languages at the time of their differentiation and relates these developments to issues in phonological theory.... By demonstrating that a nonlinear representation of the syllable together with the notion of constraint interaction can account for a wide range of data, this study takes a position on the nature of phonological representation and on a model of language change. In its attention to the history of selected problems of Slavic linguistics the book also offers a detailed survey of the field" (frontispiece).

72. **Literature, Culture, and Society in the Modern Age. Part II: In Honor of Joseph Frank**. Edited by Edward James Brown. vols. 1-2. Stanford, Calif.: Dept. of Slavic Languages and Literatures, Stanford University, 1991. Contributions en anglais et en russe.

This two-volume festschrift in honor of Joseph Frank contains 38 essays and a bibliography of Frank's works. The essays, all by Slavic literary scholars (with a few exceptions), focus on 19th- and 20th-century Russian literary figures including Dostoevsky, Turgenev, Belyj, Ahkmatova, Mandelstam, Pasternak, Zoshchenko, Nabokov, Gogol, Solzhenitsyn, and Bitov. Nonslavic articles deal with literary figures such as Cervantes, Conrad, Büchner, Mallarmé, Joyce, and Celan.

73. Chester, Pamela. **Engendering Slavic Literature**. xvii, 249p.: illus. Bloomington: Indiana University Press, 1996. Includes bibliographical references and index.

This collection of 11 essays includes non-Russian Slavic literary topics in addition to Russian ones. The authors "approach texts written by both women and men, setting their writings and careers in their temporal and social contexts" (p. viii). They maintain that by paying attention to issues of gender they also become aware of other "crucial categories of human difference" (p. viii). The chronological coverage is 19th and 20th centuries.

74. Danow, David. **Models of Narrative: Theory and Practice**. 1st ed. 202p. New York: St. Martin's Press, 1997. Includes bibliographical references.

Danow explores several authors' works (Dostoevsky, Tolstoy, Pasternak, Marquez, Bulgakov, Hawthorne, O'Connor, Endo, and Babel) and analyzes them in terms of literary models. In his parlance, "a model may be conceived as a predetermined configuration of ideas that serve as an explanatory or heuristic device" (p. 1). In this volume he intends to "outline the bare lineaments of this seminal but largely ignored topic" and explore "what amounts to not only a common mode of approach in both scientific and humanistic endeavor but a highly productive mode of human conceptualization, deserving far greater attention" (p. 1).

75. **The Great Bear: A Thematic Anthology of Oral Poetry in the Finno-Ugrian Languages**. Edited by Lauri Honko, Senni Timonen, and Michael Branch. Translated by Keith Bosley. 787p. New York: Oxford University Press, 1994. Includes bibliographical references.

This volume includes folklore concerning the bear as it has appeared among the Hungarians, Estonians, Latvians, Komis, Udmurts, Khanty, Karelians, and other peoples whose language is of Finno-Ugric origin. This extensive study, over 700 pages, contains not only translations but also commentary on thematic strands that appear throughout the folk literature. These links in the folk literature contribute evidence to the idea of Finno-Ugrian affinity. Unfortunately, the volume does not include an index.

76. **O Rus!: Studia Litteraria Slavica in Honorem Hugh McLean**. Edited by Simon Karlinsky, James L. Rice, and Barry P. Scherr. 530p. Oakland, Calif.: Berkeley Slavic Specialties, 1995. Includes bibliographical references.

This collection of articles in honor of Hugh McLean's 70th birthday covers a wide area of Slavic Linguistics and Literature contributed by colleagues and former students. A bibliography of Hugh McLean's writings from 1949 to 1994, compiled by Molly Molloy, is also included.

77. Lord, Albert Bates. **The Singer Resumes the Tale**. Edited by Mary Louise Lord. xiii, 258p. Ithaca, N.Y.: Cornell University Press, 1995. Includes bibliography and index.

Although Albert Lord died in 1991, his wife, Mary Louise Lord, brought together the various collections of notes and chapters that he intended to be the body of this book. It continues the critical work he began in *The Singer of Tales*, published in 1960. In this volume Lord resumes his close examination of oral literature, a transnational genre.

78. Schenker, Alexander M. **The Dawn of Slavic: An Introduction to Slavic Philology**. xviii, 346p.: illus., maps. *Yale Language series*. New Haven, Conn.: Yale University Press, 1995. Includes bibliographical references and index.

Schenker's aim is to mediate between the immense body of scholarly literature in many languages and the beginning student of the earliest period of Slavic culture. In the first chapter he provides a historical setting for Slavic languages; in the second he covers language, one element of philology, and includes everything from linguistic reconstruction and phonetic laws to word order, lexical borrowing, and late Proto-Slavic dialect isoglosses. In Chapter 3 he discusses early writing and focuses on several examples of it. In an appendix he provides other useful material on the rise of Slavic philology, a chronological table of the development of Slavic, an Orthodox Church calendar, and samples of early Slavic writing.

Military Affairs

79. Cross, Robin. **Citadel: The Battle of Kursk**. ix, 272p., [16] p.: illus., maps, ports. New York: Sarpedon, 1993. First published in 1993 by Michael O'Mara Books, London. Includes bibliographical references (pp. [261]-262) and index.

Robin Cross has used an examination of the Battle of Kursk to examine the methods of command used by Hitler and Stalin. The last major German offensive of World War II illustrates Hitler's failing mental stability and Stalin's iron will. The author has also used this critical military battle to illustrate the nature of the war on the Eastern front and how it was viewed by soldiers on both sides.

80. **The European Rupture: The Defence Sector in Transition.** Edited by Mary Kaldor and Genevieve Schmeder. vii, 256p. Cheltenham, Eng.: Edward Elgar, 1997. Includes bibliographical references.

This is a collection of essays on the consequences of the end of the cold war for the defense sector. The book was the result of a program on the theme of security and economy held at the World Institute for Development Economics Research. The first three chapters of the book describe the background to the problem of defense in the region and examine the relationship between defense and economics. It is also in these first few chapters that the new issues that have resulted from the downfall of communism and the resultant economic transition in much of Europe are described. The second part of the book is a series of case studies: Britain, France, Germany, the former Czechoslovakia, Hungary, and Russia. The contributors to the book are Mary Kaldor, Genevieve Schmeder, Ulrich Albrecht, Petra Opitz, Yudit Kiss, Yevgeny Kusnetsov, and Alexander Ozhegov.

81. Müller, Rolf-Dieter, and Gerd R. Ueberschär. **Hitler's War in the East, 1941-1945: A Critical Assessment**. x, 405p. Providence, R.I.: Berghahn Books, 1997. Includes bibliographical references.

This valuable bibliography and research summary intends to provide the user with a comprehensive look at a complicated and multifaceted subject. It is arranged in five parts: (a) policy and strategy; (b) the military campaign; (c) the ideologically motivated war of annihilation in the East; (d) the occupation; and (e) the results of the war and coming to terms with them. Each section begins with a research summary and is followed by a classified enumerative bibliography of works in that area.

82. Ulrich, Marybeth P. **Democratizing Communist Militaries: The Cases of the Czech and Russian Armed Forces**. xiii, 292p.: illus. Ann Arbor: University of Michigan Press, 1999. Includes bibliographical references (pp. 259-81) and index.

In this work Marybeth Ulrich examines the changing military institutions in Russia and the Czech Republic. "The main thesis of this study is that political systems matter and are indeed, determinants of patterns of civil-military relations" (p. 2). Ulrich believes that a new level of military professionalism is necessary if the military is to become an effective institution in the changing environments in these two countries. Taking a topical approach, the author begins with a discussion of the theory behind democratic civil-military relations. She then explores such issues as democratization programs in the region, the needs of the military in these societies, and the effectiveness of the military. The book includes two appendixes on military contacts conducted in each of these countries.

The Arts

83. **Socialist Realism Without Shores**. Edited by Thomas Lahusen and Evgeny Dobrenko. vi, 369p. *Post-Contemporary Interventions*. Durham, N.C.: Duke University Press, 1997. Includes bibliographical references and index.

This collection of essays is enlarged from its first issuance in a special number of the *South Atlantic Quarterly* (Vol. 94, No. 3, summer 1995). The added essays address socialist realism beyond the Soviet camp, and look at Chinese, East German, Hungarian, French, Polish, and even American socialist realism.

Society, Social Issues, Sociology

84. **Between Plan and Market: Social Change in the Baltic States and Russia**. Edited by Blom Riamo, Harri Melin, and Jouko Nikula. ix, 182p. Berlin: Walter de Gruyter, 1996. Includes bibliography, notes, and contributors.

An introductory essay by the editors and eight other essays by various contributors make up this volume. The purpose of the work is to describe and analyze the "changes that are happening in this region in the class structure and work organizations, in issues of ethnicity, culture and civil society. Problems of social networks and the different forms of capital, as defined in Bourdieu's sense, are also covered in the project" (p. 1). Individual articles focus on obstacles to capitalist development, social stratification, the working-class movement, social change and marginality, the emergence of civil society, privatization, and women and rural development.

85. Crowe, David. **A History of the Gypsies of Eastern Europe and Russia**. xvi, 317p.: map. New York: St. Martin's Press, 1994. Includes bibliographical references (pp. [291]-309) and index.

The Gypsies or Roma originally entered Eastern Europe during the Middle Ages from northern India. In spite of the fact that there were significant contributions by the Roma to the cultures of Eastern Europe and Russia, they were always treated with disrespect. Crowe examines the presence of Gypsies in Bulgaria, Czechoslovakia, Hungary, Romania, Russia, and Yugoslavia, and outlines their history and social and cultural contributions to the areas where they migrated.

86. French, R. A. **Plans, Pragmatism and People: The Legacy of Soviet Planning for Today's Cities**. xi, 233p.: illus. *Pitt Series in Russian and East European Studies*, no. 26. Pittsburgh, Pa.: University of Pittsburgh Press, 1995. Includes bibliographical references (pp. 207-25) and index.

"In broad terms, the thesis of this book is that a socialist city did indeed develop, but that its characteristics and thus its distinctiveness are an amalgam, on the one hand of socialist features deriving from Marxist theory which postulates a very high level of centralized state power and planned operation of the economy, and on the other hand of surviving elements of earlier capitalism and new elements of rediscovered capitalism, the whole amalgam being heavily affected by those uncontrolled and surely ideologically uncontrollable elements, the individual and technology" (p. ix).

87. **Family, Women, and Employment in Central-Eastern Europe**. Edited by Barbara Lobodzinska. xxiv, 315p.: tables. *Contributions in Sociology*. Westport, Conn.: Greenwood Press, 1995. Includes bibliographical references (pp. [285]-300) and indexes.

The contributors to this volume present views from within socialist countries and those of Westerners who have addressed similar concerns outside of a socialist society. "The analysis focuses on the social changes that took place after the 1989 shift and on those aspects of family and women's life that are different from those in the Western democracies. The authors' scrutiny addresses the following points: legislation, the economy, social and family services, political participation, employment, income, educational priorities, agriculture and farming on family farms, health care, and changes in attitudes" (p. xix).

88. Ray, Larry J. **Social Theory and the Crisis of State Socialism**. xi, 288p.: illus. *Studies of Communism in Transition*. Cheltenham, Eng.: Edward Elgar, 1996. Includes bibliographical references (pp. 249-81) and index.

Following a multichapter analysis of the fall of state socialism in Eastern Europe from a theoretical point of view, the author proposes "a theory of the social dynamics of integration, legitimization and change in bureaucratic-socialist societies which both accounts for the crises in general, and explains their nationally-specific forms" (p. 13).

89. Shavit, David. **Hunger for the Printed Word: Books and Libraries in the Jewish Ghettos of Nazi-Occupied Europe**. xi, 178p.: illus. Jefferson, N.C.: McFarland, 1997. Includes bibliographical references (pp. 155-73) and index.

David Shavit has worked on the subject of the ghetto libraries for some years. In this book he uses that research to present a lengthy analysis of the development, growth, and survival of ghetto libraries in Warsaw, Lodz, Kovno, Vilna, and Theresienstadt. He begins with a general description of Jewish libraries. He then discusses the Jewish ghettos of Eastern Europe. Subsequent chapters are devoted to the ghetto libraries of individual cities. The book demonstrates the survival of a society's culture even under the most severe circumstances. "It is not my intention to build up a myth about the role played by libraries, books, and reading in the ghettos. What was organized with the great effort may today seem extremely meager or of little significance. . . . It is doubtless a fact that mental activity helped some of the inmates to overcome, at least temporarily, the physical elements of their existence" (p. 153).

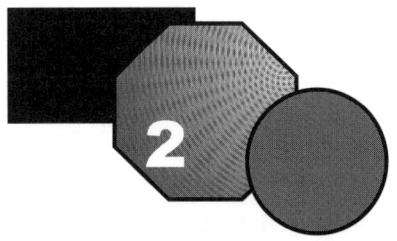

Russia, the Soviet Union, and the Russian Federation

General Reference Works

90. Benson, Morton. **Dictionary of Russian Personal Names: With a Revised Guide to Stress and Morphology.** 174p. Cambridge, Eng.: Cambridge University Press, 1992. Includes bibliographical references (pp. 173-74).

"This Dictionary has been compiled to meet the need for a reference work on the stress and morphology of Russian personal names. It indicates the stress of approximately 23,000 surnames and describes general rules that enable users to determine the stress of surnames not listed. It also fully describes the declension of surnames, with their stress shifts, and lists the most frequently used Russian given names and their principal diminutives" (frontispiece).

Bibliographies

91. **Russian Modernism: The Collections of the Getty Research Institute for the History of Art and the Humanities.** David Woodruff and Ljiljana Grubisic. 215p.: illus. (some col.). Santa Monica, Calif.: Getty Research Institute for the History of Art and the Humanities, 1997. Includes bibliographical references and index.

This 866-item bibliography covers "Russian Modernist periodicals, monographs, and ephemera in the collection of the Getty Research Institute for the History of Art and the Humanities; it does not include the Research Institute's complete holdings in the area of Russian art and literature" (p. 1). Each item includes a complete bibliographic description, as well as notes on the contents and distinctive bibliographic features. All items are arranged alphabetically by author or title.

92. Boilard, Steve D. **Reinterpreting Russia: An Annotated Bibliography of Books on Russia, the Soviet Union, and the Russian Federation, 1991-1996**. xxii, 281p. *Magill Bibliographies*. Lanham, Md.: Scarecrow Press, 1997. Includes author index.

By compiling this annotated bibliography, the author intends "to advance understanding of Russia by listing, categorizing, and describing some 600 recent books concerning Russia" (p. xx). Besides a brief introduction, each of the five sections making up the book (Reference Works and General History, Medieval Russia, imperial Russia, the USSR, and the Russian Federation) includes an introduction setting that period in context. Each of the last three sections has subsections entitled "Politics and Government," "Society and Culture," "Economics and Industry," and "Foreign Policy and Military Affairs." There is an author, title, and brief subject index. Each annotation is descriptive of the contents of the work. Unfortunately, the author has neglected to include series statements in his bibliographic citations.

93. Kavass, Igor I. **Demise of the Soviet Union: A Bibliographic Survey of English Writings on the Soviet Legal System, 1990-1991**. xxiv, 288p. Buffalo, N.Y.: W. S. Hein, 1992. Includes bibliographical references and index.

This bibliography is a sequel to Igor Kavass' earlier compilations *Soviet Law in English* and *Gorbachev's Law*. As with his earlier volumes, Kavass has included descriptions of books, articles, papers, and other publications in English. The entries are arranged by author in the first section and the same entries are arranged by subject in the second section. Each section is preceded by a "checklist" of the terms used, i.e., a list of author names precedes Section 1, a list of subject headings precedes Section 2. Many entries have annotations. Some annotations include information on the exact contents of collections of essays. The introductory information contains a list of legal resources that may be of particular interest to the researcher.

94. Pozdeeva, I. V., and Zora Kipel. **Church Slavonic, Glagolitic, and Petrine Civil Script Printed Books in the New York Public Library: A Preliminary Catalog**. 431p., [43] p. New York: The Slavic and Baltic Division, 1995. At head of title: *Draft*. The New York Public Library.

The Church Slavonic collection at the New York Public Library has previously been described in brief publications. It is a testament to the significance of that collection that this detailed descriptive has appeared. This catalog consists of two listings. The first, in Russian, is Pozdeeva's description of the materials. The second is the transliterated cataloging for each item in the collection. The name and place of publication are in Latin characters. The index to the marginalia is in Russian.

Biographies

95. Ekedahl, Carolyn McGiffert, and Melvin A. Goodman. **The Wars of Eduard Shevardnadze**. xxiii, 331p.: illus., maps. University Park: Pennsylvania State University Press, 1997. Includes bibliographical references (pp. [319]-324) and index.

Shevardnadze was Gorbachev's foreign minister. Together they were responsible for developing glasnost and perestroika in order to change what they had characterized as a rotten system. The authors "describe and analyze Shevardnadze's contribution to the effort to restructure Soviet domestic policy and revolutionize foreign policy. . . . [They] also assess his responsibility for the Soviet collapse and the leadership role he played in the independent state of Georgia that emerged after the collapse" (pp. xi-xii).

96. Hamburg, Gary M. **Boris Chicherin and Early Russian Liberalism, 1828-1866**. ix, 443p. Stanford, Calif.: Stanford University Press, 1992. Includes bibliographical references (pp. [415]-431) and index.

Chicherin was a major figure in Russian intellectual history in the last half of the 19th century. His interests included Russian history, European comparative politics, the history of political thought, metaphysics, the philosophy of law, and chemistry. He was also notable as one of the most powerful liberal thinkers in the decades preceding the Russian Revolution. This volume traces both his development as an intellectual and his impact on early Russian liberalism.

97. Howard, Edward Lee. **Safe House: The Compelling Memoirs of the Only CIA Spy to Seek Asylum in Russia**. 299p. Bethesda, Md.: National Press Books, 1995. "An enigma book." Includes index.

This is the story of Edward Howard, who was accused by the CIA of betraying the U.S. intelligence community in Moscow. Howard defected to Russia. In this book he makes the argument that he was actually used by the Russians to divert attention from their real double agent. An appendix includes documents supporting the author's claim.

98. Knight, Amy W. **Beria, Stalin's First Lieutenant**. xvi, 312p., [9] p. of plates: illus., map. Princeton, N.J.: Princeton University Press, 1993. Includes bibliographical references (pp. [281]-294) and index.

Knight declares that the present study may be considered a revisionist history "because, in examining the career of one political figure, it questions some common assumptions about Stalinism" (p. 9). In carrying out her task she not only describes and analyzes Beria's rise during the Stalin era, but also tries to examine his own personal motivations and his relations with Stalin and other powerful figures.

99. Lebed, Aleksandr. **General Alexander Lebed: My Life and My Country**. 385p. Washington, D.C.: Regnery; Distributed to the trade by National Book Network, 1997. Includes index.

In the early chapters of this volume General Lebed recounts his youth, his training as a cadet, and his desire to become a military officer. Most of the volume, however, is devoted to the campaigns in Afghanistan and in the Caucasus, where he served from the 1980s to the early 1990s. In the 1990s, especially after the fall of the Soviet Union, he emerged as a political figure in the newly created Russian Federation.

100. Lenin, Vladimir Il'ich. **The Unknown Lenin: From the Secret Archive**. Edited by Richard Pipes and David Brandenberger. Translated by Catherine A. Fitzpatrick. xx, 204p., [8] p. of plates: illus. *Annals of Communism*. New Haven, Conn.: Yale University Press, 1996. Includes bibliographical references and index.

The documents appearing in this volume were not published in Lenin's complete works or the publication entitled *Leninskii sbornik*, except if the documents appeared but were censored. The 113 documents, culled from several archives in Russia, present a complex view of the "unknown Lenin." They include letters, draft resolutions, telegrams, depositions, policy documents, private notes, reports, and memorandums. An appendix includes communications from various people (Frunze, Trotsky, Chicherin, et al.) to Lenin.

101. Levin, Aryeh. **Envoy to Moscow: Memoirs of an Israeli Ambassador, 1988-92**. xx, 417p., [16] p. of plates: illus., ports. *Cummings Center series*. London: Frank Cass, 1996.

These fascinating memoirs of the Israeli ambassador in Moscow during the fading of the Soviet state witness the political, cultural, and economic events of that tumultuous time. Levin had a 40-year career as a diplomat, serving several Israeli posts over the world. Of particular importance here is his recounting of the immense Jewish emigration from Russia after 1991.

102. McCauley, Martin. **Who's Who in Russia Since 1900**. xxiv, 268p.: maps. London: Routledge, 1997. Includes bibliographical references (pp. 267-68).

This book provides a general biographical guide for the student of Russia in the 20th century. The biographical entries provide basic information on the lives and careers of those listed here. The volume includes a glossary and chronology and numerous maps. However there is no index. There is an extensive introductory essay on the history of Russia in this century. However, there is no information on the selection criteria. "*Who's Who in Russia Since 1900* is a unique reference guide which examines the leading political, economic, cultural, military, scientific and sporting personalities in Russia and the Soviet Union from 1900 to the present" (back cover).

103. Solovev, Vladimir, and Elena Klepikova. **Boris Yeltsin: A Political Biography**. 320p.: illus. London: Weidenfeld & Nicolson, 1992. Includes bibliographical references (pp. 295-302) and index.

This political biography of Yeltsin is divided into three parts. Part 1 covers the period from 1985 to March of 1989 as Yeltsin the politician was born. Part 2 chronicles the parallel lives of Gorbachev and Yeltsin. The third part extends to the winter of 1991 as the new Russia emerges.

104. Thielmann, John H. **Escape to Freedom**. iii, 176p.: illus., maps. Mountain View, Calif.: J. H. Thielmann, 1995. Includes bibliographical references (p. 176).

This autobiography relates the author's childhood in Russia and his family's escape in 1929 through Siberia, China, Korea, and eventually to California, where they finally settled.

105. Yeltsin, Boris Nikolayevich. **The View from the Kremlin**. xix, 316p.: illus., ports. London: HarperCollins, 1994. Translated from the Russian.

Catherine Fitzpatrick has translated Boris Yeltsin's journal written between August 1991 and October 1993; it covers one of modern Russia's most turbulent periods. It is arranged chronologically and includes an appendix with biographical information on major figures of the period and some extracts from the "Archives of the General Secretary." The translator has made every attempt to maintain the tone of the original manuscript. "Clearly, *The View from the Kremlin* is not the last word on the events it describes. It is, however, a permanent record of a period of historic upheaval in Russia as seen by the man chosen by his people as their leader" (p. vii).

106. Zhirinovskii, Vladimir. **My Struggle: The Explosive Views of Russia's Most Controversial Political Figure**. 144p. New York: Barricade Books, 1996.

This autobiographical account of V. Zhirinovskii's rise to prominence also includes insight into the political and economic views of the author.

107. **My Russia: The Political Autobiography of Gennady Zyuganov**. Edited by G. A. Zyuganov and Vadim Medish. xiii, 198p.: illus. Armonk, N.Y: M. E. Sharpe, 1997. Articles and excerpts from earlier books; also includes the full text of his book *Russia and the Contemporary World*. Includes index.

Gennady Zyuganov is a Russian communist politician who ran for president in the 1996 election campaign. This book is more a compendium of articles and short books that he has written rather than a conventional autobiography. It provides insight about the political and economic platform of this well-known political figure, as well as his reflections about his loss in the 1996 election.

Handbooks and Encyclopedias

108. **Inside the New Russia: Your Source of Information.** 333p.: illus., maps. Broken Arrow, Okla.: SC Publishing, 1994. Includes bibliographical references (pp. 332-33).

This is primarily a guide to Russia's many ethnic groups. "The book helps the reader to understand who the people of the CIS are and why they became the nation they are today" (p. 6). The book has three parts. The first is an introduction on religion and the Bible in Russia. Part 2 is a collection of demographic statistics on the republics of the CIS. Part 3 is comprised of short essays on each of Russia's ethnic groups, arranged alphabetically.

109. **The Cambridge Encyclopedia of Russia and the Former Soviet Union.** Edited by Archie Brown, Michael Charles Kaser, and Gerald Stanton Smith. 2nd ed. xi, 604p.: illus. (some col.), col. maps. Cambridge, Eng.: Cambridge University Press, 1994. Rev. ed. of: *The Cambridge Encyclopedia of Russia and the Soviet Union*, 1982.

This encyclopedia is a successor volume to *The Cambridge Encyclopedia of Russia and the Soviet Union*, which was published in 1982. Rather than being just a new edition, this volume can be considered a new work. It has increased the number of contributors by almost 20 percent, and has extended its thematic coverage. In addition, the effects of changes that have taken place over the intervening 12 years are also included. Particular attention is devoted to the last 10 years of the Soviet era and to the beginnings of the post-Soviet era. Individual sections cover the physical environment, the peoples, religion, history, art and architecture, language and literature, cultural life, the sciences, politics, economy, society, military power, and international relations.

110. Friedrich, Paul, and Norma Diamond. **Encyclopedia of World Cultures, Volume VI: Russia and Eurasia/China.** xlvii, 527p., [5] p.: maps. *Encyclopedia of World Cultures*, VI. New York: G. K. Hall, 1994. Includes bibliographical references and index. Filmography (p. 522).

This volume is one in a series with a most ambitious goal. The set will provide information to a wide range of readers, those seeking general information as well as the specialist. In this volume the first 414 pages are devoted to Russia and Eurasia and 111 groups are described. Each entry is contributed by an expert on that group.

In every entry or "cultural summary" a number of areas are described. Summaries begin with a list of ethnonyms or alternative names for the culture, including those given by outsiders. The section on orientation discusses the location of the culture physically, demographically, and its linguistic affiliation. Summaries also cover the history of the culture, a discussion of their settlements and economy, kinship, marriage and family structure, sociopolitical organization, religion, and expressive culture. Each summary ends in a selected bibliography. There are several maps in the volume that locate exactly each culture described. Another feature of the series is that the volumes each include a glossary of technical terms, an ethnonym index, and a filmography.

111. Milner-Gulland, Robin. **The Russians**. xvii, 260p.: illus., maps. Oxford, Eng.: Blackwell Publishers, 1997. Includes select bibliography, chronological table to 1917, and index.

This handbook, one of a series on the Peoples of Europe, covers basic topics on Russia. Individual chapters deal with Rus as land and people, Rus as people and as state, belief systems, literature, and art. The author points out that this volume is a complement to her *Cultural Atlas of Russia* (1989) that devotes more attention to political history.

Libraries, Archives, and Museums

112. Butler, Lois J., and Lubomyr R. Wynar. **Guide to Information Resources in Ethnic Museum, Library, and Archival Collections in the United States**. xiii, 369p. *Bibliographies and Indexes in Ethnic Studies*, 7. Westport, Conn.: Greenwood Press, 1996. Includes alphabetical indexes of original names and geographical indexes organized by state and city.

Between 1993 and 1995, a "comprehensive national survey of ethnic and other institutions was conducted by the compilers. The results of that survey are presented in this book. Over 70 ethnic groups are represented here. Each entry includes the name, type of institution, address and phone/fax numbers, sponsoring organizations, personnel contact person, scope, availability and fees, visitors, staff, operating budget, publications, collection, and a brief annotation. This is a very helpful resource with a variety of uses. It certainly fulfills its stated purpose of providing "comprehensive and current coverage of the description of these ethnic resources that are authentic sources of information about America's diverse cultural groups" (p. x).

Description and Travel

113. Akchurin, Marat. **Red Odyssey: A Journey Through the Soviet Republics**. 1st ed. viii, 406p.: illus., map. New York: HarperCollins, 1992. Includes index.

This is a fascinating memoir of a Muscovite's trip through Transcaucasia, Soviet Central Asia, and the Volga River region.

114. De Villiers, Marq. **Down the Volga: A Journey Through Mother Russia in a Time of Troubles**. 1st American ed. xvi, 317p.: maps. New York: Viking, 1992. Includes bibliographical references (pp. [306]-312) and index.

The author made a journey down the Volga River in the summer of 1990 in order to see the country from its heart. The description of his 3,500-mile journey is a snapshot of a particular place at an important time in its history. His stated purpose is to show why Russia endures, even in the midst of its time of troubles.

115. Durden-Smith, Jo. **Russia: A Long-Shot Romance**. xii, 318p. New York: Alfred A. Knopf, 1994.

Durden-Smith is a writer and filmmaker. This book is about his experiences in Russia on several visits between April 1989 and October 1992.

116. Fisher-Ruge, Lois. **Survival in Russia: Chaos and Hope in Everyday Life**. vii, 187p.: illus. Boulder, Colo.: Westview Press, 1993.

Lois Fisher-Ruge is a foreign correspondent working in Germany and Moscow. In this book she examines living conditions in Russia today. Much of her book is devoted to social issues such as the economy, education, crime, and social welfare. "Lois Fisher skillfully interweaves, anecdote, conversation and observation to round out the picture of a society in turmoil" (p. 187).

117. Kapuscinski, Ryszard. **Imperium**. x, 331p. New York: Alfred A. Knopf, 1994.

This book is a personal report of journeys that the author made over 60 years. It is arranged in three parts. The first part is a narration of his journeys in Russia from 1939 to 1967. Part 2 covers the years 1989-1991, when the Soviet empire was in decline. The third part, covering the years 1992-1993, is a collection of reflections, observations, and notes that arose in the margins of [his] travels, conversations, and readings.

118. Kramer, Mark. **Travels with a Hungry Bear: A Journey to the Russian Heartland**. xii, 320p.: illus., maps. Boston: Houghton Mifflin, 1996. "A Richard Todd book."

The author set out to discover why a country with farms stretching the length of a continent had such difficulty producing food. "The spectacle of an empire that could loft astronauts or blow up the planet but couldn't supply its bakers was troubling and puzzling" (p. xi). Kramer traveled around Russia beginning in 1989 and thought he had finished his book only to be compelled to return after the events of August 1991. He focuses on the everyday activities and functioning of the farm. The author relied on interpreters during his travels to gather information. Mark Kramer was a writer for the *New York Times* magazine.

119. Krause, Aurel, and Arthur Krause. **To the Chukchi Peninsula and to the Tlingit Indians, 1881/1882: Journals and Letters by Aurel and Arthur Krause**. xiii, 230p.: illus. Fairbanks: University of Alaska Press, 1993. Includes bibliographical references (pp. 227-30).

These travel journals and letters were written by Aurel and Arthur Krause in 1881 when they left Berlin and traveled to the Chukchi Peninsula. Their journal ethnography was published separately in German in 1885 and subsequently translated and published in English in 1956. The translated documents appearing in this volume round out their expedition by narrating details of their travels and firsthand descriptions of the lives and customs of the Tlingit Indians.

120. Taplin, Mark. **Open Lands: Travels Through Russia's Once Forbidden Places**. 1st ed. 376p.: illus., map. South Royalton, Vt.: Steerforth Press, 1997. Includes bibliographical references (pp. [351]-357) and index.

After Russia and the United States signed the "Open Lands" agreement in 1992, citizens from both countries were allowed unrestricted travel throughout both countries. Taplin had been in Russia in the mid-1980s and been subject to the travel constraints then in place. This narrative describes his travels after 1992, to the formerly "forbidden" places in the former Soviet Union.

121. Young, James. **Moscow Mule**. 245p. London: Arrow, 1997. Originally published London: Century, 1996.

This is an unusual travelogue of Moscow in the early 1990s. Young gives no context for the trip in an introduction. In some ways it reads like a novel, an interesting novel that captures you from its first page.

Anthropology and Folklore

122. Bly, Robert, and Marion Woodman. **The Maiden King: The Reunion of Masculine and Feminine**. 1st ed. xviii, 264p. New York: Henry Holt, 1998. Includes bibliographical references (pp. [235]-246) and index.

In this book Robert Bly and Marion Woodman explore the Russian talk of the "Maiden Tsar" from the point of view of a poet and analyst. While they do not discuss the Russian context for this story, they do discuss many interesting aspects of this complex folk symbol.

123. Hellberg-Hirn, Elena. **Soil and Soul: The Symbolic World of Russianness**. 289p.: illus. Aldershot, Hants, Eng.; Brookfield, Vt.: Ashgate, 1998. Includes bibliographical references (pp. 257-78) and index.

"In the book, a number of stereotypes and signs of Russia, such as the double headed eagle, the tsar, bread-and-salt, troika, the Orthodox cross, etc., are presented as a consistent set of metaphors, revealing a symbolic world made by and for the Russians in order to sustain and reinforce their group identity" (back cover). The author, a native Russian who emigrated to Sweden, relies on a body of existing ethnographic work as well as her personal knowledge of Russian identity in this study.

124. Kaarsberg, Hans S., John Richard Krueger, and Arash Bonmanshinov. **Among the Kalmyks of the Steppes on Horseback and by Troika: A Journey Made in 1890: The Travelogue and Ethnography of a Danish Physician in Russia**. 124p.: illus. *Publications of the Mongolia Society*. Bloomington, Ind.: Mongolia Society, 1996.

When Hans Kaarsberg traveled from Denmark to the Steppes of Russia in the 19th century, ethnography was a new science. Much of his original 600-page volume was more of a traveler's account of the region than an ethnography. John Krueger has extracted those passages that fall into the latter category and translated them for this volume. Along with the text the translator has included a biography of Dr. Kaarsberg, a glossary of terms, and a brief commentary. The original text also included numerous photographs and some drawings. A few of the drawings have been reproduced here.

125. Mastiugina, T. M., L. S. Perepelkin, Vitalii Viacheslavovich Naumkin, and I. D. Zviagelskaia. **An Ethnic History of Russia: Pre-Revolutionary Times to the Present**. xiii, 244p. Westport, Conn.: Greenwood Press, 1996. "Prepared under the auspices of the Russian Center for Strategic Research and International Studies."

"This book describes the ethnic composition of Russia's population and the country's different 'national' territories; the authors, moreover, probe into the ethnic history of the Russian State, revealing the roots of ethnic and inter-regional problems" (p. xii). The authors are all Russian scholars of ethnology. Here they take a thematic approach to their subject discussing prerevolutionary ethnographies, changes in Russia's federative structure, classification of Russia's nationalities, and demographic processes in Russia. Finally, the authors examine the major national and socioeconomic problems facing Russia.

126. Peskov, Vasily. **Lost in the Taiga: One Russian Family's Fifty-Year Struggle for Survival and Religious Freedom in the Siberian Wilderness**. 1st ed. xv, 254p.: illus., maps. New York: Doubleday, 1994.

Written in the form of intermittent journal entries, this is the story of the Lykovs, a Russian family of Old Believers who lived in complete isolation in the coniferous forests of Siberia, some 100 kilometers for the nearest traces of humanity. The story begins in 1982 with the author's first visit to the family, and ends in 1992, the time of his last visit to the one remaining daughter.

127. **Gates of Mystery: The Art of Holy Russia**. Edited by Roderick Grierson. 1st ed. 336p.: illus. (some col.). Fort Worth, Tex.: InterCultural, [1993?]. Includes bibliographical references (pp. 328-29) and index.

This volume draws on the collection of the Russian Museum in St. Petersburg, perhaps the largest collection of Russian icons and liturgical art, to present a history of Russian religious art. Along with the numerous illustrations, each chapter of the book contains a lengthy essay by a specialist. These discuss the themes common to iconographic works, the techniques used to produce icons, and other important subjects in the study of iconography. The contributors are Evgeniia Petrova, Roderick Grierson, Sergei Averintsev, Simon Franklin, John Meyendorff, Olga Popova, Engelina Smirnova, Liudmila Likhacheva, Dariia Maltseva, and Robin Cormack. The book includes a glossary of terms.

The Arts

128. Stites, Richard. **Culture and Entertainment in Wartime Russia.** vi, 215p.: illus. Bloomington: Indiana University Press, 1995. Includes bibliographical references and index.

Many aspects of the history of World War II as it was experienced in the Soviet Union have been explored. In this volume a number of scholars have contributed studies on popular culture in Russia during that period. "The main focus of this volume is the resurfacing into public life of emotional and even spiritual expression, recently suppressed or distorted in the media during the 1930s" (p. 4). The essays cover radio popular music, theater, film, the press, classical music, and frontline entertainment. Contributors are Richard Stites, Jeffery Brooks, Louise McReynolds, James von Geldern, Harlow Robinson, Robert A. Rothstein, Harold Segel, Argyrios K. Pisiotis, Peter Kenz, Roszlinde Sartorti, and Nina Tumarkin.

129. **Mass Culture in Soviet Russia: Tales, Poems, Songs, Movies, Plays, and Folklore 1917-1953.** Edited by James Von Geldern and Richard Stites. xxix, 492p. Bloomington: Indiana University Press, 1995. Includes selected bibliography.

This volume includes materials originally gathered for a seminar offered at Stanford. The intent was to include materials from the official culture and the underground cultural movements. The time period covered encompasses some of the major historical events of the century: the revolution, the civil war, the Purges, World War II, and the postwar period. "The focus of the collection is not on great works of literary art, which have been available in translation for decades, but rather on the entertainment genres that both shaped and reflected the social, political, and personal values of the regime and the masses. Each entry is provided with a brief contextual introduction, giving its historical background and significance" (pp. xii-xiii). The four sections of the volume reflect the enormous cultural changes of each era: "The Revolution and the New Regime, 1917-1927," "The Stalinist Thirties," "Russia at War," and "The Post War Era." The materials selected range from historical works, e.g., "History of the CPSU," to film scenarios ("The Little Red Devils") to anecdotes.

General Studies

130. **Art of the Soviets: Painting, Sculpture, and Architecture in a One-Party State, 1917-1992.** Edited by Matthew Cullerne Bown and Brandon Taylor. viii, 231p., [4] p. of col. plates: illus. Manchester, Eng.: Manchester University Press, 1993. Includes index.

The 13 essays in this volume, in addition to the introduction, explore different aspects of art and architecture during the Soviet period. The essays cover topics such as Lenin's plan for monumental propaganda, allegory and iconography in Socialist Realist painting, the Soviet pavilion in Paris, Aleksandr Gerasimov, painting in non-Russian republics, the art of memory and retrospectivism, Ilya Glazunov, nonconformist art in Leningrad, and independent culture, as well as others.

131. Brumfield, William Craft. **Lost Russia: Photographing the Ruins of Russian Architecture**. ix, 132p.: illus., maps. Durham, N.C.: Duke University Press, 1995. Includes bibliographical references (pp. 129-30) and index.

The intention of this book is to provide a glimpse of Russian culture that is invisible to most eyes, the architectural monuments of the heartland. Photographs include those of "late medieval churches, with severe exteriors and fresco-covered interiors; of neoclassical estate houses and churches from the late 18th and 19th centuries; of historic Russian provincial towns, which have their own quiet beauty even in a state of dilapidation, as they usually are; and of Russia's remarkable log architecture" (p. viii).

132. Condee, Nancy. **Soviet Hieroglyphics: Visual Culture in Late Twentieth-Century Russia**. xxv, 179p. Bloomington: Indiana University Press, 1995. Compilation of seven articles translated from Russian. Includes bibliographical references and index.

"The chapters of this volume are all concerned in one way or another with visual culture, with objects or texts that engage us in a primarily visual apprehension. These include documentary and feature film; television news, game shows, advertisements, and soap operas; billboards, painting, board games, statues, cartoons and currency" (p. vii). The essays in this volume were contributed by Victoria E. Bonnell, Katerina Clark, Nancy Condee, Gregory Freidin, Helena Goscilo, John Kachur, Susan Larsen, Eric Naiman, Anne Nesbet, Vladimir Padunov, and Mikhail Yampolsky.

133. **Tekstura: Russian Essays on Visual Culture**. Edited by Alla Effimova and Lev Manovich. xxxi, 231p.: illus. Chicago: University of Chicago Press, 1993. Collections of essays, most are previously unpublished translations from the Russian.

This is a collection of essays on the many facets of Russia's visual culture. The contributors cover topics as diverse as theater and architecture. The contributors are V. N. Voloshinov, Sergei Eisenstein, Mikhail Bakhtin, Yury Lotman, Vladimir Paperny, Zinovy Zinik, Grigory Sternin, Boris Groys, Mikail Yampolsky, Mikhail Epshstein, Alexander Rappaport, Alexander Zchkarov, and Gennady Revzin. An enormous range of theoretical opinions are expressed in this one volume on Russian culture.

134. **Constructing Russian Culture in the Age of Revolution, 1881-1940**. Edited by Catriona Kelly and David Shepherd. xii, 358p.: illus. Oxford, Eng.: Oxford University Press, 1998. Includes bibliographical references (pp. [318]-329) and indexes.

This book attempts to present a more complete view of Russian culture than has been available previously by drawing more attention to the connections between literature and history. The chronological focus of this volume is the period from about 1881 to 1917. The chapters are arranged in three parts. Part 1, Prologue, consists of three essays on important key concepts (lichnost, obshchestvennost, sobornost, narodnost, and literaturnost) that are woven throughout the remaining materials. Part 2, Cultural Transformation and Late Imperial Russia, is the main part of the book. Part 3, Epilogue, Constructing a New Russia, Change and Continuity in the Aftermath of the Revolution, provides a deft summing up of the first two parts.

135. Lincoln, W. Bruce. **Between Heaven and Hell: The Story of a Thousand Years of Artistic Life in Russia**. xi, 511p., [24] p. of plates: illus. (some col.), ports. (some col.). New York: Penguin Books, 1998. Originally published New York: Viking Penguin, 1998. Includes bibliographical references and index.

"How did a country with such a tormented past bring such stunning works of art into being? To answer this question, W. Bruce Lincoln explores 10 centuries of artistic endeavor in a land uniquely suspended between East and West, past and future, sacred and secular" (book jacket). Professor Lincoln looks at all art forms as he explores Russia's artistic history, beginning with Kievan Rus and continuing to the present days. The author focuses on the context that molded Russian art, emphasizing the close relationship between art and politics. In so doing, he presents an explanation for the unique development of Russia's artistic forms.

136. Margolin, Victor. **The Struggle for Utopia: Rodchenko, Lissitzky, Moholy-Nagy, 1917-1946**. xiii, 261p.: illus. Chicago: University of Chicago Press, 1997. Includes bibliographical references and index.

As Margolin states in his introduction, "Each of the essays in this book focuses on a separate issue that involves one or more of the artists. By looking at how the three men operated in a set of specific circumstances, I hope to provide a better understanding of the larger questions about the relation of art and social life that frame this study" (p. 4).

137. **Laboratory of Dreams: The Russian Avant-Garde and Cultural Experiment**. Edited by Olga Matich and John E. Bowlt. xvii, 359p.: illus. Stanford, Calif.: Stanford University Press, 1996. Includes bibliographical references.

In the introduction to this collection of essays on the Russian avant-garde, Bowlt describes it thus: "The avant-garde ethos, then was not concerned merely with the destruction of old aesthetic and social norms and with new configurations of colored geometries and dissonant phonemes. It was an energetic force pointing to the transformation of the world by overcoming disciplinary, thematic, and biological frontiers" (p. 10). The essays collected here were originally presented at a conference in 1990 and are here arranged in four major areas and a postscript. The parts are (1) life creation: the search for a new body; (2) scientific discovery and cultural innovation; (3) word and image: manipulating semiotic systems; and (4) socialist realism as radical experiment.

138. Milner, John. **A Dictionary of Russian and Soviet Artists, 1420-1970**. 483p.: illus. (some col.). Woodbridge, Suffolk, Eng.: Antique Collectors' Club, 1993. Includes bibliographical references (pp. 482-83).

This impressive dictionary of Russian and Soviet artists includes a 20-page essay on the history of Russian art. Following this introduction, entries on Russian and Soviet artists from 1420 to 1970 are included. Each entry includes the full name, birth and death dates, a brief description, a major secondary work (article or book) devoted to the artist, and an indication of the collections that feature the work of the artist. Black-and-white, as well as color, illustrations of well-known or unusual works are present throughout the dictionary.

139. Roberts, Peter. **George Costakis: A Russian Life in Art**. xv, 223p., [16] p. of plates: illus. (some col.). New York: George Braziller, 1994. Includes bibliographical references and index.

George Costakis was a Greek national. However, he was born in Russia and maintained an active interest in Russian avant-garde art. This is the story of his collection of rare Russian avant-garde paintings. This book is drawn from recordings of Costakis describing his experiences in Russia. Peter Roberts transcribed taped conversations he had while Costakis was ill in 1987. The book tells the story of the method of collection, but more importantly of the school of art itself during Russia's turbulent Soviet period.

140. Todorov, Vladislav. **Red Square, Black Square: Organon for Revolutionary Imagination**. xi, 200p. Albany: State University of New York Press, 1995. Includes bibliographical references (pp. 189-93) and index.

The topic and theme of this work is best expressed in the author's own words. "I conceive my work as an action performed with the sclerotic end of the Communist endeavor. I perform with the end(s) of the doctrine. And the 'ornamental mannerism,' as I name the style manifested throughout the book, comes to expose my aesthetic attitude toward the dead-ends of modernism" (p. 8). The author believes that the communist system reduced modernist style to socialist realism and describes that process in this study.

141. Von Geldern, James, and Louise McReynolds. **Entertaining Tsarist Russia: Tales, Songs, Plays, Movies, Jokes, Ads, and Images from Russian Urban Life, 1779-1917**. xxvii, 394p.: illus. Bloomington: Indiana University Press, 1998. Includes bibliographical references.

This is an anthology of music, tales, plays, movie scripts, and jokes. They have been compiled to give the student of Russian history a glimpse of a side of life in the country rarely studied. "This anthology is intended to introduce readers to imperial Russia's emerging popular and commercial urban culture, and the groups that produced and consumed it" (p. xiii). The materials are arranged chronologically. Within the chronological divisions they are further arranged by medium. The chronological divisions 1779-1825, 1825-1860, 1861-1881, 1882-1905, 1906-1917 correspond to major historical milestones. Each section includes a brief introduction. The book includes a glossary of terms to assist the reader. The book lacks an index and bibliography.

142. **World Congress for Soviet and East European Studies (4th) 1990: Harrogate, England. New Perspectives on Russian and Soviet Artistic Culture**. Edited by John O. Norman. xiv, 158p., [32] p. of plates: illus. New York: St. Martin's Press, 1994. Includes bibliographical references and index.

The papers in this volume were originally given at the Fourth World Congress for Soviet and East European Studies, 1990. The essays included here cover a broad range of topics: estate design, Russian architecture, folk art, and painting in the Early Soviet period, to name only a few. "While this volume reveals the unusual degree to which the state has attempted to define and monopolize the Russian/Soviet cultural agenda, it also demonstrates the consistent ability of talent and creative vision to advance its own agenda, voice the aspirations of those spiritually or physically disposed by both Russian and Soviet variants of an imperial system, participate in the larger world community" (p. xv). The contributors are Milka Bliznakov, William Brumfield, Anthony Cross, James Curtis, Musya Glants, Alison Hilton, Catherine Nepomnyashchy, John Norman, Elena Ovsiannikova, and Priscila Roosevelt.

Architecture

143. **Russian Housing in the Modern Age: Design and Social History**. Edited by William Craft Brumfield and Blair A. Ruble. xiv, 322p.: illus. *Woodrow Wilson Center series*. Cambridge, Eng.: Cambridge University Press, 1993. Includes index.

"*Russian Housing in the Modern Age: Design and Social History* is a multidisciplinary study of the various forms of housing that have been built throughout the twentieth century in Russia" (frontispiece). Contributors are Robert Edelman, William Craft Brumfield, Milka Bliznakov, Vladimir Paperny, Stephen Kotkin, Judith Pallot, Blair A. Ruble, and Aleksandr Vysokovskii.

144. Shvidkovskii, D. O. **The Empress and the Architect: British Architecture Gardens at the Court of Catherine the Great**. vii, 273p.: illus. (some col.). New Haven, Conn.: Yale University Press, 1996.

The aim of this book is to carry out a detailed study of the significance of Anglo-Russian architectural links that were strongly forged during the reign of Catherine II. Individual chapters are devoted to Charles Cameron, a famous British architect of the time who spearheaded the Russian-British connection; the artistic worlds of Tsarskoye Selo; Pavlovsk; orientalism in Russian neo-classical architecture; Russian neo-gothic in the age of classicism; and Adam Menelaws and William Hastie.

Fine Arts

145. **Chagall: A Retrospective**. Edited by Jacob Baal-Teshuva. 374p.: illus. (some col.). Paris: Hugh Lauter Levin Associates, 1995. Includes bibliographical references (pp. 9-10).

This wonderful volume, published 10 years after Chagall's death in 1985, offers a chronologically arranged retrospective of his work. What makes it all the more interesting for the reader is that in addition to presenting his various works alongside each other by period, the editor has included speeches, excerpts of articles, and memoirs by Chagall and others in the art world to introduce each section. Titles of some of the sections include "The Russian Years," "Chagall in Paris," "The Circus, the Ballet, and the Opera," "Chagall's Ceramics, Sculpture, and Stained Glass," "Tapestries and Mosaics," "The Biblical Message," and "Remembering Chagall."

146. Barooshian, Vahan D. **V. V. Vereshchagin: Artist at War**. xvii, 198p., [8] p. of plates: illus. (some col.), ports. Gainesville: University Press of Florida, 1993. Includes bibliographical references (pp. [163]-185).

In the last quarter of the 19th century Vereshchagin was one of the most famous artists in the Western world. He had exhibits in Paris, London, Berlin, Vienna, New York, Chicago, Philadelphia, Baltimore, and other major cities. As a realist, many saw him as the foundation for an American school of painting. This is the first extensive study of Vereshchagin in English that also includes the study of the painter's life in the context of the social, political, economic, and cultural aspects of the time.

147. Bown, Matthew Cullerne. **Socialist Realist Painting**. xviii, 506p.: illus. (some col.). New Haven, Conn.: Yale University Press, 1998. Includes bibliographical references (pp. 468-79) and index.

This volume presents a comprehensive examination of Socialist Realist painting from its origins in art and revolutionary thought prior to 1917 to its collapse in the late 1980s. The contents progress in chronological fashion beginning with Russian painting and revolutionary aesthetics before the October 1917 revolution. Each of the chapters covers approximately five 15-year spans with the exception of the final chapter that is devoted to the decline of Socialist Realism, which began in 1964 and finally ended in 1991. Each chapter is replete with reproductions of many examples of Socialist Realist masterworks, and the text expertly guides the reader through the interpretation of the paintings and the social context in which they were made.

148. Kaganov, Grigorii Zosimovich. **Images of Space: St. Petersburg in the Visual and Verbal Arts**. xxv, 206p.: illus., map. Stanford, Calif.: Stanford University Press, 1997. Includes index.

There have been many studies about the architecture and landscape of St. Petersburg. What is unusual in this study is that it examines not the buildings and geographic features but the spaces that result from those features. "And so this book is about the interpretation of this unique space of Petersburg in Russian and Soviet art. It is about the changes in artistic 'spatial conception' (Florensky's term) that were inwardly linked with the development of our culture and that manifested themselves in poetry and prose, in architecture and fashion, in interior design and easel painting" (p. xvi). The book includes numerous illustrations and a map of St. Petersburg.

149. Malevich, Kazimir, and Serge Fauchereau. **Malevich**. 128p.: illus. London: Academy Editions, 1992. Translation of Malevich.

This is primarily a volume of plates reproducing works of Kazimir Malevich. Malevich was an avant-garde artist in prerevolutionary Russia who managed to continue his work after the revolution. This book includes a brief biographical sketch that places Malevich work in context. There are some 50 pages of plates. Each plate is accompanied by a description of the painting that places the work in some historical perspective.

150. Milner, John. **Kazimir Malevich and the Art of Geometry**. x, 237p.: illus. (some col.). New Haven, Conn.: Yale University Press, 1996. Includes bibliographical references (p. 230) and index.

Even though Malevich created the "most celebrated geometric painting of the twentieth century" (p. ix) (he called it Quadrilateral and it is known as the Black Square), he was concerned with geometry throughout his entire career, even in its earliest days. This book examines the various ways that Malevich incorporated geometry into his paintings, from the images themselves, to the proportions of the canvases upon which he painted. He also shows from where he drew his inspiration and to whom his own influence redounded.

151. Rifkin, Benjamin. **Semiotics of Narration in Film and Prose Fiction: Case Studies of "Scarecrow" and "My Friend Ivan Lapshin."** xii, 249p.: illus. New York: P. Lang, 1994. Includes bibliographical references (pp. 227-39) and index.

Benjamin Rifkin focuses on the transfer of dialogue from print media to film. He focuses on two works, "Scarecrow" and "My Friend Ivan Lapshin." "In the chapters below, I examine the semiotic information conveyed in the narration and especially in the narrator's discourse of the literary texts and demonstrate how this information is conveyed (or not conveyed) and by means of what devices (including lighting, camera angles, use of color, nature of shots, editing, music and other sound in the soundtrack, visual elements of the background, among others) in the filmic texts" (p. xi). After a discussion of the challenges of comparing the two media, Rifkin treats each work in a separate chapter. He concludes with a discussion of the semiotic model and the comparison of prose and film. Along with the bibliography the author has included two appendixes, one of photographs from the film, and the other, film credits. Benjamin Rifkin is a professor of Russian at the University of Wisconsin-Madison.

152. Swanson, Vern G. **Hidden Treasures: Russian and Soviet Impressionism, 1930-1970s**. ix, 205p.: col. illus. Scottsdale, Ariz.: Fleischer Museum, 1994. Includes bibliographical references (pp. 195-[196]) and index.

This wonderful collection of Soviet paintings "covers a range of subject matter that include bucolic vistas and industrialized scenes along with sensitive portraits and still lifes. Many of the works glorify the common laborer: steel workers, farmers, milkmaids, builders and loggers. Others depict landscapes, family and social life and a few portray political figures, although any political message is obscured or lost altogether" (p. viii). The volume includes essays with accompanying illustrations of the development of Russian and Soviet impressionism, a chronology of Soviet art, and biographies of the most noteworthy artists.

Music

153. Bartlett, Rosamund. **Wagner and Russia**. xx, 405p.: illus. *Cambridge Studies in Russian Literature*. Cambridge, Eng.: Cambridge University Press, 1995. Includes bibliographical references and index.

Rosamund Bartlett examines the influence Wagner has had on Russian culture. "Beginning with the first mention of Wagner's name in the Russian press in 1841 and ending almost 150 years later when the composer was finally rehabilitated during the years of glasnost, this study provides the first detailed account of Wagner's visit to Russia in 1863, and a history of the productions of his works in Russia both before and after the Revolution (including radical stagings by Meyerhold and Eisenstein). The book pays special attention to Wagner's important influence on the Russian modernist movement, focusing particularly on his impact on the leading Symbolist writers, Vyacheslav Ivanov, Andrey Bely and Aleksandr Blok" (frontispiece).

154. Cushman, Thomas. **Notes from Underground: Rock Music Counterculture in Russia**. xxiv, 403p. *SUNY Series in the Sociology of Culture*. Albany: State University of New York Press, 1995. Includes bibliographical references (pp. 373-89) and index.

This case study of rock counterculture in a society reveals many facets of the innovation and creativity that can occur in the midst of changing social circumstances. Cushman studied a community of rock musicians in St. Petersburg, Russia, from the time when rock music first entered Soviet society in the 1960s through perestroika and into the post-Soviet world. "It is a study of a Russian musical counterculture, a community united by a common way of life and a common commitment to the production and dissemination of rock music as a means of cultural opposition and as a means of claiming autonomous space and identity in Russian society" (p. xi).

155. Dubal, David. **Remembering Horowitz: 125 Pianists Recall a Legend**. xxix, 383p., [16] p. of plates: illus., ports. New York: Schirmer Books; Prentice Hall, 1995. Includes indexes.

This unusual volume contains reminiscences by 125 pianists about Horowitz and the impression his playing made on them and his influence on both their lives and their careers. Each mini-memoir contains a brief biographical sketch of the pianist.

156. Egorova, Tatiana K. **Soviet Film Music: An Historical Survey**. xiii, 311p.: illus., music. *Contemporary Music Studies*, vol. 13. Australia: Harwood Academic, 1997. Includes filmography and index.

The making of films in Russia provided Soviet composers a venue in which they could experiment with their music. It also produced some very successful collaborations between directors and composers: Eisenstein-Prokofiev, Kozintsev-Shostakovich, and Tarkovsky-Artemyev. "This fascinating volume is the first attempt at a historical analysis of Soviet film music—a unique and fully formed phenomenon" (back cover). The book is arranged into chronological sections.

157. Martyn, Barrie. **Nicolas Medtner: His Life and Music**. viii, 274p.: illus. Aldershot, Hants, Eng.: Scholar Press; Ashgate, 1995. Includes bibliographical references and indexes.

Medtner, a pianist, was overshadowed by his contemporaries Scriabin and Rachmaninoff. This volume "attempts to clarify the facts of his career and, through an examination of the works, dispel at least some misapprehensions about his music" (p. xi).

158. Prokofiev, Sergei. **Selected Letters of Sergei Prokofiev**. Edited by Harlow Robinson. xx, 348p. Boston: Northeastern University Press, 1998. Includes index.

These collected letters underline a fact already well established in standard biographies of Prokofiev that his primary devotion was to music, and nothing else. Any suspicions about his political interests or self-serving acts are put to rest here. As his biographer states: "If Prokofiev had a tragic flaw, it was his inability to see beyond his own closed world of music, a certain tunnel vision. Driven, egotistical, and applying the highest artistic standards to himself and others, he was really guilty of only one crime: a single-minded and, yes, perhaps even blind devotion to his craft" (p. xv).

159. Roberts, Peter Deane. **Modernism in Russian Piano Music: Skriabin, Prokofiev, and Their Russian Contemporaries**. 2 vols. *Russian Music Studies*. Bloomington: Indiana University Press, 1993. Includes bibliographical references and index.

"Peter Deane Roberts reviews the political and social situation in Russia during 1910-1929, the works of the earlier Russian Nationalist School, and the cultural heritage of folk music, which directly influenced composers in the twentieth century. He also discusses the relationship between Russian music and the work of Western composers, and the influence of Russian music of this period on later musical developments in the West" (back cover). Dr. Roberts teaches piano and music theory in England.

160. Schonberg, Harold C. **Horowitz: His Life and Music**. 427p., [16] p. of plates, ports. New York: Simon & Schuster, 1992. Includes index.

This comprehensive biography by Schonberg adds to a rather scant literature on Horowitz. Other than information from interviews and past magazine articles there has been written only one other biography and a volume of reminiscences by a friend. The volume contains four appendixes containing a listing of the Horowitz recordings, plus a discography of Horowitz containing a chronological section and an index and release section.

161. Taruskin, Richard. **Defining Russia Musically: Historical and Hermeneutical Essays**. xxxii, 561p.: illus., music. Princeton, N.J.: Princeton University Press, 1997. Includes bibliographical references and index.

In this complex work Taruskin repeatedly poses the question in each essay: "But how, precisely, did [Chaikovsky's and Scriabin's and Stravinsky's and Shostakovich's] songs work technically?—precisely in order to understand both the means by which the composers realized their intentions ('how [Chaikovsky's and Scriabin's and Stravinsky's and Shostakovich's] songs worked their physical effects') and also the way in which the composers were responding to issues and circumstances that, one can only presume lay below the threshold of their conscious intending as they went about the act of composing" (p. xxxi).

162. Tchaikovsky, Peter Ilich. **To My Best Friend: Correspondence Between Tchaikovsky and Nadezhda Von Meck, 1876-1878**. Edited by Edward Garden and Nigel Gotteri. Translated by Galina von Meckl. xxi, 439p., [8] p. of plates: illus., ports., music. Oxford, Eng.: Oxford University Press, 1993.

In 1876 Tchaikovsky's life and career were at a turning point. He had grown dissatisfied with his life at the Moscow Conservatoire and was beginning work on what was to be his operatic masterpiece "Eugene Onegin." It was then that he began a correspondence with a wealthy Russian noblewoman Nadezhda Meck. This volume contains translations of their letters that span the second half of the composer's life. The editors have included a "Synopsis of Letters" at the beginning of the volume. Each letter is briefly summarized in this section. The letters are arranged chronologically.

163. **Intersections and Transpositions: Russian Music, Literature, and Society**. Edited by Andrew Baruch Wachtel. xvi, 301p. *Studies in Russian Literature and Theory*. Evanston, Ill.: Northwestern University Press, 1998. Includes bibliographical references.

The interrelation between Russian musical and literary genres is well established. This collection of essays "serves as an introduction to the great variety of approaches being used by Slavicists and historians to treat the topic of Russian music in broad cultural perspective" (p. xvi). The essays themselves are presented in two sections, "music in art" and "music in life."

Dance

164. Brown, Howard, editor and designer. **Nureyev**. 177p. London: Phaidon, 1993.

Despite the absence of any narrative text, this volume of photographs gives a visual history of Nureyev's development from the first picture taken of him in 1954 in Ufa as a 16-year-old to his return to Ufa in 1987. The pictures include both formal and informal shots of the renowned dancer.

165. Drummond, John. **Speaking of Diaghilev**. [xii], 382p. London: Faber & Faber, 1997. Includes index.

John Drummond's main interest in writing this volume was to analyze artistic authority as it manifests itself in the life and works of Diaghilev. He publishes here, for the first time, interviews with a number of people who knew and/or worked with Diaghilev. These include Tamara Karsavina, Anne Benois-Tcherkessova, Lydia Sokolova, Alicia Markova, Igor Markevich, and Nicholas Nabokov. The book is filled with anecdotes about Diaghilev's meetings with these and other artists who influenced the Russian artistic world. The book includes a listing of all the productions of the Ballets Russe.

166. Gordeeva, Ekaterina, and E. M. Swift. **My Sergei: A Love Story**. 292p.: illus. (some col.). New York: Warner Books, 1996.

Sergei Mikhailovich Grinkov was a two-time Olympic pairs skating champion. This touching memoir by his wife provides insight into the life of this remarkable man, who unexpectedly died from a heart attack at age 28.

167. Lazzarini, Robert. **Maximova and Vasiliev at the Bolshoi**. 174p.: illus. London: Dance Books, 1995.

This volume traces the careers of Ekaterina Maximova and Vladimir Vasilev, two of the first Russian ballet dancers of this century. The book is in many ways an illustrated history of their careers, with its numerous photographs. A list of the choreography and production of Vasiliev and the repertoires of both dancers are included.

168. Scholl, Tim. **From Petipa to Balanchine: Classical Revival and the Modernization of Ballet**. xii, 167p.: illus. London: Routledge, 1994. Includes bibliographical references (pp. 155-64) and index.

"This work examines the Russian ballet's classical revival of an anomalous feature of Russian arts and letters (especially of St. Petersburg), the first decades of the twentieth century, when turn-of-the-century Russian artists looked increasingly to the art of the past to invigorate and reorder their work. . . . The artists discussed in this study looked to examples of past art they considered models; the resulting revival is rightly considered 'classical.' " (p. ix).

169. Schouvaloff, Alexander. **The Art of Ballets Russes: The Serge Lifar Collection of Theater Designs, Costumes, and Paintings at Wadsworth Atheneum, Hartford, Connecticut**. 352p.: illus. (some col.). New Haven, Conn.: Yale University Press in association with the Wadsworth Atheneum, 1997.

This is primarily a catalog of stage designs, costume designs, and other depictions of the Ballets Russe. Much of the catalog is based on the collection originally belonging to Serge Lifar that is presently owned by the Wadsworth Atheneum. There are individual chapters devoted to artists and designers affiliated with the Ballets Russe and others inspired by Diaghilev.

170. Solway, Diane. **Nureyev, His Life**. 1st ed. x, 625p., [32] p. of plates: illus. New York: William Morrow, 1998. Includes bibliographical references (pp. [599]-601) and index.

Solway's biography of Nureyev (billed as the most traveled dancer in history) is probably the most comprehensive one published to date. In doing research for the book she interviewed more than 200 fellow dancers and others in the many cities Nureyev visited and lived.

171. Stuart, Otis. **Perpetual Motion: The Public and Private Lives of Rudolf Nureyev**. 317p., [16] p. of plates: illus. New York: Simon & Schuster, 1995. Includes bibliographic references and index.

This full-length biography covers Nureyev's life from childhood to death from AIDS. The volume also includes two appendixes: one, on the ballets in which he danced from 1963 to 1991, and the second, roles he played from his first student performance at the Kirov Ballet school in 1956 to his last at the Budapest State Opera in 1991.

172. Surits, E., scientific editor. **The Great History of Russian Ballet: Its Art and Choreography**. 207p. Bournemouth, Eng.: Parkstone Press, 1998. Includes index.

The Russian ballet was formed over two centuries ago by immigrants from France and Italy. This richly illustrated history covers the development of the Russian ballet from its first performance through the present day. The description is chronological and after each chronological section there is a section of brief biographies of the major dancers and other primary figures for that period.

173. Tsivian, Yuri. **Early Cinema in Russia and Its Cultural Reception**. xxii, 273p.: illus. New York: Routledge, 1994. Rev. ed. of: *Istoricheskaia Retseptsiia Kino*, 1991. Includes bibliographical references (pp. [249]-264).

Tsivian examines the cinema history of prerevolutionary Russian cinema. In so doing, he shows how postrevolutionary cinema was formed by and reacted to the revolution. In addition, he analyzes the reception of cinema by audiences in Soviet Russia and expands it to include "the whole experience of film viewing in Russia at the turn of the century" (p. x). He pays special attention to aspects such as cinema architecture and the social composition of the cinema; projection technique, acoustics, and reception of moving image; narrative categories; and narrative devices.

174. **Petrushka: Sources and Contexts**. Edited by Andrew Wachtel. ix, 169p., [8] p. of plates: illus. (some col.). Evanston, Ill.: Northwestern University Press, 1998. Includes bibliographical references (pp. 157-60) and index.

Wachtel and the other authors who have contributed chapters to this collection have used Petrushka as a case study to examine a broader phenomenon. Their intention "is to place Petrushka (and, by extrapolation, the early Ballets Russes in general) in a context to which it rightfully belongs, that of Russian modernist culture. Through a careful examination of the sources of the ballet's libretto, costumes and sets, and score, the four authors attempt to show that on every level, Petrushka is a response primarily to Russian artistic trends and can best be understood in a Russian context" (p. 2).

175. Wiley, Roland John. **The Life and Ballets of Lev Ivanov: Choreographer of The Nutcracker and Swan Lake**. ix, 306p., [16] p. of plates: illus. Oxford, Eng.: Clarendon Press, 1997. Includes bibliographical references (pp. [287]-291) and index.

This study examines both the life of Ivanov and his choreographical work with ballets, including the Tulip of Haarlem, The Nutcracker, and Swan Lake. Ivanov is obscure, and Wiley's study attempts to determine why and also to correct mistaken impressions about his work.

Film

176. Bordwell, David. **The Cinema of Eisenstein**. xv, 316p.: illus. Cambridge, Mass.: Harvard University Press, 1993. Includes bibliographical references and index.

This study examines the entire career of Eisenstein. Bordwell places Eisenstein in the context of Soviet artistic culture focusing on ways in which he blended theory and practice. After this firm foundation he proceeds to describe and analyze the silent films, film theory in the silent era, practical aesthetics and pedagogy of film, cinema as synthesis in the context of film theory from 1930 to 1948, the late films (*Alexander Nevsky* and *Ivan the Terrible*), and finally the reinterpretation and use of Eisenstein in both Soviet and Western film culture.

177. Horton, Andrew. **Inside Soviet Film Satire: Laughter with a Lash**. xi, 171p. Cambridge, Eng.: Cambridge University Press, 1993. Includes filmography, list of contributors, and index.

This collection of 16 essays by Soviet and American scholars examines humor and satire expressed in Soviet cinema. The essays are arranged in three parts: the long view: Soviet satire in context; middle distance shots: the individual satire considered; close-ups: glasnost and Soviet satire.

178. Horton, Andrew. **The Zero Hour: Glasnost and Soviet Cinema in Transition**. xiv, 287p.: illus. Princeton, N.J.: Princeton University Press, 1992. Includes bibliographical references.

"This book concerns the nature and changing role of Soviet cinema during the transitional period of 1985-1991, in which glasnost (openness) finally led to substantial cultural and political perestroika." The authors' work "traces the development, the dimensions, and the dangers and cinematic rewards of these changes in Soviet culture and cinema" (p. 3). Among the topics covered are Soviet youth and changing values, Soviet women in film, glasnost in documentary film, Soviet popular genres and the new film language, and ethnic cinemas.

179. Lawton, Anna. **Kinoglasnost: Soviet Cinema in Our Time**. xv, 288p. *Cambridge Soviet Paperbacks*, 9. Cambridge, Eng.: Cambridge University Press, 1992. Includes endnotes, bibliography, filmography, and index. Filmography (pp. 270-78).

Lawton "examines the fascinating world of Soviet cinema under glasnost and perestroika. She shows how the reforms that shook the foundations of the Bolshevik state profoundly affected economic and social structures and have been reflected by changes that revolutionized the film industry and the films the industry produced" (frontispiece).

180. **The Red Screen: Politics, Society, Art in Soviet Cinema**. Edited by Anna Lawton. vi, 360p. New York: Routledge, 1992. Includes index and notes on contributors.

This volume is a collection of essays, generated from papers presented at the Conference on Soviet Cinema, held at the Kennan Institute for Advanced Russian Studies in 1986. The essays are arranged in two parts, based on chronology. The first, "From Potemkin to the Elbe," contains seven essays and the second part, "From the Thaw to the New Model," contains 13.

181. Shlapentokh, Dmitry, and Vladimir Shlapentokh. **Soviet Cinematography 1918-1991: Ideological Conflict and Social Reality**. xv, 278p. *Communication and Social Order*. New York: Aldine de Gruyter, 1993. Includes index.

"The following work will explore the role of ideology and politics in Soviet movies, concentrating on the influences of certain ideologies on the movie industry. It examines the political activity of filmmakers in the seventy-plus years between 1917, when the Bolsheviks came to power, and 1991, when the Soviet empire collapsed" (p. xiii). To accomplish this, the authors have divided the study into five parts on theory, on Soviet period and its effect, the role of ideology, the Stalin period, and the rejection of ideology. "Within the framework of an introduction that lays out the conceptual terminology used to describe that shifting ideological landscape, the authors analyze both the social groups appearing in the films and the relations of film directors and other film makers to state censorship and ideological control" (back cover).

182. Tarkovskii, Andrei Arsenevich. **Time Within Time: The Diaries, 1970-1986**. viii, 407p., [16] p. of plates: illus., ports. London: Faber & Faber, 1994. Includes index.

Andrei Tarkovskii was one of Russia's finest film directors. Although he only made seven major films, each increased his national and international reputation. These diaries cover the last years he spent in the Soviet Union before emigrating to the West. "These diaries and notebooks make compelling reading, giving us an insight into his personal life through the warmth and spontaneity of his writing" (back cover).

183. Youngblood, Denise Jeanne. **Movies for the Masses: Popular Cinema and Soviet Society in the 1920s**. xix, 259p., [16] p. of plates: illus. Cambridge, Eng.: Cambridge University Press, 1992. Includes bibliographical references and index.

In this study, popular Soviet films of the 1920s are analyzed. Focusing on popular culture, Dr. Youngblood demonstrates that the interest in popular films cuts across political loyalties and class divisions. "Denise J. Youngblood discusses acting genres, the cinema stars, audiences and the influence of foreign films and she examines three filmmakers—Iakov Protazanov, Boris Barnet, and Fridrich Ermler—who are widely assumed in the West to be of considerable importance but about whom little is actually known" (frontispiece). Dr. Youngblood has divided her study into three parts: contexts, practice, and alternatives. The book includes a filmography listing the films cited in the text with their director, year of production, and a translated title.

Theater

184. Clayton, J. Douglas. **Pierrot in Petrograd: The Commedia Dell'Arte/Balagan in Twentieth-Century Russian Theatre and Drama**. x, 369p.: illus. Montreal: McGill-Queen's University Press, 1993. Contains bibliography and index.

After an introductory chapter in which the author examines the international phenomenon known as commedia dell'arte, he then explores, in various aspects, the manifestation of this phenomenon in Russia. Individual chapters focus on commedia dell'arte and the crisis in theater, Pierrot in Petersburg from 1903 to 1917, Russian Harequinades and Russian Pirandellos, the film as Balagan, and, finally, the film as metahistory. The six appendixes contain translations of six short plays, translated for the first time into English and some of which have never been published.

185. Schuler, Catherine. **Women in Russian Theatre: The Actress in the Silver Age**. xi, 260p.: illus. *Gender in Performance*. London: Routledge, 1996. Includes bibliographical references and index.

Women in Russian Theatre is the first study of Russian actresses in English. Catherine Schuler has drawn on newly opened files to investigate the way in which actresses affected Russian modernist theater. "*Women in Russian Theatre* offers case studies of the popular actresses and actress-entrepreneurs of the age of Stanislavski, the Moscow Art Theatre and Vsevolod Meierhold.... It is with clarity and insight that Schuler considers how the social, political and aesthetic context contribute to the 'apogee of the actress' at this time" (frontispiece).

186. **Wandering Stars: Russian Emigre Theatre, 1905-1940**. Edited by Laurence Senelick. xx, 241p. Iowa City: University of Iowa Press, 1992. Studies in Theatre History and Culture.

The 13 papers included in this volume were originally presented at the Symposium on Russian Emigre Theatre, held at the Harvard Theatre Collection on Feb. 13-15, 1991. All but two of the papers presented are included. The topics are far-ranging within the focus of the conference and include, for example, "The American Tour of Orlenev and Nazimova, 1905-1906," "Nikita Balieff and the Chauve-Souris," "Maria Germanova and the Moscow Art Theatre Prague Group," "Boleslavsky in America," and "Michael Chekhov and Russian Existentialism." The editor, Laurence Senelick, provides an introduction that sets the topic of the conference in context. In addition, two appendixes are included: "Russian Drama and Performance in the U.S. Prior to the MAT Tour of 1923" and "The Moscow Art Theatre Prague Group Repertoire in London."

187. Smeliansky, Anatoly. **The Russian Theatre After Stalin**. xxxviii, 232p. Cambridge, Eng.: Cambridge University Press, 1999. Includes bibliographical references (pp. 217-23) and index.

Anatoly Smeliansky is associate head of the Moscow Art Theatre. As such he is in a unique position to analyze the history of contemporary Russian theater. He draws on his own experiences and archival material, much of which has previously been unavailable. The book is arranged chronologically beginning in 1953. "Smeliansky chronicles developments from 1953 and the rise of a new Soviet theatre, and moves through the next four decades, highlighting the social and political events which shaped Russian drama and performance. The book also focuses on major directors and practitioners, including Yury Lyubimov, Oleg Yefremov, and Lev Dodin, and contains a chronology, glossary of names, and informative illustrations" (frontispiece).

The Economy

188. Ruble, Blair A. **Money Sings: The Changing Politics of Urban Space Post-Soviet Yaroslavl**. xv, 158p.: illus., maps. *Woodrow Wilson Center series*. Washington, D.C.: Woodrow Wilson Center Press, 1995. Includes bibliographical references and index.

In this study of the city of Yaroslavl during the recent years of political and economic transition in Russia, Blair Ruble examines the political struggles over the use of urban space. Such struggles illuminate the interaction of economic, physical, social, and political factors that shape a society. "This volume, which details housing privatization, historic preservation, and urban planning, demonstrates important lessons about the bureaucratic and political dynamics of systemic change in post-Soviet Russia, the economic transition to the market, and the importance of economic factors in shaping the contemporary city" (frontispiece).

General Studies

189. **Structural Adjustment Without Mass Unemployment?: Lessons from Russia**. Edited by Simon Clarke. xiii, 355p.: illus. Cheltenham, Eng.: Edward Elgar, 1998. Includes bibliographical references and index.

This collection of essays is the result of a conference held at the University of Warwick in September 1996. The purpose of the conference was to report on research into the Russian labor market. There was no attempt to impose a uniform approach on the final papers of the participants. Rather, the papers collected here represent the variety in opinion on problems in the Russian labor market. Contributors are Simon Clarke, Veronika Kabalina, Irina Kozina, Inna Donova, Marina Karelina, Guy Standing, Pavel Smirnov, Galina Monousova, Tatyana Chetvernina, Maarten Keune, Kathleen Young, and Nick Manning.

190. Dmitrieva, Olga. **Regional Development: The USSR and After**. xi, 211p. New York: St. Martin's Press, 1996. Includes bibliographical references and index.

Dmitrieva carried out the studies contained in this book over several years while working at the Laboratory of Regional Diagnostics of the St. Petersburg University of Economics and Finance. Individual chapters cover the political, historical, and religious background; objectives, instruments, and results of regional policy; the regional development model and regional structure in the USSR on the eve of disintegration; social and economic systems in Central Asia; and disintegration and macroeconomic policy impacts of regional development from 1988 to 1992.

191. Flakierski, Henryk. **Income Inequalities in the Former Soviet Union and Its Republics**. 87p. Armonk, N.Y.: M. E. Sharpe, 1993.

Henryk Flakierski takes the initial steps toward a comprehensive understanding of pattern of income distribution in the Soviet Union. In this volume he focuses on the 1980s. He uses the new statistical data that became available under Gorbachev. "The present study, though it is by no means complete, seeks to provide a better understanding of the issues involved, and at the same time to reconsider and rethink income inequalities in the Soviet Union as a factor that contributed to the demise of the Communist region" (p. 1). The author is a professor of economics at York University.

192. Fortescue, Stephen. **Policy-Making for Russian Industry**. xi, 216p. *Studies in Russian and East European History and Society series*. London: Macmillan, 1997. "In association with Centre for Russian and East European Studies [of the] University of Birmingham." Includes bibliographical references (pp. 205-11) and index.

"The purpose of this book is to make some sense of various, largely contradictory views of the contemporary Russian economy" (p. vii). Fortescue attempts to examine the many theoretical approaches to Russia's changing economy with the intent of identifying the most fitting theoretical structure by the end of the book. He examines the different sectors of the Russian economy—agriculture, energy, industry, finance, commerce, and trade. The book is structured around the categories of policymakers in Russian society.

193. Kosals, Leonid IAnovich. **Why Doesn't Russian Industry Work?** New York: I. B. Tauris, 1994. Includes index.

Leonid Kosals believes that it is difficult for those in the West to understand the innovations that go on in Russia. In this book he explains the nature of innovation in Russia. He begins by describing the transformation that has been taking place in the Russian economy since the downfall of the Soviet system. Next, he examines the innovations and innovators in Russian enterprises today. In these chapters he discusses methods of production enterprises, innovative activity among employees, the general climate of innovation in Russia, and the lack of economic immunity in a centralized economy. Finally, he describes the reasons for stagnation in the innovative process in Russia.

194. **Emerging Market of Russia: Sourcebook for Investment and Trade**. Edited by V. L. Kvint and Jacqueline Gallus. 1 vol. (various pages): illus., map. New York: John Wiley, 1998. Includes bibliographical references and index.

The purpose of this book is to provide up-to-date information for "business executives and entrepreneurs that are already doing business with Russia or who are seriously considering opportunities within this market" (p. xvi). It consists of 62 chapters that are arranged within the following sections: general information; political structure, government, and administration; economic structure; financial system; business environment; legal system; foreign trade and investment; tax system; regional economies; and infrastructure.

195. Layard, Richard, and John Parker. **The Coming Russian Boom: A Guide to New Markets and Politics**. xvii, 380p.: illus., map. New York: Free Press, 1996. Includes bibliographical references and index.

Layard, an economic advisor, and Parker, a journalist for *The Economist*, explore the many questions that have arisen with regard to Russia's future. Appropriately each of their chapters, save the last, "Executive Summary and Future Scenarios," are presented in the form of a question—e.g., "Too much shock therapy?" and "Can Russia beat the Mafia?"

196. Minakir, Pavel A., and Gregory L. Freeze. **The Russian Far East: An Economic Handbook**. xlvii, 495p. Armonk, N.Y.: M. E. Sharpe, 1994. Includes three appendixes, index, maps, and list of tables.

This volume translated from the Russian provides the student and researcher with a voluminous amount of information on economics, geography, population, natural resources, international economic cooperation, and the changing markets in the Far East. Its four parts provide, in both textual and tabular form, individual chapters on natural resources and population, economic development, economic reform and the system of economic regulation, and an appendix containing a statistical overview, a list of organizations active in foreign trade and investment, basic laws, and decrees and normative acts regulating international trade and wages.

197. Smith, Alan. **Russia and the World Economy: Problems of Integration**. x, 253p. London: Routledge, 1993. Includes bibliography (pp. 239-45) and index.

Smith examines "the historic, economic and political obstacles that will have to be overcome if Russia is to become fully integrated into the world economy and the implications of this process for the advanced industrial economies" (p. xi).

Statistics

198. **USSR Crime Statistics and Summaries: 1989 and 1990**. Translated by Joseph Serio, 114p.: illus. Chicago: Office of International Criminal Justice, 1992. Includes index. Translations of: *Sostoianie prestupnosti v SSSR rezultaty borby s nei v 1989 godu* and *Statisticheskie dannye o sostoianii pravoporiadka v SSSR*, 1990.

This volume collects the statistics on crime for the period 1989-1990. The policies of perestroika and glasnost caused many changes in Russia. One area that was affected was the collection and publication of statistical data. This resulted in a reformulation of Soviet society's self-image. The statistics in this volume indicate many of the serious problems found in the system. "These statistics reveal the increasing lawlessness and breakdown of authority in Soviet society. . . . The situation has been very confused, and it is difficult or impossible to determine which laws take precedence. This confusion and disregard for authority has resulted in the precipitous increase in crime reflected in these data for 1989 and 1990" (p. viii). The statistics are arranged by category including property crime, organized crime, drug addiction, etc. There are extensive appendixes providing the raw data used for the summaries.

199. Harrison, Mark. **Accounting for War: Soviet Production, Employment, and the Defense Burden, 1940-1945**. xxxiv, 338p. *Cambridge Russian, Soviet and Post-Soviet Studies*, 99. Cambridge, Eng.: Cambridge University Press, 1996. Includes appendixes, endnotes, bibliography, and index.

"In this book Mark Harrison rebuilds and analyses the Soviet economy's wartime statistical record, examining its prewar size and composition, and wartime changes in GNP, employment, the defense burden, and the role of foreign aid. Complementing classic long-run growth studies the book compares the Soviet experience with that of other great powers. It emphasizes the severity of current costs and capital losses arising from the war, . . ." (frontispiece). This detailed study begins with a description of the methodology, and then turns to a review of the official Soviet description of the state of their economy immediately after the war. Harrison then looks at Western precedents for the "reconstruction" of the Soviet statistics. In the next two sections the author "proceeds with the substantive work of rebuilding series for industrial production (chapter 4), and GNP (chapter 5)" (p. 4). This is followed by a study of the role of foreign aid in the reconstruction of the economy and a review of indications of capital losses suffered by the Soviets as a result of the war.

Economic History

200. **The Economic Transformation of the Soviet Economy, 1913-1945**. Edited by R. W. Davies, Mark Harrison, and S. G. Wheatcroft. xxv, 381p.: illus., maps. Cambridge, Eng.: Cambridge University Press, 1994. Includes bibliographical references and index.

These 12 essays examine "the main quantitative features of the economic development of the Russian Empire and the Soviet Union from the eve of the First World War in 1913 to the end of the Second World War in 1945" (p. xvii). Intended as a textbook, this collection covers the crucial period in Russian industrialization. It addresses questions of establishing the main quantitative features of economic growth. It has chapters on statistics, national income, population, employment and industrial labor, agriculture, industry, transport, technology, foreign economic relations, World War I and the war on communism, and World War II.

201. **The Destruction of the Soviet Economic System: An Insiders' History**. Edited by Michael Ellman and Vladimir Kontorovich. xxiv, 326p. Armonk, N.Y.: M. E. Sharpe, 1998. Includes bibliographical references and index.

"This book is concerned with the economic history of the collapse of the Soviet civilization, with its centrally planned economy, one-party government, and official ideology, that occurred between 1985 and 1991" (p. xi). The description of the collapse of the Soviet system is provided by eyewitnesses who where involved in the functioning of the economic institutions of the Soviet Union.

202. Gregory, Paul R. **Before Command: An Economic History of Russia from Emancipation to the First Five-Year Plan**. viii, 188p.: illus. Princeton, N.J.: Princeton University Press, 1994. Includes bibliographical references (pp. [167]-184) and index.

"This book is about the quantitative economic history of the 1920s and of the late tsarist period. . . . The lack of attention to the quantitative analysis of these periods is striking. The presumption of failure was arrived at without serious analysis of the most common indicators of economic performance. This book will present counterevidence suggesting more favorable performance of both the tsarist and NEP economies" (p. 13). The author has included two appendixes providing extensive statistical data to support his conclusions.

203. Hanson, Stephen E. **Time and Revolution: Marxism and the Design of Soviet Institutions**. xv, 258p. Chapel Hill: University of North Carolina Press, 1997. Includes bibliographical references (pp. 243-51) and index.

"Stephen Hanson traces the influence of the Marxist conception of time in Soviet politics from Lenin to Gorbachev. He argues that the history of Marxism and Leninism reveals an unsuccessful revolutionary effort to reorder the human relationship with time and that this reorganization had a direct impact on the design of the central political, socio-economic, and cultural institutions of the Soviet Union from 1917-1991" (back cover). Stephen Hanson is an assistant professor of political science at the University of Washington.

204. Hunter, Holland, and Janusz Szyrmer. **Faulty Foundations: Soviet Economic Policies, 1928-1940**. xvi, 339p.: illus. Princeton, N.J.: Princeton University Press, 1992. Includes bibliographical references.

Although Soviet economic policies appeared to be very successful in their early years, by the 1960s it was apparent that Soviet economic performance was less than stellar. In attempting to discern what went wrong, the authors focus on the period 1928-1940, when they believe faulty foundations were laid for the new economy. The first three chapters are introductory background. The second set of chapters (Chapters 3-10) looks at the development of economic policies in agriculture, foreign trade, defense outlays, and monitoring of capital growth. In the third part (Chapters 11-14), the authors explore alternative models and speculate on possible outcomes for alternate economic policies.

205. Kaplan, Herbert H. **Russian Overseas Commerce with Great Britain During the Reign of Catherine II**. xxx, 309p.: illus., maps. Philadelphia: American Philosophical Society, 1995. Maps on lining papers.

Kaplan's thesis is that "Catherine, while following the general commercial policies adopted by her predecessors, recognized the interdependent nature of the British-Russian commercial relationship, and that she sought to exploit this to make Russia an independent commercial and maritime power and to make herself a major player in greater European political affairs" (p. xxvi). Based on sources in Russian and British archives, this book is arranged in four parts: (1) "The Continuity of Commercial Policy: Elizabeth—Peter III—Catherine II"; (2) "Russian Commodity Exports and Great Britain's Economic Development: From the Seven Years' War to the Armed Neutrality"; (3) "War and Commerce on the High Seas: Conventions, Commodities, Contraband"; and (4) "The Balance of Trade and Culture."

206. Rutland, Peter. **The Politics of Economic Stagnation in the Soviet Union: The Role of Local Party Organs in Economic Management**. xv, 297p.: illus. *Soviet and East European Studies*, no. 88. Cambridge, Eng.: Cambridge University Press, 1993. Includes bibliographical references (pp. 285-94) and index.

Peter Rutland believes that the Soviet economy was incapable of absorbing the reforms introduces by Gorbachev in the 1980s. His analysis has led him to the conclusion that the highly integrated political, economic, and social systems in Russia had as their ultimate goal political stability. To reform one area of the system was to wreak havoc on the others. He explores this thesis in the book by examining the use of party functionaries to intervene in various sections of the economy. He has used case studies to support his analysis. He begins with an overview of the Soviet economy. The remaining chapters focus on particular sectors of the economy, with case studies of constructing energy, transport, consumer goods, and others. "These case studies show a deeply rooted tension between economic and political approaches to problem solving in the Soviet economy" (p. xii). The volume includes a glossary of Soviet terms and two appendixes. The first discusses the obkrom and oblast data and how they were analyzed for this study. The second looks at the information taken from *Ekonomicheskain Gazeta* as source material.

207. **Merchant Moscow: Images of Russia's Vanished Bourgeoisie**. Edited by James L. West and Iurii A. Petrov. 189p. Princeton, N.J.: Princeton University Press, 1998. With the collaboration of Edith W. Clowes and Thomas C. Owen.

This collection of 13 essays and a conclusion presents a focused history of part of the Russian bourgeoisie of the 19th century—the merchant class. Through photographs and essays the volume provides a fascinating portrait of this slice of Russian society. The essays are arranged in five sections: (1) from street fair to department store: business culture and practices; (2) icon and business card: merchant culture, ritual, and daily life; (3) beyond the boardroom: social hierarchies—gender, class, and education; (4) a city of one's own: reshaping culture and space; and (5) merchant dreams: self-image and utopian vision. It also contains some introductory short essays on merchant Moscow in historical context, a note on Old Belief, and a note on photography in Russia.

Economic Theory and Planning

208. Aslund, Anders. **Russian Economic Reform at Risk**. 212p.: illus. New York: St. Martin's Press, 1995. Includes bibliographical references and index.

"Leading academics, ministers of state and practitioners combine theory with practice to present the latest views on the underlying economic trends in Russia, which often appear in conflict with everyday political events" (back cover). The essays included here were first presented at a conference at the Stockholm School of Economics, June 16-17, 1994. The contributors focused on those issues that have put stress on the economic reforms.

209. Barnett, Vincent. **Kondratiev and the Dynamics of Economic Development: Long Cycles and Industrial Growth in Historical Context**. xiv, 251p.: illus. *Studies in Russian and East European History and Society series*. New York: St. Martin's Press in association with the Centre for Russian and East European Studies, University of Birmingham, 1998. Includes bibliographical references.

Nikolai Dmitrievich Kondratiev was one of Russia's most important economic theorists. His importance rests not only in his work on Soviet-style planning but as a contributor to other areas of economic theory. "This book investigates Kondratiev both from a history of economic thought perspective and from an economic history/policy of the USSR standpoint" (p. 1). The author will consider some of the work of Kondratiev's colleagues and the affect they might have had on his own work. This book is intended as the first volume in a history of Russian economic thought.

210. Campbell, Robert Wellington. **The Failure of Soviet Economic Planning: System, Performance, Reform**. xii, 185p.: illus. Bloomington: Indiana University Press, 1992. Includes index.

Robert Campbell wrote the essays collected in this volume during a period of some 20 years. They describe the Soviet economic system and its failings. Together they elucidate the reasons the Soviet economic system collapsed. Campbell believes that there will be continuing interest in this topic. "It is this author's hope that a retrospective look will contribute to our understanding not only of the classic Soviet economic system but of economic systems generally, and the process of reform" (p. xi). The essays are grouped in three sections. The first examines the Soviet economy in the context of economic theory. Section 2 looks at the process of decision making in the Soviet system. In the final section are two essays on the question of reform.

211. **Enterprise Restructuring and Economic Policy in Russia**. Edited by Simon Commander, Qimiao Fan, and Mark E. Schaffer. xv, 290p. *EDI Development Studies*. Washington, D.C.: The World Bank, 1996. Includes index.

The basis of this book is a large survey of firms carried out by the World Bank in mid-1994 that included over 400 industrial firms. The survey examined both aggregate demand and supply shocks, including the negative effects of the withdrawal of CMFA support. Individual authors interpret the survey by looking at three major aspects: (1) employment, wages, and the provision of social benefits; (2) financial aspects of enterprise restructuring; and (3) corporate governance and competition.

212. Day, Richard. **Cold War Capitalism: The View from Moscow, 1945-1975**. xvi, 355p. Armonk, N.Y.: M. E. Sharpe, 1995. Includes bibliography (pp. 331-48) and index.

Day's thesis is that "a study of Soviet political economy helps to explain both the perceptual origins of the conflict and the tenacity with which it was waged." He reaches the conclusion that "by the mid-1970s Soviet leaders were convinced that they were gaining the upper hand. During the brief period of détente, America was acknowledged to be the dominant force in the capitalist world, but its relative strength appeared to be in decline." The main question he asks is: "How did Soviet specialists in the capitalist countries interpret western developments to Soviet political leaders?" (p. xi). He is unique in having studied Soviet perceptions from the point of view of political economy.

213. **Decision-Making in the Stalinist Command Economy, 1932-37**. Edited by E. A. Rees. xv, 331p. *Studies in Russian and East European History and Society series*. New York: St. Martin's Press, 1997. Includes bibliographical references (pp. 316-21) and index.

"This work examines the formulation and implementation of the Second Five-Year Plan, focusing on decision-making primarily at the level of the economic ministries or commissariats. It provides a series of institutional case studies of decision-making in the USSR in the Stalinist era focusing on the evolving relationship between the economic commissariats, Gosplan and the party and government organs. The work concentrates on a relatively short time-span, examining the interrelationship between institutions, and the internal processes of decision-making within institutions. The work, based on newly available archival material, analyzes the evolution of the Soviet economic system, from within" (p. 1).

Perestroika

214. **Transforming Russian Enterprises: From State Control to Employee Ownership**. Edited by John Logue, Sergey Plekhanov, and John Simons. xviii, 285p. *Contributions in Economics and Economic History*, 168. Westport, Conn.: Greenwood Press, 1995. Includes bibliography (pp. 271-75) and index.

This collection of 16 essays is arranged in three parts: (1) reforming the Russian economy: historical and theoretical perspectives; (2) case studies in Russian employee ownership; and (3) lessons of American and Russian models of ownership and management in employee-owned enterprises. This topic is timely because as of the publication date over 70 percent of the Russian firms privatized have done so through majority employee ownership.

215.   Nelson, Lynn D., and Kuzes, Irina Y. **Property to the People: The Struggle for Radical Economic Reform in Russia**. xi, 267p. Armonk, N.Y.: M. E. Sharpe, 1994. Includes bibliographical references (pp. 235-60) and index.

Nelson and Kuzes attempts to analyze the economic reforms Yeltsin established in 1992 and their long term affects. The authors drew on data from research done at Moscow Institute for Sociology to identify themes and establish a general picture of public opinion. They drew on published survey-research material selectively. What emerges in this study is the authors' attempt ". . . to illuminate structural connections and clarify decision-making processes that could inform our understanding of state-directed change under conditions quite different from those that have characterized several other inquiries into the state as a causal force" (p. 7). The data the authors used is presented in tabular form in an appendix to the book.

Agriculture

216.   Ioffe, G. V., and Tatyana Nefedov. **Continuity and Change in Rural Russia: A Geographical Perspective**. ix, 315p.: illus., maps. Boulder, Colo.: Westview Press, 1997. Includes bibliographical references and index.

The authors attempt to answer several research questions that deal with the state of Russian agriculture, the resilience of the Russian countryside over time, and the "major characteristics and dimensions of national, macro-regional, provincial, and local rural space in Russia" (p. 14). Individual chapters cover specific topics that include social peculiarities and spatial distinctions of Russian agriculture early in the 20th century, agricultural output and production factors prior to the 1990s, the chernozem countryside, the nonchernozem zone, the provinces of Belgorod and Yaroslavl, urbanites in the countryside, and large mechanized farms, among others.

217.   Libert, Bo. **The Environmental Heritage of Soviet Agriculture**. x, 228p.: illus. *Sustainable Rural Development series*, no. 2. Wallingford, Oxon, Eng.: CAB International, 1995. Includes bibliographical references and index.

"The main focus of this book is to describe and analyze the effects of Soviet and post-Soviet agricultural practices on the environment and health, and the effects of agricultural practices, industry and urbanization on the status of soil and other natural resources important for agriculture. The book provides a thorough review of these problems and also responds to several reports claiming that the situation is irremediable" (back cover). The author examines land management, irrigation practices, humus balance, plant nutrients and pollution, the use of pesticides and antibiotics, and neglect. The book includes an appendix describing textually and statistically the agricultural regions of the former Soviet Union.

218. **Land Reform in the Former Soviet Union and Eastern Europe.** Edited by Stephen K. Wegren. xxiii, 268p.: illus. *Routledge Studies of Societies in Transition*, 5. London: Routledge, 1998. Includes bibliographical references and index.

Wegren and his collaborators have recognized that there is an urban bias to most Western studies of land reform. This collection of essays is presented to address that shortcoming and to achieve several other goals: "The first goal was to address the relative dearth of book-length studies on land reform and to do so in ways that would be useful across disciplines. . . . A second goal was to provide a yardstick for measuring how far former bloc nations had come in reforming their agricultural system which had been based on the Soviet collectivization model. . . . A third goal was to assemble what we know about land reform in former bloc nations in order to understand how far reforms still have to go" (p. xiv).

Industry, Management, and Manufacturing

219. **Social Dimensions of Soviet Industrialization.** Edited by William G. Rosenberg and Lewis H. M. Siegelbaum. xix, 296p.: illus. *Indiana-Michigan Series in Russian and Eastern European Studies.* Bloomington: Indiana University Press, 1993. Papers from a seminar sponsored by the Social Science Research Council on Twentieth-Century Russian and Soviet Social History, held at the University of Michigan, Ann Arbor, in April 1988. Includes bibliographical references (pp. 285-89) and index.

The question of industrialization in Russia is a multifaceted one. The contributors to this volume are focusing on the social aspects of this problem, but even that is an enormous field of research. "The essays presented have essentially touched on four general themes: the nature and role of social mobility in its various dimensions during the 1930s; the evolving relationships between the 'new' and the 'old' workers and related changes in worker 'identity'; the management of industrialization. . . ; and the deeper . . . question of culture and its impact on the course of events" (p. x). Contributors include Sheila Fitzpatrick, Stephan Merle, Stephen Kotkin, R. W. Davies, Don K. Rowena, Hiroaki Kurimoto, Lewis H. Siegelbaum, David Sheerer, Peter Solomon, Katerina Clark, Geoff Eley, and Moshe Lewin. A "Guide to Further Reading" by Stephen Coe is included to assist those who would like to read further on the subject.

220. Shearer, David R. **Industry, State, and Society in Stalin's Russia, 1926-1934.** xiv, 263p.: illus. Ithaca, N.Y.: Cornell University Press, 1996. Includes bibliographical references (pp. 247-58) and index.

Shearer intends to explain the development of the Soviet industrial state that formed in the 1930s. Such an explanation is fraught with many contradictions. "Indeed, the new state that took shape in the chaos of the industrialization drive was unruly and unstable, the more so as its creators tried to plan and gain control over it. This contradiction between the centralization of power and the loss of control, and between rational planning and wholly unplanned consequences, is one of the central problems of Stalinism that needs explaining" (p. 20).

Labor and Trade Unions

221. What About the Workers?: Workers and the Transition to Capitalism in Russia. Compiled by Simon Clarke. 248p. London: Verso, 1993. Includes bibliographical references (pp. 242-48).

Political struggles for power in Russia have received a great deal of attention in the press. The authors of this book, Simon Clarke, Peter Fairbrother, Michael Burawoy, and Pavel Krotov, argue that the future of Russia will not be decided in the halls of the Kremlin. They believe that the future of Russia will be decided in its businesses and factories. "In short, this book is about the subversive undercurrent of social life, the class struggle" (p. 3). The essays here are based on the fieldwork of the contributing authors. They cover a broad range of topics: state socialism, worker control in industry, trade unions, the 1989 miners' strike, the strikes of 1991, and privatization.

222. Aves, Jonathan. **Workers Against Lenin: Labor Protest and the Bolshevik Dictatorship.** 220p. London: Tauris Academic Studies, 1996. Includes bibliographical references (pp. 205-11).

Aves explores the role of the workers' strikes in 1921 in the decision of the Communist Party to move away from the radical application of communist principles in building a socialist society. His study is not confined to Moscow and Petrograd, but extends to the Donbas and the Urals as well.

223. Conflict and Change in the Russian Industrial Enterprise. Edited by Simon Clarke. 289p. *Management and Industry in Russia series*, 2. Brookfield, Vt.: Edward Elgar, 1996. Includes bibliographical references and index.

This is the second volume in a series on the Russian industrial enterprise in transition. The first volume was devoted to formal and informal relations and Volume 3 will be devoted to labor in transition. Nine papers by recognized experts are presented. The first of these papers, by Simon Clarke, provides an overview of the problem and a summary of the topics covered by the other eight presenters. Clarke argues that within Marxism-Leninism conflict was bound to arise but that the party was seen as the embodiment of right and reason. Thus, such conflict had to be, by its very nature, the irrational result of "ignorance, venality or weakness, to be corrected by punishment, re-education, or even some small corrections to the Party program in the light of the further findings of science" (p. 2). These ideological structures did not dissolve with the end of the Soviet Union, he maintains, but were reembodied in neoliberalism. These case studies address "fundamental issues of conflict and change and the future development of Russia" (p. 3).

224. Clarke, Simon. **Management and Industry in Russia: Formal and Informal Relations in the Period of Transition**. x, 224p. *Management and Industry in Russia*. Aldershot, Eng.: Edward Elgar, 1995. Includes index.

This is the first volume in a series of three devoted to the Russian industrial enterprise. The essays are intensive longitudinal case studies that focus on two to four enterprises since the end of 1991. The topic covered in this volume is the relation between formal and informal relations in production. All the essays have been translated from the Russian by the editor. Clarke states that the formalism of the scientific organization of labor "could not possibly be adequate to the everyday reality of production" (p. 1). "In practice production was only possible because the formal norms were regularly violated and ignored, production at every level being dominated by informal norms and relationships in which the personal qualities of individual workers and managers could play a decisive role" (pp. 1-2). The essays explore this tension between informal norms and the rigid normative framework that exercised control.

225. Connor, Walter D. **Tattered Banners: Labor, Conflict, and Corporatism in Postcommunist**. xx, 231p. Boulder, Colo.: Westview Press, 1996. Includes bibliographical references (pp. 193-217) and index.

Its laboring class did not give up some features of the Soviet economy easily. In particular, the job security of the old economy and benefits, meager though they may have been, are sorely missed. In this book Walter Connor examines Yeltsin's attempts to deal with this problem. "Connor examines Russia's emergent labor politics in the critical first years of the post-Soviet period, focusing on the problems Yeltsin encountered in attempting to adopt a 'corporatist' solution to the conflicts of interest that have arisen between labor, employers, and the state" (p. 219). Connor looks at the trade unions and their response to working conditions in the new Russian state. He also examines the institutional structure during this period of transition.

226. Filtzer, Donald A. **Soviet Workers and De-Stalinization: The Consolidation of the Modern System of Soviet Production Relations, 1953-1964**. xv, 318p. Cambridge, Eng.: Cambridge University Press, 1992. Includes bibliographical references (pp. 302-9) and index.

"Filtzer argues that the main concern of Khrushchev's labor policy was to re-motivate an industrial population left demoralized by the Stalinist terror. This meant persuading workers to surrender their defensive shop-floor tactics of lax discipline and poor-quality work. . . . In his conclusions, Filtzer shows how the labor problems of the Khrushchev years were the same as those which confronted Mikhail Gorbachev and his ill-fated perestroika. Thus he argues that reform of the Soviet system is impossible within existing property relations" (frontispiece).

227. Hughes, James. **Stalinism in a Russian Province: A Study of Collectivization and Dekulakization in Siberia**. xi, 271p.: maps. New York: St. Martin's Press in association with the Centre for Russian and East European Studies, 1996. Includes bibliographical references (pp. 258-63) and index.

This study continues the author's previous book *Stalin, Siberia and the Crisis of the New Economic Policy*. "In this book the focus of analysis has been taken forward to examine the aftermath of the grain crisis and the evolution of the primary programmatic pillar of the Stalin revolution: the formation and implementation of the policies of forced collectivization and dekulakization" (p. ix).

228. Straus, Kenneth M. **Factory and Community in Stalin's Russia: The Making of an Industrial Working Class**. xiv, 355p.: illus. *Pitt Series in Russian and East European Studies*. Pittsburgh, Pa.: University of Pittsburgh Press, 1997.

In focusing on Soviet working-class formation, structure, and consciousness, Straus, in Part 1, examines the background of working-class formation in late imperial Russia and the early years of the Soviet Union and provides a case study of the Hammer and Sickle Steel Plant in Moscow. In Part 2 he moves to the Stalinist policy and its social chaos. He analyzes recruiting workers, attaching workers, training workers, and the effects of shock work and socialist competition. In Part 3 he looks at the urban factory community as a site of social stabilization and the making of the new Soviet working class.

Unemployment

229. **Poverty in Russia: Public Policy and Private Responses**. Edited by Jeni Klugman. xiv, 281p. *EDI Development Studies*, 1020-105X. Washington, D.C.: The World Bank, 1997. Includes bibliography and index.

The contributions to this volume, which evolved from a series of background papers commissioned by the World Bank for poverty assessment in 1991, provide "rigorous quantitative analyses of the impact of transition on the well-being of individuals and households in Russia" (p. v). The papers are arranged in two sections: (1) dimensions of poverty: health and unemployment; and (2) public policy and private responses. Of particular concern is the impact of social support, family safety nets, and public opinion about social issues.

230. Silverman, Bertram. **New Rich, New Poor, New Russia: Winners and Losers on the Russian Road to Capitalism**. xv, 159p. Armonk, N.Y.: M. E. Sharpe, 1997. Includes bibliographical references (pp. 139-54) and index.

"This study reveals that Russia has chosen a different road to capitalism. Guided by free market ideology, market reforms have resulted in dramatic declines in living standards that limit the forward movement of liberalization" (p. xiii). Topics covered include free market ideology and the specter of inequality, critical responses to radical reform, the rise of mass poverty, women as losers, wage earners as winners and losers, and entrepreneurship and the economic elite.

Resources and Their Utilization

231. Firth, Noel E. **Soviet Defense Spending: A History of CIA Estimates 1950-1990**. 1st ed. xix, 291p.: illus. *Texas A&M University Military History series*, 58. College Station: Texas A&M University Press, 1998. Includes bibliographical references (pp. [265]-281) and index.

"This book tells the story of the Central Intelligence Agency's (CIA) more than forty-year effort to estimate Soviet defense spending. It examines why and how the work was done, results of the estimating effort, and how the estimates were used. The book also addresses some of the criticisms of CIA estimates and what we have learned, since the collapse of the Soviet Union, about Soviet military outlays during the Cold War" (p. 3).

232. **Doing Business in Central Russia: Reference Book**. Edited by Igor Zornikov and Charles Swan. 267p.: illus. Voronezh, Voronezh University Press, 1992. "Spravochnoe izdanie"—Colophon.

This small directory is largely devoted to the services and businesses available in the Voronezh region. The first section does reprint laws on foreign entrepreneurs for Russia. The rest of the volume is devoted to the directory of services in Voronezh.

Business and Entrepreneurial Activity

233. **The International Review for Chief Executive Officers: Russia and the New Republics**. v.: illus. London: Sterling, 1994. Vols. for 1994 published in two parts.

Two volumes of this three-volume work are devoted entirely to Russia and the new republics. They include articles and in-depth studies from a variety of contributors that deal with all aspects of doing business in Russia. A sample of subjects covered include money markets, banking, capital and credit, telecommunications, acquiring a Russian enterprise, the chamber of commerce in Russia, the fuel and power industry, profile of poverty, and defense conversion in the FSU.

234. Burandt, Gary, and Nancy Giges. **Moscow Meets Madison Avenue: The Adventures of the First American Adman in the USSR**. 1st ed. xiv, 222p.: illus. New York: Harper Business, 1992.

Gary Burandt recounts his experiences establishing the first Russian advertising agency. While this book is not intended as a guide to the establishment of such businesses, it is meant to illustrate certain kinds of problems in emerging economies. The book is arranged topically. Gary Burandt is an executive with an international advertising agency.

235.   Hertz, Noreena. **Russian Business Relationships in the Wake of Reform**. xvi, 210p.: illus. London; New York: Macmillan; St. Martin's Press, 1997. "In association with St. Antony's College, Oxford." Includes bibliographical references (pp. 194-203) and index.

In this book, Hertz deals with a number of the key aspects of economic reform in Russia. He examines changes in the concentration of industries in various sectors of the economy, the degree to which competitive pressures are being felt and what is driving them, whether or not business relationships are protecting firms from outside influences, the role of the state in the new environment, and a number of other issues. Hertz is interested in determining whether or not a market economy can be designed. Further, he will try to determine if emulation of the Anglo-American model should be the goal. He uses a number of case studies to examine these questions. The appendixes contain a list of the key concepts in privatization, a list of the interview questions used in the case studies, sample supply and sale contracts, and sample employment contracts.

236.   Holden, Nigel, Cary L. Cooper, and Jennifer Carr. **Dealing with the New Russia: Management Cultures in Collision**. xiv, 290p. Chichester, Eng.: John Wiley, 1998. Includes bibliography and index.

This book is written for those who are exploring the Russian and CIS market for investments and other business opportunities. It complements other books on the topic but concentrates on a theme the author thinks is underdeveloped relationship building with Russian business counterparts. The first six chapters explore the various characteristics of Russian business and the social/economic context in which Russian business managers operate. Chapters 7-10 pay more attention to personal communication. Learning how to communicate with Russian business managers, the author believes, is the best way to develop success for business ventures in this new market.

237.   Lapidus, Mikhail Khlovenovich, et al. **Business in the Russian Free Market**. 232p. Kansas City, Mo.: MIR House, 1995. Includes bibliographical references (p. 232).

The authors have written a book to bridge the gap between the current state of relative ignorance about the Russian business climate and structure and its reality. Individual units cover a variety of topics that fill in such knowledge. They describe and analyze the economic and historical story of Russia's development, the state system and economic status of Russia, the transition of state property to the private sector, economic relations with foreign countries, the banking system, the financial, insurance, and real estate markets, the tax system, and money payments in Russia. It will be useful for anyone trying to understand the Russian business climate as it existed in 1995.

238. Poe, Richard. **How to Profit from the Coming Russian Boom: The Insider's Guide to Business Opportunities and Survival on the Frontiers of Capitalism**. xxvi, 305p. New York: McGraw-Hill, 1993. Includes index.

Poe argues against the common wisdom that Russia's extraordinary business opportunities are available only to highly trained and financed personnel. He "helps the reader understand that much of what is happening in Russia and much of what is valuable in Russia never finds its way into the Western press or into the official reports published by the Russian government itself. . . . He also gives specific suggestions on how to get things done in Russia. He examines closely a large number of actual ventures in Russia and walks the reader through the processes which were involved in identifying, structuring, negotiating, implementing, managing, and operating these ventures successfully" (p. xix).

Finance and Credit

239. Abel, Istvan. **Money and Finance in the Transition to a Market Economy**. 27 leaves. *Discussion Paper/Budapest Bank*, 1992. No. 1. Cheltenham, Eng.: Edward Elgar, 1998. Includes bibliographical references (pp. 191-207) and index.

The essays in this volume focus on key questions relating to monetary policy and the financial sector in transition economies in Eastern Europe. Specific topics covered include credit market failure, constraints on enterprise liquidity, fiscal and monetary policy, economics of bankruptcy, industrial restructuring, banking reform and bad loans problem, and stabilization and convertibility in the transition.

Dismantling of the Command Economy

240. **After the Cold War: Russian-American Defense Conversion for Economic Renewal**. xvii, 133p. *Geonomics Institute for International Economic Advancement series.* New York: New York University Press, 1993.

In order to achieve some progress in defense conversion and economic restructuring, 60 private individuals from the United States, Russia, and Canada met in October 1992. One of the results of their meeting was the Bread Loaf Charter, reproduced in this volume, which sets out a series of problems that must be overcome in this area. This set of essays looks at several aspects of the problem in depth. The essays give an overview of defense conversion in both the United States and Russia and provide a viewpoint from the Russian ministries, from the Russian enterprises, and from American business. The collection also includes several appendixes that contain a Joint Russian-U.S. Declaration on Defense Conversion (June 17, 1992, summit), Law on Conversion of the Defense Industry in the Russian Federation (March 1992), and the Supreme Soviet Resolution Law on Conversion.

241. Åslund, Anders. **How Russia Became a Market Economy**. xiii, 378p. Washington, D.C.: The Brookings Institution, 1995. Includes endnotes and index.

This book is based on the author's work as an economic advisor to the Russian government from November 1991 to January 1994. Åslund does not intend to give policy advice but instead analyzes events and their causes in order to "clarify what actually happened when Russia attempted a radical transformation to a market economy based on private ownership and the rule of law" (p. 1). Åslund concludes that "the main goal of the Russian economic transition has been accomplished: Russia has become a market economy" (p. 3).

242. Goldman, Marshall I. **Lost Opportunity: Why Economic Reforms in Russia Have Not Worked**. xii, 290p. New York: W. W. Norton, 1994. Includes bibliographical references (pp. 277-80) and index.

Goldman methodically examines how Yeltsin rose to power and accepted the task of reforming the Russian economy. He then turns to the role of economic advisors, the suitability of shock therapy as a reform strategy, and, in order to gain some perspective, analyzes economic reform in Germany, Japan, Eastern Europe, and China.

243. Nelson, Lynn D. **Radical Reform in Yeltsin's Russia: Political, Economic, and Social Dimensions**. xiii, 256p. Armonk, N.Y.: M. E. Sharpe, 1995. Includes index.

"This study examines political, institutional, and organizational factors that shaped Russian economic reforms from late 1991 until mid-1994, and further inquires into the implications of the reforms for both economic and non-economic institutions in Russia" (p. ix). Topics include the political dimension of economic reform, structural and cultural factors, contrasting economic priorities, and coordination issues in Russia's privatization program. It includes two appendixes. The first discusses the difficulties and methodology of data collection in 1993 in Russia and the second presents the results of surveys in tabular form.

244. **Defense Conversion, Economic Reform and the Outlook for the Russian and Ukrainian Economies**. Edited by Henry S. Rowen, Charles Wolf, and Jeanne Zlotnick. 262p.: illus. London: Macmillan, 1994. Includes bibliographies and index.

The papers presented here were originally read at a symposium on defense conversion and economic reform conducted by the RAND Corporation and the Hoover Institution on War, Peace and Revolution. The contributions, which are focused on the Russian and Ukrainian economies, are arranged in four parts: (1) current setting; (2) economic reform and defense conversion; (3) defense concepts, planning, and budgeting; and (4) foreign assistance and the reform process.

245. Ticktin, H. Hillel. **Origins of the Crisis in the USSR: Essays on the Political Economy of a Disintegrating System**. ix, 192p. Armonk, N.Y.: M. E. Sharpe, 1992. Includes bibliographical references and index.

The political economy of the Soviet Union was the focus of Gorbachev's effort to restructure the Soviet system in the 1980s. Hillel Ticktin has analyzed this process in this book. He takes advantage of the newly available material on the Russian economy and political system. "The task of this book is, therefore, to take part in the discovery of the nature of the laws governing the USSR. In this endeavor it tries to describe the changing social relations in the country" (p. 6). Ticktin examines the role of the Soviet elite, the intelligentsia, the working class, and the role of perestroika in the collapse of the Soviet Union.

Foreign Economic Relations

246. Davydov, O. D. **Inside Out: The Radical Transformation of Russian Foreign Trade, 1992-1997**. viii, 224p., [8] p. of plates: illus. New York: Fordham University Press, 1998.

This volume is directed primarily toward professional economists and those involved with Russia's foreign trade. It describes and analyzes the entire course of foreign trade in Russia from 1992 to 1996, including its successes and failures. Individual chapters cover foreign trade and economic reforms, regulating foreign trade, exports, Russia in the World Trade Organization, Russia and the Commonwealth of Independent States, and Russian relations with Europe, the United States, the Asian Pacific Region, and developing countries.

247. Hewett, Edward A. **Open for Business: Russia's Return to the Global Economy**. xii, 164p. Washington, D.C.: The Brookings Institution, 1992. Includes bibliographical references and index.

This study "analyzes Gorbachev's foreign economic strategy, [and] provides a window for understanding the disintegrative forces that stymied his reforms and eventually defeated him, undermining the country he sought to preserve" (p. vii).

248. Kuznetsov, Andrei. **Foreign Investment in Contemporary Russia: Managing Capital Entry**. xiv, 188p. New York: St. Martin's Press, 1994. Includes index and bibliographic references.

This book deals with an aspect of moving Russia to a market economy. The author explores contemporary Russia's policy toward foreign investment. Individual chapters cover the challenges of post-communist transition, the national competitiveness paradigm, Russia's previous experience as a capital-importing country, investment climate and investment risk, setting priorities for capital entry regulations, and the political economy of free economic zones.

249. Stone, Randall W. **Satellites and Commissars: Strategy and Conflict in the Politics of Soviet-Bloc Trade**. xviii, 283p. *Princeton Studies in International History and Politics*. Princeton, N.J.: Princeton University Press, 1996. Includes bibliographical references (pp. [261]-279) and index.

Stone sums up the argument and thrust of his study thus: "I claim that the East European states were pursuing their individual interests when they undermined cooperative agreements that would have yielded benefits for all. Moreover, I argue that the paralysis of Soviet policy was the product of rational adaptation by myriads of low-level officials to the constraints imposed by Soviet institutions. The failures of these institutions cannot be understood apart from the incentives that they imposed on the officials who betrayed them" (p. xi). A great deal of the research for this book is based on interviews with principal agents involved in the agreements studied.

250. Tourevski, Mark, and Eileen Morgan. **Cutting the Red Tape: How Western Companies Can Profit in the New Russia**. xxiii, 310p. New York: Free Press, 1993. Includes bibliographical references (pp. 293-300) and index.

Based on research with Russian firms, this book is a practical guide to doing business in post-communist Russia. Although it is slightly dated, many of the suggestions are still viable. Individual topics address the human dimension of doing business, advantages and obstacles to doing business, potential opportunities in trade and investment, sociocultural dynamics, discrepancies between law and reality, and negotiation with Russian businesspeople.

251. Valencia, Mark J. **The Russian Far East in Transition: Opportunities for Regional Economic Cooperation**. xi, 243p.: illus., maps. Boulder, Colo.: Westview Press, 1995. Includes bibliographical references and index.

These eight essays "examine the opportunities for multilateral economic cooperation between the Russian Far East (RFE) and Northeast Asia—Northeast China, Mongolia, North Korea, South Korea, Taiwan, and Japan" (p. 1). Three appendixes supplement the discussion with more detailed and specialized analyses.

Privatization

252. **Economic Transformation in Russia**. Edited by Anders Aslund and James Millar. viii, 190p.: illus. New York: St. Martin's Press, 1994.

This volume was based on a conference held in 1993 in Stockholm with economists who were interested in economic reform in Russia. Topics covered include stabilization policy, dilemmas of monetary and financial policy, foreign trade regulation, privatization, state enterprises during transition, the conditions of life, Poland as a useful model for Russia, and a liberal perspective on economic reforms.

253. **The Privatization Process in Russia, Ukraine, and the Baltic States: Economic Environment, Legal and Ownership Structure, Institutions for State Regulation, Overview of Privatization Programs, Initial Transformation of Enterprises**. Edited by Roman Frydman, Andrzej Rapaczynski, and John S. Earle. xiii, 276p.: illus., maps. Budapest, Hungary; New York: Central European University Press, 1993. Includes bibliographical references.

"The volume of reports presented here is the second in a series to be produced by the Privatization Project of the Central European University. The Project is designed to create a regional framework for the promotion and improvement of public policies in the area of privatization in Eastern Europe. (including former Soviet republics)" (p. x). The book is divided into five geographic sections, each devoted to one nation. Each section includes an overview; a description of the economic environment; a discussion of present forms of ownership; and an overview of privatization and commercialization. No index is included.

254. **Privatization, Conversion, and Enterprise Reform in Russia**. Edited by Michael McFaul and Tova Perlmutter. xi, 228p.: illus. Boulder, Colo.: Westview Press, 1995. Includes bibliographical references. "Published in cooperation with the Center for International Security and Arms Control at Stanford University"—CIP's pub. info.

The papers in this volume were first presented as papers at a conference on economic reform in Russia at Stanford University in November 1993. The papers are grouped into four sections. Part 1 examines Yeltsin's economic policies in 1992 and 1993. In Part 2 the contributors look at how these policies have affected business practice by studying the ways in which managers and directors of businesses have tried to save their resources. Part 3 focuses on the defense industry. In Part 4 the issues raised in the earlier sections are examined in the context of conversion, privatization, and market transition in specific enterprises. The contributors are Alexander Radygin, Sergei Sinelnikov, Michael McFaul, Irina Starodubrovskaya, Katharina Pistor, Mari Kuraishi Horne, Clifford Gaddy, Jacques Sapir, John A. Battilega, Tarja Cronberg, and David Bernstein. The book includes a glossary of terms, a summary of privatization programs, and a list of Soviet and Russian legislation relevant to enterprise reform.

255. Smith, Alan. **Challenges for Russian Economic Reform**. vi, 275p. Washington, D.C.: Published by the Brookings Institution for the Royal Institute of International Affairs, London, 1995. At head of title: Russian and CIS Programme, the Royal Institute of International Affairs.

This collection clearly and methodically presents the problems facing Russian economic reform. In an introductory chapter Alan Smith deftly summarizes the content of the other four parts, each of which are subdivided into three or four facets. Part 1 deals with regions, local power, and the potential for economic change. Part 2 explores monopoly and competition policy. Privatization in the CIS is the subject of Part 3, and the final part analyzes trade and payments between the former Soviet republics.

Education and Culture

256. Jahn, Hubertus F. **Patriotic Culture in Russia During World War I**. xii, 229p. Ithaca, N.Y.: Cornell University Press, 1995. Includes bibliographical references (pp. 209-21) and index.

Jahn explores the various manifestations of patriotic culture during World War I in Russia. He does not attempt to examine all forms of cultural production and thus excludes literature and the fine arts and concentrates instead on various forms of popular entertainment and mass culture. His sources include posters, postcards, cartoons, memoirs, journals, and archives.

257. **Russian Cultural Studies: An Introduction**. Edited by Catriona Kelly and David Shepherd. xiv, 428p.: illus. New York: Oxford University Press, 1998. Includes bibliographical references and index.

In *Russian Cultural Studies: An Introduction* the contributors provide an overview of Russian cultural develpment from 1917 to the present. The essays are arranged in five parts: (1) the politics of culture; (2) theatre, music visual arts; (3) cinema, media, the Russian consumer; (4) identities: populism, religion, emigration; and (5) sexuality, gender, youth culture. A chronology of cultural events from 1917 to the present is also included. The volume is intended as a companion to *Constructing Russian Culture in the Age of Revolution: 1881-1940*. The two volumes provide an analysis of the development of a culture in the throes of violent change.

258. **Re-Entering the Sign: Articulating New Russian Culture**. Edited by Anesa Miller-Pogacar and Ellen E. Berry. xi, 364p. Ann Arbor: University of Michigan Press, 1995. Includes bibliographical references.

These essays include a broad range of writings from formal scholarly articles to manifestos. Their aim is to describe and analyze the current culture and its implications for thought and living in the modern world. The essays are arranged in three parts: (1) culture and society; (2) literature and textuality; and (3) cinema. The editors "speak of discouragement, pessimism, and exhaustion, expressing concern for damages visited in the past and pitfalls remaining for the future" (p. 20).

259. Okenfuss, Max J. **The Rise and Fall of Latin Humanism in Early-Modern Russia: Pagan Authors, Ukrainians, and the Resiliency of Muscovy**. vi, 290p. Leiden, N.Y.: E. J. Brill, 1995. Includes bibliographical references (pp. [243]-279) and index.

Max Okenfuss examines the influence of Western writings in early modern Russia in this book. Okenfuss believes that the influence of these works has been exaggerated in the traditional historical literature. "Rather most of Muscovy resisted Latin and endured because its culture was satisfyingly complex, had psychological resonance, and was centered on a firmly held Christian faith" (p. 8). The author is looking at the intellectual elite in this study and the degree to which Western literature had become a part of their intellectual heritage. His method is to study the publishing output and compare it to that of the West. Okenfuss also reviews book ownership after members of the elite complete their education. While he is aware of the limitations of this approach, he believes it does help to evaluate the degree to which Western philosophy and writing became a part of the Russian intellectual movement. Okenfuss' bibliography clearly demonstrates the depth of his research. He divided his study into four parts. The first examines the book culture in Muscovy in general terms. The second and third follow the changes of that culture throughout the 18th century. The final part looks at the long-term effects of Latin culture in Russian society.

General Studies

260. Compton, Susan P. **Russian Avant-Garde Books 1917-34**. 175p.: illus. (some col.), ports. London: The British Library, 1992. Includes bibliography (pp. 164-65) and indexes.

The author uses the covers and contents of books and journals in order to shed some light on the contemporary interpretation of the utopian ideas that were expressed in Russia in the 1920s. These books and journals provided a vehicle for avant-garde ideas to be expressed and to be imported into a country where such ideas were increasingly seen as subversive. Compton's study provides an introduction to the cultural history of the 1920s and 1930s, the new partnerships between writers and designers, and how these ideas played themselves out in the theater, and in art and architecture.

261. **Soviet Education Under Perestroika: Papers from the IV World Congress for Soviet and East European Studies, Harrogate, UK, 1990**. Edited by John Dunstan. xiii, 230p. London: Routledge, 1992. Selected papers from the congress. Includes bibliographical references and index.

This collection of essays explores Soviet education at the end of an era. Topics covered include the progressive tradition in Soviet schooling, perestroika in the general school, the coming of the computer age in Soviet education, arts teaching, atheism and religious education, reform for teaching children with learning difficulties, vocational education, reinventing Soviet higher education, ethnic education, and prospects for comparative education between the East and West.

262. Dunstan, John. **Soviet Schooling in the Second World War**. xviii, 264p.: map. New York: St. Martin's Press in association with the Centre for Russian and East European Studies, University of Birmingham, 1997. Includes bibliographical references and index.

While there has been much written about education in the Soviet Union, there has not previously been a volume devoted exclusively to the postwar years. This book is intended to fill that lacuna. "It focuses upon the largest sector of Soviet education, the general schooling of children and young people from the start until, at the latest, the age of 18" (p. xi). The book is divided into three parts. The first lays the groundwork for the study, describing educational practice and conditions before the war. Part 2 examines the war years, changes in curriculum, and the experiences of children raised during those tumultuous years. The final section is limited to the reconstruction period late in the war. The book includes a glossary of abbreviations.

263. **Democracy in the Russian School: The Reform Movement in Education Since 1984**. Edited by Ben Eklof and Edward Dneprov. vi, 269p.: illus. Boulder, Colo.: Westview Press, 1993. Includes bibliographical references and index.

This series of essays on different aspects of the reform movement in Russian education since 1984 begins with an introductory piece by the editors on democracy in the Russian school since 1984. The other essays are then arranged in three parts: (1) the educational system under fire; (2) the VNIK program; and (3) opposition in power. Many of the articles are by Russians actively engaged in research on Russian educational practices.

264. **Education and Society in the New Russia**. Edited by Anthony Jones. xvii, 341p. Armonk, N.Y.: M. E. Sharpe, 1994. Includes bibliographical references and index.

This set of 14 essays explores the interplay of education and society in the New Russia, i.e., from 1985 onward. After an introductory essay that describes and analyzes the educational legacy of the Soviet period, the essays focus on (1) new structures and new curriculums; (2) professional education; and (3) education and social issues.

265. Kelly, Aileen. **Toward Another Shore: Russian Thinkers Between Necessity and Chance**. 400p. *Russian Literature and Thought*. New Haven, Conn.: Yale University Press, 1998. Includes bibliographical references (pp. [353]-397).

A major premise of this book is that the critique of utopian thought by writers such as Tolstoy and Dostoevsky has relevance for our own time. Kelly describes and analyzes the key ideas of Russian intellectuals such as Dostoevsky, Tolstoy, Turgenev, Chicherin, Bakunin, Herzen, and others and how their ideas relate both to the society and culture of their time and that of today.

266. Ries, Nancy. **Russian Talk: Culture and Conversation During Perestroika**. xii, 220p.: illus. Ithaca, N.Y.: Cornell University Press, 1997. Includes bibliographical references (pp. 203-14) and index.

Ries describes her fascinating study thus: "My aim in this book is not to provide a comprehensive sociology of the permutations of culture and expression in Russia during and after perestroika. If such an undertaking were possible, it would be outdated even before it was written. Instead, I try to illustrate something of the complex intervocality of various historical and human vantage points, as expressed through the daily narratives and practices of Russians themselves, and to tease out and abstract from these narratives the social and ideological orientations they convey and reproduce" (p. 3).

267. **A Hidden Fire: Russian and Japanese Cultural Encounters, 1868-1926**. Edited by J. Thomas Rimer. xi, 289p. Stanford, Calif.; Washington, D.C.: Stanford University Press/Woodrow Wilson Center Press, 1995. Includes endnotes, select bibliography, and index.

Aside from three papers specifically commissioned for this volume, the remaining studies were originally presented at a conference in 1991 in Sapporo, Japan. The 20 essays are arranged in seven sections that reflect the main themes of the conference: fictional literature; the performing arts; mutual images; Russia and Japan; cultural contacts; historical context; and some final considerations. It also includes a select bibliography of works cited in the papers presented.

268. Volkov, Solomon. **St. Petersburg: A Cultural History**. xxiv, 598p.: illus. New York: Free Press, 1995.

This translation from the Russian offers a broad but detailed examination of the cultural history of St. Petersburg beginning with a description of how the city was built and including information and reflection on how the mythos of the city was created, the city during the periods of Pushkin, Gogol, and Dostoevsky, the Silver Age, a city of revolution, of terror, of famine, and so on to the modern day. Part memoir and part history, Volkov's book is central to an understanding of one of the greatest cities in Europe.

269. **World Congress for Soviet and East European Studies (4th) 1990: Harrogate, England. School and Society in Tsarist and Soviet Russia: Selected Papers from the Fourth World Congress for Soviet and East European Studies, Harrogate, 1990**. Edited by Ben Ekloff. xii, 254p., [8] p. of plates: illus. New York: St. Martin's Press, 1993. Includes bibliographical references and index.

These papers were originally presented at the Fourth World Congress for Soviet and East European Studies in July 1990. They cover a wide range of topics relating to the Russian educational system and the environment in which it existed. Selected topics include N. A. Korf as the designer of the Russian elementary school classroom; Tolstoi and peasant learning; theater in the village school; patriarchal authority, discipline, and the Russian school; teachers, politics, and the peasant community; and others.

Mass Communications

270. Androunas, Elena. **Soviet Media in Transition: Structural and Economic Alternatives**. xii, 167p. Westport, Conn.: Praeger, 1993. Includes bibliographical references (pp. 159-60) and index.

Rather than looking at specific minor details of the mass media, Androunas instead provides a schema for analyzing the mass media in the Soviet Union. What she offers here is "an analysis of the media system in the context of the political, economic, and ethnic developments under perestroika of the Soviet society."

271. Bonnell, Victoria E. **Iconography of Power: Soviet Political Posters Under Lenin and Stalin**. xxii, 363p., [8] p. of plates: illus. (some col.). Berkeley: University of California Press, 1997. Includes bibliographic references and index.

Soviet political propaganda has been the focus of numerous studies. Victoria Bonnell examines political propaganda as it developed and was manifest in poster art. "In essence, I was captivated by the role of posters in the symbolic representation of power. As the research proceeded, I became more and more interested in the contemporary reception of the messages conveyed by visual propaganda" (p. xix). Rich with supporting illustrative material, the author examines a complex subject using the icon as her unifying theme. The chapters are arranged topically and include the iconography of the worker, representations of women generally and peasant women specifically, and Bolshevik "demonology."

272. DeLuca, Anthony R. **Politics, Diplomacy and the Media: Gorbachev's Legacy in the West**. x, 165p. Westport, Conn.: Praeger, 1998. Includes bibliographical references.

"This book is not a popular biography of Gorbachev but an account of his political leadership and the controversy over his political significance and legacy. It also discusses the importance of Gorbachev's having taken the Soviet people beyond the threshold of a new political discourse and the way in which his rhetorical approach and style transformed the political dialogue within the Soviet Union and the Soviet Union's relationship with the rest of the world" (p. x).

273. Ellis, Frank. **From Glasnost to the Internet: Russia's New Infosphere**. xxiii, 259p. New York: St. Martin's Press, 1999. Includes bibliographical references and index.

This is a study of the transformation of Russia's mass media from the creation of the Soviet dictatorship to the open environment of the Internet. The book was originally a series of lectures delivered by the author for members of the Reuters News Agency. These lectures have been expanded for this book. The book is divided into three parts. The first examines the way that censorship attacked the system it was meant to protect. Part 2 focuses on contemporary problems for the media: new media legislation, crime, and the Chechen War. In the final part the author looks at the implications of Russia's entry into the Global Information Infrastructure. The book includes a glossary, a chronology of events from 1902 to 1997, and the full text of medial legislation of the Russian Federation. There is also a bibliography of Internet sources.

274. G. N. Vachnadze. **Secrets of Journalism in Russia: Mass Media Under Gorbachev and Yeltsin**. x, 437p. Commack, N.Y.: Nova Science Publishers, 1992. Includes index.

This fascinating book has three interrelated topics: "(1) a narration about those who in the 1990s have sought to dismantle the Stalinist system in the press and book publishing, in radio and television; (2) an analysis of the development of audio- and video-technology, satellite and cable television, communications and computerization; (3) the interrelationship of the problems of a free press and human rights in Russia" (p. x).

275. Goban-Klas, Tomasz. **The Orchestration of the Media: The Politics of Mass Communications in Communist Poland and the Aftermath**. xiii, 289p. International Communication and Popular Culture. Boulder, Colo.: Westview Press, 1994. Includes bibliographical references (pp. 267-78) and index.

The author's aim is to describe and analyze the Polish mass media in its sociopolitical setting. He describes the process of setting up and then tearing down the state-run media system in Poland, examines the stakeholders in the media system during various periods, and finally identifies current problems in setting up a new democratic media system in Poland.

276. Murray, John Damian. **The Russian Press from Brezhnev to Yeltsin: Behind the Paper Curtain**. viii, 280p. *Studies of Communism in Transition*. Aldershot, Eng.: Edward Elgar, 1994. Includes bibliographical references (pp. 263-72) and index.

John Murray has made an in-depth examination of the evolution of the Russian press from the later years of the Soviet Union, through the changes of glasnost, and bringing the reader to the state of the media today. Over 100 pages of the book are taken up with interviews with members of the press from the Soviet and post-Soviet periods. He has also supplied the reader with an appendix of circulation statistics on some of the most popular newspapers in the country. This is one of the only studies on this rapidly changing area of the Russian media.

277. Turpin, Jennifer. **Reinventing the Soviet Self: Media and Social Change in the Former Soviet Union**. x, 154p. Westport, Conn.: Praeger, 1995. Includes bibliography and index.

Using discourse analysis and applied sociological theory, the author examines the Soviet press before and during glasnost and the press' role in the dissolution of the Soviet Union in 1991. The initial two chapters deal with general topics: media theory and analysis, and Soviet media for a global audience. Then Turpin devotes the next four chapters to a closer examination of *Soviet Life* and *Moscow News* under Brezhnev and Gorbachev. She concludes with a final chapter that summarizes her findings.

Geography and Demography

278. Kaiser, Robert John. **The Geography of Nationalism in Russia and the USSR**. xviii, 471p.: maps. Princeton, N.J.: Princeton University Press, 1994. Includes bibliographical references (pp. [417]-446) and index.

Robert Kaiser examines the reasons behind the emotional attachments people form to geographic regions. In the past, studies of ethnic groups have lacked a geographic focus. "This book is a preliminary attempt to explore the dynamic societal processes that restructured human communities as nations, and geographic places as homeland" (p. xviii). The study is divided into two parts. The first explores the theoretical and historical framework around the problem. Part 2 focuses on national territoriality as it has evolved in the postwar period. The appendixes provide information on the Soviet federal system and native language instruction in the USSR.

279. Kolstø, Pål. **Russians in the Former Soviet Republics**. xii, 340p.: maps. Bloomington: Indiana University Press, 1995. Includes bibliographical references (pp. 317-30) and index.

Kolstoe's objective "has been to supply background material on how the Russian Diaspora phenomenon has arisen and developed, as well as to analyze its effects on post-Soviet politics today. In the historical parts, an attempt is made to identify the driving forces behind the migratory patterns of the Russians seen under the tsars and the commissars, and a separate chapter discusses the social and political status of the Russians living in the non-Russian republics during the Soviet period. The common assumption that the Russians represented a privileged upper class is somewhat modified" (p. 5).

280. Matthiessen, Peter, and Boyd Norton. **Baikal: Sacred Sea of Siberia**. 89p.: col. illus., map. Vancouver, B.C.: Douglas & McIntyre, 1992.

Lake Baikal, which holds 20 percent of all fresh water on the planet, is depicted in this volume both in pictures and in the words of Peter Matthiessen, who visited Baikal. The volume also includes a forward by poet Yevgeny Yevtushenko.

281. Pilkington, Hilary. **Migration, Displacement, and Identity in Post-Soviet Russia**. [xi], 252p.: illus. London: Routledge, 1998. Includes bibliographical references (pp. [207]-240) and index.

After the collapse of the Soviet Union, about 25 million Russians found themselves displaced and identified as minorities in former republics. Many were forced to repatriate. Pilkington uses empirical data gathered from approximately 200 interviews with forced migrants and refugees to explore the phenomenon of reintegration from the perspective of those who were displaced. The issues raised here are relevant to wider problems with migration, displacement, and identity on a global scale.

282. Semenov-Tian'-Shanskii, Petr Petrovich. **Travels in the Tian'-Shan': 1856-1857**. Edited by Colin Thomas, Liudmila Gilmour, and Marcus Wheeler. xliii, 269p., [20] p. of plates. *Works Issued by the Hakluyt Society*, ser. no. 189. London: Hakluyt Society, 1998. Includes bibliographical references (pp. xxvi-xxx) and index.

This heavily annotated translation recounts Petr Semenov's journey to the Tian'-Shan' in 1856. A member of the Geographical Society, Semenov had long been interested in the region. In 1853 following an illness he left Russia for Germany to recuperate. There he advanced his study of Central Asia in discussion with Humboldt on the area. Though not well equipped by today's standards the translator feels Semenov made a substantial contribution to the field. "Yet this procedural approach was firmly rooted in the belief that academic geography began with the acquisition of primary data, subsequently classified according to recognized taxonomic methods, and made available for future detailed quantitative analysis and interpretation in relation to other elements of the ecosystem" (p. xxiii). This volume includes reproductions of the pencil sketches by Pavel Kosharov of Central Asia. There is an extensive bibliography and an index of plants, places, and a general index.

Government and State

Bibliographies

283. Kartsev, Vladimir Petrovich, and Todd Bludeau. **!Zhirinovsky!** xii, 198p.: illus. New York: Columbia University Press, 1995. Includes bibliographical references (pp. [175]-182) and index.
This biography of the flamboyant and abrasive leader of the Liberal Democratic Party of Russia not only describes his life and the founding of his political party. It also examines the phenomenon of bezpredel (anything goes) that is omnipresent in Russia since the fall of communism in 1991 and the ways that Zhirinovsky exploits this phenomenon for his own political gain.

284. Kavass, Igor I. **Law in Russia and the Other Post-Soviet Republics: A Bibliographic Survey of English Language Literature, 1992-1995**. xii, 784p. Buffalo, N.Y.: W. S. Hein, 1997. Includes bibliographical references and index.
Kavass has compiled an annotated bibliography of English-language publications that deal with legal issues in the former Soviet Republics from 1992 to 1995. The bibliography is arranged in three parts. Parts 1-2 contain annotated bibliographies arranged by author and subject, respectively. Part 3 is an appendix describing the main sources considered to be useful for researching the topics falling within the book's scope.

285. Solovev, Vladimir, and Elena Klepikova. **Zhirinovsky: Russian Fascism and the Making of a Dictator**. xxii, 256p., [8] p. of plates: illus. Reading, Mass.: Addison-Wesley, 1995. Includes bibliographical references (pp. 235-45) and index.
The focus of this work is not Zhirinovsky the man. The authors are concerned with the political and social phenomena surrounding Zhirinovsky's popularity and its significance for Russia's future. The book begins tracing Zhirinovsky's rise and follows his career from 1991 through early 1995. It also traces a growing fascist movement

General Studies

286. The Soviet Nationality Reader: Disintegration in Context. ix, 635p. Boulder, Colo.: Westview Press, 1992.

"Most of the chapters in this volume are devoted to pre-Gorbachev nationalities problems in order to define the context in which the USSR's nationalities crisis has unfolded" (p. 4). The essays are arranged in seven sections on history and ideology; federalism; elites and ethnic stratification; economy; languages; nationalism and nationalist movements; or coping with the nationalities crisis. The contributors include Barbara Anderson, John Armstrong, Donna Bahry, Mark Beissinger, Walker Connor, John Danlop, Helene Carrere d'Encausse, Gregory Gleason, Paul Goble, Grey Hodnett, Stephan Kux, Gail Lapidus, John Miller, Alexander Motyl, Carol Nechemias, Richard Pipes, Jonathon Pool, Teresa Rakowska-Harmstone, Phillip Roeder, Gertrude Schroeder, Brian Silver, Ronald Suny, Roman Szporluk, and V. Stanley Vardys.

287. The New Russia: Troubled Transformation. Edited by Gail Warshofsky Lapidus. viii, 280p.: illus., maps. Boulder, Colo.: Westview Press, 1995. Includes bibliographical references and index.

This collection of essays on the Russian transition to democracy was the result of research conducted at the Berkeley-Stanford Program in Soviet and Post-Soviet Studies. The contributors to this volume represent various viewpoints. The essays examine Russia's transition in the economy, politics, foreign policy, and defense. The contributors are Gail Lapidus, Richard Ericson, Edward Walker, Victor Zaslavsky, Andrei Kortunov, David Holloway, Michael McFaul, George Breslauer, and Alexander Dallin. The volume includes a glossary of significant terms.

288. Russian Pluralism—Now Irreversible? Edited by Uri Ra'anan, Keith Armes, and Kate Martin. 230p. New York: St. Martin's Press, 1992. Includes index.

"The scholars and practitioners who collaborated in the production of this work attempted to address the sociopolitical organisms that would have to be fully developed and secured in Russia so that genuine democratization could ensue" (p. 2). The authors focused on four elements they felt must be firmly in place for pluralism to be established and flourish: open political debate and organization; a just legal system; an independent media; and freedom of religion. The essays in this volume are divided into four sections that focus on each of these areas. Contributors are Keith Armes, Nina Belyaeva, Yelena Bonner, Nicholas Daniloff, Mark Elliott, Kent R. Hill, Robert T. Huber, Vitaly Korotich, Kate Martin, Uri Ra'anan, Richard Schifter, Savik Shuster, Vera Tolz, and J. Michael Waller.

289. White, Stephen, Graeme Gill, and Darrell Slider. **The Politics of Transition: Shaping a Post-Soviet Future**. x, 277p. Cambridge, Eng.: Cambridge University Press, 1993. Includes bibliographical references (pp. 230-73) and index.

"This book, by three of the West's leading scholars of Soviet and post-Soviet affairs, traces the politics of transition in the late 1980s and early 1990s from its origins to its uncertain post-communist future" (frontispiece). The book is arranged topically. The authors examine the effects of transition on the electoral system, the government, the republics, public opinion, the Communist Party, and the party system in general. The final chapter focuses on the viability of a democratic system imposed from above.

Law

290. Braun, Marina, and Galina Clothier. **English-Russian Dictionary of American Criminal Law**. xiii, 327p. Westport, Conn.: Greenwood Press, 1998. Includes copies of legal forms in Russian and English.

This criminal law dictionary is the first part of a larger project that will cover other areas of the law. The need for such a dictionary has been acutely felt especially since the end of the cold war by court interpreters, instructors, and students of legal translation, compilers of certification material, as well as attorneys and law enforcement personnel who deal with Russian-speaking clients.

The dictionary does not contain all words pertaining to criminal law, but is limited to the most frequently used words (both specifically legal terms as well as jargon and slang used in legal, court, and law enforcement settings). In addition to definitions, each entry also supplies examples of the term's usage in complete sentences in both English and Russian.

The appendix contains 17 examples of court-related documents with their Russian translations. These documents include such things as Miranda rights, petition to wave jury trial, a summons notice, etc.

This dictionary and its planned counterparts should prove especially useful for those working with Russian émigré communities in the United States.

291. Feldbrugge, Ferdinand Joseph Maria. **Russian Law: The End of the Soviet System and the Role of Law**. xii, 486p. *Law in Eastern Europe*, 45. Dordrecht, Martinus Nijhoff, 1993. Includes bibliographical references (pp. 473-76) and index.

F. J. M. Feldbrugge presents the reader with a study of Russian law as it is today. "The central assumptions of this book are that Russian law is in many ways the product of Soviet law and that Soviet law can only be understood as part and parcel of the Soviet system" (p. xi). The author begins with a description of the fundamental aspects of the subject. He then turns to detailed descriptions of the constitutional order, economic law, and social laws. The final chapter contains translations of the Constitutions, the Agreement on the Creation of a Commonwealth and other important legislation of the perestroika era.

292. **Democratization in Russia: The Development of Legislative Institutions**. Edited by Jeffrey W. Hahn. xxiv, 303p.: illus. *Contemporary Soviet/Post-Soviet Politics*. Armonk, N.Y.: M. E. Sharpe, 1996. Includes bibliographical references and index.

The papers compiled in this volume represent the culmination of four years of research by a team of Russian and American scholars. Their goal was to explore the evolution of the legislative institutions in Russia. The papers are divided into three sections: "Legislative Development at the National Level," "Legislative Development at the Local Level," and "The Lessons of Legislative Development in Russia." Students may find some of the appendixes especially helpful. One describes the structure of the government, another the legislative process for a bill in the Duma, another provides the text of the election laws in English, and still another gives a chronology of the reforms of the political system. Contributors to this volume include Jeffrey W. Hahn, Lilia Shevtsova, Timothy J. Colton, Jerry F. Hough, Thomas F. Remington, Kathryn Stoner-Weiss, Blair A. Ruble, Michael L. Mezey, Lev A. Okunkov, Yurii A. Tikhomirov, and Aleksandr Postnikov.

293. Hendley, Kathryn. **Trying to Make Law Matter: Legal Reform and Labor in the Soviet Union**. viii, 265p. Ann Arbor: University of Michigan Press, 1996. Includes bibliographical references (pp. 237-56) and index.

"This study is concerned with the social and political forces and factors that promote (or impede) the realization, in varying degrees, of a legal order in which law can be said to matter in this reciprocal sense. More specifically, it is a study of the effort to institutionalize the rule of law in the Soviet Union—to make law matter in a reciprocal rather than a coercive sense—and the attendant obstacles" (p. 3). Hendley's book is divided into four parts. The first compares the role of law in industrialized societies to its role in socialist societies. Part 2 is a case study of the implementation of a 1980 law. In Part 3 the author focuses on the gap between law in theory and law in practice in the Soviet Union. In the final section Hendley presents her argument for the necessary changes if the role of law in "post-feminist" society is to change.

294. **Reforming Justice in Russia, 1864-1996: Power, Culture, and the Limits of Legal Order**. Edited by Peter H. Solomon. x, 406p. Armonk, N.Y.: M. E. Sharpe, 1997. "Based upon . . . papers prepared for the conference 'Reforming Justice in Russia: An Historical Perspective,' which was held at Massey College, University of Toronto, 31 March-2 April 1995"—Acknowledgments. Includes bibliographical references and index.

Originally presented at a conference at the University of Toronto in 1995, these papers are the result of collaboration between American and Russian legal scholars. The 16 papers are arranged in three sections, preceded by an introduction. The introductory essay covers courts and their reform in Russian history. The remaining three sections explore varieties of justice in imperial Russia; courts, law, and Soviet power; and justice and the Russian transition.

295. Wagner, William G. **Marriage, Property, and Law in Late Imperial Russia**. xiv, 413p. *Oxford Historical Monographs*. Oxford, Eng.: Clarendon Press, 1994. Includes bibliographical references (pp. [384]-388) and index.

William Wagner examines the evolution of civil law and its affect on Russian society in the postemancipation period in this book. Wagner has divided his study into two parts. The first focuses on the family: the role of traditional law and the limits of legislative changes and its possibilities. In the second part he discusses the restructuring of property and inheritance law in this period. He examines the same themes as in Part 1.

296. **Information Sources in Law**. Edited by Jules Winterton and Elizabeth Moys. 2nd ed. London: R. R. Bowker/K. G. Saur, 1997. Includes bibliographical references and index.

This second edition of *Information Sources in Law* has been completely revised. "It provides a guide to a wide range of specialist legal literature of over 30 European countries from Portugal to Russia. It covers both primary and secondary materials including statutes and subsidiary legislation, codes and commentaries, law reports, encyclopedias, directories, bibliographies, and indexes" (back cover). There are individual sections for each country. Each of these provides a general overview on the legal history of the country and provides information on legislation, translations of legislation, codes, commentaries, treaties, law reports, judgments, computer-based systems, encyclopedias, directories, bibliographies, indices, dictionaries, current information sources, and ends with a list of all works cited. There is a detailed index and an opening section on general sources.

Politics and Government, Special Studies

297. Gooding, John. **Rulers and Subjects: Government and People in Russia 1801-1991**. xii, 387p. London; New York; Sydney; Auckland: Arnold, 1996. Includes bibliographical references and index.

Gooding's book is by and large a general history of Russia from 1801 to 1991. Its main purpose, however, is to describe and analyze the relationship between the ruling class and the masses they ruled. "It discusses rulers and the ruling class which served them, institutions of state, government policies and problems, the doctrines and myths which were the invisible chains binding subjects to rulers, the passivity of the many and the rebellions in thought and deed of the few" (p. xi). He focuses on economic policy and conditions, as well as international affairs, only when they are directly relevant to his main theme of rulers and subjects.

298. Ryan, Tracy A., and Igor Oleynik. **Russian Government Today: Fall '94**. 490p., 5 folded leaves of plates: illus., map. Washington, D.C.: Carrol Publishing, The International Center, 1993.

Although it is outdated, this is a valuable source for the description of Russia's governmental structure. The volume is divided into sections on each of the arms of government: parliamentary, executive, regional, and commercial. Each section is subdivided into parts reflecting its organizational units. Each subsection begins with a chart showing the organizational structure of that office. This is followed by a description of the powers and responsibilities of that office and rules for elections. There is also a directory of those in office in 1994. The index of names and of key words make this an especially useful source for those interested in Russian political organization.

299. Warhola, James W. **Politicized Ethnicity in the Russian Federation: Dilemmas of State Formation.** iv, 152p. Lewiston, N.Y.: Edwin Mellen Press, 1996. Includes bibliographical references (pp. [133]-141) and index.

The Russian Federation faces many of the same challenges that confronted the Soviet Union. Not least among these is the distribution of power between the central government and the local powers, as well as the sociopolitical identity of the various ethnic groups within its borders. The author of this study feels Russia is in an excellent position to develop a solution to its problem. "This may be made possible by certain traits one has acquired over centuries of historical experience as a nation; as a result of monumental contributions to world culture; as a repository of enormous natural and human resources; and as a major actor in global affairs" (p. 10). The author describes nation-state developments in Russia, the politico-geographical challenges of Russia, ethnicity in that country's political relations and ethnic minority areas, and the changing state structure.

1917 to 1991

300. Anderson, Richard. **Public Politics in an Authoritarian State: Making Foreign Policy During the Brezhnev Years.** xvi, 266p. Ithaca, N.Y.: Cornell University Press, 1993. Includes bibliographical references and index.

"The central question investigated by this book is whether political competition among Brezhnev-era Politburo members shaped Soviet foreign policy in a manner comparable to the effects of electoral competition on the foreign policy of an electoral polity. I answer that question by investigating whether going public over foreign policy generated rewards for Politburo members comparable to the advantages that elected officials obtained with tenure in office and leverage in policy bargaining" (pp. 3-4). Anderson's analysis is chronologically arranged beginning in 1964 and ending with the establishment of détente in 1970-1972.

301. Blank, Stephen. **The Sorcerer As Apprentice: Stalin As Commissar of Nationalities.** 295p. Westport, Conn.: Greenwood Press, 1994. Includes bibliographical references (pp. [229]-285) and index.

In this study Stephen Blank looks for the origins of Soviet nationality policy and its ties to imperial Russia's policies. He focuses on a few years when Stalin was responsible for the nationalities policies in the early Soviet Union. His study is arranged topically, examining first the origins of Narkomnats, its early days of operation, and its expansion. He then focuses on its reorganization in 1921 and the effects of NEP on nationalities policies. Blank then turns to local branches and their organization from 1918 to 1923, the development of cultural policies, and the crisis that arose in nationality policy at the end of this period. A great deal of the discussion focuses on the Muslim leader Sultangaliev and the issues he raised concerning the preservation of ethnic identity in a socialist society. The book includes an appendix listing the delegates to Sultangaliev's trial.

302. Brown, Archie. **The Gorbachev Factor**. xv, 406p.: illus. Oxford, Eng.: Oxford University Press, 1996. Includes bibliographical references.

This is not a book about Gorbachev. The author has something different as a focus here. "Its main concern is to understand and interpret Gorbachev's contribution to the dramatic changes which took place in the Soviet Union and in that state's relations with the outside world in the second half of the 1980s and the beginning of the 1990s—a time in which East-West relations were transformed and Communist power came to an end in Eastern Europe" (p. ix). The author examines the economic, political, and foreign policy changes as well as presenting a discussion of the coup and the collapse of the Soviet Union. The book includes a glossary.

303. Carrere d'Encausse, Hélène. **The End of the Soviet Empire: The Triumph of the Nations**. xii, 292p. New York: Basic Books, 1993. "A New Republic book." Includes bibliographical references (pp. [287]-289) and index.

D'Encausse describes and analyzes the final years of the Soviet empire. She explores the relations between the Communist Party elite and the individuals, and ethnic populations were increasingly yearning for independence and nationhood. Her book attempts to illuminate the deceptively simple question: "After the age of revolutions, with the end of the empire, is this the age of nations?" (p. xii).

304. Chuev, Feliks Ivanovich. **Molotov Remembers: Inside Kremlin Politics: Conversations with Felix Chuev**. xxiii, 438p. Chicago: I. R. Dee, 1993. Includes index.

Viacheslav Mikhailovich Molotov held many critical positions in the Soviet government under Stalin, filled high posts in the party, headed the foreign ministry, and met almost all major figures of the 20th century. He did not leave any memoirs. Even if he had, the Soviet ban on his writings and works about him would have left them unpublished. For the last 17 years of his life, Molotov met regularly with Felix Chuev. In this book, Chuev has re-created many of those interviews with Molotov. The interview is divided into four thematic sections: "International Affairs," "With Lenin," "With Stalin," and "Since Stalin." The book includes a chronology of Molotov's life.

305. D'Agostino, Anthony. **Gorbachev's Revolution**. ix, 384p. New York: New York University Press, 1998. Includes index.

This is a study of Gorbachev's rise to power and his fall. "A statesman who played the key role in liquidating one revolution and in making another, he is likely to be thought at the same time a traitor at home and a hero abroad, a man who ended up by disowning conquerors and conquests, claiming to see in them a source of weakness rather than strength" (p. 354). The author examines the many obstacles the Russian leader was forced to overcome in his attempt to reform Russia including the political opposition at home. This is a chronologically arranged history of the period.

306. Davies, Sarah. **Popular Opinion in Stalin's Russia: Terror, Propaganda and Dissent**. xix, 236p. Cambridge, Eng.: Cambridge University Press, 1997. Includes bibliographical references.

The years 1934-1941 is the period known as the "Great Terror." Despite the repression of the Stalin regime Soviet citizens still criticized the government. Sarah Davies has drawn on archival materials to analyze the public opinion of the time. She has compiled her findings in this book. "The book examines many themes, including attitudes toward social and economic policy, the terror, and the leader cult, shedding light on a highly important part of Russia's social, political, and cultural history" (p. i). The chapters of the book are divided into three sections: "Economy and Society"; "Politics and Terror"; and "The Leader Cult." The author has included a chronology and glossary.

307. Grachev, A. S. **Final Days: The Inside Story of the Collapse of the Soviet Union**. xviii, 222p. Boulder, Colo.: Westview Press, 1995. Uniform title: *Dalshe bez menia*. Also published in French as *L'histoire vraie de la fin de l'URSS*.

"As press secretary to Mikhail Gorbachev, Andrei Grachev witnessed and recorded many events unobserved by the general public. In this engaging and compelling book, he recounts these episodes in vivid detail, interpreting them in the context of the time" (p. 214). The book includes an appendix containing an English transcript of Mikhail Gorbachev's resignation speech.

308. **Executive Power and Soviet Politics: The Rise and Decline of the Soviet State**. Edited by Eugene Huskey. xiv, 281p. *Contemporary Soviet/Post-Soviet Politics*. Armonk, N.Y.: M. E. Sharpe, 1992. Includes bibliographical references and index.

Huskey and his contributors argue that an understanding of the Soviet government is central to an understanding of Soviet politics and society. However, this topic has not received adequate attention over the past quarter century in scholarship devoted to Soviet politics. The papers in this volume hope to "revive an understanding of and interest in state institutions in the Soviet Union and its successor states" (p. xiii). The 11 chapters are in four sections: (1) the state in imperial Russia and the USSR, (2) the state and the economy, (3) the state and security, and (4) the state and the future.

309. Kremenyuk, Victor. **Conflicts in and Around Russia: Nation-Building in Difficult Times**. xiv, 159p. Westport, Conn.: Greenwood Press, 1994. Includes bibliographical references and index.

Victor Kremenyuk has studied the United States and its policies for many years. He was, therefore, somewhat surprised when he was approached to write on his own country. He chose the timely topic of Russia's internal ethnic problems. Timely, as the various issues surrounding the interaction of Russia's many ethnic populations have become a serious problem after the fall of the Soviet Union. Kremenyuk has been a participant in the joint project on Ethnic Conflict Management in the former Soviet Union for several years. He has divided the study into two sections. The first views the problems in Russia as it struggles to stabilize its democratic system. The second part examines Russia's contemporary problems from the point of view of the failing empires. Two appendixes are included that chronicle the major conflicts of the USSR from 1988 to 1991 and of Russia in 1992.

310. Löwenhardt, John, James R. Ozinga, and Erik van Ree. **The Rise and Fall of the Soviet Politburo**. xix, 244p.: illus. New York: St. Martin's Press, 1992. Includes bibliographical references and index.

The three authors who collaborated on this project intend to provide the historical, sociological and institutional context of the Politburo's decision-making process. Individual chapters are devoted to the origins of the Politburo, the Politburo under Lenin, under Stalin, under Khrushchev, under Brezhnev, Andropov, and Chernenko, under Gorbachev, and its mode of operation. The volume also presents a complete list of the Politburo's composition at selected dates in its history.

311. Mastny, Vojtech. **The Cold War and Soviet Insecurity: The Stalin Years**. xi, 285p. New York: Oxford University Press, 1996. Includes bibliographical references (pp. 201-62) and index.

Mastny studies the workings of Soviet insecurity during Stalin's reign and the implications and consequences it had for the cold war. As such it is a history of the beginnings of the cold war, the foundation for which was laid in Washington as well as Moscow.

312. McCannon, John. **Red Arctic: Polar Exploration and the Myth of the North in the Soviet Union, 1932-1939**. xii, 234p., [8] p. of plates: illus., maps. New York: Oxford University Press, 1998. Includes bibliography (pp. 211-25) and index.

The Soviet Arctic, defined here as the two million square miles north of the 62nd parallel and east of the Urals, was the occasion of a still-living socialist realist myth. The author describes and analyzes the Russians in the Arctic, devoting individual chapters to the historical background of Russians in the Arctic from 1500 to 1932, the rise of Glavsevmorput (1932-1936), major expeditions in the Arctic from 1932 to 1939, the myth of the Arctic in Soviet culture, and the manufacturing of the Arctic myth and the decline of Glavsevmorput in the latter 1930s.

313. **Cracks in the Monolith: Party Power in the Brezhnev Era**. Edited by James R. Millar. xv, 243p.: illus. Armonk, N.Y.: M. E. Sharpe. Includes bibliographical references and index.

These essays are all a product of the data obtained through the Soviet Interview Project, which attempted to gather a large cross-sectional sample of opinions, perceptions, and concrete data from recent émigrés from the Soviet Union. This particular volume examines the role of the party in the Brezhnev era and analyzes the party's role, its influence, and its contribution to other bureaucratic institutions such as the legal system, enterprise management, and other sectors. Specific topics covered are politics and productivity in

Soviet industry, the manager and the primary party organization secretary, the struggle for control over statistics, the party and the economic bureaucracy, public perceptions and dilemmas of party reform, the impact of party controls at the grassroots level, and the CPSU under reform.

314. **Nationalism and the Breakup of an Empire: Russia and Its Periphery.** Edited by Miron Rezun. x, 197p. Westport, Conn.: Praeger, 1992. Includes bibliographical references (pp. [179]-183) and index.

"The theme of this book portrays the long struggle of this empire with its seat of government at the Center, and analyses both the disintegration of that Center and the collapse of its periphery" (p. ix). The material for the essays included here is taken from Russian, Latvian, Ukrainian, Georgian, Azeri, Uzbek, Turkish, and Chinese sources. The contributors focus on the role of nationalism in the collapse of the Soviet empire. The essays are arranged into five parts that reflect various centers of national identity: the Center, the European Periphery, the Caucasian Periphery, the Muslim Periphery, and a final section on international responses to the rise of nationalism. Contributors include: Miron Rezun, Larry Black, Fuat Borovali, Gordon Brown, Juris Dreifelds, Kurt Nesby Hansen, Bohdan Harasymiw, David Jones, Stephen Jones, Allan Laine Kagedan, and Lawrence Shyu.

315. Sakwa, Richard. **Russian Politics and Society**. 2nd [enl. and rev.] ed. xvii, 501p.: maps. London; New York: Routledge, 1996. Includes bibliographical references (pp. [430]-493) and index.

In this second edition, which has been substantially revised, Sakwa outlines the major elements of Russian political society since 1989. His chapters are arranged in six parts: (1) the fall of communism and the rebirth of Russia; (2) political institutions and processes; (3) federalism, nationalism, and regionalism; (4) economy and society; (5) foreign policies; and (6) the struggle for democracy. Three appendixes provide a chronology of important events in the post-Soviet period, election results since 1989, and a translation of the Russian constitution.

316. Solnick, Steven Lee. **Stealing the State: Control and Collapse in Soviet Institutions**. xiv, 337p.: illus. *Russian Research Center Studies*, 89. Cambridge, Mass.: Harvard University Press, 1998. Includes bibliographical references and index.

"This book asks why the reforms of the perestroika era caused Soviet institutional structures to break down rather than to adapt or evolve.... It is motivated by two broader goals: to employ insights from the non-Soviet literature on institutions to create a model of Soviet disintegration and to use the Soviet case in turn to enrich and extend general theories of institutional behavior" (p. 2). The first two chapters of the book provide the reader with a general framework for the study. Chapter 3 discusses the author's hypothesis that policies affecting youth are a particularly strong measure of analysis for hierarchical organizations of the Soviet type.

317. Sternthal, Susanne. **Gorbachev's Reforms: De-Stalinization Through Demilitarization**. 223p. Westport, Conn.: Praeger, 1997. Includes bibliographical references (pp. [213]-215) and index.

"This book examines how Gorbachev engaged the military in dismantling Stalin's most prominent legacy: the militarization of Soviet domestic and foreign policy. Gorbachev's objective of freeing Soviet society and economy from the stranglehold of the military could be rationalized and legitimized only by an improvement in the international environment, which at the time marked one of the tensest periods in the Cold War" (p. 16).

318. Willerton, John P. **Patronage and Politics in the USSR Cold War and Revolution**. xv, 305p. *Soviet and East European Studies*, no. 82. Cambridge, Eng.: Cambridge University Press, 1992. Includes bibliographical references (pp. 283-88) and index.

"In patronage and politics in the USSR Professor John Willerton offers major new insights into the patronage networks that have dominated elite mobility, regime formation and governance in the Soviet Union during the past twenty-five years. Using the biographical and career details of over two thousand national leaders and regional officials in Azerbaidzhan and Lithuania, John Willerton traces the patron-client relations underlying recruitment, mobility and policymaking" (frontispiece).

319. Zubok, Vladislav Martinovich. **Inside the Kremlin's Cold War: From Stalin to Khrushchev**. xv, 346p., [16] p. of plates: illus. Cambridge, Mass.: Harvard University Press, 1996. Includes bibliographical references (pp. [285]-338) and index.

"This book is our personal inquiry into the Kremlin's view of the Cold War. Growing evidence from the Russian side can help us to understand what shaped the behavior of the Soviet monolith toward the world, its confrontation with the United States, and its expansion in Europe, Asia, Africa, and Latin America" (pp. xi-xii). The author examines the roles of Stalin, Molotov, Zhdanov, Beria, Malenkov, and Khrushchev in the history of the cold war. The author is a senior fellow at the National Security Archive.

1991 to Present

320. **Russia's Democratic Moment?: Defining US Policy to Promote Democratic Opportunities in Russia**. Edited by William C. Martel and Theodore C. Hailes. xxiv, 319p. *Air War College Studies in National Securities*. Maxwell Air Force Base, Ala.: Air University Press, 1995. Includes bibliographical references.

This collection of essays addresses fundamental questions about democracy in Russia: (1) what must Russia accomplish to become a democracy?; (2) what progress has Russia made in democratic reform?; (3) does democratic reform depend on President Yeltsin or other specific personalities?; (4) what specifically can the United States do as Russia strives to become a prosperous democracy?; and (5) what pitfalls does Russia face in creating a democratic society? The essays are arranged in three parts: democratic reform of government and politics; democratic reform of economy and society; and democratic reform of military and foreign policy.

321. **Shaping Actors, Shaping Factors in Russia's Future.** ix, 141p. *Forward Studies series.* New York: St. Martin's Press, 1998. Prepared by the European Commission's Forward Studies Unit. Includes bibliographical references (pp. 137-38) and index.

This study by the Forward Studies Unit of the European Commission has as its aim understanding "the deeper socio-economic-political and psychological structures governing the Russian transformation process" (p. ix). The methodology consists of mapping out all the actors and factors that influence Russia's development. Based on that analysis, the study then develops several possible scenarios that the Russian future may witness.

322. Arbatov, Aleksei Georgievich. **Managing Conflict in the Former Soviet Union: Russian and American Perspectives.** xv, 556p.: maps. Cambridge, Mass.: MIT Press, 1997. Includes bibliographical references and index.

This volume consists of six case studies that focus on post-cold war conflict in the former Soviet territory and in Russia. These areas are: the Baltic, Crimea, Kazakhstan, Moldova, Georgia, and the North Caucasus. In each study there is both a careful and well-documented analysis from a moderate Russian perspective. In order to provide an understanding point of view these Russian accounts are followed by a commentary from an American scholar. Several themes emerge from this exercise: (1) Yeltsin's support of nationalism in the republics as a weapon in his struggle with Gorbachev; (2) the situation of minority populations; (3) the importance of laws governing citizenship and language in managing ethnic conflict; (4) pressures of the deployment of Russian troops in those regions; and (5) the limited impact of international organization.

323. **Russia's Future: Consolidation or Disintegration?** Edited by Douglas W. Blum. ix, 173p. Boulder, Colo.: Westview Press, 1994. Includes bibliographical references and index.

The essays presented here are intended to explore the nature of the evolving economic and political order in Russia. Of particular concern is the issue of consolidation versus disintegration of the various forces operative in Russian society. "At the most basic level is the question of how Russia defines itself as a society, and how it conceives of its place in relation to other states in the international system. Such essential values and self-definitions are likely to have an important influence on patterns of institution building and to impart a general direction to domestic and foreign policy" (p. 1). Individual topics covered include political party development, the Russian parliament, the economy, labor relations, regional fragmentation, the Russian military, and foreign policy.

324. **New Thinking in Soviet Politics**. Edited by Archie Brown. xii, 115p. New York: St. Martin's Press, 1992. Contains revised papers from a panel discussion at the Fourth World Congress for Soviet and East European Studies, held at Harrogate, in July 1990. Includes bibliographical references and index.

These essays attempt to provide a fresh approach to thinking about various problems of the former Soviet Union (political system, economy, national question, foreign policy, and world communism) in the immediate aftermath of the Soviet Union's collapse. They are of interest not only for their positions, but also useful in comparison to what actually happened over the subsequent decade.

325. Cooper, Leo. **Russia and the World: New State-of-Play on the International Stage**. vii, 222p. New York: St. Martin's Press, 1999. Includes bibliographical references (pp. 213-19) and index.

Leo Cooper's book examines the changing role of Russia in today's geopolitical environment. "Dr. Cooper starts by providing a history of the USSR and its collapse, as a way of setting the scene for the contemporary domestic conflicts. He then considers the all-important role of the military.... He highlights the role of the economy.... The unifying and bonding effect of NATO expansion on Russian culture, and its ramifications for global politics, is justifiably one of Dr. Cooper's principal focus in this study, as he examines the factors leading to increasing nationalism—the rise of 'the Russian Idea'—in recent years" (p. viii).

326. **Democratic Changes and Authoritarian Reactions in Russia, Ukraine, Belarus, and Moldova**. Edited by Karen Dawisha and Bruce Parrott. xviii, 386p.: illus. *Democratization and Authoritarianism in Post-Communist Societies*, 3. Cambridge, Eng.: Cambridge University Press, 1997. Includes index.

As Volume 3 in the series Democratization and Authoritarianism in Post-Communist Societies, this book provides up-to-date essays on the democratization of several countries that made up the former Soviet Union. This volume in particular focuses on the various democratic changes and authoritarian reactions to them in Russia, Ukraine, Belarus, and Moldova by presenting eight essays by individual contributors. The first two essays, by the editors, and which are included in each volume, present perspectives on post-communist democratization and an analysis of research concepts and methodologies relating to the investigation of democratization and political participation. The other essays cover democratization and the related aspects of political participation, political parties, and authoritarianism, depending on the country covered.

327. Devlin, Judith. **The Rise of the Russian Democrats: The Causes and Consequences of the Elite Revolution**. x, 294p. *Studies of Communism in Transition*. Aldershot, Eng.: Edward Elgar, 1995. Includes bibliographical references (pp. 261-85) and index.

In this study, Judith Devlin analyzes Russia's developing democratic movement. She believes that the failure of this movement to take root in Russian society is largely due to the structure of the movement itself. Devlin tries to demonstrate that the diversity of its supporting coalition prevented it from building a strong following in Russia. The author draws on newspapers, archives, and interviews in making her argument.

328. Dunlop, John B. **The Rise of Russia and the Fall of the Soviet Empire**. 1st pbk. print, with new postscript. xi, 388p. Princeton, N.J.: Princeton University Press, 1995. Includes bibliographical references (pp. [327]-369) and index.

"The six chapters that comprise this study seek to describe and to explain the causes behind the kaleidoscopic change that occurred in the former Soviet Union's largest and most populous republic during the period of 1985-1991" (p. ix). The first two chapters examine the roles of Gorbachev and Yeltsin as each struggled to keep pace with the changes they set in motion. The following chapters look at the two main political groupings—democrats and statists—and the enormous political shifts that took place in 1991. The epilogue and prologue bring the reader up to 1995 in political events.

329. Eckstein, Harry, Richard Ahl, Russell Bova, and Phillip G. Roeder. **Can Democracy Take Root in Post-Soviet Russia?: Explorations in State-Society Relations**. xi, 420p.: illus. Lanham, Md.: Rowman & Littlefield, 1998. Includes bibliographical references (pp. 383-409) and index.

This volume is the first of several that in general explore the ways in which theories of democratization can inform the study of transitions in post-communist societies. This particular volume "constitutes a general examination of the dynamics of state-society relations with particular emphasis on Russia" (p. ix). General topics considered include congruence theory, democratic theories and authority patterns, political culture and authority patterns, political inclusion, and state-society relations.

330. Ehrhart, Hans-Georg, Anna Kreikemeyer, and A. V. Zagorskii. **Crisis Management in the CIS: Whither Russia?** 257p. *Demokratie, Sicherheit, Frieden*, Bd. 92. Baden-Baden, Ger.: Nomos, 1995. Includes bibliographical references.

The breakup of the Soviet Union saw the rise in armed conflicts in the states that had newly achieved independence. The source of the conflicts often was to be found between competing ethnic interests in the region. The interest of nations no longer played a role. The essays in this volume are a product of a workshop conducted by experts on the region and leading Russian researchers, held in 1994. The book is divided into five sections. The first includes a number of case studies on conflict in the regions. There are studies on Abkhazia, South-Ossetia, the Dniestr region, Nagorno-Karabakh, and Transcaucasia. Section

2 examines the role of Russia in the conflict, past and present. "Collective Security and National Interest" is the topic of Section 3. The essays in Section 4 examine the issue of collective security. The final essay draws general conclusions for the future of stability in the region.

331. Fish, M. Steven. **Democracy from Scratch: Opposition and Regime in the New Russian Revolution**. x, 300p. Princeton, N.J.: Princeton University Press, 1995. Includes bibliographical references (pp. [273]-287) and index.

"This book is not about 'perestroika,' 'glasnost,' or 'reform,' though these phenomena did provide crucial openings for the emergence of the organizations and movements that will be the subjects of examination. Nor is it about Mikhail Gorbachev, though it does focus mainly on the period of his rule. Rather, it investigates the organized, independent revolutionary opposition in Russia" (p. 4). In one of his chapters the author examines these phenomena in four provincial cities: Ekaterinburg, Tula, Volgograd, and Orel.

332. **Russia and Chechnia: The Permanent Crisis: Essays on Russo-Chechen Relations**. Edited by Ben Fowkes. viii, 188p. New York: St. Martin's Press, 1998. Includes bibliographical references and index.

This is a collection of essays on Russia's long-standing problems in the Chechen region. The essays collected here look at the deportation of the Chechen people, the battle for Grozny, and the debate over Sheikh Shamil. The book includes a chronology of the recent conflict in the region. The contributors are Ben Fowkes, Bulent Gokay, William Flemming, and Pontus Siren.

333. Frazer, Graham, and George Lancelle. **Absolute Zhirinovsky: A Transparent View of the Distinguished Russian Statesman**. xlvi, 157p. New York: Penguin Books, 1994.

Graham Frazer and George Lancelle have compiled a number of Zhirinovsky's writings in this book. In so doing, they hope to create a picture of his extreme policies. Many of the quotations are simply bizarre. "We Russians have not forgotten how you English betrayed us in the Second World War. We will nuke you too" (back cover). The book begins with a lengthy description of Zhirinovsky's rise to power.

334. Gay, William. **Capitalism with a Human Face: The Quest for a Middle Road in Russian Politics**. xxix, 234p. *Studies in Social, Political, and Legal Philosophy*. Lanham, Md.: Rowman & Littlefield, 1996. Includes bibliographical references (pp. 215-27) and index.

This book is the product of collaboration between a Russian political scientist and an American philosopher. They set out to define a centrist position for political and economic reform. They advocate a new notion of centrism for Russia: one that combines democratic politics and a market economy without abandoning the social guarantees on which many Russians have long relied and without which their political and economic life is likely to remain in turmoil" (back cover).

335. **Elites and Leadership in Russian Politics: Selected Papers from the Fifth World Congress of Central and East European Studies, Warsaw, 1995**. Edited by Graeme Gill. xi, 190p. *Selected Papers from the Fifth World Congress of Central and East European Studies, Warsaw, 1995.* London: Macmillan, 1998.

These papers were originally presented at the Fifth World Congress of Central and East European Studies in 1995. The topics covered include: parliamentary review of ministerial appointments; Yeltsin's regional cadres policy; post-Soviet clientelist norms at the Russian federal level; the nomenklatura in post-communist Russia; elites, institutions, and democratization in Russia and Eastern Europe; elites and the Russian transition; and Russia as a post-communist country.

336. **Local Power and Post-Soviet Politics**. Edited by Jeffrey W. Hahn and Theodore H. Friedgut. *Contemporary Soviet/Post-Soviet Politics.* Armonk, N.Y.: M. E. Sharpe, 1994. Includes bibliographical references and index.

This collection of essays is devoted to a description and analysis of local power in post-Soviet Russia. The essays are divided into two parts. Part 1, local studies, includes an examination of the politics of Leningrad/St. Petersburg, political change resulting from the elections of 1990, the changing role of the local budget in Yaroslavl, a study of Saratov and Volgograd provinces, institutions, elites and local politics, and perestroika in the provinces. Part 2, systemic studies, covers main currents in the development of Russian local self-government, local support for market reform, the attitudes of local politicians, and federalist discord and accommodation.

337. **In Search of Pluralism: Soviet and Post-Soviet Politics**. Edited by Anthony Jones and Carol R. Saivetz. ix, 174p.: illus. *John M. Olin Critical Issues series.* Boulder, Colo.: Westview Press, 1994. Includes bibliographical references and index.

The contributors to this volume evaluate the climate in which political pluralism is developing in Russia and how that climate is shaping this important aspect of political life. Essays focus on civil society, the new press, urban Soviet politics, the nature of the Russian deputies, Central Asia, and business. Each contributor has analyzed pluralism in the context of one of these topics. Contributors are Stephen White, Mervyn Matthew, Theodore H. Friedgut, Jeffrey W. Hahn, Peter Clement, Elizabeth Teague, Michael E. Urban, Anthony Jones, and Carol R. Saivetz.

338. Krancberg, Sigmund. **A Soviet Postmortem: Philosophical Roots of the "Grand Failure."** xv, 166p. Lanham, Md.: Rowman & Littlefield, 1994. Includes bibliographical references and index.

This analysis of the failure of the Soviet system examines the sociological effects of Marxist-Leninist ideology. "Analyzing the realities of the Soviet regime, the author reveals the extent to which Soviet political culture was an artificial imposition with only slender roots in the life of Soviet society. The book concludes with an examination of the collapse of the Soviet empire and the problems that now beset the Commonwealth of Independent States" (back cover).

339. Laird, Roy D. **The Soviet Legacy**. xi, 223p. Westport, Conn.: Praeger, 1993. Includes bibliographical references (pp. [213]-214) and index.

"This work is an attempt to accomplish two major purposes. The first is to produce an analytical discussion of the accelerating collapse of the Soviet Union, starting with the elevation of Mikhail Gorbachev to the post of general secretary of the Communist Party of the Soviet Union (CPS6) in 1985 and ending with the death of the Union in December 1991. The second purpose is to explore the legacy of the USSR as of the end of the first quarter of 1992" (p. ix). To accomplish these purposes, the author has divided his book into two parts. Each part focuses on one of these goals. The individual chapters in the first part follow a chronological arrangement. The chapters in Part 2 are topically arranged, discussing first social welfare and then turning to public opinions.

340. **From Union to Commonwealth: Nationalism and Separatism in the Soviet Republics**. Edited by Gail W. Lapidus, Victor Zaslavsky, and with Philip Goldman. xii, 127p.: map. *Cambridge Soviet Paperbacks*, 6. Cambridge, Eng.: Cambridge University Press, 1992. Includes bibliographical references and index.

"In this volume, leading scholars from the United States, Canada, and Russia examine the forces that underlay the rise of national movements in the Soviet Union and their challenge to the stability and territorial integrity of the Soviet State" (frontispiece). Contributors are Leokadia Mikhailorna Drobizhera, Philip Goldman, Gail Warshofsky Lapidus, Galina Vasilerna Starovosteva, Ronald Grigor Suny, and Victor Zaslavsky.

341. Löwenhardt, John. **The Reincarnation of Russia: Struggling with the Legacy of Communism, 1990-1994**. xii, 238p.: map. Durham, N.C.: Duke University Press, 1995. Includes bibliographical references (pp. [213]-229) and index.

In this book John Löwenhardt discusses the rapid changes the Russian political system has undergone in the years since the overthrow of the Soviet Union. "Building on analysis of the failure of the Soviet system, Löwenhardt compares the emergence of Russia as a newborn state with other countries that have undergone transitions from authoritarianism toward democracy. Although it is often claimed that Russia is a unique case, the author argues that the lessons of other nations are relevant to the Russian situation" (back cover).

342. **Russia—A Return to Imperialism?** Edited by Kate Martin and Uri Ra'anan. viii, 216p. New York: St. Martin's Press, 1996. Includes bibliographical references and index.

The contributors to this volume discuss what they feel is an unmistakable trend in Russia's political development toward imperialist tendencies. The authors look at neo-imperial themes in doctrine and in practice in Russian politics. They also examine the targets of this imperialism and the Western response to this disturbing trend in Russian government.

343. McAuley, Mary. **Russia's Politics of Uncertainty**. xvii, 351p.: maps. New York: Cambridge University Press, 1997. Includes bibliographical references (pp. 329-39) and index.

McAuley analyzed the behavior of several political actors and observed how they reacted to the new environment of uncertainty brought on by the demise of the Soviet regime. The actors that she chose were rulers in regions and republics during the period 1991-1994. Among the regions studied were the national republics, Tatarstan and Sakha, Krasnodar krai, Perm, Tomsk, and St. Petersburg. In conducting such a study she is interested primarily in the strategies the new rulers chose in negotiating with the center of power, and secondly she attempts to explain outcomes that actually occurred.

344. **Directory of Russian MPs: People's Deputies of the Supreme Soviet of Russia-Russian Federation**. Edited by Martin McCauley. lii, 326p.: illus. Harlow, Eng.; Detroit, Mich.: Longman; Distributed exclusively in the United States and Canada by Gale Research, 1992. Listing of deputies as of April 1992.

Martin McCauley has produced a unique biographical resource. There are profiles of all the members of Parliament that have drawn on previously inaccessible data. "Profiles of each MP typically give you origins, background and career, family situation and interests, election platform and result, key political positions and votes, contact details. In addition to the biographical entries, the book includes, an introduction explaining what the parliament is and what it has done, data on its key votes and factions and groups, summary details on MPs by nationality and constituency" (back cover). There is no index.

345. McDaniel, Tim. **The Agony of the Russian Idea**. x, 201p. Princeton, N.J.: Princeton University Press, 1996. Includes bibliographical references.

McDaniel examines cycles of breakdown in Russia, the dilemmas of tsarist modernization, and the logic of Soviet communism, all as a prelude to the failure of Yeltsin's reforms. As he concludes, "Yeltsin's government could have attempted to break with this classical logic of the failure of reform in Russia. To do so they would have had to have presented a vision of Russia's future that provided a bridge to the past. From the Russian idea they might have taken modified ideals of equality, belief, community, and the responsibility of government for social welfare" (p. 186). The opportunity was missed.

346. McFaul, Michael. **Post-Communist Politics: Democratic Prospects in Russia and Eastern Europe**. xix, 132p. *S/S*, 0736-7136. Washington, D.C.: Center for Strategic and International Studies, 1993. Includes bibliographical references (pp. 125-32).

McFaul lays out the comparative context for democratic transition in Eastern Europe in order to elucidate Russia's potential path. In this brief study, published two years after the August 1991 coup, McFaul explores Russia's transition from communism, the birth of political parties, definitions of horizontal and vertical power, and comparative conclusions.

347. Mikheyev, Dimitry. **Russia Transformed**. xiv, 288p. Indianapolis: Hudson Institute, 1996. Includes endnotes and index.

Russia has undergone massive economic, political, and social changes in the last decade. The changing economic and sociopolitical environment is underlain by the same 1,000-year-old culture. How has it been affected by Russia's transformation? This is the question Dimitry Mikheyev sets out to answer in this book. The author begins with a historical overview and then turns to an examination of Russia's social composition. Mikheyev next looks at key political figures in the transformation with special attention paid to Boris Yeltsin. This is followed by a review of the struggle going on within the political elite. Changes in the economy and shifting social conditions are examined within the context of the effect of economic and political reforms. The concluding chapter focuses on the prospects for the survival of democracy in Russia.

348. Petro, Nicolai N. **The Rebirth of Russian Democracy: An Interpretation of Political Culture**. ix, 226p.: illus. Cambridge, Mass.: Harvard University Press, 1995. Includes bibliographical references (pp. [185]-216) and index.

Petro's intent is to describe and analyze the transformations of the Russian state from totalitarian society to democratic society. He wanted to go beyond a simpleminded reassessment of Sovietology as practiced in the West to produce something that would serve as a guide for the future development of Russian politics. He explores the current political culture and the failure of Sovietology, constrained autocracy in Russian history, the role of the Russian church, the forging of an alternative national identity, and the reemergence of civil society as seen in the development of alternative political organizations.

349. **Russia in Search of Its Future**. Edited by Amin Saikal and William Maley. xii, 239p. Cambridge, Eng.: Cambridge University Press, 1995. Includes index and list of contributors.

These 13 conference papers are divided into four parts: Politics, Economics, International Relations, and Culture and Society. Rather than deliver a prophecy of future events, these authors examine "selected developments in Russia's politics, economy, foreign relations and culture and society which are destined to play a substantial role in shaping Russia's future into the next century" (p. 5).

350. Sergeyev, Victor. **Russia's Road to Democracy: Parliament, Communism, and Traditional Culture**. xi, 227p. *Studies of Communism in Transition*. Brookfield, Vt.: Edward Elgar, 1993. Includes bibliographical references (pp. 211-21) and index.

The fall of the Soviet Union has raised many questions about the development of society. Not least of which is "what is the 'natural' evolution of any society?" The author of this study notes that there had been an assumption that democracy was the normal course for political systems to follow. Totalitarian systems were, in some way, a deviation from the norm. The events in Russia have called this view into question. Victor Sergeyev will analyze this problem in the context of the development of the USSR Congress of People's Deputies. He has divided the book into three parts: "The Soviet Leviathan"; "The USSR Supreme Rally"; and "A New Behemoth, or The Not Very Long Parliament."

351. **Russian Culture at the Crossroads: Paradoxes of Postcommunist Consciousness**. Edited by Dmitri N. Shalin. ix, 341p.: illus. Boulder, Colo.: Westview Press, 1996. Includes bibliographical references and index.

"Multi-textual, polyphonic, and contradictory, the current Russian cultural discourse is richly reflected in these essays by a diverse group of authors from Russian and American academic and cultural circles. Each chapter focuses on a particular cultural domain, surveying the historical origins of Russian beliefs and behaviors, exploring their Soviet and post-Soviet permutations, and highlighting the range of choices that Russians are facing at this critical juncture" (p. 329). The volume includes 11 essays. These provide an overview of the historic context of Russia's cultural development.

352. Urban, Joan Barth, and V. D. Solovei. **Russia's Communists at the Crossroads**. xi, 209p. Boulder, Colo.: Westview Press, 1997. Includes bibliographical references (pp. 195-97) and index.

This book covers the development of the Communist Party from the last years of the Soviet regime through the 1996 elections. After the banning of the Communist Party and its activities in 1991, the communist movement was reborn. Urban and Solovei show how the Communist Party of the Russian Federation developed, explain the events leading up to the constitutional crisis of 1993, the role of Ziuganovism, and the further political evolution of the CPRF and its electoral strategy for the 1996 elections.

353. Urban, Michael, Vyacheslav Igrunov, and Sergei Mitrokhin. **The Rebirth of Politics in Russia**. xiii, 429p. Cambridge, Eng.: Cambridge University Press, 1997. Includes bibliographical references and index.

In endeavoring to explain the rebirth of politics in Russia, the authors "trace the process from the pre-political period of dissident activity, through perestroika and the appearance of political groups and publications, elections, the formation of political parties and mass movements, counter-revolution and coup d'etat, the victory of democratic forces and the organization of a Russian state; to the struggle of power in the post-communist epoch, a violent end of the first republic and the contentious relations engulfing its successor" (frontispiece).

354. **Developments in Russian and Post-Soviet Politics**. Edited by Stephen White, Alex Pravda, and Zvi Gitelman. 3rd ed. xix, 359p.: illus., maps. Durham, N.C.: Duke University Press, 1994. Includes bibliographical references and index.

This volume is the revised edition of a 1992 publication of the same title. Every chapter has been updated to incorporate the political changes that have taken place since that earlier edition was published. New contributors have participated in this project, bringing expertise in areas previously of little importance for Russia. "Our aim, however, remains the same: to offer an interpretative framework for what is now a group of political systems whose evolution—in an age of nuclear weapons and telecommunications—matters almost as much to the outside world as to their own citizens" (p. xi). The essays are grouped into four parts. The first looks at the political system and the presidency, the Duma, political parties, and the changing role of the citizen. Part 2 examines public policies and the economy, privatization, social problems, and foreign policy. Part 3 is devoted to the nationalities problem. The final section examines the changing shape of the Russian political system. Contributors are Mary Buckley, Simon Clarke, Zvi Gitelman, Ronald J. Hill, Leslie Holmes, Alex Pravda, Thomas F. Remington, Peter Rutland, Richard Sakwa, Robert Sharlet, Darrell Slider, Stephen White, and John P. Willerton.

Political Parties

355. McFaul, Michael, and Sergei Markov. **The Troubled Birth of Russian Democracy: Parties, Personalities, and Programs**. xiv, 317p. *Hoover Institution Press Publication*, no. 415. Stanford, Calif.: Hoover Institution Press, 1993. Consists chiefly of interviews with various Russian personalities. Includes bibliographical references (pp. [267]-308) and index.

Before the collapse of the Soviet Union in August 1991, the power and influence of the Communist Party had already started to wane. Other political parties and movements had begun to take shape. This book, based on interviews by the authors, attempts to study the formation and current (as of 1991) platforms of the most prominent political parties in Russia at the time. An introductory chapter analyzes the origins of party formation in Russia from 1985 to 1992. The remaining chapters consist of interviews with the leaders of the most active parties at that time.

Communism, Communist Party

356. Árnason, Jóhann Páll. **The Future That Failed: Origins and Destinies of the Soviet Model**. x, 239p. London: Routledge, 1993. Includes bibliographical references (pp. [222]-227) and index.

"This book aims to link the Communist experience to the theoretical debates on modernity. . . . The author tries to show that a revised concept of totalitarianism can be used to clarify the distinctive characteristics of the Soviet model as a pattern of modernity and thus to open up new perspectives of modernization theory" (frontispiece).

357. **Bukharin in Retrospect**. Edited by Theodor Bergmann, Gert Schaefer, and Mark Selden. xxv, 251p. *Socialism and Social Movements*. Armonk, N.Y.: M. E. Sharpe, 1994. Includes bibliographical references and index.

Bukharin was the leading theoretician of socialism. Unfortunately for his sake, he advocated a fundamentally different path than was advocated by Stalin. After his rehabilitation in 1988 a conference was held and this volume bears the fruits of that gathering. The essays are gathered in three parts: (1) the revolutionary politician: human greatness and tragedy; (2) the economist: alternative strategies; and (3) the political theorist: state, party, bureaucracy. The 19 essays cover almost every conceivable aspect of Bukharin's thoughts and writings.

358. Daniels, Robert Vincent. **The End of the Communist Revolution**. viii, 222p. London: Routledge, 1993. Includes bibliographical references (pp. 191-209) and index.

Daniels hopes both to understand the context of the end of communism and "to explain the most recent and spectacular changes, whose causes and consequences cannot be properly comprehended apart from this background" (p. vii). In the early chapters of the book he explores the changes that took place in the Soviet Union from the selection of Mikhail Gorbachev as general secretary of the party in 1985 until the breakup of the Soviet Union in 1991. There were two major forces at work, perestroika from the top and a political and economic change from below. He then explores the system that preceded perestroika and takes a long view of the "entire Communist era as a process of revolution, that is, a natural sequence of events working itself out through a series of stages, the most enduring of which was the Stalinist post-revolutionary dictatorship. The notion of process in turn gives a new meaning to perestroika and the collapse of Communism. These events represent the terminal stage of the revolution and a return to the missed opportunities of 1917" (p. 3).

359. Evans, Alfred B. **Soviet Marxism-Leninism: The Decline of an Ideology**. 237p. Westport, Conn.: Praeger, 1993. Includes bibliographical references and index.

A review of most Western literature on developments in Soviet ideology leads to the conclusion that little changed after Stalin. In fact, as events proved, Soviet Marxism-Leninism had reached a critical stage by the time Gorbachev came to power. "The perspective offered by this book not only reaffirms that conclusion but also suggests that pressures for change in the official Soviet ideology had been evident ever since it had taken shape as the intellectual rationale for the mature Stalinist system by the middle of the 1930s" (p. 2). Alfred Evans traces the evolution of Soviet Marxism-Leninism from Khrushchev through Gorbachev in this volume beginning with an overview of Marx's stages of communism and Lenin's views on socialist construction. He then follows developments in the ideology as the Soviets sought to restructure the ideology to meet political necessity. He ends with a discussion of the price the Soviets paid in the collapse of Marxism-Leninism.

360. Gill, Graeme. **The Collapse of a Single-Party System: The Disintegration of the CPSU**. xi, 258p. *Cambridge Russian, Soviet and Post-Soviet Studies*, 94. Cambridge, Eng.: Cambridge University Press, 1994. Includes bibliographical references (pp. 246-50) and index.

"Graeme Gill attempts to focus on the fate of the Communist Party during the Gorbachev era. Rather than looking at perestroika as a whole, or even examining Gorbachev as a leader, this book narrows its study to one organization that had been crucial to the Soviet Government in the twentieth century, the Communist Party. When it came under challenge and it could no longer use the weapon of suppression, the party was unable to mount a serious defense of its position and role. Confronted from the top by Gorbachev's call to reform itself and by his changes to the political arena, and from the bottom by new political forces taking advantage of that arena, the party's unity collapsed and with it any sense of purpose or possibility of survival" (frontispiece). The book is arranged topically, first discussing the administrative party system in Russia and the problems that arose when reform became an issue. The next chapters examine the various methods that were attempted to accommodate the new environment of reform, the personnel solution, institutional reform, and internal reform programs, slowly arriving at a reform program out of control.

361. Gill, Graeme, and Roderic Pitty. **Power in the Party: The Organization of Power and Central-Republican Relations in the CPSU**. ix, 222p. New York: St. Martin's Press, 1997. Includes select bibliography and index.

The authors' aim is to examine the informal structure of power, especially within the party itself. After an apparent weakening in the power of the party in 1989, there seemed to be a resurgence in the elections to the Duma in 1995. To some this was evidence that the party had maintained control, especially outside major cities. The authors focus on the nature of organization of the Communist Party, especially as it relates to Uzbekistan, Tajikistan, Kazakhstan, Ukraine, and Belarus.

362. Gluckstein, Donny. **The Tragedy of Bukharin**. vii, 293p. London: Pluto Press, 1994. Includes bibliographical references (pp. 253-84) and index.

The fate of Bukharin's theories is a strange one. Discredited by the communists in 1929, he came back into vogue in the mid-1980s when market socialism was adopted by the regime. Then in 1991 he was again discredited, when Yeltsin wanted nothing more to do with communist theorists. Gluckstein argues that "Bukharin is too important a historical and political figure to be used and abused in this way. He is much more than a mere political cipher for market socialists. His theoretical arguments touched on many of the issues of today" (p. 2). The author reviews and analyzes Bukharin's theories within the context of the political culture that existed at the time.

363. Liebich, André. **From the Other Shore: Russian Social Democracy After 1921**. xi, 476p., [8] p. of plates: illus. *Harvard Historical Studies*, 125. Cambridge, Mass.: Harvard University Press, 1997. Includes bibliographical references (pp. 437-63) and index.

Although the Russian Social Democratic Labor Party (Mensheviks) ceased to exist legally after 1922, they continued their activities underground and in exile for some time after that. This book is a study of the Russian social democratic movement after 1921. Of particular concern are "Menshevik perceptions of the Soviet Union and their influence on Western attitudes. These perceptions provide an answer to a recurrent question: What would be the content of a critique of the Soviet Union from the left? Trotsky's reply is best known, but the Mensheviks' answer is more credible and more thoroughly considered inasmuch as it was developed in debate among themselves and with foreign socialists, and it remains, in fact, paradigmatic" (p. 4).

364. McDermott, Kevin, and Jeremy Agnew. **The Comintern: A History of International Communism from Lenin to Stalin**. xxv, 304p. New York: St. Martin's Press, 1997. Includes bibliographical references (pp. 272-83) and index.

The Comintern or Communist International was originally intended as a body intent on fomenting world socialist revolution. Sometime during its relatively brief life from 1919 to 1943 it evolved into "a compliant instrument of the Soviet state" (p. xx). This evolution and its causes are the subject of this book. The chapters of the book have been arranged in chronological order with one exception. Chapter 5 is devoted to the history of the Comintern from 1919 to 1939 in East Asia and was contributed by Michael Weiner. The volume includes a section of reprinted documents and a biographical glossary.

365. Mikheev, Dmitrii. **The Rise and Fall of Gorbachev**. xiv, 178p. Indianapolis: Hudson Institute, 1992. Includes bibliographical references.

"*The Rise and Fall of Gorbachev* takes a step toward filling the gap in our knowledge of the Russian mentality, and especially that of the Soviet apparatchik. Written by an exiled Soviet dissident, the book provides a provocative introduction to that mentality, delineating several important schemata through which Russians view the world" (p. xiii).

366. Robinson, Neil. **Ideology and the Collapse of the Soviet System: A Critical History of Soviet Ideological Discourse**. x, 227p. *Studies of Communism in Transition*. Aldershot, Eng.: Edward Elgar, 1995. Includes bibliographical references and index.

The author of this study notes, that when perestroika was being analyzed, ideology was generally treated as an unimportant aspect of reform. This study challenges that thesis. Robinson believes that perestroika was an ideologically motivated attempt to resolve long-standing problems in the Soviet system. "It is argued that using ideology and coping with its effects was an integral aspect of Soviet political life because of the relationship of the party to ideology. This is demonstrated in an analysis of the historical ideological justifications of the party's leadership before perestroika which seeks to show the instability of the party's power because of the party's constant need to redefine and justify its leadership and because of the contradictions that were contained within ideology used in this process" (p. vii).

367. Stalin, Joseph, 1879-1953. **Stalin's Letters to Molotov, 1925-1936**. xviii, 276p.: illus. *Annals of Communism*. New Haven, Conn.: Yale University Press, 1995. Includes bibliographical references and index.

Molotov was one of Stalin's most trusted advisors in the 1920s and 1930s, even if he was himself in danger of being killed by Stalin just before the dictator's death. These letters, turned over to the Central Party Archive by Molotov in 1969, finally came to light with the opening of the Soviet archives in 1991. Most of the letters are from 1926 to 1931 with only a scattering from 1932 to 1936. There are no letters from 1928 and 1934. Each letter is annotated and a glossary of personal names with information about each one is appended.

Perestroika, Glasnost

368. Boettke, Peter J. **Why Perestroika Failed: The Politics and Economics of Socialist Transformation**. viii, 199p. London: Routledge, 1993. Includes bibliographical references and index.

"There are two general questions which the various chapters in this book attempt to answer. First, if socialism as an economic system was so inefficient, how could it have lasted for seventy-four years? Second, if market reforms are so desirable, why have all the transforming economies experienced an acute economic decline during the reform period? Both of these questions will be answered through a series of propositions which taken as a whole provide the critical answers" (p. 3). This is a thoughtful economic analysis of the failure of Gorbachev's experiment.

369. **The Soviet Empire Reconsidered: Essays in Honor of Adam B. Ulam**. Edited by Sanford Raymond Lieberman. xii, 262p. Boulder, Colo.: Westview Press, 1994. Includes bibliographical references.

Adam Ulam is Professor Emeritus of History and Government at Harvard University. The essays collected in this Festschrift reflect his lifelong interest in Russia's political development. The contributors have focused on a number of themes: "Many reflect on the past, reassessing it in the light of archival materials that have become available since the collapse of the Soviet Union. Others examine the legacies of the Soviet past in view of their implications for the present, while still others attempt to discern the potential, long-term impact of the collapse of the Soviet Union on military foreign policies" (p. 7). The contributors are Mark. R. Beissinger, Norman Naimark, David E. Powell, Carol R. Saivetz, Angela Stent, Sarah M. Terry, and Mikahil Typkin.

370. Miller, John. **Mikhail Gorbachev and the End of Soviet Power**. xviii, 267p. New York: St. Martin's Press, 1993. Includes bibliographical references (pp. 237-53) and index.

John Miller explores the factors that contributed to the downfall of the Soviet system and Mikhail Gorbachev. Miller focuses on domestic affairs and the politics of the Soviet Union. He avoids foreign relations, believing they did not play a significant role in this process. The book is arranged topically beginning with an overview of Soviet history. This is followed by a profile of Gorbachev as a person and a leader. Miller then discusses

Gorbachev's reforms in the final two years of the Soviet Union's existence. The book includes a glossary and a chronology of events from 1982 to 1991.

371. Moskoff, William. **Hard Times: Impoverishment and Protest in the Perestroika Years: The Soviet Union 1985-1991**. xi, 243p. Armonk, N.Y.: M. E. Sharpe, c1993. Includes bibliographical references (pp. 237-39).

William Moskoff traces the downfall of the Soviet system during the years of perestroika in this book. Moskoff believes that perestroika was a complete failure contributing to the economic collapse of the country. Since it is the lives of the average individuals that most clearly reflect the economic conditions of the country as a whole, Moskoff has focused his study on them. The book discusses the "Shortage Economy," prices, income, standard of living and unemployment during this period. It also looks at the backlash—strikes and a new level of labor militancy that developed during these years.

372. Orttung, Robert W. **From Leningrad to St. Petersburg: Democratization in a Russian City**. 1st ed. xiii, 332p.: illus., maps. New York: St. Martin's Press, 1995. Includes bibliographical references (pp. [277]-286) and index.

With the well-worn phrase that all politics is local, the author examines a local movement in St. Petersburg (then Leningrad) in 1987 whereby local citizens tried to preserve a treasured historical hotel. This was the first time that the public had expressed itself in such a manner. The examination of this case study enables the reader to understand how the design of new democratic institutions is probably the key variable in effecting democratic institutions.

373. **The USSR 1987-1991: Marxist Perspectives**. Edited by Marilyn Vogt-Downey. xvi, 544p. Atlantic Highlands, N.J.: Humanities Press, 1993. Includes bibliographic references and index.

This volume contains 60 articles by various authors who provided a Marxist analysis of Soviet Marxism in the years 1987-1991. Most of the authors of these articles "adhere to the methods, ideals, and heritage of Trotsky" (p. 8). The articles are arranged in five sections: (1) perestroika, glasnost, and the workers; (2) rebellion of the non-Russians; (3) history is knocking at the door; (4) politics and the people; and (5) a new stage opens. An introduction by the editor puts these articles in the context of a Marxist philosophical heritage.

374. Zinoviev, Aleksandr. **Perestroika in Partygrad**. Translated by C. Janson. 192p. London: Peter Owen, 1992. Translation of: *Katastroika*.

This odd little novel's narrator spars with the reader, purports to tell a story of perestroika in a town shut off from the public, and generally exhibits great satisfaction in the process.

Police Terror, Espionage, Propaganda

375. Adler, Nanci. Victims of Soviet Terror: The Story of the Memorial Movement. xviii, 155p.: illus. Westport, Conn.: Praeger, 1993. Includes bibliographical references (p. [151]) and index.

Memorial is a movement that started in the late 1980s in order to force recognition and admission of Russia's intolerant and oppressive past. One of its most powerfully symbolic acts was to encircle the Lubyanka prison with a human chain in 1989. Adler's study documents the history of this organization, which began as a "quasi-conspiratorial circle" and is now seen as "one of the quiet moral pillars of democratic Russia" (p. xiii).

376. Bardach, Janusz, and Kathleen Gleeson. Man Is Wolf to Man: Surviving the Gulag. xvi, 392p.: illus., maps. Berkeley: University of California Press, 1998.

Janusz Bardach presently lives as a renowned specialist in congenital facial deformities. But in Stalin's Russia, the Russia of the Great Purges, he was a pioneer in Kolyma. In this autobiographical account he describes his life there and how one survived its many horrors.

377. Intimacy and Terror. Edited by Veronique Garros, Natalia Korenevskaya, and Thomas Lahusen. xx, 394p.: illus. New York: New Press, 1995. Includes bibliographical references.

This volume presents diaries from the 1930s. The goal was to compose a picture of the daily lives of ordinary citizens during the years of the great purges. The compilers have included nine diaries, some reproduced in their entirety, others in fragments. The book begins with a chronology and a chronicle of the year 1937 as recorded by Izvestiia. Each of the following chapters is devoted to one of the diaries. The materials have numerous notes acting as explanatory text. Each section is preceded by a brief biographical sketch.

378. Khlevniuk, Oleg Vital'evich. In Stalin's Shadow: The Career of "Sergo." xi, 193p. Armonk, N.Y.: M. E. Sharpe, 1995. Includes bibliographical references and index.

In this volume Oleg Khlevniuk examines Ordzhonikidze's role in Stalin's government. "While keeping Ordzhonikidze as his focal point, Khlevniuk examines the career of Sergo to probe larger questions of Soviet political history" (p. viii). The author examines Stalin's relationship with the Politburo and the limits of his power. He also discusses the conflicts between Stalin and his closest friends and advisors. Khlevniuk has drawn on materials from the newly opened Soviet government archives. This book first appeared in Russian in 1993. The author is an editor of the journal *Svobodnaia Mysl*.

379. Parrish, Michael. The Lesser Terror: Soviet State Security, 1939-1953. xxii, 424p., [8] p. of plates: illus., ports. Westport, Conn.: Praeger, 1996. Includes bibliographical references (pp. [361]-391) and index.

Although most people think of the time of the purges as being the most bloody during Stalin's rule, the period after World War II until Stalin's death in 1953 witnessed the continued strength of repression. Parrish focuses on Abakumov, who was head of the Ministry of State Security, and in many respects the book is a biography of him. But it is also much more than this; it is also "a history of massive crimes committed by the Soviet state during 1939-1953, usually initiated by Stalin and always carried out with his approval and consent."

380. Sevander, Mayme, and Laurie Hertzel. **They Took My Father: A Story of Idealism and Betrayal**. xii, 190p.: illus. Duluth, Minn.: Pfeifer-Hamilton Publishers, 1992.

This book recounts a little-known chapter in the repression of the 1930s that took place in the Soviet Union. It is concerned with settlements in Karelin. These settlements were made up largely of Finns and Americans of Finnish descent. They thought they were being given the opportunity to establish a homeland. Many fell victim to Stalin's purges. This book tells the story of Soviet Karelia in the 1930s through the life of one family.

381. Shelley, Louise I. **Policing Soviet Society: The Evolution of State Control**. xx, 269p.: illus. London: Routledge, 1996. Includes bibliographical references (pp. [255]-260) and index.

Shelley looks at the history and development of the Soviet militia and its implications for the current Russia and its successor states. In the course of her investigation she poses and answers several questions central to the understanding of the militia. "Why, she asks, were the militia and the rest of the sophisticated Soviet control apparatus unable to prevent the collapse of the USSR? Does Soviet law enforcement provide an undemocratic legacy for the successor states? This fascinating book fills a vital gap in literature on the Soviet legacy" (frontispiece).

382. Smith, Kathleen E. **Remembering Stalin's Victims: Popular Memory and the End of the USSR**. xv, 220p.: illus. Ithaca, N.Y.: Cornell University Press, 1996. Includes bibliographical references and index.

"This book addresses state-society conflict over human rights abuses in the former Soviet Union. It investigates why de-Stalinization became a double-edged sword for reformers within the leadership and a rallying point for democratic activists in the broader society" (p. xii). In the course of her study Smith examines liberalization and the settling of accounts, selective de-Stalinization during Khrushchev's thaw, glasnost and the reemergence of the Stalin question, anti-Stalinism and the dissidents, the birth of the Memorial Society, the decline of anti-Stalinism, and the end of Soviet rule and prospects for settling accounts.

383. Waller, J. Michael. **Secret Empire: The KGB in Russia Today**. x, 390p. Boulder, Colo.: Westview Press, 1994. Includes bibliographical references (pp. [361]-372) and index.

"In this provocative book, J. Michael Waller demonstrates that in reality the leaders and officers of the KGB have been able to maintain their power and privilege through 'new' security and intelligence services, the emerging democratic political process, and the developing market economic system" (p. 373). The theme of the book is the effect of civilian control on the security force. The author argues that because the security forces were not forced to become more accountable after the 1991 putsch, Yeltsin inherited a powerful but independent KGB, which he was able to use to strengthen his own position. Waller argues that this security force may be a threat to Russia's fledgling democracy.

Diplomacy and Foreign Relations

General Studies

384. **Nations Abroad: Diaspora Politics and International Relations in the Former Soviet Union**. Edited by Charles King and Neil J. Melvin. 240p. Boulder, Colo.: Westview Press, 1998. Includes bibliographical references and index.

This collection of essays explores the relation of ethnic groups in the Diaspora, and trans-border ethnic populations with internal politics and international relations. Groups covered include Russians, Jews, Armenians, Ukrainians, Kazakhs, the Volga Tatars, and Poles. A concluding chapter ties the knowledge gained in the preceding essays to remarks on Diasporas, international relations, and the shape and context of post-Soviet Eurasia.

385. **Russia and Europe: An End to Confrontation?** Edited by Neil Malcolm. xi, 240p. London; New York: Pinter Publishers for the Royal Institute of International Affairs, London, 1994. Includes bibliographical references and index.

"The purpose of this book is to analyze the origins and the driving forces of the changes which have taken place in relations between Russia and the rest of Europe and to examine the prospects for the future." The contributors' essays have been organized into four groups. The first three essays examine the changes Gorbachev has put in place in the context of Russia's past. The next four essays focus on the task of dismantling the cold war. Economic issues are discussed in the following two papers. The last chapter discusses possibilities for Russia's future.

386. Mendelson, Sarah Elizabeth. **Changing Course: Ideas, Politics, and the Soviet Withdrawal from Afghanistan**. xiii, 140p. *Princeton Studies in International History and Politics*. Princeton, N.J.: Princeton University Press, 1998. Includes bibliographical references and index.

Mendelson has investigated how Soviet decision makers changed thinking about foreign policy in the 1980s. He attributes this change to the earlier predominance of "old thinkers" giving ground to the propositions of "new thinkers." He proposes that "the withdrawal from Afghanistan and other subsequent reversals of foreign policy resulted because the Gorbachev coalition gained control of political resources and placed what had been misfit ideas about both domestic and foreign policies squarely on the political agenda. The Gorbachev coalition shifted the internal balance of power in favor of reformists and 'new thinkers' through a series of political strategies previously unused by Soviet political elites attempting reform" (p. 4).

387. **Rethinking Russia's National Interests**. Edited by Stephen Sestanovich. xii, 115p. *Significant Issues series*, vol. 16, no. 1. Washington, D.C.: Center for Strategic and International Studies, 1994. Includes bibliographical references.

"A distinguished international group of scholars, former government officials, and political leaders focuses on the rival conceptions of Russia's military, economic, political, and even ideological interests. The issues examined include Russia's new foreign policy goals, the concept of economic sovereignty, resurgent nationalism, relations with other former Soviet states, and the fate of Russians now living outside Russia" (back cover). The papers collected here were originally presented at a 1992 Moscow conference.

388. Smart, Christopher. **The Imagery of Soviet Foreign Policy and the Collapse of the Russian Empire**. 180p. Westport, Conn.: Praeger, 1995. Includes bibliographical references and index.

"This work aims to contribute both to the study of Soviet foreign policy in particular, and to the field of international relations in general. This area of state behavior involves more than just public relations, propaganda, negotiation, or active measures. Above all, this study should help in better understanding the rhetoric of the leadership" (p. 12). The author compares the images of the Soviet Union defined and projected by the regimes of Krushchev, Brezhnev, and Gorbachev.

To 1917

389. **Britain and Russia in the Age of Peter the Great: Historical Documents**. Edited by Simon Dixon et al. Translated by Simon Dixon. xxv, 255p., [20] p. of plates: illus. *SSEES Occasional Papers*, no. 38. London: School of Slavonic and East European Studies, 1998. Includes bibliographical references (pp. xvi-xviii) and index.

This set of documents is a collaborative venture between British and Soviet scholars. Its occasion was the celebration of the 300th anniversary of Peter the Great's visit to England and to issue a volume "of documents illustrating relations between Britain and Russia from the time of Peter's Grand Embassy of 1697-1698 until the death of the tsar in 1725" (p. xix). The 272 documents, consisting of reports, letters, instructions, and the like, are arranged in chronological order.

390. **England and the North: The Russian Embassy of 1613-1614.** Edited by Maija Jansson and Nikolai Rogozhin. Translated by Paul Bushkovitch. xxxvi, 236p., [1] leaf of plates: illus. *Memoirs of the American Philosophical Society*, vol. 210. Philadelphia: American Philosophical Society, 1994. Includes appendixes, bibliographic references, and index.

The Russian embassy of 1613-1614 to James I of England has traditionally been perceived as an economic mission. The documents translated here, however, provide a different view and suggest that the purpose was much broader, including political ends as well. In addition to the documents translated into English is a lengthy introduction that interprets the mission in the light of the accompanying evidence.

391. LeDonne, John P. **The Russian Empire and the World, 1700-1917: The Geopolitics of Expansion and Containment.** xix, 394p.: maps. New York: Oxford University Press, 1997. Includes bibliographical references (pp. 379-85) and index.

"This book has a dual purpose. It is intended to be, first of all, a comprehensive survey of the major events in the history of tsarist Russian foreign relations between 1700, when the Northern War with Sweden began, and 1917, when the Romanov dynasty collapsed" (p. xi). LeDonne notes that three of the basic works on Russian foreign policy are out of print, leaving a gap in the literature. His study has been influenced by these earlier works. However, he has modified the approach of the earlier scholars to accommodate the geopolitical model he has developed to explain the methods and goals of Russian foreign policy. LeDonne's book is divided into five parts: Russia and Its Western Frontier, Russia and Its Southern Frontier, Russian and Its Eastern Frontier, Containment by the Germanic Powers, and Containment by the Coastland Powers.

392. **Imperial Russian Foreign Policy.** Edited by Valerii Nikolaevich Ponomarev and Hugh Ragsdale. xv, 457p. *Woodrow Wilson Center series*. Washington, D.C.: Woodrow Wilson Center Press, 1993. Some contributions translated from Russian. Includes bibliographical references and index.

The contributors to this volume all participated in a conference in October 1990 at the Kennan Institute. The essays are divided into six sections: "The Origins of Imperial Russian Foreign Policy"; "Imperial Russia and the Western Borderlands in the Eighteenth Century"; "Imperial Russia in the Coming of the Crimean War"; "Imperial Russian Foreign Policy in Nineteenth-Century America"; "Adventure and Disaster in the Late Empire"; "Conclusions and Perspectives."

1917 to Present

393. Chandler, Andrea. **Institutions of Isolation: Border Controls in the Soviet Union and Its Successor States 1917-1993.** xv, 205p. Montreal: McGill-Queen's University Press, 1998. Includes bibliographical references and index.

This is the study of the use of the border controls as a mechanism of repression and isolationism. The author explores why any political system would impose such restrictions on its society and what it hoped to achieve. "Chandler provides a comprehensive examination of border controls from the Bolshevik Revolution of 1917 to the collapse of the USSR in 1991 and shows the continued importance of border controls for the newly independent Soviet successor states" (frontispiece).

394. **"Northern Territories" and Beyond: Russian, Japanese, and American Perspectives**. Edited by James E. Good, Vladimir I. Ivanov, and Nobuo Shimotomai. xxxiv, 368p.: map. Westport, Conn.: Praeger, 1995. Includes bibliographical references (pp. [341]-352) and index.

This study has been compiled by a group of scholars that are concerned with relations between Moscow and Tokyo. "In this book an attempt has been made to go back to the origins of the conflict in Russian-Japanese relations to discuss their current status, and to look past a horizon that is currently clouded by the problem of the Northern Territories" (p. xii). The book is divided into four parts: "History of the Territorial Dispute to 1986"; "Rethinking the Relationship: 1986-1993"; "Beyond the Cold War"; "Regional Security and the Future of the Trilateral Relationship." The book includes a chronology of events from 1985 to 1994.

395. Jacobson, Jon. **When the Soviet Union Entered World Politics**. xi, 388p.: maps. Berkeley: University of California Press, 1994. Includes bibliographical references (pp. 355-77) and index.

In his examination of Soviet foreign relations during the period 1917-1945, Jacobson argues that "foreign relations were central to the political imagination of the Bolsheviks and to their actual political behavior from the day they came to power even during the era of 'socialism in one country' " (p. 7). He shows how they managed to emerge from the precarious position of revolution in 1917 to becoming a major world power by the end of the Second World War.

396. **Peacekeeping and the Role of Russia in Eurasia**. Edited by Lena Jonson and Clive Archer. x, 229p. Boulder, Colo.: Westview Press, 1996. Includes bibliographical references and index.

This collection of articles is arranged in four parts. Part 1 is an introduction that comprehensively describes and analyzes Russia and peacekeeping in Eurasia. Part 2 deals with Russian interventionism in Eurasia. Part 3 contains case studies of Russian peacekeeping in some of the republics and autonomous regions. Part 4 covers multilateral security organizations for peacekeeping in Eurasia.

397. **Soviet Foreign Policy in Transition**. Edited by Roger E. Kanet, Deborah Nutter Miner, and Tamara J. Resler. xvi, 308p. Cambridge, Eng.: Cambridge University Press, 1992. Includes index.

These 15 essays were originally presented at the Fourth World Congress of Soviet and East European Studies in 1990. They are arranged in four parts: (1) the Soviet Union and the international political system; (2) the Soviet Union and Europe; (3) the Soviet Union and the developing world: global trends; and (4) the Soviet Union and the developing world. The volume concludes with regional and country case studies and a conclusion.

398. Kozhemiakin, Alexander V., and Roger E. Kanet. **The Foreign Policy of the Russian Federation**. xii, 208p. London; New York: Macmillan; St. Martin's Press, 1997. Based on papers presented at the annual meetings of the American Association for the Advancement of Slavic Studies held in Honolulu, Hawaii, in November 1993.

In November 1993 a roundtable panel on the emerging foreign policy in Russia was held at the annual meeting of the American Association for the Advancement of Slavic Studies. This volume incorporates essays by the participants of that panel and other scholars. "Our objective is to provide a current assessment of the major development in Russian foreign policy since the collapse of the Soviet Union at the end of 1991" (p. vi). Contributors include Susanne Birgerson, Aurel Braun, William Ferry, Robert Freedman, Roger Kanet, Alexander Kozhemiakin, Paul Marantz, Peter Shearman, and F. Seth Singleton. Each chapter provides an overview of Soviet policy in the region, a review of current policy in the region, and a discussion of future directions of Russia policy. Areas that are discussed include Central Europe, the Balkans, Asia, the Middle East, and the Third World.

399. Malcolm, Neil, et al. **Internal Factors in Russian Foreign Policy**. 356p.: illus., map. Oxford; New York: Published for the Royal Institute of International Affairs by Oxford University Press, 1996. Includes bibliographical references (pp. [333]-343) and index.

"This book is an attempt to analyze the way internal forces are influencing Russian foreign policy in the new, still rapidly evolving post-Soviet environment" (p. 1). This is a collection of essays bound together thematically. All examine the political elements of foreign policy. The six essays discuss the context of foreign policy change in Russia, policy thinking, policy making, the affect of public politics on foreign policy, military factors and foreign policy, and the future of foreign policy development in Russia. The contributors are Neil Malcolm, Alex Pravda, Margot Light, and Roy Allison.

400. McFadden, David W. **Alternative Paths: Soviets and Americans, 1917-1920**. x, 448p. New York: Oxford University Press, 1993. Includes bibliographical references (pp. 340-418) and index.

In the years immediately following the revolution, the Soviets and Americans struggled to establish some diplomatic and economic contacts. "This book is a detailed investigation of all these contacts: the successes, the setbacks, and frustrations. The numerous encounters by these earliest practitioners of Soviet-American diplomacy and the processes by which they struggled to find common ground to deal with common problems provide a revealing glimpse into a very different kind of diplomacy than is traditional" (p. 8).

McFadden traces these early forays into diplomacy beginning with the initial attempts to establish a relationship in 1917 and 1918, through the years of the civil war and the attempts to establish peace in 1918 and 1919, to the first attempts to establish economic relations in 1919 and 1920.

401. Nation, R. Craig. **Black Earth, Red Star: A History of Soviet Security Policy, 1917-1991**. xvi, 341p. Ithaca, N.Y.: Cornell University Press, 1992. Includes bibliographical references and index.

Nation's goal in this volume is, borrowing the words of Robert Legvold to: "put aside 'simple assumptions and begin to deal directly with the notions that actually shape the Soviet approach to the primary issues of power, security, and order' by using the past as 'a hill from which to judge the evolution of Soviet perspective' " (p. xi). Each of his eight chapters focuses on sequential periods of policy making from 1917 to 1921 and the age of world revolution to 1982-1991, with new thinking and new dilemmas.

402. Peppard, Victor, and James Riordan. **Playing Politics: Soviet Sport Diplomacy to 1992**. x, 184p. *Russian and East European Studies*, vol. 3. Greenwich, Conn.: JAI Press, 1993. Includes bibliographical references (pp. 165-80) and index.

This study analyzes the role of sports in diplomacy in Russia. The authors of this book have set themselves several goals. First, they wish to provide a history of Russian and Soviet sport diplomacy. Second, the authors try to establish the theoretical basis of Soviet sport diplomacy. Third, they explore the interaction between the Soviet Union and the United States in the context of sport diplomacy. Fourth, the authors analyze the affect of the Soviet entry into the Olympic movement. Finally, they examine the future of sports in the former Soviet Union.

403. Procyk, Anna. **Russian Nationalism and Ukraine: The Nationality Policy of the Volunteer Army During the Civil War**. xvi, 202p. Edmonton: Canadian Institute of Ukrainian Studies Press, 1995. Includes index.

In this book the author has "reconstructed the dynamics of the relationship between the various Ukrainian governments and the leadership of the White movement in the South, the VA, during the civil war years" (p. ix). She focuses on the Bolshevik Volunteer Army's nationality policy and challenges several widespread interpretations of the civil war and the motivations of the whites, including that the primary task was to resurrect the old order in Russia. Most of the questions addressed relate directly to the VA's nationality policy and its underlying ideology.

404. Schild, Georg. **Between Ideology and Realpolitik: Woodrow Wilson and the Russian Revolution, 1917-1921**. 173p. *Contributions to the Study of World History*, 0885-9159; No. 51. Westport, Conn.: Greenwood Press, 1995. Includes bibliographical references and index.

This study examines the complex relations between the United States and Russia at the time of the Russian Revolution. While the focus is on U.S. policy and the forces that shaped it, much of the volume deals with the international effects of the revolution. The author is particularly concerned with the considerations that guided Wilson in his policy making. "Political, economic and military necessities dictated that some of the most important American (and Soviet) foreign policy decisions of the years 1917 through 1919 were based on considerations of realpolitik rather than ideology" (p. 7). The author takes a chronological approach to his subject beginning with an overview of World War I and the Russian Revolution.

405. Siegel, Katherine Amelia Siobhan. **Loans and Legitimacy: The Evolution of Soviet-American Relations, 1919-1933**. x, 211p., [8] p. of plates: illus. Lexington: University Press of Kentucky, c1996. Includes bibliographical references and index.

"This book investigates the early Soviet campaign for American trade and recognition, as well as the American response, official and unofficial. It suggests that the pre-recognition era, like the post-Cold War era, embraced a Russian-American relationship that was evolving rather than rigidly polarized" (p. xi). The author examines the military, economic, and political facets of the problem from both sides. The study is arranged chronologically.

406. Skak, Mette. **From Empire to Anarchy: Postcommunist Foreign Policy and International Relations**. xii, 340p. New York: St. Martin's Press, 1996. Includes bibliographical references (pp. 290-314) and index.

In investigating the transition from empire to newly free states, Skak provides the reader with an introduction to state structure. He develops this in succeeding chapters in his case studies. Intending this volume to be a text for university students, he devotes a great deal of attention to the Soviet Union, to Russia's recent transition, and includes individual chapters on Lithuania and Hungary.

407. Van Dyke, Carl. **The Soviet Invasion of Finland, 1939-40**. xiv, 270p.: illus., maps. *Cass Series on Soviet Military Experience*, 3. London: Frank Cass, 1997. Includes bibliographical references (pp. 225-57) and index.

The Soviet invasion of Finland in the winter of 1939-1940 was the last major military operation conducted by the Red Army before the Nazi's activities in 1941. Van Dyke investigates several questions about the invasion, including: "What motivated Stalin to launch an undeclared war against Finland? What lessons did the Soviet high command learn from the experience?" (p. xi). He also provides a summary of the diplomatic and other lessons learned from the war.

With the United States

408. Boyle, Peter G. **American-Soviet Relations: From the Russian Revolution to the Fall of Communism**. xiv, 321p. London: Routledge, 1993. Includes bibliographical essay and index.

Boyle examines central episodes in US-Soviet relations since 1917 including the American intervention in Russia between 1918 and 1920, diplomatic recognition of the Soviet Union in 1933, World War II, the cold war, the Cuban missile crisis, and others. He develops the theme that "American policy toward the Soviet Union has been shaped partly by a rational calculation of the perceived threat to the United States and partly by a wide variety of internal forces within the United States, such as political considerations, economic interests and emotional factors, which, often in a somewhat irrational fashion, have been a constant part of the process which has determined US policy toward the Soviet Union" (p. vii).

409. Crockatt, Richard. **The Fifty Years War: The United States and the Soviet Union in World Politics, 1941-1991**. xviii, 417p.: maps. London: Routledge, 1995. Includes bibliographical references (pp. 384-98).

Crockatt's study is "a history of US-Soviet relations between 1941 and 1991, viewed in a global perspective. It is thus neither simply a study of bilateral superpower relations nor a comprehensive world history. The theme is rather the ways in which the United States and the Soviet Union have adapted, or failed to adapt, to global change" (p. xiii). He has divided his study into five parts: perspectives; the emergence of a bipolar world, 1941-1953; globalism and the limits of bipolarity, 1953-1964; détente and its limits, 1965-1981; and cold war versus international politics: the denouement, 1981-1991.

410. Dunn, Dennis J. **Caught Between Roosevelt and Stalin: America's Ambassadors to Moscow**. xii, 349p.: illus. Lexington: University Press of Kentucky, 1998.

Dunn examines the careers of five U.S. ambassadors to Moscow between the years 1933 and 1945. He explores the relationship of these men to Roosevelt and Stalin for several reasons. First, it provides a good perspective by which to study Roosevelt's policy toward Stalin; second, it also helps to explain Stalin's policy toward the United States; third, it provides a way of measuring the value of the institution of ambassador; and fourth, it provides a close look at the lives of these pivotal individuals during a crucial period in world history.

411. Foglesong, David S. **America's Secret War Against Bolshevism: U.S. Intervention in the Russian Civil War, 1917-1920**. x, 386p.: illus., maps. Chapel Hill: University of North Carolina Press, 1995. Includes bibliographical references (pp. [347]-369) and index.

This study of Wilson's secret war against Bolshevism during the First World War shows that "at the beginning of the Soviet-American conflict, amid popular demands for a new, open diplomacy, the Wilson administration epitomized a limited, secretive, and ineffective style of intervention, one that unsuccessfully sought to evade the constraints of democracy at home as it pursued American interests and promoted American values abroad" (p. 298).

412. **The Limited Partnership: Building a Russian-US Security Community**. Edited by James E. Goodby and Benoit Morel. xvii, 317p. Oxford, Eng.: Oxford University Press, 1993. Includes bibliographical references and index.

This volume recommends policies that Russia and the United States could take together in order to achieve co-operative security. This would enable the two nations to move from adversarial positions to a partnership. The essays are arranged in four parts: (1) introduction; (2) regime transition: from cold war to co-operative security; (3) military power and international stability; and (4) building a new security relationship.

413. Hutchings, Robert L. **American Diplomacy and the End of the Cold War: An Insider's Account of U.S. Policy in Europe, 1989-1992**. xviii, 456p.: illus. Washington, D.C.: Woodrow Wilson Center Press, 1997. Includes bibliographical references (pp. 419-35) and index.

Hutchings was a White House advisor during the demise of the Soviet Union in the late 1980s and early 1990s. His book is thus partly a political memoir and partly a scholar's analysis of the events that took place during that time. By design the book concentrates on areas in American diplomacy where the author had personal direct involvement viz. "Central and Eastern Europe before, during, and after the revolutions of 1989, Germany during the period of unification and thereafter, and broad strategies toward Europe and the Soviet Union throughout the period" (p. xi).

414. Larson, Deborah Welch. **Anatomy of Mistrust: U.S.-Soviet Relations During the Cold War**. xi, 329p. *Cornell Studies in Security Affairs*. Ithaca, N.Y.: Cornell University Press, 1997. Includes bibliographical references (pp. 315-17) and index.

Larson analyzes why the superpowers failed to achieve more cooperation in the international arena than was possible. She shows that "the United States and the Soviet Union were able to cooperate when each trusted the other to comply, or when one side made a series of unilateral concessions to alleviate mistrust" (p. 5). In examining how trust was established in a number of cases she also considers "whether factors other than changes in beliefs about the other side's intentions and motives might have altered the two sides' interest in cooperation" (p. 6).

415. Lynch, Allen. **The Cold War Is Over—Again**. xv, 208p. Boulder, Colo.: Westview Press, 1992. Includes bibliographical references.

Lynch wants the reader to reconsider the essential character of East-West relations and particularly the centrality of U.S.-Soviet relations. "The book's underlying theme is that contrary to the general understanding, the 'cold war' in East-West relations was actually put to rest between the early 1960s and the 1970s, when Eastern and Western governments codified the division of Germany and Europe. The revolutionary events of 1989 thus overturned not the Cold War order but rather the post-cold war order in East-West relations, much to the surprise and consternation of nearly every government involved, including the United States" (p. 1).

416. Nelson, Keith L. **The Making of Détente: Soviet-American Relations in the Shadow of Vietnam**. xviii, 217p. Baltimore: Johns Hopkins University Press, 1995. Includes bibliographical references (pp. [195]-207) and index.

Nelson explores détente between the Soviet Union and the United States. His thesis is that "at the end of the 1960s, analogous developments combined to persuade the leading groups in both the United States and the Soviet Union that they no longer possessed the resources required to achieve their basic objectives and that collaboration with each other was a relatively safe way to bring needs and resources into balance. Thus the decision of the leaders to pursue détente was, in effect, an effort to increase their capacities and to maximize their control without serious side effects" (p. xviii).

417. Neumann, Iver B. **Russia and the Idea of Europe: A Study in Identity and International Relations**. xviii, 253p. London: Routledge, 1996. Includes bibliographical references (pp. 223-42) and index.

"In *Russia and the Idea of Europe* Iver Neumann discusses whether the tensions between Romantic nationalist views and Europe-orientated liberal views can ever be resolved. The issue of nationalism is examined as one of the most powerful and alarming of Russian responses to the pressures exerted by European models" (frontispiece). Neumann traces the tensions between Russian and European political philosophies from the Napoleonic Wars to the present. The author believes that while Russia is attracted to the more economically flourishing European models, it is also drawn by the lure of the imperial role it might play in Asia.

418. Saul, Norman E. **Concord and Conflict: The United States and Russia, 1867-1914**. xviii, 654p.: illus., maps. Lawrence: University Press of Kansas, 1996. Includes bibliographical references (pp. 601-34) and index.

"This volume continues the history of the Russian-American experience begun in *Distant Friends: The United States and Russia, 1763-1867*, from the purchase of Alaska to the beginning of World War I. As in the case of its predecessor, this work falls between the traditional scholarly monograph and the general survey. The goal is to demonstrate the extent and nature of relations over a time frame that allows analysis of change and continuity and of nuances in political, economic, social, and cultural affairs. Above all, the intention has been to show how perceptions that each people had of the other developed and changed over time" (p. xi).

419. Shavit, David. **United States Relations with Russia and the Soviet Union: A Historical Dictionary**. xviii, 233p. Westport, Conn.: Greenwood Press, 1993. Includes bibliography and index.

David Shavit has provided a valuable resource on the history of U.S.-Russian relations for English speakers. It includes a chronology highlighting significant events in U.S.-Russian relations, a list of heads of diplomatic missions in Russia, and a list of individuals by profession and occupation. The dictionary entries include bibliographical references. Among the entries are articles on events, policies, summit meetings, treaties, individuals, institutions, organizations, and business firms. Cross-references are indicated by an asterisk before the name/topic. The work focuses on the United States, thus there is no dictionary entry for Khrushchev, Lenin, or Stalin, but many American presidents are listed, up to and including George Bush. Nevertheless, for the student of Russian/Soviet history it is a valuable resource. The book introduces many concepts and provides bibliographical resources on a wide range of concepts in English.

420. Westad, Odd Arne. **Cold War and Revolution: Soviet-American Rivalry and the Origins of the Chinese Civil War, 1944-1946**. x, 260p.: maps. New York: Columbia University Press, 1993. Includes bibliographical references (pp. [223]-245) and index.

While the focal point of this book is China, it is discussed in the context of the effect of its relationships with Russia and the United States. It is also examined in terms of how U.S.-Soviet relations shaped Chinese politics. The author believes that only a multifocused analysis can fully explain events in China during the second half of the 20th century. Much of this study is devoted to a discussion of the control exercised by the United States and the Soviet Union in the world and their relationship with one another.

421. **Witnesses to the End of the Cold War**. Edited by William C. Wohlforth. xvi, 344p. Baltimore: Johns Hopkins University Press, 1996. Includes bibliographical references and index.

"This book is a contribution to understanding the most consequential international event of the past half-century: the ending of the Cold War between the United States and the Soviet Union" (p. vii). The first six chapters are transcripts of the so-called "Princeton Conference" held in 1993. The four chapters that follow focus on key issues raised by the conference: personality and leadership, the causes and effects of changing perceptions, and the implications for various theories of international relations. The appendixes are a chronology of U.S.-Soviet relations from 1983 to 1989 and a selection of declassified documents.

422. Wohlforth, William Curti. **The Elusive Balance: Power and Perceptions During the Cold War**. x, 317p. *Cornell Studies in Security Affairs*. Ithaca, N.Y.: Cornell University Press, 1993. Includes bibliographical references and index.

In examining power in world politics and the role of the Soviet Union in the balance of power, Wohlforth investigates "how members of the Soviet political elite thought about the problem of power in world politics, mainly during the years between 1945 and 1989" (p. 1). In so doing he intends to aid the understanding of the influence of power in world politics in general. His book explores balance-of-power theory and Soviet foreign policy, the origins of thinking about power politics, the context of the postwar system, various crises, détente, and lessons from the cold war's last battle and its end.

With Western and Third World Countries

423. Adomeit, Hannes. **Imperial Overstretch: Germany in Soviet Policy from Stalin to Gorbachev: An Analysis Based on New Archival Evidence, Memoirs and Interviews**. 609p. *Internationale Politik Und Sicherheit, 48.* Baden-Baden, Ger.: Nomos Verlagsgesellschaft, 1998. Includes bibliography.

In this study of postwar Germany and Soviet foreign relations with that nation, the author has made use of materials newly accessible in the archives. He probes such questions as the causes of the division of Germany, the Soviet reaction to German unification, and its consent to German membership in NATO. The book focuses on the Soviet role in all these events. "It is therefore concerned with party and government leaders in Moscow, their political ambitions, the ideological stereotypes they shared, the institutional pressures they faced and the systemic constraints with which they had to contend" (p. 11). The book is divided into four parts, each reflecting a different era in Soviet-German relations: the postwar Soviet empire; expansion of that empire in the 1960s through the 1980s; the economic crisis of the 1980s; and the collapse of the Soviet Union. The book includes biographical notes and a list of interviews used in this study.

424. Baranovsky, Vladimir. **Russia and Europe: The Emerging Security Agenda**. xviii, 582p. New York: Oxford University Press, 1997. Includes bibliographical references and index.

"The main tasks of this study are to highlight the major conflict-generating issues in Russia's interaction with Europe and the ways in which they could be addressed; to assess the most important trends in Russia's security thinking and policy-making vis-à-vis Europe; to speculate on Russia's role in the post-Cold War European setting; and to consider the implications of developments in Russia and Russia's policy for preserving stability on the continent of Europe" (p. xiii). Scholars from Russia, Europe, and North America wrote the 24 essays that make up this collection.

425. Cross, Anthony. **Anglo-Russica: Aspects of Cultural Relations Between Great Britain and Russia in the Eighteenth and Early Nineteenth Centuries: Selected Essays**. x, 269p. Oxford: Berg, 1993. Includes index.

Anthony Cross has devoted most of his scholarly career to the study of Anglo-Russian relations. This collection of his essays was first published between 1969 and 1990 and covers the history of Anglo-Russian relations from the beginning of the 18th to the middle of the 19th century. "It covers a wide variety of topics, such as mutual perception and awareness, the creation of images and stereotypes, translations and fictional representations, travel accounts and newspaper reports. Some essays deal with particular areas of British awareness of Russian culture (e.g., folk song) or of individual writers (such as the fabulist Ivan Krylov); others recount individual British encounters with Russia (e.g., George Borrow or the Governess Lucy Atkinson)" (back cover).

426. Dannreuther, Roland. **The Soviet Union and the PLO**. ix, 222p. *St. Antony's series*. New York: St. Martin's Press, 1998.

The main purpose of this study is to assess the Soviet role in the Arab-Israeli conflict by concentrating on the relations between the Soviet Union and the PLO. The author sets up a framework for the Soviets' engagement in the conflict and then traces the Soviet-PLO relationship in five- and six-year chunks from 1964 through 1991.

427. Ginat, Rami. **The Soviet Union and Egypt, 1945-1955**. xii, 268p. London: Frank Cass, 1993. Includes bibliographical references (pp. [243]-259) and indexes.

"This deals with the political history of the Middle East, with special reference to Egypt. It aims to expose and analyze the events which led to the involvement and subsequent domination of the Soviet Union in Egypt and other Arab countries" (p. xi). The author describes and analyzes Soviet doctrine concerning the Arab world, the Egyptian communist movement and its role in the internal political arena up to 1955, the relationship between communism and Islam, the USSR's first steps in the Egyptian and Middle Eastern arena, the Soviet response to Western attempts to form a Middle East Defense Organization from 1947 to 1952, Soviet-Egyptian relations under Nasir, Egyptian arms deals with the Soviet Bloc and their implications, and Soviet-Egyptian economic relations under the military regime of 1952-1955.

428. **The Soviets, Their Successors and the Middle East: Turning Point**. Edited by Rosemary Hollis. xiii, 206p.: illus., maps. *RUSI Defense Studies series*. New York: St. Martin's Press, c1993. Includes bibliographical references and index.

The contributors to this volume investigate the relations between the Soviet Union and its former states and the powers in the Middle East. In Part 1, the essayists explore the policy shift among the Soviet Union, Israel, and the PLO in the 1980s and the changing priorities in the 1980s in the Gulf area. In Part 2, the focus is on the Soviet Union, and Iraq's invasion of Kuwait. In Part 3, the contributors concentrate on Russia's new priorities and the Middle East and the role of Central Asia.

429. Loth, Wilfried. **Stalin's Unwanted Child: The Soviet Union, the German Question, and the Founding of the GDR**. xiii, 234p. New York: St. Martin's Press, 1998.

This study of the origins of the German Democratic Republic and the Soviet Union's role in that process is based on many new sources. Among the surprising findings are that "Stalin wanted no GDR. He wanted neither a separate state in the Soviet Occupation Zone nor a socialist state in Germany at all. Instead, he sought a parliamentary democracy for all of Germany, one which would rob fascism of its social base and one which would allow the Soviet Union access to the resources of the Ruhr industrial area" (p. xi).

430. **The Decline of the Soviet Union and the Transformation of the Middle East**. Edited by Paul Marantz and David Howard Goldberg. vii, 240p. Boulder, Colo.: Westview Press, 1994. Includes bibliographical references and index.

The essayists in this volume examine various effects that the disintegration of the Soviet Union had on the Middle East. In the first of three parts, the contributors explore how the Soviet Union's changing foreign policy affected developments in the Middle East. The focus is on Gorbachev's Middle East policy, the Gulf War, policy toward Israel and the United States, and the rediscovery of the United Nations. In Part 2 they concentrate on the internal dimensions, such as the Commonwealth of Independent States, and the new Muslim nations of Central Asia. In Part 3 they look at key actors, both individual elites as well as groups such as the PLO. A concluding chapter assesses the ramifications of the decline of the Soviet Union and a transforming Middle East.

431. Neilson, Keith. **Britain and the Last Tsar: British Policy and Russia, 1894-1917**. xv, 408p.: maps. Oxford, Eng.: Clarendon Press, 1995. Includes bibliographical references (pp. [373]-399) and index.

One of Neilson's main conclusions is that "Russia was the most significant long-term threat to British interests in the twenty years before the First World War and that a driving force, perhaps the driving force, in British diplomacy was the effort to reach an accommodation with Russia" (p. xiii). His discussion and analysis is arranged in three parts: (1) setting the stage; (2) rivalry 1894-1905 (which touches on problems with China, Armenia, Central Asia, and the Russo-Japanese war); and (3) reconciliation, 1906-1917 (which covers the forging of the Anglo-Russian Convention and the formation of the Anglo-Russian alliance in the First World War).

432. Nekrich, A. M. **Pariahs, Partners, Predators: German-Soviet Relations, 1922-1941**. Edited and translated by Gregory L. Freeze. xiv, 308p. New York: Columbia University Press, 1997. Includes bibliographical references (pp. [295]-308) and index.

Nekrich examines German-Soviet relations between the wars, starting from the Rapallo Treaty through June 1941. This is still a hotly debated area of historical research. New revelations from the archives after the collapse of the Soviet regime have shed considerable light on this period. Nekrich makes excellent use of these documents, but the ideological debate continues. The volume includes a foreword by noted scholar Adam Ulam.

433. Nimmo, William F. **Japan and Russia: A Reevaluation in the Post-Soviet Era**. xxx, 207p.: maps. *Contributions in Asian Studies*, no. 3. Westport, Conn.: Greenwood Press, 1994. Includes bibliographical references (pp. [195]-198) and index.

"This book deals with the efforts of Japan and Russia to find a solution to their differences held over from World War II and examines the events that gave rise to the territorial problem, along with a general outline of Russo-Japanese relations beginning with tsarist Russia, continuing through the Soviet period and ending with the post-Soviet era" (p. xxx). The author has presented his analysis chronologically beginning with the imperial period, the source of many of the 20th-century disputes between the two nations. The book includes a general chronology of events that begins in 1855 and runs through 1993.

434. Paasi, Anssi. **Territories, Boundaries, and Consciousness: The Changing Geographies of the Finnish-Russian Border.** xx, 353p.: illus., maps. *Belhaven Studies in Political Geography.* Chichester, Eng.: John Wiley, 1996.

"This book provides a theoretically informed analysis of the social and historical construction of territories, boundaries and socio-spatial consciousness, particularly in the case of the Finnish state and the Finish-Soviet/Russian boundary" (p. xvii). Paasi provides the reader with a history of the evolution of Finno-Russian borders.

435. **Allies at War: The Soviet, American, and British Experience, 1939-1945.** Edited by David Reynolds, Warren F. Kimball, and A. O. Chubarian. xxiv, 456p. *The Franklin and Eleanor Roosevelt Institute Series on Diplomatic and Economic History,* 7. New York: St. Martin's Press, 1994.

This collection of essays by Russian, British, and American scholars explores the social, economic, diplomatic, and political history of these three countries' cooperation during the Second World War. The essays are arranged in four parts, and in each part an essay is devoted to each of the countries and a fourth to a synthesis of those three. The four parts focus on strategy, the economy, the home front, and foreign policy.

436. **Regional Power Rivalries in the New Eurasia: Russia, Turkey, and Iran.** Edited by Alvin Z. Rubinstein and Oles M. Smolansky. xii, 290p.: map. Armonk N.Y.: M. E. Sharpe, 1995. Includes bibliographical references and index.

These individual essays "examine the relationships between Russia, Turkey, or Iran and one or more of the countries of Transcaucasia or Central Asia, as well as the emerging bilateral relationships between Russia and Ukraine, on the one hand, and Turkey or Iran, on the other." The essays are arranged in four sections: Old Rivals, New Relationships; CIS and Iran; The Turkish Factor; and A Russian "Monroe Doctrine" in the Making? A concluding chapter is authored by the two editors.

437. Shumaker, David H. **Gorbachev and the German Question: Soviet-West German Relations, 1985-1990.** xii, 202p. Westport, Conn.: Praeger, 1995. Includes bibliographical references (pp. [187]-194) and index.

Did Gorbachev actually applaud German unification in 1990, having planned this outcome from the beginning? Or instead did Gorbachev and his regime never envision German unification and never found it compatible with Russian interests? When it did occur, had the Russians lost control over all related events and simply come to accept the inevitable? In exploring these two theses, Shumaker outlines the basic tenets of Russian-German relations in the late 1980s.

438. **The Russians Aren't Coming: New Soviet Policy in Latin America.** Edited by Wayne S. Smith. xii, 196p. Boulder, Colo.: L. Rienner Publishers, 1992. Includes bibliographical references and index.

The essays in this book were written in 1991. At that time it was clear that Soviet policy in the West was undergoing major revision. The scholars who contributed to this study focus on the revisions relevant to the Soviet foreign policy in Latin America. The first section discusses the effects of the realization that the "World Revolution" was a dead concept. The subject of the new policies in the region is then discussed. The remaining sections contain essays on Cuba and Central America. The contributors are Aaron Belkin, James G. Blight, Karen Brutents, Julio Carranza Valdes, David Lewis, Kiva Maidanik, Sergo Mikoyan, Georgi Mirsky, Estervino Montesino Segui, Valery D. Nikolayenko, Jack Perry, Ilya Prizel, Donna Rich-Kaplowitz, Wayne S. Smith, and Thomas G. Weiss.

439. Stent, Angela. **Russia and Germany Reborn: Unification, the Soviet Collapse, and the New Europe.** xviii, 300p.: illus. Princeton, N.J.: Princeton University Press, 1999. Includes bibliographical references (pp. [281]-291) and index.

In one fell swoop the Soviet Union lost an empire and Germany assumed a position of leadership in Europe that it had not held for some time. This volume places these unexpected events in a broader historical context. The three themes that are woven throughout this book are the "centrality of the triangular Soviet-East German-West German relationship in defining the politics of the Cold War . . . how Germany was united and how the decision-making process within the Kremlin operated during this period . . . and the impact of German unification and Soviet disintegration on post-communist European security" (pp. x-xii).

440. **Soviet Relations with India and Vietnam.** Edited by Ramesh Chandra Thakur and Carlyle A. Thayer. 315p.: illus. London: Macmillan, 1992. Includes bibliographical references and index.

"This book presents an analysis of the political, military and economic relationships between three Asian powers: India, Vietnam and the Soviet Union" (p. 1). The authors have arranged their study topically beginning with an overview of Soviet policy toward the Third World and Asia and political relations in the region. They then devote separate chapters to a discussion of political interests, military relations, and economic relations. A special section focuses on nuclear arms in the region. Another is limited to discussion of India and Vietnam. Two appendixes are included. The first contains the Indo-Soviet Treaty; the second, the Soviet-Vietnam Treaty.

441. Vasil'ev, Aleksei Mikhailovich. **Russian Policy in the Middle East: From Messianism to Pragmatism.** 1st English ed. xiii, 384p. Reading, Eng.: Ithaca Press, 1993. Includes bibliographical references and index.

Aleksei Vasil'ev traces the evolution of Russian policy in the Middle East from the Khrushchev era to the years of Gorbachev's far-reaching changes. He examines the effects of four factors on the development of this policy, or at least the perceived development:

socioeconomic realities, bureaucratic structures, individual personalities of the participants, and the author's biases.

442. Volodarskii, Mikhail I. **The Soviet Union and Its Southern Neighbours: Iran and Afghanistan, 1917-1933**. xii, 196p. London: Frank Cass, 1994.
During the earlier years of the Bolshevik regime, one of the inviolable strategic objectives was the inspiration and provocation of "global revolution." This study examines the Bolshevik's early Soviet Middle East policy, especially as it relates to Iran and Afghanistan and the influence and effect of the New Economic Policy on that program.

443. Wehling, Fred. **Irresolute Princes: Kremlin Decision Making in Mid-East Crises, 1967-1973**. 1st ed. 225p. New York: St. Martin's Press, 1997. Includes bibliographical references (pp. [203]-213) and index.
Although the focus of the examples is on the leaders of the former Soviet Union, Wehling relates the behavior of Soviet leaders to the broader context of decision making and the dilemma of managing contradictory goals, or value conflict. The first two chapters concentrate on theoretical issues related to the problem and put forth commonly accepted models for Soviet behavior. Chapters 3-5 test the analytical framework developed earlier in three case studies of regional crises. The sixth chapter summarizes the findings of the case studies. The final chapter discusses the implications of the findings for the understanding of value conflict, deterrence, and crisis management.

With Communist Countries

444. Cox, David. **Retreating from the Cold War: Germany, Russia and the Withdrawal of the Western Group of Forces**. xiv, 185p. London: Macmillan, 1996. Includes index.
This book is an account of the withdrawal of troops from East Germany. For the author this also signaled the end of the cold war as well. While not his goal, the withdrawal was the result of Gorbachev's reforms. The book is arranged chronologically. There are three appendixes on commanders in chief, chronology of events, and a reprint of the "Treaty on the Final Settlement of Germany." The selected bibliography consists largely of English-language publications with a few foreign citations in a separate section.

445. Elleman, Bruce A. **Diplomacy and Deception: The Secret History of Sino-Soviet Diplomatic Relations, 1917-1927**. xviii, 322p.: illus., maps. Armonk, N.Y.: M. E. Sharpe, 1997. Includes bibliographical references and index.
In delving into the diplomatic relations between China and the Soviet Union in the first 10 years of Soviet rule, the author reviews the diplomatic situation prior to 1919, looks at the opening of Sino-Soviet diplomatic negotiations (the Karakhan Manifesto),

and examines carefully the origins of the United Front policy. He then covers each of the major events leading up to the defeat of the United Front policy in 1927, including the entrance of Outer Mongolia into the Communist Bloc, the assertion of Soviet control over the Chinese Eastern Railway, China's revocation of the Boxer indemnity, the restoration of Russian territorial concessions, the resumption of Russian extraterritoriality, and the effect of the formation of the Chinese Communist Party on Soviet foreign policy. The three appendixes contain the 1925 Soviet-Japanese secret agreement on Bessarabia, essential information about the Communist Party's secret work, and the March 23, 1935, Soviet-Japanese Secret Protocol.

446. Gaiduk, Ilya V. **The Soviet Union and the Vietnam War**. xx, 299p. Chicago: I. R. Dee, 1996. Includes bibliographical references (pp. 251-54) and index.

In order to understand Soviet foreign policy toward Vietnam during the Second Indochina war, Gaiduk explores the various factors, trends, and motives that had an influence on Soviet decision making during those years. Chronologically the study covers from 1964 to 1973. It is based largely on materials recently available in the Soviet/Russian archives.

447. Goncharov, S. N., John W. Lewis, and Xue Litai. **Uncertain Partners: Stalin, Mao, and the Korean War**. xi, 393p., [18] p. of plates: illus. *Studies in International Security and Arms Control*. Stanford, Calif.: Stanford University Press, 1993. Includes bibliographical references (pp. [351]-380) and index.

The three authors of this book, from Russia, China, and the United States, cast new light on the history of the Sino-Soviet relationship. They believe that this history was "above all the product of competing security concepts and national interests and was dominated by the strategic designs and political acuity of Mao Zedong and Joseph Stalin" (p. vii).

448. Naimark, Norman M. **The Russians in Germany: A History of the Soviet Zone of Occupation, 1945-1949**. xv, 586p.: illus. Cambridge, Mass.: Belknap Press of Harvard University, 1995. Includes bibliographical references (pp. [475]-571) and index.

The purpose of Naimark's work is to study the Soviet occupation of Germany after the Second World War and the influence the Soviets had on the politics and culture of the occupied zone in the years following. Individual chapters explore the transition from Soviet to German administration; Soviet soldiers, German women, and the problem of rape; reparations, removals, and the economic transformation of the Zone; the Soviet use of German science; the Soviets and the German left, the Tiul'panov question, and Soviet policy making in Zone 3; building the East German police state; and the politics of culture and education.

449. Nemets, Alexander. **The Growth of China and Prospect for the Eastern Region of the Former U.S.S.R.** 111p. Lewiston, N.Y.: Edwin Mellen Press, 1996. Includes bibliographical references (pp. [99]-103) and index.

While China's economic development is the main focus of this work, over half of this study analyzes the role of the Russian Far East and its development. The main conclusion that Alexander Nemets reaches is that China is coming to control much of what was once the Soviet Union. In so doing, it is rising to the status of "superpower" itself. The author sees that this is coupled with the rising level of the standard of living as the basis for the establishment of democracy in China and the regions it comes to control economically.

The book is divided into chapters focusing on various economic areas. First, physical regions: Dongbei, Russian Far East in general, Kazakhstan; and next, geopolitical structures and changes in the Russian Far East.

450. Paine, S. C. M. **Imperial Rivals: China, Russia, and Their Disputed Frontier.** xxi, 417p.: illus., maps. Armonk, N.Y.: M. E. Sharpe, 1996. Includes bibliographical references (pp. 370-402) and index.

"How the Russo-Chinese frontier evolved from being a remote periphery to a central concern for both countries is the subject of this work" (p. 1). At the end of the 20th century the Sino-Russian border was the longest militarized border in the world. The past 150 years had witnessed countless territorial disputes. After an introduction that identifies the international, regional, bilateral, and domestic issues, Paine arranges his investigation into four parts, each of which covers a specific chronological period: (1) from Manchuria to Sinkiang, 1858-1864, and the demise of traditional Chinese diplomacy; (2) Sinkiang, 1871-1888, a turning point in Chinese foreign policy; (3) Manchuria, 1896-1905, Russian railroad imperialism and the Russo-Japanese War; and (4) Outer Mongolia, 1911-1924, shifting spheres of influence.

451. **The Soviet Union in Eastern Europe, 1945-89.** Edited by Odd Arne Westad, Iver B. Neumann, and Sven G. Holtsmark. viii, 234p. New York: St. Martin's Press, 1994. Includes bibliographical references and index.

The essays in this volume were originally presented at an international conference held in Oslo in 1992. They deal with the post-World War II relations between the Soviet Union and East European countries up to and including the revolutions of 1989-1991. Individual essays cover such topics as Czechoslovakia, the Soviet Union, and the Marshall Plan; the 1948 Soviet-Yugoslav conflict and the formation of the "Socialist Camp" model; language, politics, and ethnicity in Moldova; Soviet-Romanian relations; East European mass media; the Kremlin's impact on the peaceful revolution in East Germany; civil resistance in the revolutions of 1989-1991; and Soviet foreign policy toward its European allies.

Breakup of East European Satellites

452. Fowkes, Ben. **The Disintegration of the Soviet Union: A Study in the Rise and Triumph of Nationalism**. 281p.: illus. New York: St. Martin's Press, 1997. Includes bibliographical references and indexes.

The theme of Fowkes' book is the problem faced by the Russian and Soviet empires in their quest to integrate the non-Russian periphery into a single, monolithic state. In pursuing his theme Fowkes covers the following topics: the evolution of Soviet nationality policy, the interplay of modernization and Russification under Stalin and later, the corporatist compromise and the varieties of national resistance, Mikhail Gorbachev and the rising tide of national unrest, the explosion of the Soviet galaxy, and the failure of the August coup.

453. Karklins, Rasma. **Ethnopolitics and Transition to Democracy: The Collapse of the USSR and Latvia**. xxiii, 206p.: illus. Washington, D.C.: Woodrow Wilson Center Press, 1994. Includes bibliographical references (pp. 183-97) and index.

Ethnicity has political consequences, as has been so clearly demonstrated in south-central Europe. It has also played a major role in those countries making the transition from nondemocratic to democratic regimes. In this book Rasma Karklins looks at some of the instances where ethnicity has played a positive role in this transition. Karklins takes Latvia as his case study, demonstrating at least one instance in which ethnic pluralism supported civil and political pluralism. The book is arranged topically beginning with a discussion of ethnopolitical theory. In later chapters the theoretical groundwork established in this chapter is applied to explain the changes in the regime in the Soviet Union. Karklins also examines the connections between political and ethnic pluralism, ethnicity and political mobilization, and the international dimensions of ethnopolitics.

454. O'Ballance, Edgar. **Wars in the Caucasus 1990-1995**. xxviii, 238p. New York: New York University Press, 1997. Includes bibliographical references and index.

The wars referred to here are the result of the quest for independence of the former Soviet republics of Armenia, Azerbaijan, Georgia, and the autonomous republic of Chechnya from control by the Russian Federation. O'Ballance provides an introductory chapter on the dissolution of the Soviet Union and then in subsequent chapters follows a primarily chronological path of describing the independence movements of Armenia, Azerbaijan, Georgia, and Chechnya. His focus is on the politics, both internal and international, that informed these independent national struggles.

455. **The Sources of Russian Foreign Policy After the Cold War**. Edited by Celeste A. Wallander. xi, 233p. *John M. Olin Critical Issues series*. Boulder, Colo.: Westview Press, 1996. Includes bibliographical references and index.

These papers were originally presented at public forums in both Cambridge, Massachusetts, and in Washington, D.C. Individual essays focus on the sources of Russian conduct in foreign policy; democratization, war, and nationalism in the post-communist states; Russian nationalism and the national interest in foreign policy; foreign policy preferences of Russian defense industrialists; the interaction of Russian and European domestic and foreign policies; Russian identity and foreign policy in Estonia and Uzbekistan; competing theoretical approaches to the post-Soviet energy sector; and ideas, interests, and institutions in Russian foreign policy.

History

456. Williams, Robert Chadwell. **Russia Imagined: Art, Culture and National Identity, 1840-1995**. xvi, 394p. New York: P. Lang, 1997. Includes bibliographical references (pp. [323]-394).

This is a collection of the essays of historian Robert Williams on Russia and its relation with the West. Essays included here cover such topics as Russians in Germany, the work of Vasily Kandinsky, early Soviet theater, Bolshevism in the West, the cultural revolution of the 1930s, the works of Vladimir Nabokov, Russian fascism, the sale of Russian art by the Bolsheviks, and the writings of George Florovsky. "These essays represent my forays into various aspects of Russian history over the past thirty years.... My hope is that these essays, taken together, will help the reader journey through the history of Russia's relations with the West, imagined and read, as well as throughout the career of one historian" (pp. xi-xii).

Bibliographies, Encyclopedias, Source Materials

457. **Revelations from the Russian Archives: Documents in English Translation**. Edited by Ronald Bachman and Diane P. Koenker. Translated by Ronald Koenker and Diane P. Bachman. xxv, 808p.: illus. Washington, D.C.: Library of Congress, 1997. Includes bibliographical references and index.

This representative collection of documents released from the Soviet archives bears witness to the activities of Soviet leaders during their regime. The documents are arranged in two parts and 15 chapters. In Part 1, Internal Workings of the Soviet System, the editors have included documents portraying the apparatus of repression and terror, intellectuals and the state, the Communist Party apparatus, economic development, religion, Chernobyl, and perestroika and glasnost. In Part 2, "the Soviet Union and the United States" are documents pertaining to economic cooperation, the Communist Party of the U.S.A., wartime policies and wartime alliance, prisoners of war, cold war, the Cuban missile crisis, peaceful coexistence and détente, and Afghanistan. The editors have thoughtfully included a list of commonly used abbreviations and terms, as well as short biographical sketches of prominent personalities.

458. Acton, Edward, and Vladimir Iu. Cherniaev. **Critical Companion to the Russian Revolution, 1914-1921**. xvi, 782p.: maps. Bloomington: Indiana University Press, 1997. Includes index.

"The volume consists of free-standing essays organized into seven sections: The Revolution As Event; Actors and the Question of Agency; Parties, Movements, Ideologies; Institutions and Institutional Cultures; Social Groups, Identities, Cultures and the Question of Consciousness; Economic Issues and Problems of Everyday Life; and Nationality and Regional Questions—together with an Index which includes supplementary material on some 500 participants touched upon en passant" (p. 3). The material in this collection is intended to appeal to the uninitiated reader as well as to the specialist. The themes of the essays range from traditional questions such as issues of food supply to more contemporary concerns with the role of ritual. Western and Russian works are included in this volume. A glossary and list of abbreviations can also be found in this volume.

459. Gilbert, Martin. **Atlas of Russian History**. 1 vol. New York: Oxford University Press, 1993. Rev. ed. of: *Russian History Atlas*. Martin Gilbert, 1972. Includes bibliographic references and index.

This revised edition of Gilbert's earlier work has maintained the original structure and content. An additional section of maps has been added entitled "The End of the Soviet Union." The 14 maps in this section like the other maps in the volume draw on a wide range of material. Each presents the geographic boundaries of a specific area in or related to the Soviet Union. Each has been annotated to include historical information on the map to give the student of Russian history an overview of a particular period and historical event. All works consulted for the maps are included in the bibliography.

460. Paxton, John. **Encyclopedia of Russian History: From the Christianization of Kiev to the Break-Up of the U.S.S.R.** x, 483p.: maps. Santa Barbara, Calif.: ABC-CLIO, 1993. Rev. ed. of: *Companion to Russian History*, 1983.

This broad-ranging encyclopedia contains over 2,500 entries on people, places, ideas, movements, books, arts, and other cultural and historical entities. Many of the entries have bibliographic suggestions for future reading. In each entry bold-faced words indicate other entries within the encyclopedia. It also includes a chronology, selected bibliography, and maps.

461. Poe, Marshall. **Foreign Descriptions of Muscovy: An Analytic Bibliography of Primary and Secondary Sources**. 230p. Columbus, Ohio: Slavica Publishers, 1995. Includes index and five appendixes.

This bibliography is intended to address the problems of the source most often used in the past by scholars seeking citations to traveler's descriptions of early Muscovy. That work, *Friedrich von Adelung's Kritisch-Litterarische Ubersicht der Reisenden in Russland bis 1700*, has several difficulties that Marshall Poe has tried to avoid in this work. In particular, his arrangement and appendixes are aimed at more comprehensive coverage, correcting inaccuracies in citations in von Adelung's book, classifying works by genre, and adapting more complete bibliographic information. Poe begins with a history of Western literature on Muscovy. This is followed by a four-part bibliography covering bibliographic materials, secondary studies on the political and literary context of Western studies on Muscovy, secondary studies of foreign "Muscovitica," and a chronological guide to the materials in the bibliography. While bibliographic entries in the bibliography of bibliography section are rather sparse, the entries in the chronological list—Section 4—are quite complete. The appendixes allow several points of access. However, there is no unified name index.

462. Price, Morgan Philips. **Dispatches from the Revolution: Russia, 1915-18**. xii, 181p. Chicago: Pluto Press, 1997. Includes bibliography (pp. 177-78) and index.
Morgan Philips Price was eminently qualified to become one of the best foreign eyewitnesses to the Russian Revolution. His family had business interests in the timber trade, he spoke Russian fluently, and he had traveled extensively. This volume contains a collection of his dispatches to the *Manchester Guardian*, his book *My Reminiscences of the Russian Revolution*, and other sources for the period 1915 through August 1918.

463. Sano, Iwao Peter. **One Thousand Days in Siberia: The Odyssey of a Japanese-American POW**. xvii, 210p. Lincoln: University of Nebraska Press, 1997.
This is a memoir of a Japanese prisoner of war who was captured and imprisoned in Siberia during WWII.

464. **The Legacy of History in Russia and the New States of Eurasia**. Edited by S. Frederick Starr. xiii, 313p.: maps. *International Politics of Eurasia*, vol. 1. Armonk, N.Y.: M. E. Sharpe, 1994. Includes bibliographical references and index.
"This volume analyzes the legacy of history and its impact on the foreign relations and political identity of the new states" (p. xi). This collection of essays is the first volume in a series devoted to the analysis of the transformation of the Soviet Union into independent republics. Contributors to this volume include: S. Frederick Starr, Karen Dawisha, Bruce Parrott, Kadir Z. Alimov, Yaroslav Bilinsky, Richard G. Hovannisian, Firuz Kazemzadeh, Edward L. Keenan, Zenon E. Kohut, Romuald J. Misiunas, Serhii M. Plokhy, Alfred J. Rieber, Sergei A. Romanenko, and Tadeusz Swietochowski. The essays are divided into three sections: Russia; Western Newly Independent States; and Southern Newly Independent States. Each section begins with a map of the region.

General Studies, Readers

465. Ascherson, Neal. **Black Sea**. xi, 306p.: maps. London: Jonathan Cape, 1995. Includes bibliographical references (pp. 285-89) and index.

This is a description of the people and recounting of the history of the Black Sea area. "This is not just a place but a patter of relationships which could not have been the same in any other place, and this is why Black Sea history is first of all the history of the Black Sea" (p. 11). The book includes a chronology of major events in the region from 850 B.C.-A.D. 1994.

466. Carrère d'Encausse, Hélène. **The Russian Syndrome: One Thousand Years of Political Murder**. Translated by Caroline Higgit. xvii, 477p.: illus. New York: Holmes & Meier, 1992. Translation of: *Le Malheur Russe*. Includes bibliographical references (pp. 438-64) and index.

In his foreword Adam Ulam characterizes the central premise to Hélène Carrère d'Encausse's book as follows: "If pre-Revolutionary Soviet Russia's misfortune was to be seized by fanatical sectarians, who soon evolved into cynical bureaucrats, then what fatally changed the character of old Russia and delayed its development into a modern state was another historical catastrophe—the Mongol yoke" (p. xiii). In her own preface, the author states that it was the legacy of officially sanctioned violence that would be Russia's curse. D'Encausse traces Russia's violent past from the time of Kievan dominance to the present day.

467. Hosking, Geoffrey A. **Russia, People and Empire, 1552-1917**. xxviii, 548p.: maps. London: HarperCollins, 1997. Includes bibliographical references (pp. 493-530) and index.

"The theme of this book is how Russia obstructed the flowering of Rus', or if you prefer it, how the building of an empire impeded the formation of a nation" (p. xix). Geoffrey Hosking feels that most Western historians have not taken the problem of national identity in Russia seriously and sets out to examine that theme. The author has not taken a strictly chronological approach to the treatment of his subject. Rather the book is divided into four parts. The first discusses the origins and lasting characteristics of the Russian empire. The third part focuses on the effects the empire had on Russia's social classes. Parts 2 and 4 take a more traditional chronological approach. The volume includes a chronology of Russian history.

468. **Christianity and the Eastern Slavs: Russian Culture in Modern Times**. Vol. II. Edited by Robert P. Hughes and Irina Paperno. vviii. *California Slavic Studies*, Vol. 17. Berkeley; Los Angeles; London: University of California Press, 1994.

This is the second volume of papers delivered at a conference held in May 1988 at the University of California at Berkeley. "The papers gathered in Volume II concern various issues in the history of culture from the eighteenth to the twentieth century: cultural institutions and cultural life (Section 1) and ideological paradigms and cultural mythology

(Section 2)" (*Christianity and the Eastern Slavs*, Vol. I, p. 7). Volume 2 has contributions by Gary Marker, Michael S. Füer, Reginald E. Zelnik, Stephen K. Batalden, Stephen L. Behr, Hugh McLean, William Mills Todd III, Bernice Glatzer Rosenthal, Olga Matich, Ronald Vroon, Johana Renate Doring-Smirnov, Henryk Baran, Boris Gasparov, Irina Paperno, and Steven Cassedy. Essays are in Russian and English.

469. **Kaliningrad: The European Amber Region**. Edited by Pertti Joenniemi and Jan Prawitz. xi, 281p. Aldershot, Eng.: Ashgate, 1998. Includes index.

This anthology of papers is aimed at providing an integrated view of Kaliningrad. The contributors felt that there had previously been no studies that presented a general picture of social, economic, political, environmental, and military conditions in the region. "It is argued that in the context of Kaliningrad, the old and traditional often seem to be in stark contrast with the new and incoming. . . . However, there are also reasons to claim that the oblast, at least in principle, may become competitive within the new European political and economic order" (back cover).

470. **Reinterpreting Russian History: Readings, 860-1860s**. Edited by Gary Marker and Daniel H. Kaiser. xvii, 445p.: illus. New York: Oxford University Press, 1994. Includes bibliographical references.

This collection of texts is meant to fill several needs. First and foremost this selection of materials is meant to reflect the new emphasis in Russian historical studies on society and culture. "Supplemented by over 70 illustrations, selections are introduced by placing them in the context of the work's major themes: state structure, the economy, society and culture and every day life" (back cover). The readings are arranged chronologically.

471. Matthews, Mervyn. **The Passport Society: Controlling Movement in Russia and the USSR**. xiv, 118p. Boulder, Colo.: Westview Press, 1993. Includes bibliographical references and index.

"In this historical analysis of Russia's systems for controlling the movement and residence patterns of its citizens, Mervyn Matthews examines the social, political, and economic purposes and effects of the internal passport and residence permit as used by the centralized Russian and Communist governments" (p. 119). Matthews believes that the internal passport system is a hindrance to socioeconomic development. The book includes an appendix with the results of a survey on public attitudes toward the passport taken in 1989-1990.

472. Pokhlebkin, Vil'iam Vasilevich. **A History of Vodka**. Translated by Renfrey Clarke. xvi, 222p. London: Verso, 1992. Includes bibliographical references (pp. 210-22).

This book was written as the result of an international movement aimed at preventing the Soviet government from using the name "vodka" for their product. The government was placed in the position of having to prove that vodka originated in Russia. Since traditional documentation was lacking, the author uses an unused methodology for historians today.

He relies on an analysis of the terminology of distilling and of the word "vodka" itself. He also focuses "on the conditions in which vodka might have appeared." The first two chapters of the book review the history of alcoholic beverages in Russia. Chapters 3 and 4 examine the terminology associated with distilling and vodka production. The last chapter looks at the relationship between vodka and state ideology from the tsars and through the Soviet period. The book includes several appendixes by the author: "The Gastronomic Significance of Vodka, and How It Should Be Consumed"; "Modern Vodka of Russia . . ."; "The Effects of Alcohol on the Human Body"; and others.

473. Treadgold, Donald W. **Twentieth Century Russia**. 8th ed. xvi, 498p.: maps. Boulder, Colo.: Westview Press, 1995. Includes bibliographical references (pp. 451-71).

"Donald Treadgold traces the wrenching transformations of Russian society in the opening decades of this century, marking the emergence of Russian Marxism from an obscure radical movement and chronicling its success as a vehicle for the seizure and maintenance of political power. He then examines the development of the policy and practice of the Soviet government over the course of its seventy-year history. Revised and updated to include an account of the countries of the former Soviet Union since the collapse of communism. *Twentieth Century Russia* presents a seasoned scholar's interpretation of modern Russian history" (p. 473).

Historiography and Archaeology

474. Baron, Samuel H. **Plekhanov in Russian History and Soviet Historiography**. 274p. *Pitt Series in Russian and East European Studies*, no. 23. Pittsburgh, Pa.: University of Pittsburgh Press, 1995. Includes some correspondence in French and Russian (pp. 156-87), bibliographical references (pp. 253-65), and index.

The 11 essays compiled in this volume trace Plekhanov's views of Russian history and the reception they received in Russia and the West. These essays have been published over a number of years, from 1957 to 1986. Taken together, Baron's essays provide the reader with a complete picture of Plekhanov's work. While Plekhanov languished in obscurity during the Stalin era, his work has been resurrected.

475. Byrnes, Robert. **V. O. Kliuchevskii**. xxi, 301p.: illus. Bloomington: Indiana University Press, 1995. Includes bibliographical references (pp. [261]-293).

V. O. Kiluchevskii was the son of a poor parish priest in Pauza. He became the most influential historian of Russia's past. "This volume describes the career and scholarship of V. O. Kliuchevskii (1841-1911), whom many specialists consider Russia's most distinguished historian and whose teaching, writing, and training of young scholars have markedly affected the way Russians and others view Russia's past" (p. xvii). Byrnes follows the development of Kliuchevskii's career through his years of teaching at Moscow University, the formulation of his historiographic approach and the development of his nationalistic approach, and the development of his nationalistic views. The book includes a bibliographic essay that discusses Professor Byrnes' sources in some detail. There is also a list of abbreviations.

476. Cohen, Ariel. **Russian Imperialism: Development and Crisis**. xiv, 180p. Westport, Conn.: Praeger, 1996. Includes bibliographical references (pp. [169]-175) and index.

This is a study of the collapse of the Soviet Union. "The purpose of this book, therefore, will be to analyze the development of the Russian/Soviet Empire and its decline during Gorbachev's regime, from both political science and comparative history perspectives" (p. xiii). The author traces the development of the multiethnic empire and its decay under Gorbachev. Cohen has written this book to appeal to both the specialist and the general reader. His early chapters provide the background to the region.

477. Dukes, Paul. **World Order in History: Russia and the West**. x, 198p. New York: Routledge, 1996. Includes bibliographical references (pp. 172-88) and index.

Dukes argues that historians' ideas about the world "have been influential in transforming nations' sense of themselves.... [He] demonstrates how successive historians and other analysts attempt to make sense of the world in which they live, often appropriating intellectual ideas spawned in different contexts in order to do so" (frontispiece). He pursues this argument with particular reference to Russia and the Western world. Individual chapters cover Montesqieu and constitutional order, Marx and revolutionary order, from European toward Atlantic order, 1900-1922, and some approaches to world order, 1923-1962.

478. Golub, Spencer. **The Recurrence of Fate: Theatre and Memory in Twentieth-Century Russia**. xiii, 277p.: illus. *Studies in Theatre History & Culture*. Iowa City: University of Iowa Press, 1994. Includes bibliographical references (pp. 201-62) and index.

Spencer Golub looks at the pattern of Russian history. "The theme of this book is Russian theatrical memory in the period circa 1900-1980. I intend to illustrate how by creating rather than simply retrieving memory, the Russian state and intelligentsia directed history to conform to the recurring patterns and tragic conventions of fate" (p. 1). Drawing on the historical methodology of Iurii Lotman, Golub explores theatricality in the creation of history. The book is arranged topically, focusing on such themes as myth-making, male-female disguise and totalitarianism in culture, among others.

479. **Food in Russian History and Culture**. Edited by Joyce Stetson Toomre and Musya Glants. xxvii, 250p.: illus. *Indiana-Michigan Series in Russian and East European Studies*. Bloomington: Indiana University Press, 1997. Includes bibliographical references and index.

This volume resulted from a conference held in 1993 at the Russian Research Center at Harvard University. The call for such a conference is a reflection of the extremely high degree of interest in culinary history in the last two decades. "The chapters in this collection provide fresh insights by looking at the availability and consumption of foods at different periods in Russian history and by analyzing Russian attitudes toward food and its attendant symbolism" (p. xii). Contributors are Mauricio Borrero, Pamela Chester, Cathy A. Frierson, Musya Glants, Darra Goldstein, Leonid Heretz, Ronald D. LeBlanc, Horace G. Lunt, George E. Munro, Halina Rothstein, Robert A. Rothstein, Snejana Tempest, and Joyce Toomre.

Pre-Petrine Muscovy/Russia

480. Birnbaum, Henrik. **Novgorod in Focus**. 192p. Columbus, Ohio: Slavica Publishers, 1996. Includes bibliographic references and index.

Henrik Birnbaum has published extensively on the history of Novgorod, most notably his 1981 book entitled *Lord Novgorod the Great*. The present volume contains several essays on Novgorod's cultural history. "Though not reshaped into a sequence of consistently successive chapters for the purpose of producing a genuine monograph, the various essays included have nonetheless been so arranged as to reflect a certain chronological and thematic coherence" (p. 11). Birnbaum discusses Christianity in Novgorod, it's political, social, and cultural life, the Hansa, and Novgorod's role in Russian history.

481. Dimnik, Martin. **The Dynasty of Chernigov: 1054-1146**. xxiv, 485p., [12] p. of plates: illus., maps. Toronto: Pontifical Institute of Mediaeval Studies, 1994. Includes bibliographical references (pp. [440]-465) and index.

Martin Dimnik examines the history of the descendents of Yaroslav "the Wise." Yaroslav had introduced a new form of succession, which divided his kingdom into patrimonial domains for his sons. "This book examines how faithfully the Svyatoslavichi adhered to Yaroslav's 'testament' and how their fortunes suffered when other families broke Yaroslav's precepts" (frontispiece). Dimnik has divided his book into three parts, each devoted to one of the generations succeeding Yaroslav. In each section he looks at the ruling princes and their relationships with one another, with church, and with rulers of other principalities. The book contains three appendixes on The Monastery at Tmutarakan, The Princess of Novgorod, 1088-1096, and The Prince Monk Nikola. Maps of the area and a genealogical table are also included.

482. **Christianity and the Eastern Slavs: Slavic Cultures in the Middle Ages**. Vol. I. Edited by B. Gasparov and O. Raevskaia-Kh´iuz. 374p. *California Slavic Studies*, 16. Berkeley: University of California Press, 1993. English and Russian; summaries in English. Includes index.

This is the first volume in a set of three containing papers from two international conferences held at the University of California in May 1988. "Volume I is devoted to the period from Kievan Rus' to the seventeenth century in the history of the Eastern Slavs. The papers that comprise the three sections of the volume deal with issues in the history of Christianization, the linguistic problems associated with the adoption of Christianity in the Medieval period and at later stages, and the influence of the Christian tradition on cultural paradigms established in the period following Christianization" (pp.

6-7). All three volumes focus on Russia, Ukraine, and Belarus with an emphasis on Russia. Essays contributed are by John Meyendorff, Aleksandr Panchenko, Henrik Birnbaum, Fairy Von Lilienfeld, John Fennell, Donald Ostrowski, Jaroslaw Pelenski, Paul Robert Magosci, Dean S. Worth, Harvey Goldblatt, Francis J. Thomson, Pavel Sigalov, Boris Uspenskii, Gail Lenhoff, Priscilla Hunt, Maria Pliukhanova, and Guy Picarda. Contributions are in English and Russian—Russian essays are followed by an English summary.

483. Ostrowski, Donald G. **Muscovy and the Mongols: Cross-Cultural Influences on the Steppe Frontier, 1304-1589**. xvi, 329p. New York: Cambridge University Press, 1998.

Ostrowski shows that Muscovy did not arise without any outside influences. In his book he explores the external and indigenous origins and influences on Muscovy. "During the early period of Muscovy (1304-1448) the dominant outside influences came from Byzantium and through the Qipchaq Khanate. The author shows how these imported institutions and practices were modified by Muscovite ecclesiastical and secular leaders, and, in some cases, combined with already existing institutions and practices to meet specifically Muscovite needs. At the same time, Ostrowski also illustrates the different cultures which influenced ecclesiastical and secular institutions" (frontispiece).

484. Perrie, Maureen. **Pretenders and Popular Monarchism in Early Modern Russia: The False Tsars of the Time of Troubles**. xvii, 269p.: illus., maps. Cambridge, Eng.: Cambridge University Press, 1995. Includes bibliographical references (pp. 251-61) and index.

There were more than a dozen pretenders to the Russian throne in the early 17th century. Perrie traces the careers of these pretenders and offers explanations of their success. She argues that support for the false tsars and tsarevitches was influenced not only by the ingenious tales they told to justify their claims, but also by religious-miraculous notions of Christ-like rulers risen from the dead, and by "popular monarchist" views of the true tsar as the scourge of the boyars. Her conclusion draws comparisons and contrasts between the Russian pretenders and royal impostors who appeared elsewhere in early modern Europe.

485. **Muscovy and Sweden in the Thirty Years' War, 1630-1635**. Edited by Boris F. Porshnev and Paul Dukes. Translated by Brian Pearce. xv, 256p. Cambridge, Eng.: Cambridge University Press, 1995. Includes index.

In 1967, Boris Porshnev's Russian-language study of mid-17th-century European politics was published. This was only the first part of what was intended as a larger work. Brian Pearce has translated Chapters 1 and 4 to 8 of this work and they are renumbered here. Paul Dukes has edited this volume and written an introduction placing this work in its larger historical context. "In placing this work in the context of Porshnev's larger undertaking, Professor Dukes' substantial introduction assesses Porshnev's critics and evaluates his contributions to our understanding of the Thirty Years' War and of relations between Eastern and Western Europe at the time" (frontispiece).

486. **The "Domostroi": Rules for Russian Households in the Time of Ivan the Terrible**. Edited and translated by Carolyn Pouncy. x, 266p.: illus. Ithaca, N.Y.: Cornell University Press, 1994. Includes bibliographical references and index.

The Domostroi is a guide to running a household in imperial Russia. As such, it is a window into the day-to-day lives of Russia's upper class. This extensively annotated translation puts the document in context, explaining its significance in the larger context of Russian society, its readership, and providing the reader with all explanatory data to make the document more accessible. For anyone interested in Russian history of the imperial period, this translation with its glossary of terms and extensive bibliography will be a welcome source of information on Russian life.

487. Pritsak, Omeljan. **The Origins of the Old Rus' Weights and Monetary Systems: Two Studies in Western Eurasian Metrology and Numismatics in the Seventh to Eleventh Centuries**. xii, 172p.: illus., map. *Harvard Series in Ukrainian Studies*. Cambridge, Mass.: Distributed by Harvard University Press for the Harvard Ukrainian Research Institute, 1998. Includes bibliographical references and index.

This study on the early monetary system of Old Rus' is divided into two parts. The first examines the monetary system in use in early medieval Western Eurasia. Part 2 is made up of essays on the coins of Old Rus'. The book is liberally illustrated with photographs of coins.

488. Santich, Jan Joseph. **Misso Moscovitica: The Role of the Jesuits in the Westernization of Russia, 1582-1689**. xi, 255p. *American University Studies, Series IX History*, 178. New York: P. Lang, 1995. Includes index and bibliography.

Based on a dissertation completed in 1992, this book traces the role that the Jesuits played in the Westernization of Muscovy in the 16th and 17th centuries. The author concludes that: "The Jesuits did have an active, though indirect, role in the Westernization of Muscovy. Although the Jesuit missions failed in their primary objective, which was to bring about the union of the Muscovite Orthodox Church with the Roman Catholic Church, Jesuit participation in three Polish-Lithuanian military adventures caused a sharp Muscovite reaction against themselves, Catholics in general and Poles in particular" (p. x). The book also includes appendixes that contain Latin transcriptions of six unpublished documents relating to the Jesuits' effort.

489. Stevens, Carol Belkin. **Soldiers on the Steppe: Army Reform and Social Change in Early Modern Russia**. xii, 240p.: map. DeKalb: Northern Illinois University Press, 1995. Includes bibliographical references (pp. [217]-232) and index.

"This book is about the decisive and far-reaching consequences of military revolution on seventeenth-century Russian provincial life. . . . Each effort at military reform led to ever-widening and intersecting circles of change" (p. 5). Focusing on the southern military-administrative regions of Belgorod and Sevsk, the author shows how Russian military reform was influenced by factors such as the availability of food, and the status and conditions of farmers.

490. Tiberg, Erik. **Moscow, Livonia and the Hanseatic League, 1487-1550.** 290p. *Acta Universitatis Stockholmiensis. Studia Baltica Stockholmiensia*, 15. Stockholm: Almqvist & Wiksell International, 1995. Revision in English of the author's 1973 dissertation. Includes bibliographical references (pp. 268-81) and indexes.

Erik Tiberg explores the established historiography on Moscow and its attempts to gain a foothold the trading centers with the West. Tiberg is interested in the period after Moscow conquered Novgorod. "The central part of this work is an examination of Ivan III's and Vasilij III's policy toward the Hanse and Livonia 1487-1514. It appears that Moscow used her coveted trade in order to isolate (eventual) enemies, especially Lithuania—Poland. On both sides of this central part the relations between the Livonian towns and the rest of the Hanse are investigated from the middle of the 14th to the middle of the 16th century" (p. iv). The book is divided into four sections: Early history of area; Moscow, Livonia and the Hanse 1487-1514; Moscow, Livonia and the Hanse 1515-1557; and Conclusion. The book includes appendixes with treatises of the time.

Imperial Russia

491. Anisimov, E. V. **The Reforms of Peter the Great: Progress Through Coercion in Russia**. xi, 327p.: illus., maps. Armonk, N.Y.: M. E. Sharpe, 1993. Includes bibliographical references (pp. 309-12) and index.

Evgeni Anisimov is a contemporary Russian historian. He is a senior research scholar of the Russian Academy of Sciences. In this volume he addresses the role of Peter the Great in shaping the Russian state. Anisimov believes that an analysis of Peter's reforms exposes them as a basic part of the Russian totalitarian state that was to flourish and survive into the Soviet period. "The book comprises four basic parts. The first is devoted to Peter's personality and analyzing its makeup, for therein lay the essence of all that later took place in Russia. How Peter implemented his ideals and ideas, what goals he pursued in the different spheres of life, and what it all amounted to make up the following parts of the book" (pp. 8-9).

492. Banerji, Arup. **Merchants and Markets in Revolutionary Russia, 1917-30**. xxiii, 237p. *Studies in Russian and East European History and Society series*. New York: St. Martin's Press in association with the Centre for Russian and East European Studies, University of Birmingham, 1997.

Banerji examines internal trade in the Soviet Union during the New Economic Policy (NEP) of the 1920s. He provides a background (Part 1) by describing and analyzing private trade before NEP and then goes on to cover private traders and their relationship to the state, taxation on private traders, and means of credit. In Part 2 he turns to the existing markets and their effect on trade, focuses on private trade in industrial products and traders, and the problems encountered with grain shipments to nongrain-producing regions. A concluding chapter describes the demise of private trade and the collapse of the NEP.

493. Bernstein, Laurie. **Sonia's Daughters: Prostitutes and Their Regulation in Imperial Russia**. xiii, 344p., [7] p. of plates: illus. Berkeley: University of California Press, 1995. Includes bibliographical references (pp. 311-31) and index.

Bernstein explores the causes and state of prostitution and its control by the state in imperial Russia. She describes and analyzes the regulation of prostitution by the Ministry of Internal Affairs, the sociology of prostitution in 19th-century Russia, the reasons that drove women into prostitution, how the privileged classes interacted with prostitutes, how the state attempted to reform regulation of prostitution, and the attempts by the Russian-educated elites to abolish regulation altogether.

494. **Imperial Decline: Russia's Changing Role in Asia**. Edited by Stephen J. Blank and Alvin Z. Rubinstein. vi, 296p. Durham, N.C.: Duke University Press, 1997. Includes index.

Russia's international position has been diminished since the demise of the Soviet regime. Nevertheless, it continues to influence the stability of East Asia. "The essays included in this volume examine the major changes that have occurred under Boris Yeltsin in Russia's relations with China, Japan and the two Koreas and speculate about their consequences for Russia's future in the region and with the United States" (pp. 3-4). All essays in this volume focus on four questions: (1) How have the changes in Russia affected Asian countries? (2) How has the changing environment in Russia affected its opinions? (3) What are the key issues in foreign relations between Russia and Asian countries? (4) How does Russia's relations in Asia affect its relations with the United States? Contributors include Oles Smolansky, Stephen Blank, Bruce Elleman, Rajan Menon, Alvin Rubinstein, Hongchan Chun, Charles Ziegler, Harry Gelman, and Harry Torfimenko.

495. Conroy, Mary Schaeffer. **In Health and in Sickness: Pharmacy, Pharmacists and the Pharmaceutical Industry in Late Imperial, Early Soviet Russia**. viii, 703p.: illus. *East European Monographs*, 386. Boulder, Colo.: East European Monographs; New York: Distributed by Columbia University Press, 1994. Includes bibliographical references (pp. 642-70) and index.

Mary Conroy believes that Russian pharmacies and the pharmaceutical industry represent the Russian policy in microcosm. She also observes that they have not been the focus of historical study in the past. "There is no history of Russian pharmacies and the pharmaceutical industry in English.... However, pharmacists and pharmaceuticals were as or more numerous than intellectual and cultural leaders. Further, pharmacists heterogeneity made them a mirror of society" (p. 1). The author begins with a topical arrangement discussing the regulations that governed the industry, education for pharmacists, public vs. socialized pharmacies, pharmacists and nationality, women pharmacists in imperial Russia, public health issues, drug use, and professionalization. The second part of the book follows a chronological arrangement tracing the history of the industry from 1898 to 1920.

496. Cross, Anthony Glenn. **By the Banks of the Neva: Chapters from the Lives and Careers of the British in Eighteenth-Century Russia**. xv, 474p.: illus., map. Cambridge, Eng.: Cambridge University Press, 1997. Includes bibliographical references and index.

This work complements Cross' earlier book, *By the Banks of the Thames: Russians in Eighteenth-Century Britain* (1980), where he looked at the activities of Russians in Britain subsequent to the visit there by Peter I. In this volume he explores the activities of the British in Russia in the 18th century. It focuses especially on the development of the British community in St. Petersburg during the city's 1st century as the capital of an ever-expanding empire. Individual chapters examine the activities of the British within various fields of commerce, the navy, the medical profession, science and technology, and the arts. It concludes with a survey of travelers and travel accounts.

497. De Madariaga, Isabel. **Politics and Culture in Eighteenth-Century Russia**. vii, 304p. London: Longman, 1998. Includes bibliographical references and index.

The essays in this volume reflect some 25 years of scholarly research. They were written throughout Professor De Madariaga's career and show the evolution of her study of 18th-century Russia. They have been arranged into three sections. The first covers the nature of the Russian government and its relation to security. The second group is concerned with the methods the government used to deal with social and administrative problems. The last section includes essays on Catherine II and her relationship to Russian society and the philosophers.

498. **Russia's Great Reforms, 1855-1881**. Edited by Ben Eklof, Larisa Georgievna Zakharova, and John Bushnell. xvii, 297p.: illus. *Indiana-Michigan Series in Russian and East European Studies*. Bloomington: Indiana University Press, 1994. Includes bibliographical references (pp. 281-88) and index.

"The present collection of essays, based largely on papers presented at a conference held at the University of Pennsylvania in May 1989, before the breakup of the Soviet Union, is the first attempt to examine within a single compass the abolition of serfdom in Russia, the many other reforms associated with the historic act, and the social and economic environment with which the reforms interacted" (p. vii). As Ben Eklof notes in his introduction, this collection is not concerned with current events and historical parallels. Rather, the contributors are focusing on the historical context in which the Great Reforms took place. The essays are grouped into two sections: state and reform and state and society. The various contributors take a number of theoretical approaches to the topic. Contributors are Alexander K. Afanasev, John Bushnell, David Christian, Ben Eklof, Daniel Field, Peter Gatrell, Abbot Gleason, Samuel D. Kassow, Jacob W. Kipp, Adele Lindenmeyer, Valeriia A. Nardova, Joan Neuberger, Fedor A. Petrov, Alfred J. Rieber, Natalia F. Ustantseva, and Larisa Zakharova.

499. Frierson, Cathy A. **Peasant Icons: Representations of Rural People in Late Nineteenth-Century Russia**. x, 248p., [12] p. of plates: illus. New York: Oxford University Press, 1993. Includes bibliographical references (pp. 197-237).

In the late 19th century, Russia's elite had become concerned with understanding the peasantry. After the serfs were freed in 1861 it was necessary for the ruling classes to better understand those they ruled. To learn about the peasants, they turned to the literature of their day, official and popular. "This book is an exploration of those texts, of the various images of the Russian peasant they produced, of the sources and morphology of those images and thus of the larger debate or discourse that took on a life of its own in post-Emancipation Russia" (pp. 3-4).

500. Gatrell, Peter. **Government, Industry and Rearmament in Russia, 1900-1914: The Last Argument of Tsarism**. xvii, 399p. *Cambridge Russian, Soviet and Post-Soviet Studies*, 92. Cambridge, Eng.: Cambridge University Press, 1994. Includes index, bibliography, maps, and notes.

In this book, Peter Gatrell focuses on the struggle between Russian government and Russian society for control of policy issues governing the armaments industry in the years immediately preceding World War I. Gatrell has divided the book into two sections. The first examines the "Political, economic and defense imperatives" (p. xiii) from 1900 to 1907. Here he discusses the effects of the building revolution at home in 1905 and the Russo-Japanese War as crises lending urgency to the government's sense that it must rearm. In the second part of the book Gatrell turns to the process of rearmament: industrial recovery, the emergence of a private arms trade, and the economic impact of rearmament. "Peter Gatrell provides a comprehensive account of the attempts made by government and business to confront these challenges, examining the organization and performance of a key industry, and showing how decisions were reached about the allocation of resources, and the far-reaching consequences these decisions entailed" (frontispiece).

501. Hartley, Janet M. **Alexander I**. vii, 256p.: maps. *Profiles in Power*. London; New York: Longman, 1994. Includes bibliographical references (pp. 220-32) and index.

This informative history of Alexander I is intended both for general readership and for students and scholars. It is part of a series of *Profiles in Power* that examines key historical figures. As such it does not present a biography of the tsar, but instead focuses on his exercise of power during his rule. An extensive bibliographical essay at the end of the volume provides sufficient scholarly apparatus for further investigation.

502. Hogan, Heather. **Forging Revolution: Metalworkers, Managers, and the State in St. Petersburg, 1890-1914**. xiv, 319p. Bloomington: Indiana University Press, 1993. Includes bibliographical references and index.

During the last years of the 19th century, Russia attempted to industrialize and catch up with the more industrially developed West. This led to a growth of an urban working class and the beginnings of new industrial structures. This type of change created upheaval in the metalworking industry at a time when the new industrialists tried to "naturalize" work flows. In this study, Hogan examines the metalworking industry in the late-19th-century, early-20th-century context of labor activism and labor-management conflict.

503. Hughes, Lindsey. **Russia in the Age of Peter the Great**. xxix, 602p., [16] p. of plates: illus., map. New Haven, Conn.: Yale University Press, 1998. Includes bibliographical references and index.

Lindsey Hughes has produced a detailed study not just of Peter the Great but of the Russia he built. "The present study gives due weight to the 'traditional' areas of foreign policy, army and navy, economy and government, but it also examines neglected topics such as women and the intriguing subject of pretence and disguise" (p. xiii). Hughes has also discussed, and in many cases challenges, some of the generally held misconceptions about Peter's reign: that he secularized Russian society, that foreign influence was dominant during the period, and others. The book includes many useful features such as the Romanov family tree, a chronology of events during Peter's reign, and a list of holidays during the Petrine year.

504. Jones, Adrian. **Late-Imperial Russia: An Interpretation: Three Visions, Two Cultures, One Peasantry**. 457p.: maps. New York: P. Lang, 1997.

Jones examines the "intellectual, political, socio-economic and socio-cultural development of the most important social groups in Russian society: the peasantry and the intelligentsia" (p. 14). This is a complex interdisciplinary study intended for the scholar of Russian history.

505. Kamenskii, A. **The Russian Empire in the Eighteenth Century: Searching for a Place in the World**. xii, 307p.: illus. *New Russian History*. Armonk, N.Y.: M. E. Sharpe, 1997. Includes bibliographical references (pp. 287-96) and index.

This history of Russia in the 18th century was translated from the Russian by a prominent American historian of that period. His endorsement by effort speaks well for this endeavor. Kamenskii has emerged as one of a group of new historians who can be called a pioneer in that he is helping to free Russian historians from the stultifying Soviet ideology that has crippled Russian historical writing for more than 70 years.

506. Kivelson, Valerie A. **Autocracy in the Provinces: The Muscovite Gentry and Political Culture in the Seventeenth Century**. xx, 372p.: illus., maps. Stanford, Calif.: Stanford University Press, 1996. Includes bibliographical references (pp. [335]-362) and index.

"This is a book with a clear agenda: to explore and display the possibilities for social, cultural and political development under the rule of an autocratic state" (p. xv). The author begins her detailed study with an overview of the gentry class in 17th-century Russia. Kivelson then focuses on specific areas of the lives of the gentry that were affected by their government: inheritance and marriage laws, interaction with state and community officials, and the role of kinship in provincial politics. The author then examines the political culture of Muscovy in the early 17th century, finally turning to the transformation of Muscovite political culture in the mid-17th century. The book includes a glossary and appendixes on the provincial gentry who participated in politics in the period.

507. Klier, John. **Imperial Russia's Jewish Question, 1855-1881**. xx, 534p.: illus., maps. Cambridge, Eng.; New York: Cambridge University Press, 1995. Includes bibliographical references (pp. 501-24) and index.

John Klier has researched the development of public opinion on the Jewish Question in "Imperial Russia." This book is the result of his study. "Simply put, what did interested parties understand by the expression of 'Jewish Question', and how did they propose to resolve it? In turn what impact did public opinion have in the Jewish policies of imperial Russia during the Reform Era?" (p. xiii). Klier examines materials published in the periodical press, books, and pamphlets as he seeks to define the Russian view of the problem.

He has divided the book into three parts. The first deals with the "Era of the Great Reforms" during which many social issues were debated in the press. In the second part, Klier looks at the movement of the Jewish question from a theoretical issue to a practical problem. In Part 3 he examines the 1870s and the turbulence brought to society by modernization. The role of the Jews in this process was "consistently viewed in a negative light" (p. xviii).

508. Klier, John, and Lambroza Shlomo. **Pogroms: Anti-Jewish Violence in Modern Russian History**. xx, 393p.: illus., maps. Cambridge, Eng.: Cambridge University Press, 1992. Includes bibliographical references (pp. 373-86) and index.

This collection of essays traces the history of the late-19th-century Russian persecution of the Jews. The conference from which these papers were taken was held at a time when renewed anti-Semitism in the Soviet Union was calling attention to this problem. In this volume the pogroms of 1881-1884, 1903-1906, and 1919-1921 are examined by various scholars. "Using new approaches to the study of Russian history, the contributors examine each wave of violence in turn. They look at the role of violence in Russian society; the prejudices, stereotypes, and psychology of both the educated society and the rural masses; the work of the tsarist regime, especially the police and the army as agents of order and control; and the impact of the pogroms on the sense of Jewish identity and security in the Empire" (frontispiece). A bibliographical essay concludes the volume.

509. Leibovich, Anna Feldman. **The Russian Concept of Work: Suffering, Drama, and Tradition in Pre- and Post-Revolutionary Russia**. xiv, 166p. Westport, Conn.: Praeger, 1995. Includes bibliographical references and index.

Anna Leibovich focuses on the Russian perception of work from the 1890s to the 1930s in this book. But this is not a study of labor history in Russia. Leibovich examines the Russian worker and his personal attitude toward labor. "The focus of this work is on Russian culture and its pervasive effect on socioeconomic and related political behavior. The study is confined to ethnic male Russians" (p. 1).

510. Leonard, Carol S. **Reform and Regicide: The Reign of Peter III of Russia**. 232p. *Indiana-Michigan Series in Russian and East European Studies*. Bloomington: Indiana University Press, 1993. Includes bibliographical references and index.

Carol Leonard examines the reign of Peter III in this study of pre-Catherinian political culture. While there has been little attention focused on Peter's reign in the past, Leonard believes that it laid the foundations for the Enlightenment that was to follow. "His rationalist vision reflected the fundamental aspirations of post-seventeenth-century secular rulers, mobilization of the economy and expansion of the powers of the state, with awareness that this entailed increasing the ability of the population to pay taxes" (p. 1). Leonard examines the question of emancipation and the nobility, secularization of ecclesiastical estates, taxation, and foreign policy.

511. Lieven, D. C. B. **Nicholas II: Twilight of the Empire**. xii, 292p., [16] p. of plates: illus. New York: St. Martin's Press, 1994. Includes bibliographical references and index.

Many books have been written about Nicholas II. In recent years the works of Robert Massie and Edvard Radzinsky captured a great deal of public interest. But neither of these books nor any others on Nicholas have examined him as a ruler. "This book is very much a study of the reign as well as the man. It attempts to understand Nicholas's personality but also the system of government over which he presided and the empire which he ruled" (p. x). The author has tried to compare the reign of Nicholas to other monarchs of his time. While most of the book is arranged chronologically, the final chapter compares the downfall of the Russian monarchy to the downfall of the Soviet regime.

512. Lindenmeyr, Adele. **Poverty Is Not a Vice: Charity, Society, and the State in Imperial Russia**. xiv, 335p.: illus. Princeton, N.J.: Princeton University Press, 1996. Includes bibliographical references (pp. [305]-328) and index.

In this study of poverty in imperial Russia, Lindenmeyr examines both state and local governments approach to the issue of poverty relief from the late 17th century through the revolution. He also includes an analysis of the role of private charitable societies and their work in relief for the poor. Finally, it is also a study of the relationship of Russia to the West. As the author states: "the history of charity in the imperial period is a case study of how Russians regarded the West, and how they attempted to adapt Western ideas to Russian reality. At the same time, ideas about traditional Russian charitable beliefs and practices contributed to the search for a distinct national identity that dominated much Russian thought in the nineteenth and early twentieth centuries" (pp. 5-6).

513. Martin, Alexander M. **Romantics, Reformers, Reactionaries: Russian Conservative Thought and Politics in the Reign of Alexander I**. x, 294p.: illus. DeKalb: Northern Illinois University Press, 1997. Includes bibliographical references (pp. [257]-282) and index.

"The personal nature of politics and its interaction with public opinion determine the structure of this study. In the absence of real parties or articulate ideologies, the history of political thought and action of the early nineteenth century traces a dialectical relationship between individuals and their social milieu. Thus the story of conservatism from 1800 to the 1820s is that of different generations and socio-cultural milieu that are best studied through representative figures who both typified and shaped their collective outlook" (p. 12). In keeping with this view, Martin focuses on many of the main personalities in the conservative movement of Alexander's reign: Shishkov, Glinka, Karamzin, and many others. The book is arranged chronologically.

514. Nekrasov, George. **North of Gallipoli: The Black Sea Fleet at War, 1914-1917**. 167p., [56] p. of plates: illus. *East European Monographs*, 343. Boulder, Colo.: East European Monographs; New York: Distributed by Columbia University Press, 1992. Includes bibliographical references (pp. 163-67).

"World War I progressed on land, in the North Sea, in the Middle East—all of which is fairly well documented. We seem to know very little about the events in the Black Sea, another land locked sea. . . . What went on in the Black Sea? The answer is the subject of this book" (p. v). George Nekrasov has not attempted a definitive study of World War I in this book. Rather, he wishes to raise questions and focus the attention of naval historians on the events of World War I in the Black Sea.

515. Owen, Thomas C. **Russian Corporate Capitalism from Peter the Great to Perestroika**. xii, 259p.: illus. New York: Oxford University Press, 1995. Includes bibliographical references and index.

Thomas Owen examines the history of corporations in Russia in this study. "The study of corporations under the tsarist regime has some relevance for an understanding of post-Soviet capitalism because it makes clear the strength of anti-capitalist attitudes in Russian culture, not only under Soviet Marxism, but under the tsarist regime as well" (p. vii). The first four chapters of the book trace the development of corporate business in Russia from 1700 to 1990. In Chapter 5 the author focuses on the effects of the Russian government's xenophobia on capitalism in the country. The final chapter examines the various forms of capitalism in Russia today. The book includes several appendixes supplying the reader with a variety of data on Russian corporations.

516. Prousis, Theophilus Christopher. **Russian Society and the Greek Revolution**. xi, 259p.: maps. DeKalb: Northern Illinois University Press, 1994. Includes bibliographical references and index.

This book examines the Russian reaction to the Greek Revolution against the Ottoman Turks in the 1820s. It is the first attempt at a comprehensive treatment of the subject. "It complements the scholarly literature on Russian historical and cultural ties to the Greek East, the lands and peoples associated with Byzantium and Eastern Orthodoxy" (p. viii). One of the goals of the work is to examine the philhellenism in Alexandrine Russia that emerged as a reaction to the revolution.

517. Raeff, Marc. **Political Ideas and Institutions in Imperial Russia**. xiii, 389p. Boulder, Colo.: Westview Press, 1994. Includes bibliographical references (pp. 361-88) and index.

Marc Raeff is one of the most distinguished historians of imperial Russia in the West. In this volume, 20 of his essays on the political culture of the imperial period are collected. They have been written between 1951 and 1991 and demonstrate the evolution of Raeff's thought. They also provide any interested reader with a general picture of political culture from these that supported the autocracy to those that opposed it. The book includes a bibliography of the author's works from 1946 to 1993.

518. **Imperial Russia: New Histories for the Empire**. Edited by David L. Ransel and Jane Burbank. xxiii, 359p. *Indiana-Michigan Series in Russian and East European Studies*. Bloomington: Indiana University Press, 1998. Includes index.

This collection of essays grew out of three workshops. These workshops had the goal of encouraging scholars to look at Russian history from a new perspective. Scholars from many universities, disciplines, and generations have contributed to this work. "The goal of this volume is to raise questions and to encourage scholars to re-envision imperial Russian history liberated from schools, parties, and single story lines. The essays incorporate new research and new topics, results of a revitalized attention to Russia's past that has engaged historians and others in recent years" (p. xi). No particular methodology is consistently followed in the essays included here. Neither is their consistency in theoretical approach. The essays are grouped into three topical sections. The first includes works on autocratic rule. The second contains essays on the "Imperial Imagination." The final section covers both central Russia and the outlying areas. Contributors to this volume are Thomas M. Barrett, Jane Burbank, Gregory L. Freeze, Steven L. Hoch, Valerie A. Kivelson, Nathaniel Knight, Irina Paperno, David L. Ransel, Douglas Smith, William Sunderland, Kevin Thomas, Cythia Hyla Whittaker, and Richard Wortman.

519. Rawson, Don C. **Russian Rightists and the Revolution of 1905**. xvi, 286p. *Cambridge Russian, Soviet, and Post-Soviet Studies*. Cambridge, Eng.: Cambridge University Press, 1995. Includes bibliographical references (pp. 269-76) and index.

This is the first comprehensive study of rightist movements in Russia. Professor Rawson attempts to show the ways in which the rightist movement affected events during the revolution of 1905. The book is arranged thematically beginning with an overview of the national rightist organizations. The discussion then turns to the development of regional rightist groups, special interest groups, and the strategies of the right. "Professor Rawson demonstrates how the rightists attempted to resolve the impasse between autocracy and constitutionalism that Russia had reached by the end of 1905. The study concludes that the rightist organizations, while never a match for the opposition parties, mobilized a substantial segment of public sentiment and helped induce the autocracy to reassert its authority" (frontispiece).

520. Roosevelt, Priscilla R. **Life on the Russian Country Estate: A Social and Cultural History**. xvi, 361p.: illus. (some col.), maps. New Haven, Conn.: Yale University Press, 1995. Includes bibliographical references (pp. 344-52) and index.

"The object of this book is to describe both the world of the estate and the different visions it embodied; to determine which attitudes inspired estate building and how it took shape; to explore how estate life was lived, what emotions this life generated, and how they were conveyed in literature and art; and to examine the relationship of the estate to the larger environment, both geographical and cultural" (p. xii). Richly illustrated, this in-depth examination arranges its chapters in three sections: (1) the aristocratic playground; (2) the patriarchal enclave; and (3) the cultural Arcadia.

521. Ruane, Christine. **Gender, Class, and the Professionalization of Russian City Teachers, 1860-1914**. x, 258p.: illus. *Pitt Series in Russian and East European Studies*, no. 24. Pittsburgh, Pa.: University of Pittsburgh Press, 1994. Includes bibliographical references and index.

The Great Reforms of Alexander II changed many things in the Russian empire. One of the effects of the reforms was to create the conditions for the development of a professional class in Russia. In the first three chapters of this study of teachers as professionals in Russian society, Christine Ruane examines the formation of the urban teachers' identity. The last three chapters focus on the attempts of urban teachers to publicize their newfound professional consciousness. "The voices and deeds of individual men and women teachers remain muffled in this study. Yet, as a group, city teachers' collective stories and actions provide an essential case study of the emergence of the teaching profession and of their role in Russian civil society" (p. 20). The book includes a statistical appendix of data on city teachers.

522. Steinberg, Mark. **Moral Communities: The Culture of Class Relations in the Russian Printing Industry, 1867-1907**. x, 289p. *Studies on the History of Society and Culture*, 14. Berkeley: University of California Press, 1992. Includes bibliographical references (pp. 263-81) and index.

Mark Steinberg feels that printers are an especially instructive socioeconomic group for the analysis of social relationships in postreform Russia. "I treat here both words and behavior and the relationship between what people said and what they did (and what they said they did) as necessary evidence of attitudes and values" (p. 5). In this volume he traces the group through the prerevolutionary years as they developed their own activist movement. The volume includes an appendix on employer activists in St. Petersburg and Moscow between 1880 and 1904.

523. **Reform in Modern Russian History: Progress or Cycle?** Edited by Theodore Taranovski and Peggy McInerny. xiii, 436p. *Woodrow Wilson Center series*. Washington, D.C.: Woodrow Wilson Center Press, 1995. Papers from a conference entitled "Reform in Russia and Soviet History—Its Meaning and Function," held May 5-May 7, 1990, organized by the Kennan Institute for Advanced Russian Studies of the Woodrow Wilson International Center for Scholarship. Includes bibliographical references and index.

The papers included here were originally presented at a conference at the Kennan Institute for Advanced Russian Studies. In presenting a comparative study of the problems and prospects of reform in modern Russian history, "the book raises important methodological and historiographic questions regarding the content, scope, and significance of various reform efforts, ranging from the Great Reforms of Tsar Alexander II to attempts to salvage the Soviet system undertaken by Khrushchev and Gorbachev. One of the key issues raised is whether various attempts to modernize the political and social system were a series of cyclical failures or demonstrate a pattern of progressive development" (frontispiece).

524. Waldron, Peter. **Between Two Revolutions: Stolypin and the Politics Renewal in Russia**. viii, 220p. DeKalb: Northern Illinois University Press, 1998. Includes bibliographical references and index.

Peter Waldron's *Between Two Revolutions* is a study of the process of implementing reform and why it fails. "This book examines the programme of reform that Stolypin attempted to implement and seeks to explain the reasons for his failure. . . . Stolypin had to cope with an inheritance that rendered reform problematical; he bequeathed a legacy of failure that brought revolution closer" (pp. 2-3). Waldron begins with a discussion of Stolypin's program of reforms. He then examines those elements of society and the institutions that worked against change in imperial Russia.

525. Weber, Max. **The Russian Revolutions**. Edited and translated by Gordon C. Wells and Peter Baehr. vi, 287p. Ithaca, N.Y.: Cornell University Press, 1995. Includes bibliographical references (pp. [270]-279) and index.

In 1905, intrigued by the political developments in Russia and unsatisfied with the treatment they received in the German press, Weber decided to write his own account of the crisis. The essays translated here are the result of that effort. "In them Weber examines, among other things, the prospects for liberalism in Russia and the constitutional façade erected by the forces of autocracy to frustrate both civil freedom and parliamentary reform" (p. 1).

526. Weinberg, Robert. **The Revolution of 1905 in Odessa: Blood on the Steps**. xvi, 302p.: illus., map. Bloomington: Indiana University Press, 1993. Includes bibliographical references (pp. [277]-294) and index.

The role of ethnicity and workers in general played an important role in the 1905 revolution and its manifestation in Odessa. So argues Weinberg in this history of the 1905 revolution in Odessa. He examines a broad spectrum of workers, labor organizations, and politics before 1905, the workers' movement, and popular unrest from January to June of that year. The major Jewish pogrom that occurred and the final confrontation of the strike in December of that year are all described and analyzed in this study.

527. White, John Albert. **Transition to Global Rivalry: Alliance Diplomacy and the Quadruple Entente, 1895-1907**. xxiii, 344p. Cambridge, Eng.: Cambridge University Press, 1995. Includes bibliography, index, and chronology.

The years before World War I saw the formation of world alliances. While historians here traditionally looked at the role of the alliance between Britain, France, and Russia in this period, John White calls attention in this work to the alliances of these same nations with Japan in this period. In so doing, the author demonstrates that the First World War was truly global in nature. White has previously published a study of *Diplomacy of the Russo-Japanese War*. In this work he extends his previous study to consider the role of Russia and Japan in the establishment of the contemporary world order. The work is arranged chronologically and includes several appendixes. These contain reprinted documents of the period such as "British Proposals to Russia (1904)," "Russo-Japanese Agreement, July 30, 1907," etc.

528. Wirtschafter, Elise Kimerling. **Structures of Society: Imperial Russia's "People of Various Ranks."** xvii, 215p.: maps. DeKalb: Northern Illinois University Press, 1994. Includes bibliographical references (pp. [193]-208) and index.

"This study began as an examination of terminology, specifically usages and meanings of the category raznochintsy and their relationship to the larger problem of social categorization. After focusing on the developmental (legal, administrative, institutional, economic, and cultural) sources of the various definitions of raznochintsy, it became a discussion of the underlying dynamics of social categorization and delimitation in imperial Russia" (p. xiii). Wirtschafter examines the problem thematically considering historiography, legal issues, the origins of the raznochintsy, their connection with the building of the Russian state, their role in society, and their self-definition. The book includes an appendix on the meanings of the category raznochintsy.

529. Wortman, Richard. **Scenarios of Power: Myth and Ceremony in Russian Monarchy**. v.: illus. *Studies of the Harriman Institute*. Princeton, N.J.: Princeton University Press, 1995. Includes bibliographical references and index.

Wortman catalogs and analyzes the various means by which ritual and ceremony were used in imperial Russia both to consolidate power and to communicate the ruling elite's elevated estate to the masses and to foreign powers. It also helped to shape the behavior and expectations of the heirs to the throne. The ceremonies involved ranged from coronation and funeral extravaganzas to parades, trips through the empire, architecture, and bureaucratic formalities.

530. Zuckerman, Fredric Scott. **The Tsarist Secret Police in Russian Society, 1880-1917**. xvii, 345p., [1] folded leaf of plates. New York: New York University Press, 1996. Includes bibliographical references.

Fredric Zuckerman explores the entrenchment of the secret police in Russian society in the late 19th and early 20th centuries. In this history he examines what the populace perceived to be a threat worthy of the sacrifice of their personal freedoms. The book is divided into parts. The first provides the historical context of the discussion, tracing the development of the secret police from 1800 to 1902. In Part 2, Zuckerman turns to the lives of the detectives, secret agents, and police chiefs that were the secret police. Part 3 examines the foundations of the modern police state. In Part 4 the author looks at the revolutionary movement and its effect upon the development of the secret police. The book includes a glossary and a graphic of the chain of command in the Russian political police.

Revolution and Civil War

531. Cawthorne, Nigel. **Iron Cage**. ix, 310p. London: Fourth Estate, 1993. Includes bibliographical references (pp. 282-94) and indexes.

Nigel Cawthorne explores the question of what became of those British soldiers held by the Soviets during World War II.

532. Clements, Barbara. **Bolshevik Women**. xiv, 338p.: illus., ports. Cambridge, Eng.: Cambridge University Press, 1997. Includes bibliographical references (pp. 321-29).

Barbara Clements has made extensive study of the female members of the Bolshevik Party. In her initial research for this book, she compiled a database of known female members of the party. This provided her with detailed information on "typical" characteristics of members. She selected four members from the two founding generations: Inessa Armand, Evgenilla Bosh, Konkorida Samoslova, and Elena Stasova. These four she researched in detail. This book is the result of that research. "It examines their lives from childhood to old age and assesses their motives, their experience, and their contributions to their movement and their nation. My intention has been not only to fit the Bolshevicki into their times but also explain, whenever possible, the choices they made" (p. 17). An appendix to the book provides details on her database and its formulation.

533. Coopersmith, Jonathan. **The Electrification of Russia, 1880-1926**. xii, 274p.: illus. Ithaca, N.Y.: Cornell University Press, 1992. Includes bibliographical references and index.

Jonathan Coopersmith attempts to discover how successful the early Soviet government was at implementing full-scale electrification as it tried to establish its technological infrastructure. In his analysis, Coopersmith sees technology as "part of a 'seamless web' with society" (pp. 1-2). As such, it is analyzed within the context of the economic and social structure of the time. These elements, he believes were as influential in its development as any technological factor.

"Three themes flow through this book—the omnipresent foreign role in Russian electrification, the political constituency for the electrification process, and the economic, technical, and administrative environment in which it was attempted" (p. 5). These themes are explored in three chronologically arranged sections; 1880-1914, 1914-1920, and 1920-1926. In each section the focus of the discussion is on the political and economic factors affecting the development of electrification as well as legal and organizational elements.

534. Dune, Eduard Martynovich, translator. **Notes of a Red Guard**. Edited by Diane P. Koenker and S. A. Smith. xxxvi, 285p.: illus., maps. Urbana: University of Illinois Press, 1993. Includes bibliographical references (pp. [271]-273) and index.

Dune's memoir is an exception to the usual pattern of revolutionary writings that more often than not extolled the Bolshevik regime and all of its actions. "Dune was an enthusiastic participant in the revolutionary events of 1917-21, but also a lifelong opponent of the Stalinist regime. This memoir consequently offers the authentic voice of a fiercely independent thinker, but one who was an equally fierce supporter of the ideal of the 1917 revolution. There is nothing else like this on the revolution and the civil war" (p. xiii).

535. Figes, Orlando. **A People's Tragedy: The Russian Revolution, 1891-1924**. 1st American ed. xx, 923p. New York: Viking, 1997. Includes bibliographical references and index.

Orlando Figes has compiled a complete history of the Russian Revolution. This is the first attempt at a comprehensive history of this pivotal historical event in a single volume. Figes begins with the 1890s and follows events and the development of the revolutionary movement and takes the reader up to Lenin's death in 1924. The author believes that previous studies have been too limited in their chronological focus. This, he feels, has led too often to the conclusion that the outcome of the revolution was inevitable. "There were a number of decisive moments, both before and during 1917, when Russia might have followed a more democratic course. It is the aim of *A People's Tragedy*, by looking at the revolution in the longue duree, to explain why it did not at each of these in turn" (p. xvi). This massive work will give any serious student of Russian history a most complete picture of one of the defining events of the 20th century.

536. Fitzpatrick, Sheila. **The Cultural Front: Power and Culture in Revolutionary Russia**. xx, 264p. *Studies in Soviet History and Society*. Ithaca, N.Y.: Cornell University Press, 1992. Includes bibliographical references and index.

"This book explores the subject of power and culture in Soviet Russia. It focuses on the relationship between the Bolshevik (Communist) party and the Russian intelligentsia in the three and a half decades that began with the Bolshevik Revolution of 1917 and ended with Stalin's death in 1953.... What they were really struggling for, who was struggling, and what was the outcome are the big questions that this book addresses" (p. ix). Fitzpatrick pursues a number of aspects related to this topic chronologically. Some chapters had been published as separate essays previously. The book includes a glossary.

537. Geifman, Anna. **Thou Shalt Kill: Revolutionary Terrorism in Russia, 1894-1917**. xii, 376p.: illus. Princeton, N.J.: Princeton University Press, 1993. Includes bibliographical references (pp. [357]-365) and index.

There have been a number of studies on the early terrorist movement such as those of Adam Ulam and S. S. Volk. Anna Geifman focuses on the violent years in Russia from 1905 to 1917. "The primary objective of this study is to analyze the extent and significance of the sudden unprecedented escalation of terrorism after approximately twenty years only incidentally disturbed by gunfire and the explosion of dynamite" (p. 3). Geifman examines various terrorist groups of the time: socialist revolutionaries, social democrats, anarchists, and the criminal element who capitalized on the situation. The author has not drawn on archival material for this study but has relied upon published sources for this work.

538. Golder, Frank Alfred. **War, Revolution, and Peace in Russia: The Passages of Frank Golder, 1914-1927**. Edited by Terence Emmons and Bertrand M. Patenaude. xxvi, 369p. *Hoover Institution Press Publication*, no. 411. Stanford, Calif.: Hoover Institution Press, 1992. Includes bibliographical references and index.

Frank Golder is remembered primarily for collecting the unique Slavic collection now in the Hoover Institute at Stanford. He was a scholar studying Russian-American relations at the turn of the century. Golder also traveled extensively in Russia and kept a detailed diary of these journeys. His trips to Russia took place between 1914 and 1927. Thus his diary is a firsthand description of the death of imperial government and the creation of the Stalinist dictatorship. This volume compiles Golder's diaries and relevant letters of the time. It provides the Western reader with a unique view of some of the most critical events of the 20th century.

539. Goldfrank, David M. **The Origins of the Crimean War**. xiv, 344p.: maps. *Origins of Modern Wars*. London; New York: Longman, 1994. Includes bibliographical references (pp. 305-21) and index.

David Goldfrank is a professor of history at Georgetown University. In this study, he revisits the question of the causes of the Crimean War. His analysis leads him to place responsibility for this conflict with the various rulers and politicians in Russia, Britain, France, and Austria. He also looks at the conditions that exacerbated the crisis in Europe and led to the war. "In this important study, David Goldfrank has examined the archives of a dozen countries, including Russia, to present a fresh account of the subject. He shows that the European diplomatic roots of the war stretch far beyond the 'Eastern Question' itself and are intimately linked to the domestic concerns of the participants" (back cover).

540. **Memories of Revolution: Russian Women Remember**. Edited by Anna Horsbrugh Porter, Frances Snow, and Elena Welch. ix, 138p.: illus., map. London: Routledge, 1993. Includes index.

This is a collection of oral histories from 10 women, all of whom lived through the Russian revolution and its aftermath. All but one of the women were "whites" and all but one of the "whites" eventually left Russia for exile abroad. All of the women were from the privileged classes and their stories are immediate since they are told in the present tense.

541. Judson, William V. **Russia in War and Revolution: General William V. Judson's Accounts from Petrograd, 1917-1918**. xxxiv, 334p.: illus. Kent, Ohio: Kent State University Press, 1998. Includes bibliographical references (pp. 307-15) and index.

William Judson was one of the West's most famous observers of the Russian Revolution. Judson was an official observer of the Russo-Japanese War of 1905 and was in Russia in 1917 throughout the collapse of the provisional government and the Bolshevik takeover. His reports have been used by many scholars as source material for the events of those years. Georger Konnake and William Appleman Williams both drew on his detailed descriptions and assessments of Russia's military. This volume includes Judson's documentation of his meeting with Trotsky in 1917, previously unpublished. While Judson's papers have been extensively quoted elsewhere, the compiler feels that its new publication has special relevance in a time when Russian-American relations are changing. The bulk of the papers collected here are largely drawn from the years of the revolution. The volume includes brief biographical sketches of major figures.

542. Pereira, N. G. O. **White Siberia: The Politics of Civil War**. xii, 261p.: illus., maps, ports. Montreal: McGill-Queen's University Press, 1996. Includes bibliographical references (pp. 221-53) and index.

Pereira does not claim to have written the definitive, or even a comprehensive, history of Siberia. "Rather it is a detailed analysis of the White movement in Siberia, its internal struggles no less than its contest with the Reds, and the reasons for and the consequences of its defeat" (p. 5). After an introductory chapter on the physical setting, background, and regional development, he examines the similarities and differences with the revolution in European Russia, the resistance to Bolshevik rule, the democratic counterrevolution and White Union, the rise and fall of Kolchak's regime, and the aftermath and consolidation of power.

543. Read, Christopher. **From Tsar to Soviets: The Russian People and Their Revolution, 1917-21**. vi, 330p.: maps. New York: Oxford University Press, 1996. Includes bibliographical references (pp. 301-22) and index.

Christopher Read provides an overview of Russian society at the time of the revolution in the book. "In particular, the main focus of the present volume is to restore the autonomous revolutionary activity of the ordinary population to its rightful place in the overall interpretation of the revolution. . . . [It is about] an episode in the continuing struggle of ordinary people in the Russian Empire to become conscious actors contributing to decisions affecting their lives" (p. 5). The book is arranged chronologically and surveys much of the existing research on the revolution.

544. Reed, John. **John Reed and the Russian Revolution: Uncollected Articles, Letters, and Speeches on Russia, 1917-1920**. Edited by Eric Homberger and John Biggart. xxxiv, 320p. New York: St. Martin's Press, 1992. Includes bibliographical references and index.

"The present volume collects John Reed's articles, transcripts of speeches, unpublished manuscripts and material from his notebooks on the Russian Revolution. It complements *Ten Days That Shook the World* (1919), Reed's contemporary account of the Russian Revolution in 1917" (p. ix). The essays are arranged chronologically, with sections devoted to 1917, 1918, 1919-1920. Each section begins with a chronology of Reed's life during that year. Reed's life was transformed by the Russian Revolution as is clearly evident by the material collected here. These essays present a Westerner's view not only of the events of the revolution but also of the character of Russian people, a character that led to the overthrow of a monarchical system.

545. Shkliarevsky, Gennady. **Labor in the Russian Revolution: Factory Committees and Trade Unions, 1917-1918**. xxi, 282p. New York: St. Martin's Press, 1993. Includes bibliographical references.

In this study Gennady Shkliarevsky examines two types of workers' organizations: factory committees and trade unions. The critical year of 1917-1918 is the focus. The author will demonstrate that during this period two critical changes befell these organizations. The factory committees lost their independence and the labor movement became a single-party institution. These changes signified a shift to a monopoly on power. "In many respects, the elimination of pluralism in the labor movement paralleled and had a feedback effect upon the process of consolidation and centralization of power carried out by the Bolshevik leadership in all spheres of national life" (p. xx). The book follows a chronological arrangement.

546. Smele, Jon. **Civil War in Siberia: The Anti-Bolshevik Government of Admiral Kolchak, 1918-1920**. xix, 759p.: illus., maps. Cambridge, Eng.; New York: Cambridge University Press, 1996. Includes bibliographical references (pp. 683-750) and index.

This study examines the war between Lenin's newly established regime and his opponents, the "White," Army which was established on the borders of Russia and assisted by foreign allies. "In particular, it details the history of the white movement in Siberia, and the fortunes of its leader, Admiral Alexander Kolchak, the 'Supreme Ruler' of Russia" (frontispiece). The author believes that the defeat of the White Army was due as much to geography and climate as to failures of policy and leadership.

The body traces the history of the White Army from its formation in 1918 to its defeat in 1919 and Kolchak's arrest. The book is extremely detailed with extensive citations from primary and secondary source material. The bibliography alone is nearly 100 pages in length and is organized by subject. The author has included an appendix with an organizational table of the anti-Bolshevik government in Siberia 1918-1920.

547. **Cultures in Flux: Lower-Class Values, Practices, and Resistance in Late Imperial Russia**. Edited by Mark D. Steinberg and Stephen Frank. vi, 214p. Princeton, N.J.: Princeton University Press, 1994. Includes bibliographical references (pp. [205]-210) and index.

"This collection of essays examines the dynamic cultural world of Russia's lower classes during the last decades of the pre-Revolutionary order. The authors recall neglected or forgotten stories about popular life and culture" (p. 3). So the editors describe this collection of 10 essays on Russian culture on the verge of revolution. The essays include studies of death rituals, popular culture, amusement parks, folk songs, the popular press, worker authors, and hooliganism. All examine these topics in the context of the average common man, the individual, the peasant, the worker, the soldier.

548. Steinberg, Mark D. **The Fall of the Romanovs: Political Dreams and Personal Struggles in a Time of Revolution**. xviii, 444p.: illus. *Annals of Communism*. New Haven, Conn.: Yale University Press, 1995. Includes bibliographical references (pp. 419-22) and index.

This volume provides a rare look at the materials that were previously classified in the Russian archives. Each chapter of this volume includes an introduction and translations of archival materials with extensive annotations. The chapters cover the following broad topics: "Revolution"; "Under Arrest at Tsarskoe Selo"; "Siberian Captivity"; and "Death in Yekaterinburg." There are a number of supplementary materials in the volume including a glossary of personal and institutional names, a genealogy of the imperial family, and a chronology. The book also includes reproductions of many rare photographs of the royal family.

549. Tolz, Vera. **Russian Academicians and the Revolution: Combining Professionalism and Politics**. xiv, 236p. *Studies in Russian and East European History and Society series*. New York: St. Martin's Press, 1997. Includes bibliographical references and index.

Vera Tolz examines the effects of the revolution on members of the Russian Academy of Sciences. Her purpose, in part, is to analyze the effects of the revolution on a prerevolutionary professional group in Russia. However, Tolz sees academicians as unique among professional people in Russian society. "In contrast to other professional groups, the academicians regarded themselves as members of the international scientific community, and this direct link with abroad had a strong impact on their behavior as well as on the Bolsheviks' attitude toward the academy" (p. viii). The book is divided into two parts. The first presents an overview of the status and life of the academician in prerevolutionary Russian society. Part 2 functions as a set of case studies, examining the biographies of a group of academicians: Nikolai Iakovlevich Marr, Sergie Fedorovich Ol'denburg, Ivan Petrovich Pavlov, Aleksei Nikolaevich Krylov, and Vladimir Ivanovich Vernadsky. The book includes an appendix listing the full members of the Russian Academy of Sciences in 1917.

550. Von Geldern, James. **Bolshevik Festivals, 1917-1920**. xiv, 316p.: illus. *Studies on the History of Society and Culture*, 15. Berkeley: University of California Press, 1993. Includes bibliographical references (pp. 259-303) and index.

"The purpose of this book is to provide an overview of mass festivals during the Civil War (1917-20) and to discuss some of the theoretical issues raised by their study. The intended audience is broad. Combining the roles of historian and theoretician has been difficult; the chapters are arranged chronologically but with the intent of building a theoretical argument at the same time" (p. 6). This study is supplemented by its many useful illustrations.

551. Wood, Elizabeth A. **The Baba and the Comrade: Gender and Politics in Revolutionary Russia**. 318p. *Indiana-Michigan Series in Russian and East European Studies*. Bloomington: Indiana University Press, 1997.

Wood describes how the new Soviet regime attempted to bring women into the public sphere and involve them in politics. She argues that "the baba, the female figure considered to be illiterate, superstitious, and generally 'backward,' served as an important foil for the ideal of the comrade. The comrade would construct a new world, transforming human nature and building a new, Soviet civilization. . . . 'The self-centered, narrow-minded, and politically backward female [baba] becomes an equal, a fighter, and a comrade' " (p. 1).

RSFSR and USSR

552. **Stalinist Terror: New Perspectives**. Edited by J. Arch Getty and Roberta T. Manning. viii, 294p. Cambridge, Eng.: Cambridge University Press, 1993.

This collection of essays focuses on the severely repressive policies implemented by Stalin in the 1930s. Rather than concentrate entirely on personality, they describe and analyze context, economics, and specific groups. The essays are arranged in four parts: (1) persons and politics; (2) backgrounds; (3) case studies; and (4) impact and incidence. Collectively they represent a fascinating look at a well-studied phenomenon, but enriched by the latest findings from Soviet archives.

553. Bacon, Edwin. **The Gulag at War: Stalin's Forced Labour System in the Light of the Archives**. xii, 190p. New York: New York University Press, 1994. Includes bibliographical references and index.

When the Russian archives allowed scholars to begin examining the documents on the Soviet Gulag, they opened the doors to new areas of historical research. Edwin Bacon's book is a product of such research. Bacon focused on the years during World War II in the Gulags since the bulk of material demanded that he pick some period. "Study of the war years demonstrated both the Gulag's role as a vital source of human resources— particularly evident in the conscription of many inmates into the armed forces—and the fact that even with the need for manpower at its peak, there were those inmates for whom the Soviet state's primary intention was isolation and death" (p. 4). Bacon begins his study with an overview of previous studies and then turns to the newly disclosed information from the archives. He then reviews Gulag administration, the question of the number of prisoners held or executed, labor use, and life in the Gulag. The book includes appendixes with statistical data and a description of the administrative structure of the Gulag.

554. Barros, James, and Richard Gregor. **Double Deception: Stalin, Hitler, and the Invasion of Russia**. 307p. DeKalb: Northern Illinois University Press, 1995. Includes bibliographical references.

Barros and Gregor investigate the still perplexing question: "Why did Moscow's leaders fail to comprehend that one of the greatest 'surprise' attacks in military history was imminent?" (p. ix). The surprise attack was, of course, the attack by Germany on Soviet Russia on June 22, 1941. The authors conclude that the failure was not one borne by the intelligence services, but by Stalin himself. To support their hypothesis the authors have used recently divulged archival and other primary sources.

555. Carrère d'Encausse, Hélène. **The Great Challenge: Nationalities and the Bolshevik State, 1917-1930**. xiv, 262p.: maps. New York: Holmes & Meier, 1991. Translation of: *Le grand Ddi*. Includes bibliographical references and index.

Ethnic divisions and violence in the former Soviet Union have captured international attention in recent years. While this often seems an unexpected development, Hélène Carrère d'Encausse has written of this problem for many years. "Madame d'Encausses' book is a reliable guide to the events that led to the present predicament. She traces with superb command of the facts the diverse devices which the communists employed in the futile attempt to neutralize the forces of ethnicity and mold their subject peoples into a submissive mass" (p. xiv). This work first appeared in French in 1987. It is translated here by Nancy Festinger. The book is divided into four parts: The Terms of the Debate; Nationalism; A Tough Compromise: Diversity and Unity; and The Cultural Revolution.

556. Clark, Katerina. **Petersburg, Crucible of Cultural Revolution**. xii, 377p. Cambridge, Mass.: Harvard University Press, 1995. Includes bibliographical references (pp. [313]-363) and index.

There is a certain dynamic in any revolution whereby ideologies constrain the "extra-historical" agendas of the revolutionaries. "In this book I examine this dynamic by focusing on the quest of Petersburg intellectuals to establish a quintessential revolutionary culture during the fateful years of war and revolution, 1913-1931" (p. ix). Clark takes a chronological approach to her subject beginning with the prerevolutionary years and developing her thesis as she describes the construction of Soviet culture.

557. Clarke, Simon, Peter Fairbrother, and Vadim Borisov. **The Workers' Movement in Russia**. v, 431p. *Studies of Communism in Transition*. Aldershot, Eng.: Edward Elgar, 1995. Includes bibliographical references and indexes.

This is a history of three different organizations and their relationship to the workers' movement as a whole: The Independent Miners' Union in Kuznetsk; Sotsprof; the Federation of Air Traffic Controllers Union. "Our aim in this book is therefore to locate the new workers' movement in Russia in its connections with the workers it claims to represent as well as with the national and local political authorities to whom it addresses its demands and whose development it seeks to influence" (p. 2). The book begins with an overview of the new workers' movement in Russia developing after 1989. The authors then examine the 1989 miners' strike in Kuzbass. The following three chapters are each devoted to one of the organizations listed above. In the last chapter, the authors turn again to the question of the workers' movement, its nature, and chances for survival in the new Russia.

558. Coleman, Fred. **The Decline and Fall of the Soviet Empire: Forty Years That Shook the World, from Stalin to Yeltsin**. xvii, 459p.: map. New York: St. Martin's Press, 1996. Includes bibliographical references (pp. 431-44) and index.

Fred Coleman has taken on the daunting task of analyzing the failure of the Soviet system. He has been a correspondent in Russia since the 1960s and has experienced a great number of the major events in that country's history firsthand. He is led to four important conclusions: (1) The fall of communism was inevitable; (2) Communism in Russia could not be reformed; (3) By overestimating the Soviet threat, the United States failed in its best efforts to resist communism; (4) The lessons from our failures in the handling of policy with regard to the Soviet Union are important for our future diplomatic relations with other countries. Coleman begins with Khrushchev's years in power and ends with Yeltsin's first four years in power. The author draws on his personal experience, archived material, and numerous Western sources in Russia.

559. Corti, Eugenio. **Few Returned: Twenty-Eight Days on the Russian Front, Winter 1942-1943**. xiv, 253p.: map. Columbia: University of Missouri Press, 1997. Includes bibliographical references.

This is the personal account of the Italian army's withdrawal from Russia. It recounts conditions there at the end of the war as seen by a common soldier.

560. Davies, R. W. **Soviet History in the Yeltsin Era**. viii, 264p. New York: St. Martin's Press, 1997. Includes bibliographical references.

This volume is in three distinct, but related, parts. Part 1 contains the politics of history during the years 1989 to 1996. Part 2 covers the battle for the archives and access to them that occurred during this time. Part 3 describes how the teaching of Russian history in Russia is being enriched by archival discoveries and changes brought about by the politics of history. Two appendixes also provide interesting information about the era. The first gives print runs of newspapers and periodicals from 1985 to 1995, and the second is a brief listing of major events in Russian and Soviet history during this period.

561. Fitzpatrick, Sheila. **Everyday Stalinism: Ordinary Life in Extraordinary Times: Soviet Russia in the 1930s**. x, 288p., [8] p. of plates: illus. New York: Oxford University Press, 1999. Includes bibliographical references.

Sheila Fitzpatrick examines the world of ordinary man in the most extraordinary of times. This is a study of "everyday life" at the height of Stalin's terror. This is also a book about urban life in Russia. Fitzpatrick looks at the privileged and the poor to produce a picture of a society permeated at all levels by its government. She focuses on the evolution of Homo Sovieticus whose most valued skill was the "hunting and gathering of scarce goods" (p. 2).

562. Fitzpatrick, Sheila. **Stalin's Peasants: Resistance and Survival in the Russian Village After Collectivization**. xx, 386p. New York: Oxford University Press, 1994. Includes bibliographical references (pp. 335-74) and index.

In this study Sheila Fitzpatrick focuses on the period from 1929 to 1941. The subject of the study is the Russian peasant as he/she experienced the process of collectivization. "Collectivization, imposed by the state with little regard for specific local conditions, not only gave peasants throughout Russia the same basic institutional structure (the kolkhoz), but also generated similar cultural patterns of resistance and adaptation" (p. 18). Sheila Fitzpatrick is Bernadotte E. Schmitt Professor in History at the University of Chicago.

563. Ginzburg, Lidia. **Blockade Diary**. xiv, 114p. London: Harvill Press, 1995. Translated from the Russian.

Lidia Ginzburg was seldom in the good graces of the Soviet literary establishment. Many of her works were published many years after they had been written. In this work, Ginzburg describes the painful experiences of those who lived through the 900-day siege of Leningrad during World War II. "From her own experience of the blockade and using facts, conversations and impressions collected over many years, Lidia Ginzburg has created a remarkable every-man hero in whom she distills the collective experience of life under siege" (book jacket). The book has now appeared in translation by Alan Myers.

564. **The Holocaust in the Soviet Union: Studies and Sources on the Destruction of the Jews in the Nazi-Occupied Territories of the USSR, 1941-1945**. Edited by Jeffrey S. Gurock and Lucjan Dobroszycki. xii, 260p. Armonk, N.Y.: M. E. Sharpe, 1993. Includes index.

The essays in this volume present a picture of the Nazi attempt to destroy the Jewish population in its Soviet territories. The essays are grouped into four parts. The first part provides the reader with background. Drawing on archival material the authors have compiled a brief study of the Soviet reaction to the Holocaust. In Part 2 the contributors examine the official Soviet policy during the Holocaust that affected the Jewish population. Part 3 recounts the Holocaust in specific regions of the Soviet Union, particularly the Baltic. The final part is an analysis of the sources available for study of the Holocaust.

565. Hardeman, Hilde. **Coming to Terms with the Soviet Regime: The "Changing Signposts" Movement Among Russian Émigrés in the Early 1920s**. x, 319p. DeKalb: Northern Illinois University Press, 1994. Includes bibliographical references (pp. [281]-309) and index.

Smenovekhovstvo is a tendency to call for reconciliation with the Bolsheviks in order to steer the evolution of the Soviet regime toward more "acceptable" forms. It came from a programmatic collection called Smena vekh, which influenced the émigré community into the mid-1920s. This book "deals with the genesis, the ideas, and the principal exponents of smenovekhovstvo. In addition, it portrays the place the movement occupied both in the émigré community and in Soviet Russia, as well as the way in which the Soviet authorities approached the movement" (p. 16).

566. Hochschild, Adam. **The Unquiet Ghost: Russians Remember Stalin**. xxvii, 304p.: illus., map. New York: Viking, 1994. Includes bibliographical references (pp. 289-96) and index.

Adam Hochschild probes the memories of the children of Russia's great purges in this book. "I wanted to talk with Russians of every sort to see how they were remembering, judging and coming to terms with that period—and to talk not only with people in Moscow, but with men and women across this entire vast country all the way to the icy heart of darkness itself, Kolyma" (p. xxvii). The reminiscences he collects here are presented in regional groups: Moscow, Siberia, and Kolyma. Hochschild is a writer living in San Francisco. He is the author of *Half the Way Home*.

567. Hoffmann, David Lloyd. **Peasant Metropolis: Social Identities in Moscow, 1929-1941**. xiii, 282p.: illus., maps. *Studies of the Harriman Institute*. Ithaca, N.Y.: Cornell University Press, 1994. Includes bibliographical references (pp. [251]-273) and index.

The revolution and the rebuilding of the Russian economy caused massive upheaval in the society. There was a great deal of migration to the cities. David Hoffmann examines the migration traditions and village networks that determined settlement patterns. "Only through an examination of the process of in-migration and the particular conditions of

Soviet industrialization is it possible to identify features of peasant-culture (in partial or metamorphosized form) which provided new city dwellers with a basis for understanding the city and the place they occupied in it" (p. 5). Hoffmann notes the intense interaction between urban officials and peasant migrants in Moscow. The author focuses on how the peasants adapted and how the evolutions of their social identity prevented the Soviet officials from creating the loyal working class they sought.

568. Kotkin, Stephen. **Magnetic Mountain: Stalinism As a Civilization**. xxv, 639p.: illus., map. Berkeley: University of California Press, 1995. Includes bibliographical references (pp. 599-608) and index.

Stephen Kotkin has used Magnitogorsk as a case study for the analysis of the development of Stalinism in the USSR. He believes it offers a microcosm of the USSR. This study is consequently not limited to one discipline but spans such fields as economics, politics, culture, and sociology. The book is divided into two parts. The first examines industrialization and urbanization in the USSR. Part 2 explores the new society that developed out of the rapidly changing Soviet society. Kotkin has drawn on a large number of primary sources in preparing this study. The book includes an outline of Soviet organizational structure.

569. Morris, M. Wayne. **Stalin's Famine and Roosevelt's Recognition of Russia**. ix, 224p. Lanham, Md.: University Press of America, 1994. Includes bibliographical references and index.

Morris examines the horrors of collectivization and famine in the 1930s in Russia and the inadequately explored silence of the West. Morris believes with other historians such as Robert Conquest and James Mace that the answer lies with Roosevelt's attempts to end the policy of nonrecognition of the Soviet Union. This book explores that silence, looking beyond Roosevelt to other Western sources for an answer. The book includes several appendixes that contain documents illustrating the information that the State Department had concerning the famine during the 1930s.

570. Naiman, Eric. **Sex in Public: The Incarnation of Early Soviet Ideology**. xi, 307p. Princeton, N.J.: Princeton University Press, 1997. Includes bibliographical references and index.

"*Sex in Public* examines the ideological poetics and the rhetoric of power in the Soviet Union during the 1920s, a period of anxiety over the historical legitimacy of Soviet ideology and Bolshevik power" (book jacket). The author has used a wide range of sources from Party Congress papers, literary works, pamphlets, film, crime reports, etc. From these various sources Naiman constructs a unique explanation for the Soviet preoccupation with crime, disease, and sex in the early years of the regime.

571. **The Stalin Phenomenon**. Edited by Alec Nove. vi, 216p. New York: St. Martin's Press, 1993. Includes bibliographical references and index.

This collection of essays attempts to further the understanding of Stalin's years in power. Five well-known scholars have contributed their views on Stalin to this volume. Alec Nove, R. W. Davies, Sheila Fitzpatrick, J. Arch Getty, and Sergo Mikoyan do not share the same opinion on Stalinism. But all seek to answer questions about Stalin's role in history. The various essays examine economic aspects of Stalinism, his politics and Western perspectives on him, as well as broader examinations of Stalinism.

572. Raack, R. C. **Stalin's Drive to the West, 1938-1945: The Origins of the Cold War**. viii, 265p.: illus. Stanford, Calif.: Stanford University Press, 1995. Includes bibliographical references (pp. [235]-258) and index.

This is the first examination of the Stalin-Hitler pact and its consequences that was undertaken with access to documents and archives from behind the Iron Curtain. The focus of the work is "on the work of Hitler and Stalin, and later, on Stalin and his Western allies, on the demolition of traditional Europe, and on the effort to reconstruct it during and after the war" (p. 9).

573. Rees, E. A. **Stalinism and Soviet Rail Transport, 1928-41**. xiv, 307p.: port. London: Macmillan, 1995. Includes bibliographical references (pp. 289-95) and indexes.

This is an attempt to rethink the development of the Stalinist state. E. A. Rees does this by examining both the political science and economic history approach to Stalin's government. "This work provides an institutional case-study of decision-making in the USSR in the Stalinist era, focusing on the Commissariat of Ways of Communication (Narodnyi Kommissariat Putei Soobshchenia, known also as NKPS or Narkomput), which was responsible for the administration of the rail transport system" (p. 1). The study is chronologically arranged beginning with the years of "Forced Development, 1928-1930." Rees then traces the development of the railway system and demonstrates how its development reflected the state of Russia as a whole. The appendixes to the book include statistical data on the railway system.

574. Ruder, Cynthia Ann. **Making History for Stalin: The Story of the Belomor Canal**. xvi, 248p.: illus. Gainesville: University Press of Florida, 1998. Includes bibliographical references (pp. [235]-243) and index.

The White Sea-Baltic Canal project holds an interesting place in the history of Soviet labor and literature. It emphasized the policy of "reforming" society and the use of collective labor for modernization. In literature it was commemorated in what became an infamous work of literature, *The History of the Construction of the Stalin White-Baltic Canal*. Cynthia Ruder has chosen this as the focus for this study. "In reconstructing the history of the Belomor project and its attendant literary works, I hope to encourage a deeper understanding of the mechanisms at work in the development and implementation of Stalinist culture and to reopen the discussion of the Belomor incident" (p. xi). Ruder has approached her topic thematically, first examining the question of how the history of the canal's construction was rewritten. She then looks at the creation of the history . . . itself. This is followed by an analysis of the use of literature as historical narrative. Ruder then turns to an examination of the various literary descriptions of the Belomor Canal and the emergent historical "truth" they defined.

575. Service, Robert. **A History of Twentieth-Century Russia**. xxxiii, 653p.: illus., maps. Cambridge, Mass.: Harvard University Press, 1998. Includes bibliographical references (pp. 555-[613]).

This comprehensive history covers Russia from the early years of the century and the fall of the Romanovs through the year 1997. This detailed and extensive study will provide the student of Russian history with a thought-provoking analysis of Russia's 20th century.

576. Soifer, Valerii. **Lysenko and the Tragedy of Soviet Science**. xxiv, 379p.: illus. New Brunswick, N.J.: Rutgers University Press, 1994. Includes bibliographical references (pp. [309]-358) and indexes.

This translation of Soifer's extensive study of Lysenko and his effect on Soviet science was originally published in Russian. Soifer believes that Lysenko's legacy has had long-lasting and severely detrimental effects on the Soviet educational and scientific communities. He also tries to identify the origins of Lysenkoism. "I have argued that Lysenkoism was by no means a result of the erroneous, unscientific views of one individual, supported by the leaders of the official ideology and the machinery of state, but a social phenomenon in conditions ostensibly of planned science but actually of harsh and unceasing Party dictatorship over the scientists" (p. 4). Soifer has included biographical sketches to make this work more accessible to the nonspecialist.

577. Stephan, John J. **The Russian Far East: A History**. xv, 481p. Stanford, Calif.: Stanford University Press, 1994. Includes index and select bibliography.

John Stephan has produced in one volume the first comprehensive history of the Russian Far East. Many contributions to the study of the region have been made focusing on specific areas. This is the first work that looks at all sides of the study of the area: geography, foreign policy, anthropology, and personal history. Stephan has drawn largely on Russian sources for this study, supplementing them when possible with Western, Japanese, Chinese, and Korean materials. The work is arranged chronologically beginning with a section on the geography and prehistory of the region, laying the groundwork for a discussion of the Chinese influence in the region. The first section then turns to an analysis of the "Russian Entree" into the region. Part 2 examines the establishment and the results of Russian control in the imperial period. Part 3 turns to a study of the Soviet period and the changes taking place in the area. The book ends with a section of appendixes; these include an administrative chronology, population tables, and biographical notes.

578. **Making Workers Soviet: Power, Class, and Identity**. Edited by Ronald Grigor Suny and Lewis H. Siegelbaum. xiii, 399p.: illus. Ithaca, N.Y.: Cornell University Press, 1994. Includes bibliographical references and index.

The essays in this book originated at a 1990 conference held at Michigan State University. "Drawing on such diverse sources as propaganda art, the trade union press, workers' memoirs, and materials in recently opened Soviet archives, this is the first book to examine the shifting identity of the 'working class' in late tsarist and early Soviet societies. New essays by fifteen leading historians show how Russian workers responded to attempts to make them Soviet" (back cover).

579. Viola, Lynne. **Peasant Rebels Under Stalin: Collectivization and Culture of Peasant Resistance**. xii, 312p. New York: Oxford University Press, 1996. Includes bibliographical references (pp. 291-303) and index.
Viola's ultimate aim is to "understand something of the politics of the revolution by exploring the politics of the peasantry. . . . This book is a study of peasant resistance, broadly defined, that seeks to document not only the vast struggle waged by the peasantry during collectivization, but also the manifestation in the USSR of universal strategies of peasant resistance in what amounted to a virtual civil war between state and peasantry" (p. viii). The author sets out to demonstrate that resistance to Stalin's policies was more widespread and organized than previously had been supposed. She relies on data from the Russian archives to support her argument.

580. Watson, Derek. **Molotov and Soviet Government: Sovnarkom, 1930-41**. xxiii, 274p.: illus. New York: St. Martin's Press in association with the Centre for Russian and East European Studies, University of Birmingham, 1996. Includes bibliographical references and index.
"This study is focused on the evolution of Sovnarkom and its political history when Molotov was chairman: a period which spans Stalin's economic revolution, the Great Terror and the approach of the Great Patriotic War" (p. xii). The first chapters of the book examine the early years of Sovnarkom's existence under the leadership of Rykov. Chapters 3-5 discuss the operation and institutional history of the organization. The final two chapters analyze the role of Sovnarkom in the politics of the 1930s. The book includes an appendix with a diagram of Sovnarkom's structural changes. There is also an extensive bibliography.

581. Young, Glennys. **Power and the Sacred in Revolutionary Russia: Religious Activists in the Village**. xiv, 307p.: illus., maps. University Park: Pennsylvania State University Press, 1997. Includes bibliographical references (pp. [281]-297) and index.
This is a study of the relationship between religion, laity, and Communist Party activists during the turbulent years following the revolution, 1921-1928. Glennys Young feels that the existing studies of this topic have treated the peasantry as "passive recipients" of the actions of government officials. "This study is unique, therefore, in that it examines

in detail the other side of the process. It shows how religious belief and practice of Russian villagers actually shaped both rural and national politics during the period of New Economic Policy. Thus, religious belief and practice served as an active agent of political mobilization and transformation" (p. 4). The book is arranged chronologically beginning with an introductory chapter that discusses the "political consequences of religious belief" (p. 9) from 1861 to 1917. The rest of the book follows the evolution of both the political consequences and the belief structure throughout the NEP.

582. **Bitter Legacy: Confronting the Holocaust in the USSR**. Edited by Zvi Gitelman. viii, 332p. Bloomington: Indiana University Press, 1997. Includes bibliographical references and index.

"This volume describes and analyzes how the Holocaust was perpetrated in the USSR and how it was treated after the war in Soviet scholarly publications and popular literature. Political calculations determined the Soviet treatment of the Holocaust, though that treatment was by no means uniform" (p. vii). In this collection of essays the contributors explain how the Holocaust has been represented in the USSR. Contributors to the volume are Mordechai Altshuler, Shalom Cholawski, Zvi Gitelman, Mykhailo Koval, Yosef Litvak, Michael MacQueen, Shimon Redlich, Daniel Romanovsky, Sara Shner-Neshamit, Shmuel Spector, Hans-Heinrich Wilhelm, and Sima Ycikas.

Military Affairs

General Studies

583. Blacker, Coit D. **Hostage to Revolution: Gorbachev and Soviet Security Policy, 1985-1991**. xviii, 239p. New York: Council on Foreign Relations Press, 1993. Includes index.

Blacker attempts "to construct a concise explanation for the causes and consequences of the Gorbachev revolution, particularly as it affected the related issues of military reform, arms control, regional and international security, and civil-military relations" (p. 1). He examines the Brezhnev legacy, military doctrine and the restructuring of the armed forces, arms control and regional security, perestroika, and the Soviet military, and concludes with an analysis of Gorbachev, security policy, and the Soviet collapse.

584. Holden, Gerard. **Russia After the Cold War: History and the Nation in Post-Soviet Security Politics**. 205p. *Studies from the Peace Research Institute Frankfurt*, 27. Frankfurt am Main, Ger.: Campus Verlag; Boulder, Colo.: Westview Press, 1994. Includes bibliographical references.

"The study describes the disintegration and restructuring of the Soviet/Russian military system between 1991 and 1993. It examines the uses of history and nationalism, during this period, in the relegitimization of the Russian state, and their influence on its foreign and security policy" (front cover). Gerard Holden is a researcher at the Peace Research Institute, Frankfurt.

585.   Kokoshin, Andrei Afanas'evich. **Soviet Strategic Thought, 1917-91**. xiii, 225p. *CSIA Studies in International Security*. Cambridge, Mass.: MIT Press, 1998.

Kokoshin focuses on three major themes: (1) the relationship between policy and strategy in Soviet military doctrine; (2) threats to Soviet security and the probability of a future war; and (3) offense and defense in Soviet military strategy. He provides a concluding chapter on Russia's national security and military power and its implications for assessing the present-day dimensions of the national security problem, and the development of a new armed forces for Russia.

586.   Reese, Roger R. **Stalin's Reluctant Soldiers: A Social History of the Red Army, 1925-1941**. xii, 267p.: illus. *Modern War Studies*. Lawrence: University Press of Kansas, 1996. Includes bibliographical references (pp. 239-51) and index.

Not intended to be a comprehensive history of the Red Army, this book instead "explores several important but neglected social-historical themes of the Soviet military that are essential to understanding why the Soviet Union, a rising industrial power with the world's largest and most mechanized army, came close to being eliminated as a geopolitical entity in only a matter of six months" (p. ix). The book is organized thematically, with chapters devoted to organization and training of the regular army and territorial forces; daily life, conditions of service, and discipline; the political administration and the army; the Red Army Officer Corps; the effects of the purges; and the last 18 months of the Red Army and its predictable disaster.

To 1917

587.   Cockfield, Jamie H. **With Snow on Their Boots: The Tragic Odyssey of the Russian Expeditionary Force in France During World War I**. 1st ed. xi, 396p.: illus. New York: St. Martin's Press, 1998. Includes bibliographical references (pp. [377]-385) and index.

During the First World War several countries sent expeditionary forces to fight on the Western Front. The least known of these was the Russian Expeditionary Force, which consisted of two brigades that fought as a unit in France from 1916 until the Russian Revolution in 1917. In spite of the mutiny by several of the men in that year, many remained in France to fight until the armistice in November 1918. Cockfield provides here a regimental history, describing their saga and exploring the larger context in which their actions took place.

588. Fuller, William C. **Strategy and Power in Russia, 1600-1914**. xx, 557p.: maps. New York: Free Press, 1992. Includes bibliographical references and index.

Fuller indicates that this is not a comprehensive military history of Russia in the time period indicated. Rather, "this book is an interpretative study of the ways in which tsarist statesmen and governments tried to employ force or the threat of force to achieve their political objectives over the roughly three hundred years from the founding of the Romanov dynasty in the early seventeenth century to the outbreak of World War I in 1914. It is therefore a study of high strategy as the great Prussian theorist Clausewitz defined it, that is, as the connection between military means and political ends" (p. xiv). Individual chapters are devoted to Russian military weakness in the 17th century, Peter the Great and the advantages of backwardness, Russian imperialism and military power in the 18th century, the War of 1812, policy and strategy of Nicholas I, and other topics.

589. Menning, Bruce. **Bayonets Before Bullets: The Imperial Russian Army, 1861-1914**. x, 334p.: illus. *Indiana-Michigan Series in Russian and East European Studies*. Bloomington: Indiana University Press, 1992. Includes bibliographical references (pp. [309]-327) and index.

"This study traces the organization and military art of the Imperial Russian Army through two wars and two phases of the industrial revolution" (p. 1). Menning focuses on military theory and practice as he examines Russia's military activities in the years before the revolution. The book is chronologically arranged.

1917 to Present

590. Currie, Kenneth M. **Soviet Military Politics: Contemporary Issues**. xxiv, 253p. *Issues in Soviet and East European Studies*. New York: Paragon House, 1992. Includes bibliographical references and index.

Currie focuses here on Soviet military politics. This entails an examination of the military's role in the Soviet political system. In the first of two parts, Chapters 1-3, he examines military policy, doctrine, and strategy. In Part 2, Chapters 4-7, he emphasizes civil-military relations, military professionalization, and the impact of military reform. A concluding epilogue looks at the effect of the coup on the Soviet military and its influence in political matters.

591. Galeotti, Mark. **Afghanistan, the Soviet Union's Last War**. xi, 242p.: maps. London: Frank Cass, 1995. Includes bibliographical references and index.

In this study, Mark Galeotti seeks to understand the impact the Afghanistan war had on Soviet society and politics. He has drawn on war veterans' newspapers, correspondence and conversations with veterans, and the results he obtained using a questionnaire in making his assessment of the situation. His book is divided into four parts: "The Veterans," "The Victims of War," "The War and Society," and "The War and the Professional Soldiers." Galeotti does not see the war as a pivotal event in the downfall of the Soviet Union. "It was part and parcel of the catastrophes, blunders, tensions, and crises which brought the Soviet system down, from Chernobyl to food queues, the Tbilisi massacre to the collapse of the Eastern Bloc. Perhaps at most it added a particularly red hue and some dramatic imagery to the collage" (pp. 232-33).

592. Herspring, Dale R. **Russian Civil-Military Relations**. xxiv, 230p. Bloomington: Indiana University Press, 1996. Includes bibliographical references (pp. [193]-223) and index.

Speculating that the development of Russian civil-military relations over the next five years is the most important issue in Russian politics today, Herspring examines the political-military culture of both the Soviet and post-Soviet periods. He "examines some of the models developed by Western social scientists to explain civil-military relations at key times during the Soviet period, notably the 1920s, when Soviet power was being established, and the 1980s, when Gorbachev tried to regain civilian control over military-security issues" (p. xi). He attempts to see how useful these models were in predicting ensuing events and identifies key variables that have affected civil-military relations in the past.

593. Nichols, Thomas. **The Sacred Cause: Civil-Military Conflict Over National Security, 1917-1992**. xiii, 259p. Ithaca, N.Y.: Cornell University Press, 1993. Includes bibliographical references and index.

Thomas Nichols examines the roll of the Soviet military in Soviet society. "It is my hope . . . that the fluid nature of Russian politics will not detract from the essential premise of this book, for it is one that bears directly on the Russian future: that the structure of civil-military politics in the Soviet era was inherently conflictual, in that it pitted an ideologically indoctrinated officer corps against an increasingly pragmatic Party elite, which in turn served to create a military of unstable and conflicted loyalties" (p. ix). Nichols follows the development of the relationship between civil and military factions in politics beginning with Stalin. He examines the changes that took place under Khrushchev and Brezhnev and the ultimate consequences seen under Gorbachev.

594. Noggle, Anne. **A Dance with Death: Soviet Airwomen in World War II**. 1st ed. xiv, 318p.: illus. College Station: Texas A&M University Press, 1994. Includes bibliographical references (pp. 13-14).

Anne Noggle served in the American Air Force in World War II and has written about her experiences. For this book she interviewed 69 women who have served in the Soviet Army Air Force. Noggle feels that these interviews provide an insight into the "Soviet mind." "This is not a history but an account—personal, and at times emotional—of what it was like to spend nearly four years flying combat, from the early days of devastation and retreat to the victory paid for with so many millions of lives" (p. xi).

595. Philbin, Tobias R. **The Lure of Neptune: German-Soviet Naval Collaboration and Ambitions, 1919-1941**. xxi, 192p.: illus., maps. *Studies in Maritime History*. Columbia: University of South Carolina Press, 1994. Includes bibliographical references and index.

"This study investigates German and Soviet naval activities in the inter-war period and is intended to illuminate Soviet and German naval intentions and interface vis-à-vis their defense policies and political systems" (p. xiii). Philbin has divided his book into three parts. The first establishes the background in Soviet-German relations and particularly the military relations that existed between the two nations from 1917 to 1939. Part 2 focuses on the first years of World War II. In Part 3 the author looks at military operations during the war.

596. Reinhardt, Klaus. **Moscow—The Turning Point: The Failure of Hitler's Strategy in the Winter of 1941-42**. Translated by Karl B. Keenan. xiv, 481p.: maps. *Studies in Military History*. Oxford: Berg, 1992. Includes bibliographical references and index.

"Using a wealth of source material, the author sets out to refute the widely held view among historians and military experts that the German defeat at Stalingrad in the winter of 1942-43 marked the turning point in the war. He shows how Hitler's attempt to crush the Soviet Union in a Blitz campaign was doomed to failure from the outset and how defeat outside Moscow compromised his plans for successful conclusion to the war" (frontispiece). The chapters are arranged chronologically and the author has included an extensive selection of maps.

Navy

597. Heise, Volker, Steven E. Miller, and Andreas Fürst. **Europe and Naval Arms Control in the Gorbachev Era**. xvi, 341p. Stockholm: Oxford University Press, 1992. Includes bibliographical references and index.

The goal of this volume is "to begin to fill a significant gap in research in the naval arms control field. Instead of addressing the issue in global terms or from a superpower perspective, naval arms control is examined from a European viewpoint, focusing on the following questions: What role might naval arms control have in the interests and perceptions of European states? What opportunities for and obstacles to naval arms control exist in Europe? Which security problems might be solved and which created by naval arms control measures?" (p. xii). The 16 chapters are arranged in geographical sections: the Norwegian Sea, the Baltic region, the Mediterranean region. Many of the chapters contain appendixes featuring key translated documents, and appendixes at the end of the volume provide information about the extent of naval forces in these regions in 1991.

598. Phillips, Edward J. **The Founding of Russia's Navy: Peter the Great and the Azov Fleet, 1688-1714**. ix, 214p. Westport, Conn.: Greenwood Press, 1995. Includes bibliographical references (pp. [201]-206) and index.

Rather than a history of battles won and lost, "the book explores the creation of the tsar's navy as an evolving process of gathering and mobilizing available political, economic, social, and cultural resources to surmount technical, organizational, and financial challenges. This inquiry seeks to shed new light on the impact of the past as a precedent for reform, the impact of the rule as an instrument of reform, and the impact of the West as a model for reform, the central-most questions about this era of profound change" (p. viii).

599. Yoder, H. S. **Planned Invasion of Japan, 1945: The Siberian Weather Advantage**. xvi, 161p.: illus., 1 folded map. Philadelphia: American Philosophical Society, 1997. Includes bibliographical references (pp. 139-42) and index.

An invasion of Japan was planned by the Joint Chiefs of Staff to take place in November 1945. In order to ensure the greatest success, a group of naval weather observers were stationed in Eastern Siberia in Khabarovsk to observe weather conditions in preparation for the invasion. This volume recounts the establishment of that weather base and relations between Soviet and U.S. military personnel that occurred as a result.

Special Studies

600. Arnold, Anthony. **The Fateful Pebble: Afghanistan's Role in the Fall of the Soviet Empire**. xiv, 225p.: map. Novato, Calif.: Presidio, 1993. Includes bibliographical references (pp. 211-19).

Anthony Arnold argues in this study that the Soviet loss in Afghanistan played a significant role in the destruction of the Soviet Empire. Arnold sees that Empire as having been supported by three crucial elements—the party, the military, and the KGB. In this book he demonstrates how an un-winnable war in Afghanistan undermined the stability of those three basic political supports. The book is arranged topically and includes a glossary of terms.

601. Baev, Pavel K. **The Russian Army in a Time of Troubles**. xiii, 204p. London; Thousand Oaks, Calif.; New Delhi: Sage Publications, 1996. Includes bibliography, name index, and subject index.

Baev seeks to understand what happened to the Russian military with the fall of communism after 1991 and what possible courses it will take in the years ahead. Beginning with a historical perspective on Russia's security agenda and a special focus on the issue of territoriality, he then examines the Russian/Soviet army's involvement with politics, Russia's security interests, and the role of the army in protecting them. He then moves on to analyze the feasibility of political control over the Russian army, external contacts of the Russian army (e.g., NATO), the general issue of conflict management in the former Soviet Union, and the performance of the army in a peacekeeping role, including the

Chechen war. The concluding chapter places Russia's peacekeeping activities in a broader European context.

602. Barylski, Robert V. **The Soldier in Russian Politics: Duty, Dictatorship and Democracy Under Gorbachev and Yeltsin**. xii, 510p. New Brunswick, N.J.: Transaction Publishers, 1998. Includes bibliographical references and index.

"*The Soldier in Russian Politics* examines military dimensions of contemporary Russian politics. It is both a political history and a political-sociological analysis" (p. 1). The author attempts to place the role of the military and the changes in Russia in their proper context. He feels that little attention has been given to what he feels was a significant contribution to the politics that led to the downfall of the Soviet Union. The book is divided into three parts: "The Military and the End of the Soviet State"; "The Military and the New Russian State"; and "Testing the Russian State's Viability."

603. Heinämaa, Anna. **The Soldiers' Story: Soviet Veterans Remember the Afghan War**. Translated by A. D. Haunix. 131p. *Research series (University of California, Berkeley. International and Area Studies)*, no. 90. Berkeley: International and Area Studies, University of California at Berkeley, 1994. Original title: *Sotilaitten tarina*.

This volume collects the reminiscences of the soldiers who fought in the Soviet-Afghan war. "It is not the purpose of this book to prove anything. We have not attempted to seek out the guilty or to present political or historical voice to those who, unwillingly or unintentionally, came to participate in one of world history's undeclared wars" (p. viii). The book includes interviews conducted from 1990 to 1991. Those interviewed were between 25 and 30 years old and from a variety of nationalities. The book is divided into chapters, each devoted to one of the interviewees. There is no commentary, leaving readers to reach their own conclusions. The epilogue of the book is a series of letters from soldiers to their families.

604. **Russian Security After the Cold War: Seven Views from Moscow**. Edited by Teresa Pelton Johnson and Steven E. Miller. xi, 208p. Washington, D.C.: Brassey's, 1994.

"These essays constitute a broad overview of the efforts of major figures in Moscow's foreign-policy debate to come to grips with the security challenges confronting Russia. While this book is something of a snapshot of quickly moving events, nevertheless virtually all of the authors represented here are still active players, and the views of each reflect an influential constituency in the current Russian debate" (p. viii).

605. Lambeth, Benjamin S. **The Warrior Who Would Rule Russia: A Profile of Aleksandr Lebed**. xvii, 125p.: port. London: Brassey's, 1997. Originally published Santa Monica, Calif.: RAND Corp., 1996.

This report was prepared for the U.S. Air Force by the RAND Corporation. "It offers a detailed portrait of Retired Russian army Lieutenant General Alexsandr I. Lebed, who rose to prominence three years ago as the commander of Russia's 14th army in Moldova and has since been appointed security adviser by the recently reelected Boris Yeltsin" (p. iii). Because of his role at the time of the writing of the report, it was believed that he warranted careful attention by American military leaders and defense planners.

606. Lockwood, Jonathan Samuel, and Kathleen O'Brien Lockwood. **The Russian View of U.S. Strategy: Its Past, Its Future**. 233p. New Brunswick, N.J.: Transaction Publishers, 1993. Rev. ed. of: *The Soviet View of U.S. Strategic Doctrine*, 1983. Includes bibliographical references (pp. 221-29) and index.

In using open-source Soviet writings, the Lockwoods attempt to analyze the Russian perception of U.S. nuclear strategy. Their study is arranged in five parts, with three appendixes. In Part 1 they provide a doctrinal overview of the development of U.S. strategic doctrine and the evolution of Soviet strategic doctrine. In Part 2 they examine the massive retaliation period (named by John Foster Dulles' strategy of "massive retaliation") that lasted from 1954 to 1960. In Part 3 they describe the flexible response period (1961-1968) and in Part 4 the realistic deterrence period (1969-1982). In Part 5 they follow the evolution of policy and policy perceptions from the Strategic Defense Initiative to the collapse of communism (1983-1991). Their three appendixes contain information relating to comparative US/USSR ICBM/SLBM/Bomber deployments, a chronology of major events, and the impact of ballistic missile defense on operational warfare.

607. Zisk, Kimberly Marten. **Engaging the Enemy: Organization Theory and Soviet Military Innovation, 1955-1991**. x, 286p. Princeton, N.J.: Princeton University Press, 1993. Includes bibliographical references.

This study examines the role of military officers in introducing innovations into the Soviet military. It does this from within a case study methodology that uses Soviet reactions to three major changes in military doctrine promulgated by the United States or NATO. These three changes were: "the American and NATO adoption of the Flexible Response doctrine in the 1960s; the American adoption of the Schlesinger Doctrine in 1974; and the combination of the American adoption of the AirLand Battle doctrine and the NATO adoption of the Follow-on Forces Attack (FOFA) doctrine in the early 1980s" (p. 7).

Nuclear Arms

608. Holloway, David. **Stalin and the Bomb: The Soviet Union and Atomic Energy, 1939-1956**. xvi, 464p.: illus. New Haven, Conn.: Yale University Press, 1994. Includes bibliographical references and index.

"This book examines Soviet policy in relation to atomic energy from the discovery of nuclear fission at the very end of 1938 to the mid-1950s, when the Soviet Union tested thermonuclear weapons. It asks why the Soviet Union built nuclear weapons, and how it did so; what the implications of the nuclear project were for Soviet society and politics; and what effect nuclear weapons had on Soviet foreign and military policy. It tries to set the Soviet nuclear project in its comparative context, and also to show how it was affected by, and in turn influenced, other nuclear projects" (pp. 1-2).

609. Turbiville, Graham Hall. **Weapons Proliferation and Organized Crime: The Russian Military and Security Force Dimension**. 53p. *INSS Occasional Paper: Proliferation series*, 10. Colorado Springs, Colo.: USAF Institute for National Security Studies, U.S. Air Force Academy, 1996. "June 1996." Includes bibliographical references (pp. 46-53).

This brief study outlines weapons proliferation in the former Soviet Union in the context of the rule of organized crime, the military, and security organizations in that proliferation. The author contends that this is an international threat. "Russian military and security forces are the principle source of arms becoming available to organized crime groups, participants in regional conflict, and corrupt state officials engaged in the black, gray, and legal arms markets in their various dimensions" (p. ix). In this study, Turbiville examines the problem thematically, beginning with a discussion of the Russian criminal environment. This is followed by discussions of military crime and the relationships between military crime and conventional arms trade. Turbiville also examines the question of military criminal activity and weapons of mass destruction, and nuclear and chemical arms and their proliferation.

Russian Language

General Studies

610. Comrie, Bernard, Gerald Stone, and Maria Polinsky. **The Russian Language in the Twentieth Century**. 2nd ed. (Rev. and ed. of: *The Russian Language Since the Revolution*.) xi, 385p. Oxford, Eng.: Clarendon Press, 1996. Includes bibliographical references and index.

This is a second edition of a work originally published in 1978. The purpose of the book "is to trace and illustrate the main changes that have taken place in the Russian language since the beginning of the twentieth century, and particularly of those between 1917 and the late 1980s, a time which can be identified as the Soviet period. . . ."

After a comprehensive introduction, individual chapters are devoted to pronunciation, stress and intonation, morphology, syntax, vocabulary, sex, gender and the status of women, modes of address and etiquette, and orthography and punctuation.

Dictionaries and Glossaries

611. Lubensky, Sophia. **Random House Russian-English Dictionary of Idioms**. 1st ed. xxvii, 1017p. New York: Random House, 1995. Includes bibliographical references (pp. 835-48) and index.

An idiom, defined by the author, is "a nonfree combination of two or more words that acts as a semantic whole" (p. xiii). The dictionary contains over 13,000 Russian idioms. Each entry includes a grammatical description, definitions, usage notes, English equivalents, and variables and patterns. The introduction gives a complete and detailed guide to use and structure.

Textbooks and Grammars

612.   Offord, Derek. **Using Russian: A Guide to Contemporary Usage**. xxx, 407p. Cambridge, Eng.: Cambridge University Press, 1996. Includes glossary, list of words and affixes, and index.

This book is aimed at the advanced learner "who has studied the basic grammar of the language and is now striving for a more comprehensive and sophisticated knowledge" (p. xiii). Individual chapters cover varieties of language and register, problems of meaning, problems of translation from English into Russian, vocabulary and idiom, language and everyday life, verbal etiquette, word formation, inflection, prepositions, and syntax.

613.   **World Congress for Soviet and East European Studies (4th) 1990: Harrogate, England. The Golden Age of Russian Literature and Thought: Selected Papers from the Fourth World Congress for Soviet and East European Studies**. Harrogate, 1990. Edited by Derek Offord. xiii, 174p. New York: St. Martin's Press, 1992. "Published in association with the International Council for Soviet and East European Studies"—Verso t.p. Includes bibliographical references and index.

This collection of essays resulted from the Fourth World Congress for Soviet and East European Studies. The essays cover a variety of subjects in the area of literature. Several selections appear in translation here. "While the quality of contributors' papers has been the main criterion for their selection for inclusion in this volume, an attempt has also been made to strike a balance between fresh work on major authors (Pushkin, Lermontov, Turgenev, and Dostoevsky), important work on minor authors (Marlinsky, Pisemsky, and Boborykin), and studies that relate to thinkers (Chaadaev, Herzen, and in part, Bakunin)" (p. ix). The essays are arranged in a loose chronological order.

Russian Literature

Bibliographies, Biographies, Encyclopedias

614.   Aroutunova, Bayara. **Lives in Letters: Princess Zinaida Volkonskaya and Her Correspondence**. 204p., [20] p. of plates: illus. Columbus, Ohio: Slavica Publishers, 1994. Pictures on lining papers.

These translated letters of Princess Volkonskaya cover the years 1812-1838. She was a lady-in-waiting to the Dowager Empress and married Prince Volkonskii in 1811.

She developed a romantic liaison with Tsar Alexander that lasted several years. Among the letters translated here are ones from Mme. De Stael, Baratynsky, Kozlov, Glinka, Turgenev, Vyazemsky, Zhukovsky, the tsar, and Cardinal Ercole Consalvi. Also included are several letters to Prince A. N. Volkonskii. Each letter is preceded by a commentary on the occasion of the letter and followed by notes that elucidate specific references. Together the correspondence gives a fascinating view of the aristocratic life in early-19th-century Russia.

615. Carlisle, Olga Andreyev. **Under a New Sky: A Reunion with Russia**. xix, 248p. New York: Ticknor & Fields, 1993.

This fascinating memoir by acclaimed writer Olga Andreyev Carlisle, granddaughter of Leonid Andreyev, is a series of vignettes from her youth to the early 1990s. In them she relates her life in Paris as a child and her experiences in meeting Pasternak, Chukovsky, Sakharov, Askoldov, and other literary and cultural figures. It concludes with her visit to Russia just before the 1991 coup, after a 22-year forced exile. Written with a deep compassion and understanding, her memoir is an adventure in itself.

616. **Reference Guide to Russian Literature**. Edited by Neil Cornwell and Nicole Christian. 972p. Chicago: Fitzroy Dearborn, 1998. Includes index.

This weighty tome is intended to be a comprehensive guide to the main writers of Russian literature and to their best-known works. The 273 writers and 293 works span the chronological limits of Russian literature, from the Kievan period to the present-day post-communist writing of the Russian Federation. The editors acknowledge their bias toward 19th- and 20th-century authors. In terms of coverage the selection breaks down as approximately 10 percent 18th century and earlier, 33 percent 19th and early 20th century, and the remaining 57 percent 20th century.

The entries, each of which was written by one of the 180 contributors, are arranged in alphabetical order. Each entry contains a short biographical sketch (no illustrations), a list of publications and related critical studies, and, where applicable, published bibliographies of the author's works and related criticism. In each author's section there is always a critical appraisal essay and in most cases an essay about a major work of the author.

These individual author entries are preceded by a rich introduction that contains a general reading list (most of which are in English), a chronology of main historical and literary events, a glossary of 51 terms with brief (one- to two-sentence) definitions, followed by a series of a dozen essays covering topics such as Old Russian Literature, Aleksander Pushkin: From Byron to Shakespeare, Women's Writing in Russia, Russian Literary Theory, and Russian Literature in the Post-Soviet Period. The volume is well equipped with a title index and notes on contributors and advisors.

This impressive work is sure to be useful for anyone studying Russian literature, at whatever stage. The introductory essays serve as a solid overview of the subject, and the bibliographies and essays on each writer are well done and will whet the appetite of the beginner, as well as consolidate the knowledge of the specialist.

617. **Dictionary of Russian Women Writers**. Edited by Marina Ledkovskaia-Astman, Charlotte Rosenthal, and Mary Fleming Zirin. xli, 869p. Westport, Conn.: Greenwood Press, 1994. Includes bibliographical references (pp. [813]-822) and index.

This impressive dictionary is "The first in any language to cover the lives and works of Russian women writers, who, despite their significant historical and cultural contributions, are by and large missing from the canon of Russian Literature" (p. xxiii).

The biographical/critical entries are presented in alphabetical order. Each of these is written by one of the approximately 100 contributors to this valuable reference work. In addition to biographical and critical information, each entry also includes extensive bibliographies by and about the authors. The entries are prefaced by an introductory essay by the editors that sets women's writing in Russia in context.

618. Urbanic, Allan. **Russian Émigré Literature: A Bibliography of Titles Held by the University of California, Berkeley Library**. 329p. Oakland, Calif.: Berkeley Slavic Specialties, 1993. Entries in romanized Russian; prefatory matter in English.

This comprehensive catalog of Russian émigré literature held at the University of California at Berkeley consists of an alphabetical listing of titles by their library main entry. There are, additionally, a personal name index that contains additional authors and editors whose names did not appear as entries in the main listing, a corporate name index based on the same principle, a subject index based on the same principle, and a subject index based on the Library of Congress subject headings. Entries are in brief form and contain author, title, and place and date of publication, as well as the UC Berkeley call number.

General Studies and Histories

619. **Russian Eyes on American Literature**. xiv, 310p. Jackson: University Press of Mississippi, 1992.

This collection of essays sets several precedents. "It is the first effort to explore many of the major developments in the whole of American writing, from colonial times to the present, by Russian critics free from the rigorous ideological limitations of the Soviet system. Finally, it is the first collection of essays in American letters by Russian critics written specifically for readers in the English-speaking world" (p. viii). This collection is the result of the first collaboration between the Gorky Institute of World Literature in Moscow and an American university press.

620. Austin, Paul M. **The Exotic Prisoner in Russian Romanticism**. xii, 214p. New York: P. Lang, 1997. Includes bibliographical references and index.

Paul Austin believes that the influence of the West on Russia profoundly affected the development of its culture. "The literature resulting from the conjuncture of European literary fashion, and expanding empire and the scientific enquiry produced a new vision of the self-conscious hero and heroine. Out of the plethora of stories and poems came characters aware that their captivity was frequently as much psychological as physical" (p. xi). Austin looks at the works of Pushkin and Lermontov in this context.

621. **Russian Literature and the Classics**. Edited by Peter I. Barta, David H. J. Larmour, and Paul Allen Miller, 191p. Amsterdam: Harwood Academic, 1996. Includes bibliographical references.

Editors Peter Barta, David Larmour, and Paul Miller explore the influence of Western classical literature on Russian literature of the 19th and 20th centuries. The works of Derzhavin, Dostoevsky, Belyi, Vyacheslav Ivanov, Vasili Grossman, Aleksandr Kushnev, and Joseph Brodsky are discussed.. "While by no means claiming to offer a comprehensive approach, the authors focus on various aspects of the influence which the Classics have had on Russian literature at particularly significant junctures—the beginning of the nineteenth century; the age of the great Russian realist novel; the 'Silver Age'; Stalin's terror; the 'Thaw' after 1965; and the period just before the collapse of Soviet society" (back cover). Contributors include Charles Byrd, Naomi Rood, Mary Jo White, Pamela Davidson, Frank Ellis, David N. Wells, and Dan Ungurianu.

622. Brown, Deming. **The Last Years of Soviet Russian Literature: Prose Fiction, 1975-1991**. x, 208p. Cambridge, Eng.; New York: Cambridge University Press, 1993. Includes bibliographical references (pp. 191-95) and index.

Brown provides a "comprehensive survey of developments in Russian prose over the last fifteen years of the Soviet regime. . . . Special attention is given to the evolving patterns of publication during the period: the rehabilitation of suppressed writers and the first publication of writings that had formerly belonged to the literary underground" (frontispiece). It also includes a bibliography of English translations of Soviet Russian prose of authors whose works have been translated in the past 20 years.

623. Dobrenko, Evgenii Aleksandrovich. **The Making of the State Reader: Social and Aesthetic Contexts of the Reception of Soviet Literature**. x, 374p. Stanford, Calif.: Stanford University Press, 1997. Includes bibliographical references (pp. 332-63) and index.

What factors shaped the readers of the early Soviet period? How did the sociopolitical changes of the Soviet era shape the social space of the reader? Evgenii Dobrenko examines these questions in this work. He focuses on socialist realism. "This book examines the social and aesthetic prerequisites for the reception of Socialist Realism, that is, a new horizon of reading" (p. vii). The chapters are arranged topically, discussing the institutional attempts to mold the reader, the type of reader of the revolutionary era, and the use of the educational system and the libraries in the attempt to shape the reader. The final chapter describes "The Ideal Reader." The text was translated by Jesse Savage.

624. Finke, Michael. **Metapoesis: The Russian Tradition from Pushkin to Chekhov**. xv, 221p. Durham, N.C.: Duke University Press, 1995. Includes bibliographical references (pp. [203]-217) and index.

Michael Finke compares the works of five Russian authors in this book. In each of the works discussed, the author commented on his own poetics. Finke is using a theoretical model first prepared by Roman Jakobson. "From it derives this book's guiding principles: that the significance of metapoetic discourse cannot be understood, first, in isolation from other communicative functions at play in the writing and reception of a given literary text, nor, second, without a general and historical understanding of the role of metapoesis in the broader arena of discourse to which it belongs" (p. xii). Finke compares the works of Gogol, Dostoevsky, Tolstoy, Pushkin, and Chekov. He has selected works he feels have not received enough critical attention. In each case the author engages in a good deal of "self-reflexive literature."

625. Friedberg, Maurice. **Literary Translation in Russia: A Cultural History**. vii, 224p. University Park: Pennsylvania State University Press, 1997. Includes bibliographical references and index.

Friedberg's book emphasizes the ideological dimension of translating "a literary pursuit that is elsewhere not considered particularly susceptible to political pressures" (p. 15). He provides a historical background to translation in Russia from 988, theoretical controversies that surround the translating activity, the centrality of translating to literary authors (considering that many of them did translation), and the effect of translations on the literary process.

626. Friedrich, Paul. **Music in Russian Poetry**. xvii, 344p. *Middlebury Studies in Russian Language and Literature*, vol. 10. New York: P. Lang, 1998. Includes bibliographical references (pp. [297]-321) and indexes.

"This innovative work from Paul Friedrich surveys the Russian lyric scene from the mid-18th century through the Modern period; in terms of the poet's own ideas as well as the author's interpretations. Such themes as poetic craft, musicality, creativity, socio-political context, and multilingualism as musical competence, are discussed and interrelated through their variations in 21 of Russia's finest lyric poets and then integrated through two 'recapitulations' " (back cover). Friedrich has included such poets as Sumarokov, Dezhavin, Krylov, Pushkin, Tyutchev, Lermontov, Fet, Blok, Khlebnikov, Akhmatova, Pasternak, Tsvetaeva, and Esenin.

627. **Christianity and the Eastern Slavs: Russian Literature in Modern Times, Vol. III**. Edited by Boris Gasparov, Robert P. Huges, Irina Paperno, and Olga Raevsky-Hughes. viii, 332p. *California Slavic Studies*, 18. Berkeley; London: University of California Press, 1995. Vol. 3. Russian Literature in Modern Times, Edited by Boris Gasparov . . . [et al.], 1995.

This is the third volume in a series that collects papers delivered at two international conferences held in 1988. The earlier volumes, *Slavic Cultures in the Middle Ages* and *Russian Culture in Modern Times*, were issued in 1993 and 1994, respectively. This volume includes essays by Liza Knapp, Alexander Zholkovsky, Lewis Bagby, Aage Hansen-Love, Joan Delaney Grossman, Tomas Venclova, David M. Bethea, Irene Mansing-Delic, Vladimir E. Alexandrov, Savah Pratt, Peter Alberg Jensen, Lazar Fleishman, and Olga Raevsky-Hughes. The essays are arranged chronologically and are in English and Russian. "Volume III contains papers that focus on literary texts and literary movements; the three sections are devoted to the nineteenth century, the age of Modernism (ca. 1890-1920), and the period from 1920 to 1960" (*Christianity and the Eastern Slavs*, Vol I, p. 7).

628. Hooker, Mark. **The Military Uses of Literature: Fiction and the Armed Forces in the Soviet Union**. 245p. Westport, Conn.: Praeger, 1996. Includes bibliographical references and index.

"*The Military Uses of Literature* is a study of a little known, made-to-order genre of Soviet literature that was written to fill the order of socialist realism fiction about the Armed forces placed by the Main Political Directorate of the Army and Navy (MPD)" (p. ix). The book has two parts. The first examines the history of the MPD's demand for a particular portrayal of military life. The later chapters discuss the realities of military life and the development of the genre in a post-war society.

629. Kraeger, Linda, and Joe E. Barnhart. **Dostoevsky on Evil and Atonement: The Ontology of Personalism in His Major Fiction**. 199p.: illus. Lewiston, N.Y.: Edwin Mellen Press, 1992. Includes bibliographical references (pp. [160]-170) and index.

Linda Kraeger and Joe Barnhart examine the role of evil in Dostoevsky's works in general and the *Brothers Karamazov* in particular. In all cases they look at his works as they relate to and challenge religious beliefs.

630. Lachmann, Renate. **Memory and Literature: Intertextuality in Russian Modernism. Roy Sellars, and Anthony Wall**. xxv, 436p. *Theory and History of Literature*, 87. Minneapolis: University of Minnesota Press, 1997. Includes bibliographical references, endnotes, and index.

Against the background of Russian formalism and Czech structuralism, Lachmann presents a view of literature "as the epitome of cultural memory" (p. xi) and thereby moves away from the conception of literature as an assembly of works. But literature for Lachmann is not a representation of cultural memory, but instead "it enacts the operations of memory, thus opening up a means of access to observing how and perhaps even why culture comes about" (p. xiii). Her raw material is the literary corpus of Russian modernism.

631. Marsh, Rosalind J. **History and Literature in Contemporary Russia**. xi, 289p. New York: New York University Press, 1995. Includes bibliographical references (pp. 220-75) and index.

Rosalind Marsh has chosen recent historical fiction as the focus of this study. She examines historical fiction published since 1985 but limits her study to works that fictionalize the people and events of the 20th century. Marsh discusses the first reassessments of history that appeared in 1985-1986 and the changes that came about with glasnost. She then turns to two central writers, Shatrov and Rybakov. She then reviews works on a variety of historical themes; collectivization, the Stalin terror, Lenin, the civil war, the revolution, and the late tsarist period. "The last part of the book will therefore attempt to analyze why the condition of both history and literature in Russia has changed so radically since the euphoric early days of glasnost. The conclusion will investigate the achievements and limitations of the newly published historical fiction, then focus on the difficulties and challenges still facing Russian writers and historians under Yeltsin's presidency" (p. 3).

632. Martinsen, Deborah A. **Literary Journals in Imperial Russia**. xiv, 265p. Cambridge, Eng.; New York: Cambridge University Press, 1997. Includes bibliographical references (pp. 250-57) and index.

This collection of essays on the history of Russian literary journals analyzes the major social forces and issues that shaped literary journals during the period. In addition, "detailed accounts are provided of individual journals and journalists, and descriptions are offered of the factors that contributed to their success" (frontispiece). Individual essays are grouped in four parts: 18th century, early 19th century, mid-19th century, and silver age. An excellent introductory essay sets this literary form in context.

633. Morson, Gary Saul. **Narrative and Freedom: The Shadows of Time**. xiv, 331p.: illus. New Haven, Conn.: Yale University Press, 1994. Includes bibliographical references and index.

Gary Morson examines the interaction of narrative and temporality in the works of Dostoevsky and Tolstoy, among others. Morson is a proponent of Bakhtinian analysis. "The book is divided into seven chapters, each of which alternates discussions of temporality and narrative with illustrations drawn from literary works" (p. 9). This is a complex work, but is not intended solely for the specialist in Russian literature. Morson has tried to make the Russian examples accessible to those not familiar with this literature.

634. **The Cambridge History of Russian Literature**. Edited by Charles A. Moser. Rev. ed. x, 709p. Cambridge, Eng.: Cambridge University Press, 1992. Includes bibliographical references (pp. 615-52) and index.

This revised edition of Moser's history contains 11 essays by Russian literary scholars on the following topics: the literature of old Russia, 988-1730; the 18th century; the transition to the modern age; the 19th century: romanticism; the 19th century: the natural school and its aftermath; the 19th century: the age of realism and modernism; turn of the century: modernism, 1885-1925; the 20th century: era of socialist realism, 1925-1953; the 20th century in search of new ways: 1953-1980; and Russian literature in the 1980s.

635. Peterson, Ronald E. **A History of Russian Symbolism**. xiii, 254p. *Linguistic and Literary Studies in Eastern Europe*, vol. 29. Amsterdam: John Benjamins Publishing, 1993. Includes bibliographical references and index.

Russian symbolism had its beginnings in the early 1890s with the authors Merezhkovsky, Hippius, Sologub, Balmont, Bryusov, and others. Peterson's analysis proceeds chronologically, covering the first steps of this movement, through individualism and decadence, modernism in art and literature, and symbolism as a unified movement in the 1904-1906 period. He continues to examine its proliferation, the internal polemics, mystical anarchism, the years of crisis and transition (1909-1910), and the decline and its "demise" in the revolution. A final chapter covers the symbolists' fates and their influence.

636. Platt, Kevin M. F. **History in a Grotesque Key: Russian Literature and the Idea of Revolution**. x, 293p. Stanford, Calif.: Stanford University Press, 1997. Appendixes contain poems and notes in Russian and English.

"My study begins with a simple question concerning the periods of social transformation in modern Russian history: what special possibilities for literary creation arise in such periods of rapid transition from one set of social institutions to another, from one world to another?" (p. 3). Kevin Platt examines four periods of revolutionary change: the Petrine reforms of the early 18th century; the Great Reforms of the second half of the 19th century; the postrevolutionary period of the early 20th century; and the disintegration of the Soviet government. From each period Platt selects the works of Leskov, Khvoschchinskaia, Zamiatin, Platonov, and Kibirov as demonstrative of the changes the society was experiencing. He limits himself solely to the Russian experience. He begins with a discussion of the revolutionary grotesque. Platt then turns to a chronologically arranged discussion of each of the authors. The volume includes two appendixes with translations of the anonymous 18th-century work "On the Condition of the World: To the Sun" and Kibirov's "To Serezha Gandlevsky: About Certain Aspects of the Present Sociocultural Situation."

637. Porter, Robert. **Russia's Alternative Prose**. xiii, 218p. Oxford: Berg, 1994. Includes bibliographical references (pp. 193-205) and index.

"This volume is an up-to-date, scholarly, and lucid examination of major works of some of the Russian writers who have come to prominence since 1985, when Gorbachev rose to power and effectively abolished all literary controls. . . . The author contends that 'alternative prose' in Russia deserves serious critical attention, and that in discarding the 'civic mindedness' of a former era, it is aligning itself more with Western literature and is rediscovering pre-Stalinist literary trends" (back cover). The author focuses on such writers as Aleshkovsky, Sorokin, Narbikov, Petrushevskaia, Tolstaya, Erofeev, Popov, and Limonov.

638. Rancour-Laferriere, Daniel. **The Slave Soul of Russia: Moral Masochism and the Cult of Suffering**. xii, 330p. New York: New York University Press, 1995. Includes bibliographical references and index.

Daniel Rancour-Laferriere believes there are many patterns of masochistic behavior in Russian society. "What I am proposing to do here is to construct a psychoanalytic model of the mentality behind both slavish behavior and its cultural signification in Russia" (p. 4). The book's nine chapters discuss elements of masochism in many areas of Russian life and how they have affected cultural development.

639. Shneidman, N. N. **Russian Literature, 1988-1994: The End of an Era**. xii, 245p. Toronto; Buffalo, N.Y.: University of Toronto Press, 1995. Includes bibliographical references and index.

Shneidman's purpose is "to investigate the effect of the recent changes in Eastern Europe, and, in particular, of the dissolution of the Soviet Union, on Russian literature" (p. ix). His study covers the years from 1988 to 1994 and is intended as a general introductory survey of the topic. It supplements his earlier work "Soviet Literature in the 1980s: Decade of Transition," published in 1989. Individual chapters cover politics, literature, and society; the Russian literary scene; the old guard; and the intermediate generation: the new writers of perestroika.

640. Tavis, Anna A. **Rilke's Russia: A Cultural Encounter**. xix, 195p. Evanston, Ill.: Northwestern University Press, 1994. Includes bibliographical references (pp. 181-90) and index.

Rainer Rilke's writings have been interpreted in a variety of ways. Anna Tavis views his writings as an interpretation of Russian culture. "Constructed thematically, this study draws on earlier biographical and critical material and contributes a portrait of the writer as a worthwhile interpreter of Russian culture. It reclaims the poet's approach as a valid though idiosyncratic representation of Russian life at the turn of the last century" (p. xviii). The author here examines Rilke's works in the light of other studies of his writings such as those of Patricia Brodsky and Daria Reshetylo-Rothe. The first chapter describes Rilke's "cultural marginality" in Prague. In Chapter 2 Tavis argues for the validity of a foreign cultured interpreter as opposed to the more traditional stance of the native interpreter. In Chapters 3 and 4 the author looks at Rilke's journeys to Russia and the effect on his work. Rilke's attitudes toward Russian religion and its pictorial storytelling arts are examined in Chapter 5. In Chapters 6 and 7 Rilke's attitudes toward Tolstoy are the focus. In particular, Tavis looks at the essay written by Rilke in response to Tolsoty's "What Is Art?" The final two chapters focus on the last year of Rilke's life.

641. Vishevskii, Anatolii. **Soviet Literary Culture in the 1970s: The Politics of Irony**. x, 326p.: illus. Gainesville: University Press of Florida, 1993. Includes bibliographical references (pp. 121-29) and index.

This book is part criticism and part anthology. In the first part, consisting of three chapters, Vishevskii describes and analyzes various types of irony that appeared in 1970s Soviet literature and culture. Vishevskii argues that in the 1970s Soviet intellectuals in particular were especially attuned to irony. They found it in all its force in Siberian prose and Georgian film. Chapter 1 deals with irony in Siberian short stories. Chapter 2 explores irony in Georgian cinema, the chansons, and the stand-up comedy of Mikhail Zhvanetsky. Chapter 3 is devoted to ironic prose, especially that prose that appeared in the back pages of newspapers and periodicals. Part 2 of the book is an anthology of a sample of the works described in Part 1.

642. Wachtel, Andrew. **An Obsession with History: Russian Writers Confront the Past**. xi, 276p. Stanford, Calif.: Stanford University Press, 1994. Includes bibliographical references and index.

Andrew Wachtel believes that Russians have a unique attitude toward their own history. Wachtel identifies three central features of this view. First, Russians see their historical experience as unique—absolutely different from any other people. Second, Russians believe they can overcome their history. Third is the belief that Russia will play some unique role in the history of mankind. In this book, Wachtel traces those ideas in Russia's 19th- and 20th-century literatures. He has selected Karamzin's *History of the Russian State*, works by Pushkin, Tolstoy's *War and Peace*, Dostoevsky's *Brothers Karamazov*, and Solzhenitsyn's *Red Wheel*. "My analysis of this tradition has a dual purpose: on the one hand, I think that it provides a window onto the peculiar Russian attitude toward history; on the other, I believe that it will allow us to read some major works of Russian literature in an entirely new light" (p. 7).

643. Wachtel, Michael. **Russian Symbolism and Literary Tradition: Goethe, Novalis, and the Poetics of Vyacheslav Ivanov**. xi, 247p. Madison: University of Wisconsin Press, 1994. Includes bibliographical references (pp. 231-42) and index.

"It is the thesis of this book that the Russian Symbolists' creativity was based on a type of reception diametrically opposed to that posited by (Harold) Bloom" (p. 4). Wachtel feels that the symbolist movement was in many ways retrospective in nature. He sets out to demonstrate this by examining the works of Vyacheslav Ivanov. The book is divided into two parts: "Ivanov and Goethe" and "Ivanov and Novalis."

644. Waddington, Patrick. **From the Russian Fugitive to the Ballad of Bulgarie: Episodes in English Literary Attitudes to Russian from Wordsworth to Swinburne**. 320p. *Anglo-Russian Affinities series*. Oxford: Berg, 1994.

Waddington presents the views and reactions of four English 19th-century poets, Wordsworth, Tennyson, Browning, and Swinburne, to Russia and Russian culture. Individual chapters are devoted to each author, and the analysis of each is focused on that specific author. Appendixes include Wordsworth's *The Russian Fugitive* and Browning's *Ivan Ivanovitch*.

645. Wes, Marinus Antony. **Classics in Russia 1700-1855: Between Two Bronze Horsemen**. viii, 366p. *Brill's Studies in Intellectual History*, vol. 33. Leiden, Ger.; New York: E. J. Brill, 1992. Translation of: *Tussen twee bronzen ruiters*.

In this book Marinus Wes studies the influence of Western classical literature on Russian literary development. To this point, no other scholar has attempted a systematic, historical study of this topic. Wes covers the period from 1700 to 1855. In this work he focuses on the introduction of classical studies in Russia and their profound influence on Pushkin, Gogol, Goncharov, and others.

646. Woodward, James B. **Form and Meaning: Essays on Russian Literature**. 368p. Columbus, Ohio: Slavica Publishers, 1993. Includes bibliographical references (pp. [326]-368).

These essays of Woodward are revised versions of previously published pieces that have appeared in the past 25 years in several journals. The studies themselves critique five different genres and cover 14 Russian and Soviet writers, poets, and dramatists, from Pushkin to Aitmatov. Most of the chapters are devoted to individual works.

647. Ziolkowski, Margaret. **Literary Exorcisms of Stalinism: Russian Writers and the Soviet Past**. xi, 190p. Columbia, S.C.: Camden House, 1998.

"The goal of this study is to contextualize several recurrent images that figure prominently in literature devoted to the Stalin era written, with few exceptions, since 1953 and first published either in Russia or abroad. These images by no means exhaust the repertoire of Russian writers concerned with this period, but they are among the most important and frequent. Central to the critical endeavor undertaken here is the analysis of the fictional portraiture of Stalin, which exploits a wide array of repeated motifs that underscore a generally hostile representation of the dictator" (p. x).

Anthologies

648. **Contemporary Russian Poetry: A Bilingual Anthology**. Translated by Gerald Stanton Smith. xxxiii, 353p. Bloomington: Indiana University Press, 1993. Includes bibliographical references (pp. [336]-342) and indexes.

"This anthology brings together the work of twenty-three poets writing in Russian during the 1970s and 1980s, a period that will probably prove to be no more self-contained than any other in the convoluted continuum of the history of literature" (p. xxv). So Gerald Smith begins his introduction to this bilingual anthology. The poets are arranged chronologically to give the reader an idea of the direction in which the genre developed during these years. The anthology includes works by Boris Slutsky, Vladimir Kornilov, Evgenii Rein, Dmitrii Bobyshev, Bella Akhmadulina, Lev Loseff, and Joseph Brodsky to name only a few. The "Notes on the Poets and the Poems" includes biographical sketches on each author. The compiler has also included a bibliography for further reading.

649. **The Edificatory Prose of Kievan Rus'.** Translated by William R. Veder. lvi, 202p. Cambridge, Mass.: Distributed by Harvard University Press for the Ukrainian Research Institute of Harvard University, 1994. Translated from Old Russian and other Slavic languages.

This volume contains modern English translations of the Izbornik of 1076 and the Homilies of Grigorij the Philosopher. The first is the third oldest of the dated Slavic books and is an encyclopedic handbook of theological, historical, biblical, and legal learning. The Homilies is an obscure cycle of sermons addressed to an anonymous congregation in Rus'. They were written within 14 years of one another. The texts are preceded by an informative introductory essay by William Veder.

650. Andrew, Joe. **Russian Women's Shorter Fiction: An Anthology, 1835-1860.** xvii, 469p. Oxford, Eng.: Clarendon Press; Oxford University Press, 1996. Includes bibliographical references.

These 10 translated works by six Russian women authors date from 1837 to 1858. Andrew's purpose in translating these works is to "provide the reader with an in-depth introduction to a critical period in the development of Russian women's writing" (p. vii). The six authors included here are: Elena Gan, Mariya Zhukova, Nadezhda Durova, Nadezhda Khvoschchinskaia, Avdotya Panaeva, and Nadezha Sokhanskaya.

651. **The Portable Twentieth-Century Russian Reader.** Edited by Clarence Brown. Rev. and upd. ed. xviii, 615p. London: Penguin Books, 1993. Previous ed.: 1985.

This 1993 revision of the original 1985 edition includes alterations in notes to reflect the revised circumstances that eventuated from the 1991 coup, and a new selection from the work of Mikhail Bulgakov. The selections themselves "list" toward the early and middle parts of the century and include the works of 21 authors. In addition to the general introduction by Clarence Brown, each of the author's selections is prefaced by a brief introduction that gives biographical and critical details.

652. **The Penguin Book of New Russian Writing: Russia's Fleurs Du Mal.** Edited by V. V. Erofeev and Andrew Reynolds. Translated by Victor Erofeyev. xxix, 381p. London: Penguin Books, 1995.

This anthology of contemporary Russian writers introduces the Western reader to the new Russian avant-garde. Twenty-one leading writers are included in this volume. Among them are Varlaam Shalamov, Victor Astafiev, Andrei Sinyavsky, Victor Erofeyev, Tatyana Tolstaya, and Vladimir Sorokin. A biographical section is included at the end of the volume that also includes notes for the selections used in this volume. "The new Russian literature as evidenced by this collection is characteristically raw, abrasive and skeptical, calling everything into question, including the 'Boring West' " (back cover).

653. Gessen, Masha. **Half a Revolution: Contemporary Fiction by Russian Women**. 1st ed. 269p.: illus. Pittsburgh, Pa.: Cleis Press, 1995.

This anthology of recent fiction by Russian women contains the novellas and short stories of nine authors. These authors emerged after changes began to develop in Russia in the mid-1980s. Each selection contains a brief introduction by the editor. The volume contains the works of Nina Gorlanova, Galina Volodina, Irina Polyanskaya, and other contemporary authors.

654. Hollingsworth, Paul. **The Hagiography of Kievan Rus'**. xcv, 267p.: map. *English Translations*, 2. Boston: Distributed by Harvard University Press for the Ukrainian Research Institute of Harvard University, 1992. Includes bibliographical references (pp. [233]-248) and indexes.

This volume includes translations into English of six principal hagiographic works written in Russia prior to 1240, the advent of the Mongolian period. They are not only important in their role in the development of early Slavic literature, but they are also essential for studying the formation of Christian culture in the Russian medieval period. Included here are "Lesson Concerning the Life and Murder of the Blessed Passionate-Sufferers Boris and Gleb"; "Life of Feodosij"; "Tale and Passion and Encomium of the Holy Martyrs Boris and Gleb"; "Tale of the Miracles of the Holy Passion-Sufferers of Christ Roman and David"; "Life of Avraamij of Smolensk"; "Memorial and Encomium for Prince Volodimir of Rus'." The editor/translator has also provided an excellent introductory essay and other critical apparatus.

655. **Conscience Deluded: Stories by Russian Women**. Edited by Ayesha Kagal and Natasha Perova. xviii, 247p. Kali International Fiction. New Delhi: Kali for Women, 1994. Translated from Russian.

This is a collection of short stories by Russian women from the postperestroika era. The stories range in their themes from the coming of age of a young Jewish girl in Russia, to the hospital conditions faced by Russian women. "Men are missing in many of these stories. They are longed for, sought after, dreamt about, but remain elusive . . ." (p. xviii). The 10 authors in this book vary in style and use a variety of literary devices. The authors represented here are: Nina Iskrenko, Ludmilla Ulitskaya, Galina Scherbakova, Irina Polyanskaya, Nina Sadur, Marina Palei, Svetlana Vasilenko, Yekaterina Sadur, Ksenia Klimova, and Lydia Ginsburg.

656. **Present Imperfect: Stories by Russian Women**. Edited by Ayesha Kagal and Natasha Perova. v, 202p. Boulder, Colo.: Westview Press, 1996. Originally published as: *Conscience Deluded*. New Delhi: Kali for Women, 1994.

This collection includes the writings of Ulitskaya, Vasilenko, Ginsburg, Scherbakova, Nina Sadur, Klimova, Palei, and Yekaterina Sadur. "While many of these writers share a feminist outlook, their perspectives are vastly disparate and often steeped in a peculiarly post-Soviet irony. . . . Yet, common to all are recurrent and interwoven motifs of self-discovery, sexual power, emotional attachment, social alienation, and vulnerability to uncontrollable forces" (p. 202). Western edition of *Conscience Deluded*.

657. Kelly, Catriona. **An Anthology of Russian Women's Writing, 1777-1992**. xxv, 535p. Oxford; New York: Oxford University Press, 1994. Poetry, prose, and drama is in the original Russian and an English translation.

There have been a number of anthologies of Russian women's writing in recent years. "Read from the beginning, the anthology provides a brief history of Russian women's writing, both in its discontinuities and in its continuities" (p. xiv). The editor had as her goal to have the works in this volume elucidate the history of women's writing, and she selected works for inclusion largely on this basis. Kelly used a strict definition of literary text in selection, excluding film scripts, domestic manuals, writing for children, letters, etc. The works are arranged in chronological order. The principles guiding translations for the volumes were that the translations were intended as equivalents. Brief biographical sketches on the authors precede each translation. The notes assist the reader with unfamiliar concepts.

658. **Women's View**. Edited by Natasha Perova and Andrew Bromfield. 238p.: illus., ports. Moscow: Glas, 1992. Spine title: *New Russian Writing*.

Prior to the fall of the Soviet Union there was no women's "movement" and only one official organization for women. Since 1991, however, a genuine women's movement and women's literature have developed. This anthology presents a good cross section of the types of writing that reflect Russian women's views of the world and their search for identity in the new Russia.

659. Popkin, Cathy. **The Pragmatics of Insignificance: Chekhov, Zoshchenko, Gogol**. viii, 289p.: illus. Stanford, Calif.: Stanford University Press, 1993. Includes bibliographical references (pp. [259]-275) and index.

What merit is there in telling a tale whose focus is the most insignificant of daily events? How "tellable" is such a story? In her examination of the works of Chekhov, Zoshchenko, and Gogol, Cathy Popkin sets out to examine these and other issues. In her chapters on Chekhov and Zoshchenko, which begin the book, the author examines "ways in which incidents normally considered small and unimportant can be interpreted as events of enormous significance . . ." (p. 11). In the remaining chapters, Gogol's style is examined. "As I consider the types of 'irrelevancies' Gogol looses on his reader . . . , I will be concerned principally with the function of this stylistic excess in the context of the narrative transaction, performing not a stylistic analysis, but rather asking what this persistent characteristic . . . does to the text and its reception" (p. 14).

660. Popov, Evgeny. **Merry-Making in Old Russia**. Translated by Robert Porterviii. 218p. *Writings from an Unbound Europe*. Evanston, Ill.: Northwestern University Press, 1997. Includes translators notes: "Most of these stories were first published as *Zhdu liubvi ne verolomnoi* by Sovetskii pisatel' in 1989."

A set of short stories by Siberian author Evgeny Popov is collected in this volume. All the stories were written and are set in the Soviet period. Most were unpublished until after the fall of the Soviet Union. "The language of Popov's fiction combines Soviet cliché with time-honored Russian vernacular. Yet the pathos and parody thus engendered run much deeper than political satire; the author is as likely to poke fun at the Russian classics as at the Five-Year Plan" (p. viii).

661.   Rzhevsky, Nicholas. **An Anthology of Russian Literature from Earliest Writings to Modern Fiction: Introduction to a Culture**. xiv, 587p. Armonk, N.Y.: M. E. Sharpe, 1996. Includes bibliographical references (pp. 581-87).

This anthology is intended for use in an undergraduate course dealing with Russian culture. Although all the selections are literary, what follows each section is a guide to how that selection was transformed into other cultural artifacts, film, art, music, opera, etc. The 39 selections are subdivided into six sections: cultural beginnings, the emerging self, the search for identity, the subversions of secularization, new aesthetic languages, and thresholds—Soviet culture and beyond. In addition, following each section is a selected bibliography of primary and secondary sources specific to the work in question.

662.   Segel, Harold B. **Twentieth-Century Russian Drama: From Gorky to the Present**. Updated ed. xvi, 527p.: illus. PAJ Books. Baltimore: Johns Hopkins University Press, 1993. Includes bibliographical references (pp. [507]-514) and index.

The 20th century was a rich period in the history of Russian drama and has long awaited a wide-ranging study. Harold Segel has compiled an overview of the drama of this period. His view of this literature is one of literature written for the theater. His focus is on the drama as literature and only touches on production when directly relevant. Segel covers the drama after Chekhov, beginning with Gorky. This volume was originally published in 1979. This updated edition takes the reader up through 1989. The book is arranged chronologically. It includes an appendix listing translations into English of Russian dramas.

Critical Studies

663.   Aiken, Susan Hardy, et al. **Dialogues = Dialogi: Literary and Cultural Exchanges Between (Ex) Soviet and American Women**. xviii, 415p.: illus. Durham, N.C.: Duke University Press, 1994. Includes bibliographical references (pp. [393]-407) and index.

Many works seek to make explicit the changes in Russian society that have since led to the fall of the Soviet regime. This volume attempts to expose some of these societal changes by comparing the literary works of Russian and American women writers. The book is divided into four sections, each of which compares the portrayal of a particular theme in a short story. The first section compares the works of two established writers of an older generation. Next, the editors have chosen two works that explore the question of sexuality in each society. Section 3 contains two stories dealing with the lives of marginalized groups in both countries. The final section has essays written by representatives of indigenous peoples of the two countries. The editors have selected I. Grekova and Tillie Olsen, Ludmilla Petrushevskaia and Toni Caoe Bambara, Elena Makarova and Jayne Anne. Along with the short stories in each section are essays by the co-authors on the theme of that section. This is followed by the transcribed discussion between the co-authors.

664. **Freedom and Responsibility in Russian Literature: Essays in Honor of Robert Louis Jackson**. Edited by Elizabeth Cheresh Allen and Gary Saul Moroson. x, 306p. *Studies in Russian Literature and Theory, Yale Russian and East European Publications*, no. 12. Evanston, Ill.: Northwestern University Press, 1995. Includes footnotes and list of contributors.

This collection of literary criticism has been published in honor of Robert Jackson. Jackson is, perhaps, best known for his work on Dostoevsky. There are several scholars who have contributed essays on Dostoevsky to this volume, but it is not limited to criticism of this author. There are also essays on Zhukovskii, Baratynskii, Turgenev, Tolstoy, Chekhov, Solovev, Gorky, Pasternak, Tsvetaeva, and Nabokov. The essays are arranged chronologically. They all somehow reflect the themes of freedom and responsibility. "Whatever their specific topic, these essays each manifest a determination to exercise the critical independence and integrity exemplified by Robert's work" (p. 5).

665. **Russian Narrative and Visual Art: Varieties of Seeing**. Edited by Roger B. Anderson and Paul Debreczeny. viii, 211p.: illus. Gainesville: University Press of Florida, 1994. Includes bibliographical references and index.

"All the essays included in the present volume deal with interplay between verbal and visual art forms, revealing the internal tensions within the cultural matrix of different periods" (p. 6). There is no attempt here to cover this topic in a comprehensive way. The goal was, rather, to focus on systems of symbols in various areas of Russian culture that will only emerge if both the literary and artistic realms are explored. The essays discuss subjects as varied as the roles of romantic landscape, the country house in art and literature, and modernist poetics. There are discussions of the works of Gogol, Dostoevsky, Chekhov, Serov, Tsvetaeva, Filonov, Kollwitz, and Bulgakov. The contributors are James West, Priscilla Reynolds Roosevelt, Gary Cox, Roger Anderson, Paul Debreczeny, Allison Hilton, Antonia Filonov Gove, and Juliette R. Stapanian-Apkarian.

666. Andrew, Joe. **Narrative and Desire in Russian Literature, 1822-49: The Feminine and the Masculine**. vii, 257p. New York: St. Martin's Press, 1993. Includes bibliographical references (pp. 251-54) and index.

This work is, in some sense, a sequel to an earlier work of Andrew's: *Women in Russian Literature, 1780-1863*, but narrower in chronological scope (1822-1849). The texts he examines are, for the most part, those that lie outside the traditional canon. Throughout Andrew deals with setting, plot, and character to explore conceptions of gender and genre in early-19th-century Russian literature.

667. Beaudoin, Luc J. **Resetting the Margins: Russian Romantic Verse Tales and the Idealized Woman**. xii, 248p.: illus. *Berkeley Insights in Linguistics and Semiotics*. New York: P. Lang, 1997. Includes bibliographical references (pp. [219]-242) and index.

The author examines the Romantic verse tale, focusing on Baratynsky and Pushkin, in order to investigate "the question of Romantic philosophy in its linguistic and gender manifestations" (p. xi). Works analyzed include Baratynsky's *Eda*, *The Ball*, and *The Gypsy Girl* and Pushkin's *Eugene Onegin*.

668. Bitov, Andrei. **A Captive of the Caucasus**. 323p. New York: Farrar, Straus & Giroux, 1992.

Much of Andrei Bitov's writing was censored in the Soviet Union. This translation presents two of his works that have previously only appeared in a less than complete form. This volume includes "Lessons of Armenia" and "Choosing a Location." Bitov's style of writing lends itself well to publications of works in tandem, as his writings normally not only proceed from one another but comment on each other. In the first work, Bitov describes his journey in America and his feelings of alienation from his homeland, Russia. Then second story "is an intellectually spirited inquiry into the persistent idea of homeland and the individual's identity, cultural and creative" (book jacket). This book is translated by Susan Brownsberger.

669. Booker, M. Keith, and Dubravka Juraga. **Bakhtin, Stalin, and Modern Russian Fiction: Carnival, Dialogism, and History**. xiv, 181p. Westport, Conn.: Greenwood Press, 1995. Includes bibliographical references (pp. [167]-176) and index.

There have been many studies on the writings of Bakhtin in recent years, such as the works by Katerina Clark, Michael Holquist, Gary Morson, and Carle Emerson. Booker and Juraga are not attempting a definitive study of Bakhtin's writings. Rather, they present a survey of his work and career. They believe this "complex body of work is informed by a number of key concepts, including carnival, dialogism, and historicism" (p. xiii). The early chapters of this book serve as an introduction to these concepts. In the second chapter, the writings of Aksyonov are used to illustrate many of the comments made by Bakhtin on Russian literature. The works of other Russian writers are given a "Bakhtinian" reading in the remaining chapters. These include Ilf and Petrov, Zoshlhenko, Aleskovsky, and Bitov. "Together, the readings in this study are intended to provide a useful illumination of the attempts of Bakhtin—and modern Russian writers of fiction—to cope with the difficulties of modern Russian history and to maintain a sense of Russian cultural tradition amid the many events that have distributed that tradition in this century" (p. xiv).

670. Booker, M. Keith. **Joyce, Bakhtin, and the Literary Tradition: Toward a Comparative Cultural Poetics**. 273p. Ann Arbor: University of Michigan Press, 1995. Includes endnotes, bibliographic references, and index.

This work is an explanation of comparative cultural poetics. Using the literary critic Mikhail Bakhtin as a theoretical resource, it presents an "intertextual dialogue" between Joyce and specific literary predecessors: Homer, Rabelais, Dante, Goethe, Shakespeare, and Dostoevsky. Many issues raised by the author have a direct relation to contemporary critical debates over the nature of modern literary history.

671. Brandist, Craig. **Carnival Culture and the Soviet Modernist Novel**. xi, 264p. New York: St. Martin's Press, 1996. "In association with St. Antony's College, Oxford."

Brandist examines "the relationship between Russian, and later Soviet, popular holiday culture and the novel in the period from the late 1920s to the Second World War" (p. vii) and describes "the influence of institutional framework, relations of power and class-based social and cultural practices on the artistic production of certain Soviet writers" (p. vii). Among the authors analyzed are Blok, Bely, Olesha, Platonov, Kharms, Bulgakov, and Vaginov. His analysis is divided into two parts: (1) Carnival and the Russian Literary Intelligentsia and (2) Carnival and the Soviet Modernist Novel.

672. Clowes, Edith W. **Russian Experimental Fiction: Resisting Ideology After Utopia**. xvi, 236p. Princeton, N.J.: Princeton University Press, 1993. Includes bibliographical references (pp. 223-31) and index.

As Clowes states in her introduction, "This book explores the challenge that literary play poses to ideological fixation" (p. ix). The study is in three parts. In Part 1 she explores the clash between experimental fiction and ideological fixation. Part 2 looks at various aspects of the meta-utopian experiment in fiction, and in Part 3 Clowes analyzes specific works in depth. A concluding chapter places Russian meta-utopian fiction in a European context.

673. Cornwell, Neil. **James Joyce and the Russians**. xiii, 175p. London: Macmillan, 1992. Includes endnotes, bibliographic references, and index.

This study intends to extend the awareness of Joyce's allusions to Russia and Russian writing and to describe his relationship with three Russian cultural figures who were his contemporaries: Andrei Bely, Vladimir Nabolkov, and Sergei Eisenstein. A final section considers Russian and Soviet responses to Joyce.

674. **Literature, Lives, and Legality in Catherine's Russia**. Edited by Anthony Cross and G. S. Smith. viii, 174p. Cotgrave, Eng.: Astra, 1994.

The papers published in this volume represent approximately one-third of those presented at the fourth meeting of the Study Group on Eighteenth-Century Russia held in 1989. The collection includes three lectures, a complete panel (on Shcherbatov), three of the papers on the French Revolution, and single papers from other historical and literary panels.

675. de Scherbinin, Julie W. **Chekhov and Russian Religious Culture: The Poetics of the Marian Paradigm**. xiii, 189p.: illus. Studies in Russian Literature and Theory. Evanston, Ill.: Northwestern University Press, 1997. Includes bibliographical references (pp. 153-84).

In Russian Orthodoxy two images of womanhood are often held up as central to the view of female identity, the Virgin Mary and Mary Magdalene. "I argue in this book that Chekhov fully grasped the authority that the Christian paradigm of the two Marys wielded in Russian culture" (p. 2). De Scherbinin follows Chehkov's use of this imagery as it develops in his work. She begins with background information on the use of the "Marian imagery" by other authors prior to Chekhov. She then focuses on the development of this imagery in Chehkov's early work. The last four chapters consider this device in specific works by Chekhov including "Peasant Woman: The Teacher of Literature" and "My Life." A brief appendix lists the Russian titles of the works by Chekhov consulted for this study.

676. Eidelman, Dawn D. **George Sand and the Nineteenth-Century Russian Love-Triangle Novels**. 175p. Lewisburg, Pa.; London; Cranbury, N.J.: Bucknell University Press, Associated University Presses, 1994. Includes bibliographical references (pp. 157-70) and index.

Eidelman explores the borrowings by Russian authors of the love triangle theme from three of George Sand's works: *Jacques* (1834), *Mauprat* (1837), and *Horace* (1842). After two introductory chapters on the erotics of reading, and women and fiction, she analyzes the love triangle theme that arises in each of the aforementioned novels and are manifest in selected Russian fiction of the 19th century.

677. **World Congress for Soviet and East European Studies**. Edited by J. D. Elsworth. xiii, 200p. New York: St. Martin's Press, 1992. "Published in association with the International Council for Soviet and East European Studies"—Verso t.p. Includes bibliographical references and index.

The papers contained in this volume were first presented at the Fourth World Congress for Soviet and East European Studies in 1990. Authors covered are Konevskoi, Voloshin, Viacheslav Ivanov, Livshits, Gorky, Sologub, Belyi, and Zamyatin.

678. **The Silver Age in Russian Literature: Selected Papers from the Fourth World Congress for Soviet and East European Studies, Harrogate, 1990**. Edited by John Elsworth. xiii, 200p. New York: St. Martin's Press, 1992. Includes index.

This volume contains a selection of papers from the Fourth World Congress for Soviet and East European Studies. Contributors include: Joan Grossman, Vladimir Kupchenko, Natalie Roklina, Vera Dadmantova, Denis Mickievicz, Ronald Vroon, Andrew Barratt, Milton Ehre, Lena Szilard, Robert Maguire, and John Malmstad. Six of the essays are devoted to poets and to prose writers. The poets are presented first. Some writers who have previously received little critical attention are discussed here, such as Ivan Konevskoi.

There are also essays on Voloshin, Viacheslav Ivanov, Livshits, Gorky, Sologub, Belyi, and Zamyatin.

679. Erlich, Victor. **Modernism and Revolution: Russian Literature in Transition**. 314p. Cambridge, Mass.: Harvard University Press, 1994. Includes bibliographical references (pp. [281]-304) and index.

Erlich examines the major Russian literary texts of the period from the revolution until 1930 in order to see what light they shed on "two seemingly incompatible perspectives" (p. 13). One perspective is that the 1920s in Russian literature and art was one of "diversity and vitality, of excitement and experimentation" (p. 12). This is the traditional view. The other perspective was voiced eloquently by Nadezhda Mandelstam in her memoir *Hope Against Hope*. In contrasting this traditional view she says: "But in reality it was the twenties in which all the foundations were laid for our future—the casuistical dialectics, the dismissal of old values, the longing for unanimity and self-abasement" (quoted by Erlich, p. 12). His well-reasoned and careful exposition of this tension is the subject of this work.

680. Freidenberg, O. M. **Image and Concept: Mythopoetic Roots of Literature**. xvi, 492p. *Sign/Text/Culture: Studies in Slavic and Comparative Semiotics*, 2. Amsterdam: Harwood Academic, 1997. Includes bibliographical references.

This posthumous translation of Freidenberg's work is an experiment in historical aesthetics. Her main thesis is that: "the appearance of ancient poetic categories originates in the appearance of concepts, since the ancient concept is only a form of the image; and in this form of the image the concept has the function of 'transferal' [perenesenie], translation of concrete meanings of the image into abstract meanings, 'transferring' [perenosnye: figural, metaphorical] meanings, which gives rise to metaphors and poetic figurality" (p. 29). The focus of the criticism is on Greek tragedy, but the criticism is by Boris Pasternak's cousin, correspondent, and confidante. After publishing her first major work in 1936 the author was silenced when her book was confiscated prior to publication.

681. Fusso, Susanne. **Designing Dead Souls: An Anatomy of Disorder in Gogol**. 195p. Stanford, Calif.: Stanford University Press, 1993. Some passages in Russian and some in transliterated Russian.

Using an analysis of the structure of Gogol's nonfiction writings, Susanne Fusso attempts an explanation of his most famous piece of fiction, *Dead Souls*. "For the purposes of this study, Gogol's historiographical principles are of interest not as ways of modeling history but as formal structures that are related to analogous structures in his literary works." Fusso concentrates on an analysis of Gogol's *Arabesque* for comparative purposes. The book is topically arranged.

682. Gardiner, Michael. **The Dialogics of Critique: M. M. Bakhtin and the Theory of Ideology**. 258p. London: Routledge, 1992. Includes bibliographical references.

Instead of concentrating on Bakhtin as a literary theorist as most writers on Bakhtin tend to do, Gardiner sees him as a social thinker. "Gardiner introduces Bakhtin's core concepts dialogism, polyphony, carnival through an examination of the Bakhtin Circle's major writings. He scrutinizes Bakhtin's insights into the nature of the text, showing how they engage with Marxist theories of ideology, the hermeneutic tradition as represented by Gadamer, Habermas, and Ricoeur, and the poststructuralism of Barthes and Foucault. The book concludes with a critical assessment of Bakhtin's contribution to ideological and cultural criticism and an appraisal of his legacy for the purposes of Ideologiekritik" (frontispiece).

683. **Cultural Mythologies of Russian Modernism: From the Golden Age to the Silver Age**. Edited by B. Gasparov, Robert P. Hughes, and Irina Paperno. 494p. *California Slavic Studies*, 15. Berkeley: University of California Press, 1992. English and Russian.

The papers in this volume were originally delivered at a conference at the University of California at Berkeley in May 1987. The papers are organized here into three sections: "Cultural Myth of Pushkin"; "Pushkin As an Institution"; and "Pushkin in the Twentieth Century: Readings, Texts and Subtexts." Contributions are in English and Russian.

684. Gillespie, David C. **Iurii Trifonov: Unity Through Time**. x, 248p. Cambridge, Eng.; New York: Cambridge University Press, 1992. Based on work done for author's doctoral thesis in 1984-1985.

The work of Iurii Trifonov changed dramatically during his career. "This study, however, takes as its starting point Trifonov's interest in history and the passage of time, and attempts to show how this interest informs all his writing from his earliest, Stalin Prize-winning period to the self-consciously modernist later works" (frontispiece). Gillespie's study follows Trifonov's development chronologically. The book includes an extensive bibliography that lists Trifonov's major publications and minor writings, the latter often published in obscure journals.

685. **Russian Subjects: Empire, Nation, and the Culture of the Golden Age**. Edited by Monika Greenleaf and Stephen Moeller-Sally. xiii, 449p. *Studies in Russian Literature and Theory*. Evanston, Ill.: Northwestern University Press, 1998. Includes index.

This is a collection of essays by some of the foremost scholars in the field of Russian literary criticism. Studies by Harsha Ram, Monika Greenleaf, Ronald LeBlanc, Judith Kornblatt, Sally Kux, Stephen Baehr, and Melissa Frazier cover a range of subjects. The volume is divided into three parts, "Translatio Poetae: Poetics of Empire"; "Alternative Histories"; and "Encroaching Modernity: The Public and the Subject." *Russian Subjects* extends the borders of its purview back to the reign of Catherine the Great, when the myth of an internationalist, grandly imperial Golden Age and the institutions necessary to foster it were first established; and forward to the first two decades of Nicholas I's reign, when a jostling assortment of writers and a burgeoning public press would rush to embody the new rallying cry of nation, originality, popular voice, and the changing configurations of Russian "subjectivity."

686.   Heier, Edmund. **Literary Portraiture in Nineteenth-Century Russian Prose**. 331p. Köln, Ger.: Böhlau Verlag, 1993. Includes bibliographical references (pp. [315]-327) and index.

This book is concerned with direct literary portraiture, "which is a verbal portrait consisting of a direct description of the physical appearance of a character" (p. 3). After discussing the features of direct literary portraiture, as well as the theories of physiognomist Johan Caspar Lauater, Heier examines portraiture in the works of Pushkin, Lermontov, Turgenev, Goncharov, Dostoevsky, and Tolstoy.

687.   Hoisington, Sona Stephan. **A Plot of Her Own: The Female Protagonist in Russian Literature**. x, 164p. Evanston, Ill.: Northwestern University Press, 1995. Includes bibliographical references (pp. 129-64).

This collection of essays takes a "revisionist" approach to the study of the female protagonist in Russian literature. ". . . it takes issue with the old 'unconscious' assumption of critics, male and female alike, that women characters in fiction (even if idealized) are marginal . . ." (p. 1). These studies discuss Pushkin, Dostoevsky, Tolstoy, and Bulgakov. Contributors include Elizabeth Klosty Beaujour, Jane T. Coslow, Thea Margret Durfee, Caryl Emerson, Helena Goscilo, Sona Stephan Hoisington, Amy Mandekler, Gary Saul Morson, Harriet Mureau, and Gary Rosenshield.

688.   **Out Visiting and Back Home: Russian Stories on Aging**. Edited and translated by Thomas H. Hoisington. xiv, 230p. Evanston, Ill.: Northwestern University Press/Hydra Books, 1998.

"All in, *Out Visiting and Back Home* is designed to acquaint English-speaking readers with the best in contemporary Russian short fiction and to give them varied insight into the aging process not as an abstraction belonging to gerontologists, but as a complex of mental and physical changes all of us defect in ourselves as we inevitably mature and grow older" (p. xiv). This anthology includes works by Denis Dragunsky, Friedrich Gordenstein, Nina Katerli, Vasily Belov, Vasily Shukshin, Vladimir Makanin, Ludmila Petrushevskwya, Tatyana Tolstaya, Anatoly Kim, and Ludmila Ulitskaya.

689.   Holmgren, Beth. **Women's Works in Stalin's Time: On Lidiia Chukovskaia and Nadezhda Mandelstam**. x, 225p.: illus. Bloomington: Indiana University Press, 1993. Includes bibliographical references (pp. [213]-221) and index.

This work is intended to describe and evaluate two important writers and their texts. Both Lidiia Chukovskaia and Nadezhda Mandelstam were impressive both for their writing and their cultural activism. Holmgren evaluates their work, both literary and activist-cultural in the context of Stalin's rigid sociocultural policies. A concluding chapter explains what these women meant for both women writers and women activists in the post-Stalin era.

690. Hutchings, Stephen C. **Russian Modernism: The Transfiguration of the Everyday**. xiii, 295p. *Cambridge Studies in Russian Literature*. New York: Cambridge University Press, 1997. Includes bibliographical references (pp. 278-88) and index.

In this study of Silver Age narrative, Stephen Hutchings examines the Russian idea of "byt" or everyday life. "Drawing on semiotics and theology, Stephen C. Hutchings argues that byt emerged from a dialogue between two traditions, one reflected in western representational aesthetics for which daily existence figures as natural and normative, the other encapsulated in the Orthodox emphasis on ionic embodiment" (frontispiece). Hutchings sets himself three goals: (1) To demonstrate that "byt" as a "culturally significant category" (p. 7) arises in the Silver Age. (2) To identify Russia's contribution to European modernism (p. 7). (3) Finally, to explore the link between Silver Age literature and 19th-century Russian realism. To accomplish this the author will examine the works of Chekhov, Sologub, Belyi, Rozanov, and Remizov. He moves from a general discussion of the concept of everyday life in European literature to its particular manifestation in Russian literature. He then narrows his study to an examination of special literary works ending with a characterization of the Russian revolutionary era as it manifested itself in politics and aesthetics.

691. Isenberg, Charles. **Telling Silence: Russian Frame Narratives of Renunciation**. viii, 179p. Evanston, Ill.: Northwestern University Press, 1993. Includes bibliographical references (pp. 147-74) and index.

This book contains studies of frame narratives in works by four Russian authors: Turgenev, Dostoevsky, Tolstoy, and Chekhov. Isenberg attempts to "discover the qualities of the frame narrative of renunciation" (p. vii) through close readings of these works. An introductory chapter explores various aspects of frame narratives and its relationships to genre issues. A concluding chapter "reframes" the subject of frame narratives through a reading of Vladimir Makanin's 1976 story, "Story About a Story."

692. Kelly, Catriona. **A History of Russian Women's Writing, 1820-1992**. xii, 497p. Oxford, Eng.: Clarendon Press, 1994. Includes bibliographical references (pp. [447]-483) and indexes.

This is the first single volume of Russian women's writing to be published. "Written from a bold feminist perspective, the book combines a broad historical survey with close textual analysis. Sections on women's writing in the periods 1820-1880, 1881-1917, 1917-1954, 1953-1992 are followed by essays on individual writers" (back cover). There are sections on Mariya Zhukova, Karolina Pavlova, Elena Gan, Olga Shapir, Nadezhda Teffi, Anna Akhmatova, Sofiya Parnok, Marina Tsvetava, Vera Bulich, Natalya Baranskya, Elena Shavarts, Olga Sedakova, and Nina Sadur. The bibliography is divided into sections on bibliographies and reference sources on women writers, publications by

Russian women writers, and woman's history in Russia, providing the reader with a wealth of resources.

693. **Socialist Realism Revisited: Selected Papers from the McMaster Conference**. Edited by Nina Kolesnikov and Walter Smyrniw. 139p. Hamilton, Ont.: McMaster University, 1994. Includes index.

The nine papers collected in this volume are a representation of the more than 30 that were originally presented at a conference at McMaster University in 1993. Five of the papers are on general topics related to socialist realism—e.g., utopianism, linguistic relativism, and the language of ideologies; the other four are more specific and concern the drama of Czech socialist realism, genre, novelistic portraits of Stalin, and socialist realism in Polish literature.

694. Kornblatt, Judith Deutsch. **The Cossack Hero in Russian Literature**. xiii, 229p. Studies of the Harriman Institute. Madison: University of Wisconsin Press, 1992. Includes endnotes, selected bibliography, and index.

Kornblatt's book consists of 12 chapters in two parts. Part 1 focuses on the 19th century and Part 2 on the 20th. She analyzes "the development of the Cossack myth, and the dynamic relationship of that myth to changing reality in nineteenth- and twentieth-century Russia" (p. x). Pushkin, Gogol, Babel, Sholokhov, and Nabokov are among the authors examined.

695. Kujundzic, Dragan. **The Returns of History: Russian Nietzscheans After Modernity**. xii, 219p. Albany: State University of New York Press, 1997. Includes bibliographical references (pp. 205-14) and index.

Dragan Kujundzic applies the traditions of Russian Nietzscheanism to his readings of Mikhail Bakhtin and Yuri Tynianov. The result is an unusual look at Russian formalist writing. He tries to show, as the subtitle suggests, that these writers were "striving after modernity" and at the same time were a product of that modernity they sought. The author has divided the volume into six sections beginning with a general discussion about Nietzsche and Russian formalism. This is followed by specific discussions of parody, temporality, genre, history, and Stalinism.

696. Laird, Sally. **Voices of Russian Literature**. xxviii, 231p.: ports. Oxford, Eng.: Oxford University Press, 1999. Includes bibliographical references (pp. [213]-225) and index.

Sally Laird has interviewed 10 of Russia's most important contemporary literary figures for this volume. "They range from Fazil Iskandev, who began his career in the 1950s, to Vikto Pelevin, who published his first work when the Soviet Union was on the brink of collapse. Together, they offer an insider's account of the fate of Russian literature over the last four decades, from the post-Stalin Thaw, through the repression of the Brezhnev years, to the heady revival of literature under glasnost and the radical recasting of the writer's role in the post-communist marketplace" (p. xiii). Each interview begins with a bio-bibliographical sketch. The volume includes a chronology of major events in Soviet literary history and a bibliography of works by each of the authors interviewed.

697.   Layton, Susan. **Russian Literature and Empire: Conquest of the Caucasus from Pushkin to Tolstoy**. xi, 354p.: maps. Cambridge, Eng.; New York: Cambridge University Press, 1994. Includes bibliographical references (pp. 339-47) and index.

This is a study of the role the Caucasus has played in Russian writing. It is a literary study rooted in historical context. Susan Layton explores not only the attitudes of the authors for whom the Caucasus became a literary vehicle, she also analyzes changing reader response as well. "While showing how literature often underwrote imperialism, the book carefully explores the tensions between the Russian state's ideology of a European mission to civilize the Muslim mountain peoples, and romantic perceptions of those tribes as noble primitives whose extermination was no cause for celebration" (frontispiece). Layton follows the changing perceptions and attitudes through their literary portrayal beginning with Pushkin and continuing through Tolstoy. In her conclusion, the author looks to Russian literature's changing view of Asia in the 20th century.

698.   Leighton, Lauren G. **The Esoteric Tradition in Russian Romantic Literature: Decembrism and Freemasonry**. viii, 224p. University Park: Pennsylvania State University Press, 1994. Includes bibliographical references and index.

Lauren Leighton examines what she calls "thaumaturgy" or the performance of wonders that defines the relationship between literature and esotericism. "In this study of the application of thaumaturgy to the creation of literary texts I attempt to discover the role of the esoteric tradition in Russian romantic literature" (p. 2). Leighton focuses on the works of Bestuzhev, Pushkin, Rayevsky, Ryleyev, and Zhukovsky among other authors of the time.

699.   Levin, Iuri D. **The Perception of English Literature in Russia: Investigations and Materials**. Translated by Catherine Phillips. xi, 258p. Nottingham, Eng.: Astra, 1994. Includes index.

This is a translation of Iuri Levin's study of the influence of English literature on Russian culture and society. Levin focuses on, but is not limited to, the influence of Swift and Shakespeare. The book is divided into two parts. The first section contains three essays on the enlightenment. Here he discusses English periodicals in Russian literature, Jonathan Swift, and the influence of English poetry on Russian sentimentalism. Section 2 looks carefully at Shakespeare in Russian literature.

700. **Readings in Russian Modernism: To Honor Vladimir Fedorovich Markov**. Edited by Vladimir Markov, Ronald Vroon, and John E. Malmstad. 405p.: illus. Moscow: Nauka, 1993. Title on added t.p.: *Kul'tura russkogo modernisma*. English and Russian.

This volume is a collection of essays in honor of the 73rd birthday of Vladimir Markov. Markov is considered to be the foremost expert on Russian modernism. This volume collects writings by many of his students and colleagues. These include: Henryk Baran, Henrik Birnbaum, N. A. Bogomolov, Diana Lewis Burgin, George Cheron, Thomas Eekman, E. G. Etkind, Aleksandar Flaker, Lazar Fleishman, B. M. Gasparov, Aage A. Hansen-Löve, Vyach Ivanov, Simon Karlinsky, Emily Klenin, Anna Lawton, Barbra Lönnquist, John E. Malmstad, Jean-Claude Marcade, Olga Matich, Nils Åke Nilsson, Katherine Tierman O'Connor, Rodney Patterson, K. Ju. Postoutenko, Omry Ronen, M. I. Shapir, Rochelle Stone, K. F. Taranovsky, Roman Timenchik, Ronald Vroon, Willem G. Weststeijn, Dean S. Worth, and Alexander Zholkovsky.

701. Marsh, Rosalind J. **Gender and Russian Literature: New Perspectives**. xvi, 353p. Cambridge, Eng.; New York: Cambridge University Press, 1996. Includes bibliographical references and index.

"This collection of original essays by leading western and Russian specialists gives an overview of key issues in Russian women's writing and of important representations of women by men, between 1600 and the present. This volume contributes to the contemporary feminist project of rediscovering many hitherto unjustly neglected Russian women writers and sheds further light on the literary construction of women's identity by Russian men. It combines a study of the history and biography of women writers with close readings of literary texts, and explores certain controversial issues in Russian women's literary studies . . ." (frontispiece).

702. Masing-Delic, I. Irene. **Abolishing Death: A Salvation Myth of Russian Twentieth-Century Literature**. viii, 363p. Stanford, Calif.: Stanford University Press, 1992. Includes bibliographical references and index.

In this study Irene Masing-Delic examines the literature of turn-of-the-century Russia to the 1930s. Her examination will include the works of Maksim Gorky, Fyodor Sologub, Aleksandr Blok, Nikolai Ognyov, and Nikolai Zabolotsky. "My goal is to examine the entire structure of a literary myth in twentieth-century pre-and post-revolutionary Russian literature positing earthly immortality and also to elucidate its formation by looking at its religious, philosophical, and ideological sources" (p. 2). The author begins by examining the myth itself and then turns to a consideration of each author's works.

703. May, Rachel. **The Translator in the Text: On Reading Russian Literature in English**. xii, 209p. Studies in Russian Literature and Theory. Evanston, Ill.: Northwestern University Press, 1994. English and Russian. Includes bibliographical references (pp. 187-203) and index.

There are many schools of literary criticism, many approaches to the study of the novel. In this book, Rachel May looks at the interplay between the text of the novel and the changes necessarily imposed on that text in the process of translation. "In keeping with its project of crossing and exploring boundary lines within and around texts, this book addresses several traditionally separate audiences. By considering together questions of production, reception and interpretation of translated texts, I hope to include translators, readers and teachers among my audience" (p. 2). Professor May draws on numerous examples of translation from the works of Turgenev, Dostoevsky, Gogol, Trifonov, Zoshchenko, Solzhenitsyn, and Tertz. Two appendixes explore translations of Bulgakov's *Master and Margarita* and some examples of English translation.

704. Morris, Marcia A. **Saints and Revolutionaries: The Ascetic Hero in Russian Literature**. x, 256p. Albany: State University of New York Press, 1993. Includes bibliographical references (pp. 227-41) and index.

"An examination of literary works spanning more than seven centuries, this volume studies the ascetic hero and asceticism, exploring the elusive interplay between religion, politics, and belles lettres in Russia" (back cover). Morris identifies the religious context of the writings of Kievan Rus', examining the *Kievan Crypt Paterilon*, *The Life of Avraamii Solenskii*, *Epifanni's Life of Sergis Radonezhskii*, and other writings. In particular, Morris looks at the religious themes of apocalypticism and deification. Later in the volume the author looks at the 19th- and early-20th-century revivals of the same themes in the writings of Gogol, Tolstoy, Dostoevsky, Chernyschevsky, and Gorky.

705. Murav, Harriet. **Russia's Legal Fictions**. 263p. Ann Arbor: University of Michigan Press, 1998. Includes bibliographical references and index.

Murav examines literary works and literary figures in 19th- and 20th-century Russian literature in order to understand "legal and political forms of power and authority insofar as they figure in the literary author's construction of his or her own authority" (p. 6). Authors involved in the study are: Sukhovo-Kobylin, Suvorin, Dostoevsky, Solzhenitsyn, and Siniavskii.

706. Nakhimovsky, Alice S. **Russian-Jewish Literature and Identity: Jabotinsky, Babel, Grossman, Galich, Roziner, Markish**. xiv, 251p. Baltimore: Johns Hopkins University Press, 1992. Includes bibliographical references (pp. [215]-246) and index.

In the first chapter Nakhimovsky provides a historical overview of Russian Jewish writing. The remaining chapters are each devoted to a single author. Those concerned are Vladimir Jabotinsky, Isaac Babel, Vasily Grossman, Alexander Galich, Felix Roziner, and David Markish. The aim of her study is to observe how Russian Jewish writers express their own self-identity and how it has changed in the past 100 years.

707. Pachmuss, Temira. **A Moving River of Tears: Russia's Experience in Finland**. 289p.: illus. *American University Studies. Series XII, Slavic Languages and Literature*, vol. 15. New York: P. Lang, 1992.

This study has two purposes. First, the author presents it as "an exposition of information, surveying the Russian endeavor throughout the nineteenth century to unite Russian and Finnish literatures" and second, "to reveal the Russian literary endeavor in Finland, 1808-1840." The writers and events covered are presented chronologically. Individual chapters, for example, examine the "graces" of Finland (Stjernval, Musina-Puskina, and Patkul'), the aspirations, frustrations, and accomplishments of Yakov Grot in Finland, Russian women writers in the age of modernism at the turn of the century, and other topics. Two appendixes, "Russian Newspapers and Journals in Finland" and "The Journal of Concord," provide additional information for the reader.

708. **Creating Life: The Aesthetic Utopia of Russian Modernism**. Edited by Irina Paperno and Joan Delaney Grossman. x, 288p. Stanford, Calif.: Stanford University Press, 1994. Includes bibliographical references (pp. [231]-279) and index.

These seven essays all wrestle with one of the "accursed questions" of modern literature, the relations of art and life. This problem was central to the creators of symbolism, the movement that launched modernism in Russia. The intent of the volume is to provide "a comprehensive, but not an exhaustive, treatment of the modernist aesthetic utopia" (p. 9). Authors studied in the essays include Vladimir Solov'ev, Andrey Belyi, Viacheslav Ivanov, Valeryi Briusov, Dmitry Merezhkovsky, Alexander Blok, and Zinaida Gippius.

709. Parthé, Kathleen. **Russian Village Prose: The Radiant Past**. xiv, 194p. Princeton, N.J.: Princeton University Press, 1992. Includes bibliographical references (pp. [149]-187) and index.

Parthé's purpose is "to characterize the Village Prose movement as a whole through the identification of those parameters which make up its 'code of reading' " (p. x). The first chapter articulates the characteristics of village prose, a movement that came to a close in the late 1970s. Chapters 2-5 look in more depth at features such as genre, generational and cyclical time, and memory and loss. Chapter 6 covers critical reactions to village prose and Chapter 7 is devoted to the end of the movement. Two appendixes include an English translation of Aleksei Leonov's "Kondyr" and a critical analysis of it.

710. Peterson, Nadezhda L. **Subversive Imaginations: Fantastic Prose and the End of Soviet Literature, 1970s-1990s**. xii, 216p. Boulder, Colo.: Westview Press, 1997. Includes bibliographical references (pp. 197-209) and index.

Peterson's work is about the end of Soviet literature and the emergence of a new Russian literature that overtly engages with fantasy. The author's 10 chapters "explore the literary and social roots of fantastic prose, seeking its motivation and purpose in relationship to socialist realism" (p. 7).

711. Polonsky, Rachel. **English Literature and the Russian Aesthetic Renaissance**. xii, 249p.: illus. *Cambridge Studies in Russian Literature*. Cambridge, Eng.: Cambridge University Press, 1998. Includes bibliographical references and index.

"This is the first study of the Russian reception of English literature from Romanticism to Aestheticism, focusing particularly on the reception by Russian poets of Shelley, Ruskin, Pater, Frazer, and Wilde. Framing this account is a pioneering exploration of the intellectual background to these influences in comparative scholarship, illuminating a common interest in myth, folklore, anthropology and the origins of language" (frontispiece). The book is divided into two parts. The first examines the early influence of English literature through the works of Shelley and Poe. The second part looks at the traces of Wilde's writings in Russian literature. Polonsky did not intend this as a comprehensive study of the topic. Rather, it is intended as an introduction to interaction between two great literary traditions.

712. Pomorska, Krystyna, Elena Semeka-Pankratov, Morris Halle, Catherine V. Chvany, and Elzbieta Ettinger. **Studies in Poetics: Commemorative Volume: Krystyna Pomorska (1928-1986)**. 588p. Columbus, Ohio: Slavica Publishers, 1995. Includes bibliographical references (pp. 586-88).

Krystyna Pomorska was a well-known scholar of Russian literature. As a translator of poetry as well as a respected analyst of Russian literary genres of the 20th century, she contributed a great deal to her field. This volume contains articles by her colleagues, students, and friends. The articles are organized into three sections: the semiotics of culture, structural poetics, and linguistics and poetics. Articles are published here in the language in which they were submitted. Thus, the volume includes several essays in Russian. The contributors include Henryk Baran, Elizbieta Chodakowska Ettinger, Samuel Keyster, and Jindrich Toman.

713. Roberts, Graham. **The Last Soviet Avant-Garde: OBERIU—Fact, Fiction, Metafiction**. xiii, 274p. *Cambridge Studies in Russian Literature*. New York: Cambridge University Press, 1997. Includes bibliographical references and index.

"This is the first comprehensive study of the group of avant-garde Soviet writers active in Leningrad in the 1920s who styled themselves OBERIU, 'The Association for Real Art.' Graham Roberts re-examines commonly held assumptions about OBERIU, its identity as a group, its aesthetics and its place within the Russian and European literary traditions" (frontispiece). Roberts considers the writings of Vvedinsky, Vaginov, Kharms, Zabolotsky, Bakhterev, and other members of the group.

714. Robin, Régine. **Socialist Realism: An Impossible Aesthetic**. xxxvii, 345p. Stanford, Calif.: Stanford University Press, 1992. Translation of: *Le réalisme socialiste*. Includes bibliographical references (pp. 303-35) and index.

Robin's book is in three parts. Part 1, "Cacophony at the First Writer's Congress of 1934 on the Subject of 'Socialist Realism,' " focuses on the difficulties of formulating an aesthetic stance for a bankrupt idea. Part 2 provides the historical background to the genre. In Part 3, Robin examines the theoretical basis for Socialist Realism. The author has provided the students of Russian literature a long overdue examination of an important period in the history of Russian literature.

715. Rogers, Thomas F. **Myth and Symbol in Soviet Fiction: Images of the Savior Hero, Great Mother, Anima, and Child in Selected Novels and Films**. 344p.: illus. San Francisco: Mellen Research University Press, 1992. Includes bibliographical references and index.

Jungian philosophy reached its greatest popularity in the West after the Soviet Union had become a closed society. For this reason, Jung's theories have not been tested against the backdrop of Russian society. Thomas Rogers believes this offers a rare opportunity for scholars. He examines the works of 10 Soviet artists: Zamyatin, Babel, Olesha, Pilnyak, Platonov, Bulgakov, Rasputin, Aytmatov, and Taukovsky. He has selected this particular group as one that shares an "allegorical read of life." Each chapter is devoted to an artist and his works. Rogers outlines the archetype created by these authors and demonstrates the similarity between them.

716. Ronen, Omry. **The Fallacy of the Silver Age in Twentieth-Century Russian Literature**. xxi, 114p. Amsterdam: Harwood Academic, 1997.

"In this monograph Ronen continues his outstanding research into intertextual links among different Russian authors. . . . It is devoted to a concrete problem in the metalinguistic study of the terminology of modern Russian literary history. The stock phrase Silver Age is described in its different (partly evaluative, i.e., axiological) uses by different Russian authors. Through this network of connections Ronen uncovers important features of literary relations" (pp. xi-xii). Ronen examines works by Berdiaev, Akhmatova, Tsvetaeva, Mandelstam, Gumilev, Piast, and others.

717. **Nietzsche and Soviet Culture: Ally and Adversary**. Edited by Bernice Glazer Rosenthal. xvi, 421p.: illus. *Cambridge Studies in Russian Literature*. New York: Cambridge University Press, 1994. Includes index.

This collection of essays examines the impact of Nietzschean thought on Soviet culture. "It addresses key peculiarities of the Soviet reception of Nietzsche—the role of the pre-Revolutionary interest in the occult, the way revolution figured as an allegorical subject, the intertwining of art and ideology in the obsession with creating a new culture, the continuing Russian interest in Nietzsche as a religious thinker, and the manner in which censorship affected the dynamic of reception and influence" (frontispiece). Contributors include Bernice Rosenthal, Bengt Jangfeldt, Henryk Baran, Elaine Rusinko, Maria Carlson, James von Geldern, Gregory Freidin, Milka Bliznakov, Irina Paperno, Isabel A. Tirado, Mikhail Agursky, Margarita Tupitsyn, Edith Clowes, Clare Cavanagh, Boris Groys, and Menahem Brinker.

718. Ryan-Hayes, Karen L. **Contemporary Russian Satire: A Genre Study**. xi, 289p. *Cambridge Studies in Russian Literature*. Cambridge, Eng.; New York: Cambridge University Press, 1995. Includes bibliographical references (pp. 273-83) and index.

This study of Russian satire examines five texts, Iskander's *Rabbits and Boa Constrictors*; Erofeev's *Moscow-Petushki*; Limonov's *It's Me Eddie*; Dovlatov's *Ours*; and Voinovich's *Moscow 2042*. All are works of this century and together, arranged chronologically, the author believes they show the development of general norms. These have become the models of today's Russian satire. "Each work under examination is placed within the wider European literary context as well as within the Russian tradition and it's representative of a different subgenre of satire" (frontispiece). The author has selected works representative of various "subgenres" in order to present a clear picture of the genre as a whole.

719. Shentalinskii, Vitalii, and John Crowfoot. **The KGB's Literary Archive**. x, 322p., [8] p. of plates. London: Harvill Press, 1995. Includes index.

The aim of Socialist realism was to "produce talented but servile literature." As this book points out, the effect was an abject failure because most of the talented writers in Stalin's time were either shot or sent to prison camps. Shentalinskii here reveals previously untold truths about the life and death of 20th-century Russia's best writers by detailing his search in archival sources controlled by the KGB.

720. Shepherd, David. **Beyond Metafiction: Self-Consciousness in Soviet Literature**. xii, 260p. Oxford, Eng.: Clarendon Press; Oxford University Press, 1992. Originally presented as the author's thesis (doctoral—University of Manchester, 1990).

Metafiction (fiction about fiction) can be traced back to Laurence Sterne in the 18th century. In Chapter 1 Shepherd discusses several issues, both theoretical and historical, that concern metafiction in general and its applicability to Soviet literature in particular. In subsequent chapters, he deals with texts in which questions of writing predominate (Chapters 2-3), and in which questions of the writer are more important (Chapters 4-5). In Chapter 6 he theorizes about "the most important general issues raised by the analysis of specific works" (p. 27).

721. Sicher, Efraim. **Jews in Russian Literature After the October Revolution: Writers and Artists Between Hope and Apostasy**. xxiv, 282p.: illus. Cambridge, Eng.; New York: Cambridge University Press, 1995. Includes bibliographical references (pp. 218-72) and index.

Rather than being a book about Jewish culture in the Soviet Union, this book instead is a series of essays describing how some major Jewish authors (e.g., Issac Babel, Osip Mandelstam, Boris Pasternak, and Ilia Ehrenburg) "created art out of their accommodation with the Revolution and with themselves" (p. xix). These individual case studies are introduced by a "general discussion of the writing self against the background of acculturation and apostasy among Russian-speaking Jews in Russia before and after the Revolution"

(p. xix). An extensive set of scholarly endnotes provides further bibliographic guidance and selected exposition of other themes.

722. Simmons, Cynthia. **Their Fathers' Voice: Vassily Aksyonov, Venedikt Erofeev, Eduard Limonov, and Sasha Sokolov**. 218p. *Middlebury Studies in Russian Language and Literature*, vol. 4. New York: P. Lang, 1993. Includes bibliographical references and index.

Cynthia Simmons focuses on the works of Vassily Aksyonov, Venedikt Erofeev, Eduard Limonov, and Sasha Sokolov in this study of post-Stalinist literature. She examines their vision of literature and its role in society. Simmons sees these writers as the first to test the limits of "glasnost." The author tries to establish the connection between "alternative prose" of the 1990s and Russia's pre-Soviet literary heritage.

723. Singleton, Amy C. **No Place Like Home: The Literary Artist and Russia's Search for Cultural Identity**. x, 193p. Albany: State University of New York Press, 1997. Includes bibliographical references (pp. 175-88) and index.

Amy Singleton explores the loss of cultural identity as it relates to the demise of the "Great Russian Writer" (p. 144). In particular she focuses on specific works by Gogol (*Dead Souls*), Goncharov (*Oblomov*), Zamiatin (*We*), and Bulgakov (*The Master and Margarita*). Each of these works reflects changes in the perception of Russian cultural identity. "The novel, like the home, encompasses by nature the ambiguities inherent in the search for identity while acting as a medium of self-expression. In the four works included in this study . . . an uncertain attitude toward the aesthetic representation and realization of a Russian cultural self is manifest in the heroes' torturous search for ideal forms of democracy and self-expression" (pp. 3-4).

724. Smith, Les W. **Confession in the Novel: Bakhtin's Author Revisited**. 167p. Madison, Wis.: Fairleigh Dickinson University Press, 1996. Includes bibliographical references (pp. [151]-164) and index.

Modern physics has changed our view of the material world. Les Smith believes that changes in the scientific world carry over to the world of literature. In this study of the works of Bakhtin, Dostoevsky, O'Connor, and DeLillo he is concerned with the conflict between the author and his main character. "As a topic for study, confession in the novel provides an intensive example of how ideologies in general might relate to fiction. In a sense, as I argue below, all novels become confessional through the mediation of narrative form" (p. 14).

725. Tolczyk, Dariusz. **See No Evil: Literary Cover-Ups and Discoveries of the Soviet Camp Experience**. xxi, 361p. *Russian Literature and Thought*. New Haven, Conn.: Yale University Press, 1999. Includes bibliographical references (pp. [311]-348) and index.

Dariusz Tolczyk examines the portrayal of Soviet prison life in the sanctioned Soviet press from the 1920s to the mid-1960s. "The author considers how Soviet novelists and poets in the 1920s dealt with the Leninist notion that ethics are entirely utilitarian and realitive; analyzes the official glorification of the gulag in the early 1930s in such works as White Sea Canal, . . . and examines why the subject of the camp became taboo from 1937 to the Khruschevian thaw of the early 1960s" (book jacket). Tolczyk presents his subject chronologically.

726. Voronskii, Aleksandr Konstantinovich. **Art As the Cognition of Life: Selected Writings, 1911-1936**. Translated and edited by Frederick S. Choate. xxv, 526p.: illus. Oak Park, Mich.: Mehring Books, 1998. Includes index.

Voronskii was a major figure in postrevolutionary Soviet intellectual life and editor of one of the most influential literary journals of the 1920s. He was a supporter of Trotsky and the Left in opposition to Stalinism. He was eventually expelled from the party, arrested and sent into exile, rearrested, and finally executed. This anthology of his writings includes a wide variety of pieces all focusing on Russian intellectual life from 1911 to 1936.

727. Weiner, Adam. **By Authors Possessed: The Demonic Novel in Russia**. xi, 318p. *Studies in Russian Literature and Theory*. Evanston, Ill.: Northwestern University Press, 1998. Includes bibliographical references (pp. 295-311) and index.

In this book Adam Weiner looks at some of the works of Gogol, Dostoevsky, Belyi, and Nabokov. He is interested in the vision of the demonic in the works of these authors. "The novelists I treat in what follows are all at base good artists and moral artists—which did not prevent them from creating demonic works. A demonic novel, while not necessarily a bad novel, is, however, one with a crack in its moral base" (p. 9). Weiner explores this theme in depth in this work.

728. Wigzell, Faith. **Russian Writers on Russian Writers**. xvii, 194p.: illus. Oxford; Providence, R.I.: Berg, 1994. Includes bibliographical references and index.

In this work a group of essays are collected that focus on the writer as critic. "the intention is to illumine the theme of writer on writer in the Russian context, at the same time highlighting many of the ways in which the comment of writer on writer can function" (p. xvii). The essays discuss a number of authors' works on other authors. Some of those included are Fet, Chekhov, Merezhkovskii, Ivanov, Tsvetaeva, Joseph Brodsky, Trifonov, and Zinov'ev.

729. Zholkovskii, A. K. **Text Counter Text: Rereadings in Russian Literary History**. xi, 370p.: illus. Stanford, Calif.: Stanford University Press, 1994. Includes bibliographical references (pp. [337]-359) and index.

As the author notes, "the book is about twentieth-century Russian literature rereading its classical era and pressing the past masters (and on occasion a master's own past, as in the chapter on Pasternak) into the service of more recent needs—avant-gardist, revolutionary, post-revolutionary, dissident, émigré" (p. 2).

Individual Authors

730. **The Life and Work of Fedor Abramov**. Edited and translated by David Gillespie. xiv, 138p. *Studies in Russian Literature and Theory*. Evanston, Ill.: Northwestern University Press, 1997. Includes endnotes and bibliographical references.

Abramov was one of the leading representatives of the village prose movement of the 1960s and 1970s. The movement "lamented the disappearance of the old Russian village in the modern, industrial world, and the spiritual and moral values associated with it" (p. vii). These essays by Russian and American authors analyze various aspects and works of Abramov's literary output. The editor has also included translated excerpts from Abramov's diaries that portray the dilemma facing Abramov of artistic freedom and official restraints.

731. Mozur, Joseph P. **Parables from the Past: The Prose Fiction of Chingiz Aitmatov**. xv, 212p. *Pitt Series in Russian and East European Studies*, no. 22. Pittsburgh, Pa.: University of Pittsburgh Press, 1995. Includes bibliographical references (pp. 203-5) and index.

Aitmatov published many of his works in Soviet literary journals in the years following the Khrushchev cultural thaw. Even though he was a Khirghiz, he was widely admired throughout the Soviet Union. In this critical study of the author's works, he examines his development and his noticeable change in the 1980s from an establishment writer to one who increasingly drew inspiration from the folk literature of his native land. His study proceeds chronologically, with several chapters focusing on works such as *Farewell, Gul'sary, The White Ship, The Day Lasts More Than a Hundred Years*, and *The Place of the Skull*.

732. Akhmatova, Anna Andreevna, and Ronald Meyer. **My Half Century: Selected Prose**. xvi, 439p.: illus. Ann Arbor, Mich.: Ardis, 1992. Includes bibliographical references (p. [429]) and index.

Characterized by Akhmatova as the "story of my life and the fate of my generation," this unfinished collection of prose pieces covers memories about prominent literary and cultural figures, essays on Pushkin, reviews and public addresses, and letters. An afterword by Emma Gershtein sets this work in context.

733. **Akhmatova Centennial Conference: Anna Akhmatova, 1889-1989.** 281p.: illus. Oakland, Calif.: Berkeley Slavic Specialties, 1993. English and Russian. Includes bibliographical references.

The June 1989 conference held in Bellagio marked the 100th anniversary of the birth of Anna Akhmatova. This volume includes 17 papers by scholars from many countries with topics as varied as the contributors. Most contributors are in English.

734. Amert, Susan. **In a Shattered Mirror: The Later Poetry of Anna Akhmatova.** xii, 274p. Stanford, Calif.: Stanford University Press, 1992. Based on the author's doctoral dissertation. Includes bibliography, endnotes, and index.

Amert focuses on the late post-1935 poetry of Akhmatova, by analyzing the poetics of these works using close readings of major texts. He also examines other factors that would influence interpretation of those moral-philosophical, religious, and general aesthetic concerns out of which her poetry comes.

735. Dalos, Gyorgy. **The Guest from the Future: Anna Akhmatova and Isaiah Berlin.** 250p. New York: Farrar, Straus & Giroux, 1999. Includes bibliographical references and index.

This book recounts the meeting between Anna Akhmatova and Isaiah Berlin that took place in Leningrad in November 1945. While the meeting did not seem to affect Berlin, it profoundly changed Akhmatova. "This book is the story of a single night, the night of Isaiah Berlin's visit to Anna Akhmatova in Leningrad in November, 1945, and its unfortunate consequences, and is mainly told from Akhmatova's viewpoint. It is a love story, the story of a love that became a focal point in the life of the poet, giving meanings to events that preceded and followed" (p. 7).

736. **Anna Akhmatova and Her Circle.** Edited by Konstatin Polivanov. Translated by Patricia Beriozkina. xvi, 281p. Fayetteville: University of Arkansas Press, 1994. Includes appendix.

This volume contains personal recollections of Akhmatova by her closest friends and associates, selections of autobiographical prose by Akhmatova herself, and sketches of some of her contemporaries by other contemporaries. Originally published in Russian in 1991, the intent is to present Akhmatova from a series of viewpoints, hoping to capture the depth and complexity of the poet.

737. Ketchian, Sonia I. **The Poetic Craft of Bella Akhmadulina.** viii, 248p. University Park: Pennsylvania State University Press, 1993. Includes name index, index of works cited in English, and index of works cited in Russian.

Russia's premier contemporary Russian woman poet, Bella Akhmadulina, is examined critically in this book. Ketchian first examines the specifics of the lyric voices that appear in her poems and then moves on to analyze the poetry of the mature "garden" period, especially focusing on the collection, *The Secret*.

738. Babel', I. Isaak. **1920 Diary**. Edited by Carol J. Avins. Translated by H. T. Willettsl. viii, 126p., [8] p. of plates: illus., maps. New Haven, Conn.: Yale University Press, 1995. Translated from Russian.

This diary covers the period when Babel' covered the Polish-Soviet war as a correspondent and is popularly known as his "Red Calvary" diary, taking its designation from a cycle of short stories by the same name. The diary was never confiscated by the NKVD (precursor to the KGB), but passed into the hands of his widow in the 1950s. In the late 1980s, excerpts were finally published in Russian.

739. Bernard-Donals, Michael F. **Mikhail Bakhtin: Between Phenomenology and Marxism**. 187p. Cambridge, Eng.; New York: Cambridge University Press, 1994. Includes bibliographical references (pp. 179-84) and index.

This is a study of the writings of Mikhail Bakhtin. "In *Mikhail Bakhtin: Between Phenomenology and Marxism*, Michael Bernard-Donals examines various incarnations of phenomenological and materialist theory including the work of Jauss, Fish, Rorty, Althusser, and Pecheux and places them beside Bakhtin's work, providing a contextualized study of Bakhtin, a critique of the problems of contemporary critics, and an original contribution to literary theory" (back cover).

740. Emerson, Caryl. **The First Hundred Years of Mikhail Bakhtin**. xvi, 293p. Princeton, N.J.: Princeton University Press, 1997. Includes bibliographical references and index.

"After a reception-history of Bakhtin's published work, she [Emerson] examines the role of his ideas in the post-Stalinist revival of the Russian literary profession, concentrating on the most provocative rethinkings of three major concepts in his world: dialogue and polyphony; carnival; and 'outsideness,' a position Bakhtin considered essential to both ethics and aesthetics. Finally, she speculates on the future of Bakhtin's method, which was much more than a tool of criticism: it will 'tell you how to teach, write, live, talk, think' " (book jacket).

741. Mihailovic, Alexandar. **Corporeal Words: Mikhail Bakhtin's Theology of Discourse**. x, 291p. *Studies in Russian Literature and Theory*. Evanston, Ill.: Northwestern University Press, 1997. Includes bibliographical references (pp. 259-71) and index.

Alexandar Mihailovic has written a study of Bakhtin's work in the context of the Russian Orthodoxy that influenced it. Although Bakhtin's writings are usually analyzed as Marxist works, Mihailovic believes they also show the basis of his Orthodox background.

Examining the major essays of Bakhtin's career, he hopes to demonstrate the theological underpinnings of his work.

The book follows Bakhtin's work chronologically. Such works as *The Problems of Dostoevsky's Art* (1924), "Discourse in the Novel" (1934-1935), and "Forms of Time and the Chronotope in the Novel" (1937-1938) are discussed in turn. In all these early works Mihailovic finds Bakhtin's "systematic use of theological terms" indicative of the role religious thought plays in his analysis. Bakhtin's book *Rabelais and His World* (1940), as it has been analyzed by such scholars as Mikhail Ryklin, is also discussed. The final chapter discusses Bakhtin's last writings. Mihailovic believes that Bakhtin's theological interests were not just evidenced by his use of a theological terminology. "In a certain sense, theology in Bakhtin becomes thoroughly humanized and aestheticized, the christological metaphor emerging as a rhetorical and theoretical model rather than a devotional paradigm, a structure in whose interstices he could arrange his ideas about the anti-hierarchical drift of language and culture" (pp. 15-16).

742. Keys, Roger. **The Reluctant Modernist: Andrei Belyi and the Development of Russian Fiction, 1902-1914**. xii, 268p. Oxford, Eng.: Clarendon Press, 1996. Includes bibliographical references (pp. [239]-262) and index.

Roger Keys discusses Belyi's writing as a part of the European modernist school. The book is divided into three parts. The first examines the critical reception of modernist prose from the time of the symbolists to the present day. The second part examines "the Symbolist view of writer as prophet revealing religious or mystical truth to society through imaginatively unmediated transcendent 'symbols' and argues on the evidence of Belyi's Second Dramatic Symphony, in particular, the inherent resistance of fiction to communicating universal messages of this 'theurgic' kind" (p. vii).

In Part 3, Keys argues that in *Petersburg* and *The Silver Dove*, Belyi's writings showed a change from the view of art as a "passive reflection of otherworldly 'truths' " (p. vii). This change led to Belyi's use of perspectivism.

743. Berberova, Nina Nikolaevna. **The Tattered Cloak: And Other Novels**. 307p. London: Vintage, 1992.

This collection contains *The Resurrection of Mozart*, *The Waiter and the Slut*, *Astashev in Paris*, *The Tattered Cloak*, *The Black Pestilence*, and *In Memory of Schliemann*.

744. Bagby, Lewis. **Alexander Bestuzhev-Marlinsky and Russian Byronism**. x, 372p. University Park: Pennsylvania State University Press, 1995. Includes bibliography and index.

Bagby recognizes the importance of Bestuzhev-Marlinsky for Russian literary culture. In the 1820s and 1830s he was a "compelling life model for writers and readers" (p. vii). In the 1850s and 1860s he was admired by political activists. In this volume Bagby attempts to restore Bestuzhev-Marlinsky's part in Russian literary life so as to see him as the public of his day did. Throughout he weaves biography and critical analysis to give us an impressive picture of a prominent prose writer of the first half of the 19th century.

745. Bitov, Andrei. **The Monkey Link: A Pilgrimage Novel**. Translated by Susan Brownsberger. v, 373p. New York: Farrar, Straus & Giroux, 1995. Includes endnotes.

The three tales comprising this novel were written between 1971 and 1993. In it the author intended to pose three questions: "What is man's role in relation to other biological species? To God? To humankind?" (p. 355). As the translator comments, "this 'pilgrimage novel' is a drama of salvation—a battle between good and evil for possession of the hero's soul, and for the soul of his nation. The hero's journey is not done: it is the eternal struggle upward, toward God. But it takes place in time, our time, and its endpoint in this novel is an unforgettable moment of hope in our history" (pp. 359-60).

746. Chances, Ellen B. **Andrei Bitov: The Ecology of Inspiration**. xvi, 331p.: illus. Cambridge, Eng.; New York: Cambridge University Press, 1993. Includes bibliographical references (pp. 301-23) and index.

Intending to present "a comprehensive study of the author's writings to the scholarly community" (p. 17), Chances examines each of his writings in chronological order. In doing so she reveals Bitov's "capacity to face head-on the necessity of the quest for a life of integrity, no matter how gut-wrenching that path may be. He documents the dignity that accompanies the ability to face reality as it is rather than as one might want it to be" (pp. xiii-xiv).

747. Bethea, David M. **Joseph Brodsky and the Creation of Exile**. xvii, 317p. Princeton, N.J.: Princeton University Press, 1994. Includes bibliographical references (pp. [299]-311) and index.

Bethea does not claim to provide a definitive critical biography of Brodsky. Instead, he gives the reader a study that attempts "to frame the issue of who he is as international man of letters and how he arrived at his present role as Russian-born American poet laureate" (p. xi). To carry out his task the author shows as much who Brodsky was not as who he was by comparing him to other poets and other traditions, including John Donne, T. S. Eliot, Mandelstam, Pasternak, Tsvetaeva, and Nabokov.

748. Haber, Edythe C. **Mikhail Bulgakov: The Early Years**. ix, 285p. *Russian Research Center Studies*, 90. Cambridge, Mass.: Harvard University Press, 1998. Includes bibliographical references and index.

Edythe Haber's book on Bulgakov examines individual works by the author to elucidate his large body of work. Haber emphasizes the themes in his early writings that appear in fully developed form in *The Master and Margarita*. The author examines Bulgakov's narrative prose for the most part. The book is divided into two parts. The first provides the biographical background and discusses Bulgakov's early serious prose. In the second part of the book Haber turns to the satiric works, published between 1922 and 1926.

749. Smeliansky, Anatoly. **Is Comrade Bulgakov Dead?: Mikhail Bulgakov at the Moscow Art Theatre**. Translated by Arch Tait. viii, 374p. London: Methuen, 1993. Revised translation of: *Mihkail Bulgakov v Khudozhestvennom teatre*. Includes index and endnotes.

Smeliansky portrays Mikhail Bulgakov and the Moscow Art Theatre during his directorship there. The author poetically describes the subject of the book thus: "This is a book about a power which tried to destroy all that was alive in Russian culture. It is a book about a great Russian theatre seduced by the Stalin regime. It is a book about one man who tried under conditions of absolute unfreedom to retain his own identity and soul" (p. 5).

750. Bunin, Ivan. **Cursed Days: A Diary of Revolution**. Translated by Thomas Gaiton Marullo. xiii, 286p. Chicago: I. R. Dee, 1998. Includes bibliographical references (pp. 273-74) and index.

This is Ivan Bunin's diary from his last years in Moscow and Odessa in 1918 and 1919. As Marullo says in his introduction, this was Bunin "in his underwear"; in the diary he abandons his aristocratic prose and is wrenchingly honest about the horrors of the Soviet regime. Also included here are selections from articles written in 1919 in Odessa in which he discourses on insights he had about the Russian Revolution. Detailed annotations also aid in interpreting both texts.

751. Bunin, Ivan. **Ivan Bunin: From the Other Shore, 1920-1933: A Portrait from Letters, Diaries, and Fiction**. Edited by Thomas Marullo. x, 332p.: illus., ports. Chicago: I. R. Dee, 1995. Continues: *Ivan Bunin: Russian Requiem, 1885-1933*. Includes bibliographical references (pp. 311-12) and indexes.

This second volume of Bunin's diary, letters, and autobiographical writings tells how Bunin's 13-year exile from Russia turned from tragedy to triumph when he became a writer of international fame. In addition, this volume also sheds light on many aspects of the Russian emigration from 1917 to 1930.

752. Bunin, Ivan. **Ivan Bunin: Russian Requiem, 1885-1933: A Portrait from Letters, Diaries, and Fiction**. Edited by Thomas Marullo. x, 387p.: illus. Chicago: I. R. Dee, 1993. Includes bibliographical references (pp. 367-78) and index.

This first volume of Bunin's diary, letters, and autobiographical writings is conceived by the translator as a "journal which Bunin could willingly embrace as his, a poignant and personal commentary on the first fifty years of his life and the 'dark night' between the twilight of imperial Russia and the dawn of the new Soviet state" (p. ix).

753. Zweers, Alexander F. **The Narratology of the Autobiography: An Analysis of the Literary Devices Employed in Ivan Bunin's** *The Life of Arsen'ev*. x, 190p. *Middlebury Studies in Russian Language and Literature*, 11. New York: P. Lang, 1997. Includes bibliographical references (pp. [177]-187) and index.

As Zweers states in his introduction: "Ivan Bunin's *The Life of Arsen'ev* belongs to the category of the Nabokov autobiography since in his novel the child's world is evoked as re-experienced by the adult narrator, that is, from a purely grown-up perspective. Although Bunin does not deny that there are many autobiographical details in his novel, he insists that it would be viewed by critics as a fictitious work. Consequently, an attempt is made to sort out how the novel's contents can most appropriately be characterized" (p. x).

754. Chernyshevsky, Nikolai. **Prologue: A Novel from the Beginning of the 1860s**. Translated by Michael R. Katz. xvii, 359p. *Studies in Russian Literature and Theory*. Evanston, Ill.: Northwestern University Press, 1995. Includes endnotes and select bibliography.

This is a translation of Chernyshevsky's "other" novel. Written during his exile in Siberia, Part 1 of it was first published in 1877 and without the author's name. Both parts were finally published in Russia in 1906. By writing it Chernyshevsky "was hoping that his new work would arouse European interest in the Russian revolutionary movement" (p. ix).

755. Gilman, Richard. **Chekhov's Plays: An Opening into Eternity**. xxii, 261p. New Haven, Conn.: Yale University Press, 1995. Includes bibliographical references (pp. [245]-254) and index.

After an introductory chapter that explores truth, moral reality, and imagination in Chekhov's plays, Gilman devotes subsequent individual chapters to a critical analysis of *Ivanov*, *The Seagull*, *Uncle Vanya*, *Three Sisters*, and *The Cherry Orchard*.

756. Senelick, Laurence. **The Chekhov Theatre: A Century of the Plays in Performance**. xv, 441p.: illus. New York: Cambridge University Press, 1997. Includes bibliographical references and indexes.

In this study, Laurence Senelick has produced a comparative study of Chekhov's plays in production. "Many now consider Chekhov a playwright equal to Shakespeare, and this book studies how the reputation evolved, and how the presentation of his plays varied and altered from their initial productions in Russia to the most recent postmodern deconstructions" (frontispiece). For Senelick, the study of various styles of production is a vehicle for examining differences in social, political, and aesthetic attitudes from one country to another. The book is organized into chapters devoted to productions in different countries. It includes an index of productions.

757. Turkov, Andrei. **Anton Chekhov and His Times**. xv, 327p. Fayetteville: University of Arkansas Press, 1995. Includes endnotes.

This volume contains reminiscences of Chekov by 10 of his contemporaries including Korolenko, Stanislavksy, Gorky, and Bunin, as well as selected correspondence to Chekhov by an even wider group of friends and acquaintants.

758. Turner, C. J. G. **Time and Temporal Structure in Chekhov**. viii, 113p. *Birmingham Slavic Monographs*, no. 22. Birmingham, Ala.: Dept. of Russian Language and Literature, University of Birmingham, 1994. Includes bibliographical references (pp. 100-105) and index.

In this slim volume, C. J. G. Turner analyzes the theme of time in Chekhov's writings. He examines several manifestations of temporality in Chekhov: the past, aging, life, death, and the present. The book includes a brief bibliography on Chekhov.

759. Zubarev, Vera. **A Systems Approach to Literature: Mythopoetics of Chekhov's Four Major Plays**. 179p. *Contributions to the Study of World Literature*, 75. Westport, Conn.: Greenwood Press, 1997. Includes endnotes, bibliography, and index.

After an introductory chapter where the author "develops a concept of a comprehensive approach to mythopoetics as it applies to a literary work" (p. 12), Zubarev devotes succeeding chapters to analysis of *The Seagull*, *Uncle Vanya*, *Three Sisters*, and *The Cherry Orchard*.

760. Buchanan, Henry. **Dostoevsky's Crime and Punishment: An Aesthetic Interpretation**. 90p. Nottingham, Eng.: Astra, 1996. Includes bibliographical references (pp. [81]-87) and index.

Buchanan challenges a traditional reading of *Crime and Punishment* as a Christian novel.

761. Frank, Joseph. **Dostoevsky: The Miraculous Years, 1865-71**. xv, 523p.: illus. Princeton, N.J.: Princeton University Press, 1995. Includes bibliographical references (pp. 505-15) and index.

This is the fourth volume in a series by Frank on the life and works of Dostoevsky, with this volume covering the years 1865-1871 during which time he wrote *Crime and Punishment*, *The Idiot*, and *The Devils*, as well as two novellas. Frank's purpose for all literary biography is "to furnish readers with a context, drawn from the writer's personal life, as well as from the social, cultural, literary, and philosophical background of his or her time that will help toward a better understanding of the work" (p. xi).

762. Jackson, Robert Louis. **Dialogues with Dostoevsky: The Overwhelming Questions**. 346p. Stanford, Calif.: Stanford University Press, 1993. Includes bibliographical references (pp. [305]-336) and index.

In this work Robert Jackson does not examine Dostoevsky's influence on various writers. Rather, he looks at the common themes analyzed by Dostoevsky and many other writers. "Though questions of influence or impact of one writer upon another sometimes constitute the given of the discussion, the main focus is upon the issues—moral-psychological, aesthetic and historophilosophical—that engage these writers in their contact with each other's work or emerge from a juxtaposition of their works or ideas" (p. 4). The authors under discussion are Tolstoy, Turgenev, Chekhov, Nikolai Strakhov, Gorky, Chateaubriand, the Marquis de Sade, Gogol, Shakespheare, Nietzsche, Ivanov, Bakhtin, and of course Dostoevsky. These essays have been written over a number of years and some have been published elsewhere.

763. Knapp, Liza. **The Annihilation of Inertia: Dostoevsky and Metaphysics**. xi, 315p. Evanston, Ill.: Northwestern University Press, 1996. Includes endnotes, select bibliography, and index.

For Dostoevsky to annihilate inertia is to achieve eternal life. Knapp develops the idea of inertia as it was understood by Dostoevsky's contemporaries and by Dostoevsky himself. She then proceeds to analyze several of Dostoevsky's novels to demonstrate how he dealt with this idea in his fiction. Particular attention is paid to *Crime and Punishment*, *The Idiot*, *The Devils*, *The Adolescent*, and *Brothers Karamazov*.

764. Knapp, Liza. **Dostoevsky's *The Idiot*: A Critical Companion**. viii, 274p. *Northwestern/AATSEEL Critical Companions to Russian Literature*. Evanston, Ill.: Northwestern University Press; American Association of Teachers of Slavic and East European Languages, 1998. Includes bibliographical references.

This collection of essays examines works about Dostoevsky's *The Idiot* and early texts of the work itself. The essays are divided into three sections. The first is a general discussion of the novel and how it came to be written. Part 2 is composed of critical essays on of the book. The final section is a set of primary sources relevant to the study of the novel. This section includes sections from Dostoevsky's notebooks and letters from Anna Dostoevsky. The collection includes a bibliography of selected works relevant to *The Idiot*. Contributors to the study are David M. Bethea, Liza Knapp, Robin Feuer Miller, and Nina Pelikan Straus.

765. **Dostoevskii and Britain**. Edited by William J. Leatherbarrow. ix, 310p. Oxford; Providence, R.I.: Berg, 1995. Includes bibliographical references (pp. 293-310).

This collection of essays includes translations of Russian works and Western writings on Dostoevsky's relationship to and with Britain. "Reprinting for the first time in English a number of articles previously inaccessible as well as essays by noted contemporary scholars, this book brings together a wealth of material on Dostoevsky's visit to Britain, the extent to which he drew inspiration from British writers and thinkers, the impact he made on subsequent British culture" (back cover). There are essays on Dostoevsky and Shakespeare, Dickens, Chartist novels, and D. H. Lawrence among other topics.

766. Leatherbarrow, William J. **Fyodor Dostoyevsky—The Brothers Karamazov**. ix, 115p. Cambridge, Eng.: Cambridge University Press, 1992. Includes bibliographical references (pp. 112-15).

Rather than try to cover every conceivable aspect of this work, the author instead presents "a unified analysis centered upon the novel's preoccupation with justice, order and disorder . . ." (p. 3). It includes a chapter on the background to the novel and a much longer section that deals with the novel itself and its critical reception.

767. Meerson, Olga. **Dostoevsky's Taboos**. xvi, 232p. *Studies of the Harriman Institute/Artes Liberales*, 2. Dresden, Ger.: Dresden University Press, 1998. Includes bibliographical references (pp. [219]-227) and index.

"Olga Meerson's book, *Dostoevsky's Taboos*, ranks as one of the highlights of Dostoevsky criticism simply because it furnishes a key not only to Dostoevsky's idea of human subjectivity but to his narrative technique as well. The taboos discussed are, of course, not those of Dostoevsky himself, but those of his "heroes," haunted by traumatic insult, a psychic wound, something unspoken, . . ." (p. xi). The introductory note by Horst-Jurgen Gerigk summarizes Meerson's detailed analysis of Dostoevsky's use of the taboo. The author is Assistant Professor of Russian at Georgetown University.

768. Miller, Robin Feuer. **The Brothers Karamazov: Worlds of the Novel**. xv, 156p.: illus. *Twayne's Masterwork series*, no. 83. New York: Twayne Publishers, 1992. Includes bibliographical references.

Robin Feuer Miller is a professor of Russian and comparative literature at Brandeis University. She has written several studies on Dostoevsky. This volume is one of Twayne's Masterwork series. As with other volumes in the series, the author provides a discussion of critical themes and concepts and historical context in which the *Brothers Karamazov* was written. Miller also discusses the critical reception of this work. She has compiled a chronology of Dostoevsky's life and selected bibliography.

769. Paperno, Irina. **Suicide As a Cultural Institution in Dostoevsky's Russia**. ix, 319p. Ithaca, N.Y.: Cornell University Press, 1997. Includes bibliographical references (pp. 207-56) and index.

Paperno shows how "suicide, an individual act, becomes a cultural artifact" (p. 3). Some of the issues discussed are specific to Russia in the 19th century, while others relate to Western Europe in general. She does not try to discover why human beings commit suicide or to explain suicidal behavior. Instead, "this book is about the cultural construction of the meaning of human experience" (p. 3).

770. **The Dostoevsky Archive: Firsthand Accounts of the Novelist from Contemporaries' Memoirs and Rare Periodicals**. Introduction by Igor Volgin. Edited by Peter Sekinin. xiii, 370p., [16] p. of plates: illus. Jefferson, N.C.: McFarland, 1997. Includes bibliographical references (pp. 347-62) and index.

Many of the documents translated here are those that have recently been unearthed in the spetskhran (Special Repository) of several Soviet archives. The editor has arranged them in topical chapters that include his childhood in Moscow; his studies in the St. Petersburg Military Engineering Academy; his father's death and his first literary success; the Petrashevsky Circle; prison, army service, and exile; literary journals and innocent novels; three love stories in the 1860s in Russia and abroad; major novels; the Pushkin speech; and his last month. A detailed chronology of Dostoevsky's life is also included.

771. Straus, Nina Pelikan. **Dostoevsky and the Woman Question: Rereadings at the End of a Century**. 191p. London: Macmillan, 1994. Includes bibliographical references (pp. [179]-186) and index.

As the author notes in her introduction, this "book explores Dostoevsky's major works with a focus on his women characters, his references to rape and men's abuse of women, and his construction of the feminine. Such an approach to Dostoevsky is feminist mainly in the sense that the woman question is not subsumed within a larger frame" (p. 1). After an introductory chapter that explores the theme of Dostoevsky and the feminine, the author examines *Crime and Punishment*, *The Gambler*, *The Idiot*, *The Eternal Husband*, *The Possessed*, *The Diary of a Writer*, and *Brothers Karamazov*. A concluding chapter summarizes her findings.

772. Terras, Victor. **Reading Dostoevsky**. xii, 171p. Madison: University of Wisconsin Press, 1998. Includes bibliographical references and index.

"In this stimulating critical introduction to Dostoevsky's fiction, literary scholar Victor Terras asks readers to draw their own conclusions about the nineteenth-century Russian writer. Discussing psychological, political, mythical, and philosophical approaches, Terras deftly guides readers through the range of diverse and even contradictory interpretations of Dostoevsky's rich novels" (back cover). Terras devotes most of the chapters in this study to each of Dostoevsky's major works: *Crime and Punishment*, *The Idiot*, *The Possessed*, *A Raw Youth*, and *Brothers Karamazov*. An appendix to the study discusses the affect of translation on Dostoevsky's works.

773. Any, Carol Joyce. **Boris Eikhenbaum: Voices of a Russian Formalist**. xiii, 281p.: illus., port. Stanford, Calif.: Stanford University Press, 1994. Includes bibliographical references.

Boris Eikhenbaum was an influential Soviet critic of Russian literature and member of the group Opoiaz. Carol Any revisits his work to reassess the theory of his criticism and his place in the world of literary criticism. "I shall argue in this study that his work after 1927, especially his opus on Tolstoy, was a response to Soviet political reality, and in some measure an attempt if not to engage it in dialogue, at least to compose an alternative monologue" (p. 4). The volume is devoted to Eikhenbaum's critical three-volume study of Tolstoy written between 1928 and 1940.

774. Rubenstein, Joshua. **Tangled Loyalties: The Life and Times of Ilya Ehrenburg**. xii, 482p.: illus., ports. London: I. B. Tauris, 1996. Includes bibliographical references (pp. 451-60) and index.

Rubenstein's biography interprets the life of journalist and novelist Ilya Ehrenburg, "the renowned Soviet writer, who has shouldered the lifelong burden of always being blamed by somebody, somewhere, for something" (pp. 395-96).

775. Erofeyev, Victor. **Russian Beauty**. Translated by Andrew Reynolds. vi, 343p. London: Penguin Books, 1993. Translated from the Russian.

This is Victor Erofeyev's first novel. The story is narrated by a beautiful woman named Irine. The book describes her life as she meets and shares her bed with a variety of characters. In a 1990 interview with the *New York Times*, Erofeyev characterizes Irine as being based on him. "My experience was human, hers sexual, but both our lives stood at a crossroads of Soviet society. It is this society, then on the brink of perestroika, that I have sought to portray" (*NYT*, 2-15-90, section C, p. 21). Victor Erofeyev has published collections of essays and was the editor of the dissident publication *Metropol*.

776. **Venedikt Erofeev's Moscow-Petushki: Critical Perspectives**. Edited by Karen L. Ryan-Hayes. x, 231p. *Middlebury Studies in Russian Language and Literature*, 14. New York: P. Lang, 1997. Includes bibliographic references. Some text in Russian.

Erofeev was a mysterious figure in his lifetime (he died in 1990) and will best be remembered for his single text—*Moscow-Petushki*. The nine essays included here present various analysis of this literary text.

777. Horowitz, Brian. **The Myth of A. S. Pushkin in Russia's Silver Age: M. O. Gershenzon, Pushkinist**. x, 129p. Evanston, Ill.: Northwestern University Press, 1996. Includes bibliographical references and index.

This is a study of Mikhail Gershenzon's criticism of Pushkin and its influence on Russian literary criticism generally. "By examining Gershenzon as a Pushkinist, we get a vivid sense of the inner workings of Russian literary life during the heated period 1900-1925, a world in which literature, philosophy, politics, academe, art, and personal relationships converged" (p. 1). Horowitz examines Gershenzon's intellectual development and his philosophical interpretation of Pushkin and traces the development of his criticism of Pushkin.

778. Maguire, Robert A. **Exploring Gogol**. xxii, 409p. *Studies of the Harriman Institute*. Stanford, Calif.: Stanford University Press, 1994. Includes bibliographical references (pp. [377]-390) and index.

Robert Maguire attempts to analyze the body of Gogol's work in this study. Working in the tradition of such literary scholars as Victor Erlich, Donald Fanger, and Richard Pence, Maguire examines each of Gogol's works in turn. He does spend less time on such works as "The Overcoat" and "The Nose," believing that they have already received extensive coverage in the literature. His book includes a chronology of the major events in Gogol's life, and a bibliography of works by Gogol are cited in the text.

779. Shapiro, Gavriel. **Nikolai Gogol and the Baroque Cultural Heritage**. xiii, 259p.: illus. University Park: Pennsylvania State University Press, 1993. Originally presented as the author's thesis (doctoral)—University of Illinois at Urbana-Champaign, 1984.

Shapiro explores Gogol's "creative adaptation of the cultural heritage of the Baroque" and also examines "diverse and ingenious ways in which Gogol accommodated this heritage in his verbal art" (p. 1). Shapiro considers all of Gogol's work to be searching for connections to the Baroque: poetry, prose, drama, drawings, correspondence, and notebooks. After an introduction and a first chapter on Gogol and the Baroque milieu, he explores farms, topoi, and figurative language—topics that are covered in individual chapters. An afterword provides a concise statement of his thesis and findings.

780. Diment, Galya. **The Autobiographical Novel of Co-Consciousness: Goncharov, Woolf, and Joyce**. xiv, 199p. *Florida James Joyce series*. Gainesville: University of Florida Press, 1994. Includes bibliographical references (pp. [183]-194) and index.

This book explores the novel of co-consciousness as exemplified by Goncharov, Woolf, and Joyce. In addition to concerning itself about the autobiographical novel, it "is also about the 'mystery of the conscious' as it makes its presence felt in the three writers' sophisticated and subtle treatment of their inner conflicts through two well-developed, fully dimensional, very 'unsupernatural,' and perfectly active parts of a fictional 'split self'" (p. 3).

781. Barratt, Andrew. **The Early Fiction of Maksim Gorky: Six Essays in Interpretation**. xi, 155p. Nottingham, Eng.: Astra, 1993. Includes bibliographical references (pp. [147]-151) and index.

The author has compiled six interpretive essays on six short stories written by Maksim Gorky. Three of these essays have been published previously. In no way does Barratt claim to provide a comprehensive assessment of these works, but instead seeks "to convince the reader that Gorky is a writer who deserves the sort of detailed attention which he has singularly failed to attract from students in the West" (p. ix). Besides individual essays on Makar Chudra, My Fellow-Traveller, Chelkash, On the Raft, Malva, and Twenty-Six Men and a Girl, he has provided introductory and concluding essays to bring some coherence to his analysis.

782. Marsh, Cynthia. **File on Gorky**. 104p. *Writer-Files; Metheun Drama Book*. London: Methuen, 1993. Includes select bibliography.

This highly useful compilation of information about Gorky's plays is arranged in four sections. Section 1 is a chronology of Gorky's life and career. Section 2 contains basic information about each of the plays. Section 3 gives information about Gorky's non-dramatic works. Section 4 is a select bibliography of Gorky's work and criticism of it in English.

783. Dowler, Wayne. **An Unnecessary Man: The Life of Apollon Grigor'ev**. 286p. Toronto; Buffalo, N.Y.: University of Toronto Press, 1995. Includes bibliographical references and index.

This is a traditional biographical study of 19th-century literary critic Apollon Grigor'ev. The author is attempting to make Grigor'ev more accessible to allow readers "to judge for themselves whether Grigor'ev's detractors are right about his writings" (p. 6). The book looks at Grigor'ev's works chronologically. "This biography, therefore, aspires to do no more than make the life and thought of Apollon Grigor'ev as transparent to the readers as possible, so that they too can know and judge this man, who, according to the novelist and aesthetic Konstantin Leon'ev, 'not only resembled a Russian but was the thing in itself' " (p. 6). The book includes a bibliography of Grigor'ev's writings.

784. Ellis, Frank. **Vasiliy Grossman: The Genesis and Evolution of a Russian Heretic**. xii, 239p. Oxford: Berg, 1994. Includes bibliographical references (pp. 222-34) and index.

Ellis' study of Vasiliy Grossman is based exclusively on Western and Soviet printed sources. Completed before 1989, he was unable to take advantage of access to the archives that became easier subsequent to 1991. The analysis is straightforward. After an introductory chapter, the following chapters cover his work and life chronologically. Specifically they focus on Soviet writers and the Great Fatherland War, the war years, interpreting catastrophe: 1945-1960, progress, science and war, inside the totalitarian state, and concluding remarks.

785. Davidson, Pamela. **Viacheslav Ivanov: A Reference Guide**. 382p. New York: G. K. Hall/Simon & Schuster/Macmillan, 1996.

Davidson, herself a well-known Ivanov scholar, has done an exemplary job of producing this annotated bibliography on the noted theoretician of symbolism and critic of culture. The bulk of this scholarly work contains a selected annotated chronological listing of works about Ivanov beginning in 1903 with reviews of his collection of lyric verses, *Kormichie zvezdy* (*Pilot Stars*), and ending in 1993 with some 57 items covering his entire oeuvre. Criticism in over 10 different languages is represented with 58 percent in Russian, 24 percent in English, and under 10 percent each of Italian, German, French, Polish, Czech, Dutch, Hungarian, Lithuanian, and Serbian. All but two of the 1,111 entries have been examined *de visu*; each consists of a full bibliographic citation (with English translation) and a descriptive annotation of the contents. When applicable, Davidson provides cross-references to other works cited. The volume also includes a lengthy introductory essay on Ivanov and his critics that is divided into four periods: 1903-1924, 1925-1961,

1962-1985, and 1986-1993. In addition, a chronological list of works by Ivanov as well as an author index and detailed subject index to the entire contents are provided.

The annotations are models of clarity and informative exposition. Anyone interested in doing serious work on Ivanov cannot afford to ignore this book.

786. Goldstein, Vladimir. **Lermontov's Narratives of Heroism**. x, 244p. Evanston, Ill.: Northwestern University Press, 1998. Includes bibliographical references (pp. 222-36) and index.

"While the main body of this study analyzes Lermontov's depiction of autonomous, independent, and self-reliant characters, who 'metaphysically and religiously' assert themselves, here I shall survey the dominant cultural expectation connected with the issues of heroism and individualism as articulated by Lermontov's contemporaries and by some of his later opponents (Slavophiles, Dostoevsky, Solov'ev, Berdiaev, Vladimir Hossky)" (p. 2). The author also seeks the reasons motivating what he sees as a consistent misinterpretation of Lermontov. The book is arranged topically.

787. Barabtarlo, Gennady. **Aerial View: Essays on Nabokov's Art and Metaphysics**. x, 301p. *American University Studies, Series XXIV*. New York: P. Lang, 1993.

As Barbatarlo states in his introduction: "The sum of the essays that compose this volume presumes to show ways in which Nabokov, by perfecting stylistic and structural elements of the art, described the secrets of the hereabout ('physica') and probed the mysteries of the hereafter" (p. 1). Each of the book's seven chapters focuses on specific works by Nabokov: "Revenge," *Invitation to a Beheading*, *The Enchanter*, English short stories, the Russian *Lolita*, *Pnin*, et al.

788. Connolly, Julian W. **Nabokov's Early Fiction: Patterns of Self and Other**. xiii, 279p. Cambridge, Eng.; New York: Cambridge University Press, 1992. Includes bibliographical references (pp. 268-75) and index.

In contrast to the literature on Nabokov in the 1960s and 1970s, which attempted to decode his fiction, the last decade of criticism has looked at the ethical dimensions of his work. This book "aims to delineate Nabokov's growth as a literary artist during the first phase of his career in fiction (1924-1939) by focusing on his changing approach to one of the most significant concerns of his art: the relationship between self and other" (p. 1). Connolly looks at Nabokov's short stories of the period as well as at *Mary*, *King, Queen, Knave*, *The Defense*, *The Eye*, *Laughter in the Dark*, *Despair*, *Invitation to a Beheading*, and *The Gift*.

789. Rampton, David. **Vladimir Nabokov**. viii, 143p. *Modern Novelists*. New York: St. Martin's Press, 1993. Includes bibliographical references (pp. 134-40).

David Rampton attempts to construct a "reading guide" for the general reader in this brief study. The author presents a variety of critical explanations of Nabokov's works. The chapters present the analysis in a chronological fashion beginning with Nabokov's early writings, which appeared in the 1920s (e.g., "Mary" and "Glory"), and concluding with his publications in the 1960s and 1970s (*Pale Fire, Ada, Look at the Harlequins*). This book is one in the series Modern Novelists.

790. Shapiro, Gavriel. **Delicate Markers: Subtexts in Vladimir Nabokov's Invitation to a Beheading**. xii, 243p. illus. *Middlebury Studies in Russian Language and Literature*, vol. 19. New York: P. Lang, 1998. Includes bibliographical references and index.

This is the first monographic study entirely devoted to Nabokov's *Invitation to a Beheading*. The author has selected this work to illustrate the more general nature of Nabokov's writing. "Contrary to the prevailing critical practice of interpreting the novel along specific lines, such as political or metaphysical, Shapiro considers its diverse subtexts, the implicit meanings, thereby achieving more complex and multifaceted perspectives" (back cover). The author is Associate Professor of Russian Literature at Cornell University.

791. Wood, Michael. **The Magician's Doubts: Nabokov and the Risks of Fiction**. viii, 252p. London: Chatto & Windus, 1994. Includes bibliographical references (pp. 238-48) and index.

Rather than a detailed commentary on Nabokov's English-language works reminiscent of Nabokov's own commentary on *Eugene Onegin*, Wood here intends "an intense, even intimate dialogue with provocative texts; a report on the adventure of reading" (p. 7). Individual chapters are devoted to *The Real Life of Sebastian Knight, Bend Sinister, Speak Memory, Lolita*, and his translation of *Eugene Onegin, Pnin, Pale Fire*, and *Ada*.

792. Odoevskii, V. F. Kniaz'. **The Salamander and Other Gothic Tales**. Translated by Cornwell. 215p. London: Bristol Classical Press, 1992. Translated from Russian.

Besides being a public civil servant from 1926 to 1869, Odoevskii was also well known as a "romantic writer, children's writer, thinker, musicologist, educationalist, philanthropist, amateur scientist and general 'renaissance man' " (p. 1). The selections here are primarily from his gothic fiction.

793. Burgin, Diana Lewis. **Sophia Parnok: The Life and Work of Russia's Sappho**. xxvi, 355p.: illus. *Cutting Edge: Lesbian Life and Literature*. New York: New York University Press, 1994. Includes bibliographical references and index.

This critical literary biography of author Parnok includes the full texts of 90 of her poems, translated by Burgin. The work artfully weaves both biographical details and the author's literary output into a fascinating portrait of this gifted writer.

794. Sendich, Munir. **Boris Pasternak: A Reference Guide**. xxi, 376p. New York: G. K. Hall, 1994. Includes bibliographical references and indexes.

This guide is made up of six parts: abbreviations; introduction; Pasternak's Russian writings (1913-1990); critical literature (1914-1990); author index; subject index. The introduction provides the reader with a context for Pasternak's writing and some measure of his influence. The list of Pasternak's publications contains 556 entries and includes publications in many genres: poetry, prose, tales in verse, translations, criticism, reviews, speeches, and others. The main part of the book is the annotated bibliography of critical literature on Pasternak. It includes over 1,000 entries published primarily in Russian and English. The compiler has concentrated on more recent publications, although he does include early criticism. He has excluded criticism that focuses on the political elements in Pasternak's work or that is biographical in nature. The entries in this section and in the bibliography of Pasternak's publications are arranged chronologically. The annotated critical literature is evaluative in nature. While not comprehensive, this is an extremely valuable source for any scholar studying this influential Russian author.

795. Petrushevskaia, Liudmila. **The Time—Night**. Translated by Sally Laird. 155p. London: Virago Press, 1994.

This novel was originally published in the journal "Novyi Mir," no. 2, 1992.

796. Seifrid, Thomas. **Andrei Platonov: Uncertainties of Spirit**. xii, 273p. *Cambridge Studies in Russian Literature*. Cambridge, Eng.: Cambridge University Press, 1992. Includes bibliographical references and index.

"This study of Andrei Platonov (1899-1951) focuses on the interrelation of philosophical themes, imagery and verbal devices in his prose" (frontispiece). Thomas Seifrid examines Platonov's work as it developed throughout his life. He shows how Platonov's work was shaped by his "dialogue" with Marxist-Leninist philosophy. He also shows how Platonov developed his own style of writing while maintaining the expected elements of socialist realism.

797. Popov, Evgenii. **The Soul of a Patriot: Or Various Epistles to Ferfichkin**. Translated by Robert Porter. x, 194p. *Writings from an Unbound Europe*. London: Harvill Press, 1994. Translation of: *Dusha patriota*.

"*The Soul of a Patriot* is about many things, but at its heart it is concerned with the death throes of the 'era of stagnation,' Gorbachev's euphemism for the attenuated neo-Stalinism that pertained under Brezhnev" (p. v).

798. **Pushkin Today**. Edited by David M. Bethea. vi, 258p. Bloomington: Indiana University Press, 1993. Includes bibliography and index.

These papers were originally presented at a conference in Madison, Wisconsin, to mark the sesquicentennial anniversary of Pushkin's death and represent the broad spectrum of American scholarship on Pushkin. The 14 essays are evenly divided into two parts: "contemporary critical views" and "text and context." The first part is an introduction, of sorts, to the wealth of critical methodologies now being applied to Pushkin; the second part delves into those dark spots and obscure passages in the texts of the poet's life and works that have not yet been successfully resolved.

799. Bethea, David M. **Realizing Metaphors: Alexander Pushkin and the Life of the Poet**. xviii, 244p. *Publications of the Wisconsin Center for Pushkin Studies.* Madison: University of Wisconsin Press, 1998. Includes index.

This study was originally conceived as a short monograph on Pushkin's relations with Derzhavin, one of the greatest Russian poets before him. The first part deals with how art relates to life and vice versa for Pushkin, and the second part demonstrates how Pushkin created his life through poetry.

800. Briggs, A. D. P. **Alexander Pushkin, Eugene Onegin**. viii, 116p. Cambridge, Eng.; New York: Cambridge University Press, 1992. Includes bibliographical references (pp. 114-16).

The author provides a chronology of Pushkin's life and works along with related literary and historical events. Then five chapters are divided, respectively, to the poetry of Eugene Onegin; the story line; the unreal reputations of Eugene Onegin and Tatyana Larina; Olga, Lensky, and the duel; and It is in verse, but is it a novel? A final guide to English translations and further reading is also appended.

801. Cooke, Brett. **Pushkin and the Creative Process**. xi, 180p.: illus. Gainesville: University Press of Florida, 1998. Includes bibliographical references and index.

In this volume, Brett Cooke examines Pushkin's unique literary genius in the hope of learning more about the creative process in general. "Pushkin sought out the secrets of poetic inspiration in common, down-to-earth experiences. He created a psychology of creativity virtually on his own, one sufficient for him to do his work" (p. viii). Since Cooke believes that Pushkin's findings are not far from those of today's specialists, it seems a worthwhile exercise to examine his views of creativity.

802. Debreczeny, Paul. **Social Functions of Literature: Alexander Pushkin and Russian Culture**. xvi, 282p., [4] p. of plates: illus. Stanford, Calif.: Stanford University Press, 1997. Includes bibliographical references (pp. [255]-267) and index.

Although Debreczeny devotes most of his attention to Pushkin, he maintains that what information he has gathered about this one author should be relevant to the study of literature in general. His study is in three parts. In Part 1 he examines the reader's response to the reading of the literary text. Part 2 looks at the way an individual's response to a text is conditioned by their social environment. The third part analyzes the aura surrounding the personality of the author. His study goes beyond traditional literary history and uses psychology, anthropology, and other disciplines.

803. Druzhnikov, Yuri. **Prisoner of Russia: Alexander Pushkin and the Political Uses of Nationalism**. xii, 454p. New Brunswick, N.J.; London: Transaction Publishers, 1999. Includes bibliographical references and index.

It is perhaps an understatement to say that much has been written on Pushkin. He has been the most popular object of Russian literary studies since his death. Every aspect of his life has been examined. It is extremely difficult for scholars to identify original topics on Pushkin. Yuri Druzhnikov thinks he has found just such a subject in the focus of this book. "We are faced with a question not yet posed by Russian scholars which is relevant in this, typically Russian context.... We must determine whether Pushkin intended to go abroad, only to return again, or whether he planned to leave the country forever, that is, to migrate" (p. ix). The volume is divided into two parts. The first part discusses Pushkin's plans to go abroad. Part 2 looks at Pushkin as a "runaway."

804. Edmonds, Robin. **Pushkin: The Man and His Age**. xv, 303p., [16] p. of plates: illus. London: Macmillan, 1994. Includes bibliographical references (pp. [290]-295) and index.

Edmonds has written a life of Pushkin "studied within the parameters of his historical context" (p. xiv). The historical context also includes sensible expositions of the major literary works and how they came to be written.

805. Evdokimova, Svetlana. **Pushkin's Historical Imagination**. xviii, 300p. *Russian Literature and Thought*. New Haven, Conn.; London: Yale University Press, 1999. Includes bibliographical references and index.

Pushkin's historical writing has been discussed in a variety of works. In this volume Evdokimova attempts to examine all of his historical writings, an exercise that has not previously been undertaken. The author believes that Pushkin's view of history was ever-changing. This is reflected in his varying views of the same historical events in different works. The book is divided into three parts. Part 1 focuses on Pushkin's search for a connection between historical change and national identity. Part 2 continues the study of the role of cultural context in Pushkin's view of history. Part 3 examines Pushkin's varying views of historical phenomenon in his writings on Peter the Great. "This analysis of Pushkin's historical and meta-historical texts should extend our understanding of the poet's infinitely varied perception of history. If there is anything that unites them, it is Pushkin's believing in, and striving for, the complementarity of multiple truth" (p. xv).

806. Greenleaf, Monika. **Pushkin and Romantic Fashion: Fragment, Elegy, Orient, Irony**. viii, 412p. Stanford, Calif.: Stanford University Press, 1994. Includes endnotes and index.

Many critics have been critical of Pushkin's fragmentariness, or overall lack of a plan, in the internal structure of his compositions. Greenleaf examines Pushkin in relation to his Russian and European contemporaries with a special focus on *Boris Godunov* and the cycle of southern oriental poems.

807. Shaw, J. Thomas. **Pushkin: Poet and Man of Letters and His Prose**. 273p.: illus. Los Angeles: Charles Schlacks, Jr., Publisher, 1995. Includes bibliographical references (pp. [84]-109) and index.

In this first volume of Shaw's *Collected Works* are collected articles written over many years that appeared in a variety of publications. The articles are arranged in two parts. Part 1 contains a lengthy (p. 83) overview of Pushkin's life and works and a selected Pushkin bibliography. Part 2 contains seven articles on Pushkin's prose.

808. Shaw, J. Thomas. **Pushkin's Poetics of the Unexpected: The Non-Rhymed Lines in the Rhymed Poetry and the Rhymed Lines in the Non-Rhymed Poetry**. 369p. Columbus, Ohio: Slavica Publishers, 1993. Includes bibliography, individual work index, name index, and term index.

"This monograph will study in some detail Pushkin's poetics of the unexpected, as regards to non-rhymed lines in the rhymed poetry and rhymed lines in the non-rhymed poetry" (p. 7). The structure of the study consists of two parts that include seven chapters preceded by an introduction that lays out the general methodology of the study, and a conclusion that summarizes what has been discerned. An appendix includes tables of vertical enrichment, orchestration, and parts of speech. Part 1 (Chapters 1-2) focuses on the analysis of long narrative poems and lyrics. Part 2 (Chapters 3-7) deals with nonrhymed poems imitating folk poetry and the dramas. *Evgenii Onegin* is not included.

809. Rybakov, Anatolii. **Fear**. 1st English-language ed. vi, 686p. Boston: Little, Brown, 1992. Translation of the Russian.

Fear is the sequel to Rybakov's earlier work, *Children of the Arbat*. "*Fear* takes place against the background of the ruthless terror, unparalleled in history, in the years 1935-1937. Characters from *Children of the Arbat* encounter new ones, and their struggle against the evil of dictatorship shows that people can remain human beings—live and love, experience passion and joy—even in a morally deformed society" (p. vi).

810. Tertz, Abram. **Little Jinx**. xvi, 80p. London: Quartet Books, 1993.

As Edward Brown remarks in the preface, "This brief, heavily laden story of alienation, rejection, and absolutely blameless guilt is one of the greatest products of Sinyavsky/Tertz's perverse and tender art. . ." (p. xi).

811. Soloukhin, Vladimir Alekseevich. **A Time to Gather Stones: Essays**. xxi, 251p.: port. Evanston, Ill.: Northwestern University Press, 1993. Includes bibliographical references (pp. 237-51).

Vladimir Soloukhin grew up in rural Vladimir in the 1920s and 1930s. He witnessed the development and fall of the Soviet system and the constant attacks on the Russian intellectual community during those years. In this book, as one of the most influential writers in the post-Stalinist period, he chronicles the attempts by organized groups and individuals to save Russia's literary and cultural monuments. "In his essays Soloukhin characteristically utilizes literary information as a starting point for the discussion of broader issues, such as the relationship between culture and spirituality, and the causes for the degradation of the environment" (p. xiii). Soloukhin's book was first published in Russian in 1980.

812. Nepomnyashchy, Catharine Theimer. **Abram Tertz and the Poetics of Crime**. x, 390p. New Haven, Conn.: Yale University Press, 1995. Includes bibliographical references (pp. [361]-382) and index.

Andrei Sinyavsky wrote under the pseudonym of Abram Tertz for much of his career. In this book, Catharine Nepomnyashchy examines the "linguistic strategies and metaphors for the writer and writing, which, taken together, define Sinyavsky's vision of literature" (p. 2). The author focuses on the ramification of adopting Sinyavsky's view that if the writer is a criminal, the text must be viewed as the crime scene, and the act of writing, the crime. To elaborate this thesis Nepomnyashchy reviews a number of Sinyavsky's publications including "What Is Socialist Realism," "The Trial Begins," "Pkhents," "At the Circus," "Gramophoniacs," "Lyubimov," "In the Shadow of Gogol," "Little Tsores," and "Goodnight."

813. Feuer, Kathryn Beliveau. **Tolstoy and the Genesis of *War and Peace***. xiv, 295p.: illus. Ithaca, N.Y.: Cornell University Press, 1996. Includes bibliographical references (pp. 279-84) and index.

Kathryn B. Feuer studied the manuscript editions of Tolstoy's masterpiece and every version he wrote before compiling her analysis of *War and Peace*. "To read *Tolstoy and the Genesis of War and Peace* is to stroll through a developing landscape of Tolstoyan imagination with an expert guide" (p. xii). This study examines the evolution of the novel from its first manifestations in Tolstoy's early works to the first manuscript versions of the novel. Feuer discusses the political conception of *War and Peace* in the second part of her book. Kathryn Feuer did not survive to publish this study; the book has been edited by Robin Feuer Miller and Donna Tussing Orwin.

814. Jahn, Gary R. **The Death of Ivan Ilich: An Interpretation**. xiv, 115p.: illus. New York: Twayne Publishers, 1993.

"Involving an inventive and engaging strategy, Gary R. Jahn asks readers to approach *The Death of Ivan Ilich* from an ironic standpoint—to view what seems literal as figurative and vice-versa—with an eye toward discovering the multiple patterns of organization and allusion permeating Tolstoy's great short novel" (back cover).

815. Jones, W. Gareth. **Tolstoi and Britain**. xii, 303p. *Anglo-Russian Affinities series*, 7. Oxford: Berg, 1995. Includes bibliographical references (pp. 279-89) and index.

"The aim of this selection of articles, all dealing with the links between Tolstoi and Britain, is to convey the dynamic development of that interchange, its various facets and reach, and the reciprocal benefit gained by Britain and Russia in their example of the symbiosis of their cultures" (p. 26). To accomplish this, the editor has selected a variety of essays. He begins with a section on the influence of British literature in Tolstoy's writings. This is followed by other selections on the British reception of Tolstoy's works, both his novels and his polemical writings. Several essays are on Tolstoy's influence on British writers even those who were not among his admirers are presented next. The final section is devoted to writings on Tolstoy's influence on social policies. The essays are from a variety of writers including George Bernard Shaw and Mathew Arnold.

816. Mandelker, Amy. **Framing Anna Karenina: Tolstoy, the Woman Question, and the Victorian Novel**. xv, 241p.: illus. *Theory and Interpretation of Narrative series*. Columbus: Ohio State University Press, 1993. Includes bibliographical references (pp. 211-23).

In recent years, the traditional analysis of Tolstoy's work has been challenged. Along with Richard Gustafson and other critics, Amy Mandelker questions the division of Tolstoy's work into two periods: pre- and postconversion. "The thesis of this book is first that Tolstoy's literary-historical placement at the apex of realism is problematic, and second that Anna Karenina reflects Tolstoy's polemic with realist art and his quest for mythopoesis . . ." (p. 3). In Part 1 the author analyzes the "mythologizing" of Tolstoy's life and the effect this has had on the critical literature. Parts 2-3 explore four examples of imagery in *Anna Karenina* and how each symbolizes one of four themes of the novel: the woman question, representation, illusion, and enlightenment. This volume is one in the Theory and Interpretation of Narrative series.

817. Orwin, Donna Tussing. **Tolstoy's Art and Thought, 1847-1880**. viii, 269p. Princeton, N.J.: Princeton University Press, 1993. Includes bibliographic references and index.

Orwin tries to "reconstruct the ideas that led Tolstoy to write the masterpieces of his youth and middle age" (p. 3). In Part 1 she attempts to decipher what Tolstoy's original vision might have been. This includes examination of the Hegelian atmosphere of the 1850s and the influence of Chernyshevsky and Tolstoy's emerging understanding of nature. In Part 2 she focuses on the *Cossacks* and *War and Peace* and how the unity of man and nature played itself out in these novels. Part 3 deals with a disintegration of his initial vision under a variety of pressures and how this was incorporated into *Anna Karenina*.

818. Rancour-Laferriere, Daniel. **Tolstoy on the Couch: Misogyny, Masochism, and the Absent Mother**. viii, 270p. New York: New York University Press, 1998. Includes bibliographical references and index.

Daniel Rancour-Laferriere examines Tolstoy's attitudes toward women and sexuality in this study. "Tolstoy's contradictory feelings about women and sexuality—more prominently paraded in the *Kreutzer Sonata* than in any other of his works—will be the primary concern of this book. Tolstoy's repudiation of sex is embedded within a complex of polarized feelings about women and sexuality" (p. 3). Rancour-Laferriere focuses on the relationship between Tolstoy and his mother, his argument for sexual abstinence and its basis, and the expression of his sexual attitudes in his writing.

819. Sankovitch, Natasha. **Creating and Recovering Experience: Repetition in Tolstoy**. 245p. Stanford, Calif.: Stanford University Press, 1998. Includes bibliographical references and index.

This is a study of what Natasha Sankovitch believes to have been a basic mechanism in Tolstoy's writings—repetition. She believes that Tolstoy uses repetition to communicate the process by which human beings structure their life experiences. She has divided her analysis into four parts. "The first part is intended to sketch broadly the narratological and epistemological concerns repetition helps Tolstoy to address, the second and third to examine intratextual repetition in his fiction, and the fourth to consider intertextual ones" (p. 7).

820. Shirer, William L. **Love and Hatred: The Troubled Marriage of Leo and Sonya Tolstoy**. 400p., [16] p. of plates: illus. London: Aurum Press, 1994. Includes bibliographical references (pp. 374-86) and index.

Tolstoy died alone, away from his home, November 3, 1910. Far from his wife of 48 years. In this book, William Shirer draws on the diaries of Tolstoy and his wife to explore the unhappy last years of Tolstoy's life. This was William Shirer's final work published shortly after his death.

821. Silbajoris, Rimvydas. **War and Peace: Tolstoy's Mirror of the World**. xii, 149p.: illus. *Twayne's Masterwork series*, no. 146. New York: Twayne Publishers, 1995. Includes bibliographical references (pp. 141-44) and index.

"In *War and Peace: Tolstoy's Mirror of the World*, author Rimvydas Silbajoris explores the thesis that Tolstoy's landmark is indeed a statement about life in its totality, as if the earth were a unified organism narrating itself in the uncountable processes of living and dying" (book jacket). This volume is one in Twayne's Masterwork series. As with other volumes in the series, this book includes a chronology of the life of the author under study.

822. Tolstoy, Leo. **Soedinenie, Perevod i Issledovanie Chetyrekh Evangelii/The Gospel According to Tolstoy**. Edited and translated by David Patterson. xxxviii, 155p. Tuscaloosa: University of Alabama Press, 1992. Includes bibliographical references.

Tolstoy's *Resurrection* was intended as an introduction to three subsequent works on religion. One of these, *A Harmony, Translation and Investigation of the Four Gospels*, was written from 1880 to 1891. This work included translations of the text of the gospels and commentary on the theological works of Tolstoy's time. Each chapter in this work ended with a narrative on the text. "These summaries comprising the life and teachings of Jesus have been gathered into this volume to form *The Gospel According to Tolstoy*. We have in hand, then, an edited and translated version of the Gospel edited and translated by Tolstoy, not only as he understood them but as he wished them to be understood" (p. xi). The volume includes the preface to the first edition.

823. Williams, Gareth. **Tolstoy's Childhood**. vi, 110p. *Critical Studies in Russian Literature*. London: Bristol Classical Press, 1995. Includes bibliographical references (pp. 95-106) and index.

Gareth Williams examines Tolstoy's book *Childhood* in this slim volume. The book is divided into two parts. Part 1 looks at the critical reception of the book on its publication and up to the revolution. In the second part the author provides his own assessment of this classic piece of literature.

824. Goscilo, Helena. **The Explosive World of Tatyana N. Tolstaya's Fiction**. xii, 227p.: illus. *Writers' Worlds*. Armonk, N.Y.: M. E. Sharpe, 1996. Includes bibliographical references and index.

Tatyana Tolstaya was born in Leningrad in 1951. She began publishing in Russia in 1983. Her first book of short stories sold out immediately in Russia and was translated into English only two years later. In this study of Tolstaya's writings, Helena Goscilo discusses various works by Tolstaya, linking them thematically. In this way Goscilo examines Tolstaya's conception of love, marriage, her use of stereotypes and fantasy, and the Tolstayan perception of time. Goscilo does not attempt a unified reading of Tolstaya. "In fact, it [the book] assiduously avoids a neatly packaged, smooth interpretation, in the conviction that Tolstaya's fiction enables her to follow through to its fictional conclusions the adoption of various perspectives on phenomena ranging from imagination, memory, time, art, and spirituality to consumerism, selfishness, egotism, vanity, and the like" (pp. 7-8). The book includes an annotated bibliography of Tolstaya's works.

825. Smith, Alexandra. **The Song of the Mocking Bird: Pushkin in the Work Marina Tsvetaeva**. 211p. *European University Studies; Series XVI, Slavonic Languages and Literature;* 48. New York: P. Lang, 1994. Includes bibliographical references.

In this book, Alexandra Smith examines Tsvetaeva's writings on Pushkin. Raised in a multilingual environment, Tsvetaeva spoke German, French, and Russian. The author argues that mimicry played a major part in her writings. She believes that Tsvetaeva's writings on Pushkin directly affected the development of her own style.

826. Feiler, Lily. **Marina Tsvetaeva: The Double Beat of Heaven and Hell**. xii, 299p. Durham, N.C.: Duke University Press, 1994. Includes index and endnotes.

This is a full-length biography of Tsvetaeva, a well-known 20th-century Russian poetess.

827. Hasty, Olga Peters. **Tsvetaeva's Orphic Journeys in the Worlds of the Word**. xvi, 267p. Evanston, Ill.: Northwestern University Press, 1996. Includes endnotes and index.

The myth of Orpheus, which has been described as "poetry thinking about itself" (p. xvi), is used in Olga Hasty's book as a vehicle for examining the writings of Marina Tsvetaeva. "A consideration of the interpretive process to which Tsvetaeva subjects the myth provides a fruitful starting point for the explication of her artistic values and for the investigation of how these values are translated into specific poetic detail. In Tsvetaeva's Orpheus we discriminate definitive characteristics of the poet and observe how they function within her poetic universe. [. . .] In tracing the potential for metamorphosis that Tsvetaeva uncovers in the Orpheus myth, we trace also her creative process" (p. 8).

828. Makin, Michael. **Marina Tsvetaeva: Poetics of Appropriation**. xii, 355p. Oxford, Eng.: Clarendon Press, 1993. Includes bibliographic references and index. Based on the author's thesis (doctoral—Oxford University, 1985) presented under title: *The Inherited Text in the Poetic Works of Marina Tsvetaeva*.

This full-length study of Tsvetaeva is a substantially revised version of the author's dissertation from Oxford. Not claiming to possess "unitary theoretical rigor," it is instead a useful introduction to Tsvetaeva's poetry.

829. Razumovsky, Maria. **Marina Tsvetayeva: A Critical Biography**. 1st English ed. 363p.: illus. Newcastle upon Tyne, Eng.: Bloodaxe Books, 1994. Includes bibliographical references (pp. 339-53) and index.

"This book is the most comprehensive biography in any language of the Russian poet Marina Tsvetayeva (1892-1941). Drawing on a variety of sources, including the memoirs of Tsvetayeva's family, friends and literary contemporaries, as well as her poetry and autobiographical writings, Maria Razumovsky has been able to reconstruct the major episodes in Tsvetayeva's life, and to relate them to the literary and historical events of her time" (book jacket). This book was originally published in German in 1981. It has been translated into Russian and French in other editions. This is the first English-language edition of this thorough study of one of Russia's most influential writers.

830. Shveitzer, Viktoria. **Tsvetaeva**. Edited by Angela Livingstone, Robert Chandler, H. T. Willetts, and Peter Norman. xv, 413p. New York: Farrar, Straus & Giroux, 1993. Includes chronology, bibliographic references, and index.

This English translation of the author's *Byt i Zhtie Mariny Tsvetaevoy* is slightly abridged from the original, published in 1988. This is a full-length literary biography of Tsvetaeva.

831. Allen, Elizabeth Cheresh. **Beyond Realism: Turgenev's Poetics of Secular Salvation**. viii, 255p. Stanford, Calif.: Stanford University Press, 1992. Includes endnotes and index.

In attempting to demythologize Turgenev criticism, this monograph addresses several issues implicit in Turgenev's narratives "in order to uncover the unique literary patterns that cohere in an intricate, imaginative vision of art and human existence" (p. 4). The chapters in Part 1 examine the ethical and aesthetic aspects of the realist tradition; then in Part 2 Allen examines the particulars of Turgenev's poetics.

832. Friel, Brian. **A Month in the Country: After Turgenev**. 109p. Loughcrew, Oldcastle, County Meath; Ire.: Gallery Press, 1992.

This play is based on a literal translation of Turgenev's text by Christopher Heaney. From that, Freil composed "this very free version" (p. 7).

833. Turgenev, Ivan Sergeevich. **First Love and the Diary of a Superfluous Man**. Translated by Constance Black Garnett. v, 90p. New York: Dover Publications, 1995.

These translations of two of Turgenev's most popular tales were originally published by Constance Garnett. In addition to some slight corrections, this edition also contains new introductory notes and a few exploratory footnotes.

834. Turton, Glyn. **Turgenev and the Context of English Literature, 1850-1900**. x, 219p. London: Routledge, 1992. Includes bibliographical references (pp. 208-15) and index.

Turton's book on Turgenev has two aims: (1) "examine the texts of translations from Turgenev in the two decades where a coherent group of his works was translated—the 1850s and the 1890s" (p. 2) and the relationship of translations to the culture in which they were produced and (2) analyze the impact on English fiction, especially on the authors George Gissing and Henry James.

835. Shukshin, Vasily. **Stories from a Siberian Village**. Laura Michael and John Givens. xlviii, 253p. DeKalb: Northern Illinois University Press, 1996. Includes endnotes, glossary, and bibliographical references.

Vasily Shukshin is credited with giving new life to the art of the short story in the Soviet Union. This volume includes 25 stories set in Siberia, most of which have not appeared in English translation before. "Eccentrics and oddballs, Shukshin's protagonists are restless freedom seekers whose dreams and foibles are as broad and inexplicable as their native Siberian landscape" (back cover). The volume includes one essay by Kathleen Parthe and another by John Givens. There is also a bibliography of his major writings.

836. Erofeev, Venedikt. **Moscow Stations: A Poem**. Translated by Stephen Mulrine. ix, 131p. London: Faber & Faber in association with Brian Brolly, 1998. This translation originally published 1997.

This "poem" is an autobiographical novel. "Structurally, the novel is picaresque in character, a series of bizarre encounters and adventures in 'real time' or reflection, fitted loosely over the thirty-odd stations of the Moscow-Petushki line" (p. viii).

837.   Yevtushenko, Yevgeni. **Don't Die Before You're Dead**. 415p. London: Robson, 1995. Translated from the Russian.

A novel by the celebrated poet Yevgeni Yevtushenko. A glossary of unfamiliar terms is included to help the English-speaking reader.

838.   Goldstein, Darra. **Nikolai Zabolotsky: Play for Mortal Stakes**. xiii, 306p. Cambridge Studies in Russian Literature. Cambridge, Eng.: Cambridge University Press, 1993. Includes index, endnotes, and select bibliography.

This critical study of poet Nikolai Zabolotsky examines the artist's life as well as his work. In it the author "highlights the deep ambiguity of Zabolotsky's era by exploring the ways in which the poet was influenced both by the avant-garde and by the Soviet scientific establishment" (frontispiece). An appendix includes the OBERIU Declaration.

839.   Zalygin, Sergei Pavlovich. **The Commission**. Translated by David Gordon Wilson. xix, 358p. DeKalb: Northern Illinois University Press, 1993.

Sergei Zalygin is a Russian author who has been publishing fiction since 1941. He has endured the hardships of writing under the Soviet regime. This novel, however, was one that was accepted by the Soviet censors. Regardless of their opinion this was one of the author's most successful works. "The novel is the story of one man's struggle with the responsibility forced upon him by the historical developments of his time. Ustinov is constantly torn between his overpowering urge to live and work as he feels God intends, and the social and political duty to which he is called. Faced with historical events that would seem to lead in a straight line into the nothingness of social and ecological destruction, Ustinov and Zalygin's readers must close the circle, a task that is nothing less than a human moral duty, a 'commission' which may not be resigned" (p. xix).

840.   Carleton, Gregory. **The Politics of Reception: Critical Constructions of Mikhail Zoshchenko**. x, 228p. *Northwestern University Press Studies in Russian Literature and Theory*. Evanston, Ill.: Northwestern University Press, 1998. Includes bibliographical references and index.

This is a critical study of the works of the early-20th-century Russian author Mikhail Zoshchenko. "The question motivating this study can be summed up as follows: What is the interconnection between how he writes, how he has been read, and how, in the end, he sought to read himself? Its goal is to elucidate, in concrete terms, the strategies by which we generate meaning from such texts and how, in turn, these same texts operate upon us" (p. 14). Carleton looks at several of Zoshchenko's works including "Youth Restored," "The Blue Book," and "Before Sunrise."

841.   Scatton, Linda H. **Mikhail Zoshchenko: Evolution of a Writer**. xv, 296p.: illus. Cambridge, Eng.; New York: Cambridge University Press, 1993. Includes bibliographical references (pp. 280-91) and index.

This work is the first full-length study in English of Zoshchenko's literary career, and of his critical and political reception in society. It not only provides a critical assessment of all his work, and biographical information about the writer, but also includes an appendix that discusses his posthumous recognition and criticism in the USSR and abroad.

Special Studies, Censorship

842. Ermolaev, Herman. **Censorship in Soviet Literature, 1917-1991.** xviii, 323p. Lanham, Md.: Rowman & Littlefield, 1997. Includes bibliographical references (pp. [305]-314) and index.

Ermolaev's purpose is "to give a comprehensive picture of Soviet censorship in literature from the inception to the dissolution of the Soviet state. The emphasis is laid on detailed textual examination of literary works that were subjected to continuous or extensive censorship" (p. xiii). His study proceeds chronologically with individual chapters devoted to: birth and maturation (1917-1931); intensification (1932-1945); the peak (1946-1953); the unstable thaw (1954-1964); the freeze (1965-1984); and melting (1985-1991).

Émigré Literature

843. Glad, John. **Conversations in Exile: Russian Writers Abroad.** 315p.: illus. Durham, N.C.: Duke University Press, 1993. Translated from the Russian.

What is today's role for the Russian writer living abroad? This is the question posed by this work. The answer takes the form of a series of interviews with a number of Russian writers. All left Russia as exiles. Today, they find themselves in the role of expatriates. There are interviews in this volume with Igor Chinnov, Yury Ivask, Roman Goul, Vasily Aksyonov, Vladimir Voinovich, Joseph Brodsky, Boris Khazanov, Andrei Siniavsky, Maria Rozanova, Sasha Sokolov, Fridrikh Gorenstein, Aleksandr Zinoviev, Natalya Gorbanevskaya, Vladimir Maksimov, and Edward Limonov. Each is preceded by a brief biographical sketch. There is a glossary of names and a chronology of the Russian emigration at the back of this volume.

844. **Under Eastern Eyes: The West As Reflected in Recent Russian Émigré Writing.** Edited by Arnold B. Macmillan. xii, 163p. New York: St. Martin's Press, 1992. Includes bibliographical references and index.

This is a collection of articles that resulted from a 1989 conference on Third-Wave Russian writers. A number and variety of émigré authors are included such as Vasilii Aksenov, Anatolii Gladinin, Lev Loseff, and Zinovii Zinik. Other contributors are largely Western specialists in the subject of Russian emitter literature such as Gerald Stenton Smith, Hans Rothe, Robert Porter, Arnold Macmillan, Julian Graffy, and Nora Bukhs. One interesting contribution is by Galinia Belaia a professor at Moscow State University when this volume was published.

845. Patterson, David. **Exile: The Sense of Alienation in Modern Russian Letters**. xii, 204p. Lexington: University Press of Kentucky, 1995. Includes bibliographical references (pp. [192]-199) and index.

"The purpose of this book is to demonstrate through a study of selected Russian texts that the fundamental problem of meaning in human life is a problem of homelessness; that the effort to emerge from exile is an effort to return meaning to the word and thus to the self and to the other; and that the exile of the word is an exile of human being" (p. xi). Though David Patterson is dealing with universal themes, his discussion focuses on the works of Dostoevsky, Tolstoy, Florensky, Shestov, Solzhenitsyn, Sinyavsky, Brodsky, and Gendelev, moving from spiritual to physical exile and the different types of alienation that accompany each. Since this is a discussion of exile in general, the audience is not intended to be limited to Slavicists. Patterson describes his method as existential. The work is divided into five parts. "The World in Collision" examines the works of Dostoevsky, in particular the *Notes from the Underground Man* and *Winter Notes*. In Part 2 Tolstoy's *Ivan Illich* is the focus as well as *Resurrection*. In Part 3, "The Rupture of Religious Discourse" Patterson looks at the works of Pavel Florensky and Lev Shestov. Part 4 turns to the political exile of Alexander Solzhenitsyn and Andrei Sinyavsky. The final section is devoted to physical exile as it examines the literary works of Joseph Brodsky and Mikhail Gendelev.

Philosophy and Political Theory

846. Bakhtin, Mikhail Mikhailovich. **Toward a Philosophy of the Act**. Edited by Michael Holquist and Vadim Liapunov. Translated by Vadim Liapunov. 1st ed. xxiv, 106p. Austin: University of Texas Press, 1993. Includes bibliographical references (pp. 77-100) and index.

"*Toward a Philosophy of the Act* is a translation of an unfinished philosophical essay by M. M. Bakhtin (1895-1975) that was published in Russian in 1986 by S. G. Bocharov under the title "K filosofi postupka" (p. xvii).

847. **Beyond the Monolith: The Emergence of Regionalism in Post-Soviet Russia**. Edited by Peter J. Stavrakis, Joan DeBardeleben, J. L. Black, and Jodi Koehn. xii, 259p.: map. Washington, D.C.; Baltimore: W. Wilson Center Press; Johns Hopkins University Press, 1997. "Published in cooperation with the Institute of Central/East European and Russian-Area Studies, Carlton University, Ottawa"—P. preceding t.p.

This book is a collection of articles, originally presented at a conference at Carlton University. Its purpose is to explore those factors that have contributed to the growth of regionalism in post-Soviet Russia. "As such, the contributions to this volume fill a gap in our understanding of contemporary Russian politics and society and challenge scholars to reconsider the traditional paradigms through which Soviet Russia has been understood: If Russia's future depends on the provinces, then we must seek to understand the challenges of socio-economic transformation from the perspectives that lie outside of Moscow" (p. 4). The essays have been grouped into four sections: "Historical Setting," "Politics," "Economic Reform and Social Change," and "Ethnic Perspectives." Contributors include Don Rowney, Joan DeBardeleben, Aleksander A. Galkin, John Young, Darrell Slider, Carol Clark, D. J. Peterson, Mark Field, Cynthia Buckley, Greg Poelzer, Nail Moukhariamov, and Robert Daniels.

Marxism in Russia and in the USSR

848. Harding, Neil. **Leninism**. x, 346p. Durham, N.C.: Duke University Press, 1996. Includes bibliographical references (pp. 319-40) and index.

"This book sets out to examine critically the constitutive elements of Leninism as a world view, as a way of comprehending the economic, social, and political realities of the modern world" (p. 2). Harding's main objective is "to give an account of the mental map that Leninism provided to its followers through which they orientated themselves, came to recognize friends and were impelled to mobilize and organize themselves against their perceived enemies" (p. 2). Three appendixes include a chronology of events and Lenin's writings, a guide to Lenin's collected works, and Lenin's principal works by topic.

849. Yakovlev, Aleksandr Nikolaevich. **The Fate of Marxism in Russia**. xxi, 250p. New Haven, Conn.: Yale University Press, 1993. Includes index.

Aleksandr Yakovlev reflects on the course of his country's guiding philosophy and its downfall in the 20th century in this book. "This work is an extended essay, a series of reflections rather than a scholarly treatise engaged in a debate with other philosophers or social scientists. It is preoccupied with Soviet and Russian history and makes little effort to place the development of the Soviet state in the broader context of twentieth-century history" (p. viii). The book has several appendixes. All are lectures or speeches given by Yakovlev on Marxism in the last century in Russia.

850. Loone, Ëero Nikolaevich. **Soviet Marxism and Analytical Philosophies of History**. Translated by Brian Pearce. xvii. 280p.: illus. London: Verso, 1992. Translation of: *Sovremennaia filosofiia istorii*. Includes bibliographical references (pp. 259-71) and index.

Although this book was originally written in Russian in 1976 and published in 1980 in the Soviet Union, it was primarily aimed at a Soviet and East European readership. The author describes his work thus: "In this book contemporary philosophy of history is presented and established as theory of historical cognition and historical knowledge. The author does not advance his own theory of history, but studies historiography, the totality of writings about history" (p. 1). Loone does this from the point of view of Marxism and Marx's writings. He examines the transformation of the philosophy of history into the theory of historical cognition, the developing structure of historical knowledge, procedures for establishing historical knowledge, and methodology of historiography and the theory of socioeconomic formations. A postscript examines the Soviet Union and perestroika as a test for the Marxist philosophy of history.

Intellectual and Cultural Histories

851. **Memoirs of Peasant Tolstoyans in Soviet Russia.** Edited by William Edgerton. xxviii, 264p.: illus. *Indiana-Michigan Series in Russian and East European Studies.* Bloomington: Indiana University Press, 1993. Includes bibliographical references and index.

As the Bolsheviks began constructing their socialist state they encountered opposition from many quarters. One of the least-expected opposition groups was the Peasant Tolstoyans. Very little has been known of this group and its struggle to survive in Soviet society until 1988. In that year the memoirs of seven Tolstoyans were published in Moscow. "The memoirs and documents published in this book bear testimony not only to the distortion in Lenin's portrayal of the typical Tolstoyan but also to the Soviet failure to bury all traces of the Tolstoyan movement for good" (p. xvi). The editor has selected the memoirs of five Tolstoyans: Yelena Shershenyova, Boris Mazurin, Dmitry Morgachev, Yakov Dragunovsky, and Ivan Dragunovsky.

852. **Late Soviet Culture: From Perestroika to Novostroika.** Edited by Gene Kuperman and Thomas Lahusen. vi, 338p. *Post-Contemporary Interventions.* Durham, N.C.: Duke University Press, 1993. Includes bibliographical references and index.

Some of these essays had already appeared in a special issue of the *South Atlantic Quarterly* devoted to the Soviet Union. This present collection enlarges that former collection by seven additional essays. The purpose of the collection is that the variety of themes and approaches "will contribute to an understanding, beneath the inflation of facts, of the debates in the late 1980s and early 1990s around what still and already may be called 'late Soviet culture'" (p. 2).

853. **Russian Thought After Communism: The Recovery of a Philosophical Heritage.** Edited by James P. Scanlan. xviii, 238p. Armonk, N.Y.: M. E. Sharpe, 1994. Includes bibliographical references and index.

Recognizing that the fall of communism had widespread social and cultural effects, the authors contributing to this volume explore how this social upheaval affected Russian philosophy and fostered reinterpretations of previous giants of Russian philosophy. The essays are arranged in five parts: (1) an overview of the return to Russian philosophy after communism; (2) the 19th century revisited (Slavophilism, Fedorov, and Solov'ev); (3) the Silver Age in post-communist perspective (Berdiaev and Merezhkovskii); (4) Russian émigré thought reclaimed; and (5) finding philosophy under Soviet rule (Losev and Bakhtin).

Psychology

854. Etkind, Alexander. **Eros of the Impossible: The History of Psychoanalysis in Russia.** vii, 408p. Boulder, Colo.: Westview Press, 1997. Includes bibliographical references (pp. 351-94).

This history of psychoanalysis in Russia is more than a dry treatise on movements and theoretical positions. Instead it focuses a great deal on the personalities involved, their words and actions, the ideas that influenced their lives, and the vagaries of history that affected them. It begins at a time when the cultural elite was part and parcel of the intellectual life of Europe and ends in the period when psychoanalysis was suspect and its practitioners were imprisoned or at the very least were prevented from applying their skills.

855. Miller, Martin A. **Freud and the Bolsheviks: Psychoanalysis in Imperial Russia and the Soviet Union.** xvii, 237p. New Haven, Conn.: Yale University Press, 1998.

"This book is principally concerned with the importation of the concepts of Sigmund Freud to Russia, the establishment of a psychoanalytic presence there, and the consequences this process had for the country" (p. ix). An appendix contains Freud's letters to Nikolai Osipov, one of the founders of Russian psychoanalysis.

Religion

856. **Christianity After Communism: Social, Political, and Cultural Struggle in Russia.** Edited by Niels Christian Nielsen. xii, 171p. Boulder, Colo.: Westview Press, 1994. Includes bibliographical references.

In April 1993 a conference was held on the future of religion in Eastern Europe after communism. The papers in this volume are the result of that conference. They represent views as divergent as the backgrounds of the participants. This group consists of American Slavic scholars and theological scholars with expertise in Orthodoxy, Roman Catholicism, and Protestantism. "All of our author-participants share the conviction that something new and of crucial significance for religious life has happened and is happening in Russia. . . . Today old conflicts have surfaced—often in bitterness and religious intolerance as state-sponsored suppression of the churches has ceased" (p. vii). The essays have no unifying theme beyond the generally stated interest of the future of religion in Russia. They cover a variety of topics such as "Ethics and Economic Activity in Russia," "The New Religious Press in Russia," "Sociological Models of Religion in Post-Communist Societies," "Visions in Conflict: Starting Anew Through the Prism of Leadership Training," and "The West Wants Chaos." Such a broad spectrum gives the reader the opportunity to consider the effects of the reintroduction of religion into a society as a whole after a century of repression.

General Studies

857. **Religion and Culture in Early Modern Russia and Ukraine.** Edited by Nancy Shields Kollmann and Samuel H. Baron. viii, 213p.: illus. DeKalb: Northern Illinois University Press, 1997. "These articles are the fruit of the second workshop in Early East Slavic Culture, which was held June 19-24, 1993, at Stanford University"—Pref. Includes bibliographical references and index.

The papers contained in this volume were originally presented at the second workshop in Early East Slavic Culture, held at Stanford in 1993. The authors examine a variety of topics including backwardness in Russian peasant culture, concepts of society and social identity, court ceremony, supplicatory prayers, miracle stories, martyrdom, Russian painting, and religious reform and the emergence of the individual in 17th-century Russian literature.

858. **Russian Religious Thought.** Edited by Judith Deutsch Kornblatt and Richard F. Gustafson. x, 266p.: illus. Madison: University of Wisconsin Press, 1996. Includes bibliographical references and index.

"This volume contains essays on four seminal thinkers from the modern Russian tradition: Vladimir Soloviev, Pavel Florensky, Sergei Bulgakov, and Semen Frank" (p. 5). The contributions contained in this volume were originally given as papers at an NEH-sponsored conference. While paper presentations were given on a number of Russian religious thinkers, these four were chosen as the focal point for this volume because of the coherence of their philosophies. Contributors include: Judith Deutsch Kornblatt, Richard F. Gustafson, Maria Carlson, Steven Cassedy, David M. Bethea, Michael A. Meerson, Bernice Glatzer Rosenthal, Paul Valliere, Robert Slesinski, George L. Kline, Philip J. Swoboda, and James Scanlan.

History

859. Anderson, John. **Religion, State, and Politics in the Soviet Union and Successor States.** xi, 236p.: illus., map. Cambridge, Eng.: Cambridge University Press, 1994. Includes bibliographical references (pp. 223-30) and index.

In addition to examining the post-Stalin Soviet's policy toward religion and religious practice, this study also includes an investigation of the many factors that led to a major change in religious policy. Individual chapters cover religious policy under Khrushchev, Brezhnev and also his successors, Gorbachev, and the transformation of religious policy in the 1990s.

860. Bushkovitch, Paul. **Religion and Society in Russia: The Sixteenth and Seventeenth Centuries.** vii, 278p. New York; Oxford: Oxford University Press, 1992. Includes extensive bibliography and appendix, "Manuscript of Epifanii Slavinetskii's Sermons."

This study concerns itself with the history of religion in Russia among the landowning elite. The author has limited himself to a specific time period and a certain segment of society in the hope of covering more thoroughly a period of enormous change in the role of religion in Russian life. The author believes the traditional historical view that the late 17th century as the real beginning of Westernization is misleading. Bushkovitch believes early in the 17th century, as early as 1620, Russia was the recipient of Western influence. "For the elite the greatest changes began with the increasing influence of Ukrainian religious writings in the 1620s, a process that would redirect the elite's religious world away from ritual and miracle cults toward sermons and other moralizing writings, both at court and elsewhere" (p. 9).

Bushkovitch traces the general development of the church in the 16th and 17th centuries in the first few chapters of the book. He uses this framework to demonstrate that the evolution of Russia's religious life at this time prepared Russian society for the changes to be introduced by Peter the Great. The author attempts to show that Russia's religious development in this period, in many ways, paralleled changes in religious life in the West.

861. Corley, Felix. **Religion in the Soviet Union**. xiv, 402p.: illus. New York: New York University Press, 1996. Includes bibliographical references.

The opening of the Soviet archives to Western scholars has provided them with enormous amounts of material for examination. This volume selectively compiles some of those documents related to the treatment of the Soviet religious community by the Soviet bureaucracy. "Each of the documents in this collection—all but a handful of which have never appeared in English—has been included because it illustrates in some way the complex web of relations during the Soviet era between religious groups and the state" (p. 2). The documents are arranged into chronological chapters. Each begins with a brief introduction that places the documents in historical context.

862. Davis, Nathaniel. **A Long Walk to Church: A Contemporary History of Russian Orthodoxy**. xxiii, 381p.: illus. Boulder, Colo.: Westview Press, 1995. Includes bibliographical references (pp. 339-60) and index.

Nathaniel Davis has set himself the task of writing a secular history of the Orthodox Church. One of the questions central to his study is why the church has continued to revive after years of repression. He begins with a chronological analysis of the church's development beginning with the Bolshevik revolution and continuing throughout the century's turbulent events. He includes chapters on the clergy, the underground organization of religion, convents, theological education, and church publications on finance and the laity. Davis has made use of the formerly closed archives of Russia to compile this study. He is a professor at a California university.

863. Ellis, Jane. **The Russian Orthodox Church: Triumphalism and Defensiveness**. vi, 240p. *St. Antony's series*. New York: St. Martin's Press in association with St. Antony's College, Oxford, 1996. Includes bibliographical references (pp. 224-31) and index.

Ellis traces how the Russian Orthodox Church emerged from a position of relative obscurity and persecution into a social, cultural, and spiritual force recognized by the Soviet/Russian government. She begins with the first signs of religious freedom in the mid-1980s during the period of glasnost, and then proceeds to describe and analyze the significance of the millennium celebrations of 1988 in the USSR, the reversal of policy on religion, and other factors that enabled the Orthodox Church to achieve a new status in Russian society.

864. Evtuhov, Catherine. **The Cross and the Sickle: Sergei Bulgakov and the Fate of Russian Religious Philosophy**. x, 278p.: illus. Ithaca, N.Y.: Cornell University Press, 1997. Includes bibliographical references (pp. 253-72) and index.

Sergei Bulgakov was one of the most prominent religious philosophers of the Russian Silver Age. Evtuhov uses Bulgakov's biography and the development and maturation of Bulgakov as a religious philosopher in order to paint a broader picture of Russian religious philosophy during the Silver Age and the effects it had on society, culture, and politics.

865. **Religious Policy in the Soviet Union**. Edited by Sabrina Petra Ramet. xix, 361p. Cambridge, Eng.: Cambridge University Press, 1993. Includes bibliographical references and index.

"This book brings together fifteen of the West's leading scholars of religion in the USSR, and provides the most comprehensive analysis of the subject yet undertaken. Bringing much hitherto unknown material to light, the authors discuss the policy apparatus, programs of atheisation and socialization, cults and sects, and the world of Christianity" (frontispiece). Contributors are Sabrina Petra Ramet, John Anderson, Oxana Antic, Marjorie Mandelstam Balzar, John Dunstan, Jane Ellis, J. A. Helby, Larry E. Holmes, Samuel A. Kliger, Anatolii Levitin-Krasnov, Otto Luchterhandt, Walter Sawatsky, Myroslaw Tataryn, Paul De Vries, and Philip Walters. The book includes an appendix providing basic statistics on religious groups numbering 2,000 or more in the Soviet Union.

866. Robson, Roy R. **Old Believers in Modern Russia**. xiii, 188p.: illus. DeKalb: Northern Illinois University Press, 1995. Includes bibliographical references and index.

In this study Roy Robson examines the relationship between religion and culture by studying specific aspects of the life of Old Believers in Russia. "Specifically, it examines two major issues relating to the experience of Old Believers at the end of Russia's ancient regime. First, it seeks to prove that Old Believer traditions helped to create a 'culture of community.' Later chapters will show how this most traditional segment of Russian religious life interacted with the secular processes of modernization and change" (p. xi).

867. **Religious and Secular Forces in Late Tsarist Russia: Essays in Honor of Donald W. Treadgold**. Edited by Charles E. Timberlake. x, 366p. Seattle: University of Washington Press, 1992. Includes bibliographical references and index.

These essays all deal with some aspect of church-state relations, church history, and secularism in late tsarist Russia. Topics include: an overview introductory essay by the editor on religious pluralism in the period of reactionary ideas and the church-state relationship in tsarist Russia; the Jesuits role in founding schools; Alexander Herzen, Marxism, and Aziatchina; crime, police, and mob justice in Petrograd in 1917; as well as two tributes to Donald Treadgold, to whom this volume is dedicated.

Special Studies

868. Batalden, Stephen K. **Seeking God: The Recovery of Religious Identity in Orthodox Russia, Ukraine, and Georgia**. 299p.: illus. DeKalb: Northern Illinois University Press, 1993. Earlier versions of all except one essay were presented at the symposium on "The Recovery of Religious Identity in the Soviet Union" held at Arizona State University in March 1991.

Most of the essays in this volume were originally read as papers at a symposium on the same topic held in 1991 at Arizona State University. The primary assumption of this volume "is that the new religious consciousness, although partially occasioned by the death of communism, is firmly rooted in living traditions that antedate by centuries the relatively brief period of Soviet rule in Eurasia" (p. 4). The essays from various perspectives are concerned with the historical sources of religious identity in Orthodox culture. The essays themselves are organized in three parts: (1) popular religious culture and Orthodox identity; (2) confessional and natural identity in the Orthodox world; and (3) sources for the study of religious identity in the Orthodox East.

869. Emmons, Terence. **Alleged Sex and Threatened Violence: Doctor Russel, Bishop Vladimir, and the Russians in San Francisco, 1887-1892**. xiv, 251p.: illus. Stanford, Calif.: Stanford University Press, 1997. Includes bibliographical references and index.

The story that Emmons tells "concerns a conflict that took place in the period 1889-1892 in San Francisco between the Russian Orthodox Bishop of the Aleutians and Alaska and a Russian émigré medical doctor who went by the name Nicholas Russel" (p. xi). The story itself is of little historical significance, but does help to understand the worldview and cultural assumptions of two distinct actors in this narrative, the Dr. Russel, who was a member of the revolutionary-populist intelligentsia, and Bishop Vladimir, a conventional Russian cleric.

870. Epp, Ingrid I., and Harvey L. Dyck. **Peter J. Braun Russian Mennonite Archive, 1803-1920: A Research Guide**. xxxvii, 215p. Toronto: University of Toronto Press, 1996.

This guide provides the researcher with access to materials once a part of the State Archives of the Odessa region. That archive housed the historical records of the Mennonite communities of southern Ukraine. "Consisting of more than 130,000 pages of rare and significant sources, the Peter J. Braun Russian Mennonite archives are the most extensive collection of in-group Russian Mennonite documents surviving from the imperial period. . . . In 1990-91 it was microfilmed and the microfilm was brought to Canada. This research guide provides a historical introduction to the archive and a detailed file-by-file listing and description of its contents" (p. ix). The files are arranged chronologically. A chronology of Mennonite history in Russia is included to assist the user. The descriptions are brief but exact. Unfortunately, no index of subjects is included.

871. **The Occult in Russian and Soviet Culture**. Edited by Bernice Glatzer Rosenthal. vii, 468p.: illus. Ithaca, N.Y.: Cornell University Press, 1997. Includes bibliographical references and index.

This is a collection of essays that examines the evolution of occultism in 20th-century Russia. The essays are grouped into five sections. The first includes three essays on occultism in prerevolutionary Russia. The three essays in Part 2 focus on occultism in the early 20th century. The three essays in Part 3 examine the relationship between science and magic. Part 4 includes four essays on occultism under Stalin. Part 5 traces the occult after Stalin. The book includes several appendixes describing source materials on the occult.

Science, Technology, and Research

General Studies

872. **The Evolution of Theodosius Dobzhansky: Essays on His Life and Thought in Russia and America**. Edited by Mark B. Adams. xi, 249p.: illus. Princeton, N.J.: Princeton University Press, 1994. Selected papers from the International Symposium on Theodosius Dobzhansky, held in Leningrad in Sept. 17-19, 1990.

Dobzhansky has been called the central architect of the modern evolutionary synthesis during the interwar years who integrated diverse biological specialties into his classic book *Genetics and the Origin of Species*, published in 1937. This memorial volume contains 16 essays about Dobzhansky. They are arranged in five parts: an introduction; essays on his Russian roots, entomology, and evolutionary genetics; his relation to the Morgan lab and the breakdown of the naturalist/experimentalist dichotomy; his scientific legacy; and Dobzhansky's worldview.

873. Graham, Loren R. **Science in Russia and the Soviet Union: A Short History**. x, 321p. *Cambridge History of Science*, 10. Cambridge, Eng.: Cambridge University Press, 1993. Includes appendix (2 parts), endnotes, bibliographic essay, and index.

Well-known historian of Russian science, Graham has written this book as an introduction for the educated layman who is interested in the history of Russian science. The nine chapters are arranged in three parts: the tsarist period, Russian science and a Marxist revolution, and science and Soviet society. An appendix provides two additional chapters on the strengths and weaknesses of Russian and Soviet science. The first deals with the physical and mathematical sciences and the second with biological science, medicine, and technology.

874. Graham, Loren R. **What Have We Learned About Science and Technology from the Russian Experience?** xiii, 177p.: illus. Stanford, Calif.: Stanford University Press, 1998. Includes bibliographical references and index.

Graham's aim is to understand better science and technology as social and cultural institutions. He believes that this can be accomplished when we examine the extent to which they take on different forms in contrasting environments. The scientific establishment of the Soviet Union in the 1980s was purportedly the largest in the world, outnumbering that in the United States by 20-30 percent. In looking at Soviet science he addresses questions such as: (1) is science a social construction?; (2) are science and technology Westernizing influences?; (3) how robust is science under stress?; (4) how willing are scientists to reform their own institutions?; and (5) who should control technology?

875. Josephson, Paul R. **Totalitarian Science and Technology**. ix, 123p. *Control of Nature*. Atlantic Highlands, N.J.: Humanities Press, 1996. Includes bibliographical references (pp. 111-18) and index.

There have been several studies that have examined the development of science in a totalitarian regime. Often the view is adopted that science is usually able to remain outside the system, not relying on the political elements in a society in its decision making. The author of this study points out that this view is frequently difficult to reconcile with the facts. "This book aims at a balanced view of science in totalitarian regimes, going beyond mere attacks on their 'pseudo-science' " (p. 2). Josephson will compare the development of science under Hitler and Stalin. He demonstrates that these regimes had tremendous impact on science in their countries.

876. Krementsov, N. L. **Stalinist Science**. xvii, 371p. Princeton, N.J.: Princeton University Press, 1997. Includes bibliographical references (pp. [307]-358) and indexes.

Focusing on the period from 1939 to 1949, Krementsov examines the origin, evolution, and consolidation of the Stalinist science system. He covers the transition phase of Russian science in the period 1890-1929, the Stalinization of Russian science during the 1930s, and the most memorable intellectual artifact of Stalinist science in the field of genetics. He then analyzes the further consolidation in the 1940s, the effect of the aftermath of World War II, and the effects of the beginning of the cold war. In its final years, Krementsov shows how the ideologically dominated science affected education, research, careerism, and institutional rivalry.

877. Rimmington, Anthony, and Rod Greenshields. **Technology and Transition: A Survey of Biotechnology in Russia, Ukraine, and the Baltic States**. ix, 227p.: map. London: Pinter, 1992. Includes bibliographical references (pp. [216]-218) and index.

This book provides "a detailed survey and analysis of the most important issues in biotechnology in the Soviet Union's successor states" (p. 1) and biotechnology's impact on the economy and the management of biotechnology R & D and production. Individual chapters deal with biotechnology's impact on agriculture, on medicine, and the environment, and the commercialization of biotechnology. In addition to a chapter on the opportunities for international biotech companies, the author also provides an appendix containing a directory of biotechnology R & D and production in Russia and the former Soviet republics.

878. **The Making of a Soviet Scientist: My Adventures in Nuclear Fusion and Space from Stalin to Star Wars**. Edited by R. Z. Sagdeev and Susan Eisenhower. xi, 339p. New York: John Wiley, 1994. Includes index.

Sagdeev is an expert in plasma physics and at the time of the writing of this book was a professor of physics at the University of Maryland. For many years he was the director of the Soviet Academy of Sciences Space Research Institute. As the late Carl Sagan's introduction states, "This autobiography casts light on little-known and very important corners of the former Soviet Union" (p. xi).

879. Tropp, Eduard Abramovich. **Alexander A. Friedmann: The Man Who Made the Universe Expand**. x, 267p.: illus. Cambridge, Eng.: Cambridge University Press, 1993.

Alexander Friedmann was a relativistic cosmologist and also made contributions to hydrodynamics and meteorology. This volume originally appeared in Russian on the anniversary of his birth in 1888. It explores his childhood, education, and his work on space, time, and the geometry and dynamics of the universe.

Telecommunications

880. Campbell, Robert Wellington. **Soviet and Post-Soviet Telecommunications: An Industry Under Reform**. vii, 253p. Boulder, Colo.: Westview Press, 1995. Includes bibliographical references.

"The aim of this book is to describe and interpret the telecommunications system and telecommunications policy in the former USSR against the background of current world experience and to evaluate progress toward a more effective structure in the era of reform. The central idea is to relate the performance of the sector to the organizational and regulatory variables that affect that performance" (p. 2). Topics covered include an overview and historical background; economics; development and production of equipment; specialized services and applications; the changing environment for telecommunications under economic reform; television and radio broadcasting; prospects for expansion and modernization; and analysis and critique of telecommunications policy in the emerging situation. An appendix describes network architecture, the evolution of the inter-city network, hierarchical architecture, and equipment.

Environmental Protection

881. Bailey, C. C. **The Aftermath of Chernobyl: History's Worst Nuclear Power Reactor Accident**. 2nd ed. vii, 189p.: illus. Dubuque, Iowa: Kendall/ Hunt, 1993.

The author explains what happened at Chernobyl and what effects the disaster had, especially on the Saami people in Lapland. He also describes the effect it had on nuclear power policy in Sweden. Bailey concludes with speculation on what the long-range implications of Chernobyl are and the lessons we can learn from it.

882. Dodd, Charles K. **Industrial Decision-Making and High-Risk Technology: Siting Nuclear Power Facilities in the USSR**. xii, 211p.: illus., maps. Lanham, Md.: Rowman & Littlefield, 1994. Includes bibliographical references (pp. 187-206) and index.

Dodd examines the problem of siting of nuclear power facilities. He describes the nature of the siting problem, the stakeholders in the decision, the institutional setting for such decision making, and the various patterns of the nuclear industry development in the Soviet Union in an introductory chapter. He then proceeds to provide an overview of the Soviet energy sector, the institutional setting in the Soviet nuclear power industry to 1986, policy prior to 1986, post-Chernobyl changes in nuclear policy, new participants in the decision-making process after Chernobyl, and the legacy of Soviet decision making and nuclear power. Several appendixes provide additional factual information.

883. Feshbach, Murray. **Ecological Disaster: Cleaning Up the Hidden Legacy of the Soviet Regime**. x, 157p.: illus. New York: Twentieth Century Fund Press, 1995. Includes bibliographical references (pp. 121-46) and index.

In providing an overview of the legacy of Soviet-imposed damage to the environment, Feshbach also "charts a strategy for Western institutions to follow to help 'stop the bleeding.' " Individual chapters are devoted to Chernobyl; threats to the Arctic Ocean and the Japan and Baltic Seas; dying lakes, rivers, and inland seas; chemical and biological warfare centers and other secret facilities; and pollution of the air and land.

884. Hill, Malcolm R. **Environment and Technology in the Former USSR: The Case of "Acid Rain" and Power Generation**. xii, 261p.: illus. *New Horizons in Environmental Economics*. Lyme, N.H.: Edward Elgar, 1997.

Hill focuses on atmospheric pollution in the former USSR and the various factors, both technological and commercial, that influence the level of these emissions. After an introductory first chapter, the author provides the dimensions and context for atmospheric pollution, information on fuels and combustion processes, and how this relates to power generation. His final three chapters examine the roles of Western and Russian companies in technology transfer for reduced environmental pollution; the political, economic, and commercial factors; and conclusions and suggestions for further research.

885.   Morgenstern, W. **Mathematical Modeling with Chernobyl Registry Data: Registry and Concepts**. vi, 110p.: illus. *Veröffentlichungen Aus Der Geomedizinischen Furschungsstelle Der Heidelberger Akademie d Wissenschaften Supplememt Zu Den Sitzungsberichten Der Mathematisch-1995.* New York: Springer, 1995. Includes bibliographical references.

This study is the result of a cooperative research project conducted by the Heidelberg Academy for the Humanities and Sciences, the Russian Academy of Sciences, and the Russian Academy of Medical Sciences. The main aim of the project is to "develop mathematical methodologies needed for better information support in health policy decision-making in the area of primary health care provision for the Russian populations affected by radiation due to the Chernobyl accident" (back cover). The core of the volume is a description of general mathematical approaches in the project and the given conditions of the registry of data.

886.   **Nagasaki Symposium on Chernobyl**. Edited by S. Nihon Nagataki. xx, 272p.: illus. Amsterdam; New York: Elsevier Science, 1994. "Proceedings of 'Chernobyl Update,' 3 June 1994 at the 67th Annual Meeting of the Japan Endocrine Society; 'Chernobyl in the Future,' 4 June 1994 at the International Chernobyl Thyroid Symposium, sponsored by the Ministry of Education, Science, and Culture, Japan; and the 'Japan-NIS Chernobyl Thyroid Symposium,' 12 December 1993, sponsored by the Nagasaki University."

The purpose of this symposium was to "present and discuss the available (purely) scientific data from all over the world independent of psychological, social, economic, and political bias, and thus to make conclusions that would further medical science. The symposium consisted of two sessions, "Chernobyl Update" and "Chernobyl in the Future." The conclusions and recommendations of presenters are provided at the end of each session.

887.   **Environmental Resources and Constraints in the Former Soviet Republics**. Edited by Philip R. Pryde. ix, 366p.: illus., maps. Boulder, Colo.: Westview Press, 1995. Includes bibliographical references and index.

This collection of essays examines the real state of the environment in the former Soviet republics. "Focusing broadly on environmental systems, infrastructures, and problems, the book also surveys each republic's physical geography, ethnography, resources, history, economic bases and future needs and potential" (p. 353). Each essay in the volume is devoted to one of the republics. Taken together, these papers provide an overview of the environment in the region.

Social Conditions and Sociology

888. Recent Social Trends in Russia, 1960-1995. Edited by Irene A. Boutenko and Kirill E. Razlogov. xvii, 379p. *Comparative Charting of Social Change.* Montreal: McGill-Queen's University Press, 1997. Includes bibliographical references.

The editors of this volume have compiled sociological data that have not previously been compiled in one source. Thus, this study presents a detailed analysis of the social changes in Russia in the late 20th century. Among the data presented here is evidence of changing attitudes toward institutions such as marriage and of a rise in unemployment and a growing young professional group. There are also indications of diversification in religious beliefs and of an increase in the influence of Western cultures on Russian society. "The findings suggest that Russian and Western societies are more similar than one would imagine and contradict the popular conception that Communist Russia fell out of world history for seventy years" (frontispiece).

889. Sexuality and the Body in Russian Culture. Edited by Jane T. Costlow, Stephanie Sandler, and Judith Vowles. x, 357p.: illus. Stanford, Calif.: Stanford University Press, 1993. Includes bibliographical references (pp. [277]-346) and index.

The editors remind us that while the essays in this volume greatly expand our knowledge of sexuality in Russian culture, there is still much we do not know. The essays themselves approach the subject from different vantage points, but the introductory essay provides a framework in which to read them so that they form a coherent whole. The essays themselves are arranged in three parts: (1) the cultural history of sexual representation, (2) literary versions of sex and body, and (3) the maternal body.

890. Melvin, Neil. Russians Beyond Russia: The Politics of National Identity. 170p.: maps. *Chatham House Papers.* United Kingdom: The Royal Institute of International Affairs, 1995. Includes bibliographical references (p. 170).

In this study Neil Melvin examines the Russified settlers living outside the Russian Federation. He focuses on six former republics: Russian Federation, Estonia, Latvia, Moldova, Ukraine, and Kazakhstan. Throughout he is concerned with three main issues. First, how has the political identity of Russians living in these regions changed with changing governments? Second, what role, if any, do the Russified communities play in the emerging national identities of these regions? Third, does the study of the Russified population living outside of Russia help us understand the relationship between ethnicity, nation, and state in the ex-USSR? Each chapter of the book is devoted to one region with a concluding discussion. The book includes a brief statistical appendix showing general characteristics in the Russified population under discussion.

891. Schmemann, Serge. **Echoes of a Native Land: Two Centuries of a Russian Village**. 1st ed. 350p.: illus., maps. New York: Alfred A. Knopf, 1997. Includes bibliographical references and index.

Serge Schmemann describes life in a Russian village in this volume. The Pulitzer Prize-winning author focuses on the village of Koltsovo, previously known as Goryainovo, Karovo, and Sergieyevskoye. Schmemann selected this particular village because it was once the location of his family's estate. His story of life in this village as it passed through the imperial, Soviet, and post-Soviet periods illuminates much of life in Russia.

892. Wirtschafter, Elise Kimerling. **Social Identity in Imperial Russia**. xi, 260p.: illus., map. DeKalb: Northern Illinois University Press, 1997. Includes bibliographical references (pp. [223]-253) and index.

Wirtschafter addresses questions raised in her earlier studies of social categories, dealing especially with soldiers' children, common soldiers and noncommissioned officers, and "raznochintsy." In describing her work she says: "These groups, while enjoying limited privileges, occupied ambiguous outsider statuses within a social framework constantly redefined by an activist state. Attention to formal social categories in turn has led me to emphasize long-term patterns of development that can account for the Russian empire's ability to integrate multiple societies and cultures in an enduring, flexible, though ultimately fragile, polity" (p. ix). Here she includes landowning nobility, civil and military servicemen, clergy, commercial-industrial elites and semielites, the professions and intelligentsia, peasants, townspeople, and workers.

General Studies

893. **Social Trends in Contemporary Russia: A Statistical Source-Book**. Translated by Michael Ryan. xiii, 249p. New York: St. Martin's Press, 1993. Includes bibliographical references.

This book compiles statistics from a number of official statistical publications issued by Goskomstat (the State Committee for Statistics). Prior to glasnost, few official statistics were published on a regular basis that accurately reflected social trends in Soviet society. Since the late 1980s this has changed. Michael Ryan has compiled statistical data on ethnic population, marriages, divorces, sex, women in society, education, life expectancy, morbidity, mortality, welfare, housing, and crime. His appendixes provide additional explanatory notes, transliteration tables, and bibliographical details on the sources used.

894. Novak, Jan. **Commies, Crooks, Gypsies, Spooks, and Poets: Thirteen Books of Prague's Year of the Great Lice Epidemic**. 202p. South Royalton, Vt.: Steerforth Press, 1995.

Jan Novak, acclaimed Czech novelist, turns his creative skills to a description of late-20th-century Prague. The 13 "books" here describe his yearlong visit to his homeland with his family. During that trip he was able to assess the changes in the city since his departure and call on his knowledge of Prague's history, giving the reader a rich sense of life in Prague. Novak also describes the difficulties facing those living in post-communist Eastern Europe.

895. Pilkington, Hilary. **Russia's Youth and Its Culture: A Nation's Constructors and Constructed**. xiv, 358p. London: Routledge, 1994. Includes bibliographical references (pp. [326]-346) and index.

"In this book, Hilary Pilkington applies the methods of cultural studies research to this study of Russian youth . . . the book also aims to chart the passage of Western youth cultural studies in the twentieth century and suggests some new ways forward in the light of the study of the Russian experience." This is the first ethnographic study of Russian youth by a Western scholar. It includes a glossary of youth slang and an appendix of data on the participants in the study.

896. Randolph, Eleanor. **Waking the Tempests: Ordinary Life in the New Russia**. 431p. New York: Simon & Schuster, 1996. Includes bibliographical references (pp. 391-410) and index.

"*Waking the Tempests* is about how ordinary Russians are struggling to survive the revolution from Communism to Capitalism in the 1990s" (book jacket). Eleanor Randolph has interviewed a varied group of Russians from many sectors of society. In so doing she hoped to show how the massive changes taking place in Russia in the last decade of the 20th century have affected all levels of society. There are interviews with mail-order brides, ballerinas, priests, murderers, doctors, and real estate brokers. They are young and old, of both genders, and from various religions and social groups. All are faced with a society in a state of flux.

897. Semyonova Tian-Shanskaia, Olga. **Village Life in Late Tsarist Russia**. Edited by David L. Ransel. Translated by Michael Levine and David L. Ransel. xxx, 175p.: illus. *Indiana-Michigan Series in Russian and East European Studies*. Bloomington: Indiana University Press, 1993. Translated from Russian. Includes bibliographical references (pp. [173]-179).

The author undertook this study in the late 1890s "in order to meet the need for information about the actual life conditions, attitudes, and aspirations of the peasantry" (p. xi). The focus on a single village and families within that village was unique at the time and served to make this a classic ethnographic study in the field. Tian-Shanskaia not only is a keen observer, but also concentrates on the treatment of women and children as well as a wide range of rituals and everyday practices.

898. Worobec, Christine. **Peasant Russia: Family and Community in the Post-Emancipation Period**. xiv, 257p.: illus. DeKalb: Northern Illinois University Press, 1995. Includes bibliographical references (pp. [225]-247) and index.

"This book describes the world of the Russian peasant during the four decades after emancipation.... [It] explains who these peasants were, how they lived, how they treated each other, and how they struggled to perpetuate their society in the face of the challenges of freedom and modernization" (pp. x-xi). Individual chapters are devoted to resources and obligations, the customs of property devolution, the family life cycle and household structures, courtship, marriage, and the culture of patriarchy.

Alcoholism and Drug Abuse

899. White, Stephen. **Russia Goes Dry: Alcohol, State and Society**. ix, 250p. Cambridge, Eng.: Cambridge University Press, 1996. Includes bibliography, notes, and illustrations.

This intentionally disturbing book expertly depicts and analyzes the role of alcohol in Russian society. In the 1980s there was a heroic attempt to stem alcohol abuse. White documents this campaign and also "traces the profound influence of alcohol through Russian history, and charts the campaign from its initiation under Mikhail Gorbachev to its disappointing aftermath in the post-communist 1990s" (frontispiece). His analysis clearly presents the limitations of any orchestrated attempt to achieve social reform.

Social Problems and Social Change

900. Ball, Alan M. **And Now My Soul Is Hardened: Abandoned Children in Soviet Russia, 1918-1930**. xxi, 335p., [28] p. of plates: illus., maps. Berkeley: University of California Press, 1994. Includes bibliographical references (pp. 311-24) and index.

Ball investigates the phenomenon of bezprizornye (homeless children) that was especially acute in the first decade of Bolshevik rule. He begins with an introductory chapter on the origins of these homeless youth and proceeds from there to a broader examination of their situation. In the second part of the book he focuses on the state's response to this tragedy and its attempt to answer questions of housing and rehabilitation and eventual prevention of homelessness of children.

901. **Dear Comrade Editor**. Edited by Susan Bridger and James Riordan. 235p. Bloomington: Indiana University Press, 1992.

"No more vivid reflection of the perestroika process can be found than in letters written by readers of the Soviet press. The post-1985 period unleashed a veritable outpouring of the soul, a release of pent-up passion, sometimes a burning desire to be part of the changes, sometimes to shout abuse at authority" (p. 1). The editors, Jim Riordan and Susan Bridger, have selected a number of letters from the major publications of the perestroika period. These have been grouped by topic into chapters on "Politics," "Youth," "Women," "The Needy and the Privileged," "Rural life," "Everyday Life," "Nationalism," and "Work and Army Service." The editors present the Western reader with Soviet perceptions of this world.

902. **Soviet Civilization Between Past and Present**. Edited by Mette Bryld and Erik Kulavig. 193p.: illus. *Odense University Slavic Studies*, vol. 10. Odense: Odense University Press, 1998. Includes index.

This anthology is comprised of a number of essays by a group of European scholars. "The present anthology focuses on various aspects and manifestations of consciousness, in particular of mass consciousness, in the Soviet Union and post-Soviet Russia (with a detour to the new Lithuania)" (back cover). The essays cover a range of topics: Lenin's image in the mass consciousness; public dissent under Khrushchev; national identity in the Russian cinema; dualism in Soviet society. The contributors are Hans Henrik Brockdorff, Mette Bryld, Soren Damkjaer, David Gillespie, Natalis Kozlova, Erik Kulavig, Pernille Larsen, Irina Sandomirskaia, Olga Velikanova, and Natalia Zhuravkina.

903. **Ethnic Conflict in the Post-Soviet World: Case Studies and Analysis**. Edited by L. M. Drobizheva. xv, 365p.: illus., maps. Armonk, N.Y.: M. E. Sharpe, 1996. Includes bibliographical references (pp. 353-55) and index.

"The case studies collected in this volume cover a broad spectrum, from the battle-fields of Bosnia and Nagorno-Karabagh to the successfully managed conflicts, and negotiated settlements, of Estonia, Tatarstan and the Sakha Republic. The authors outline the contours and character of these conflicts and explain the underlying factors producing and/or mitigating conflict" (p. 3). The case studies are divided by region and include the Balkans, Central Europe, the Baltics, Ukraine, Russia, Siberia, the Volga, the Caucasus, and Central Asia. There is also a section on minorities, refugees, and migrants. This volume is one in the Women in International Security series.

904. Dutkina, Galina. **Moscow Days: Life and Hard Times in the New Russia**. Translated by Catherine A. Fitzpatrick. xiv, 238p. New York: Kodansha International, 1996. Includes bibliographical references (pp. 231-32) and index.

This honest, penetrating memoir by journalist Galina Dutkina explains social and economic conditions in post-communist Russia, focusing especially on Moscow.

905. Grant, Bruce. **In the Soviet House of Culture: A Century of Perestroikas**. xvii, 225p.: illus., map. Princeton, N.J.: Princeton University Press, 1995. Includes bibliographical references (pp. [191]-222) and index.

Grant provides a history of the cultural transformation of North Sakhalin Nivkhi during the Soviet period, as it was remembered in 1990. He compares narrative accounts of living Nivkhi with archival documents, travel accounts, and other scholarly documents. These accounts "show that Nivkhi largely negotiated their identity over the last seventy years between the variously manifested dialectics of tradition and modernity, then perestroika..." (p. 17). How these indigenous peoples managed their past " is essential for understanding what took place over the Soviet period, and for understanding rationales for current redefinition in the new geopolitical matrix of North Asia" (p. 17).

906. Hardwick, Susan Wiley. **Russian Refuge: Religion, Migration, and Settlement on the North American Pacific Rim.** xiii, 237p.: illus., maps. Chicago: University of Chicago Press, 1993. Includes bibliographical references (pp. 201-22) and index.

"Russian migration, settlement, landscape and adaptation to life on the North American Pacific rim form the central themes of this book. Research questions focus specifically on the importance of the role of religion in migration and settlement decision making by immigrant groups" (p. 3). The author selected this geographic area because it is the oldest Russian-American community, it has great diversity in its religious community, and it has seen tremendous development in recent years. Hardwick uses a "geo-ethnographic" approach for her study, relying on interviews and field observations for her data.

907. Harwin, Judith. **Children of the Russian State, 1917-1995.** ix, 222p. Aldershot, Eng.: Avebury, 1996. Includes bibliographical references (pp. 192-213) and index.

"This book charts the development of policy and services for Russian children in need of public care from the Revolution to the present day. Its particular emphasis lies on the last ten years because these are the watershed years in the history of Russian child care" (p. 1). Harwin begins with an overview of public care for children from Lenin to Brezhnev. She then examines family structure and parenting practices in the late Soviet period. At this point in the book she begins a systematic examination of the changes originating in the policies of perestroika that would have long-term effects for the nation's children. During the Yeltsin years she focuses on family support, substitute care services, social work, and social pedagogy. Finally, she discusses what lies ahead for the children of the new Russian state.

908. **Public Opinion and Regime Change: The New Politics of Post-Soviet Societies.** Edited by Arthur H. Miller, Vicki L. Hesli, and William Mark Reisinger. viii, 310p.: illus. Boulder, Colo.: Westview Press, 1993. Includes bibliographical references (pp. 292-305).

The results reported in this volume come from surveys conducted in the Soviet Union between 1988 and 1991. They are valuable not only for the light they shed on the opinions of citizens of a state that did not seek feedback from public opinion, but also because they represent baseline data for future surveys. The volume is in four parts and each contains essays and studies by individual researchers. Part 1 deals with conducting public opinion research in the Soviet Union. Part 2 reveals how citizens relate to politics: individuals, groups, and the political system. Part 3 focuses on the economy and Part 4 on foreign policy.

909. Piirainen, Timo. **Towards a New Social Order in Russia: Transforming Structures and Everyday Life.** vi, 254p.: illus. Aldershot, Eng.: Dartmouth University Press, 1997. Includes bibliographical references (pp. [247]-254).

In planning this book the author was confronted with three major questions. The first concerned various mechanisms of social change in a transitional society, the second dealt with the daily life of ordinary people that were forced to cope with rapid social change, and the third was methodological and revolved around questions dealing with how such change was to be studied. He tackled these questions by first presenting basic concepts in social change, then examining everyday encounters with the new market economy, how work and employment were transformed, and the resulting class society based on household behavior and consuming potential. He then presents mini-case studies of four families in St. Petersburg and concludes with chapters on households and public power and possible future directions.

910. **Rocking the State: Rock Music and Politics in Eastern Europe and Russia**. Edited by Sabrina P. Ramet. x, 317p.: illus. Boulder, Colo.: Westview Press, 1994. Includes bibliographical references and index.

This is the first scholarly attempt to treat all the countries of the former Soviet bloc with regard to their reception and internalization of rock music. Every country except Albania is discussed in this volume. The contributors are Olaf Leitner, Alex Kan, Nick Hayes, Sabrina Petra Ramet, Laszlo Kurt, Stephen Ashley, Sergei Zamascikov, Robert Bird, Maria Paula Survilla, and Romana Bahry. "Bringing together some of he world's leading authorities on rock music under communism, this book analyzes the rise of specific rock groups throughout Eastern Europe and the Soviet Union, examining the broader social culture in which they operated and evaluating the political ramifications of their popularity" (p. 297).

911. Wyman, Matthew. **Public Opinion in Postcommunist Russia**. xiv, 269p.: illus. London: Macmillan, 1997. "Published in association with the Centre for Russian and East European Studies, University of Birmingham." Includes bibliographical references (pp. 239-65) and index.

Assessment of public opinion and the reporting of it was unknown in Russia before perestroika. This book examines not only the development of the public opinion gathering apparatus in Russia, but explores several questions including: "How have Russians responded to the collapse of their empire? What, if anything, do they regret about the collapse of communism? What do they think of their new post-communist leaders? Who favours the introduction of capitalism, and who is against? How, if at all, do older people, who spent the majority of their lives living under communist rule, differ in their attitudes from the younger, post-communist, generation? How have attitudes shifted over time?" (pp. xiii-xiv).

Women

912. **Perestroika and Soviet Women**. Edited by Mary Buckley. xiii, 183p. Cambridge, Eng.: Cambridge University Press, 1992. Includes index.

The essays in this volume were all written before August 1991. Each of the authors discusses to some degree "the implications of reform for female labour in industry and in agriculture, the falling percentage of female deputies, new women's groups, the changing status of women's councils and the position of women in Ukraine. . . . This book presents a thorough analysis of the impact perestroika, democratization and glasnost had upon the Soviet women as workers, consumers and political actors" (frontispiece).

913. **Women's Activism in Contemporary Russia**. Edited by Linda Racioppi and Katherine O'Sullivan See. xiii, 277p. Philadelphia: Temple University Press, 1997. Includes bibliographical references and index.

The authors of this study trace the development of the women's movement in Russia. They begin with a description of the historical context in which activism has evolved in Russia. The economic, political, and social position of women are examined. There are chapters here that discuss individual women's groups such as the Union of Women in Russia and the Independent Women's Forum. There are also discussions of economic changes for women in recent years. The volume includes appendixes listing the registered women's organizations in Russia and supplying the text of an "Open letter to American Women issued on behalf of the Congress of Soviet Women, July 1993." There is also a list of sources for locating interviews with activists discussed in the book.

914. Alfeyeva, Valeria. **Pilgrimage to Dzhvari: A Woman's Journey of Spiritual Awakening**. vii, 328p. New York: Bell Tower, 1992. Includes bibliographical references.

As Russia seeks to identify its religious persona in the late 20th century, one Russian woman sets out on her own personal journey of "spiritual awakening." Valeria Alfeyeva describes the unusual paths such a journey can take in this book. The author has made many pilgrimages to monasteries all over the world. In this story of a Russian writer caught in the political and social upheaval of her country, much of her personal experience is documented.

915. Attwood, Lynne. **Red Women on the Silver Screen**. 272p., [16] p. of plates: illus., ports. London: Pandora, 1993. Includes index.

There have been many books written on Soviet cinema but little discussion about the role of women in this industry. This book provides the Western reader with perspective on a subject seldom explored. The book is arranged into three parts. The first provides the reader with an overview of Soviet history and the place of women and cinema in that history. Parts 2 and 3 are interviews conducted with Russian film critics, directors, camera operators, and scriptwriters. The author has included a select list of Russian and Soviet films at the end of the volume.

916. **No More Heroines?: Russia, Women and the Market**. Edited by Sue Bridger, Rebecca Kay, and Kathryn Pinnick. x, 220p. *Women & Politics/ Women and Politics* (Routledge [Firm]). London: Routledge, 1996. Includes index, bibliography (pp. 210-17), and appendix.

This is the first volume in a series on women and politics. The purpose of this work is "to shed some light on the complex nature of women's lives in Russia today and on the multiplicity of factors that are affecting their choices and behavior. In particular, it seeks to examine the Soviet legacy for women as Russia embarked on its economic reforms, to analyze the impact these reforms have had on women and, most of all, to explore the options which remain open to them and their responses, both as individuals and in new voluntary organizations" (p. 2). In two parts, "The Impact of Change," and "Responding to Change," individual chapters concentrate on women and unemployment, living standards, women and business, survival strategies, and sexual exploitation and the new labor market.

917. **Russia Through Women's Eyes: Autobiographies from Tsarist Russia**. Edited by Toby W. Clyman and Judith Vowles. x, 393p.: ports. *Russian Literature and Thought*. New Haven, Conn.: Yale University Press, 1996. Includes bibliographical references (pp. [381]-386).

This is a collection of translated autobiographical writings from Russian women of the 19th century. Taken together the writings collected here present the reader with a unique view of imperial Russia through the eyes of a number of women. The autobiographies reflect the views of writers, doctors, scholars, and politicians, but all women, shaped by the experiences of a woman's life in Russia of the 19th century. Each autobiography is prefaced with a brief biographical sketch.

918. **Women and Society in Russia and the Soviet Union**. Edited by Linda Harriet Edmondson. ix, 233p. Cambridge, Eng.: Cambridge University Press, 1992. Includes bibliographical references and index.

The role in society and experiences of women in the Soviet Union have been largely ignored by Western scholars until the late 1960s. Over the last 20 years the study of women and gender topics has become a major area of research. "This volume demonstrates the originality and diversity of this recent research. . . . The essays reflect the interdisciplinary nature of women's studies and include chapters on women writers, women's work, women and politics, women as soldiers, female prostitution, popular images of women and women's experiences of perestroika" (p. 1). Contributors include Catriona Kelly, Mary Schaeffer Conroy, Linda Edmondson, Barbara Norton, Richard Abraham, Marina Ledkovsky, Elizabeth Waters, Sue Bridger, and Mary Buckley.

919. Engel, Barbara Alpern. **Between the Fields and the City: Women, Work, and Family in Russia, 1861-1914**. xi, 254p.: illus., maps. Cambridge, Eng.: Cambridge University Press, 1994. Includes bibliographical references and index.

After the emancipation of the serfs in 1861, Russia began to industrialize, and many peasant women, especially around big cities like Moscow, began to interact with the market economy. Some of these women found opportunities in the urban setting, while many others found hardship. What Engel demonstrates is that "changes that slackened the hold of the patriarchal family provided new opportunities for peasant women, but they also rendered women more economically and personally vulnerable" (p. 4).

920. Goscilo, Helena. **Dehexing Sex: Russian Womanhood During and After Glasnost**. vi, 183p. Ann Arbor: University of Michigan Press, 1996. Includes bibliographical references (pp. 171-80) and index.

As Goscilo tells the reader in the introduction, "This volume contains six separate but interrelated discussions of Russian womanhood as reconstructed and deconstructed in Russian culture during the last decade" (p. 1). Individual chapters explore gender politics during glasnost, the prevailing paradigm equating women with maternity and nationhood, the subversive potential of "new women's prose," the relationship between gender and spatial categories, and the nature, structure, and marketing of pornography.

921. **Fruits of Her Plume: Essays on Contemporary Russian Woman's Culture**. Edited by Helena Goscilo. Armonk, N.Y.: M. E. Sharpe, 1993. Includes index.

This volume is a collection of articles. "The essays collected here examine women's works in order to identify the distinguishing traits of gendered cultural products and of the individual talents that gave them birth" (p. xix). There is deliberately no unifying theorized framework as the editor hoped to get a broad sample of the work in the field. Contributors include: Helena Goscilo, Svetlana Boym, Richard Chapple, Caryl Emerson, John R. Givens, Darra Goldstein, Beth Holmgren, Natal'ia Ivanova, Jevzy Kolodziej, Thomas Lahusen, Nadia L. Peterson, Stephanie Sandlev, and Nicholas Zekulin.

922. **Russia—Women—Culture**. Edited by Beth Holmgren and Helena Goscilo. xiv, 386p.: illus. Bloomington: Indiana University Press, 1996. Includes bibliographical references and index.

These essays attempt to present a broader view of culture and women. "Drawing on the latest, least myopic scholarship in (Western) women's studies and cultural studies, we picture the entity of Russian culture as an amorphous, intricate, many-layered and much-lived-in place, a rambling house of countless private and public rooms, with limitless street access, instead of the proverbial museum of cultural monuments" (p. ix).

923. Mamonova, Tatyana. **Women's Glasnost vs. Naglost: Stopping Russian Backlash**. xx, 184p. Westport, Conn.: Bergin & Garvey, 1994. Includes bibliographical references and index.

Mamonova was exiled from Russia in 1979 for her activities in establishing the neofeminist movement there. This collection of interviews with Russian women by Mamonova includes a wide cross section of women from all walks of life. Her book shows how glasnost (openness) validated their lives, but also how naglost (backlash) also haunted their newly found empowerment.

924. Millinship, William. **Front Line: Women of the New Russia.** xxi, 297p.: ports. London: Methuen, 1993. Includes bibliographical references (pp. [295]-297).

William Millinship was the Moscow correspondent for the *Observer* from 1989 to 1992. He decided to compile a series of interviews with Russians as they lived through the extraordinary changes of 1992. "I decided to interview only women for a number of reasons. In my three years traveling around Russia and other parts of the Soviet Union, I had come to respect their energy, quick understanding, thoughtfulness, strength, sense of humor and breadth of interests" (p. x). Millinship's interviews cover such topics as women, sex, health, the communist legacy, the camps, religion, privilege and the ruling class, education, the arts, and business. A brief chronology of the last 100 years is included.

925. Ruthchild, Rochelle Goldberg. **Women in Russia and the Soviet Union: An Annotated Bibliography.** xiv, 203p. New York: G. K. Hall, 1993. Includes indexes.

This bibliography includes English-language works on the lives of women in Russia and the Soviet Union. Although the compiler does not give a range of dates for the publications to be included, most seem to date from the latter part of the 20th century. This also reflects the developmental stage of the field of research. The entries are primarily descriptive, but references to criticisms are sometimes included. "This bibliography is intended to aid students, teachers, and scholars in the field of Russian/Soviet studies. A quick perusal of this book will show that there has been an increase in the number of articles and books about women in Russia and the Soviet Union published in recent years" (p. xii). The compiler has divided the entries into categories including reference works, general studies, folk culture, ancient and medieval society, 1682-1796, Catherine the Great, the emperors, the era of the great reforms, the Soviet period, autobiographies and biographies, fiction, and literary criticism.

926. **Russian Peasant Women.** Edited by Lynne Viola and Beatrice Farnsworth. 304p. New York: Oxford University Press, 1992.

This volume collects 14 essays on the life faced by the peasant women in Russia before and after the revolution. It explores a range of topics including labor, sexual life, family structure, midwifery, religion, village life, divorce, collectivization, women in agriculture, and glasnost. Contributors include Mary Matossian, Christine D. Worobec, Rose Glickman, Cathy Frierson, Beatrice Farnsworth, Samuel Ramer, Brenda Meehan-Waters, Lynne Viola, Roberta Manning, and Susan Bridger.

Special Studies

927. Boym, Svetlana. **Common Places: Mythologies of Everyday Life in Russia**. xii, 356p.: illus. London: Routledge, 1994. Includes bibliographical references (pp. 384-98).

"This book is not about Soviet politics or Russian art but about the unwritten laws of everyday existence, about everyday aesthetic experiences and alternative spaces carved between the lines and on the margins of the official discourses" (p. 5). Boym, a former Leningrader, looks at the little things of everyday life, "byt" in Russian, in order to reveal "some centuries-old mechanisms of cultural survival, arts of minor compromise and resistance" (p. 5). Her analytic sketches are arranged in four sections: mythologies of everyday life; living in common places: the communal apartment, writing in common places: graphomania; and post-communism, postmodernism. She concludes with a chapter on nostalgia for the commonplace.

928. Cullen, Robert. **The Killer Department: Detective Viktor Burakov's Eight-Year Hunt for the Most Savage Serial Killer in Russian History**. 1st ed. 258p.: illus., maps. New York: Pantheon Books, 1993.

Cullen presents a fascinating journalistic account of the hunt for Russia's most savage serial killer. Told from the point of view of the chief detective in the case, Viktor Burakov, it documents the killings and the methods used by Russian police to apprehend the killer, Andrei Chikatilo.

929. Draitser, Emil. **Taking Penguins to the Movies: Ethnic Humor in Russia**. 199p. Detroit: Wayne State University Press, 1998. Includes bibliographical references (pp. 185-92) and index.

Draitser claims that this is the first extensive work on Russian ethnic humor. He offers "not only a comprehensive collection of Russian ethnic humor of the second half of this century, but its content analysis and interpretation in sociopolitical and psychological terms" (p. 10). In the course of his study he deals with an overall assessment of the phenomenon of Russian ethnic humor, the reasons for the appearance and proliferation of Russian ethnic jokes, and other forms of ethnic humor such as nicknames, proverbs, and sayings.

930. Edelman, Robert. **Serious Fun: A History of Spectator Sports in the USSR**. xvi, 286p.: illus. New York: Oxford University Press, 1993. Includes bibliographical references (pp. 251-76) and index.

Here Edelman pays attention to spectator sports that ordinary Soviet citizens actually chose to watch, versus those that the government tried to promote as part of its worldwide propaganda machine. In part, the author's objective is to determine if there can be such a thing as a socialist spectator sport. Topics explored in this study include the history of Soviet spectator sports, the international dimension of Soviet sport, the roles of professionals and amateurs, sport as entertainment and perestroika, and professionalism in sports.

931. George, Alexandra. **Escape from "Ward Six": Russia Facing Past and Present**. xxiv, 760p.: illus. Lanham, Md.: University Press of America, 1998. Includes bibliographical references (pp. [719]-738) and index.

As the author states in the introduction, this is an eyewitness account "of change in Russia during a period of historic significance. During two lengthy stays spanning mid-1991 to the end of 1992 and autumn 1993 to mid-1995 I will take the reader through a first-hand account of life in Russia at a unique crossroads in her history." Through interviews with hundreds of intellectual elites she provides a broad discussion of the challenge that Russia faces in rebuilding its internal cultural, intellectual, social, and economic structures.

932. Handelman, Stephen. **Comrade Criminal: Russia's New Mafiya**. x, 398p. New Haven, Conn.: Yale University Press, 1995. Includes bibliographical references (pp. [387]-389) and index.

Handelman explores the new Russian underworld, the Russian mafia, and uses his exploration as a way of understanding one of the major reasons why Russia did not live up to the expectations of development and democratization that were held for it when Gorbachev resigned in December 1991. In the course of his investigations he relies on personal interviews with both criminals and the Russian law enforcement agencies, on-the-spot reporting, and available documents.

933. Krivich, Mikhail, and Ol 'gert Ol´gin. **Comrade Chikatilo: The Psychopathology of Russia's Notorious Serial Killer**. 287p.: illus. Fort Lee, N.J.: Barricade Books; distributed by Publishers Group West, 1993. Translated from the Russian by Todd Bludeau.

This is another account of the pursuit, capture, and trial of the worst serial killer in modern Russian history. What makes this story somewhat unique is that his trial was the first public criminal trial after the breakup of the Soviet Union.

934. Ledeneva, Alena V. **Russia's Economy of Favours: Blat, Networking, and Informal Exchange**. xiii, 235p.: illus. *Cambridge Russian, Soviet and Post-Soviet Studies*, 102. New York: Cambridge University Press, 1998. Includes bibliographical references (pp. 222-31) and index.

"The word blat refers to the system of informal contacts and personal networks which was used to obtain goods and services under the rationing which characterized Soviet Russia. Alena Ledeneva's book is the first to analyze blat in all its historical, socio-economic and cultural aspects, and to explore its implications for post-Soviet society. In a socialist distribution system which resulted in constant shortages, blat developed into an 'economy of favours' which shadowed an over-controlling centre and represented the reaction of ordinary people to the social constraints they faced. In social and economic terms, blat exchanges became vital to the population, and to the functioning of the Soviet system. At the same time, however, blat practices subverted the ideological and moral foundations of Soviet rule, and the study of blat provides concrete evidence of the tendency of the Soviet system to subvert itself. Finally, the book shows that the nature of the economic and political changes in contemporary Russia cannot be properly understood without attention to the powerful legacy of the blat economy" (frontispiece).

935. Lourie, Richard. **Hunting the Devil.** xxii, 263p. New York: HarperCollins, 1993. Includes index.
Lourie relates the arrest, interrogation, and trial of Andrei Chikatilo, a serial murderer in Rostov on the Don. The information in the book was taken from the official documentary record and the participants.

936. Russell, Elena. **The Golden Edge: Growing Up in Russian Alaska.** 226p. London: Jonathan Cape, 1995.
Elena Russell grew up in the 1950s in far north Alaska. The autobiography traces her life and the influence of her Russian roots on her everyday existence.

937. Rywkin, Michael. **Moscow's Lost Empire.** xiii, 214p.: maps. Armonk, N.Y.: M. E. Sharpe, 1994. Includes bibliographical references (pp. 199-203) and index.
Although the Soviet Union has disintegrated, its ethnic groups and its national problems survive. Michael Rywkin is concerned with describing those problems in this book. "The intention is to give the reader a full picture of national and ethnic issues affecting the former Soviet Union and its component republics, or rather their heirs, the post-Soviet states, at the outset of their independent existence" (p. xi). Rywkin divides his subject into four broad categories: "Regions"; "Minorities"; "Issues"; and "Policies." In each, he gives the reader a broad overview of the challenges and difficulties facing the newly independent states of the post-Soviet Union.

Handicrafts

938. Toomre, Joyce Stetson. **Classic Russian Cooking: Elena Molokhovets' A Gift to Young Housewives.** xiii, 680p.: illus. *Indiana-Michigan Series in Russian and East European Studies.* Bloomington: Indiana University Press, 1992. Includes bibliographical references (pp. [633]-648) and index.
Cookbooks often provide a glimpse into the domestic culture of a society. This classic cookbook is such a source. Originally published in 1861 Elena Molokhovets' book was an instant success and was in its 20th edition by 1897. Joyce Toomre has provided the Western student of Russian culture a unique source in this translation of Molokhovets' book. The extensive introduction and appendixes supply those unfamiliar with Russian culture with all necessary background information to take full advantage of the information and recipes in this unusual resource.

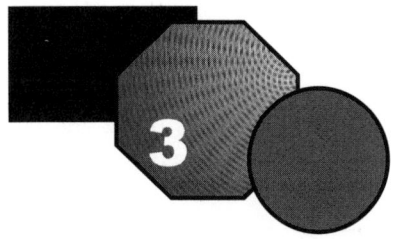

Commonwealth of Independent States, Other Former Soviet Republics, Jews, and Other Minorities

General Studies

939. **Russia's Orient: Imperial Borderlands and Peoples, 1700-1917.** Edited by Daniel R. Brower and Edward J. Lazzerini. xx, 339p.: illus., maps. Bloomington: Indiana University Press, 1997. Includes bibliographical references (pp. [317]-331) and index.

This collection of 14 articles grew out of a conference held in 1994 at the University of California at Berkeley. The collapse of the Soviet Union was the occasion for increased access to the empire's remotest regions as well as to the local archives located there. Each of these scholars has provided fresh approaches to the study of the Russian East and its borderlands.

940. **Post-Soviet Women: From the Baltic to Central Asia.** Edited by May Buckley. xvii, 316p. Cambridge, Eng.: Cambridge University Press, 1997. Includes index.

This is an interdisciplinary study of women in the post-Soviet republics of the former USSR. Specialists with varying views of their subject wrote all contributions. There is not, therefore, one unified conclusion of this book. "This volume is the first to take a systematic look at the position of women in the post-Soviet states of the former USSR. It is divided into two main parts: The first focuses on the economy, society, and polity of the Russian federation; the second gives specialists' insights into social, political, economic, and military developments in the other republics of the former Soviet Union. The book pays special attention to women's own perceptions of their lives" (p. i).

941. Chinn, Jeff, and Robert John Kaiser. **Russians As the New Minority: Ethnicity and Nationalism in the Soviet Successor States**. xii, 308p.: maps. Boulder, Colo.: Westview Press, 1996. Includes bibliographical references (pp. 287-89) and index.

Rather than rely on the more common theoretical framework of decolonization to explore nationalism in the states of the former Soviet Union, these two authors try to assess the interethnic relationships "from a less russophobic viewpoint while at the same time avoiding the opposite russocentric approach. [They] were particularly interested in applying the concept of interactive nationalism, a refinement of reactive ethnicity, as both an explanatory and predictive model for inter-ethnic behavior" (p. xi). The chapters are arranged in three parts. In Part 1 they provide a theoretical and historical background. In Part 2 they present studies of individual states (the Baltics, Belarus and Ukraine, Moldova, Kazakhstan, Central Asia, and Transcaucasia), and in Part 3 they provide conclusions and draw implications.

942. Goldenberg, Suzanne. **Pride of Small Nations: The Caucasus and Post-Soviet Disorder**. xv, 233p. London: Zed Books, 1994. Includes bibliographical references (p. xv) and index.

The purpose of this volume is to provide a wealth of information about the Caucasus. It begins with a history of the area and the return of these small republics to the world community after the downfall of the Soviet Union. After a chapter on the economic situation, Goldenberg devotes separate chapters to Georgia, Azerbaijan, Armenia, the war in Nagorno-Karabakh, and the various nationalities in the North Caucasus. The author's emphasis is on the current economic and political situation and the entry of these republics into the mainstream of world economics and politics.

943. Juviler, Peter H. **Freedom's Ordeal: The Struggle for Human Rights and Democracy in Post-Soviet States**. xvi, 283p. *Pennsylvania Studies in Human Rights*. Philadelphia: University of Pennsylvania Press, 1998. Includes bibliographical references and index.

The newly independent states of the former Soviet Union face a staggering array of challenges in virtually all areas of their societies. Not only must they rebuild their political and economic systems, they must find a way to renew their social systems. All of this must be done within the context of the legacy of the Soviet system. This book adopts the basic assumption "that democracy, human rights, and the rule of law are inseparable companions to the building and consolidation of stable, inclusive, democratic communities" (p. x). The author examines what he believes to have been the internal contradictions of the communist system and their repercussions. He also looks at the nature of authoritarianism and what its legacy is for the region.

944. Khazanov, Anatoly Michailovich. **After the USSR: Ethnicity, Nationalism and Politics in the Commonwealth of Independent States**. xxi, 311p.: illus., maps. Madison: University of Wisconsin Press, 1995. Includes bibliographical references (pp. 272-98) and index.

The first three chapters explore "the role that nationalism has played in the breakup of the Soviet Union and in undermining communist ideology in the country . . . the main characteristics of a post-totalitarian society and the role of nationalism in its ideology and practice" (p. xv), and the role of nationalism of ethnic minorities in the current Russian context. The remaining chapters tie theory to practice in looking at nationalism in Central Asia in general, Kazakhstan, Yakutia, Chechnya, and the plight of the Meskhetian Turks.

945. Liber, George. **Soviet Nationality Policy, Urban Growth, and Identity Change in the Ukrainian SSR, 1923-1934**. xvii, 289p.: maps. *Soviet and East European Studies*, no. 84. Cambridge, Eng.; New York: Cambridge University Press, 1992. Includes bibliographical references (pp. 241-75) and index.

"This book analyzes the precarious relationship between Soviet legitimacy-building and the consequences of rapid industrial development in the Ukrainian Soviet Socialist Republic, the most populous non-Russian republic in the USSR, during the 1920s and 1930s. George Liber traces the impact of rapid urban growth upon the implementation of Soviet preferential policies, korenizatsiia. . . . The author shows how the interplay between industrialization, urbanization, and korenizatsiia produced a modern, urban Ukrainian identity. This, he argues, explains why the Stalinist leadership changed its course on the nationality question in the 1930s and gave precedence to the Russians in the USSR" (frontispiece).

946. Smith, Graham. **Nation-Building in the Post-Soviet Borderlands: The Politics of National Identities**. xi, 293p.: illus., maps. Cambridge, Eng.: Cambridge University Press, 1998. Includes bibliographical references (pp. 224-83) and index.

This multiauthored work focuses on the challenges of nation-building after the fall of the Soviet state. The chapters are arranged in three parts: (1) rediscovering national histories (Ukraine, Belarus, Transcaucasia, Central Asia); (2) ethnopolitics and the construction of group boundaries (Baltic states, Ukraine, Central Asia); and (3) language and nation-building (Georgia, Uzbekistan).

Baltic Republics

947. **Lithuanian Literature**. Edited by Vytautas Kubilius, Rita Dapkute, and Diana Bartkutep. 549p. Vilnius: Vaga, 1997. Includes bibliography and index.

This collection of essays presents an overview of Lithuanian literary development. The editors have selected articles by a number of Lithuanian literary scholars and translated them. As a group they present a picture of the history of Lithuanian literature beginning in ancient times. The editors have not attempted to find materials that present detail on the cultural environment in which Lithuanian literature evolved. "This book attempts to reveal the basic tendencies in the development of Lithuanian literature. Therefore, not all authors are described here, only those who were most characteristic in the expression of certain tendencies. Only the most prominent works of an author are mentioned here, works which have played an active role in the evolution of national literature" (p. 7). The volume includes a bibliography of translations of Lithuanian works into foreign languages.

948. Crowe, David. **The Baltic States and the Great Powers: Foreign Relations, 1938-1940**. xv, 264p.: illus., map. Boulder, Colo.: Westview Press, 1993. Includes bibliographical references (pp. 239-51) and index.

With the independence of the Baltic states after the August 1991 coup, these countries finally tasted independence. "This book looks at the origins of their first attempt at nationhood and the significance of the relationship of these countries with the major powers from 1918-1940 on their history during that period" (p. xiii). Particular attention is given to the relations between Germany and the Soviet Union during this period and the ethnic and historical context of the Baltic countries themselves.

949. Hansen, Birthe. **The Baltic States in World Politics**. ix, 164p. New York: St. Martin's Press, 1998. Includes bibliographical references.

"The aim of this collaborative work has been to focus on the international dimension of Estonia's, Latvia's and Lithuania's security challenges after their reemergence as independent states in the late summer of 1991" (p. vii). The Baltic states have become the focus for several questions arising out of the demise of the Soviet Union. These include what the limits are of the new "West," the response of Russia to these international changes, the implications of the new Europe extending to the former Soviet Union, as well as questions relating to the role of the Baltic states in this new international order. The essayists in this volume address these questions.

950. Hiden, John, and Patrick Salmon. **Baltic Nations and Europe: Estonia, Latvia and Lithuania in the Twentieth Century**. Rev. ed. viii, 227p. London; New York: Longman, 1994. Includes bibliographical references and index.

The authors present the diversity of Baltic history from the Middle Ages until the end of the First World War. In 1918 all three countries saw an opportunity for independence and they took advantage of it. During the interwar period they thrived, only to lose their independence in 1940. Here the authors focus on the countries' survival in what they depict as one of the blackest periods of their collective history. In the final section of the book they turn their attention to the mid-1980s up to independence in 1991. One particular emphasis is the authors' concern with the broader conditions in which the Baltic republics had to survive and live. This study restores the Baltic republics to their rightful place in a general postwar European context.

951. **Towards a Civic Society: The Baltic Media's Long Road to Freedom Perspectives on History, Ethnicity and Journalism**. Edited by E. Lauk, Peeter Vihalemm, and Svennik Høyer. 366p.: illus., maps. Tartu: Nota Maltica, 1993. Includes bibliographical references (pp. 361-64).

The year 1991 saw the first conference on the media in the Baltic states. It was held at the University at Oslo and brought together scholars whom, although they had common scholarly interests, had never met. "Because this was such an unusual occasion, it was decided that in addition to publishing the conference papers, a book should be prepared covering the unique experience of the Baltic media and its long way to freedom" (p. 9). This volume is the result. It is intended as a text on the topic. The chapters cover a wide range of topics on the media's development with a great deal of retrospective material providing context for the discussion of the changes facing the region. Along with the essays there are some 60 pages of appendixes, which include extensive data on the region.

952. Lieven, Anatol. **The Baltic Revolution: Estonia, Latvia, Lithuania and the Path to Independence**. 2nd ed. xlvii, 454p.: illus., map, ports. New Haven, Conn.; London: Yale University Press, 1993. Includes index.

Lieven admits that his book tries to do many things. "It attempts to combine elements of a portrait of the contemporary Baltic states and their peoples, a sketch and interpretation of their history and culture, a personal report from the struggle, and elements of oral history from people whom I interviewed. It also contains a polemical argument concerning the position of the Baltic Russians, which [he thinks] involves dangers greater than the West has realized" (p. xiii). He also provides several useful appendixes, including a historical chronology from 3500 B.C. to A.D. 1985, a contemporary chronology from 1985 to 1992, information on Baltic demography and geography, data on the Soviet Baltic economies on the eve of the national revolutions (1989-1990), and a biographical guide to political figures, 1988-1992.

953. Mouritzen, Hans. **Bordering Russia: Theory and Prospects for Europe's Baltic Rim**. xii, 322p.: illus., map. Aldershot, Eng.; Brookfield, Wis.; Singapore; Sydney: Ashgate, 1998. Includes bibliographical references (pp. 295-313) and index.

The countries selected here for study (Finland, Poland, Lithuania, Latvia, and Estonia) not only border Russia, but are also "serious candidates" for inclusion in Western alliance arrangements. In the 11 chapters eight different contributors explore the various aspects of these countries, their relationships with Russia and the West, and the prospects for their future role in any alliance.

954. Redecker, Niels von. **The Baltic Question and the British Press 1989-1991**. ix, 87p. *Hamburger Beiträge Zur Geschichte Des Östlichen*, 5. Hamburg, Ger.: Kovac, 1998. Includes bibliographical references (pp. 77-87).

This study, based on the author's dissertation, concerns the role of the Baltic states in world affairs and how that role was reflected in the British press from 1989 to 1991. "The main purpose of this study is to throw some light on British perceptions of the Baltic reemergence on Europe's political landscape after five decades of Soviet embrace" (pp. 2-3).

955. Shen, Raphael. **Restructuring the Baltic Economies: Disengaging First Years of Integration with the USSR.** vi, 241p.: illus. Westport, Conn.: Praeger, 1994. Includes bibliographical references and index.

This book examines the transition in the Baltic economy from the Soviet command-style system to a market economy. Raphael Shen begins with a general profile of the three Baltic states and then examines the politics and economies in those nations for the last 50 years. Shen then turns to reforms in various areas of the economy since the fall of the Soviet Union: currency reform, price and wage reform, banking reform, and budgetary reform at the state level. The discussion next focuses on privatization, foreign investment, foreign trade, industry, and agriculture. The author examines every major area of the economy as it moves through the transitionary period of the early 1990s.

956. **The Baltic States: The National Self-Determination of Estonia, Latvia, and Lithuania.** Edited by Graham Smith. xii, 214p.: illus., map. New York: St. Martin's Press, 1994. Includes index.

This is a collection of essays on the role played by the Baltic states in the transformation of Eastern Europe and the Soviet Union. "The underlying rationale of this book is that it is only possible to understand fully the prominent contribution of the Baltic peoples to this geopolitical transformation by locating the Baltic states within the wider context of their twentieth-century struggle for national self-determination" (p. xi). The essays are grouped into two parts. The first part includes essays that establish the historical context for the changes of the late 20th century. The contributions in this section trace the history of the region from the late 19th century to the Soviet takeover. In the second part, the contributors focus on the transition in the region to independent statehood. The contributors are Asdne Aasland, Michael Bradshaw, Phil Hanson, Nicholas Hope, David Kirby, Richard Mole, Andrus Park, Denis Shaw, Aleksandras Shtromas, Graham Smith, and James D. White.

957. **Economic and Social Changes in the Baltic States in 1992-1994.** Edited by Urve Venesaar and George A. Hachey. xiii, 197, 31p.: illus. Tallinn: Institute of Economics, Estonian Academy of Sciences, 1995. Includes bibliographical references (pp. 190-97).

The material for this book was supported by a grant from the Commission of the European Communities. The data provided here cover the period 1992-1994. Their main objective was "to analyze the available information in order to get a picture of the progress of transition in the Baltic states [and] . . . the impact of economic changes on living conditions and welfare in the Baltic states" (p. iii).

Estonia

958. Arter, David. **Parties and Democracy in the Post-Soviet Republics: The Case of Estonia**. xviii, 283p.: illus. Aldershot, Eng.: Dartmouth University Press, 1996. Includes bibliographical references.

In studying parties and democracy in Estonia, Arter carried out eight visits and many interviews with selected elites. His book examines the evolution in East Europe generally from democratic transition to democratic consolidation, all within the context of radical system change in the former Soviet republics. "A basic premise of this study is that party building will materially assist in society building, that is, in developing regularized and structured patterns of civic involvement in decision making (a 'democratic society') and, by extension, in reversing the accentuated demobilization and depoliticisation of the citizenry characterizing the post-revolutionary period" (p. x).

959. **Estonian Short Stories**. Edited by Kara Purl and Darlene Reddaway. Translated by Ritva Poomp. 277p. *Writings from an Unbound Europe*. Evanston, Ill.: Northwestern University Press, 1996. Includes endnotes and biographical notes.

These translated stories are representative of the development of Estonian literary consciousness from the 1960s to the 1980s. During this period there was a transformation from the highly controlled Soviet-imposed culture to the time in the late 1980s when Estonia began to redevelop a connection to Western civilization. Stories included here are by Valton, Unt, Kross, Saat, Raudam, Mattheus, Berg, and Ehlvest.

960. Zelnik, Reginald E. **Law and Disorder on the Narova River: The Kreenholm Strike of 1872**. xiii, 308p.: illus., maps. Berkeley: University of California Press, 1995. "A Centennial book." Includes bibliographical references (pp. 297-304) and index.

The strike that occurred in 1872 was the last episode of that type that was not influenced by the leftist intelligentsia. The author's case history of the strike shows how the workers themselves moved toward a rudimentary understanding of legal norms and how the governor of Estland province supported the workers' aspirations as much as he could within the existing legal and social framework.

Latvia

961. Dreifelds, Juris. **Latvia in Transition**. xi, 216p. Cambridge, Eng.: Cambridge University Press, 1996. Includes select bibliography and index.

Not pretending to be an exhaustive examination of all aspects of post-Soviet life and politics, this work instead focuses on subjects relevant for understanding the "processes and attitudes" involved in Westernization reforms. Individual chapters deal with Latvian history and the Latvian national rebirth; the establishment of democracy, economics, reform, and demography; and language and ethnic relations.

962. Ezergailis, Andrew. **The Holocaust in Latvia, 1941-1944: The Missing Center**. xxi, 465p.: illus., maps. Riga: Historical Institute of Latvia, 1996. Includes bibliographical references (pp. [419]-440) and index.

This is a detailed history of the Holocaust in Latvia. The author feels that previous studies have been inadequate. In his view, most rely on a simple extension of the causes of the Holocaust in Continental Europe to Latvia's case. Ezergailis' work is arranged chronologically. It begins with a chapter establishing the historical context for the events of the Holocaust in Latvia. The book includes numerous appendixes with documents related to the Holocaust. It also includes a glossary of terms.

963. Plakans, Andrejs. **Historical Dictionary of Latvia**. xxvi, 192p. *European Historical Dictionaries*, no. 19. Lanham, Md.: Scarecrow Press, 1997. Extensive bibliography.

One in the series *European Historical Dictionaries*, this volume on Latvia follows the same general organization as earlier volumes. It expresses the views of its author/compiler Andrejs Plakans in its selections and coverage of topics. As with the other volumes in the series, it is divided into three parts: a detailed chronology, a dictionary section, and a bibliography organized by subject. The chronology gives brief descriptions of all major events affecting Latvia's development beginning with A.D. 800-1100 and the records of tribute payments by inhabitants of eastern Latvia, and ending with 1996 and the parliamentary election of Gontes Ulmanis to a second term. The dictionary section begins with a general introduction on the physical characteristics of Latvia, an overview of its culture, history, politics, education, demographics, and renewed independence. The author makes no pretense to comprehensive coverage. There are entries on general topics such as fascism, law, economy, and so forth, along with many entries on Latvian writers, political figures, and geographical locations. Some entries are not included, such as a description of the Hansa League. This omission, however, may be due to the book's stated focus on more recent events. Entries did not include bibliographies, although those on literary figures do include references to their works, cited in the Latvian. The bibliography is organized by subjects and lists only English-language works, articles, and books. The one organizational flaw to this work could be said to be its lack of an index.

964. Skultans, Vieda. **The Testimony of Lives: Narrative and Memory in Post-Soviet Latvia**. xxi, 217p.: illus., map. London: Routledge, 1998. Includes bibliographical references (pp. [201]-211) and index.

The author describes and analyzes Latvian narrative, especially as it occurs in biography and autobiography, and the role of memory in narrative.

Lithuania

965. Eidintas, A. Alfonsas, and Vytautas Zalys. **Lithuania in European Politics: The Years of the First Republic, 1918-1940**. 1st St. Martin's Press ed. 250p., [8] p. of plates: illus., map. New York: St. Martin's Press, 1998. Includes bibliographical references and index.

This is more than just a study of those years in the early 20th century when Lithuania was an independent republic. "The purpose of this book is to explain how Lithuanian national consciousness grew from an unstructured instinct to a firm sense of nationhood in the course of this century." The authors begin with an examination of the establishment of the state in 1918 and then discuss the evolution of its institutions. They then examine Lithuania's role in European politics in the 20th century before World War II. A discussion of the final days of Lithuania's independence is followed by a brief comparison of the Lithuanian state in 1940 and 1990. The book includes appendixes on the governments in power in Lithuania between 1918 and 1940 and a chronology of important dates in Lithuanian history.

966. Greimas, Algirdas J. **Of Gods and Men: Studies in Lithuanian Mythology**. Translated by Milda Newmax. 231p. *Folklore Studies in Translation*. Bloomington: Indiana University Press, 1992. Includes bibliographical references and indexes. Translation of: *Apie dievus ir zmones*.

This volume collects several separate studies by Algirdas Greimas on the mythology of Lithuania. The author does not try to reach any general conclusions on his subject. Some sections are meant to elucidate the methodology of mythological analysis. The author is working at a disadvantage in that the book was written during his exile in the West, and he, therefore, had no access to archival sources. Greimas discusses such mythological figures as the Kaukai, Aitvaras, and Ausrine. "Greimas establishes the semantics of the mythical concepts and figures empirically, inferring them from their use and occurrence in Lithuanian literature, folklore, and customs. Furthermore, his interpretation is not allegorical" (p. x). Algirdas Greimas was director of d'Etudes l'Ecole der Hautes Etudes en Sciences Sociales, Paris.

967. **"Come into My Time": Lithuania in Prose Fiction, 1970-90**. Edited by Violeta Kelertas. 251p. Urbana: University of Illinois Press, 1992. A collection of short stories translated from Lithuanian.

This anthology of Lithuanian prose fiction contains 15 pieces from nine writers. The editor has also included an informative and substantive introduction to Lithuanian prose fiction that discusses major themes and techniques.

968. Mathiassen, Terje. **A Short Grammar of Lithuanian**. 256p. Columbus, Ohio: Slavica Publishers, 1996. Includes bibliographical references and index.

This short grammar was written mainly for students of Lithuanian at the university level. It contains the fundamentals of phonology, morphology, and syntax. The author describes the work as synchronic and prescriptive, as opposed to a descriptive grammar. Examples in the book have been gleaned from newspapers and dictionaries.

969. Rowell, S. C. **Lithuania Ascending: A Pagan Empire Within East-Central Europe, 1295-1345**. xxi, 375p.: illus., maps. *Cambridge Studies in Medieval Life and Thought*; 4th Ser., 25. Cambridge, Eng.; New York: Cambridge University Press, 1994. Includes bibliographical references (pp. 318-60) and index.

"From 1250 to 1795 Lithuania covered a vast area of eastern and central Europe. Until 1387 the country was pagan. How this huge state came to expand, defend itself against western European crusaders and play a conspicuous part in European life are the main subjects of this book." The analyses are presented chronologically. The book includes a glossary of foreign terms, genealogical tables, a list of manuscript sources, and two appendixes. The first contains some of the sources on the fall of Kiev in Russian. The second is a chronological table of the Orthodox hierarchies from 1283 to 1461.

970. Senn, Alfred Erich. **Gorbachev's Failure in Lithuania**. 1st ed. xx, 188p. New York: St. Martin's Press, 1995. Includes bibliographical references and index.

"This study examines the interplay between Vilnius and Moscow in the decisive period of Gorbachev's time in power, from 1988 to the August coup in Moscow in 1991" (p. viii). The author feels that Gorbachev's policies ran counter to Lithuania's newfound national consciousness. They also created diplomatic difficulties for the Soviet Union and the United States. Alfred Senn examines the evolution of the crisis in Lithuania and why he considers this to have been such a failure for Gorbachev, the reformer.

971. Suziedelis, Saulius. **Historical Dictionary of Lithuania**. xxxiv, 382p. *European Historical Dictionaries*, no. 21. Lanham, Md.: Scarecrow Press, 1997. Includes bibliography and five appendixes.

This volume of the *European Historical Dictionaries* series is somewhat different from the others. The compiler has included a preface explaining his selection considerations in compiling this volume, and his intended audience. He has compiled this as a guide for the general reader, not the specialist. "This Dictionary is intended, rather as an introduction for the non-specialist who needs a guide to the most important milestones in Lithuania's past" (p. xi).

In format it is constructed along the same lines as other volumes in the series. There are several historical maps instead of one general one. An extensive chronology, and encyclopedic overview of Lithuania's past, and a dictionary section follow these. The entries reflect the compiler's intent to provide general information on Lithuania. Some statistical data is provided in the article on population.

The bibliography includes Polish, Russian, Lithuanian, and Western-language publications. A description of its organization precedes the bibliographic citations. A list of relevant periodical publication is included.

This volume also includes informational appendixes. These cover pronunciation, Lithuanian rulers, political leaders, and frequently cited place-names.

972. Vardys, Vytas Stanley. **Lithuania: The Rebel Nation**. xi, 242p.: illus., maps. *Westview Series on the Post-Soviet Republics*. Boulder, Colo.: Westview Press, 1997.

Under tsarist rule until 1915, Lithuania only tasted independence for a brief period, then was subjected to Soviet rule until 1991. Vardys' book on Lithuania presents a brief background on the country's historical roots and then examines its history from 1918 through the mid-1990s. The underlying theme of the author's work is the striving for independence, finally achieved after the demise of the Soviet empire and the new challenges that such independence brings.

Ukraine

The reader should also consult *Independent Ukraine: A Bibliographic Guide to English-Language Publications, 1989-1999* by Bohdan S. Wynar (Englewood, Colo.: Ukrainian Academic Press, 2000) for a more comprehensive annotated bibliography of citations dealing with Ukraine.

Bibliographies, Encyclopedias

973. Boiko, Maksym, and Ihor N. Boyko. **Three Landmarks of Ukrainian Bibliography, 1073-1832**. 85p.: illus. Bloomington, Ind.: Volhynian Bibliographic Center, 1993. Includes index.

Boiko provides a historical introduction to Ukrainian bibliography by discussing in detail three prominent landmarks of this discipline. The three monuments are the Izbornik, 1073, the Bibliographical Index of the New Testament, Ostrih, 1580, and writings by Pavlo Osypovych Iarkovskyi. He provides background information about each of these as well as related bibliographical events and writings.

General Studies

974. Beauplan, Guillaume Le Vasseur sieur de. **A Description of Ukraine**. Andrew B. Pernal and Dennis F. Essar. xiii, 242p.: illus., maps; 29 folded plates in case. Cambridge, Mass.: Distributed by Harvard University Press for the Harvard Ukrainian Research Institute, 1993. Includes bibliographical references and indexes.

This is the third volume of a set that included a facsimile edition of Beauplan's original work in French and a Ukrainian translation of it. This final volume consists of an English translation and a separate map case that contains selections of reprints of Beauplan's maps and a modern map for comparison. This volume, in addition to the translation, contains detailed notes to the text, subject and name index, and an index of place-names.

975. Dull, Christine, and Ralph Dull. **Soviet Laughter, Soviet Tears: An American Couple's Six-Month Adventure in a Ukrainian Village**. xi, 370p., [32] p. of plates: illus. (some col.), map. Englewood, Ohio: Stillmore Press, 1992. Includes index.

This volume is part memoir and part analysis of an American couple's six-month stay at a collective farm in Makov, Ukraine. The memoir of their impressions, and so forth, came from Christine's Dull's journal excerpts. The analysis comes from farmer Ralph's discussion of farming methods and agricultural technology. It is useful for gaining an insight into the daily life of a Soviet collective farm in 1989.

976. Lotocki, Borys. **Borys' Odyssey**. 271p.: illus. Denver, Colo.: ZZYZX, 1994.

"As a child, Borys lives in the final days of the tsarist era. As a young teenager, he enjoys the mysteries of Constantinople where he attends a Turkish school. The War brings Borys harrowing adventure and narrow escapes on his way to Europe from Turkey. He spends a year living all over Europe. He eventually marries and moves to New York to raise his family" (back cover).

977. **Ukraine and Ukrainians Throughout the World: A Demographic and Sociological Guide to the Homeland and Its Diaspora**. Edited by Ann Lencyk Pawliczko. xxxiii, 508p., [48] p. of plates: illus. Toronto: Published for the Shevchenko Scientific Society by University of Toronto Press, 1994. Includes bibliographical references.

This impressive reference work offers a survey of Ukrainians in Ukraine and in the diaspora. After two introductory chapters, Ukraine and Ukrainians Throughout the World and an Overview and Ukraine: Its Culture and History, by individual authors, the volume proceeds to provide a sociological and cultural survey of Ukrainians throughout the world. As we might imagine, the material covering Europe and North America takes up most of the volume, but ample attention is also paid to South America, Africa, Asia, and the Middle East. Each chapter is written by a specialist in the area and contains brief demographic data, and extended essays and sources are consulted.

Sociology

978. Cheney, Glenn Alan. **Journey to Chernobyl: Encounters in a Radioactive Zone**. 191p., [8] p. of plates: illus. Chicago.: Academy Chicago Publishers, 1995.

A UN inspector describes his journey to Chernobyl and his experiences while visiting there in 1991.

979. **Workers of the Donbas Speak: Survival and Identity in the New Ukraine, 1989-1992**. Edited by Lewis H. Siegelbaum and Daniel J. Walkowitz. xvi, 226p.: illus., maps. Albany: State University of New York Press, 1995. Includes bibliographical references and index.

This volume presents a collection of interviews with working men and women of the industrial city of Donetsk who speak about their struggles during the period of transformation between 1989 and 1993. After a brief introduction, the interviews are arranged in three sections, each with its own introduction. The three sections are (1) worker stories: the older generation, 1989; (2) labor politics, 1989-1992; (3) survival and identity, 1992.

History

980. Bevan, David. **A Case to Answer: The Story of Australia's First European War Crimes Prosecution**. xii, 264p.: illus., map. Kent Town, South Australia: Wakefield Press, 1994. Includes index.

In 1990 Ivan Polyukhovich was arrested in Australia for his role in the massacre of approximately 900 people in Ukraine during World War II. This book recounts the trial of Polyukhovich and all the unusual evidence brought forth to try to prove his guilt.

981. Bohdan, Vladimir A. **Avoiding Extinction: Children of the Kulak**. 547p.: illus. New York: Vantage Press, 1992.

This memoir recounts the author growing up in Ukraine, the interwar period in Eastern Europe, the trials and tribulations of war, the displaced persons' camps in Austria, and eventual emigration to the United States in 1949.

982. Gudziak, Borys Andrij. **Crisis and Reform: The Kyivan Metropolitanate, the Patriarchate of Constantinople, and the Genesis of the Union of Brest**. xv, 489p., [4] p. of plates: illus. (some col.), maps, ports. *Harvard Series in Ukrainian Studies*. Cambridge, Mass.: Harvard University Press, 1998. Includes bibliographical references (pp. [396]-439) and abstract.

The Union of Brest, its causes and significance, is the subject of the study. But the author was motivated by a broader interest in the history of Orthodoxy. "Pained and puzzled by the history of Christian disunity—particularly from the perspective of the Ukrainian religious experience—I became convinced that an examination of the relationship between the Metropolitanate of Kyiv and the Patriarchate of Constantinople provides an indespensible foundation for understanding confessional relations in the Ukrainian contest" (p. xi).

983. Hamm, Michael F. **Kiev: A Portrait, 1800-1917**. 1st pbk. print., with new preface. xviii, 304p.: illus. Princeton, N.J.: Princeton University Press, 1995. Includes bibliographical references (pp. [237]-286) and index.

Michael Hamm has used a wide range of sources to create this history of Kiev in the late imperial period of the Russian empire. He has drawn heavily on the memoir literature to capture the flavor of everyday life in the city and consulted city directories, provincial surveys, and reports of the municipal administration for factual and statistical data. Kiev is presented in a period of "transformation and renascence" as it developed during the 19th century. "*Kiev: A Portrait, 1800-1917* tells the story of a frontier town's transformation into a large metropolis; as such, it should contribute to a deeper understanding of urban development in the Russian Empire as a whole" (p. xii).

984. Hay-Holowko, Oleksa. **For Them the Bells Did Not Toll: Events of the Great Terror-Famine of 1932-1933 in Ukraine Under Soviet Russia Occupation**. iii, 210p. Winnipeg: Communigraphics/Printers' Aid Group, 1993.

This novel portrays the Ukrainian Holocaust and is described by one who experienced it firsthand.

985. Kaminski, Andrzej Sulima. **Republic Vs. Autocracy: Poland-Lithuania and Russia, 1686-1697**. 312p. Cambridge, Mass.: Distributed by Harvard University Press for the Harvard Ukrainian Research Institute, 1993. Includes bibliographical references (pp. [281]-299) and index.

This study of diplomatic relations between Russia and Poland-Lithuania is presented against the backdrop of the history of the time. After an introductory chapter that sets the apparatus of each of these powers, he analyzes the Russian residency in Poland and the Polish residency in Moscow and describes in some detail the struggle for Ukraine and the Solomon Affair, which brought Russian-Polish cooperation against the Tatars to a halt. His study is "not so much a discussion of the actual course of diplomatic relations as an analysis of the diplomatic relationship and operation of diplomatic services of the two rival powers" (p. 2).

986. Kuromiya, Hiroaki. **Freedom and Terror in the Donbas: A Ukrainian-Russian Borderland, 1870s-1990s**. xiv, 357p.: illus., maps. *Cambridge Russian, Soviet and Post-Soviet Studies*, 104. Cambridge, Eng.: Cambridge University Press, 1998. Includes bibliographical references (pp. 344-46) and index.

Kuromiya describes and analyzes the terror that befell the Russian-Ukrainian borderland, the Donbas, because, in part, of the freedom that the area enjoyed. This history traces the development of this region, often a haven for fugitives, from its foundation as a modern coal and steel center, through the revolution and encompassing the famine of 1932-1933, the Great Terror, World War II, the Holocaust, and de-Stalinization.

987. **Towards an Intellectual History of Ukraine: An Anthology of Ukrainian Thought from 1710 to 1995**. Edited by Ralph Lindheim and George S. N. Luckyj. 418p. Toronto: University of Toronto Press, 1996. Includes bibliography and index.

This useful anthology of documents dating from 1710 to 1995 intentionally gathers materials that "explore issues that intellectual history has traditionally set out to examine and explain. They touch on religious, philosophical, aesthetic, ethical, sociological, historical, and political ideas" (page preceding t.p.). They are introduced and put into context in the 50-page introductory essay by the editors. Most longer documents are excerpted.

988. Magocsi, Paul R. **The Persistence of Regional Cultures: Rusyns and Ukrainians in Their Carpathian Homeland and Abroad**. ix, 220p.: maps. Fairview, N.J.; New York: Carpatho-Rusyn Research Center, distributed by Columbia University Press, 1993. English and Ukrainian, with some text in Polish.

This collection of articles first published in their original languages (Russian, Ukrainian, and Polish) are here translated for the first time. The original articles are also included. All deal with the cultures of specific ethnic groups in various parts of Carpatho-Rus'.

989. Marples, David Roger. **Stalinism in Ukraine in the 1940s**. xix, 228p. Edmonton: University of Alberta Press, 1992. Includes bibliographical references (pp. [171]-218) and index.

Marples examines Stalinism in western Ukraine commencing with the 1939 Nazi-Soviet pact and ending with the summer of 1945 when Transcarpathian Ukraine was incorporated from Czechoslovakia. Although the sequence of chapters does not form a connected narrative, individual chapters address key questions related to the topic at hand, such as the foundations of Stalinism in Ukraine; wartime collaboration in Ukraine; Khrushchev, Kaganovich, and the 1947 crisis; the Kulak in postwar Ukraine; and Khrushchev and mass collectivization in western Ukraine, 1950-1951.

990. Nahaylo, Bohdan. **The Ukrainian Resurgence**. xix, 608p., [16] p. of plates: illus., ports. Toronto; Buffalo, N.Y.: University of Toronto Press, 1999. Includes bibliographical references (pp. 555-61) and index.

Nahaylo explains the reasons for the resurgence of Ukraine into the world stage in a relatively short period of time. He explains how the process of revival began, who led it, and how it developed into a powerful movement for national renewal and freedom. In the last chapters of the book he analyzes the first several years of Ukrainian independence and how Ukraine has dealt with the many challenges and risks that it faced. In performing this analysis the author also sheds light on the transformation of the entire Soviet empire.

991. Palij, Michael. **The Ukrainian-Polish Defensive Alliance, 1919-1921: An Aspect of the Ukrainian Revolution**. 391p. Edmonton, Alb.: Canadian Institute of Ukrainian Studies Press, 1995. Map on lining papers. Includes bibliographical references and index.

In spite of the ravages of war, revolution, and disintegration, the Bolsheviks were able to reconsolidate their power shortly after November 1917. This reemergence of Russian power threatened both Ukraine and Poland. As a result, both nations wished to prevent occupation by Soviet Russia. They did this by creating the Ukrainian-Polish alliance of 1920. This book examines the prelude to this alliance and the consequences of it for both Ukraine and Poland.

992. Read, Piers Paul. **Ablaze, the Story of Chernobyl**. xxix, 478p., [16] p. of plates: illus. London: Secker & Warburg, 1993. Includes index.

The author attempts to examine the human side of the Chernobyl accident of April 1986. Read obtained access to previously classified information, including that relating to atomic power, the trial held in Chernobyl, the report of the State Committee for Safety in the Atomic Power Industry, and various other protocols and reports. Read also investigates the environmental aspects and the resulting radiation injuries of the victims.

993. Saprykin, S. IU. **Ancient Farms and Land-Plots on the Khora of Khersonesos Taurike: (Research in the Herakleian Peninsula, 1974-1990)**. xi, 153p., [ca. 60] p. of plates: illus. Amsterdam: J. C. Gieben, 1994. Includes bibliographical references (pp. [109]-117).

This is an extended detached study of a well-defined territory in Soviet Western Crimea, which served as the hinterland of the Greek city of Khersonesos Taurike. This territory in ancient times was divided into plots and cultivated. Approximately one-half of the book covers the analysis of construction of four farmhouses. The second half of the book looks at architecture and historical background. Sixty-five plates included in the volume depict the remaining ruins as well as pictures of artifacts discovered at the site.

994. Shandor, Vikentii. **Carpatho-Ukraine in the Twentieth Century: A Political and Legal History**. xvii, 321p. Cambridge, Mass.: Distributed by Harvard University Press, 1997. Includes bibliographical references (pp. [285]-300) and index.

Shandor was an important government official in pre-World War II Central Europe. In addition, he was a prolific writer on various topics dealing with Carpatho-Ukraine. Carpatho-Ukraine was originally applied to 13 districts that encroached deeply into present-day Hungary. The Ukrainians who lived there were called Ruthenians. This designation was used in both literary works and political documents. From 1919 to 1939 this territory was part of the newly established state of Czechoslovakia and was called Subcarpathian Ruthenia. The territory eventually became part of Ukrainian SSR and officially called the Transcarpathian Oblast. The author brings his substantial experience and legal training to discuss the development of Carpatho-Ukraine from 1918 through 1945 and its unification with the Ukrainian Soviet Socialist Republic.

995. Subtelny, Orest. **Ukraine: A History**. 2nd ed. xiv, 692p., [66] p. of plates: illus. Toronto; Buffalo, N.Y.: Published by the University of Toronto Press in association with the Canadian Institute of Ukrainian Studies, 1994. Includes bibliographical references.

This is a second edition of the author's history that first appeared in 1988. In addition to updating the bibliography and making some minor corrections, this version also includes a new chapter on the events that occurred from the end of 1988 through 1991. At that time Ukraine declared its independence. As Subtelny points out, Ukraine is still in a state of flux, but this authoritative history should help to make clear the past from which modern Ukraine has emerged.

996. **German-Ukrainian Relations in Historical Perspective**. Edited by Hans-Joachim Torke and John-Paul Himka. viii, 239p. Edmonton, Alb.: Canadian Institute of Ukrainian Studies Press, 1994. "Papers presented at an international conference held in Garmisch-Partenkirchen, Oct. 13-17, 1986, and organized by the Canadian Institute of Ukrainian Studies"—T.p. verso.

The 14 articles contained in this volume were originally presented at an international conference devoted to the history of German-Ukrainian relations, held in Garmisch-Partenkirchen in 1986. The period covered by essays goes from the early 19th century to the present day, although the majority of the papers deal with World War II. The papers are of special significance because they reflect the first such articles to appear whose authors were allowed more in-depth access to Soviet archives than had previously been the case.

997. Velychenko, Stephen. **National History As Cultural Process: A Survey of the Interpretations of Ukraine's Past in Polish, Russian, and Ukrainian Historical Writing from the Earliest Times to 1914**. xxxv, 283p.: illus., maps. Edmonton, Alb.: Canadian Institute of Ukrainian Studies Press, 1992. Includes index.

This work "traces the evolution of interpretations of Ukraine's past in survey histories of Poland, Russia and Ukraine. The book provides a guide to and summary of the Polish, Russian and Ukrainian elite images of Ukrainian history but also examines the broader issue of how interpretations change" (p. xiv). In addition, two appendixes describe and analyze tsarist censorship and Ukrainian historiography (1828-1906) and Ukrainian lands in pre-18th-century cartography.

998. Velychenko, Stephen. **Shaping Identity in Eastern Europe and Russia: Soviet-Russian and Polish Accounts of Ukrainian History, 1914-1991**. 266p. New York: St. Martin's Press, 1993. Includes bibliographical references (pp. [224]-258) and index.

The main purpose of this volume is to survey "the origins and evolution of official versions of Ukraine's past to illustrate how historical writing and interpretative change occurred in Soviet-type systems" (p. 1). Velychenko's nine chapters are arranged in three parts. Part 1 provides background and context. Part 2 investigates Polish historiography and how it interpreted Ukraine, and Part 3 performs the same function for Soviet Russian historiography. An appendix covers perestroika and its interpretation.

999. Wynn, Charters. **Workers, Strikes, and Pogroms: The Donbas-Dnepr Bend in Late Imperial Russia, 1870-1905**. 289p.: illus. Princeton, N.J.: Princeton University Press, 1992. Includes bibliographical references (pp. [269]-281) and index.

In the late 19th century, a large working class grew in the Ukraine Donbas region. Much of this laboring population originated in the countryside. Peasant migrants moved to the region in this period seeking higher wages among other things. Charters Wynn examines the militant labor movement that developed in this area in this work. "It is my hope that an analysis of the labor movement in what was fast becoming Russia's industrial heartland will contribute to a more realistic conception of the dynamics of Russia's labor unrest" (p. 3). The book is divided into two parts. Part 1 provides the reader with background information on the labor force. Part 2 traces the history of the labor movement from the 1870s to December 1905. The concluding chapter places the labor movement in the larger context of Russia's revolutionary movement.

1000. Yaroshinska, Alla. **Chernobyl, The Forbidden Truth**. xvii, 135p.: illus., maps. Lincoln: University of Nebraska Press, 1995. "Bison Books." Includes bibliographical references.

Alla Yaroshinska was a journalist in the Soviet Union, living and working in Zhitomir, Ukraine, at the time of the Chernobyl nuclear disaster. She writes in this book about the damage, the deaths, fallout, and the cover-up of this unprecedented disaster. Her stories were not published in the Soviet Union until 1989, when Izvestia began publishing materials by the more "radical" press. Yaroshinska is now a member of Boris Yeltsin's council. "Why should we return to the theme of Chernobyl years later, as the now-independent states struggle for mere existence? The reason is simple: This book illustrates, as no one has before, the extent to which the Soviet regime could mislead its own people, even directly imperiling their lives" (pp. xvi-xvii).

Government and Politics

1001. **Contemporary Ukraine: Dynamics of Post-Soviet Transformation**, xxi, 290p.: illus., maps. Armonk, N.Y.: M. E. Sharpe, 1998. Includes bibliographical references and index.

The papers collected in this volume were originally delivered at a conference entitled "Soviet to Independent Ukraine: A Troubled Transformation." The conference was held at the University of Birmingham in June 1996. "The authors brought together in this volume have one common purpose—to discuss the difficult post-Soviet transformation in Ukraine and its attempt to construct a nation, build a state, democratize, and marketize" (p. xi). The contributions to the volume are grouped into five sections: "Nation and State Building," "National Identity and Regionalism," "Politics and Civil Society," "Economics and

Society," and "Foreign and Defense Policies." The volume includes a bibliography of secondary sources on Ukraine.

1002. **Ukraine and European Security**. Edited by David E. Albright and Semen Iosifovich Appatov. ix, 129p.: map. London: Royal Institute of International Affairs, 1997. Includes bibliographical references (pp. 122-29).

This volume grew out of a workshop held for European and Ukrainian security analysts in November 1996. During the workshop four fundamental topics were explored by all participants: "(1) European security issues during the coming decade and their priorities, (2) strategies for approaching these issues, (3) Ukraine's security role in Europe, and (4) Ukraine's security and the Atlantic community" (p. 6). Each of the major participants wrote papers for the workshop and these papers (17 in all) are collected in this volume, arranged under the four topics noted above.

1003. Drohobycky, Maria. **Crimea: Dynamics, Challenges and Prospects**. lvi, 250p.: maps. Lanham, Md.: Rowman & Littlefield, American Association for the Advancement of Science, 1995. Includes bibliographical references and index.

This collection of articles is the result of an international conference held in Kiev in 1994. All of them discuss various issues relating to the crisis in the Crimea. The nine essays are arranged in three sections: (1) Crimea in the Post-Soviet Order; (2) Political and Social Developments in Crimea; and (3) Crimea: National, Regional, and International Security Implications.

1004. Hopkins, Arthur T. **Unchained Reactions: Chernobyl, Glasnost, and Nuclear Deterrence**. xviii, 153p.: illus. Washington, D.C.: National Defense University Press, 1993. Includes bibliographical references (pp. 113-41) and index.

Hopkins examines the social and political effects of the Chernobyl disaster. He analyzes the accident itself and the ineptitude of the Soviet bureaucracy after the reactor accident and then sees how Soviet citizens' attitudes toward their government and toward nuclear deterrence were influenced. He suggests that the accident, occurring as it did when glasnost was in full swing, helped bring about the independence of the Soviet republics.

1005. IPHECA (Organization). **Health Consequences of the Chernobyl Accident: Results of the IPHECA Pilot Projects and Related National Programmes, Summary Report**. vi, 38p.: illus. Geneva: World Health Organization, 1995.

This WHO report summarizes a much more extensive unpublished document, also prepared by WHO. It describes the accident of April 25-26, 1986, the response by the national authorities, the activities of international organizations, and various activities by IPHECA (the International Programme on the Health Effects of the Chernobyl Accident).

1006. Kordan, Bohdan S. **Other Anxieties: Ukraine, Russia and the West**. viii, 70p.: port. Kingston, Ont.: Kashtan Press, 1994. Includes bibliographical references.

Kordan has documented the two years (1991-1992) of a critical transition for Ukraine, from one of 15 Soviet republics to independent state. Although Kordan's impressions of the events may be transitory, he also raises the same fundamental questions about Ukraine's future with which that country will have to grapple for several years to come.

1007. **Ukraine Today: Perspectives for the Future**. Edited by Halyna Koscharsky. [16], 174p. Commack, N.Y.: Nova Science Publishers, 1995. "Proceedings of the conference 'Ukraine Today—Perspectives for the Future,' June 19-21, 1992." Includes bibliographical references and index. Collection of papers in English and Ukrainian.

"This collection of papers is based mainly on the proceedings of a conference, organised by the Ukrainian Studies Centre at Macquarie University in Sydney. . . . The impetus for the conference was the recently achieved independence of Ukraine and the desire to further cultural, educational and community ties between Ukraine and Australia by providing a forum for the discussion of issues of concern associated with self-determination" (p. xi). About half the essays are in Ukrainian, the remainder in English. They are grouped into sections on historical development, public health after Chernobyl, emigration, religion, education, and culture.

1008. Kravchuk, L. M. **Our Goal—A Free Ukraine: Speeches, Interviews, Press-Conferences, Briefings**. 181 b6 s.: illus. Kiev, Rus.: Globus Publishers, 1993. Title in colophon: *Nasha meta—vil'na Ukraïna*.

Articles, excerpts from interviews, and other primary documents by Leonid Kravchuk, president of Ukraine, have been translated here into English. The documents are arranged chronologically, beginning from his inauguration speech for the Supreme Council of Ukraine on December 5, 1991, and ending with an article appearing in the journal *New Statesman* in late 1992.

1009. Krevza, Lev, Bohdan A. Struminsky, Roman Robert Koropeckyj, Dana Roby Miller, William R. Veder, Igor Struminski, and Zakhariia Kopystens'kyi. **Lev Krevza's A Defense of Church Unity; and Zakhariia Kopystens'kyi's Palinodia**. 2 vols. (xlii, 1165p.): port. Cambridge, Mass.: Distributed by Harvard University Press for the Ukrainian Research Institute of Harvard University, 1995. Includes bibliographical references and index.

The history of the Orthodox Church is complex. There are many examples in the Slavonic-Ruthenian literature of attacks of Latin Christians. The works in this volume are translations of early-17th-century texts on the polemic concerning church unity. As such, they also deal with the relations between Latin and Orthodox Christians.

These works have been meticulously translated and annotated here. The first document, "A Defense of Church Unity," was written by a member of the Uniate Basilian Order, Lev Krevza, in 1617. The second was published in 1621.

1010.   Kuzio, Taras, and Andrew Wilson. **Ukraine: Perestroika to Independence**. xiv, 260p., [12] p. of plates: illus. Edmonton, Alb.: Canadian Institute of Ukrainian Studies Press, 1994. Includes bibliographical references and index.

This book aims to investigate the forces and events that led up to the vote by the Ukrainian Parliament to declare its independence and the subsequent ratification of that decision by popular referendum on December 1, 1991. Individual chapters cover theories of nationalism and the Soviet Ukrainian context, strength and weaknesses of the natural movements, the Gorbachev period, the birth of mass politics, Ukrainian elections and the rise of a multiparty system, the rise of national communism, and the coup and aftermath.

1011.   Kuzio, Taras. **Ukraine: State and Nation Building**. xiii, 298p. *Routledge Studies of Societies in Transition*, 9. London: Routledge, 1998. Includes bibliographical references.

Kuzio, in analyzing post-Soviet developments in Ukraine, focuses on the role of nationalism in forging the new nation. Some have predicted that Ukraine, as well as other newly independent states, may collapse into ethnic conflict. Kuzio discovers that the threat of such conflict has been exaggerated and that the potential for building an inclusive political nation based upon "civic and ethnic Ukrainian attributes" is possible.

1012.   Kuzio, Taras. **Ukraine Under Kuchma: Political Reform, Economic Transformation and Security Policy in Independent Ukraine**. xxiii, 281p.: illus., maps. *Studies in Russian and East European History and Society series*. New York: St. Martin's Press, 1997. Includes bibliographical references (pp. 267-75) and index.

As Kuzio makes clear in his introduction, independent Ukraine under Kravchuk "had to undertake not two (economic and political) but four difficult transitions from a command-administrative system to a market economy, from a totalitarian system to a democracy, from an incomplete and deformed national identity to a nation, and from a subject of empire to statehood" (pp. 2-3). His book explores and analyzes the new Ukrainian Parliament; the issues, voters, myths, and legends of the 1994 presidential elections; the return of the Crimea to Ukraine; political reform, economic transformation, and structural change, and new foreign and defense policies.

1013.   Kuzio, Taras. **Ukrainian Security Policy**. xiv, 168p. Westport, Conn.: Praeger, 1995. "Published with the Center for Strategic and International Studies, Washington, D.C." Includes bibliographical references (pp. 141-57) and index.

The purpose of this volume is to describe the new geopolitical significance of Ukraine and the related political implications, both internal and external. His individual chapters cover Ukraine's political legacies, domestic sources of security policy, foreign policy and international relations, and military and nuclear policy.

1014. Medvedev, Grigorii. **No Breathing Room: The Aftermath of Chernobyl**. 213p. New York: Basic Books, 1993. Includes index.

Medvedev was a nuclear engineer and department chief in the Directorate of Nuclear Energy of the former Soviet Union. He was one of several experts summoned to deal with the Chernobyl disaster in the autumn of 1986. This, his second book on this subject, deals with the Soviet bureaucracy, its workings, and the effect this had on dealing with both the immediate effects of the Chernobyl disaster and its aftereffects, which lasted at least until 1991.

1015. Motyl, Alexander J. **Dilemmas of Independence: Ukraine After Totalitarianism**. xv, 217p. New York: Council on Foreign Relations Press, 1993. Includes bibliographical references (pp. 198-202) and index.

Much of the research for this book was carried out during two trips to Ukraine in 1992. As Motyl sees it, the fall of the Soviet Union has bequeathed two legacies to Ukraine and other successor states. "The legacy of empire encourages the forceful promotion of rapid and fundamental change; the legacy of totalitarianism negates the very possibility of that change" (p. xi). In dealing with these seemingly unreconcilable forces, Motyl gives a historical perspective of Ukraine's independence. He enumerates the problems of overcoming the legacies of empire and totalitarianism; shows how it should forge a new identity, engage a posttotalitarian Russia, transform a dependent economy, and fashion a postcolonial elite; and presents current dilemmas for the West.

1016. Pavlychko, Solomiia Dmitrievna. **Letters from Kiev**. viii, 177p., [16] p. of plates: illus. Edmonton, Alb.: Canadian Institute of Ukrainian Studies Press, 1992.

Solomiia Pavlychko works at the Ukrainian Academy of Sciences. She had visited family in Canada in 1990 only to return to a Ukraine in political and social upheaval. Her father was a prominent member of the opposition in Parliament. Pavlychko began a series of letters to her friends in Canada describing the events in Ukraine. "Her letters thus give center-stage view of the political crises of that fateful year. When she wrote the letters, she had just discovered feminism, and this informs her view of social relations and the politics of everyday life" (p. 1). The book includes numerous photographs chronologically depicting the opposition movement.

1017. Wanner, Catherine. **Burden of Dremas: History and Identity in Post-Soviet Ukraine**. xxvi, 255p.: illus., maps. *Post-Communist Cultural Studies*. University Park: Pennsylvania State University Press, 1998. Includes bibliographical references and index.

As Wanner points out in her introduction, Ukraine is the largest new state to appear in Europe in this century. After the breakup of the Soviet Union, Ukrainian leaders tried many ways in which to develop Ukraine into an autonomous, unified state. One means to do this was through culture. Wanner's book examines ways in which this came about, through schools, pop culture, the state calendar of commemorations and celebrations, and the altering of public spaces. Their aim in all this is to "exploit the potential to provide a vital link between individuals and the state via the nation. Collective histories are suggestively and emotively revised to foster solidarity and a feeling of belonging" (p. xxvii). Her study is arranged in two parts. In Part 1 (Chapters 1-3), she describes and analyzes the legacy of Soviet culture. In Part 2 (Chapters 4-7), she focuses on educational reform, festivals, commemoration and the state calendar, and the urban landscape.

1018.   Wilson, Andrew. **Ukrainian Nationalism in the 1990s: A Minority Faith**. xvii, 300p.: maps. Cambridge, Eng.: Cambridge University Press, 1997. Includes endnotes, select bibliography, and index.

Wilson argues that Ukrainian nationalism "has always been a complex and variegated phenomenon" (p. xiii). In attempting to unravel this intricate web, he examines the historical roots of regional diversity, Ukrainian nationalism in the modern era, channels of nationalist discourse (political parties, civil society, and religion), the role of national communism in shaping Ukrainian nationalism, the limits to nationalist support, and the nationalist agenda as reflected in domestic politics, Ukrainianisation and the state, and external affairs. His final chapter draws conclusions from his study and examines how possible scenarios for the future development of Ukrainian nationalism may affect the Ukrainian state as a whole.

Economics and Business

1019.   **Ukraine: An Economic Profile**. vi, 41p.: illus. (some col.), maps. [S.l: s.n., 1992. Prepared by the Central Intelligence Agency.

Based primarily on information from the Ukrainian statistical annual *Narodnoye khozyaystvo*, and other national level statistical compendiums of the former Soviet Union, Poland, and France, this volume presents summary time series data for Ukraine through 1991. Areas covered include history and government, population and the labor force, structure and performance of the economy, economic reform, foreign economic relations, and living standards and social industries.

1020.   **Ukraine: The Agriculture Sector in Transition**. xix, 150p.: illus., col. map. *A World Bank Country Study*. Washington, D.C.: The World Bank, 1994. This study is based on the findings of a World Bank mission that visited Ukraine in October 1993 and reflects developments since then.

This *World Bank Country Study* presents information about Ukraine's agricultural economy and the potential problems in carrying out agricultural developments. The mission upon which the report was completed was carried out in October 1993.

1021. Centre for Co-operation with European Economies in Transition: Organisation for Economic Co-operation and Development. **Investment Guide for Ukraine**. 147p.: forms. Paris: OECD, 1993.
The information presented in this guide, valid as of April 1, 1993, was designated to help those who are interested in doing business and investing in Ukraine. Individual chapters cover such topics as the economy, foreign direct investment legislation, incentive measures, natural legislation and regulations relevant to foreign direct investment, taxes, and investment opportunities.

1022. Shen, Raphael. **Ukraine's Economic Reform: Obstacles, Errors, Lessons**. xii, 214p.: illus. Westport, Conn.: Praeger, 1996. Includes bibliographical references (pp. [203]-209) and index.
"This study examines the effects of Ukraine's integration with the FSU for seventy-three years, investigates Ukraine's inherited economic structure and functioning vis-à-vis reform obstacles, analyzes and evaluates its reform policies since regaining independence, presents an outline of practical lessons from its unique reform experiment, and concludes with recommendations for the government of Ukraine, as well as for the governments of other newly independent republics of the FSU" (p. xii).

1023. United States Bureau of Export Administration, and U.S.-Ukraine Committee for the Conversion of the Defense Industry. **Investment Opportunities in Ukrainian Defense Conversion**. Revised "RFP" edition. iii, 151p. Washington, D.C.: The Bureau, 1994.
This volume is useful for anyone interested in investment in Ukraine with an eye toward promoting conversion of defense industries. The greatest part is devoted to a directory of enterprises that are attempting to convert from purely military products to commercial products. Subsequent chapters give an overview of the economic status of Ukraine in the mid-1900s and tables of imports and exports as a percentage of U.S. and Ukrainian bilateral trade.

Religion

1024. Bociurkiw, Bohdan R. **The Ukrainian Greek Catholic Church and the Soviet State (1939-1950)**. xvi, 310p.: illus., maps, ports. Edmonton, Alb.: Canadian Institute of Ukrainian Studies Press, 1996. Includes bibliographical references (pp. [260]-288) and index.
In this book, Bociurkiw examines the effects of Stalin's unification of the Galician metropoly of Halych and the Russian Orthodox Church. "The study analyzes the motives, means, and results of this intertwined ecclesiastical-nationality policy. It finds explanations and models for that policy not in Marxism-Leninism, but in the tsarist policies toward the Uniates in the territories annexed after the partitions of Poland in the

late eighteenth century" (p. ix). Bociurkiw's book is arranged chronologically. It includes a glossary and an extensive bibliography, organized by subject.

1025. Chirovsky, Andriy. **Pray for God's Wisdom: The Mystical Sophiology of Metropolitan Andrey Sheptytsky**. xx, 279p. Chicago: Metropolitan Andriy Sheptytsky Institute of Eastern Christian Studies, 1992. Includes bibliographical references (pp. 256-71) and index.

This study of the head of the Ukrainian Catholic Church, Metropolitan Andriy Sheptytsky (1865-1944), focuses on those aspects of his sophiological thought. The first chapter of his study covers Metropolitan Andriy's biography, giving a general background and an introduction to his literary activity. The next five chapters treat his sophiology as reflected in his work *The Wisdom of God* (1932), and to a lesser extent, in *Christian Righteousness* (1936), brief references to Sophia in his writings, other Russian sophiologists (V. Solovyov, S. Bulgakov, and P. Florensky), the sources of his sophiology, and general conclusions. An appendix contains an English translation of the introduction to his two sophiological works, miscellaneous references to *The Wisdom of God* in his other writings, and the *Prayer for Divine Wisdom*.

1026. Frick, David A. **Meletij Smotryc'kyj**. xvii, 395p.: illus., maps. Cambridge, Mass.: Distributed by Harvard University Press for the Harvard Ukrainian Research Institute, 1995. Includes bibliographical references (pp. [369]-385) and index.

This critical biography examines in some detail the life and ecclesiastical-political affairs of Smotryc'kyj. According to Frick, he was "one of the outstanding figures in the great flourishing of Orthodox spirituality that occurred in the late sixteenth and early seventeenth century" (p. xi) in response to several challenges posed by the Polish heterodox and the Society of Jesus. Two appendixes include Smotryc'kyj's letters and his critical use of biblical citations.

1027. Klassen, Pamela E. **Going by the Moon and the Stars: Stories of Two Russian Mennonite Women**. ix, 151p. Waterloo, Ont: Wilfrid Laurier University Press, 1994. Includes bibliographical references (pp. 139-45) and index.

Klassen presents the life stories, with emphasis on the religious part of their identity, of two Russian women who grew up in the Soviet Ukraine, experienced World War II, and eventually emigrated to Canada. The relatively unusual aspect of their stories is that both of them are Mennonite women. So beside the interpretation of their lives as Mennonites, the author also considers "how the construction of identity occurs in relation to the multiplicity of gender, political, religious, family, class, and ethnic plots" (p. 2).

1028. Marshall, Richard H., Jr., and Thomas E. Bird. **Hryhorij Savyc Skovoroda: An Anthology of Critical Articles**. xv, 319p. Edmonton, Alb.: Canadian Institute of Ukrainian Studies Press, 1994. Includes bibliographical references (pp. 287-310) and index.

This selection of critical essays on Skovoroda, an 18th-century Ukrainian sage, describes and analyzes the role played by him in the cultural and intellectual life of eastern Slavdom. The essays are arranged in four sections: (1) Skovoroda and society; (2) Skovoroda and literature; (3) the philosophy and theology of Skovoroda; and (4) a bibliography of works by and about Skovoroda.

Music, Architecture, and Art

1029. Leshko, Jaroslaw. **Jacques Hnizdovsky, 1915-1985: Retrospective Exhibition (Iakiv Hnizdovs'kyi, 1915-1985: Retrospektyvna Vystavka)**. 84p.: illus. (some col.) New York: Ukrainian Museum, 1995. Includes bibliographical references (p. 83).

This volume on Jacques Hnizdovsky was produced on the occasion of an exhibition of his work in 1995-1996 at the Ukrainian Museum, New York. Hnizdovsky was born in Ukraine and he had formal artistic training in Warsaw and Zagreb, and after spending a short time in Munich, he emigrated to the United States in 1949. The individual plates are accompanied by a bibliographical narration and analysis of the painter's life and art.

1030. Soroker, Yakov, and Andrii Horniatkevych. **Ukrainian Musical Elements in Classical Music**. Edited by Andrii Horniatkevych. Translated by Olga Samilenko.155p.: music. Edmonton, Alb.: Canadian Institute of Ukrainian Studies Press, 1995. Translation of: *Ukraïns'ki elementy v tvorchosti kompozytoriv-kliasykiv*.

This translation explores the ties between Ukrainian folklore and idiom and classical music. Its chapters describe several melodic phrases characteristic for Ukrainian folk music (Chapter 1), the manifestation of these phrases in classical composers (Chapters 2-4), Polish and Russian composers, and a conclusion.

Language, Literature, and Folklore

1031. Beniukh, Oles, and R. I. Galushko. **Ukrainian Phrasebook and Dictionary**. 205p. New York: Hippocrene Books, 1994.

This phrase book is aptly named, containing as it does some 100 pages of everyday phrases classified under 15 rubrics such as at the airport, hotel, restaurant, food and drink, services, transportation, etc. This is a brief pronunciation guide, but there is no description of grammar. Each expression is preceded by its English equivalent and followed by a romanized pronunciation and with stress indicated by capital letters.

1032. Bykhovets', N. M., and Iurii Oleksiiovych Zhluktenko. **English-Ukrainian Dictionary, Ukrainian-English Dictionary**. 2 vols. in 1 (693p.) Kyïv, Rus.: Femina, 1995.

This new dictionary includes some 40,000 terms defined in English and Ukrainian. It is intended for the student or general reader. Since Ukrainian is largely phonetic in its spelling, phonetic symbols are not included but stress is indicated for each word. Some general notes on grammar are also included.

1033. **Zhabka, and Other Ukrainian Folk Tales Retold in English**. Edited by Danny Evanishen. Translated by John Evanishen. 134p.: illus. Summerland, B.C.: Ethnic Enterprises Publishing Division, 1995.

This is the editor's selection of Ukrainian folktales and is the second volume of a planned four-part series.

1034. **From Three Worlds: New Ukrainian Writing**. Edited by Ed Hogan. 282p. Boston: Zephyr Press, 1996. Includes notes on translators, editors, and contributors.

In this volume the writings of current Ukrainian authors have been collected. The idea of collecting these works was born in 1993 when the editor of the journal *Glas*, Ed Hogan, heard a reading by Volodymyr Dibrova. Hogan devoted an issue of the journal to Ukrainian literature. That issue is reprinted in this volume. A number of authors are represented including Dibrova, Mykola Kumanovsky, Kostantyn Moskalets, Evhenia Kononenko, Tania D'avigon, Yevnen Pashkovsky, Valery Shevchuk, Vasyl Holoborodko, Natalka Bilotserkivets, Oksanaw Zabuzhko, Viktor Neborak, Solomea Pavlychko, Olen Lyshena, Yury Andrukhovych, Bohdan Zholdak, Yuri Vynnychuk, Oleksandr Irvantes, and Halyna Pahutiak. The volume includes prose and poetry. Poetry is published here in the original Ukrainian with parallel text in English. There is also an introductory essay on contemporary Ukrainian literature.

1035. Ilnytzkyj, Oleh Stepan. **Ukrainian Futurism: 1914-1930: A Historical and Critical Study**. xviii, 413p., [8] p. of plates: illus. (some col.). *Harvard Series in Ukrainian Studies*. Cambridge, Mass.: Distributed by Harvard University Press for the Harvard Ukrainian Research Institute, 1997. Includes bibliographical references and index.

Ukrainian Futurism was a literary and artistic movement that arose as a reaction to the Ukrainian modernist movements of the 1900s and 1910s. When the Futurist movement developed it was viewed in Ukrainian society as an attempt to glorify the exotic and as a rejection of tradition. "This work represents the first effort not only to describe the conflict between the Ukrainian avant-garde and the public, but to provide a comprehensive account of Ukrainian Futurism as a literary movement" (p. xiii). The author has divided the study into three parts. The first part traces the history of the movement from its inception. Part 2 looks at the theoretical basis of the Futurists. Part 3 examines the major practitioners of the style, authors such as Mykhail Semenko, Oleksa Slisarenko, Geo. Shrurupii, Dmytro Buzko, and Leonid Skrypnyk.

1036. Kononenko, Natalie O. **Ukrainian Minstrels: And the Blind Shall Sing**. xvi, 360p., [12] p. of plates: illus., map, ports. *Folklores and Folk Cultures of Eastern Europe*. Armonk, N.Y.: M. E. Sharpe, 1998. Includes bibliographical references and index.

This volume is the first in the series *Folklores and Folk Cultures of Eastern Europe*. Kononenko's study examines the tradition of oral poetry in Ukraine. "The focus is on the performers, the kobzari and lirnyky of the Ukrainian countryside, but the study also includes new translations of the basic songs of their repertory" (p. ix). The study is divided into two parts: "Ukrainian Minstrelsy" and "Minstrel Rites and Songs." The first part is a detailed history of the tradition and its place in Ukrainian culture. The second part is divided into sections of texts and songs. The latter is further subdivided by type of song. The book includes an appendix listing information on the minstrels, their apprenticeships, and their earnings as minstrels.

1037. Luckyj, George S. N. **Ukrainian Literature in the Twentieth Century: A Reader's Guide**. viii, 136p. Toronto: University of Toronto Press, 1992. Includes endnotes and index.

This in not intended as a literary history, but rather as a survey of "the main literary trends, the chief authors, and their works, as seen against the historical background of the present century" (p. vii). Ukrainian émigré literature is also covered.

1038. **Modern Ukrainian Short Stories**. Edited by George Stephen Nestor Luckyj. Rev. 1st ed. 230p. Englewood, Colo.: Ukrainian Academic Press, 1995. Parallel text editions in Ukrainian and English.

Arguing that the volume has not diminished since its first edition was published in 1973, the editor presents here 15 stories with parallel texts in Ukrainian and English. Although the literary scene has changed over the past 20 years, their stories still are representative of the classical, modernist period of Ukrainian literature. An appendix provides some basic information about those authors and stories included.

1039. Press, J. Ian, and Stefan Pugh. **Colloquial Ukrainian**. vii, 373p. *The Colloquial series*. London: Routledge, 1994. Includes glossary, index, and cassettes.

This textbook with accompanying cassettes provides "a complete introductory course in the Ukrainian language, but one which can still be used by someone who needs only to 'survive' " (p. 1). Each lesson begins with a dialogue and introduces grammatical points illustrated. (It also includes texts for reading, exercises, and vocabulary lists.)

1040. Selivachov, Mykhailo. **Folk Designs of Ukraine**. Translated by Yuri Tkrach. 63p.: illus., map. Doncaster, Aust.; Kiev, Rus.: Bayda Books, Ivan Honchar Museum, 1995. English translation of the Ukrainian work (nontitled) by the author.

The author is presently senior scholar at the Kiev Rylsky Institute for Art Studies, Folklore and Ethnology. This slim volume gives the historical background of Ukraine folk art, and then proceeds to discuss the various types and uses of designs, all of which is accompanied by illustrations.

1041. Shkandrij, Myroslav. **Modernists, Marxists and the Nation: The Ukrainian Literary Discussion of the 1920s**. xii, 265p. Edmonton, Alb.: Canadian Institute of Ukrainian Studies, 1992. Includes bibliographical references and index.

The subject of this study is an event commonly referred to as the literary discussion. Its significance went beyond literary affairs and is portrayed by the author as "the central event of Ukrainian intellectual history of the twenties, perhaps of the century" (p. xii). The focus here is on three principal issues: (1) the multifaced context underlying the torrent of polemical writing; (2) the events leading up to the defeat of the group around Mykola Khvylovy; and (3) the main theoretical issues running through the debates.

1042. Slavutych, Yar. **Three Narratives, Six Poems**. Edited by Roman Orest Tatchyn, Orysia Ferbey, and Watson Kirkconnell. 64p. Edmonton, Alb.: Slavuta, 1992. Poems in Ukrainian and English, on facing pages.

This third book of Slavutych's translations includes the long poetic narrations "Solovetsky Prisoner," "Plaint," and "Daughter Without a Name." Each of the works translated here is represented with the facing page in the original Ukrainian. Slavutych began writing poetry in Ukraine in 1940 and continued after the war in Augsburg and Canada.

1043. Tarnavs′ka, Marta. **Ukrainian Literature in English: Articles in Journals and Collections, 1840-1965: An Annotated Bibliography**. 176p. Edmonton, Alb.: Canadian Institute of Ukrainian Studies Press, 1992. Includes indexes.

This report is part of a series of similar reports that intends to provide "comprehensive coverage of translations from and materials about Ukrainian literature, published in the English language from the earliest known publications to the present." The present bibliography is arranged alphabetically by author. Each entry contains a full bibliographic citation as well as a brief annotation describing its contents. Two indexes, a personal name (author, co-author, editor, translator, illustration) and chronological one, provide additional access to the contents.

1044. Tarnawsky, Maxim. **Between Reason and Irrationality: The Prose of Valerijan Pidmohyl'nyj**. 222p. Toronto; Buffalo, N.Y.: University of Toronto Press, 1994. Includes bibliographical references and index.

Until now, no comprehensive analysis of the works of Ukrainian author Valerijan Pidmohyl'nyj had been published. Maxim Tarnawsky fills this gap in literary criticism with this book. "In particular, it examines Pidmohyl'nyj's writings in chronological sequence, illuminating the development of theme, structure, and style . . . the principal goal of this study is to map [his] . . . artistic central core and to delineate its gradual evolution" (p. 3). Extensive analysis is devoted to *Ostap Šaptala, Misto, Nevelycka Drama*. Tarnawsky hopes to reach the general reader and the specialist. To this end, he has devoted much of his introduction to the life of Pidmohyl'nyj and the political and literary context in which his writings were produced. He has also included a substantial bibliography of works by and about Pidmohyl'nyj.

Dissident Movement

1045. **Ukraine, From Chernobyl' to Sovereignty: A Collection of Interviews**. Edited by Roman Sol'chanyk. xxvi, 174p. Edmonton, Alb.: Canadian Institute of Ukrainian Studies Press, 1992. Includes bibliographical references and index. Translated from Ukrainian.

This volume contains transcripts of 15 interviews with central actors in the reemerging free Ukraine. Topics include the political movement "Rukh," Ukrainian-Russian relations, the democratization process, the national question, Chernobyl, and Ukrainian-Jewish relations.

Émigrés

1046. Alexandrow, Julia, and Tommy French. **Flight from Novaa Salow: Autobiography of a Ukrainian Who Escaped Starvation in the 1930s Under the Russians and Then Suffered Nazi Enslavement**. xiii, 202p.: illus. Jefferson, N.C.: McFarland, 1995. Includes index.

This autobiography begins when the author was a small girl of seven in Ukraine. The story follows her life through the war, Nazi labor camps, and eventual emigration to the United States and her life there until 1978.

1047. Ewanchuk, Michael. **Reflections and Reminiscences: Ukrainians in Canada, 1892-1992**. x, 169p.: illus., ports. Winnipeg, Man.: M. Ewanchuk, 1995. Includes bibliographical references (p. 166) and index.

In attempting to provide an overview of the Ukrainian-Canadian experience, the author has reprinted primary sources relating to Ukrainians in Canada, especially about the hierarchs of both the Ukrainian Catholic and Orthodox Churches. The sources, arranged thematically in 10 parts, include the writer's recorded conversations with Ukrainian immigrants to Canada, correspondence and interviews with pioneers and leading community activists, and secondary encyclopedic information.

1048. Hryniuk, Stella M., and Lubomyr Y. Luciuk. **Multiculturalism and Ukrainian Canadians: Identity, Homeland Ties, and the Community's Future**. vi, 89p.: illus. Toronto; Downsview, Ont.: Multicultural History Society of Ontario. Available from University of Toronto Press, 1993.

This issue of the journal *Polyphony* contains papers presented at a symposium organized by the Ukrainian Canadian Centennial Commission that was held in Toronto in November 1991. The papers presented, as well as the recorded remarks of the discussants, focused around questions relating to the ties between Ukraine and the Diaspora. The questions became thematic models for each of the three sessions entitled, respectively: (1) A question of identity? Canada's Ukrainians and multiculturalism; (2) Divided loyalties? Homeland ties in times of crisis; and (3) A new commons? The viability of Ukrainian-Canadian organizational structures in the 1990s and beyond.

1049. Knysh, George D. **Michael Sherbinin in Winnipeg: A Preliminary Study**. 88p.: illus. Winnipeg, Man.: Ukrainian Academy of Arts and Sciences in Canada, 1994. Includes bibliographical references and index.

Sherbinin was noted for many activities, including his pedagogical activities among the Saskatchewan Doukhobors, his missionary and social work among the poor sections of Chicago, and as a disciple of Lord Radstock and an acquaintance of Leo Tolstoy. In this volume Knysh ties all the separate threads of his life together and weaves a coherent tapestry of the life of this remarkable man.

1050. Nay, Marshall A. **Trailblazers of Ukrainian Emigration to Canada: Wasyl Eleniak and Ivan Pylypow**. 208p.: illus. Edmonton, Alb.: Brightest Pebble Publishing, 1997. Includes bibliographical references and index.

The bibliographies of Wasyl Eleniak and Ivan Pylypow are presented for two reasons: (1) "they helped a massive emigration of Ukrainians from the Austro-Hungarian Empire to Canada and (2) they became highly successful transplants themselves" (p. 7). They both first came to Canada in 1891. The book describes their life in Ukraine, their exploratory journey to Canada, their final emigration to Canada, and their settlement and life together.

Central Asian Republics and Peoples

1051. **Political and Economic Trends in Central Asia**. Edited by Shirin Akiner. ix, 207p. London: British Academic Press, 1994. Includes bibliographical references.

The papers included in this volume were originally presented at a conference in London in 1987. In spite of their delay in coming to print, the editor argues that they are valuable because they provide information and analysis that are not widely available in the West. Furthermore, they also offer a unique perspective on the thinking about Central Asia on the eve of fundamental change. Specific topics explored are tradition and change in Central Asia, ethnic cadres policy, political education, youth problems, agriculture, living standards, ethno-demographic problems, Soviet Muslims and their foreign co-religionists, and Muslim theological education.

1052. **Post-Soviet Central Asia**. Edited by Touraj Atabaki and John O'Kane. xv, 384p. London: I. B. Tauris in association with the International Institute for Asian Studies, 1998. Includes bibliographical references.

This volume contains the proceedings of the Fifth Conference of the European Society for Central Asian Studies that was held in Copenhagen in 1995. The 25 papers deal with present-day problems of Central Asia, particularly in the social, economic, and political realms.

1053. **The New Geopolitics of Central Asia and Its Borderlands**. Edited by Ali Banuazizi and Myron Weiner. 284p.: map. Bloomington: Indiana University Press, 1994. Includes bibliographical references and index.

These papers were originally presented at a series of workshops held at MIT. "This volume assesses the recent developments in the six post-Soviet Muslim republics of Central Asia and Transcaucasus within a geo-political rather than a national framework. Its basic premise is that both the internal developments and the international relations of these states need to be seen in the context of the larger Turko-Islamic and Iranian civilizations, to which they once belonged and with which they have now once again begun to interact, as well as in the still broader Eurasian context that includes Russia, China, Pakistan, India, Japan and the neighboring Middle Eastern states" (p. 8).

1054. Bergholz, Fred W. **The Partition of the Steppe: The Struggle of the Russians, Manchus, and the Zunghar Mongols for Empire in Central Asia, 1619-1758: A Study in Power Politics**. vi, 522p. *American University Studies. Series IX, History*, vol. 109. New York: P. Lang, 1993. Includes bibliographical references (pp. [479]-509) and index.

Bergholz examines Russia's relations with China in the context of the struggle for empire in Central Asia from 1619 to 1758. In Part 1 he looks at Russia's expansion into Siberia and its first contacts with the Mongols and China. In Part 2 he analyzes the relations of the Ch'ing dynasty with Russia. In the final two chapters (Part 3) he describes the final partition of the steppe, the seeking by the Kazakhs of protection from the Zunghar Mongols, and the eventual destruction of the Zunghar khanate.

1055. **The North Caucasus Barrier: The Russian Advance Towards the Muslim World**. Edited by Marie Broxup and Abdurakhman Avtorkhanov. xvii, 252p.: illus., maps. New York: St. Martin's Press, 1992. Includes bibliographical references and index. "Bibliographical note on selected works published in recent decades in Western European languages" (pp. 241-44).

The essays collected in this volume are on the struggle of the North Caucasus people to maintain their independence from Russia during the last 200 years. "The author of this work felt that the history of the North Caucasus, which has played a predominant part in framing Russian colonial thinking, deserves to be known outside a narrow circle of specialists, and that this strategically important region and its turbulent deeply Muslim peoples are destined to continue to play an important role in the shaping of Russian politics" (p. ix). Contributors are Abdurakhman Avtorkhanov, Marie Bennigsen Broxup, Fanny Bryan, Paul Henze, and Chantal Lemercier-Quelqueljay. The book includes a glossary.

1056. Chenciner, Robert. **Daghestan—Tradition and Survival**. xi, 307p.: illus., maps. New York: St. Martin's Press, 1997. Includes bibliographical references (pp. 295-301) and index.

This extremely handsome and well-researched volume presents an extensive, readable ethnography of Daghestan in the late 1980s and early 1990s. Individual chapters cover the strongman cult, women and sex, birth and death, food, textiles, clothing and costumes, and religion and naturalism. Several appendixes provide tables of additional factual information.

1057. **Conflict, Cleavage, and Change in Central Asia and the Caucasus**. Edited by Karen Dawisha and Bruce Parrott. xv, 423p. *Democratization and Authoritarianism in Post-Communist Societies*, 4. Cambridge, Eng.: Cambridge University Press, 1997. Includes index.

As Volume 4 in the series *Democratization and Authoritarianism in Postcommunist Societies*, this book provides up-to-date essays on the democratization of the countries of Central Asia and the Caucasus. The first two essays, by the editors, and which are included in each volume, present perspectives on post-communist democratization and an analysis of research concepts and methodologies relating to the investigation of democratization and political participation. The essays on the Caucasus deal with Armenia, Georgia, and Azerbaijan. Those on Central Asia focus on political participation in Kazakhstan, the fate of political liberalization in Kyrgyzstan, thwarted democratization in Tajikistan, the quest for stability and control in Turkmenistan, and political development in Uzbekistan.

1058. **Tajikistan: The Trials of Independence**. Edited by Mohammad Reza Djalili and Frédéric Grare. xiii, 248p.: maps. Richmond, Surrey, Eng.: Curzon, 1998. Includes bibliographical references (pp. 237-41).

The central theme of this book is the conflict that arose in Tajikistan in 1992. The 13 essays are arranged in five sections: (1) construction of a national identity; (2) division and conflict; (3) the Tajik conflict and the wider world; (4) peacemaking and peacekeeping; and (5) humanitarian dimensions. Several maps, including those portraying regional groups or clans and the drug trade, are included in an appendix.

1059. **Russia's Muslim Frontiers: New Directions in Cross-Cultural Analysis**. Edited by Dale F. Eickelman. x, 206p.: map. *Indiana Series in Arab and Islamic Studies*. Bloomington: Indiana University Press, 1993. Includes bibliographical references and index.

In 1990 workshops were held in Moscow and Leningrad on the scholarly research concerning Muslim society. Scholars from the Soviet Union and the West participated and compared the theoretical approaches that had been taken to this research in the past. This book is the result of those workshops and two subsequent U.S. conferences. These meetings were interdisciplinary, including anthropologists, political scientists, historians, and religious scholars. The essays are grouped into four sections: "International Regional Perspectives"; "Central Asia"; "Afghanistan and Iran"; and "Pakistan."

1060. **Household Welfare in Central Asia**. Edited by Jane Falkingham. xiv, 259p.: illus. London: Macmillan, 1997. Includes bibliographical references (pp. 237-49) and indexes.

There has been little published on the standard of living in Central Asia. The contributors to this work attempt to partially fill this gap in the literature. "The hallmark of the book is the quantitative analysis of different aspects of household welfare using data from a variety of sources, most notably household surveys" (pp. 1-2). The chapters are arranged into three parts. Part 1 discusses the methodology used in this study. Part 2 presents a quantification of the living standards in the region. Part 3 examines the government policies that support that standard of living.

1061. **The New States of Central Asia and Their Neighbours**. Edited by Peter Ferdinand. 120p. *New Central Asia and Its Neighbours*. New York: Council on Foreign Relations Press, 1994. "Published in North America ... for the Royal Institute of International Affairs." Originally published London: Pinter Publishers, 1994; under the title: *New Central Asia and Its Neighbours*.

The purpose of this book is to describe how the new states of Central Asia have begun to develop and to interact with their neighbors. The countries included are Kazakhstan, Kyrgyzstan, Tajikistan, Turkmenistan, and Uzbekistan. Individual chapters focus on the republics themselves; their origins, history, and more recent past; and relations with Russia, the Middle East, south Asia (India and Pakistan), and China. A concluding chapter summarizes the political, social, and economic changes that have taken place within this region in the past several years.

1062. Frank, Allen J. **Islamic Historiography and "Bulghar" Identity Among the Tatars and Bashkirs of Russia**. viii, 232p. Leiden, Netherlands; Boston: E. J. Brill, 1998. Includes bibliographical references (pp. [207]-217) and index.

In this study Allen Frank examines the role of the Volga-Ural Islamic clerisy in defining the ethnic identity of the Volga-Ural Muslims. He is particularly interested in the locally produced Turkic histories. These emerged at the end of the 8th century. "By analyzing these histories we can better understand how local historiographical traditions were reconfigured to adduce a coherent and unifying regional identity in ways that were meaningful to these Muslims" (p. 2). The book is divided into six chapters. The first gives an overview of Volga-Ural Islamic historical writings. Chapter 2 discusses the relationship between the Russian government and the Volga-Ural clerisy to the end of the 18th century. Chapter 3 examines the most popular of local histories, while the fourth chapter reviews "Bulgarist" historiography. In Chapter 5 the author reviews the commentaries on the histories. The final chapter focuses on the fate of Bulgar identity in the early 20th century.

1063. Haghayeghi, Mehrdad. **Islam and Politics in Central Asia**. xxiv, 264p.: illus., maps. New York: St. Martin's Press, 1995. Includes bibliographical references (pp. [243]-250) and index.

"This study is an attempt to put into comparative perspective the principal dynamics of Islamic revival in Central Asia" (p. xviii). In carrying out his plan, the author gives an overview of Islam under communism, investigates the changing nature of policies toward religion and especially Islam, outlines the main currents of the Islamic revival in Central Asia, and explores the nature and scope of Islamic movements in Central Asia, the Central Asian governments' response to these movements, and an assessment of ethnicity in Central Asia.

1064. Hostler, Charles Warren. **The Turks of Central Asia**. xi, 237p.: maps. Westport, Conn.: Praeger, 1993. Rev., upd. ed. of: *Turkism and the Soviets*, 1957. Includes bibliographical references (pp. [219]-233) and index.

This comprehensive study of Turkic peoples is essentially a handy reference book about Turks. Individual chapters present cogent information about the origins and physical characteristics of Turks, a historical sketch of the Turkic peoples, the emergence and development of Turkism, pan-Turkism, and a final chapter on the competition and struggle for influence among the Turks of the former USSR. Several appendixes give biographical sketches of prominent Turks and excerpts from relevant documents.

1065. Kemper, Michael, Anke von Kügelgen, and Dmitriy Yermakov. **Muslim Culture in Russia and Central Asia from the 18th to the Early 20th Centuries**. vols. 1-2: illus. *Islamkundliche Untersuchungen*, Bd. 2. Berlin: Schwarz, 1996. Includes bibliographical references. Contributions in English and German.

This is the second volume in a series on Muslim culture in Russia from the 18th to 20th centuries. In this volume the contributing authors focus on transregional and interethnic relations in the Russian empire and Central Asia. "By emphasizing transregional and inter-ethnicity we hope to avoid examining the history of the Muslim regions in a pre-national period from a national perspective" (p. 1). Because numerous topics were relevant to this study, the essays have been arranged topically. The subjects covered are "networks of scholars"; "inter-ethnic relations and Diaspora"; "Islam and politics in a non-Muslim state"; "Literature"; and "Architecture." Most essays included here are in English with some German contributions.

1066. Central Asia: Its Strategic Importance and Future Prospects. Edited by Hafeez Malik. xi, 337p. New York: St. Martin's Press, 1994. Includes bibliographical references and index.

The rise of nationalism in Central Asia in the wake of the downfall of the Soviet Union has raised many questions about the region. Not the least of these is what will Central Asia's geopolitical role be in the future. It was with these questions in mind that a conference was held at Villanova University in 1992. The papers in this volume are part of the result of that conference. The conference papers focused on three dimensions of the situation in Central Asia: "(1) the Russian conquest of Central Asia and its impact on the Turkic Muslim populations, which are indigenous to the region; (2) ethnic conflicts spawned by the collapse of the Soviet state; and (3) the emergence of new interactions among the Central Asian states, Russia, the United States, and the Southwest Asian states of Iran, Afghanistan, and Pakistan" (p. vii). The papers collected in this volume examine these questions in light of the many changes in the region.

1067. Central Asia and the World: Kazakhstan, Uzbekistan, Tajikistan, Kyrgyzstan, and Turkmenistan. Edited by Michael Mandelbaum. vii, 251p.: maps. New York: Council on Foreign Relations Press, 1994. Includes bibliographical references and index.

The eight papers in this volume consider the changing nature of foreign relations in Central Asia. Each considers a different aspect of the issue: unity in the region, the effect of the collapse of the Soviet Union; the nature of the new federation; Central Asia and the West; the growth of capitalism; security; Tajik-Uzbek relations; and Central Asia and China. This is the first book to examine these questions. The contributors are Michael Mandelbaum, Martha Brill Olcott, Daniel Pipes, Graham E. Fuller, Robert Cullen, Shafgul Isalm, Susan Clark, Barnett R. Rubin, and Ross H. Munro.

1068. Mesbahi, Mohiaddin. **Central Asia and the Caucasus After the Soviet Union: Domestic and International Dynamics.** x, 353p. Gainesville: University Press of Florida, 1994. Includes bibliographical references and index.

The papers presented here were originally read at an international conference in Tehran, Iran, in March 1992. The individual contributions are arranged in four parts. In Part 1 the contributors analyze ethnicity and Islam and the ethno-historical dynamics of Muslim societies within Russia and the CIS. Part 2 surveys the new Muslim states of the North Caucasus and Azerbaijan. In Part 3 well-known scholars the new Muslim states in Central Asia, and Part 4, consisting of four essays, examines the new geopolitics that have resulted.

1069. Peimani, Hooman. **Regional Security and the Future of Central Asia: The Competition of Iran, Turkey, and Russia**. xiv, 151p.: map. Westport, Conn.: Praeger, 1998. Includes bibliographical references (pp. [135]-141) and index.

The focus of this book is on the relations among the Central Asian countries and the main contenders for power and influence in the region: Iran, Turkey, and Russia. The role of Iran in the energy industry in the region is seen as a major factor in furthering that country's influence there. The author explores the concept of regional security, the historical background of relations among the countries, and the society, military, and economic factors that affect relationships in the region.

1070. Poliakov, Sergei Petrovich. **Everyday Islam: Religion and Tradition in Rural Central Asia**. xxvi, 155p.: illus. Armonk, N.Y.: M. E. Sharpe, 1992. Translation of: *Bytovoi islam*. Includes bibliographical references (pp. 145-46) and indexes.

This is a translation of a Soviet work on Central Asia. Sergei Poliakov is a professor at Moscow State University and was a lifelong member of the Communist Party. "He believes Central Asia to be mired down by the weight of traditionalism—that is, by 'everyday Islam': the customs, values, and economic practices of traditional rural Islamic society" (p. xiv). Poliakov was very concerned that the policies of Gorbachev were exacerbating the problems of the region by encouraging the traditional elites of the region. This is not a traditional scholarly work, nor heavily annotated. Poliakov was careful not to "name names" for fear of retaliation against those voicing unpopular opinions. The book is organized topically, discussing economic structure of the region, family structure, religion, and social dynamics. It contains a glossary to assist those readers less familiar with the region.

1071. Ro'i, Yaacov. **Muslim Eurasia: Conflicting Legacies**. xiii, 330p.: illus., maps. London: Frank Cass, 1995. Includes bibliographical references and index.

In this first volume of a joint project between the Cummings Center for Russian Studies and the Dayan Center for Middle Eastern and African Studies, the individual essayists concentrate on domestic trends and developments in the Muslim regions of the Soviet Union and the Commonwealth of Independent States. Essays approach this theme with broadly based essays, e.g., "Islam and Fundamentalism in Independent Central Asia," or in more country-specific types, e.g., "Regionalism and Clan Loyalty in the Political Life of Uzbekistan."

1072. **Central Asia in Transition: Dilemmas of Political and Economic Development**. Edited by Boris Rumer. xx, 286p.: illus., map. Armonk, N.Y.: M. E. Sharpe, 1996. Includes bibliographical references and index.

Rumer believes that two key factors will determine the fate of the new Central Asian states: "(1) geopolitics, especially the relationship with Russia and the relations among the Central Asian states themselves; and (2) the outcome of attempts to transform their economies" (p. xi). The essays compiled in this volume focus on these two factors.

Contents include essays that explore the transnational corporations in Central Asia; economic development; case studies of Uzbekistan, Kyrgyzstan, and Kazakhstan; and the experiences of translation economies in East Asia and their implications for Central Asia.

1073. Schoeberlein-Engel, John S. **Guide to Scholars of the History and Culture of Central Asia**. 313p. *Research Publications of the Harvard Central Asia Forum*, no. 1. Cambridge, Mass.: Harvard Central Asia Forum, 1995. Includes bibliographical references and indexes.

Besides being an alphabetical directory of scholars studying Central Asia, this volume can serve as a guide to research in the field. Each entry includes basic information on individual scholars and their major publications. The subject index provides an access point for locating scholarly works in particular areas. Entries also provide information on the scholar's positions and/or titles, bibliographical information, a work address, educational background, languages, interests, and representative publications.

1074. **Around the Roof of the World**. Edited by Nicholas and Nina Shoumatoff. Ann Arbor: University of Michigan Press, 1996. Includes bibliographical references and index.

These collected essays, most of which have been translated from Russian and French, all focus around Central Asia. All of the correspondents describe their areas from a personal point of view. Many of these "tours" are walking tours, some involve auto, some mountain climbing. The final chapter, written by the editors, includes a frank debate on the spirituality of this part of the world. As the editors state, "Our panorama thus expands from the natural and human into the numinous dimensions, a triad that spans the diapason of Central Asia's mountain world" (p. 12).

1075. Smith, Sebastian. **Allah's Mountains: Politics and War in the Russian Caucasus**. x, 288p.: maps. London: I. B. Tauris, 1998. Includes bibliographical references (pp. [275]-278).

"President Boris Yeltsin said he was just 'restoring constitutional order,' but a day in Grozny was enough to realize that something deep roofed was underway. Chechnya was where the curses of history and revenge raged out of control" (p. 3). Sebastian Smith witnessed much of the destruction of Grozny and could not help but wonder what had created this hatred between the Russian and Chechens. This book explores that question and the history of the relations of the Russians with the peoples of the other regions of the North Caucasus and what the future may hold for the area.

1076. Tütüncü, Mehmet. **Caucasus, War and Peace: The New World Disorder in Caucasia**. 221p.: maps. Haarlem, Netherlands: SOTA, 1998. Includes a contribution in Turkish.

"The collapse of the Soviet Union was peaceful, but its aftermath has been remarkably violent" (p. 7). So Mehmet Tütüncü introduces this collection of essays that focuses on that violent aftermath. The papers collected here were originally presented at a conference in the Netherlands in June 1997. The main issues examined here include: what the causes of the conflict are; the role of international organizations and the media; the use of conflict resolution in alleviating the conflict; and the role of women in the region. Contributors include Western scholars and experts from the region. The volume is divided into four parts, the first three focusing on the geographic areas of conflict: Karabagh, Chechnya, and Abkhazia. The final part is on general trends in the region. The book includes a brief list of suggested readings.

1077. Vachnadze, Georgii Nikolaevich. **Russia's Hotbeds of Tension**. 285p.: maps. Commack, N.Y.: Nova Science Publishers, 1994. Includes bibliographical references and index.

Georgii Vachnadze has written a study of the changing view of Russia as it is seen from the newly independent states. "Former small-time petty bosses in these outlying provinces have now become presidents, MPs, mayors and have thus gained independence from Moscow. But they are now under the influence of their constituencies" (frontispiece). The book is divided into three parts discussing the separation of the republics from the Soviet state, the vantage point from the nonorthodox republics, and new centers of power.

Other Republics

1078. Chorbajian, Levon, Patrick Donabedian, and Claude Mutafian. **The Caucassian Knot: The History and Politics of Nagorno-Karabagh**. xvi, 198p. *Politics in Contemporary Asia*. London: Zed Books, 1994. Includes bibliographical references and index.

This is an English translation of a work previously issued in French in 1991. Besides the translated text of that version, this volume also includes a 48-page introduction to the English-language edition by one of the authors, which provides a succinct summary of the issue. The three authors of this study examine Nagorno-Karabagh, the autonomous region heavily populated by Armenians but lying within the Azerbaijani republic, and the strife that had befallen the inhabitants of the region in the late 1980s and early 1990s. Individual chapters are devoted to the history of Karabagh from antiquity to the 20th century, Karabagh in the 20th century, and a conclusion. Several appendixes provide primary source documents that supplement the main text.

1079. Croissant, Michael P. **The Armenia-Azerbaijan Conflict: Causes and Implications**. viii, 172p. Westport, Conn.: Praeger, 1998. Includes bibliographical references and index.

Croissant addresses "the regional and international dynamics and implications of the Armenia-Azerbaijan conflict" (p. xiii). After presenting the historical context and the impact of geography on the region, he traces the continuing Armenian-Azerbaijani conflict as it revived in 1988 and reached escalation in 1991. Examining the roles that the major regional powers played in the conflict, he analyzes how a confluence of forces led to bloodshed and the final cease-fire in 1994. A concluding chapter assesses the prospects for and likely repercussions of renewed warfare between these two countries in the future.

1080. Dunlop, John B. **Russia Confronts Chechnya: Roots of a Separatist Conflict**. Cambridge, Eng.: Cambridge University Press, 1998. Includes index.

"In this book John Dunlop provides an understanding of the background to the Russian invasion of Chechnya in December 1994, tracing events from 4000 B.C. to the time of the invasion. The historic encounter between Chechens and Russians, first during pre-Petrine and then with imperial Russia, is carefully examined. The genocide and oppression endured by the Chechens under the communists are discussed in detail. The convulsive 'Chechen Revolution' of 1991, which brought General Dzhokhar Dudaev to power, is described, as are developments within Chechnya during 1992-1994. The author traces the negotiation process between the Russian Federation and secessionist Chechnya, elucidating the reasons for the breakdown of the quest for a peaceful resolution of the conflict" (frontispiece).

1081. Gall, Charlotta, and Thomas de Waal. **Chechnya: Calamity in the Caucasus**. xiv, 416p. New York: New York University Press, 1998. Includes bibliographical references and index.

Gall and de Waal were both eyewitnesses to the events that they relate in these pages. Both were correspondents for *The Moscow Times* and de Waal also worked for the *Times* of London. De Waal first visited Chechnya to write about the 50th anniversary of the deportations of Chechens in 1944 and Gall flew to Grozny, the capital, on the first day of Russian invasion. Not only did Gall suffer through two hostage crises, but also spent time in the mountains with Chechen guerrillas and interviewed the Chechen leader Dudaev in his mountain hideout. Their purpose in writing this book is to tell the story of this conflict and to put it in its historical context.

1082. **Transcaucasian Boundaries**. Edited by Suzanne Goldenberg, Richard N. Schofield, and John F. R. Wright. 1st ed. vii, 237p.: illus., map. *SOAS/GRC Geopolitics series*, 4. New York: St. Martin's Press, 1996. Includes bibliographical references and index.

Most of these papers, which explore the geopolitical and territorial problems of the Caucasus, were originally presented at the July 1992 School of Oriental and African Studies Conference on Transcaucasian Boundaries. Individual papers focus on topics such as nationalities and borders in Transcaucasia and the North Caucasus; Russia and Transcaucasia; Iran and Transcaucasia; the Armenian presence in mountainous Karabakh; the republic of Azerbaijan; the geopolitics of Georgia; the Georgian/South Ossetian territorial and boundary dispute; and Abkhazia: a problem of identify and ownership.

1083. Hunter, Shireen T. **The Transcaucasus in Transition Nation-Building and Conflict**. *Significant Issues series*, vol. 16, no. 7. Washington, D.C.: The Center for Strategic and International Studies, 1994. Includes bibliographical references.

Hunter examines and analyzes the tremendous challenges faced by Armenia, Azerbaijan, Georgia, as well as Nagorno-Karabakh, in the wake of the dissolution of the Soviet Union in 1991. She initially places the problem in context by describing the mixed legacies of the Transcaucasus, such as the ancient Iranian, Roman-Christian, Islamic, Turkic, Russian, and Western influences. She then turns to each of the countries/autonomous regions in turn and emphasizes those factors that she considers the most important, such as political, economic, national movements, and nationalism. Before proffering a conclusion she analyzes the role of international and regional actors and the effects of their policies on the Transcaucasus.

1084. Khodarkovsky, Michael. **Where Two Worlds Met: The Russian State and the Kalmyk Nomads, 1600-1771**. xiii, 278p. Ithaca, N.Y.: Cornell University Press, 1992. Includes bibliographical references (pp. 251-62) and index.

The Kalmyks were originally nomads that appeared near the Volga River in the early 17th century. They represented the last wave of nomadic migration from inner Asia to the steppes of the Caspian Sea. This volume relates the history of the Kalmyk people, their relations with the Russian empire, and the resulting effect on both societies in the 17th and 18th centuries.

1085. **Mongolia in the Twentieth Century: Landlocked Cosmopolitan**. Edited by Stephen Kotkin and Bruce A. Elleman. xx, 313p.: illus., maps. Armonk, N.Y.: M. E. Sharpe, 1999. Includes bibliographical references and index.

This is a collection of presentations originally delivered at a conference at Princeton University in February 1995. The conference focused on the transnational history of the Mongols in the 20th century. The papers collected here do not represent a common point of view and are not comprehensive in their coverage of the topic. The essays are grouped into three sections. The first are papers on the Sino-Soviet struggle for the region. Section 2 includes papers on international diplomacy over Outer Mongolia. The final section collects those discussions focused on the contemporary problems of Mongolia.

1086. Lieven, Anatol. **Chechnya: Tombstone of Russian Power**. xii, 436p.: illus. New Haven, Conn.: Yale University Press, 1998.

In explaining the Russians' defeat in Chechnya, Lieven seeks to do it "in terms of the Russian state, Russian society and the Russian psyche in the 1990s" (p. viii). His book is arranged in three parts: (1) the war; (2) the Russian defeat; and (3) the Chechen victory.

1087. Odom, William E., and Robert Dujarric. **Commonwealth or Empire?: Russia, Central Asia and Transcaucasus**. xviii, 290p. Indianapolis: Hudson Institute, 1995. "This book was made possible by the Office of the Assistant Secretary of Defense for International Security"—p. [xv]. Includes bibliographical references (pp. [269]-283) and index.

In this study of post-Soviet Transcaucasian and Central Asian republics, the authors conclude that no outside state is rushing into the vacuum left by the demise of the Soviet empire. Moreover, the expected influences from the Middle Eastern states that have cultural and linguistic ties to the region have also not reasserted themselves. The authors' purpose therefore is to sort out what is happening in the region by exploring the capabilities and will of the Russian military, the power of Islam, and the effects of a changing regional geography.

1088. Zhang, Yongjin, and Rouben Azizian. **Ethnic Challenges Beyond Borders: Chinese and Russian Perspectives of the Central Asian Conundrum**. xii, 240p. *St. Antony's series.* New York: St. Martin's Press in association with St. Antony's College, Oxford, 1998. Includes bibliographical references and index.

This collection of 12 essays is meant to investigate the various challenges in Central Asia, particularly as they relate to ethnicity. The essays are arranged in four parts: (1) political challenges; (2) the ethnic conundrum; (3) economic agonies; and (4) strategic and security issues. Contributors include authors from Russia, China, and New Zealand. One of its purposes is to provide to the English-speaking reader several viewpoints from both Chinese and Russian specialists that have not been available prior to this time.

Armenia

1089. **The Armenian People from Ancient to Modern Times**. Edited by Richard G. Hovannisian. 2 vols.: maps. New York: St. Martin's Press, 1997. Includes bibliography (pp. 327-49) and index.

This cooperative work by 17 Armenian specialists covers the entire span of Armenian history in two volumes. It examines all facets of Armenian life, including culture, geography, and relations with the Diaspora.

1090. Shahnuratian, Samvel. **The Sumgait Tragedy**. xiii, 343p. New Rochelle, N.Y.: Arstide D. Caratzas, 1990.

After Armenians made the peaceful demand for the reunification of the autonomous region of Nagorno-Karabakh, Azerbaijanis began to threaten and carry out minor incidents of insults and violence against Armenians living in various cities in Azerbaijan. One of the most violent and tragic of these incidents occurred in the city of Sumgait, where Armenians were attacked in their homes, some were killed, and many were raped. This volume presents translated eyewitness accounts to this modern pogrom.

Azerbaijan

1091. Atabaki, Touraj. **Azerbaijan: Ethnicity and Autonomy in Twentieth-Century Iran**. xiv, 238p.: maps. London: British Academy Press, 1993. Includes bibliographical references (pp. 221-32) and index.

Atabaki examines the brief existence of the autonomous government of Azerbaijan, which existed in 1945-1946. To do this the author presents a general historical overview of the origin of Azerbaijani ethnic identity that arose in Iran in the 19th century and amid the politics of the Ottoman Empire. In the final three chapters Atabaki analyzes the socio-political background of the autonomous government of Azerbaijan.

1092. Goltz, Thomas. **Azerbaijan Diary: A Rogue Reporter's Adventure in an Oil-Rich, War-Torn, Post-Soviet Republic**. xxx, 496p.: illus, maps. Armonk, N.Y.: M. E. Sharpe, 1998. Rev. ed. of: *Requiem for a Would-Be Republic*.

This book first appeared in 1994 in Istanbul under the title *Requiem for a Would-Be Republic*. When that book appeared, Azerbaijan did not appear to have a future as an independent state, and the tone of the book reflects the author's belief that the new republic would not survive. The boom in oil sales changed all that. The author has taken an unconventional approach, writing in the first person, and not relying on precious studies of the region or current press reports. He adopts an approach he refers to as "contact journalism." "The reason for the paucity of reference to 'others' is that I have seen far too many examples of bad sourcing in the press and in scholarly articles on Azerbaijan to believe anything not witnessed by me (or by someone whose honesty and integrity I can vouch for)" (p. xi). The book is arranged chronologically. The author has added an epilogue to account for events since 1994.

1093. Swietochowski, Tadeusz. **Russia and Azerbaijan: A Borderland in Transition**. x, 290p.: maps. New York: Columbia University Press, 1995. Includes bibliographical references (pp. [269]-282) and index.

Azerbaijan is often called the quintessential borderland, located as it is "between Europe and Asia, Islam and Christianity, Russia and the Middle East, Turks and Iranians, Shi'a and Sunni Islam. The book deals with a divided people in a divided land and a split that has resulted from European conquest of a frontier region of the Middle East. It examines the last two centuries of Azerbaijan's history, beginning with the Russian seizure of the northern part of the country in the early nineteenth century, and concluding with the achievement of the independence by the post-Soviet Azerbaijani Republic in the 1990s" (p. vii).

Georgia

1094. Eastmond, Antony. **Royal Imagery in Medieval Georgia**. xx, 268p., [16] p. of plates: illus. (some col.). University Park: Pennsylvania State University Press, 1998. Includes bibliographical references (pp. [245]-259) and index.

"This book examines the ways in which art was used to promote the power and rule of the Bagrat'ioni rulers of Georgia in Caucasia. It covers the period of the rise of the Bagrat'ioni dynasty from rulers of the minor principality of T'ao-K'larjeti in southwest Georgia in the ninth century to the rulers of the major power in eastern Anatolia and the Caucasus at the beginning of the thirteenth century. From this period survive fourteen major monumental images as well as a number of smaller images on coins and icons, which can all be used to determine the ways in which art helped to create and define perceptions of power in the country" (p. 1).

1095. Goldstein, Darra. **The Georgian Feast: The Vibrant Culture and Savory Food of the Republic of Georgia**. 1st ed. xxv, 229p.: illus., map. New York: HarperCollins, 1993. Includes bibliographical references (pp. 212-15).

One-fourth of this volume describes Georgian feasting customs and the remainder provides recipes for enjoying such feasts yourself.

1096. Rayfield, Donald. **The Literature of Georgia: A History**. xvi, 360p. Oxford, Eng.: Clarendon Press, 1994. Includes bibliographical references and index.

With this comprehensive history of Georgian literature, Donald Rayfield attempts to fill a long-standing gap in Western knowledge. The book has been developed out of a set of encyclopedia entries written by the author for another publication. In this study he has been able to elaborate on these and write an extensive and detailed history of an important literature. The author has tried to reach all readers, regardless of their expertise in the subject area. For those readers who know no Georgian, he has listed all English-language translations of the literature in the bibliography.

Belarus

1097. Marples, David R. **Belarus: From Soviet Rule to Nuclear Catastrophe**. xxi, 179p.: illus., map. New York: St. Martin's Press, 1996. Includes bibliographical references (pp. 158-69) and index.

The disaster in Chernobyl raised many questions for Belarus. This study examines some of the issues related to Chernobyl. From this starting point the author extends his analysis in this book to other issues. "It seeks to put the contemporary problems of Belarus into historical perspective. It argues that modern problems have old roots: that today's nihilistic philosophy and what to a Westerner appears as appalling pessimism about the future owes much to the way the area and the state were developed in the twentieth century" (p. xxi). The book includes a glossary.

1098. Picarda, Guy. **Minsk: A Historical Guide and Short Administrative, Professional and Commercial Directory**. 248p. Minsk: Technalohija, 1994.

This unusual book is intended for the English-speaking visitor to the Belarussian capital. It is unusual in its emphasis on the history of Minsk. The first part of the book is a brief history of the city. The next section lists the major sites of interest for visitors providing extensive architectural and historical information on each. This is followed by a section on the Minsk region. The last two sections are brief listings of contemporary facilities, entertainment, and a professional directory. Unfortunately, the book lacks an index.

1099. Zaprudnik, IA. **Belarus: At a Crossroads in History**. xxi, 278p.: illus., maps. *Westview Series on the Post-Soviet Republics*. Boulder, Colo.: Westview Press, 1993. Includes bibliographical references (pp. 247-57) and index.

This history of Belarus covers the period from the beginnings of Belarus in the 10th century up to the present day. The emphasis, however, is on Belarus in the 20th century with individual chapters on Soviet and Polish experiences in a divided Belarus, destruction by war and Russification (1941-1985), confrontation between the national intelligentsia and the communists (1985-1992), political players, the economy, and neighbors and the world during that same period. A brief appendix presents a chronology of major events in the development of Belarus.

1100. Zaprudnik, Jan. **Historical Dictionary of Belarus**. 299p. *European Historical Dictionaries*, no. 28. Lanham, Md.: Scarecrow Press, 1998. Includes bibliography and appendix.

This excellent dictionary includes history, economy, politics, religion, society, culture, and demographics. The author provides a 22-page introductory essay that covers the social, cultural, and political history of the country. Key words in each entry are in bold, indicating separate entries on those terms. The work contains a list of acronyms and abbreviations, map, and historical chronology. The appendix lists rulers of Belarus. Of special interest is the 60-page multilingual classified bibliography of works on all aspects of Belarus.

Siberian Peoples and Cultures

1101. **The Paleolithic of Siberia: New Discoveries and Interpretations**. Edited by Anatoliy Derev'anko, Demitri Shimkin, and W. Roger Powers. Translated by Inna Laricheva. 406p.: illus. Urbana: University of Illinois Press, 1998. Includes bibliographical references (pp. 381-95) and index.

This collection of essays came about from the suggestion of the late Demitri Shimkin who noted that discoveries made in Siberia were virtually unknown to foreign colleagues. One reason for this state of affairs was the language barrier. The other was that most publications on Siberia came out of regional publishing houses with small print runs. The seven chapters cover the following: (1) a short history of discoveries and the development of ideas in the paleolithic of Siberia; (2) the quaternary paleogeography of north Asia; (3) the lower paleolithic in Siberia and the Russian Far East; (4) the middle and upper paleolithic of western and central Siberia; (5) the paleolithic of the Russian Far East; (6) the physical specificities of paleolithic hominids in Siberia; and (7) human occupation of nearby regions and the role of population movements in the paleolithic of Siberia.

1102. Dodwell, Christina. **Beyond Siberia**. 159p., [16] p. of plates: illus. (chiefly col.), maps, ports. London: Hodder & Stoughton, 1993.

Christina Dodwell attempts to fill the void in the literature on Kamchatka. This impressionistic study traces her travels and encounters in this region as she attempts to put a human face to this region known only from 19th-century geographic descriptions. The book lacks a bibliography.

1103. **Between Heaven and Hell: The Myth of Siberia in Russian Culture**. Edited by Galya Diment and Yuri Slezkine. x, 278p. New York: St. Martin's Press, 1993. Includes bibliographical references and index.

This volume is a collection of essays that have as their theme Siberia's perceived dualistic nature. Contributors are Adele Barker, Galya Diment, James R. Gibson, David Gillespie, John Givens, Bruce Grant, Bruce T. Holl, Harriet Nurav, Johanna Nichols, N. G. O. Periera, Yuri Slezkine, Leona Joker, and Stephen Watrous.

1104. **Rediscovering Russia in Asia: Siberia and the Russian Far East**. Edited by Stephen Kotkin and David Wolff. xxiii, 356p. Armonk, N.Y.: M. E. Sharpe, 1995. Includes index and selected bibliography.

This volume compiles the papers given at a conference on Siberia held at Princeton University in December 1993. The interdisciplinary nature of the conference is reflected in the range of topics covered in the contributions. Topics were left to the individual's discretion. "Scholars were invited to participate on the basis of recent, hands-on research, experience in the archives, libraries, villages, and cities of Siberia, the Russian Far East, China, Korea, and Japan. This is new research by new people, the fruits of a considerable investment in developmental scholarships . . ." (p. 11). The book has been divided into five sections: "Overlapping Peripheries, Antagonistic Centers"; "Siberian Identities: Autonomy, Science, and Redemption"; "Far Eastern Identities: Settlement, Natives, and Borders"; "After Communism: Resources for Cooperation or Confrontation"; and "Northeast Asia: Re-emergence of a Transnational Region." A selected bibliography is included at the end of this volume.

1105. Lincoln, W. Bruce. **The Conquest of a Continent: Siberia and the Russians**. xxii, 500p.: illus., maps. New York: Random House, 1994. Includes bibliographical references (pp. [461]-478) and index.

Lincoln provides a lively and informative account of the conquest and integration of Siberia by the Russians. His tale proceeds chronologically with the Mongol invasion in the 13th century and ends with Siberia's modern age, just before the transformation of the Soviet empire.

1106. Slezkine, Yuri. **Arctic Mirrors: Russia and the Small Peoples of the North**. xiv, 456p.: illus., maps. Ithaca, N.Y.: Cornell University Press, 1994. Includes bibliographical references (pp. 397-445) and index.

Slezkine presents the story of the relationship between the speculations about human and Russian identity and a testing ground and images evolved those speculations. As such it is "a story of Russia's confrontation with its remotest 'living ancestors,' a study of the place of the 'small peoples' in Russian empire and in the Russian mind" (p. ix). He bases his study on the hypothesis that "cross-cultural encounters cannot be fully described in terms of domination, that colonial representations cannot be wholly reduced to the 'gross political fact' of colonialism" (p. x). The author proceeds chronologically, beginning in the 11th century and continuing through perestroika.

Jews

General Studies

1107. Greenbaum, Avraham. **The Periodical Publications of the Jewish Labour and Revolutionary Movements in Eastern and Southeastern Europe 1877-1916: An Annotated Bibliography**. xx, 100p.: illus. Jerusalem: The Dinur Center, The Hebrew University, 1998. Includes indexes. Introduction and preface also in Hebrew.

This bibliography was prepared in order to study the role of the periodical press in the Jewish labor and revolutionary movements. It lists "the periodical literature of the Jewish socialist and revolutionary movements in the Russian Empire, the Austrian Empire and the Balkans, from the beginnings in 1877 up to and including 1916" (p. 9). Each entry includes a brief title, place of publication, language, frequency, editors, organizational sponsorship, libraries where the title is held if known, source of information, and annotation. The periodicals include those in Bulgarian, Czech, German, Greek, Hebrew, Ladino, Polish, Rumanian, Russian, Turkish, and Yiddish.

Emigration

1108. Buwalda, Piet. **They Did Not Dwell Alone: Jewish Emigration from Soviet Union**. xviii, 297p.: illus. Washington, D.C.: Woodrow Wilson Center Press. Includes bibliographical references (pp. 263-68) and index.

The chronological coverage of this volume coincides with the years in which "the Netherlands embassy represented the Israeli interests in Moscow and therefore had to issue the visa that practically every Jew needed to depart." The 14 chapters are arranged in two parts, the 1970s and the 1980s. The history covers not only the diplomatic side of things, but also the entire apparatus and the people caught in its grip, from refuseniks who stayed behind and were harassed to people on the outside who helped those who wanted to emigrate to do so.

1109. Cassedy, Steven. **To the Other Shore: The Russian Jewish Intellectuals Who Came to America**. xxiii, 197p.: illus. Princeton, N.J.: Princeton University Press, 1997. Includes bibliographical references (pp. [161]-188) and index.

In telling the story about a small influential group of Jews who immigrated to the United States from Russia between 1881 and the early 1920s, the author focuses primarily "on the role the Russian culture and politics played in the formation of the character of the Russian Jewish emigre intelligentsia in America" (p. xi).

The book is in two parts. In Part 1 Cassedy relates the way that the Jewish immigrants, while still in Russia, were indoctrinated into the beliefs of the Russian revolutionary doctrines known as nihilism and populism. These beliefs brought about a crisis of identity for those who held them. Part 2 of the book tells how they applied these beliefs in their new surroundings.

1110. Cohn, Michael. **Jewish Bridges: East to West**. xiv, 126p.: illus. Westport, Conn.: Praeger, 1996. Includes bibliographical references (pp. [117]-122) and index.

"Jewish cultural migration," Cohn illuminates, "is a process of cultural adaptations by those Jews not allowed to assimilate and, at times, the geographical transference of Eastern Jewish settlements to the West with as little change as possible" (p. ix). After presenting the background of Jewish migration and the eventuating pressures on East European Jewry, Cohn then traces Jewish assimilation vis-à-vis their participation in various trades: the fur business, cloth and clothing, music and stage.

1111. Haskell, Guy H. **From Sofia to Jaffa: The Jews of Bulgaria and Israel**. 235p.: illus. Detroit, Mich.: Wayne State University Press, 1994. Includes bibliographical references (pp. 216-30) and index.

In this wide-ranging study, Haskell has divided his work into four parts. In Part 1 he examines and criticizes how Israeli social science looks at immigration and ethnicity. In Part 2 he surveys the history of Jews in Bulgaria. Part 3 recounts the story of the Jews of Bulgaria in Israel, and the final part tells of the Jews who had remained in Bulgaria. Also included are three appendixes that contain statistics, a list of informants for the study, and two complete interviews conducted during the study.

1112. Markowitz, Fran. **A Community in Spite of Itself: Soviet Jewish Émigrés in New York**. xvi, 317p. *Smithsonian Series in Ethnographic Inquiry.* Washington, D.C.: Smithsonian Institution Press, 1993. Includes bibliographical references (pp. 301-14) and index.

"This book presents an ethnographic study of Soviet Jewish émigrés in New York City, conducted five to seven years after the 1978-1980 peak of immigration. It documents a short time span in the process of Soviet Jews' confrontations with an adjustment to a new society and illustrates the directions that culture change takes within this immigrant group" (p. xi). The author begins by establishing the characteristics of Jewish culture in Russia and then goes on to describe the transferal and adaptation of that culture in the United States. The book includes two appendixes. One deals with the mechanics of emigration. The other provides profiles of the informants who participated in this study.

1113. Salitan, Laurie P. **Politics and Nationality in Contemporary Soviet-Jewish Emigration, 1968-89**. x, 180p. New York: St. Martin's Press, 1992. Includes bibliographical references and index.
Salitan analyzes Soviet-Jewish emigration policy in order to identify the factors that contribute toward that policy. Rejecting the notion that the Soviet Union was a monolithic state, she embraces the view that most policy was a result of competing elites and interest groups. Her first three chapters examine Soviet-Jewish emigration policy from this perspective. In Chapter 4 she then provides a comparative perspective by examining Soviet-German emigration policy in order to see the similarities and discontinuities between them. A final chapter and afterword sum up her findings.

1114. Soyer, Daniel. **Jewish Immigrant Associations and American Identity in New York, 1880-1939**. 291p.: illus., maps. Cambridge, Mass.: Harvard University Press, 1997. Includes bibliographical references (pp. [207]-274) and index.
Landsmanshaftn, or hometown associations, numbered over 1,000 for immigrant Jews in New York City at the beginning of the 20th century. Not particular to Judaism, these associations in general supported the acculturation process of newly arrived immigrants. They also provided their members with benefits such as medical care, income support, and burial. This study examines the landsmanshaftn phenomenon in New York from 1880 to 1939.

History

1115. Altshuler, Mordechai. **Soviet Jewry on the Eve of the Holocaust: A Social and Demographic Profile**. xx, 346p. Jerusalem: Ahva Press, 1998. Includes bibliographical references (pp. [203]-214) and index.
The Soviet population experienced enormous changes during the 1930s. Forced industrialization and collectivization impacted all sectors of the society. Mordechai Altshuler examines the effect on Soviet Jewry, drawing on statistical dates of the Soviet archives. "These precise demographic and statistical data, that can be provided only by a general census, permitted a broad analysis of the principal demographic and social processes at work among Soviet Jews during the 1930s, on the one hand, and their implications for the Holocaust, on the other" (p. x). The book is arranged topically covering geographical distribution of Jews in the army, gulag, villages, and cities; distribution by age and gender; and trends in marriage and divorce, religion, education, and social stratification. The book includes more than 100 pages of statistical tables and includes an appendix on Jews living in the annexed territories.

1116. Fishman, David E. **Russia's First Modern Jews: The Jews of Shklov**. xiii, 195p. *Reappraisals in Jewish Social and Intellectual History*. New York: New York University Press, 1995. Includes bibliographical references (pp. 169-80) and index.

Fishman maintains that "the appearance of Haskalah and acculturation in Shklov suggest a much more variegated Jewish cultural landscape in the late eighteenth century, and an earlier intrusion of modernity than has been appreciated" (p. 6). In the course of his investigation into the social history of the Jews from this Byelorussian town, he shows how they "were offered a preview of the problems which would confront Russian Jewry during the nineteenth century, and, naively and unwittingly, they rehearsed a range of positions and solutions which would be embraced by their descendants" (p. 136).

1117. Haberer, Erich E. **Jews and Revolution in Nineteenth-Century Russia**. xv, 246p. Cambridge, Eng.: Cambridge University Press, 1995. Includes bibliographical references and index.

"*Jews and Revolution in Nineteenth-Century Russia* is a carefully researched study of one hundred years of Russian-Jewish revolutionary history, exploring the origins and characteristics of Jewish participation in Russian revolutionary politics between 1790 and 1890. Focusing sharply on Jewish motivations and the qualities of Russian-Jewish activists, it drastically reverses the traditional historiographical trend of de-Judaizing and minimizing the role of Jews who joined Russian revolutionary circles, especially during the movement's Populist phase of the 1870s and 1880s. By the same token, it challenges many clichés and assumptions that have governed conventional wisdom on the radical behavior of so-called assimilationist 'non-Jewish Jews.' This revisionist approach restores a neglected yet important group of Jews to their rightful place in the historical experience of the Jewish people in Russia" (frontispiece).

1118. Judge, Edward H. **Easter in Kishinev: Anatomy of a Pogrom**. x, 186p.: illus. *Reappraisals in Jewish Social and Intellectual History*. New York: New York University Press, 1992. Includes bibliographical references (pp. 173-80) and index.

The Kishinev Rebellion and ensuing pogrom represent a painful chapter in the history of the life of Jews in Eastern Europe. Though not on the same scale as the persecution of the Jews under the Nazis, the indifference of the Christian populations of that later time is foreshadowed in their behavior in 1903. Edward Judge recounts the events of the pogrom in the context of the Russian attitude toward the Jews in the 19th century. He begins with a discussion of the "Jewish Question in Russia." He then turns to a description of conditions in Kishinev and the various events leading up to the pogrom. Judge concludes, "It laid things out for the whole world to see how terribly vulnerable were the Jews who lived in Christian Europe, and how few Christians could be expected to come to their aid in the event of a monstrous attack" (p. 146).

1119. Kaufman, Jonathan. **A Hole in the Heart of the World: Being Jewish in Eastern Europe**. vi, 328p. New York: Viking, 1997. Includes bibliographical references (pp. [321]-328). "The stories of five families; a luminous portrait of the Jewish life that persists, though transformed and tenuous, as a vital element in the European community."

Kaufman uses the lives of several actual families in Eastern Europe (East Germany, Czechoslovakia, Hungary) to describe concrete details about life as a Jew in Eastern Europe. The book is divided into four parts. In the first the author traces the history of the families and their experiences from the defeat of the Nazis in 1945 to 1948 when the Iron Curtain fell. Part 2 covers the period 1948-1968. Part 3 shifts its focus to the second generation. Part 4 carries their story to their condition after the fall of the wall in 1989. A final chapter provides reflection and speculation about the future.

1120. **From a Ruined Garden: The Memorial Books of Polish Jewry.** Edited by Jack Kugelmass and Jonathan Boyarin. 2nd exp. ed. xvi, 353p.: illus., maps. Bloomington: Indiana University Press, 1998. Published in association with the United States Holocaust Memorial Museum, Washington, D.C.

The selections contained here, drawn from over 60 Jewish memorial books devoted to the lives and deaths of Jewish communities in Eastern Europe, are concerned with Polish Jewish communities. The individual selections are arranged in broad classes: our towns, townspeople, lifeways, events, legends and folklore, Holocaust, and the townspeople abroad. For those contributing to such memorial books and those compiling them, memory became a deeply meaningful religious and political act.

1121. Melzer, Emanuel, and David Elgel. **Gal-Ed on the History of the Jews in Poland**. Series Is Gal-Ed, Book 113. Tel Aviv: Gal-Ed, 1997. Hebrew title on added t.p.: Me'asef le- toldot Yahadut Polin. Parallel text in Hebrew. English section has summaries of Hebrew articles and vice versa. "Made possible by a grant from the Memorial Foundation for Jewish Culture"—T.p. verso. Includes index to Gal-Ed, vols. 1-10. Includes bibliographical references and index.

This volume of *Gal-Ed* contains an English section and a Hebrew section. The studies contained herein touch upon several topics, including the social, economic, cultural, religious, and political aspects of Polish Jewry. There is no chronological limit on subject matter.

1122. Ro'i, Yaacov. **Jews and Jewish Life in Russia and the Soviet Union**. xiii, 432p.: illus. London: Frank Cass, 1995. Includes bibliographical references and index.

This volume of 26 essays by separate contributors explores various aspects of Jews and Jewry in Russia and the Soviet Union. The essays are grouped in eight sections: The Tsarist Legacy: Socioeconomic Trends; The Bolshevik/Soviet Approach to the Jewish Question; The Interaction Between Popular and Official Anti-Semitism; World War II and Its Aftermath; Cultural Expressions of the Soviet Jewish Anomaly; the Jewish Religion Under the Soviet Heel; Soviet Jewry and the International Arena; and Demography and Emigration: Past Trends and Prospects.

1123. Weinberg, Robert. **Stalin's Forgotten Zion: Birobidzhan and the Making of a Soviet Jewish Homeland: An Illustrated History, 1928-1996**. ix, 105p.: illus., maps. Berkeley: University of California Press; Judah L. Magnas Museum, 1998. Includes bibliographical references (pp. 97-98) and index.

The Russian imperial government and the Soviet government had sought for a method of solving their "Jewish problem." In their attempt to isolate the Jewish population from the rest of the country they arrived at the idea of the creation of a separate Jewish state. There were many ideological arguments for the creation of such a state as well as practical considerations. In theory it was seen as a way to preserve the language and culture of the Jewish people while assimilating them into the Soviet economy. The Soviets also saw this as a method of strengthening their position in their Far Eastern holdings. Practically speaking the project failed and "may have been designed to do so . . . clearly, Birobidzhan was designed to buttress Soviet claims to a territory that might be claimed by China or Japan and, perhaps, to ensure the failure of the Jewish colonies in the European republics lest they become the centers of a new Jewish nationalism or even of a 'reconstructed' Jewish people" (p. 8). This book was intended to accompany an exhibition on the subject. It is heavily illustrated and includes a selected bibliography.

Special Studies

1124. Braham, Randolph L. **Anti-Semitism and the Treatment of the Holocaust in Poscommunist Eastern Europe**. vii, 253p. *Holocaust Studies series*. New York: Columbia University Press, 1994. Includes bibliographical references.

The lectures that appear here are "devoted to an in-depth evaluation of a disturbing phenomenon—the reassertion of xenophobic nationalism and the concomitant rise of anti-Semitism in post-communist East Central Europe" (p. v). A specialist in each country writes the chapter devoted to his specialty. Individual chapters analyze the phenomenon of anti-Semitism in East Central Europe in general, Bulgaria, the Czech Republic, Germany, Hungary, Poland, Romania, Slovakia, the USSR/CIS, and Yugoslavia. They were all originally presented during the 1992 academic year as part of the Rosenthal Institute for Holocaust Studies.

1125. Brym, Robert J., and Rozalina Ryvkina. **The Jews of Moscow, Kiev, and Minsk: Identity, Antisemitism, Emigration**. Edited by Howard Spier. xvi, 142p., [4] p. of plates: illus. London: Macmillan in association with the Institute of Jewish Affairs, 1994. Includes bibliographical references (pp. 132-39) and indexes.

This volume is the result of a public opinion poll that took place in Moscow, Kiev, and Minsk between February and April 1993. Besides an estimation of the number of Jews currently in those three republics (Russia, Ukraine, and Belarus), questions in the survey centered around various issues relating to identity, anti-Semitism, and emigration. In addition to a concise summary of his findings, Brym provides an introductory chapter that places Jewry in Soviet and post-Soviet society in context.

1126. **In the Warsaw Ghetto: Summer 1941**. Edited by Willy Georg and Rafael F. Scharf. 1st ed. 111p.: illus. New York: Aperture, 1993.

These photographs of the Warsaw Ghetto and its inhabitants in 1941, along with selected passages from ghetto diaries, portray the life of Jews in this ghetto at the beginning of WWII.

1127. Kostrychenko, Gennadi. **Out of the Red Shadows: Anti-Semitism in Stalin's Russia**. 333p. *Russian Studies Series, From the Secret Archives of the Former Soviet Union*. New York: Prometheus Books, 1995. Includes bibliographical references.

Kostrychenko does not focus on Stalin's own personal anti-Semitism. Instead he examines the part and state-initiated policies of anti-Semitism that prevailed through Stalin's reign. He bases his research on the archives of the Central Committee of the Communist Party, of the KGB, and of the Federal Counter Intelligence Service.

1128. Lederhendler, Eli. **Jewish Responses to Modernity: New Voices in America and Eastern Europe**. ix, 232p. *Reappraisals in Jewish Social and Intellectual History*. New York: New York University Press, 1994. Includes bibliographical references and index.

The author makes no pretense that he is presenting an integrated account of Jewish society and culture in the 19th and 20th centuries. Instead the essays here argue, in various ways, that "there is a culture of modernity to which social, political, literary, and linguistic issues are all related . . . the key motif is the ripple effect, or afterlife, if you will, of the Haskalah, the Jewish Enlightenment (late eighteenth to nineteenth century) . . ." (p. 1). The essays encompass Jewish modernity not only in Russia and East Europe but in the Diaspora, especially in America.

1129. Maltiel-Gerstenfeld, Jacob. **My Private War: One Man's Struggle to Survive the Soviets and the Nazis**. xxii, 313p.: port. London; Portland, Oreg.: Vallentine Mitchell, 1993.

This is one of a series of Holocaust survivor's testimonies. The author recounts his experience in the Nazi occupations of Lvov and his subsequent successful attempts to elude being placed in a concentration camp.

1130. Redlich, Shimon. **War, Holocaust and Stalinism: A Documented Study of the Jewish Anti-Fascist Committee in the USSR**. Edited by K. M. Anderson et al., editorial committee. Translated by I. Altman et al., compilers. xxix, 504p., [12] p. of plates: illus. *New History of Russia series*, 1. Amsterdam: Harwood Academic, 1995. Includes bibliographical references and index.

During World War II the Soviet government established the Jewish Anti-Fascist Committee, primarily as a tool of the Soviet propaganda machine. The committee eventually became a focal point for Jewish problems and concerns in the Soviet Union. "War, Holocaust and Stalinism presents a documented history of the Jewish Anti-Fascist Committee in the Soviet Union during the Second World War, the Holocaust and the immediate post-war years to the end of 1948. It centers upon the tragic fate of Soviet Jewry under both Hitler and Stalin during this most significant period in Jewish history" (back cover). Much of the volume is taken up with the publication of documents from the Russian State Archives and the Archive of the Communist Party. The volume is a valuable resource for anyone researching the state of the Jews in Russia in the mid-20th century.

1131. Toll, Nelly S. **Behind the Secret Window: A Memoir of a Hidden Childhood During World War Two**. 1st ed. xiii, 161p.: col. illus. New York: Dial Press, 1993. The author recalls her experiences when she and her mother were hidden from the Nazis by a Gentile couple in Lvov, Poland, during World War II.

This memoir by the author of the Nazi occupation of Lvov and her concealment from the Nazis during WWII is accompanied by her drawings, made at the time.

1132. Weitzner, Jacob. **Sholem Aleichem in the Theater**. 182p. Northwood: Science Reviews, 1994. Includes bibliographical references (pp. 173-78) and index.

After a brief introduction chapter that relates how Sholem Aleichem became a writer and launched a literature (Yiddish), the author then focuses on the problems inherent in realizing the written text onstage. Subsequent chapters analyze the staging of specific plays, "Stempenyu," "The Treasure," "Tevye the Dairyman," and "The Jackpot."

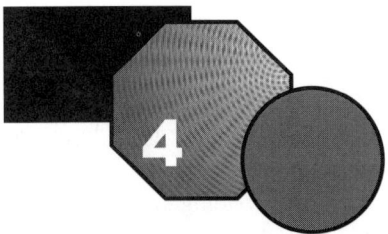

Eastern Europe

General Reference Works

1133. Eastern Europe and the Commonwealth of Independent States, 1997. 3rd ed. xiv, 926p.: maps. *Regional Surveys of the World.* London: Europa Publications, 1996.

This richly informative encyclopedia examines 27 countries in Central and Eastern Europe, the Caucasus, and Central Asia. Thirty specialists contributed to this volume. In Part 1 there are 12 essays that give a general background and assessment of issues central to the region. In Part 2 there are chapters on each of the 27 countries of the area. "The detailed, augmented and extensively updated statistical and directory sections also include information on major companies, other financial and business organizations, government and state institutions, religion, the media, environmental organizations and culture . . ." (p. v). Part 3 includes 200 political biographies of prominent personages in the region.

1134. Global Studies: Russia, the Eurasian Republics, and Central/Eastern Europe. 5th ed. v: illus., maps. *An Annual Editions Publication.* Guilford, Conn.: Dushkin, 1994.

This interesting encyclopedia-type work is one of a series covering other continents and major areas of the world. It includes basic statistics and maps for Russia, the Eurasian republics, and the Baltic states, followed by one long (approximately 100-page) essay entitled "Russia and the Eurasian Republics: Building New Political Orders." This is followed by a map of Central/Eastern Europe, a brief essay on that area, and then individual country reports covering society, politics, economics, etc. This is then supplemented by articles from the world press by noted experts on the country in question. An appendix includes a glossary of terms and abbreviations used.

1135. Crampton, Richard, and Ben Crampton. **Atlas of Eastern Europe in the Twentieth Century**. xv, 297p.: illus., maps. London: Routledge, 1996. Includes index.

This impressive atlas is arranged chronologically in seven parts. The individual parts cover, respectively: (1) before the First World War, (2) the First World War and the Versailles peace settlement, (3) the interwar years, (4) the Second World War, (5) Eastern Europe under communist domination, (6) Eastern Europe at the end of the communist period, and (7) the end of communist rule and post-communist Eastern Europe. Each section provides historical maps on each country with explanatory text, as well as numerous statistical tables. It is an excellent source for any type of library.

1136. Hupchick, Dennis P., and Harold E. Cox. **A Concise Historical Atlas of Eastern Europe**. 120p.: maps. New York: St. Martin's Press, 1996. Includes bibliographical references and index.

This historical atlas of Eastern Europe (encompassing present-day Albania, Austria, Bosnia-Herzegovina, Bulgaria, Croatia, Czech Republic, Eastern Germany, Greece, Hungary, Macedonia, Poland, Romania, Slovakia, Slovenia, federation of Serbia, and Montenegro) is presented in a series of 50 two-color (white and green) full-page-size maps. A facing page contains a two-column explanatory text. The atlas is divided into six parts: introductory maps (political, 1996, physical, demographic, cultural); Part I—Early Medieval to 13th Century; Part II—Late Medieval, 13th to 15th Centuries; Part III—Early Modern, 16th to 18th Centuries; Part IV—Period of Nationalism, 19th Century to 1918; and Part V—Modern and Contemporary, 1918-1991. It also contains a bibliography and index. The authors produced the atlas to provide students with an affordable visual aid for the study of Eastern Europe.

The atlas has a few minor defects such as inconsistencies in the labeling of bodies of water (on some maps they are labeled, on others not), the shadings of green to delineate different areas are often difficult to discern, or the mention of a geographic feature in the accompanying text—the Black Sea—but no labeling on the map. However, although there is another commercially available atlas (Paul Magocsi, *Historical Atlas of East Central Europe*, 1992 [see ARBA, 1994, item 520]) that is superior in terms of layout and detail, Hupchick and Cox's work will be more than sufficient for the occasional student of the area.

1137. Ingrao, Charles W. **A Guide to East-Central European Archives**. ix, 210p. *Austrian History Yearbook*, XXIX, 1998, Part 2. Minneapolis: Center for Austrian Studies, University of Minnesota Press, 1997.

This volume was a special issue of the *Austrian History Yearbook* devoted to archives. The volume is divided into sections each on an East European country. Each section opens with background information on the country accompanied by a map. This is followed by sections on central archives, regional archives, church archives, and private repositories. Within these sections general descriptions of the archival structure at each level are supplied. This includes the names and addresses of the main archives in each category and descriptions of the contents of the archive. The major finding aid for the archive is also listed. This volume is an excellent summary of archival resources in east-central Europe. It is unfortunate that it lacks an index.

Bibliography

1138. Magocsi, Paul R. **Carpatho-Rusyn Studies: An Annotated Bibliography**. Vol. I: 1975-1984. Vol. II: 1985-1994. *East European Monographs*, 522. Boulder, Colo.: East European Monographs; New York: Distributed by Columbia University Press, 1998. Includes index.

This chronologically arranged bibliography continues the series of bibliographies on this area beginning in 1988. "The object of the bio-bibliography is to record with relatively brief annotations books, pamphlets, and articles that deal with all aspects of Carpatho-Rusyn culture in the European homeland as well as in other parts of Europe and North America where Carpatho-Rusyns live" (p. vii). The extensive index includes entries by author, title main entries, and subject. There is an appendix that lists the total number of publications for each language listed in the book. There are similar appendixes for subject entries and languages. Newspaper articles and reviews are not included in the bibliography.

History

1139. Dolukhanov, Pavel Markovich. **The Early Slavs: Eastern Europe from the Initial Settlement to the Kievan Rus**. xiii, 237p.: illus., maps. London; New York: Longman, 1996. Includes bibliographical references (pp. 210-30) and index.

Pavel Dolukhanov examines the archaeological evidence available to revisit the question of where the Slavs originated. He uses network analysis to take a new look at the evidence as to the origin of the Slavs. "The main conclusions which follow from the materials presented in the preceding chapters may be summarized quite simply: the socio-economic development of the peoples who lived in the Russian Plain throughout Prehistory and Early History was following a pattern common to the rest of Europe, with limitations and variations imposed by the physical and social environment" (p. 198).

1140. Flam, Helena. **Mosaic of Fear: Poland and East Germany Before 1989**. xxi, 283p. *East European Monographs*, 508. Boulder, Colo.: East European Monographs; New York: Distributed by Columbia University Press, 1998. Includes bibliographical references.

Flam intends to "reconstruct some elements of the mosaic of fear in two communist regimes, the Polish and the East German, in the two-three decades before the regime break-down of 1989" (p. ix). He constructs his study from interviews carried out in both Poland and Germany as well as published sources, underground writings, pertinent fiction, literary criticism, and historiography.

1141. **Attila: The Man and His Image**. Edited by Franz H. Bäuml and Marianna Birnbaum. 131p. Budapest, Hungary: Corvina, 1993. Published under the auspices of the Center for Medieval and Renaissance Studies, University of California, Los Angeles. Includes bibliographical references (pp. 117-24) and index.

Attila is a name infamous in history. He has been portrayed in many ways historically. This volume of essays is drawn from the papers delivered at a conference on the subject of Attila and his historical image. "The twelve studies written by internationally acknowledged university lecturers from West and Central Europe and the United States include not only the historical information available on Attila, but also a wide range of the representations of his ever-changing image in art, literature and music" (back cover). The essays are arranged into four sections, each focusing on a specific area or time in which Attila's image is discussed: the historical Attila, Attila in art, portrayals of Attila in the Middle Ages and Renaissance, and Attila in the modern age. The book is lavishly illustrated.

1142. Held, Joseph. **Dictionary of East European History Since 1945**. x, 509p., [15] p. of plates: illus., maps. Westport, Conn.: Greenwood Press, 1994. Includes bibliographical references and index.

This book is unique in the universe of reference sources. It is intended for all serious students of East European history. The book is divided into sections by country. For each country a general description, map, and chronology are provided at the beginning of the section. The bulk of each section is taken up with entries on people, places, and events of significance for the late-20th-century history in the country. Cross-references are included whenever necessary. "This book is the only comprehensive one-volume dictionary on East European personalities, politicians, and history since 1945. It provides basic, up-to-date information on the events and background that have led up to the current crisis" (back cover). Each entry includes a bibliography, primarily of English-language works.

1143. Herwig, Holger H. **The First World War: Germany and Austria-Hungary 1914-1918**. xix, 490p.: maps. Modern Wars. London: Holger H. Herwig, 1997. Includes bibliographical references and index.

Herwig's history of the First World War follows a chronological outline of the events with some intervening chapters dealing with industrial and manpower mobilization. In examining the role of the Austro-Hungarian empire, he concentrates on the initial stages of mobilization and the battles in Galicia in 1914. From that point on he focuses on the attempts to preserve the independence and integrity of the Habsburg monarchy against the Russians, Italians, and its German ally.

1144. Hupchick, Dennis P. **Culture and History in Eastern Europe**. xvii, 206p. New York: St. Martin's Press, 1994.

The essays contained in this volume are intended to provide the reader with a historical and cultural perspective on what is going on in Eastern Europe. They help illuminate the peoples and events that were central in the development of post-Soviet Eastern Europe. For the most part they are expanded versions of presentations given previously.

1145. Johnson, Lonnie. **Central Europe: Enemies, Neighbors, Friends**. xi, 339p.: illus., maps. New York: Oxford University Press, 1996. Includes bibliographical references (pp. 299-314) and index.

"This book is a historical survey of Central Europe, a region that encompasses contemporary Germany, Poland, the Czech Republic, Slovakia, Austria, Hungary, Slovenia, and Croatia" (p. v). The purpose of this book is to introduce readers to the complex history of the region from A.D. 400 to 1989. The author has focused on historical patterns of conflict, cohabitation, and cooperation in the region. He has not attempted to present a comprehensive, narrative history of events in the area. Rather, Johnson seeks to give students a general picture of the diversity of the region. The book includes an epilogue describing changes in Central Europe since 1989.

1146. Judson, Pieter M. **Exclusive Revolutionaries: Liberal Politics, Social Experience, and National Identity in the Austrian Empire, 1848-1914**. xi, 304p. *Social History, Popular Culture, and Politics in Germany*. Ann Arbor: University of Michigan Press, 1996. Includes bibliographical references (pp. 275-93) and index.

"This book traces the emergence and transformation of a German liberal movement in the Habsburg monarchy. In mid-nineteenth-century Austria men and women, largely of Burger social origins, forged a political movement that challenged the legitimacy of the reigning systems of government. . . . The ensuing struggles between liberalism and its various opponents were political in the broadest sense of the word. They were as much about establishing an alternative system of values and cultural practices in Austrian society as they were about mastering specific political institutions" (p. 1).

1147. Kottanner, Helene. **Memoirs of Helene Kottanner, (1439-1440)**. Translated by Maya Bijvoe Williamson. xi, 79p. Cambridge, Eng.: D. S. Brewer, 1998. Includes bibliographical references (pp. [73]-75) and index.

Kottanner was a servant and confidante of Queen Elizabeth of Hungary (1409-1442). She "played a pivotal role in the theft of the holy crown of St. Stephen from the treasury of the royal stronghold of Visegrad on 20 February 1440. Her account tells how the crown was smuggled out of the stronghold in a pillow and rushed on a sled to the queen in her castle in Komorn, where within hours she was delivered of a baby boy, Ladislaus Posthumous (1440-1457), who three months later was crowned king of Hungary" (back cover). This account is one of the earliest pieces of historical prose written by a woman.

1148. Longworth, Philip. **The Making of Eastern Europe: From Prehistory to Postcommunism**. 2nd ed. xiii, 352p. New York: St. Martin's Press, 1997. Includes bibliographical references and index.

Philip Longworth's new edition of *The Making of Eastern Europe* has several purposes. The author's original intent of asserting "the value of historical enquiry" is still central to this study. Longworth also attempts to demonstrate the relevance of historical study in the contemporary world. Beyond this, he hoped to fuel debate among historians. He has attempted to do so in part using a unique arrangement in this study, an "anti-chronological" arrangement. Thus the book begins with the collapse of communism and ends with the origins of the Eastern European states. In this edition he updates the book and adds a new introduction.

1149. Meurs, Wim P. van. **The Bessarabian Question in Communist Historiography: Nationalist and Communist Politics and History-Writing**. viii, 458p.: illus. Boulder, Colo.: East European Monographs; New York: Distributed by Columbia University Press, 1994. Includes bibliographical references (pp. 405-44) and index.

The author approaches the Bessarabian question from several levels. Meurs provides an explanation of Soviet historiography on the topic, a short history of Bessarabia, a history of nationalities policy in the Moldavian republic, as well as the Moldavian historiography related to the question. Finally, the same question is again viewed from the Romanian perspective. Several appendixes providing chronology, a discussion on the quantification of historical writing, the Sfatul Tarii, and demography enhance the reader's knowledge about the entire problem.

1150. Pavlowitch, Stevan K. **History of the Balkans, 1804-1945**. 1st ed. 375p. New York: Longman, 1999. Includes bibliographical references and index.

This sweeping history of the Balkans (Albania, Bulgaria, Greece, Romania, the Yugoslav lands) begins with the awakening of the nationalities between 1804 and 1830 and follows the area's development through self-rule, constitutions, revolutions, crises, and reforms. A large portion of the author's analysis focuses on the period from the Congress of Berlin through the beginning of World War I. The account ends with the final days of the Second World War. The period was chosen because the rise of nationalities began in 1804 and the end of WWII brought about an entirely new group of problem survival under the communist regimes.

1151. Sedlar, Jean W. **East Central Europe in the Middle Ages, 1000-1500**. xiii, 556p.: maps. *History of East Central Europe*, vol. 3. Seattle: University of Washington Press, 1994. Includes bibliographical references (pp. 497-527) and index.

This study is Volume 3 in the *History of East Central Europe* series. The first volume was a historical atlas of the region. Volume 2 covered the beginnings of state formation in Eastern Europe. This volume covers the next time period, that which saw the greatest development and often the greatest achievement in the area. "In a word, the era from 1000 to 1500 was in many respects the Golden Age for the nationalities of East Central Europe. At one time or another during those five centuries, Bulgaria, Serbia, Hungary, Poland and Bohemia all were major states playing a leading role on the European stage" (p. ix). The book is arranged topically covering migrations into the region, state formation, the role of the monarchy, nobles and landholders, religion, government, law, commerce, foreign relations, and education. The three appendixes supply supporting information in the form of a chronology, list of monarchs, and place-name equivalents for towns and cities.

The bibliographical essay follows the subjects covered in the body of the book but is subdivided by country. It supplies a rich source of information for the student of the area.

1152. Siebel-Achenbach, Sebastian. **Lower Silesia from Nazi Germany to Communist Poland**. xx, 381p.: illus., maps. New York: St. Martin's Press, 1994. Includes bibliographical references (pp. 342-60) and index.

The author investigates the dispute over Lower Silesia between Poland and Germany. There are two interrelated themes explored by the author: "first, what actually transpired in Lower Silesia itself from 1942 to 1949, and second, how was Lower Silesia dealt with among the great powers and their allies during this period?" (p. 5). This area is of significance because of the part it played in the postwar economic development of both Poland and Germany.

1153. Swain, Geoff. **Eastern Europe Since 1945**. 2nd ed. xv, 265p. *Making of the Modern World*. New York: St. Martin's Press, 1998. Includes bibliographical references (pp. 238-55) and index.

This is an updated and expanded edition of the 1993 publication of the same title. The author has sketched the history of Eastern Europe from 1945 to 1997. No attempt has been made to be comprehensive in this analysis. "However, the main themes addressed are fairly clear cut, corresponding roughly to the chapter headings: the road to power, diverse paths to socialism, Stalinist uniformity, the impossibility of democratized communism, the attempt at economic reform, bureaucratic resistance, and economic and social collapse" (pp. 6-7). The author has used various countries to exemplify the changes in the region as a whole. The book includes a chronology of events in the region from 1945 to 1997.

1154. Todorova, Maria N. **Imagining the Balkans**. xi, 257p. New York: Oxford University Press, 1997. Includes bibliographical references (pp. 217-50) and index.

The geographic term "Balkan" has come to have a meaning, a negative meaning, in common speech. The transfer of a regional designation to common parlance is very unusual. Maria Todorova believes that it reflects an image of the region that was first born at the turn of the century and never changed. Todorova's book focuses on how this image of the Balkans arose and has been perpetuated. Here is not a study of the historiography of the region. "The question is how to explain the persistence of such a frozen image. How could a geographical appellation be transformed into one of the most powerful pejorative designations in history, international relations, political science, and nowadays, general intellectual discourse" (p. 7).

1155. Treadgold, Warren T. **A History of the Byzantine State and Society**. xxiii, 1019p.: illus., maps. Stanford, Calif.: Stanford University Press, 1997. Includes bibliographical references and index.

Warren Treadgold has written a comprehensive, detailed history of the Byzantine empire. His study is not focused on historiography, but on history. The author feels his approach is different from that taken in other studies in various ways. He does not emphasize the catastrophe of the 7th century and does focus more on the survival of the army during that period. He relies on statistics and estimates for his discussion of the empire's economic decline. The book includes an appendix of rulers of the empire from A.D. 284 to 1481.

1156. **Balkan Currents: Studies in the History, Culture and Society of a Divided Land**. Edited by Lawrence A. Tritle. 143p. *Monographs in Balkan Studies*. Los Angeles: Loyola Marymount University, 1998. Papers presented at "The Balkans Today," a symposium held at Loyola Marymount University, Oct. 15, 1994. Includes bibliographical references and index.

This volume contains studies presented at a symposium held in 1994. The aim of the conference and the papers presented was to present "occasionally conflicting views and assessments of the on-going crisis in this region following the break-up of the Yugoslav state in 1990/1991" (p. ix).

1157. Vego, Milan N. **Austro-Hungarian Naval Policy, 1904-14**. xviii, 213p., [8] p. of plates: illus., maps. London: Frank Cass, 1996.

Defining naval policy as "the sum of all the political, budgetary, social and purely military decisions by the country's highest leadership that affect a naval situation in general and the size and composition of naval forces in particular" (p. 1), Vego provides a comprehensive history of the Austro-Hungarian naval policy during the years 1904-1910. In addition to focusing on the internal components of naval policy, the author also considers the influence of external factors, such as Italy's policies regarding irredentists and other movements.

1158. Wolff, Larry. **Inventing Eastern Europe: The Map of Civilization on the Mind of the Enlightenment**. xiv, 419p.: illus., maps. Stanford, Calif.: Stanford University Press, 1994.

Wolff explores the question that intellectuals of the Enlightenment came to think of Europe as being divided into east and west. His investigation covers 18th-century travelers on the frontier; sexuality, slavery, and corporal punishment; fiction, fantasy, and vicarious voyages; political geography and cultural cartography, Voltaire's Russia; Rousseau's Poland; barbarians in ancient history and modern anthropology; and the evidence of manners and the measurement of race.

Government, Politics, and Law

1159. **Forward to the Past?: Continuity and Change in Political Development in Hungary, Austria, and the Czech and Slovak Republics**. 307p.: illus. Oakville, Conn.: Aarhus University Press, 1997. Based on a conference held in October 1994 at the University of Aarhus. Preface. Includes bibliographical references and index.

At the present time there are two extreme images of Eastern Europe. This volume aims to bridge the gap between these two positions by examining the effect of past regimes, social structures, and culture on the development of democracy in present-day Eastern Europe. The contributors "examine critically the processes of state and nation-building in relation to regime change."

1160. Agh, Atilla. **Emerging Democracies in East Central Europe and the Balkans**. viii, 359p. *Studies of Communism in Transition*. Cheltenham, Eng.: Edward Elgar, 1998. Includes bibliographical references (pp. 317-31) and index.

The author takes a comparative approach to democratization and Europeanization in this region. "This book deals with the socio-political history of the Central European and Balkan states as a process of democratization and marketization in the common framework of Europeanization" (p. 4). After an introductory paragraph that details the difficulties of a regional approach to studying democratization, he then devotes, in Part II, individual chapters to Poland, Hungary, and the Czech and Slovak republics. In Part III he examines the Balkan countries. In Part IV he draws the analysis to a close by providing a useful summary of the Europeanization of these two regions.

1161. Borneman, John. **Settling Accounts: Violence, Justice, and Accountability in Postsocialist Europe**. xii, 197p. *Princeton Studies in Culture/Power/History*. Princeton, N.J.: Princeton University Press, 1997. Includes bibliographical references (pp. [177]-188) and indexes.

Borneman investigates the attempts of post-Soviet states to deal with their criminal pasts in the first five years after the change in regimes. The principles here also apply to other countries, such as Italy and Colombia. The book "therefore presents itself as a blurred genre: part ethnography of ritual purification under the rule of law in the former East Germany, part history of a global legal transformation, part essay in comparative political-legal anthropology, part moral philosophy" (p. x).

1162. Center for Preventive Action Staff. **Toward Comprehensive Peace in Southeast Europe: Preventing Conflict in the South Balkans: Report of the South Balkans Working Group**. Edited by Barnett R. Rubin. xi, 135p.: maps. *Preventive Action Reports*, vol. 1. New York: Twentieth Century Fund Press, 1996. Includes bibliographical references (pp. 115-28) and index.

The Center for Preventive Action has as its charge the study and testing of conflict prevention. In this volume they present their conclusions on the future avoidance of conflict in southeast Europe. The book begins with an overview of the recommendations of policy changes to stabilize the region. This is followed by the supporting material and a description of field missions that took place in the region to gather data. A lengthy appendix entitled "Observing the Observers" discusses language and ethnicity as they relate to the balance of power in the region.

1163. Cottey, Andrew. **East-Central Europe After the Cold War: Poland, the Czech Republic, Slovakia and Hungary in Search of Security**. xi, 208p. London: Macmillan, 1995. Includes bibliographical references and index.

Cottey recognizes that the countries of east-central Europe have always been closely related with peace and security in Europe generally. In this volume he examines how Poland, the Czech lands, and Hungary each faced the challenges brought about by the revolutions of 1989 to 1994. The primary focus is on the national security policies of these states and how decisions are reached in this area by their national governments. After devoting successive chapters to each individual country, his final chapter assesses the security of the region since the end of the cold war and the prospects for future stability in the region.

1164. Csanadi, Maria. **Party-States and Their Legacies in Post-Communist Transformation**. xlvii, 386p.: illus. *Studies of Communism in Transition*. Cheltenham, Eng.; Northampton, Mass.: 1997. Includes bibliographical references (pp. 349-71) and index.

The author has answered questions about state socialism that have long remained unanswered—"about the relationship between the structure and the functioning of the system and between the evolution of the system and its collapse" (p. xxix). Her analysis focuses on one central point, "that the functioning of the system and its development over time reflected the structure and the operation principles of the party and the state apparatus" (p. xxx).

1165. **Reconstructing the Balkans: Geography of the New South East Europe**. Edited by Darrick R. Danta and Derek R. Hall. xx, 260p.: illus. Chichester, Eng.: John Wiley, 1996. Includes bibliographical references and index.

Adam approaches this topic in an unconventional way. In the first of four parts Adam provides an introduction to the entire topic, providing general reasons for socialism's collapse. In Part 2 (Chapters 2-6) Adam looks at the traditional, unreformed system focusing on Poland, Hungary, and the Soviet Union. In Part 3 (Chapters 7-10) he examines economic reforms that began as early as the 1960s in their relation to the collapse. In Part 4, he provides conclusions.

1166. Ekiert, Grzegorz. **The State Against Society: Political Crises and Their Aftermath in East Central Europe**. xvi, 435p. Princeton, N.J.: Princeton University Press, 1996. Includes bibliographical references (pp. [405]-430) and index.

Ekiert has carried out a detailed study of the institutional breakdown that occurred in three socialist societies in Eastern Europe after social and political crises. The countries and crises chosen were the Hungarian revolution of 1956, the reform movement in Czechoslovakia in 1968, and the rise of the Solidarity movement in Poland in 1980. One of the major questions pursued by Ekiert was why the communist regimes in Hungary and Czechoslovakia were able to restore stability and the dominance of the party after their crises, but why the Polish Communist Party was not.

1167. Elster, Jon, Claus Offe, and Ulrich Preuss. **Institutional Design in Post-Communist Societies: Rebuilding the Ship at Sea**. xii, 350p. Cambridge, Eng.: Cambridge University Press, 1998. Includes bibliographical references and index.

Jon Elster, Claus Offe, and Ulrich Preuss take a new approach to the analysis of the transition to a market economy in Eastern Europe. "They integrate interdisciplinary theoretical work with elaborate empirical data on some of the most challenging events of the twentieth century. Three groups of phenomena and their causal interconnection are explored: the material legacies, constraints, habits and cognitive frameworks inherited from the past; the erratic configuration of the new actors, and new spaces for action; and a new institutional order under with agency in institutionalized and the sustainability of institutions is achieved" (frontispiece).

1168. **Post-Communist States in the World Community: Selected Papers from the Fifth World Congress of Central and East European Studies**. Edited by William E. Ferry and Roger E. Kante. xvii, 305p. *Selected Papers from the Fifth World Congress of Central and East European Studies*, Warsaw, 1995; London: Macmillan, 1998. Includes bibliographical references and index.

This selection of essays was first delivered as papers at the Fifth World Congress of Central and East European Studies in Warsaw in 1995. The papers included here focus on issues of security and Russian foreign policy in Asia, Europe, and east-central Europe. The essays collected for this volume were not intended to provide comprehensive coverage of foreign policy issues in the region. Rather, they focus on issues central to the region.

1169. Goldman, Minton F. **Revolution and Change in Central and Eastern Europe: Political, Economic, and Social Challenges**. xiv, 497p.: maps. Armonk, N.Y.: M. E. Sharpe, 1997. Includes bibliographical references (pp. 453-69) and index.

Goldman has chronicled the economic, political, and social changes in Eastern Europe over the past decade. His first two chapters are devoted to the roots and causes of the communist collapse and problems of post-communist development in general. In individual chapters he then focuses on individual countries, covering Yugoslavia in two chapters, one to collapse and disintegration, and the other to the Bosnian civil war. The selected bibliography offers a core reading list in English of material covering this period and topic.

1170.   Holmgren, Beth. **Rewriting Capitalism: Literature and the Market in Late Tsarist Russia and the Kingdom of Poland**. xviii, 240p.: illus. *Pitt Series in Russian and East European Studies*. Pittsburgh, Pa.: University of Pittsburgh Press, 1998. Includes bibliographical references (pp. 225-36) and index.

The late 19th century saw the development of popular literature in Russia and Poland as in the West. This was a major shift away from the serious literature common in both countries that had always been a vehicle for social criticism. It is the development of this literature that is the focus of the book. "My book argues that the literature of fin-de-siècle Russia and its subordinate, the Kingdom of Poland, represent important variations on dominant Western models of interaction between culture and commerce because these literatures articulate (1) two developing European cultures similarly bifurcated between a politicized elite and uneducated, or recently educated, masses; (2) two cultures similarly critical of and self-consciously distinct from the West; and (3) two cultures enacting the enmeshed politics of imperialism and national self-determination outside the European empire, non-European colony paradigm" (p. xiii). Holmgren begins with an overview of the publishing industry in both nations. She then takes up the view of capitalists in Russian and Polish literature. The marketing of literature in each country is discussed next. In the final chapter Holmgren compares the changes in literature at the end of the 19th century to the current events in the publishing arena in Poland and Russia.

1171.   **International Commission on the Balkans. Unfinished Peace: Report of the International Commission on the Balkans**. Edited by Leo Tindemans. xxiv, 197p. Washington, D.C.: Carnegie Endowment for International Peace, 1996.

This report by the International Commission on the Balkans is intended to report on current conditions and to formulate "long-term measures to contribute to the establishment of a durable peace in that region" (p. vii). The report is in four parts. Part 1 describes the Balkan predicament, the origins of the war, the breakup of Yugoslavia, and the problems of nation-state building in a multiethnic environment. Part 2 focuses on the war and the international response to it, the logic of peace plans, and transatlantic strains. Part 3 looks at each Balkan country individually and gives country conditions, trends, and proposals. Part 4 summarizes the findings and presents conclusions and proposals for Balkan regional cooperation, reconstruction and development, democracy, civil society and the media, ethnic relations, and the treatment of minorities and security.

1172.   Kirchner, Emil J. **Decentralization and Transition in the Visegrad: Poland, Hungary, the Czech Republic and Slovaki**. 1st ed. xviii, 237p.: maps. New York: St. Martin's Press, 1999. Includes bibliographical references and index.

The contributions included here intend to complete three research aims. "Firstly, to examine the extent to which decentralization had taken place in the Visegrad states since 1990. Secondly, to explore whether the experience of local and regional development in Western Europe can serve as a guide for decentralization in the Visegrads. Thirdly, to highlight the importance of external factors, especially the EU, in the development of sub-national bodies in these countries" (p. xv).

1173. **Contemporary Nationalism in East Central Europe**. Edited by Paul Latawski. xiii, 200p. New York: St. Martin's Press, 1995. Includes bibliographical references and index.

Nationalism has been one of the main problems in parts of Eastern Europe. Yet, other countries in the region have not demonstrated any serious problems with nationalism. "This book attempts to offer a balanced look at nationalism in the region, placing contemporary problems in an historical perspective. In doing so it seeks to dispel some of the clichés and myths surrounding the phenomenon as it manifests itself in East Central Europe today" (p. viii). The contributors to this volume of essays have focused on nationalism in Bulgaria, Czechoslovakia, Hungary, Poland, Romania, and Yugoslavia. The contributors are Paul Latawski, Wojciech Roszkowski, Raymond Pearson, Duncan M. Perry, John Morison, Rebecca Ann Haynes, Frances Millard, Martyn Rady, and John R. Lampe.

1174. **Party Structure and Organization in East-Central Europe**. Edited by Paul G. Lewis. xviii, 229p.: illus. *Studies in Communism in Transition*. Cheltenham, Eng.; Brookfield, Vt.: Edward Elgar, 1996. Includes bibliographical references.

The articles contained in this volume were first presented as papers at a conference in Warsaw in 1994. Their common theme is to direct "attention to developments within the new parties of East-Central Europe and the conditions that influence their organizational growth" (p. xviii). The countries specifically covered include Hungary, the Czech Republic, Poland, Bulgaria, and Germany.

1175. Miller, William Lockley, Stephen White, and Paul Heywood. **Values and Political Change in Postcommunist Europe**. xxii, 460p.: illus. New York: St. Martin's Press, 1998. Includes bibliographical references and index.

This is an extensive study of the changes in political values that have taken place in Eastern Europe in the post-communist era. The study is based on 11 surveys of public opinion in the FSU and east-central Europe that were taken between 1993 and 1996. The five former communist countries in the study are Russia, Ukraine, Hungary, Slovakia, and the Czech Republic. The authors focus on enduring political values as opposed to political preferences and examine factors shaping political values such as public perceptions of politics, influences, and change in the region.

1176. **Building Democracy?: The International Dimension of Democratisation in Eastern Europe**. Edited by Geoffrey Pridham, George Sanford, and Eric Herring. vii, 224p. New York: St. Martin's Press, 1994. Includes bibliographical references and index.

This volume is the result of collaboration of British scholars that intends to explain the various factors that affect the international dimension of democratization in Eastern Europe. They examine theory, practice, and interregional comparisons, provide a comparison with other regions, and explore the culture of democracy, the effect of international security, and the European Community. Three final essays focus on Czechoslovakia, Hungary, and Poland as individual case studies.

1177. **The Constitutions of New Democracies in Europe**. Edited by Peter Raina. xvii, 314p. Braunton, Devon, Eng.: Merlin, 1995.

This volume contains the constitutions established as of 1995 in Bulgaria, the Czech Republic, Estonia, Hungary, Latvia, Lithuania, Poland, Romania, the Russian Federation, and the Slovak republic. The constitutions are printed here in English. There is no commentary offered.

1178. **East-Central Europe in the 1990's**. Edited by Joan Serafin. x, 256p. Boulder, Colo.: Westview Press, 1994. Includes bibliographical references.

This collection of essays examines the transition in east-central Europe and the changes in the political, economic, and social sectors of the region. "Individual chapters examine the ongoing processes of institution-building, the growth of political pluralism, ethnic strife, economic transformation, and new security dilemmas both within and across national boundaries" (back cover). The essays are grouped into three sections: an overview of the region, economic issues, and political and social issues.

1179. **Dissolution, Continuation, and Succession in Eastern Europe**. Edited by Brigitte Stern. vii, 211p. The Hague: Martinus Nijhoff, 1998. Includes bibliographical references.

Since the fall of the Soviet Union, all the countries of Eastern Europe have been faced with enormous changes in their political systems. Essentially, they are all faced with the end of one state system and the construction of another. The problems arising from this situation are the subject of this collection of essays. "The compendium broadly covers the consequences of State succession in the arenas of public international law, private international law, and international relations, addressing a wide range of concerns: currency, debt, international commercial arbitration, nationality and European security. The unifying thread amid these diverse topics is State succession, the circumstance in which these problems have arisen" (back cover).

1180. Stokes, Gale. **Three Eras of Political Change in Eastern Europe**. xiii, 240p. New York: Oxford University Press, 1996. Includes bibliographical references.

Stokes' examination of political change in Eastern Europe is divided into three parts. In Part 1 he examines the origins of East European politics. This covers the defining fault lines of Eastern Europe, the rise of nationalism, and the social origins of East European politics. In Part 2 he studies the rise and fall of Yugoslavia from 19th-century Serbia through the disintegration in the late 1980s. In Part 3 he analyzes the crisis year of 1989, the modes of opposition leading to the revolution in Eastern Europe, the lessons of East European revolutions of 1989, and possibilities for optimism about Eastern Europe.

1181. **Postcommunist Presidents**. Edited by Ray Taras. ix, 250p.: illus., maps. Cambridge, Eng.: Cambridge University Press, 1997. Includes bibliographical references (pp. 238-39) and index.

Many political scientists would agree that it is one thing to analyze how political actors choose specific political institutions and the reasons for their doing so. It is quite another to determine what difference such choices actually make. These essays explore these and other questions in Russia, Ukraine, Kazakhstan, Poland, the Czech Republic, and Hungary. There are also three essays that present general thoughts on presidentialism in post-communist Europe, the separation of powers problem, and an afterword on the making of post-communist presidencies.

1182. **Social Democracy in a Post-Communist Europe**. Edited by Michael Waller, Bruno Coppieters, and Kris Deschouwer. ix, 203p.: illus. London: Frank Cass, 1994. Includes bibliographical references and index.

The 10 essays in this volume are arranged in two parts. In Part 1 overarching themes are covered and the focus is on models and problems. In Part 2 (six essays) individual case studies are presented. A host of questions are addressed, including: "How do social-democratic parties in either part of Europe stand in relation to governmental power? Are the economic and social problems by which both sets of parties are currently being assailed to any extent shared? How far do the social-democratic programmes and organizations in Europe resemble one another?" (p. viii), and others.

1183. Zuzowski, Robert. **Political Change in Eastern Europe Since 1989: Prospects for Liberal Democracy and a Market Economy**. 165p. Westport, Conn.: Praeger, 1998. Includes bibliographical references (pp. [149]-160) and index.

Zuzowski examines political change in Eastern Europe after the collapse of communism. Rather than analyze the entire region, he chooses instead to focus on Russia, Poland, and the Czech Republic. Two introductory chapters precede this country-specific analysis. He also brings the West's approach to post-communist Eastern Europe to bear on these countries' political development. In a concluding chapter he lays out the prospects in Eastern Europe for liberal democracy and a market economy.

Foreign Relations

1184. **Postcommunist Elites and Democracy in Eastern Europe.** Edited by John Higley, Jan Pakulski, and Wlodzimierz Wesolowski. xiii, 301p.: illus. New York: St. Martin's Press, 1998. Includes bibliographical references and index.

This collection of essays examines the evolution of political elites in Eastern Europe in the post-communist era. The essays focus on changes in the elite in Russia, Germany, the Czech Republic, Slovakia, Poland, Hungary, and Bulgaria.

1185. Hulsman, John C. **A Paradigm for the New World Order: A Schools-of-Thought Analysis of American Foreign Policy in the Post-Cold-War Era.** 222p. New York: St. Martin's Press, 1997. Includes bibliographical references and index.

John Hulsman uses the Bosnian crises as a vehicle to demonstrate changes in U.S. foreign policy since the end of the cold war. While part of the book deals with foreign policy issues in general, much of it examines U.S. foreign policy regarding Eastern Europe and Russia. There is also a detailed discussion of the American response to the Bosnian crises. "This book will explore different conceptions of the past-1989 world by identifying and analyzing schools of thought that underlie the policy positions of decision-makers in the new era" (p. 1).

1186. Larrabee, Stephen F. **The Volatile Powder Keg: Balkan Security After the Cold War.** xxviii, 320p. Washington, D.C.: American University Press, 1994. Includes bibliographical references.

Based on the author's belief in 1990 that the Balkans were to become again a source of political instability in south Europe, this volume had two goals. The first goal was "to examine the basic underlying trends in the Balkans that might contribute to instability in the area and make the region a problem for Western policymakers. A second goal was to analyze the role that Western institutions might play in containing and dampening tensions in the region" (p. vii). The 14 separately authored essays are arranged in three parts: (1) domestic change and regional stability; (2) regional security problems; and (3) the role of external actors and institutions.

1187. Lévesque, Jacques. **The Enigma of 1989: The USSR and the Liberation of Eastern Europe.** ix, 267p. Berkeley: University of California Press, 1997. Includes bibliographical references and index.

The great enigma of 1989 was the Soviet Union's giving of "permission" to the collapse of East European communist regimes. Not only was war avoided, but seemingly little international tension was created. Lévesque looks at the place of Eastern Europe in Gorbachev's political project and the Soviet Union's foreign policy; the year 1989 as the apotheosis of the Soviet Union's new foreign policy, with special chapters devoted to

Poland, Hungary, East Germany, Bulgaria, Czechoslovakia, and Romania; and the aftermath including the reunification and status of Germany and the agony and the end of the Warsaw Pact.

1188. Marko, Augustín, and Pavol Martinický. **Slovak-Magyar Relations: History and Present Day in Figures**. 1st ed. 99p.: maps. Bratislava: Signum, 1995. At head of title: Slovak Society for Protection of Democracy and Humanity, Bratislava, Slovak Republic. Includes bibliographical references (pp. 91-93).

This brief study examines the minority policies in Hungary toward the Slovaks in the 20th century. This is seen as a central issue in Hungarian-Slovak relations.

Communism

1189. **The Social Legacy of Communism**. Edited by Sharon L. Wolchik and James R. Millar. xiii, 404p.: illus., map. *Woodrow Wilson Center series*. Washington, D.C.: Woodrow Wilson Center Press, 1994. Includes index.

The changes in Russia and Eastern Europe have received much attention in the scholarly literature. There have been an especially large number of studies on the economic and political transitions in the region. Less attention has been focused on the social changes that have accompanied the downfall of communism. The essays in this volume examine a number of social issues. They are grouped by topic covering ethnic issues, health and crime, social divisions, and the problems of labor. Within these areas the contributing authors have focused on specific issues such as drug abuse in Central and Eastern Europe, the religious renaissance in Russia, and unemployment, to name only a few.

Economics, Trade, and Business

1190. **The Privatization Process in East-Central Europe: Evolutionary Process of Czech Privatization**. Edited by Michal Mejstrik, Alexis Derviz, and Alena Zemplinerova. xviii, 330p. *International Studies in Economics and Econometrics*, 36. Dordrecht, Netherlands; Boston: Kluwer Academic, 1997. Includes index and bibliography (pp. 307-17).

In supporting their thesis that "partial economic reform is not possible without privatization" (p. 1), the various authors in this volume explain the conditions necessary for privatization and the results of the privatization process in Czechoslovakia and the Czech Republic.

1191. **Privatization Surprises in Transition Economies: Employee-Ownership in Central and Eastern Europe**. Edited by Milica Uvalic and Daniel Vaughan-Whitehead. xiv, 306p.: illus. Cheltenham, Eng.: Edward Elgar, 1997. Includes bibliographical references and index.

This collaborative effort presents several case studies in privatization. What is evident is that there is no one good model for privatization, and different countries should try to use as many models as practical. The case studies focus on privatization efforts in the Baltic countries, Bulgaria, the Czech Republic, Hungary, Poland, Romania, Russia, Ukraine, and the Yugoslav successor states.

1192. Adam, Jan. **Planning and Market in Soviet and East European Thought, 1960s-1992**. xviii, 320p. New York: St. Martin's Press, 1993. Includes bibliographical references (pp. 296-312) and index.

Adam's study is arranged in two parts. In Part 1 (Chapters 1-5) Adam focuses on the debates on planning and market in the 1960s that took place in the USSR, Czechoslovakia, Hungary, and Poland. In Part 2 (Chapters 6-10) he examines debates on planning and market that occurred in the 1980s and 1990-1992. In both parts he begins with a chapter that analyzes the common and contrasting features of the debates during the time period in question. His concluding chapter offers observations.

1193. **Europe's Economy Looks East: Implications for Germany and the European Union**. Edited by Stanley W. Black. xvi, 363p.: illus., map. Cambridge, Eng.: Cambridge University Press, 1997. Includes bibliographical references (pp. [403]-419) and index.

The essays in this volume arose from a conference held in Washington, D.C., in May 1995. They "present general equilibrium calculations of the worldwide effects of trade liberalization between CEECs [Central and Eastern European Countries] and the European Union (EU) on real wages and welfare; analysis of trade in 'sensitive' sectors; and measurement of Germany's role in the transition. . . . Other essays examine the effects of privatization, labor migration from the East, and alternative approaches to integration of CEECs into the EU, including quick entry, variable geometry, and free-trade areas" (frontispiece).

1194. **The Transition in Eastern Europe**. Edited by Olivier Jean Blanchard, Kenneth A. Froot, and Jeffrey D. Sachs. 2 vols. Chicago: University of Chicago Press, 1994. Includes bibliographical references and indexes. Vol. 1. Country Studies—Vol. 2. Restructuring.

The papers in these volumes provide the context for examining questions of stabilization and reform in Eastern Europe. Individual papers are devoted to Poland, Czechoslovakia, Hungary, East Germany, Slovenia, and Russia. The papers in Volume 2 examine particular issues such as labor market institutions, public finance, privatization, bankruptcy reform, and foreign trade.

1195. Bonin, John, Kalman Mizsei, Istvan Szekely, and Paul Wachtel. **Banking in Transition Economies: Developing Market Oriented Banking Sectors in Eastern Europe**. xii, 195p. Cheltenham, Eng.: Edward Elgar, 1998.

These essays present the findings and conclusions of a project team for the World Bank that focused on creating market-oriented banking sectors in transition economies. In addition to a summary chapter, other topics covered include bank privatization in Hungary, Poland, and the Czech Republic; the role of foreign banks in economies of transition; regulation of bank failures; and retail banking in Central and Eastern Europe.

1196. **Rebuilding the Financial System in Central and East Europe, 1918-1994**. Edited by Philip L. Cottrell. xii, 177p. Aldershot, Hants, Eng.: Scholar Press, 1997. Includes bibliographical references (pp. [161]-169) and index.

This series of essays focuses on central banking and commercial banking. Individual topics covered include currency reform, bank industry networks, and historical reflections on the financial system of several East European countries during the interwar period.

1197. Gerhard, Gehrig. **Economies in Transition: A System of Models and Forecasts for Germany and Poland**. 293p.: illus. *Contributions to Economics*. Heidelberg, Ger.: Physica-Verlag, 1993. Includes bibliographical references.

This book would be of primary interest to econometricians who are developing economic forecasting models. The individual chapters discuss the creation of the models used, numerical techniques used, as well as the simulation results. The models are comparative, using both Poland and Germany as their foci. This work concentrates on models for the money and labor marked for Germany and the use of Poland as an example for economies in transition.

1198. **Financial Reform in Central and Eastern Europe**. Edited by Stephany Griffith-Jones and Zdenek Drábek. x, 256p. London; New York: Macmillan; St. Martin's Press, 1995. Includes bibliographical references and index.

The essays in this collection are arranged in four parts: (1) introduction and non-banking financial flows; (2) case studies; (3) lessons from developing countries; and (4) conclusions and policy implications. The cases studies cover key issues in Czech and Slovak banking, capital accumulation for long-term economic growth in the Czech Republic, problems of financing small and medium-sized enterprises in the Czech Republic, development of the financial sector in Hungary during the transition period, and financial sector development and macroeconomic policy in Poland in 1990-1993.

1199. **East-Central European Economies in Transition**. Edited by John P. Hardt and Richard F. Kaufman. xv, 709p.: illus. Armonk, N.Y.: M. E. Sharpe, 1995. Includes bibliographical references and index.

This comprehensive study was presented to the Joint Economic Committee of Congress in 1994. It assesses the economies of Eastern Europe during the time of transition from command economies to market economies. The individual essays are separated into four sections: (1) the transition to market economies and political pluralism; (2) Western assistance and integration; (3) regional relations; and (4) country studies.

1200. Henderson, Karen. **Back to Europe: Central and Eastern Europe and the European Union**. xix, 307p.: illus., map. London; Philadelphia: UCL Press, 1999. Includes bibliographical references (pp. 285-95) and index.

The countries of Eastern Europe have faced many challenges as they redefine themselves as democratic systems. Not least among these has been their attempt to become integrated into the European Union. It is this struggle that is the focus of this volume of papers. Divided into three sections, the papers discuss three major themes: security, structural problems, and politics. "The aim of the book is to provide a comprehensive guide to the challenges of EU enlargement which presents original research as well as being easily accessible to both readers with a background in EU studies and those interested in the states of post-communist Europe" (p. viii). Contributors include: Brian Ardy, Janice Bell, Irena Brinar, Gerhard Eisl, James Gow, Heather Grabbe, Jackie Grower, Karnen Henderson, Grazme P. Herd, Kristy Hughes, Tamasz Michiewicz, Frances Millard, David Phinnemore, Michael Alexander Rupp, Helene Sjursen, Brian Slocok, and Martin Smith. The volume includes a chronology of major events from March 1957 to December 1997.

1201. Hoen, Herman Willem. **The Transformation of Economic Systems in Central Europe**. xi, 203p. *Studies in Comparative Economic Systems*. Cheltenham, Eng.: Edward Elgar, 1998. Includes bibliographical references (pp. 181-93) and index.

Hoen explores the various aspects of economic transformation of economic systems in Central Europe and concentrates on Hungary, the Czech and Slovak Republics, and Poland. He develops a theory of economic transformation, shows the mutual dependency of transformation and integration, investigates the pros and cons of "shock therapy" versus "gradualism," and suggests a political economy of transformation for the future.

1202. **Environmental Action in Eastern Europe: Responses to Crisis**. Edited by Barbara Jancar-Webster. 238p.: map. Armonk, N.Y.: M. E. Sharpe, c1993. Includes index.

This is a collection of essays on the long-standing environmental problems of Eastern Europe. "The chapters that follow address the current uneasy time of transition in a similar pattern. Each attempts to explain why and how the old regime brought such environmental destruction, why and how the opposition utilized the environmental theme to bring down the communist government, and what new legislation and organized action on the part of environmental groups are needed to remedy the existing negative environmental conditions" (p. 2). The essays are divided into two parts: "Problems and

Changes in Environmental Management" and "The Influence of Environmental Movements." The essays address problems in Poland, Hungary, the Czech Republic, Slovakia, the former Soviet Union, the Baltic states, and Slovenia.

1203. **Problems of Economic and Political Transformation in the Balkans**. Edited by Ian Jeffries. vi, 199p.: illus. London: Pinter, 1996. Includes bibliographical references and index.

This collection of essays focuses on the political and economic factors affecting change in the Balkans. The contributors believe that the former have been somewhat neglected in the literature. The essays are region or country specific. Contributors are academics and political advisors.

1204. Kofman, Jan. **Economic Nationalism and Development: Central and Eastern Europe Between the Two World Wars**. vii, 248p. Boulder, Colo.: Westview Press, 1997. Includes bibliographical references and index.

Kofman's study of economic nationalism and development is arranged in two parts. In Part 1 he presents various theoretical and research approaches to nationalism, an overview of economic nationalism, its sources and causes, and directions and instruments of economic nationalism. In Part 2 he explores the effects of economic nationalism, especially protectionism. He presents the theory and practice of protectionism, an overview of the policy of protectionism in East and Central Europe, and the experience of Poland, Czechoslovakia, and Bulgaria with protectionism. An epilogue poses questions for discussion and further hypotheses.

1205. Kornai, Janos. **Highway and Byways: Studies on Reform and Post-Communist Transition**. xv, 241p. Cambridge, Mass.: MIT Press, 1995. Includes bibliographical references and indexes.

This volume collects eight essays by Janos Kornai, all written between 1990 and 1994. "The subject of each is the search for a new road by Hungary, and in addition by the whole Eastern European region that lived under the socialist system" (p. vii). The first two essays examine the attempts to reform the existing socialist system. The remaining papers focus on post-socialist development.

1206. Kostis, Kostas P. **Modern Banking in the Balkans and West-European Capital in the Nineteenth and Twentieth Centuries**. vi, 255p. Brookfield, Vt.: Ashgate, 1999. Based on the Athens Conference on Modern Banking in the Balkans and West-European Capital, held in January 1997. Includes bibliographical references (pp. [235]-250) and index.

Some of the papers included here were originally presented at a conference in Athens in January 1997. Others were written specifically for this volume. "This volume attempts to follow the role of western, and especially West-European, capital in the constitution of modern banking systems in Balkan countries and in the economic development of these countries" (p. 2). The essays focus on the extent to which West European capital has penetrated the different Balkan countries, the use of this capital, the new techniques and ideas introduced by Western banks in transferring this capital, the facilitation of the integration of inter-Balkan financial networks, and the effect of Western European banking on the development of this area.

1207. Lavigne, Marie. **The Economics of Transition: From Socialist Economy to Market Economy**. 2nd ed. xx, 328p.: illus. New York: St. Martin's Press, 1999. Includes bibliographical references and index.

This is the second edition of a 1995 publication. The author has expanded the original discussion of the problems facing socialist nations making the change to a market economy. She has particularly expanded the discussion of the role of the European Union in Eastern Europe. "The book provides a contemporary comparative approach to the process of transformation and supplies a large amount of factual and statistical information" (back cover). The author has presented a nontechnical discussion of the economic situation in the area, in the hope of making the study accessible to the largest audience. The book includes an appendix with a great deal of statistical data.

1208. Mullineux, A. **Financial Reform in Central and Eastern Europe: Lessons from the "West," Poland and Further East**. 257p.: illus. Commack, N.Y.: Nova Science Publishers, 1995. Includes bibliographical references and index.

The 13 papers in this collection are arranged in two parts. Part 1 contains lessons from the West and other transforming economies dealing with exchange rate policies, inflation, setting up banking systems, small business financing, and privatization. Part 2 provides the lessons learned in Poland during its early phase of transformation and deals with privatization, microeconomic impact of monetary policy, and banking sector reform, all of which are instructive for other transforming economics.

1209. Myant, Martin R. **Successful Transformations?: The Creation of Market Economies in Eastern Germany and the Czech Republic**. xiii, 267p. *Studies of Communism in Transition*. Cheltenham, Eng.: Edward Elgar, 1996. Includes bibliographical references (pp. 257-61) and index.

These papers were originally presented at conferences in 1995. Their aim is to answer general questions about the success of economic transformation in Eastern Germany and the Czech Republic. For both cases "an assessment is made of the effects of past policies and of the structural changes that have taken place, with a substantial emphasis on the changes to, and within, enterprises" (p. 2).

1210. **Income Inequality and Poverty in Eastern and Western Europe**. Edited by Notburga Ott and Gert Wagner. x, 253p.: illus. *Contributions to Economics*. Heidelberg, Ger.: Physica, 1997. "The authors . . . discussed their drafts at the workshop 'Inequality in Europe' "—Preface. Includes bibliographical references.

The essays here were originally presented as papers at the conference "Inequality in Europe." Individual pieces cover topics such as welfare policies, comparative poverty research, working poor and minimum wages, poverty and social security transfers, old age poverty, and studies of poverty in specific countries.

1211. Palairet, Michael. **Balkan Economies, C. 1800-1914: Evolution Without Development**. xvi, 415p.: illus., maps. Cambridge, Eng.: Cambridge University Press, 1997. Includes bibliographical references.

This fascinating economic history of the Balkans explores the Balkan economies during the Ottoman period to 1878 in Part 1 and then moves to analyze economic decline and political freedom from 1878 to 1914 in Part 2. This book explores "the economic experience of the Balkan territories through the observations of contemporaries" and sets these observations "within a deductive framework of economic logic" (p. xiii).

1212. Palmieri, Deborah Anne. **Russia and the NIS in the World Economy: East-West Investment, Financing and Trade**. xv, 182p. Westport, Conn.: Praeger, 1994. Includes bibliographical references (pp. [169]-172) and index.

This collection of essays examines Russia's changing role in the world economy. "The goal of this book is to conjoin vital issue areas with research by scholars that can genuinely shed light on Russia's domestic economic developments and its international economic relations with the West" (p. viii). The essays discuss such topics as foreign economic relations, foreign investment in Russia, Russian export protectionism, the commodity exchange, and marketization. Contributors are Deborah Anne Palmieri, Ariel Cohen, Eileen M. Crumm, Margaret B. McClean, Jamus Clay Moltz, Paula M. Ross, William E. Schmickle, and Eric A. Stubbs. The appendix is a chronology of major Soviet and post-Soviet economic decrees.

1213. Schlegelmilch, Kai. **Green Budget Reform in Europe: Countries at the Forefront**. xxxi, 443p.: illus. Berlin: Springer, 1999. Includes bibliographical references.

The first part of this book focuses on green budget reform experiences in Western and Eastern Europe. It includes individual papers on specific issues and countries (Austria, Denmark, Sweden, the Netherlands, Switzerland, Poland, and Hungary). The second part of the book concentrates on a case study of green budget reform in Slovenia.

1214. Shen, Raphael. **Economic Reform in Poland and Czechoslovakia: Lessons in Systemic Transformation**. xiv, 268p. Westport, Conn.: Praeger, 1993. Includes bibliographical references (pp. [261]-264) and index.

This is a comparative study of the economic changes occurring in Poland and Czechoslovakia. Each country has chosen a different pace for economic reform; however, the author believes the methods used to accomplish these reforms have not varied much from country to country. Shen further contends that the differences between the two countries' economic successes are a reflection of cultural and societal variations between the two. "The tentative conclusion is that systemic transformation must take into due consideration the key variables—cultural, social, and political as well as economic—that will either positively or negatively respond to significant policy measures" (p. xiv). The author begins with historical overviews of the two economies from 1945 to 1989 that focus on economic performance and past reforms. He then looks at reform measures in specific areas of the economy: banking, foreign investment, foreign trade, property, and industry. The book includes a chronology covering events from 1989 to 1992.

1215. Stephan, Johannes. **Economic Transition in Hungary and East Germany: Gradualism and Shock Therapy in Catch-Up Development**. xv, 293p.: illus. *Studies in Economic Transition*. New York: St. Martin's Press, 1999. Includes bibliographical references (pp. 257-81) and index.

By drawing on the experiences of economic shock therapy in Hungary and East Germany, this book "intends to provide an investigative study into the economics of systemic transformation and catch-up development" (p. 3). Topics covered include economic integration and socialist legacies, the German Monetary Union and currency reform, German unification and prospects for catch-up development, the development of the financial sector in Hungary, monetary stabilization policies in Hungary, and Hungarian foreign trade and catch-up development.

1216. Strong, Ann Louise, Thomas A. Reiner, Thomas A. Strong, and Janusz M. Szyrmer. **Transitions in Land and Housing: Bulgaria, the Czech Republic, and Poland**. 1st ed. vi, 298p.: maps. New York: St. Martin's Press, 1996. Includes bibliographical references (pp. [289]-296) and index.

"This study of changing patterns of ownership in land and housing and the formation of real estate markets in Central and Eastern Europe during the post-1989 'transition' focuses on three nations: Bulgaria, Czechoslovakia and the successor Czech Republic, and Poland." The authors of this study used the information gathered on their field trips to the region in 1992-1994 to supplement data from printed resources. An analysis of the process of privatization is at the heart of this study. The authors conclude that it is this process that is at the heart of the change to a market economy in the region. They focused on the years 1989-1995 while the region was going through its most extreme social, political, and economic changes. The volume includes appendixes with statistical data on the economies of the countries under analysis.

1217. Winters, L. Alan. **Eastern Europe's International Trade**. xvi, 189p.: illus. Manchester, Eng.: Manchester University Press, 1994.

In examining the effects of economic liberalization on international trade, the authors address three sets of questions: "the likely extent and direction of Eastern Europe's international trade; the trading relationships between the EC and the East European countries; and the factors influencing the composition of East European trade" (p. xiv). Some of their results were previously published in scholarly journals and other publications.

1218. Zloch-Christy, Iliana. **Eastern Europe and the World Economy: Challenges of Transition and Globalization**. xv, 293p.: illus. Cheltenham, Eng.: Edward Elgar, 1998.

This set of essays examines the various issues involved in the transition from socialism to a market economy. The essays are arranged in four parts: (1) the developed economies (industrial governance structures, economic nationalism, and the world economy); (2) the East European economies (privatization, integration, etc.); (3) international organizations and the transitional economies in Eastern Europe (admission to the European Union, the World Trade Organization); and (4) selected aspects and perspectives (industrial policy, relevance of the Japanese experience, venture capital and economic development, economic linkage policies, and a case study of Hong Kong).

Language and Literature

1219. Franks, Steven. **Parameters of Slavic Morphosyntax**. xvi, 409p.: illus. *Studies in Comparative Syntax*. New York: Oxford University Press, 1995. Includes bibliographical references and index.

"The primary goal of this study is to explore accounts of syntactic diversity among the Slavic languages unifying analyses of similar phenomena across the different languages. Most of the problems to be addressed deal with issues of phrase structure and case assignment" (p. ix).

1220. Hannan, Kevin. **Borders of Language and Identity in Teschen Silesia**. xx, 255p.: illus., maps. *Berkeley Insights in Linguistics and Semiotics*, Vol. 28. New York: P. Lang, 1996. Includes bibliographical references (pp. [223]-251) and index.

In Teschen Silesia German, Czech and Polish have had a great influence on the dialects of that region. This study examines the sociolinguistic aspects of language change in that area and does so with a firm grounding in diachronic and synchronic linguistics. The author devotes individual chapters to the geography of the region, as well as ethnography and other elements that help to create linguistic borders in the area.

1221. Kraszewski, Charles S. **The Romantic Hero and Contemporary Anti-Hero in Polish and Czech Literature: Great Souls and Grey Men**. v, 325p. Lampeter, Eng.: Edwin Mellen Press, 1998. Includes bibliographic references and index.

Charles Kraszewski has studied and translated the literatures of Poland and the Czech Republic. In this book he takes a comparative look at the role of the hero in each of those literatures. "The purpose of this book is to study major heroic and anti-heroic texts of Polish and Czech literature in an effort to determine the close relationship of the contemporary works of authors such as Havel and Herbert to the romantic texts of poets like Mickiewicz and Macha and to discover the national and general relevance of heroic and anti-heroic literature, both for the eras in which they were created, and for subsequent generations" (p. 1). Other authors included in this study include Slowacki, Kajetan, Krasinski, Norwid, Borovsky, Exben, Nemcova, Gombrowicz, Baranczak, Zahradnicek, and Holan.

1222. Longinovic, Tomislav. **Borderline Culture: The Politics of Identity in Four Twentieth-Century Slavic Novels**. xiii, 197p. Fayetteville: University of Arkansas Press, 1993. Includes bibliographical references (pp. [187]-192).

Tomislav Longinovic examines the works of Mikhail Bulgakov, Witold Gombrowicz, Danilo Kis, and Milan Kundera in this study. He is concerned with identifying common themes, imagery, and other elements that might indicate their common Slavic origins. Longinovic is attempting to show the "borderline" nature of all that is Slavic at the end of the 20th century. The author uses psychoanalytic terminology to describe the influence of political mechanisms of the formation of cultural identity. After his introductory chapter describing in detail the author's methodology in this study, he presents the reader with four chapters, each devoted to an individual author. The final chapter is concerned with the current rise of nationalism in today's Slavic world.

1223. **A New Slavic Language Is Born: The Rusyn Literary Language of Slovakia**. Edited by Paul Robert Magocsi. xv, 68p. *East European Monographs*, 184. Boulder, Colo.: East European Monographs; New York: Distributed by Columbia University Press, 1996. Includes bibliographical references. English and Slovak.

In 1995 the act of codifying the Carpatho-Rusyn literary language took place in Bratislava Slovakia. This volume contains the presentations that took place at a scholarly seminar in Bratislava immediately following the event. It contains the declaration and introductions, three scholarly articles on the Rusyn language, as well as an appendix of other material given on the day of codification.

1224. **South Slavic Writers Since World War II**. Edited by Vasa D. Mihailovich. 474p.: illus. *Dictionary of Literary Biography*, vol. 181. Detroit: Gale Research, 1997. Includes index.

This volume of the *Dictionary of Literary Biography* follows the conventions of previous volumes in that its purpose is to place major figures in the larger perspective of literary history and offer appraisals of how these figures work. In general the volumes of the series present so-called career biographies and provide reliable information about the authors chosen for inclusion. Like its companion volume (vol. 147 in the series) that covered South Slavic writers before World War II, this one by the same editor, Vasa Mihailovich, offers the reader an interesting biographical and critical assessment of the most influential and interesting writers bounded by the chosen parameters of time and place.

After a brief introduction by Mihailovich that sets the context for the biographies that follow, each of the writer's entries from Ivan Aralica to Vitomil Zupan are arranged alphabetically and not separated by country of origin. Each national (based on language) literature is well represented. Included are writers from Serbia, Croatia, Macedonia, Slovenia, and Bulgaria. Each biography is written by a well-known critic in the field.

The entries are structured similarly. Each begins with a bibliography of book-length works and, when appropriate, selected periodical publications. Following this is the biography, often with illustrations in addition to the mandatory picture of the author. Each ends with a bibliography of secondary sources on the author in both English and other languages. At the end of the volume is a "Checklist of Further Readings" in various languages, a list of contributors with their institutional affiliations, and a cumulative index to the authors contained in all the previous DLB volumes including this one.

This is a solid reference work and deserves to be on the shelves of every major research library.

1225. **Eastern and Central Europe**. Edited by James Naughton. xvi, 439p.: illus., maps. *Traveler's Literary Companion*. Lincolnwood, Ill.: Passport Books, 1996. Includes bibliographical references and index.

In this volume of *Traveler's Literary Companion* the editor takes the reader on a literary tour of this part of Europe. Poland, the Czech Republic, Slovakia, Hungary, Romania, Bulgaria, Albania, and the lands of the former Yugoslavia are all a part of this guide. Each section covers one region. Each contains an introduction to the country with an overview of its geography, culture, and political system. This is followed by literary "extracts," brief bibliographical sketches of major writers. There is also a "book list" in each section. This volume provides an introduction to anyone interested in the literature of the area.

1226. **Linguistic Minorities in Central and Eastern Europe**. Edited by Christina B. Paulston and Donald Peckham. xiv, 289p.: map. Clevedon, Eng.: Multilingual Matters, 1998. Includes bibliographical references and index.

This collection of articles focuses on the languages of Eastern Europe and the former Soviet Union. The book begins with an introductory chapter. The remaining chapters are arranged geographically; each describes the linguistic features of the minorities in a specific region or country. "If the chapters are considered together, however, trends and generalizations of linguistic minorities in central and eastern Europe emerge and lend themselves very well to contrast and comparison of ethnic minorities in other parts of the world, and so to theory testing at a higher level of abstraction" (p. viii). The countries or regions considered are Austria, the Balkans, Bulgaria, the Caucasus, the Czech Republic, Hungary, Latvia, Romania, Russia, and Slovakia. Poland has been excluded because of its extensive ties to the West.

1227. **The Literature of Nationalism: Essays on East European Identity**. Edited by Robert B. Pynsent. viii, 282p. *Studies in Russia and East Europe*. London: Macmillan, 1996. Includes bibliographical references and index.

These essays explore the many aspects of nationalism in Eastern Europe today. They cover topics that include: the debate between tradition and modernity in the shaping of a Romanian identity; sociohistorical perspectives on attitudes to Hungarian; Zeromski and the crisis of Polish nationalism; Czech nationalism and women writers of the fin de siècle; Tin Ujevic and the Yugoslav ideal; a Bulgarian biography of Mussolini and others.

1228. Schaarschmidt, Gunter. **A Historical Phonology of the Upper and Lower Sorbian Languages**. 175p. *Historical Phonology of the Slavic Languages*, 6. Heidelberg, Ger.: Universitatsverlag C. Winter, 1998. Includes bibliographical references and indexes.

While Sorbian languages have been the subject of many linguistic studies, there has been no systematic analysis of the language. This work attempts to fill this gap. "The historical phonology of Upper and Lower Sorbia is presented as a series of 'synchronic slices' connected by sound changes that are dated using all available evidence. Especially for the period before the 16th century, i.e., the beginning of a written tradition lasting to the present days, this evidence is drawn to a large extent from a systematic reexamination of the findings in onomastic research" (p. 7).

National Minorities

1229. Dadrian, Vahakn N. **The History of the Armenian Genocide: Ethnic Conflict**. 3rd rev. ed. xxviii, 452p. Providence, R.I.: Berghahn Books, 1997. Includes bibliographical references (pp. [428]-446) and index.

"The present study has two principal goals: (1) to examine the World War I Armenian genocide through the vast corpus of official Ottoman-Turkish documents, as well as those of imperial Germany and imperial Austria, Turkey's wartime political military allies; (2) to subject that genocide to a critical analysis from a historical perspective" (p. xv). Vahakn Dadrian believes the Turko-Armenian conflict was simply a mechanism used by the Ottoman Turks to end forever the Turko-Armenian conflict that had haunted the region. Dadrian's book is heavily documented and includes an appendix describing possible sources in Nazi Germany on the Armenian genocide.

1230. McCarthy, Justin. **Death and Exile: The Ethnic Cleansing of Ottoman Muslims, 1821-1922**. xv, 368p.: maps. Princeton, N.J.: Darwin Press, 1995. Includes bibliographical references (pp. 347-57) and index.

This is a history of mortality and forced migration of Muslim people in the Balkans, Anatolia, and the southern Caucasus prior to 1922. The author examines the most important motivations and causes behind this phenomenon and provides data in illustrating the persecution of Muslims during this period.

1231. Sugar, Peter F. **Nationality and Society in Habsburg and Ottoman Europe**. 1 vol. (various pagings). *Collected Studies series. Studies in East-Central Europe 1500-1900*. Brookfield, Vt.: Variorum, 1997. Includes bibliographical references and index.

These 10 essays were all previously published from 1958 through 1991. They either appeared as journal articles, conference papers, or chapters in books, and deal with questions of nationality or society in Central Europe. Their subject area is broad and covers the influence of the Enlightenment and the French Revolution in 18th-century Hungary, external and domestic roots of Eastern European nationalism, railroad construction, the development of the Balkan village, and others.

1232. Taji-Farouki, Suha. **Muslim Identity and the Balkan State**. x, 250p. New York: New York University Press, 1997. Includes index.

The contributors to this study all examine, to one degree or another, the relationship "between the Balkan Muslim communities and the states in which they live, as well as their self-definition in relation to these states" (p. 1). In addition to the general theme of Muslim identity, two chapters at the end of the book explore the relation of Turkey and Turkish-Islamic loyalties to the development of Muslim identity in the Balkans.

1233. **National Identities and Ethnic Minorities in Eastern Europe: Selected Papers from the Fifth World Congress of Central and East European Studies**. Edited by Ray Taras. xii, 228p. New York: St. Martin's Press, 1998. Includes bibliographical references and index.

These essays were originally presented at the Fifth World Congress of Central and East European Studies held in Warsaw in 1995. Among the topics dealing with ethnicity are the psychology of overlapping identities, redefining national identity after communism, the new interpretation of ethnicity in Central and Eastern Europe, the ethnic identity of the Polish population in Belarus, and other ethnic/nationalist frictions.

Holocaust

1234. **Women in the Holocaust**. Edited by Dalia Ofer and Lenore J. Weitzman. vii, 402p. New Haven, Conn.: Yale University Press, 1998. Includes index.

"This book shows how questions about gender lead us to a richer and more finely nuanced understanding of the Holocaust. They help us envision the specificity of everyday life and the different ways in which men and women responded to the Nazi onslaught. The discussion of women's unique experiences provides a missing element of what we must now see as an incomplete picture of Jewish life during the Holocaust" (p. 1).

1235. Apple, Slovie Solomon. **They Were Strangers: A Family History**. 1st ed. 213p. New York: Vantage Press, 1995. Includes bibliographical references (p. 213).

This poignant memoir recounts the story of a Russian Jewish family and what they endured because of anti-Semitism in Russia and Europe.

1236. Braham, Randolph. **Destruction of Romanian and Ukrainian Jews During the Antonescu Era**. xvi, 413p. *East European Monographs*, 483. Boulder, Colo.: East European Monographs; New York: Distributed by Columbia University Press, 1997. Includes bibliographical references.

The papers in this volume were originally presented at a conference held in Washington, D.C., in 1996 on the Fate of Romanian and Ukrainian Jews Under the Antonescu Regime. The essays are arranged in four parts: an analytical overview of anti-Semitism and responses to it, the "genocidal drive against Romanian and Ukrainian Jews during the Antonescu era" (p. viii), the "foreign" factor in the history of the Holocaust in Romania, and finally the various myths and history reinterpretation campaigns led by Romanian chauvinistic nationalists.

1237. Braham, Randolph, and Scott Miller. **The Nazis' Last Victims**. 200p. Detroit, Mich.: Wayne State University Press, 1998. Includes bibliographical references and index.

After the Germans invaded Hungary in March 1944, it took only three months to identify Jews, confiscate their property, ghettoize them, and deport them to Auschwitz. This process evolved over 12 years in Germany and Poland. The individual scholarly essays give several perspectives to these tragic events in Hungary, including stories of escape and the difficulty of dealing with recollections and reactions after the war.

1238. Capra, Dominick L. **History and Memory After Auschwitz**. ix, 214p.: illus. Ithaca, N.Y.: Cornell University Press, 1998. Includes bibliographical references and index.

Capra focuses on "the interactions among history, memory, and ethicopolitical concerns as they emerge in the aftermath of the Shoah. Each chapter approaches these questions from a distinctive perspective that is meant to interact in a thought-provoking but nontotalizing manner with the angle of vision in other chapters" (p. 2).

1239. Deaglio, Enrico. **The Banality of Goodness: The Story of Giorgio Perlasca**. Translated by Gregory Contixiv. 165p. *The Erma Konya Kess Lives of the Just and Virtuous series*. Notre Dame, Ind.: University of Notre Dame Press, 1998. Includes bibliographical references (pp. 161-63).

Deaglio has provided part narration and part diary of Giorgio Perlasca, who repeatedly volunteered his services to save Jewish lives. Well known in Italy, he stands beside Raoul Wallenberg, Irene Opdyke, Helena Melnyczuk, and others who risked their own lives to save Jews during the Holocaust.

1240. Drix, Samuel. **Witness to Annihilation: Surviving the Holocaust, a Memoir**. xvi, 249p.: illus. Washington, D.C.: Brassey's, 1994. Includes index.

This painful memoir by Dr. Drix relates his experiences in the Janowska concentration camp, which was located near the city of Lwów, Poland, present-day Lviv, Ukraine.

1241. Elias, Ruth. **Triumph of Hope: From Theresienstadt and Auschwitz to Israel**. Translated by Margot Bettauer Dembo. 1st ed. x, 274p.: illus., maps. New York: John Wiley, 1998. "Published in association with the United States Holocaust Memorial Museum."

This memoir traces the author's youth in Ostrava, Czechoslovakia, and the effect of the Second World War, her imprisonment in both Theresienstadt and Auschwitz, and her eventual emigration to Israel after the war.

1242. Fischler-Martinno, Janina. **Have You Seen My Little Sister?: Joseph's Little Sister**. vi, 277p.: illus. *The Library of Holocaust Testimonies*. London: Vallentine Mitchell, 1998.

This memoir relates the story of the author as a victim of the Holocaust in Poland. At age 11, in 1941, she was drawn into the Krakow ghetto. In 1943 she escaped with the help of her brother. They both survived and were reunited in Krakow in 1945.

1243. Gillan, Garth J. **Rising from the Ruins: Reason, Being, and the Good After Auschwitz**. xi, 140p. Albany: State University of New York Press, 1998. Includes bibliographical references (pp. 129-33) and index.

This collection of essays is divided into two parts. The first covers from ancient times to the end of the Second World War. The second part focuses on the prelude to the communist period, the communist period itself, and post-communism. The essays are meant to put into a historical context the current development and transition to a democratic state.

1244. Gold, Ruth G. **Ruth's Journey: A Survivor's Memoir**. xvi, 293p.: illus., maps. Gainesville: University Press of Florida, 1996. Includes bibliographical references.

This memoir recounts the ordeals of Ruth Glasberg Gold, her transport to a concentration camp by the Nazis from her native Romania, and her survival of the war. She then moved to Israel, then to South America, and finally settled in Miami at the age of 50.

1245. Grunbaum, Irene. **Escape Through the Balkans: The Autobiography of Irene Grunbaum**. xxiii, 191p.: illus., maps. Lincoln: University of Nebraska Press, 1998. Includes bibliographical references (pp. [181]-191).

This memoir, discovered after the author's death, describes what Irene Grunbaum experienced during the war, although much of her life prior to moving to the Balkans and after she had emigrated to Brazil remains a mystery.

1246. Grynberg, Henryk. **Children of Zion**. xi, 178p. Jewish Lives. Evanston, Ill.: Northwestern University Press, 1998. Includes bibliographical references.

Grynberg calls this a "documentary tale." It consists of fragments of interview records that were compiled in Palestine in 1943 on the basis of Jewish children (primarily between the ages of 11 and 18) evacuated from the Soviet Union to Palestine. It is a terrifying tale, made the more terrifying by the simple prose of its witnesses.

1247. **Anatomy of the Auschwitz Death Camp**. Edited by Yisrael Gutma and Michael Berenbaum. xvi, 638p. Bloomington: Published in association with the United States Holocaust Memorial Museum, Washington, D.C. by Indiana University Press, 1998. Commissioned by the U.S. Holocaust Research Institute.

This was the first attempt to comprehensively study the Auschwitz death camp. It brings together the works of scholars who have spent their lives studying the Holocaust, but have never before collaborated in that study. As a comprehensive study, this is an interdisciplinary work with studies by experts in medicine, psychology, sociology, and history. Every essay is original to this work, although the research may have appeared elsewhere. The essays are divided into six sections: the camp as an institution; the mechanisms of execution; the personnel of Auschwitz; the lives of those interred at the camp; the resistance to Auschwitz; and the view of the outside world. Every section is preceded by a brief summary of all its essays.

1248. Handler, Andrew. **A Man for All Connections: Raoul Wallenberg and the Hungarian State Apparatus, 1944-1945**. 144p. Westport, Conn.: Praeger, 1996. Includes bibliographical references and index.

Raoul Wallenberg saved many Hungarian Jews during the Holocaust. He remains an enigmatic figure with little known concerning his life history or fate after the war. Andrew Handler survived the Holocaust in Hungary and grew up hearing much of the heroism of Wallenberg. In this slim volume he tries to provide a more complete picture of this heroic man.

1249. Hativni, David W. **The Book and the Sword: A Life of Learning in the Throes of the Holocaust**. 1st ed. 197p. New York: Farrar, Straus & Giroux, 1996.

This memoir, by a Romanian Jew, describes that part of the Holocaust experienced by the author in Romania and his eventual resettlement in New York after the war.

1250. Isacovici, Salomon, and Juan M. Rodriguez. **Man of Ashes**. Translated by Dick Gerdesxvi. 244p. Lincoln: University of Nebraska Press, 1999.

This memoir by Salomon Isacovici relates how he awoke one morning in 1940 as a Hungarian, having gone to bed the night before as a Romanian. Isacovici begins his story with his youth and follows it through imprisonment in Birkenau and Auschwitz, his liberation by the Americans, and the eventual rebuilding of his life in postwar Romania.

1251. Lagerwey, Mary D. **Reading Auschwitz**. 182p. *Ethnographic Alternatives Book series*, vol. 5. Walnut Creek, Calif.: AltaMira Press, 1998. Includes bibliographical references (pp. 161-78) and index.

Mary Lagerwey's study is part of a series that consciously tries to "blur the boundaries between the social science and humankind," thus it is not a traditional ethnography. Culture is not the decisive factor in behavioral decisions. Auschwitz provides a unique, if tragic, context for such a study. Certainly few other settings could so exemplify the breakdown of cultural standards. Lagerwey reexamines the memoirs of Holocaust survivors and one victim. She constantly interjects her own reactions to those readings. "Her guest comes to understand some of the particularities of the experience. By comparing examples of other male and female narratives, she coaxes readers to view stories of the Holocaust through a gender lens" (p. 8). The readings are presented sequentially. Mary Lagerwey is an Assistant Professor of Nursing with a background in sociology. The book includes an appendix of memoirs of Auschwitz published in English.

1252. Ofer, Dalia, and Hannah Weiner. **Dead-End Journey: The Tragic Story of the Kladovo-Sabec Group**. xxii, 231p.: illus., maps. *Studies in the Shoah*, 14. Lanham, Md.: University Press of America, 1996. Includes bibliographical references.

This book is a translation of a Hebrew book originally published in 1991. "This book tells the story of over one thousand Jewish refugees and their unfinished voyage to Mandatory Palestine. They set out from central Europe in November 1939; in April 1941 they were trapped by Nazi invaders. For twenty months, these Jews found themselves in Yugoslavia.... Their fate was the fate of European Jewry and its Holocaust: first, forced emigration; ultimately, the mass murder of the Final Solution" (p. xiii). The appendixes include letters, songs, and other documents that portray the lives of the refugees in Yugoslavia.

1253. Olere, David. **Witness: Images of Auschwitz**. 112p.: illus. (some col.). N. Richland Hills, Tex.: WestWind Press, 1998. Includes bibliographical references (p. 110).

This unsettling volume consists of poems and drawings of death camp experiences. The 45 drawing/text sets are arranged in two parts. Part 1 is entitled "From the hell train straight to the gas chamber"; Part 2 is "Every day life, every day death in the camp." Olere was an artist who was born in Warsaw in 1902, who moved to Berlin and then to Paris to pursue his art. He was arrested in Paris and sent to several camps, including Auschwitz, where he worked emptying the gas chambers and burning corpses in the ovens. He died in Paris in 1985.

1254. Pankowsky, Hanna D. **East of the Storm: Outrunning the Holocaust in Russia**. xiv, 218p.: ill, map. Lubbock: Texas Tech University Press, 1998. Includes index.

This is the personal narrative of Hanna Pankowsky, who with her family escaped the Nazis by going east to Russia. The work chronicles her experiences from 1939 to 1947, when she finally emigrated to Mexico. She currently lives in Texas.

1255. Peck, Jean M. **At the Fire's Center: A Story of Love and Holocaust Survival**. xiii, 243p. Urbana: University of Illinois Press, 1998. Index.

Peck interviewed two couples, the Hornsteins and the Ornsteins, who were friends in prewar Hungary. From the 80 hours of interviews she wrote this account of love and suffering during the time of the Holocaust in Poland and Hungary.

1256. Shachan, Avigdor. **Burning Ice: The Ghettos of Transnistria**. xii, 510p. *East European Monographs*, 447. Boulder, Colo.: East European Monographs; New York: Distributed by Columbia University Press, 1996. Includes bibliographical references (pp. 483-85) and index.

Burning Ice is the story of the destruction of the Jews in Bessarabia during World War II. The author, Avigdor Shachan, took part in the death marches there and swore to relate the fate of his people to the world. Beyond this, he seeks to find the answers to three questions: Did the Romanian authorities plan the mass murders in advance? How many Jews were killed in Transnistria? What caused the terror and hatred of the Romanians against the Jews when they had lived in that region for hundreds of years?

1257. Spiegel, Isaiah. **Ghetto Kingdom: Tales of the Lodz Ghetto, David H. Hirsch, and Roslyn Hirsch**. xxvii, 128p. *Jewish Lives*. Evanston, Ill.: Northwestern University Press, 1998. Includes bibliographical references.

Isaiah Spiegel was born in Lodz and survived the ghetto there and Auschwitz. His family were all victims of the Holocaust. The stories collected here were written in the Lodz ghetto and later revised. "In using his creative powers to transform the suffering and death of his people into stories that preserve their memory, Spiegel succeeds in affirming the humanity and dignity the Germans were so intent on destroying."

1258. Tuszynska, Agata. **Lost Landscapes: In Search of Isaac Bashevis Singer and the Jews of Poland**. 192p. New York: William Morrow, 1998.

Agata Tuszynska was born and raised in Poland. Yet Polish Jewry held no place in the country she knew. In this book she tries to find the Poland Isaac Bashevis Singer described in his many books by retracing his life.

1259. Weissbrod, Abraham. **Death of a Shtetl**. v, 129p., [21] p. of plates: illus. New York: L. Milch, 1995.

This book first appeared in Yiddish in 1948. This English translation is the work of another survivor from the same town. *Death of a Shtetl* describes the destruction of the Jewish population of a small town through personal narratives in Eastern Galicia during World War II. The Jews of this town were either slaughtered or sent to death camps. Few survived. This book is the work of those who did. "We join in Abraham Weissbrod's desire that this book serve as a memorial to the Jewish victims who perished in and near Skalat and also as a legacy to our children, grandchildren, and to future generations who must undertake the difficult task of educating themselves about this tragic period in our long history" (p. ii).

1260. **In the Shadow of the Swastika: A Jewish Resistor's Story**. Edited by Hermann Wygoda. xvi, 167p.: illus. Urbana: University of Illinois Press, 1998. Includes index.

Hermann Wygoda is a Polish Jew whose parents, siblings, and son were murdered in the gas chambers of the Nazi concentration camps. He ended up commanding an Italian partisan unit. As Michael Berenbaum, who writes the foreword to his book, states: "Wygoda is unusually dispassionate. There is little room for melancholy within this work, for moments of sentimentality. He is precise in his observations of himself and others. He is unusually candid about the luck that led to his survival and keen in his understanding of the skills that permitted him to emerge" (p. vii).

The Society, Sociology

1261. **Freedom for Publishing: Publishing for Freedom. The Central and East European Publishing Project**. Edited by Timothy Garton Ash. 201p. Budapest, Hungary; New York: Central European University Press, 1995. Includes bibliographical references.

This book tracks the brief history of the CEEPP, Central and East European Publishing Project. The volume begins with Timothy Garton Ash's personal account of the work of the project. Elizabeth Winter has contributed a catalog of the activities of the CEEPP. Richard Davy contributed an essay on the state of publishing in the Czech Republic, Slovakia, Poland, and Hungary.

1262. Couroucli, Maria. **The Balkans, Ethnic and Cultural Crossroads: Educational and Cultural Aspects**. 87p. Germany: Council for Cultural Co-operation (CDCC), 1997. Published also in French as: *Les Balkans, carrefour d'ethnies et de cultures: les aspects éducatifs et culturels*.

This is a report of a workshop held in Sofia in May 1995. It brought together 15 European experts, two members of the Council of Europe secretariat, and about 50 Bulgarians. "The aim of the workshop was to provide information, and draw the attention of teachers and teacher trainers to the problem of re-emerging nationalism, racism and xenophobia in Europe. It proposed to do so by analyzing these issues within the historical context of the Balkans, a typical European multicultural area" (p. 9). The volume offers a summary of the debates along four themes and papers presented at the workshop.

1263. Ivo Banac. **National Character and National Ideology in Interwar Eastern Europe**. xxvi, 254p. New Haven, Conn.: Yale Center for International and Area Studies, 1995. "Articles . . . read and discussed at the International Conference on National Character and National Ideology in Interwar Eastern Europe, which was convened at the Inter-University Center of Post-Graduate Studies in Dubrovnik, Croatia, from May 31 to June 4, 1989"—p. xi. Includes bibliographical references.

"On a global scale, the sentiment of national belonging is among the most potent of social forces, and it has been so for at least two centuries. Political action taken in the name of national liberation or national development has been responsible for secessions, wars both internal and international, the breakup of multinational empires, movements of decolonization, increased prosperity for some once-oppressed national groups, and new oppression for other groups." The contributors to this volume come from North America and Western and Eastern Europe. Individual essays are devoted to Poland, Czechoslovakia, Hungary, Romania, Croatia, Bulgaria, and Macedonia.

1264.   Langman, Juliet, and László Kürti. **Beyond Borders: Remaking Cultural Identities in the New East and Central Europe.** vii, 180p.: illus. Boulder, Colo.: Westview Press, 1997. Includes index.

These case studies present analyzes of the ethno-political movements currently existing in east-central Europe. The authors recognize that these movements are "socially constituted, contested, and negotiated as well as historically bounded in the arena of international geopolitics." Individual case studies concentrate on Poland, Moldova, Bulgaria, Albania, Macedonia, Hungary, and Austria.

1265.   **The Reformation in Eastern and Central Europe.** Edited by Karin Maag. xi, 235p.: illus., maps. *St. Andrews Studies in Reformation History.* Aldershot, Eng.: Scholar Press, 1997. Includes bibliographical references and index.

The 13 papers in this volume were originally presented at a conference at St. Andrews in April 1995. They cover a wide range of topics relevant to understanding the reformation in Eastern and Central Europe. Included are papers covering protestant literature in Bohemian private libraries, the writing of national history, pre-Reformation changes in Hungary at the end of the 15th century, Calvinism and estate liberation movements in Bohemia and Hungary, mural paintings, ethnicity and religious identity, the image controversy in negotiations between Protestant theologians and Eastern Orthodox churches, church building and discipline, morals courts, and others.

1266.   **Gender Politics and Post-Communism: Reflections from Eastern Europe and the Former Soviet Union.** Edited by Magda Mueller and Nanette Funk. x, 349p.: illus. *Thinking Gender.* New York: Routledge, 1993. Includes bibliographical references and index.

"This collection is a joint venture of women from post-communist countries and Western feminists. The essays, mainly by post-communist women, discuss the gender politics of the turbulent transformation to post-communism and help to make sense of the transformation as a whole" (p. 1). The essays are intended to clarify for Westerners the position of women in Eastern Europe, thereby avoiding divisiveness between feminists internationally. The essays are grouped by country. The contributors represent women from a variety of professional groups: academics, politicians, and writers.

1267. Ramet, Sabrina P. **Social Currents in Eastern Europe: The Sources and Consequences of the Great Transformation.** 2nd ed. xvi, 598p. Durham, N.C.: Duke University Press, 1995. Includes bibliographical references and index.

This is a second expanded edition of Sabrina Petra Ramet's study of the social changes in Eastern Europe as they move from their communist-dominated past. "My idea in writing this book was that diverse social currents (mainly ethnic, religious, trade unionist, civic, feminist, musical-cultural, and youth) do not exist in isolation; on the contrary they overlap, interact, and often follow parallel lines of development" (p. xi). Ramet seeks in this book to examine the interrelationships between these cultural elements and to demonstrate how social changes create challenges for political authorities. This new edition contains five new chapters and two other chapters have been expanded. The book is organized into six sections: "Introduction"; "Dissent and Parallel Society in the 1980s"; "Religious and Ethnic Currents"; "A New Generation"; "Collapse of the Old Order"; and "Building New Systems." Several appendixes include data from public opinion polls.

1268. **Ana's Land: Sisterhood in Eastern Europe.** Edited by Tanya Renne. xi, 240p. Boulder, Colo.: Westview Press, 1997. Includes bibliographical references.

This interesting collection of articles explores the various facets of feminism in major countries of Eastern Europe. The countries covered are: Poland, Slovakia and the Czech Republic, Hungary, Romania, Bulgaria, Serbia, Croatia, and Slovenia. Each of the essays is written by women from those countries. The content of the volume is best described thus: "The ways in which the women in each Eastern European country negotiate their politics and projects reveal the flavor of feminism and its acceptance in their societies. The situation of women in each country appears similar, yet the situation of feminism and feminist-friendly concepts varies greatly. There is a clear spectrum in the region of feminism and progress in putting forward women's concerns.

1269. Scott-Stokes, Natascha. **The Amber Trail: A Journey of Discovery by Bicycle from the Baltic Sea to the Aegean.** viii, 199p.: maps. London: Weidenfeld & Nicolson, 1993. Includes bibliographical references (pp. 197-99).

Natascha Scott-Stokes describes her encounters with East Europeans as she travels by bicycle through Poland, Czecho-Slovakia, Hungary, Serbia, and Macedonia. She uses the ancient amber trade route as the path for her journey.

1270. Splichal, Slavko. **Media Beyond Socialism: Theory and Practice in East-Central Europe.** xiv, 177p. *International Communication and Popular Culture.* Boulder, Colo.: Westview Press, 1994. Includes bibliographical references (pp. 153-63) and index.

"This book offers some theoretical insight and empirical examination of present changes to help understand media controversies arising from recent political economic developments" (p. xi). The five chapters in this book provide a thorough examination of the subject. Splichal begins with an overview of the subject. Chapter 2 investigates the effect democratization has had on the media in east-central Europe. Chapter 3 focuses on privatization and the media in the region. Chapter 4 examines the state's reaction to privatization and its attempts to maintain its control on the media. In the final chapter the author attempts to look at what may be ahead for the media. Slavko Splichal is a professor of communication science and the sociology of information processes at the University of Ljubljana in Slovenia.

The Arts and Culture

1271. **The Magical and Aesthetic in the Folklore of Balkan Slavs: Papers of an International Conference.** Edited by Dejan Ajdačić. 171p.: illus. Belgrade: Library Vuk Karadžić, 1994. Includes bibliographical references.

This volume compiles the papers delivered at the conference "The Magical and Aesthetic in the Folklore of Balkan Slavs." The conference was held in October 1993. The papers cover an array of topics from animals in folk magic to imagery in legends. Contributors include Nikos Chausidis, Ljubinko Radenković, Boris Putilov, Mirjana Detelić, Hatidža Krnjević, Oxana Mikitenko, Albena Georgieva, Violeta Piruze-Tasevska, Dejan Ajdačić, Biljana Sikimić, Plamen Bochkov, Viktor Gusev, Dragoslâv Dević, Oliviera Vasić, Vasilka Kuzmanova, Jasminka Dokmanović, Lyubomir Mikov, Naum Tselakovski, Iveta Todorova Pirgova, Milena Benovska S'bkova, Eugenia Mitseva, and Radost Ivanova.

1272. **Five Filmmakers: Tarkovsky, Forman, Polanski, Szabó, Makavejev.** Edited by Daniel J. Goulding. xi, 289p.: illus. Bloomington: Indiana University Press, 1994. Filmography (pp. [272]-280). Includes bibliographical references (pp. [264]-271) and index.

The contributors to this book are all writing about filmmakers who began their careers in Eastern Europe. Some of these filmmakers have since come to the West. Others have frequently worked in collaboration with Western film companies. "Each of these filmmakers, in his own unique way, has challenged the ideological and cultural boundaries that once separated East from West, and has helped to open the way for a newer generation of talented filmmakers from former East-bloc countries who wish to participate (and are participating) in growing numbers of cross-cultural film productions" (p. vii). Each of the five chapters is devoted to one filmmaker. A filmography is included for each. The contributors are Vida T. Johnson, Graham Petrie, Peter Hames, Herbert Eagle, David Paul, and Daniel Goulding.

1273. Hanak, Peter. **The Garden and the Workshop: Essays on the Cultural History of Vienna and Budapest.** Budapest, Hungary: Europa Institut, 1998. Includes bibliographical references (pp. [213]-240) and index.

The essays in this volume are dedicated to Peter Hanak, noted Hungarian historian and innovator of Hungarian historiography. Most of the essays, by former colleagues, focus on Hungarian history and culture.

1274. Moravánszky, Ákos. **Competing Visions: Aesthetic Invention and Social Imagination in Central European Architecture, 1867-1918**. xv, 508p., [16] p. of plates: illus. (some col.). Cambridge, Mass.: MIT Press, 1998. Includes bibliographical references and index.

Ákos Moravánszky has spent many years studying patterns and styles in Central European architecture. "The structure of this book reflects my intention to set architectural development against its cultural background. Since it is not a historical survey, it does not tell a chronological story" (p. xi). Each chapter examines a different aspect of the cultural environment in which architecture of the late Hapsburg era developed. Moravánszky discusses such themes as the role of the city, art nouveau, the search for a national style, and social reform. The book is lavishly illustrated.

Science and Technology

1275. **Controlling Pollution in Transition Economies: Theories and Methods**. Edited by Randall Bluffstone. xxiv, 279p. *New Horizons in Environmental Economics*. Lyme, N.H.: Edward Elgar, 1997. Includes bibliographical references and index.

The environmental offenses of the Soviet system have become well known since the downfall of that empire. Much improvement has taken place in Eastern Europe as emerging economies begin to take shape. Economists have discussed the need for the integration of more cost-effective environmental policies with existing structures suggesting a variety of instruments like the pollution charge. "A major goal of this book is to document the emerging experience to integrate this instrument, which often existed but worked ineffectively under communism, into revised regulatory structures" (pp. xvii-xviii). This collection of essays includes contributions by scholars from all over Eastern Europe.

1276. **The Technology of Transition: Science and Technology Policies for Transition Countries**. Edited by David A. Dyker. viii, 292p. Budapest, Hungary; New York: Central European University Press, 1997. Includes index.

This is an economic analysis of the difficulties facing the East European nations in their attempt to revitalize their technology sectors as they make the transition to market economies. "Dyker and his contributors, by contrast, argue that macroeconomic balance will not—by itself—produce the innovations and technological dynamism necessary for sustained growth in East European economies" (back cover). The essays are divided into four sections: "Setting the Scene," "Transferring the Technology," "Building the Institutions," and "Technology Transfer and International Trade."

1277. **The Environmental Challenge for Central European Economies in Transition**. Edited by Bedrich Moldan and Jurg Klarer. 304p. Chichester, Eng.; New York; Weinheim; Brisbane; Singapore; Toronto: John Wiley, 1997. Includes bibliographical references and index.

From over 40 years of communist rule, the countries of Eastern Europe had inherited some of the worst environmental problems in the world. After six years of transition had been completed, the contributors to this volume assessed their progress in environmental protection in the context of this dynamically changing economic, political, and social arena. After a regional overview in Chapter 1, the book devotes separate chapters to Bulgaria, the Czech Republic, Hungary, Latvia, Poland, and the Slovak republic.

The Downfall of Communism

1278. Beyme, Klaus von. **Transition to Democracy in Eastern Europe**. viii, 186p.: illus. London: Macmillan in association with International Political Science Association, 1997. Includes bibliographical references (pp. 170-84) and index.

The author explores various theoretical approaches to democratization in Eastern Europe and the factors that lay at the base of such theories. These factors include civil society, nationalism, cooperation of old and new elites in post-communist systems, the transformation of a planning system to a market system, institution building, political parties, and political culture in general.

1279. **Environmental Security and Quality After Communism: Eastern Europe and the Soviet Successor States**. Edited by Joan DeBardelebeen and John Hannigan. vi, 188p. Boulder, Colo.: Westview Press, 1995. Includes bibliographical references and index.

It has been known in the West for some time that Eastern Europe and the Soviet Union were on the brink of an environmental disaster. The environmental crisis in the region is bound to affect the international community either through the creation of regional instability or the effects of environmental accidents. "The chapters in this volume explore the linkages between environmental quality and security in the countries of the former Soviet bloc. Based on papers presented at a conference at Carleton University (Ottawa) in February 1993, the contributions have been updated to reflect development through the end of 1993" (p. 5). The first section of the book examines direct connections between environmental quality and security. Later essays look at indirect connections. The volume includes a glossary of acronyms and terms.

1280. Gianaris, Nicholas V. **Geopolitical and Economic Changes in the Balkan Countries**. xii, 227p.: illus. Westport, Conn.: Praeger, 1996. Includes bibliographical references (pp. [205]-213) and index.

Gianaris examines "the historical background and the recent economic and political changes in the troubled Balkan countries from the standpoint of ethnic conflicts, developmental trends, and potential cooperation among themselves, as well as with the European Union" (p. xii). Individual chapters are devoted to Greece, Turkey, the former Yugoslavia, Albania, Bulgaria, and Romania.

1281.   Hupchick, Dennis P. **Conflict and Chaos in Eastern Europe**. 1st ed. xi, 322p.: maps. New York: St. Martin's Press, 1995. Includes bibliographical references (pp. [303]-305) and index.

Dennis Hupchick's essays in this volume examine the dramatic events in Eastern Europe in the late 1980s and early 1990s. This volume is a sequel to the author's earlier volume, *Culture and History in Eastern Europe*. In that work, Hupchick established a conceptual framework for the analysis of the collapse of the Soviet regime. Here the author uses case studies to expand on his earlier work. He discusses the way marriage has been affected since the downfall of the Soviet regime. He also looks at the problems in Transylvania, Macedonia, and Bosnia.

1282.   **Between Disintegration and Reintegration: Former Socialist Countries and the World Since 1989**. Edited by Takayuki Ito and Shinichiro Tabat. v, 444p. Sapporo, Japan: Slavic Research Center, Hokkaido University, 1994. In English and Russian. Includes bibliographical references.

This volume collects some of the papers given at an international symposium held in Sapporo, Japan, September 2-3, 1993. The title of the symposium was "International Reintegration of the Former Soviet and East European Countries." The essays are divided into six sections entitled: "Getting Out of Communism"; "Russia and the CIS: Continuing Disintegration or New Integration?"; "The Russian Economy: Reformed or Betrayed?"; Yugoslav Entanglements"; "East Asia Facing the Soviet Collapse"; and "Emerging Security Framework in Europe."

1283.   Klein, Patricia. **Struggling with the Communist Legacy: Studies of Yugoslavia, Romania, Poland and Czechoslovakia**. xiii, 256p.: illus., maps. Boulder, Colo.: East European Monographs; New York: Distributed by Columbia University Press, 1998.

"The papers in this volume focus on the transitions taking place in Eastern Europe as a result of the collapse of communism. . . . The crises and chaos that resulted from this abrupt change from a stable communist society form the theme of the book" (p. xi). The essays are divided into three sections: "The Making of Yugoslavia's Successor States"; "The Balkan States"; and "Other Post-Communist Countries." Numerous maps and charts are included.

1284.   Lane, David Stuart. **The Rise and Fall of State Socialism: Industrial Society and the Socialist State**. viii, 233p.: illus., maps. Cambridge, Eng.: Polity Press, 1996. Includes bibliographical references (pp. [203]-225) and index.

"The objective of this book is to set in perspective the socialist project which began with the Russian Revolution of October 1917 and culminated with the dissolution of the USSR in December 1991" (p. 4). David Lane examines the rise of socialism in Russia, Eastern Europe, China, and Cuba. He also looks at its decline in these regions. He defines four phases of development in communist States: seizure of power, development, reform, and collapse. For each geographic region he examines the evolution of socialism within the context of these four phases.

1285. Lendvai, Paul. **Blacklisted: A Journalist's Life in Central Europe**. xvi, 213p., [8] p. of plates: ports. London: I. B. Tauris, 1998. Translation of: *Auf schwarzen Listen*. Includes index.

This fascinating volume is the author's memoir of his youth in Hungary, and his eventual emigration to Vienna and life as a journalist. The memoir is in three parts. The first covers his imprisonment, trial, and experiences in communist Hungary prior to 1956 and his emigration to Vienna. Part 2 is concerned with his life in Vienna and his new perspective on Hungary and the cold war. The third part is devoted to his views and experiences as a journalist from the late 1970s through the early 1990s. His impressions of the fall of communism are particularly noteworthy.

1286. Quinn, Frederick. **Democracy at Dawn: Notes from Poland and Points East**. 1st ed. xxi, 250p.: illus. *Eastern European Studies*, no. 5. College Station: Texas A&M University Press, 1998. Includes index.

Frederick Quinn was working for the Office of Democratic Institutions and Human Rights in Warsaw when he wrote this book. His purpose is to present the Western reader with a more realistic view of life in the changing societies of Eastern Europe. "Mr. Quinn is not a sociologist, yet in his book performs an important prescriptive function that most sociologists no longer perform. He gives us concrete facts, insights into 'Habits of the Heart'; and in general, an empathetic understanding of some of the people in formerly communist nations from Poland to Romania, Moldova, Ukraine, and Kazakhstan, to name a few" (p. xiii).

1287. Ramet, Sabrina P. **Nihil Obstat: Religion, Politics, and Social Change in East-Central Europe and Russia**. xi, 424p. Durham, N.C.: Duke University Press, 1998. Includes index.

Drawing on interview research in Germany, Austria, Slovenia, Croatia, Bosnia, Serbia, and Macedonia and published sources in almost all Slavic languages, Sabrina Ramet examines the relationship between religion and politics in east-central Europe in the late 20th century. "Sabrina P. Ramet discusses development as far back as the eleventh century to explain the patterns that have evolved to show how they still affect contemporary interecclesiastical relations as well as relations among church, state and society" (back cover). The five parts of the book begin with an overview of the region. In the next three sections Ramet looks at various areas in the region, starting with the north and Germany, Poland, Czechoslovakia, and Hungary. She then turns to the Balkans and the former Soviet Union. The last part focuses on a discussion of post-communist trends in the region.

Albania

1288. Andrews, Mary Catherine, and Gulhan Ovalioglu. **Albania and the World Bank: Building the Future**. iii, 88p. Washington, D.C.: The World Bank, 1994. Color map on lining paper.
This brief study describes the projects initiated by the World Bank and the Albanian government as they set about the task of rebuilding the Albanian economy. The book is divided into chapters covering specific sectors of the economy. Each has been targeted with a particular project to revitalize the economy. These projects are focused on the infrastructure, agriculture, health services, housing, and the private sector.

1289. Biberaj, Elez. **Albania in Transition**. xvii, 377p. Boulder, Colo.: Westview Press, 1998. Includes bibliographical references.
This work examines the radical changes in Albania, primarily in politics and the economy, which have taken place during the last decade. Elez Biberaj examines the course of those changes, providing the reader with a basic historical and political context. "A basic assumption of this book is that Albania and the Albanians are not peripheral to the West; rather, strategic issues are involved" (p. 7). Working from this premise Biberaj follows the changes that have taken place, focusing on the years between 1992 and 1996. He looks at the role of the Democratic Party, economic and social changes, foreign policy, and the nationality question. He has drawn extensively on primary Albanian sources, Western publications on Albanian development, and his own interviews with officials, journalists, etc.

1290. **The Changing Shape of the Balkans**. Edited by F. W. Carter and H. T. Norris. xiii, 180p.: illus., maps. Boulder, Colo.: Westview Press, 1996. Originally published [S.l.]: UCL Press, 1995. Includes bibliographical references and index.

This is a collection of essays that issued from a seminar held at the School of Oriental and African Studies in December 1991. "The book's aim is to enlighten the reader on the more specific aspects of changes in the northern and western parts of the Balkan peninsula resulting from the break-up of Yugoslavia, a country concocted as a home for all southern Slavs after the First World War" (p. vii). The articles all center on the theme of geopolitical problems of the region. Special attention is given to the role of religion in the region, the many divisions of the area, and the divisive nature of the ethnic groups in the Balkans. Contributors include Mark Wheeler, H. T. Norris, Natasha Milanovich, C. Sorabji, John B. Allcock, George Joffe, Mladen Klemencic, Michel Foucher, George Prevelakis, and Hugh Pulton.

1291. Costa, Nicolas J. **Albania, a European Enigma**. xi, 188p. New York: Columbia University Press, 1995.

Costa traces the protracted economic and political crises that have plagued Albania since its emergence as a nation-state in 1912 through its involvement in the Yugoslav imbroglio in the early 1990s. Aside from standard documentary sources, he has also relied on interviews with Ramiz Alia, the successor to Enver Hoxha in 1985, and Abas Ermanji, former military commander of the nationalist Balli Kombetar forces.

1292. Hall, Derek. **Albania and the Albanians**. xxvi, 304p. London: Pinter, 1994. Includes bibliographical references (pp. 273-300) and index.

"This seminal reference work on Albania provides a background understanding of the evolution of Albania and the Albanian nation, with a view to better understanding its likely role in the common European home of the twenty-first century" (back cover). Derek Hall of the University of Sunderland focuses on Albania's history, natural resources, economic and cultural development, and a range of other factors. He looks at Albania's future in light of all of Albania's changing history. An appendix lists alternative place-names.

1293. Human Rights Watch. **Human Rights in Post-Communist Albania**. vii, 156p. New York: Human Rights Watch, 1996. "This report was researched and written by Fred Abrahams"—p. [iv].

Like similar volumes issued by Human Rights Watch, this one provides a comprehensive overview of the human rights situation in the focus country. After an introduction and set of recommendations to the government of Albania, it gives a historical background and description of the legal system. It then details specific areas of concern. For Albania these are accountability and impunity, political participation and the electoral process, freedom of expression in the media, ill-treatment, deaths in custody and arbitrary arrests, minority rights, the rights of women, the rights of homosexuals, U.S. government policy, European policy, and a concluding chapter. Three appendixes provide translations of their law on genocide, law on the verification of moral character, and law on the press.

1294. Hutchings, Raymond. **Historical Dictionary of Albania**. xvi, 275p.: maps. *European Historical Dictionaries*, no. 12. Lanham, Md.: Scarecrow Press, 1996. Includes bibliography (pp. 261-75).

This comprehensive historical dictionary includes more than strictly historical terms. It has biographical, ethnographic, geographical, political, diplomatic, and economic entries relating to Albania. It should be considered a first source for ready reference for this country.

1295. Jacques, Edwin E. **The Albanians: An Ethnic History from Prehistoric Times to the Present**. xviii, 730p. Jefferson, N.C.: McFarland, 1995. Includes bibliographical references and index.

Edwin Jacques attempts to fill a gap in the Western literature on the people of Albania. There has long been little information on the Albanians and their history. This volume begins with the appearance of the Albanians in Western Europe and traces their history to 1992. Jacques has directed his work at scholarly and general audiences alike. It has an extensively indexed map to assist the uninitiated reader.

1296. Lani, R., et al. **My Albania: Ground Zero**. Edited by Bob Brewer. Translated by Ilir Ikonomi. 88p.: illus. New York: Lion of Tepelena Press, 1992. Translated from Albanian.

This is a collection of material drawn from newspapers, journals, archival materials, and a variety of other sources. "The pieces included here offer a roadmap that reveals how internal and external forces coalesced to move Albania from Ceausescu's death in 1989 to the free elections of March 1992. But they do more than merely chronicle events. The reports inform with an emotional power deriving from their eyewitness immediacy" (p. 2). The short volume is divided into parts: articles, photo essays, cartoon portfolio, full text interviews, and iconography.

1297. Orel, Vladimir. **Albanian Etymological Dictionary**. xlii, 670p. Boston; Leiden, Netherlands: Koninklijke Brill nv., 1998. Includes indexes.

Vladimir Orel's *Albanian Etymological Dictionary* is the result of 20 years of research. While drawing on the works of Gustav Myer, Eqrem Labej, Norbert Jokl, Max Vasmer, and Eric Hamp, the author had added many new explanations based on his research of Balkan etymology. The introduction provides the user with a short history of Albanian historical phonetics. Each entry includes the meaning of the term along with this etymology. The extensive bibliography and indexes will be of interest to the serious student of linguistics. There are over 3,000 entries.

1298. Post, Susan E. Pritchett. **Women in Modern Albania: Firsthand Accounts of Culture and Conditions from over 200 Interviews**. ix, 302p. Jefferson, N.C.: McFarland, 1998. Includes index.

This is not a scientific sociological analysis of women in Albania. It is rather a collection of the stories of several women of contemporary Albania told in their own words. The compiler/author found herself in Albania in 1993. She had traveled there with her husband who had been transferred by his business to this tiny European country. Post was extremely interested in the country and its culture. In particular, she sought to understand the conditions under which women lived in Albania. To investigate this topic she interviewed a number of women. While there was no scientific selection process, she did try to identify women of roughly the same socioeconomic level, political orientation, geographical location, and with the same religious background. The book is divided into sections that begin with an overview of a topic such as living conditions, urban and rural, and this is followed by a number of interviews focusing on the same topic. Post looks at such factors as age and common lifestyles and careers.

1299.   Sherer, Stan. **Long Life to Your Children!: A Portrait of High Albania**. 230p.: illus., maps. Amherst: University of Massachusetts Press, 1997. Includes bibliographical references.

The writers spent three months in High Albania, a section of the country that includes the city of Shkoder. They wanted to "understand and explain how the various components of this society viewed their present lives and the future at this crucial time in its history" (p. 7). The result of their investigation is a series of personal vignettes, narrated by the inhabitants themselves. The volume is richly illustrated with black-and-white photographs of the residents of Shkoder and its surrounding villages.

1300.   Sugarman, Jane C. **Engendering Song: Singing and Subjectivity at Prespa Albanian Weddings**. xix, 395p.: illus., maps; music; 1 sound disc (digital; 4 3/4 in.). *Chicago Studies in Ethnomusicology*. Chicago: University of Chicago Press, 1997. Includes bibliographical references and index.

This is a formal study of weddings and singing in Albania. The author has centered the work around several observations made during her fieldwork. Primary among these was that song and music held a unique and central place in the life of Albanians. In this ethnomusicological study the author draws on research done in Albania and in Canada. The book includes a discography of South Albanian music.

1301.   Vickers, Miranda, and James Pettifer. **Albania: From Anarchy to a Balkan Identity**. x, 324p.: maps. New York: New York University Press, 1997. Includes bibliography (pp. 307-8).

This book is based on research carried out both in Britain and in Albania, where a large number of those involved in the events described have been interviewed. After a brief introduction, it begins with the crisis of the one-party state after the death of Enver Hoxha and covers the events through the May 1996 elections. It also includes seven appendixes that provide additional information relevant to the events described.

1302. Zickel, Raymond, and Walter R. Iwaskiw. **Albania: A Country Study**. 2nd ed. xxxviii, 288p. *Area Handbook series*, DA Pam; 550-98. Washington, D.C.: Library of Congress, Federal Research Division, 1994. Includes bibliography (pp. 251-60) and index.

Like all volumes in this excellent series, this one devoted to Albania contains a voluminous amount of information presented in an easy-to-read format. Individual chapters include historical setting, the society and its environment, the economy, government and politics, and national security.

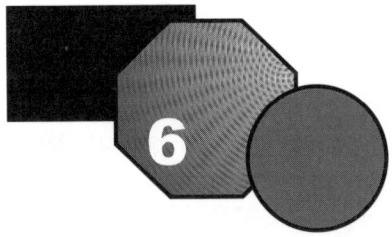

Bulgaria

History

1303. Bar-Zohar, Michael. **Beyond Hitler's Grasp: The Heroic Rescue of Bulgaria's Jews**. 1st ed. xiii, 298p. Holbrook, Mass.: Adams Media Corporation, 1998. Includes bibliographical references and index.
This book traces the escape of Bulgarian Jews from Hitler's ultimate solution.

1304. Bozhkov, Atanas. **Bulgarian Contributions to European Civilization**. 421p.: illus. (some col.). Sofia: Bulvest 2000, 1994. Translated from the Bulgarian. Includes bibliographical references.
In this monumental work, art historian Bozhkov attempts a synthesis of much of his previous work. Here he shows the contributions of Bulgarian art and culture to European civilization from the Middle Ages to the present day. In doing this he also makes the reader aware of contemporary Bulgarian artists living abroad. He not only traces artistic motifs, but also compares works of art, ideas, and symbols in his quest to present as full a picture as possible of Bulgarian culture.

1305. Crampton, R. J. **A Concise History of Bulgaria**. xv, 259p.: illus., maps. *Cambridge Concise Histories*. Cambridge, Eng.: Cambridge University Press, 1997. Includes bibliographical references (pp. [248]-251) and index.
"This book provides a general introduction to the history of Bulgaria and the Bulgarians. The text and illustrations trace the rich and dramatic story from the days when Bulgaria was the center of a powerful mediaeval empire, through the long centuries of Ottoman rule, to the cultural renaissance in the nineteenth century and the political upheavals of our own century" (frontispiece).

1306. Deirez, Raymond. **Historical Dictionary of Bulgaria**. lvii, 466p. *European Historical Dictionaries*, no. 16. Lanham, Md.: Scarecrow Press, 1997. Includes bibliography.

Raymond Deirez has studied many aspects of Bulgarian culture and history. His early research included Slavonic philology, Bulgarian literature, and history. Later he obtained his Ph.D. by writing on Grigor Purlichev and the origin and evolution of national consciousness in the Balkans. He has drawn on all areas of his expertise to produce this excellent *Historical Dictionary of Bulgaria*. As with the other volumes of the *European Historical Dictionaries* series, this 19th volume is divided into three different sections: a chronology, dictionary, and bibliography.

The chronology is very detailed and is divided into major historical and political periods beginning with "Antiquity (Before 618 A.D.)." The remaining sections designate political periods of Bulgaria's history: The First Bulgarian Empire, Byzantine Rule, Second Bulgarian Empire, Ottoman Rule, National Awakening, Kingdom of Bulgaria, Communist Rule, and the Post Communist Period. This is followed by a list of Bulgaria's rulers from A.D. 641 to the present. There is also a list of the names of all prime ministers from 1879 to the present.

The dictionary selection begins with a general encyclopedic overview of Bulgaria covering geography, climate, resources, population, state, and history. The dictionary entries, as in other volumes, include general topics, such as education, ethnic minorities, and demography as well as entries specific to Bulgarian history and culture. Within each entry, key terms are printed in boldface. Entries do not include bibliographies. However, entries on writers list major works, giving both their Bulgarian titles and the English translation.

The bibliography is 100 pages long and is divided by subject. It begins with a bibliographic essay referring the reader to other resources. The bibliography includes books and articles. This is a valuable resource for anyone seeking information on Bulgarian history.

1307. Hall, Richard C. **Bulgaria's Road to the First World War**. 374p. *East European Monographs*, 460. Boulder, Colo.: East European Monographs; New York: Distributed by Columbia University Press, 1996. Includes bibliographical references.

Richard Hall examines national aspirations that developed in Bulgaria in the late 19th and early 20th centuries. The author considers the effect national unity in Bulgaria had on neighboring Balkan states. Hall takes a chronological approach to his study. He does focus on the role of key individuals such as Ivan Geshov and Stoyan Danev as well as Tsar Ferdinand. The book's extensive bibliography is divided into sections according to the type of publications and is further subdivided by country.

1308. Marazov, Ivan, Alexander Fol, Margarita Tacheva-Khitova, and Ivan Venedikov. **Ancient Gold: The Wealth of the Thracians: Treasures from the Republic of Bulgaria**. 256p. New York: Harry N. Abrams, 1998. Catalog accompanying a traveling exhibition opened in Feb. 1998. Includes bibliographical references (pp. 246-49) and index.

This exhibition catalog of ancient Thracian treasures toured the United States in 1997. The artifacts depicted here came from the peoples who inhabited the central part of the Balkan Peninsula. Each of the sections is written by an expert in the field and includes color photographs of the monuments exhibited. Individual chapters focus on Thrace and the Thracians; Between Ares and Orpheus: Myth, Kingship, and Art in Ancient Thrace; Thracian Royal Tombs; and the Thracian Cosmos. This mini-history of Thracian artistic treasures is then followed by the exhibition catalog.

1309. Pundeff, Marin V. **Bulgaria in American Perspective: Political and Cultural Issues**. 334p. *East European Monographs*, 398. Boulder, Colo.: East European Monographs; New York: Distributed by Columbia University Press, 1994. Includes bibliographical references.

This volume is essentially a group of collected essays by the author on the history of Bulgaria and the contemporary condition of Bulgarian culture and politics. They deal with Bulgarian nationalism, Bulgarian-American relations, Bulgarian historiography, and Bulgaria's political evolution since 1879.

1310. Thompson, E. P. **Beyond the Frontier: The Politics of a Failed Mission, Bulgaria 1944**. 111p.: map. Stanford, Calif.: Stanford University Press, 1997. Includes bibliographical references.

E. P. Thompson gave a series of lectures at Stanford University in 1981. These focused on an unusual subject for Thompson, a historian of the 19th century. He chose as his topic the partisan effort in Bulgaria during World War II. Thompson had a personal interest in this subject as his brother had been killed while assisting the partisans as part of his assignment working for Churchill's Special Operations Executive. Unfortunately, Thompson never finished his work on those lectures. What is published here is based on his notes and on the correspondence between E. P. Thompson and his brother during the war. The book includes a brief bibliography.

1311. **Voices from the Gulag: Life and Death in Communist Bulgaria**. Edited by Tzvetan Todorov. Translated by Robert Zaretsky. viii, 178p. University Park: Pennsylvania State University Press, 1999. Includes bibliographical references and index.

In 1990, a Bulgarian documentary aired that told the brutal story of Bulgaria's prison camps under Todor Zhivkov. The film used a number of interviews with prisoners and those who worked in the camps. "The present work is the result of an initiative taken in Sofia by the literary agency Medium. They placed at my disposal the transcript of the film, along with several published works that treat the subject of the concentration camps" (p. xiii). The author has divided the interviews into three groups: "The Inmates," "The Other Side," and "Among the Families." He begins with an introductory essay and historical summary. This book was originally published in France in 1992 and is here presented in a translation by Robert Zaretsky.

Economics, Trade, and Business

1312. Bristow, John A. **The Bulgarian Economy in Transition**. xiii, 248p.: illus. *Studies of Communism in Transition*. Cheltenham, Eng.: Edward Elgar, 1996. Includes bibliographical references (pp. 235-42) and index.

Up until 1991 anglophone scholars have not paid much attention to the Bulgarian economy, preferring instead to focus on Russia, Hungary, Poland, and Czechoslovakia. Bristow describes and analyzes the economic transition process in Bulgaria. As the author states: "The emphasis is on trying to understand what is going on rather than on devising simple solutions to complex problems" (p. xii). After an introductory chapter that sets the scene, he covers liberalization and stabilization policy, recent macroeconomic developments, aspects of industry and agriculture, international economic relations, reform of financial institutions, fiscal reform, and privatization.

Language and Literature

1313. **Post-Theory, Games, and Discursive Resistance: The Bulgarian Case**. Edited by Alexander Kiossev. xxi, 190p. Albany: State University of New York Press, 1995. Includes list of contributors and index.

This collection of essays contains works by Bulgarian intellectuals that were written in the late 1980s and early 1990s. They reflect the pent-up dicer of these thinkers to interact with the rest of the world's ideas.

Government, Politics, and Law

1314. **Bulgaria at the Crossroads**. Edited by Jacques Coenen-Huther. vi, 261p. New York: Nova Science Publishers, 1996. Includes bibliographical references and index.

The main purpose of this volume "is to shed light on both the characteristics that Bulgarian society has in common with other past-totalitarian societies and the peculiarities of the Bulgarian situation" (p. 2). The individually authored articles, all by sociologists, are arranged in four parts: (1) the difficult way out of totalitarianism; (2) social change and the rise of a new political culture; (3) a multicultural society and its collective memory; and (4) problems of the transition toward a market economy.

1315. Bell, John D., ed. **Bulgaria in Transition: Politics, Economics, Society and Culture After Communism**. xii, 345p.: illus. *Eastern Europe After Communism*. Boulder, Colo.: Westview Press, 1998. Includes bibliographical references and index.

The 13 excellent articles in this volume explore the difficulties with the Bulgarian transition from communism. The articles are arranged in five broad topical areas: politics and law, the economy and the environment, ethnic and religious issues, culture, and foreign relations.

1316. Melone, Albert P. **Creating Parliamentary Government: The Transition to Democracy in Bulgaria**. xxi, 323p. *Parliaments and Legislatures series*. Columbus: Ohio State University Press, 1998. Includes bibliographical references (pp. 293-306) and index.

Melone focuses on the "fascinating story of the negotiations and struggles in the early 1990s that transformed the Bulgarian political regime from a Soviet-style puppet state to a freestanding democracy" (p. xi). He examines the process by which this democratization took place in three parts. In Part 1 he devotes four chapters to the National Roundtable talks and the agreement that eventuated for the election for the Grand National Assembly. Part 2 looks at the activities of the Grand National Assembly in adopting a new constitution and other related activities. Part 3 examines the politics of consolidation that arose in the Parliament because of interinstitutional conflict.

1317. **Bulgaria in Transition: Environmental Consequences of Political and Economic Transformation**. Edited by Krassimira Paksaleva, Philip Shapira, John Pickles, and Boian Koulov. xxi, 267p.: illus., maps. *Studies in Green Research*. Aldershot, Hants, Eng.: Ashgate, 1998. Includes index.

This is a collection of essays on the way in which Bulgaria has moved from its communist to post-communist state and the effect the transition has had on the environmental policies of the country. The essays collected here are the results of the Program on Peace and International Cooperation of the John D. and Catherine T. MacArthur Foundation that funded the collaborative project to study the effects of the political transition in Bulgaria on its environment. The essays are grouped into two parts. The first part examines the context in which the transition took place, for example, the state of the environment and environmental policy under the old regime. Part 2 focuses on restructuring the system at the local level.

1318. Zloch-Christy, Iliana. **Bulgaria in a Time of Change: Economic and Political Dimensions**. xi, 221p. Aldershot, Hants, Eng.: Avebury, 1996. Includes bibliographical references and index.

Some, but not all, of the articles appearing in this book were presented at a conference in 1994 by both American and Bulgarian scholars. The articles are arranged in four parts, reflecting the various aspects of development and transition over the past decade. The parts are: (1) Bulgarian state and society in retrospect; (2) the process of transformation after 1989; (3) transformation of the economy and legal structure; and (4) relations with the world.

The Society, Sociology

1319. Creed, Gerald. **Domesticating Revolution: From Socialist Reform to Ambivalent Transition in a Bulgarian Village**. xvi, 304p.: illus., map. University Park: Pennsylvania State University Press, 1997. Includes bibliographical references (pp. [279]-295) and index.

The Bulgarians faced many challenges in the 1940s. Not least of these was collectivization of the farms. Once accomplished, the Bulgarian rural population found some measure of security in socialist agricultural structure. It was no wonder that they faced the changes of the 1990s with some trepidation. "In *Domesticating Revolution*, Gerald Creed explains this unexpected outcome through a detailed study of economic reforms in one Bulgarian village from the beginning of collectivization in the 1940s to de-collectivization efforts in the 1990s" (back cover). The author is an anthropologist and takes an anthropological approach to his study.

1320.   Eminov, Ali. **Turkish and Other Muslim Minorities of Bulgaria**. 218p. New York: Routledge, 1997. Includes bibliographical references.

Eminov traces the effects of Bulgarian nationalism on minority policy, especially relating to Muslims from 1878 to 1989. Topics covered include the status of Islam and Muslims in Bulgaria, the major Muslim minorities in Bulgaria, the education of Turkish speakers in Bulgaria, Bulgarian, Turkish and the linguistic effects of nationality policy, and post-1989 politics and Muslim minorities.

1321.   Rice, Timothy. **May It Fill Your Soul: Experiencing Bulgarian Music**. xxv, 370p.: illus., 2 maps. Chicago: University of Chicago Press, 1994. Includes discography (p. 347), bibliographical references (pp. 349-57), and index.

In this book Timothy Rice examines the tradition of Bulgarian folk music. Aside from the history and development of the musical tradition of Bulgaria, he examines the cognitive processes associated with learning music. Rice focuses on the Varimezov family in this study. This volume comes with a compact disc. The author relies on his own experiences learning to play Bulgarian folk music and those of his teachers to gain an understanding of the knowledge necessary to play Bulgarian music.

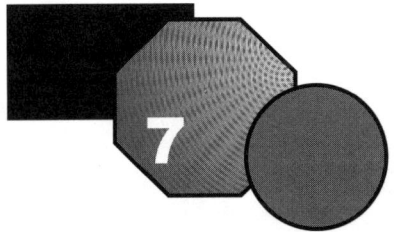

Czech and Slovak Republics

General Reference Works

1322. **Prague**. Translated by Susie Lun. 220p. Santa Barbara, Calif.: ABC-CLIO, 1996. Includes indexes.

This bibliographic guide to Prague is arranged by topic. The 533 annotated entries are arranged under the following rubrics: the city and its people; geography; guide books; travelers' accounts; prehistory and archaeology; life in Prague; history; population; language; religion; social conditions; social services; health and welfare; education; statistics; politics and government; economy; transport; science and technology; environment; literature; the arts; architecture and urban planning; food and drink; the media; and cultural institutions. A map of Prague is also included.

1323. Kirschbaum, Stanislav J. **Historical Dictionary of Slovakia**. lxxxvi, 213p. *European Historical Dictionaries*, no. 31. Lanham, Md.: Scarecrow Press, 1998. Includes bibliographical references (pp. 195-211).

This comprehensive, but handy, historical dictionary contains lots of information necessary for all aspects of historical research on Slovakia. Prior to the listing of terms and definitions, Kirschbaum has presented a chronology of events occurring on Slovakian territory and a brief (30-page) history of the country. After the section containing historical terms he includes chronologically arranged lists of rulers and other dignitaries and a substantial classified bibliography of books and articles relating to Slovakia.

1324. Kovtun, George J. **Czech and Slovak History: An American Bibliography**. xxiv, 481p.: illus. Washington, D.C.: Library of Congress, 1996. Includes bibliographical references and index.

This is the first bibliography to compile publications on Czech and Slovak history published primarily in America. The compiler used the collection of the Library of Congress for monographic selections. Articles were selected from some 70 periodical titles. The bibliography includes publications issued through 1993. George Kovtun decided to exclude the many publications on the events of the Velvet Revolution and the following developments. The volume is divided topically with a section on collections, biographies and memoirs, Jan Hus, Jan Amos Komensky, Tomas G. Masaryk, and Jews and Jewish affairs. Entries in all sections are arranged alphabetically by author or editor.

History

1325. Bednar, Zdenek F. **Where Is My Home?: A Theology of Hope As the Outcome of Despair: A Survivor of Nazism, Communism and Exile Remembers the Forces That Shaped His Faith**. xi, 340p.: illus., ports. Allison Park, Pa.: Pickwick Publications, 1998. Includes bibliographical references.

Written in the author's typical narrative theology style, this memoir is primarily a faith journey of a man who survived several despotic regimes and exile.

1326. **Prague in Black and Gold: Scenes from the Life of a European City**. Edited by Peter Demetz. 1st ed. xviii, 411p.: maps. New York: Hill & Wang, 1997. Includes bibliographical references (pp. 379-95) and index.

"I am not foolish enough to believe that I can offer a Prague history as it really happened, but I hope to counter some of the traditional narratives with other stories that do not hide my polemical intentions. I wish to sketch a few selected chapters of a paradoxical history..." (pp. xi-xii). Peter Demetz is a Professor Emeritus of Yale University born in Prague. He attempts to show the reader the varied, multiethnic history that Prague has had for the last 1,000 years.

1327. Gargett, Robert H. **Cave Bears and Modern Human Origins: The Spatial Taphonomy of Pod Hradem Cave, Czech Republic**. xx, 265p.: illus. Lanham, Md.: University Press of America, 1996. Includes bibliographical references (pp. [239]-258) and index.

Robert Gargett begins this study from the premise that premodern hominid may have been significantly, cognitively different from modern man. If this is true it might explain some of the ambiguous analysis of middle paleolithic sites previously offered. Gargett uses the site of the Pod hradem cave in the Czech Republic. Much of this study focuses on the theory and method of site analysis. There are two appendixes that present the reader with detailed data on the site.

1328. Hochman, Jiri. **Historical Dictionary of the Czech State**. xxxix, 203p.: illus., maps. *European Historical Dictionaries*, no. 23. Lanham, Md.: Scarecrow Press, 1998. Includes bibliographical references (pp. 153-80).

This handy volume "covers not only the present situation but also the times of the old Czech principality and kingdom both as a sovereign state and as a part of the Austrian, later Austro-Hungarian, Empire then Czechoslovakia, both as an independent country before World War II and then under German and Soviet domination. It also considers the basic components of Bohemia, Moravia and Ruthenia as well as Slovakia. While attention is paid primarily to history and politics, other aspects of the country, namely economic, social, religious and cultural ones, are equally worthy of note. A chronology, introduction and specific entries cover all. There are also a comprehensive bibliography and useful appendixes, including a full text of Charter 77" (p. vii).

1329. Holy, Ladislav. **The Little Czech and the Great Czech Nation: National Identity and the Post-Communist Transformation of Society**. x, 226p. *Cambridge Studies in Social and Cultural Anthropology*, 103. Cambridge, Eng.: Cambridge University Press, 1996. Includes notes, bibliography, and index.

Politics is usually not considered by anthropologists to be a part of the cultural structure of a people. It is often considered as part of the more "rational" elements of a society with a utilitarian function. Ladislav Holy analyzes politics here as a purely cultural phenomenon in order to investigate the Czech experience under the Soviets. "The aim of this book is to investigate the specific ways in which Czech cultural meanings and in particular the notion of Czech identity and the accompanying nationalist sentiments have affected life under communism, its overthrow, and the political and economic transformation of post-communist society" (p. 2). To accomplish this Holy looks at self-stereotypes, national traditions, the imaging of the nation, the political process, and nation and state in Czech culture.

1330. Iggers, Wilma. **Women of Prague: Ethnic Diversity and Social Change from the Eighteenth Century to the Present**. viii, 381p.: illus. Providence, R.I.: Berghahn Books, 1995. Includes bibliographical references (pp. [368]-373) and index.

Much has been written about Prague and its many famous residents such as Kafka. However, there is little in the literature on the women who inhabited the city. Wilma Iggers has drawn on an array of autobiographical literature to fill this gap. "I hope, as much as is possible between the covers of one book, to bring a number of women from the different ethnic groups to life, to show their everyday thoughts and concerns and how they experienced the changes that took place around them" (p. 2). Each chapter of this book is devoted to an individual and begins with an overview of the subject's life. Sources for each chapter are included at the end of the volume.

1331. Kirschbaum, Stanislav J. **A History of Slovakia: The Struggle for Survival**. 1st St. Martin's Griffin ed. xvi, 350p.: maps. New York: St. Martin's Griffin, 1996. Includes bibliographical references (pp. [321]-336) and index.

Professor Stanislav Kirschbaum has written the first popular history of Slovakia in English. Kirschbaum's training is as a political scientist. His primary interest has been in Slovak politics in Czechoslovakia. In this book, he looks at Slovak history as the struggle of the Slovaks to survive. "The story I tell is one that shows how they have individually and collectively developed and faced the challenges of invasion, foreign statehood, and in the later periods of their history, also assimilation. This struggle appears first in the social and economic development of Central Europe, later in a political conflict with state authorities" (p. ix). The book is arranged chronologically. There are several historical maps and an extensive bibliography.

1332. Klassen, John M. **Warring Maidens, Captive Wives and Hussite Queens: Women and Men at War and Peace in Late Medieval Bohemia**. xii, 291p.: illus., map. *East European Monographs*, 527. Boulder, Colo.: East European Monographs; New York: Distributed by Columbia University Press, 1999. Includes bibliographical references (pp. 271-87) and index.

John Klassen reexamines the effect of the Hussite revolution on the position of women in 15th-century Czech society. "The goal of this study was to examine all accessible aspects of Czech society and culture in the fifteenth century. In order to get as wide as possible a survey of women's words and activities, I examined the judicial proceedings, private letters and property transactions, and official records of several towns, many of which are contained in the multi-volume Archiv Česky, the fundamental pillar of Czech historical scholarship" (p. 6). After a thorough discussion of the existing literature, the author concludes with František Smahel that the Hussite movement was not able to elevate the status of women. The study is divided into four parts. The first introduces the subject and provides the context for the historiographical discussion. The second focuses on the family in Bohemia, its legal status, and its relation to the judicial system. Part 3 describes the role of women in the Hussite revolution. Part 4 looks at women in government, focusing on urban sources and those that recount the lives of noble and royal women.

1333. Komenda-Soentgerath, Olly. **In the Shadow of Prague**. Translated by Tom Beck. ix, 99p.: illus. London; Boston: Forest Books, 1996.

Many Germans were born and raised in the Czech Republic before World War II. They would grow up bilingual, an integral part of cities such as Prague. The war and Hitler's conquest of the region changed all that. The Czech were very bitter after the war and tried to drive all Germans out of Prague. Olly Komenda-Soentgerath experienced all this and describes those eventful days in this slim volume.

1334. Krejcí, Jaroslav, and Pavel Machonin. **Czechoslovakia, 1918-92: A Laboratory for Social Change**. xviii, 266p.: maps. New York: St. Martin's Press in association with St. Antony's College, Oxford, 1996. Includes bibliographical references and index.

This work is concerned with the attempt to build a composite ethnic nation and create a functioning political and economic framework. It is divided into three parts. Part 1 examines ethnopolitics and the problems of a multiethnic state and parliamentary democracy, as well as the interplay of nationalism and communism. Part 2 focuses on the economic context and the rise and fall of the socialist experiment. Part 3 concentrates on social metamorphoses and gives a history of such changes from the 1920s through 1992.

1335. Leff, Carol Skalnik. **The Czech and Slovak Republics: Nation Versus State**. xvii, 295p.: maps. *Nations of the Modern World: Europe*. Boulder, Colo.: Westview Press, 1997. Includes bibliographical references (pp. 281-82) and index.

After two introductory chapters that provide the historical context of Czechoslovakia in post-communist transition, Leff then builds a framework for understanding what she calls the triple transition of democratization, marketization, and national transformation. This transition has "reconfigured the dynamics between state and nation. . . . The book offers a valuable case study of a country coming back to Europe, but it also provides an opportunity for analyzing the influence of communism on what had been a significant interwar European state" (p. 283).

1336. Lukes, Igor. **Czechoslovakia Between Stalin and Hitler: The Diplomacy of Edvard Benes in the 1930s**. xii, 318p.: illus. New York: Oxford University Press, 1996. Includes bibliographical references (pp. 277-309) and index.

The signature event of the crisis of the 1930s was the Four-Power Agreement that was signed at Munich in September 1938. "This book deals with the European crisis of the 1930s by focusing on the hitherto neglected Czechoslovak and Soviet perspectives" (p. v).

1337. **Prague in the Shadow of the Swastika: A History of the German Occupation, 1939-1945**. Edited by C. A. MacDonald and Jan Kaplan. 215p.: illus. (some col.). London: Quartet Books, 1995. Col. maps on endpapers.

This richly photo-illustrated history of the occupation of Prague by the Nazis begins with the German invasion in 1939 and ends with the Russian liberation of Prague in 1945. The study is based on primary and secondary sources in several languages. The photographs come from private collections and the Kaplan/MacDonald Archive. The combination of text and photographs portrays the horror and terror endured by Czech citizens during the occupation.

1338. Murphy, Daniel. **Comenius: A Critical Reassessment of His Life and Work**. x, 294p. Portland, Oreg.: Irish Academic, 1995. Includes bibliographical references and index.

Jan Amos Komensky or Comenius was a 17th-century writer. Through his writings the world came to know the traditions, particularly the liberal educational traditions, of Moravian Christianity. "The present study therefore completes a trilogy, being the third in a series of works on educators who share a common liberal-religious philosophy and who, as it happens, also share a similar Slavic ancestry" (p. 3). After a brief introduction, Daniel Murphy begins with a biographical portrait of Komensky. He then examines the cultural and historical roots of his educational philosophy. In Chapter 4 he presents the "Comenian Vision of Universal Education." Chapters 5-7 examine the principles of pedagogic philosophy in Komensky's thought and his views on higher education.

1339. Ripellino, Angelo Maria. **Magic Prague**. Translated by Michael Henry Heim. vii, 333p., [32] p. of plates: illus., map, ports. London: Picador, 1995. Originally published London: Macmillan, 1994.

This is a translation of Angelo Ripellino's 1973 work. It paints a picture of Prague through the centuries, exploring its politics, culture, history, and literature.

1340. Sayer, Derek. **The Coasts of Bohemia: A Czech History**. xv, 442p.: illus., maps. Princeton, N.J.: Princeton University Press, 1998. Includes bibliographical references and index.

As Sayer states in his first chapter, "This book is about Czechs and their Czechness; a little nation, by their own estimate, of scant consequence in the councils of the great" (p. 17). Although this is a history of Bohemia, much of the focus is on culture in the lives of Czechs and the influence of this culture both within Bohemia and in Europe.

1341. Skilling, H. Gordon. **T. G. Masaryk: Against the Current, 1882-1914**. xv, 248p. University Park: Pennsylvania State University Press, 1994. Includes bibliographical references (pp. 179-222) and index.

This is not a comprehensive biography of Masaryk's life. It only covers his life up to 1914. "The book is unique in focusing attention on Masaryk as a persistent nonconformist prior to the First World War. For three decades he was an unrelenting critic of conventional wisdom, established institutions, customary practices and habits in Bohemia and in Austria-Hungary as a whole" (p. xii).

1342. Stein, Eric. **Czecho/Slovakia: Ethnic Conflict, Constitutional Fissure, Negotiated Breakup**. xxiii, 386p. Ann Arbor: University of Michigan Press, 1997. Includes bibliographical references (pp. 365-77) and index.

Eric Stein was one of those picked to help draft a new Czecho-Slovak constitution after the Velvet Revolution in 1989. This book is based on that experience. He describes and analyzes the process within the context of nationalism and ethnic conflict and uses a dramatic framework (Prologue, Acts 1-4, Epilogue) to present his findings. He proceeds chronologically, presenting the setting and actors, and takes into account the asymmetry of the Czech and Slovak state and the "threshold issues" that are present with any constitutional reform. As a concluding chapter he reviews the sources of ethnic conflict and of separation and various strategic elements of constitutional negotiations.

1343. **Bohemia in History**. Edited by Mikul'as Teich. xiv, 389p.: illus., maps. Cambridge, Eng.: Cambridge University Press, 1998. Includes bibliographical references and index.

This collection is unique among the English-language resources on the Czech Republic. All the essays were contributed by scholars working in the Czech lands today. The essays all focus on major themes in Czech history. The 18 essays cover sociopolitical themes, the arts, sciences, education, and interethnic relations among other topics. Contributors include Jan Havránek, František Kavka, Dusan Kovac, Helena Krejcova, Jan Křen, Jiri Kroupa, Robert Kvaček, Josef Maček, Vladimir Macura, Zdenek Merinsky, Jaroslav Meznik, Milan Otáhal, Josef Petráń, Lydia Petráňová, Irena Seidlerová, Jiří Sláma, František Smahel, Mikul'as Teich, Alice Teichová, Otto Urban, and Josef Válka.

1344. Trapl, Milos. **Political Catholicism and the Czechoslovak People's Party in Czechoslovakia, 1918-1938.** 151p. *East European Monographs*, 409. Boulder, Colo.: East European Monographs; New York: Distributed by Columbia University Press, 1995. Includes bibliographical references and index.

Between the two World Wars of the 20th century the Czechoslovak Republic was in a period of political stability. There have been a number of studies of this period. This volume will look at the Czech Catholic political movement. "I aimed this work especially at the characterization of Czech political Catholicism in the period of its interwar evolution and above all at its most important and prominent section, the Czechoslovak People's Party" (p. 4). This is a specialized study of a previously little explored political group.

1345. Triska, Jan F. **The Great War's Forgotten Front: A Soldier's Diary and a Son's Reflections.** xii, 182p.: illus., maps. *East European Monographs*, 500. Boulder, Colo.: East European Monographs; New York: Distributed by Columbia University Press, 1998. Includes bibliographical references (pp. 177-82).

In this powerful personal narrative, a Czech cabinetmaker relates his experiences on the Austrian side of the Austrian-Italian front during World War I. As the foreword by David Kennedy states: "At all points he attentively recorded not only the drama of combat and the accumulating signs of political decline, but also the prosaic aggravations and joys of the soldier's life from wretched weather, bad food, and ubiquitous lice to occasionally kind officers, wondrous discoveries of caches of wine, and ineffable precious visits to his wife and child" (p. xii).

Economics, Trade, and Business

1346. Dedek, Oldrich. **The Break-Up of Czechoslovakia: An In-Depth Economic Analysis**. 208p. Aldershot, Eng.; Brookfield, Vt.: Avebury, 1996. Includes bibliographical references (pp. 205-8).

This study of the breakup of Czechoslovakia looks at the history of the state and the consequences of its division. Since all the contributors to this study are economists, its focus is the economy. There are four parts to this book, the first of which is a chronology of the Czech state from 1918 to 1989. Part 2 examines the major economic and political events in Czechoslovak history after 1989. In the third part the author examines the policies adopted to minimize the trauma that arose from the implications the breakup has had for the future of the region. The book lacks an index.

1347. **Managing in Emerging Market Economies: Cases from the Czech and Slovak Republics**. Edited by Daniel S. Fogel. viii, 237p.: illus. Boulder, Colo.: Westview Press, 1994.

This set of case studies intends to describe the difficulties in managing enterprises in emerging market economies in the period 1989-1993. The focus is on the Czech and Slovak Republics. The studies are arranged in four parts: (1) the economic situation of Central and Eastern Europe; (2) managerial behavior and entrepreneurship; (3) privatization and meeting market demands; and (4) conclusion. Individual industries covered are chemicals, steel, airlines, and technology. In addition, specific management topics are also considered such as transformation management, downsizing, institution building and organizational design, unions, and total quality management.

1348. **OECD Staff: Labour Market and Social Policies in the Slovak Republic**. 176p. Paris: OECD, 1996. Includes bibliographical references. At head of title: Centre for Co-operation with the Economies in Transition. Published in French under the title: *Politiques emploi et politiques sociales en Republique Slovaque*.

This review examines labor market and social policies in the Slovak Republic. It stresses macroeconomic developments, the labor market structure and trends, long-term unemployment, social security programs and income support, and labor market policy.

1349. Pavlinek, Petr. **Economic Restructuring and Local Environmental Management in the Czech Republic**. xiv, 423p.: illus. Lewiston, N.Y.: Edwin Mellen Press, 1997. Includes bibliographical references and index.

As the Czech Republic makes the transition from a command economy to a market one, several changes invariably are taking place in the economic, political, and social spheres. Here Pavlinek investigates the "importance of geographical variability and geographical scale on the processes associated with the transition" (p. 1). By stressing the geographic scale and geographical variability associated with the transition, he hopes to contribute to a greater theoretical understanding of this complex process.

1350. **The Czech Republic and Economic Transition in Eastern Europe.** Edited by Jan Svejnar. xxvii, 434p. San Diego, Calif.: Academic Press, 1995. Includes index.

"*The Czech Republic and Economic Transition in Eastern Europe* is the first in-depth, comparative analysis of the Czech Republic's economic transition after the fall of the Communist bloc. Edited by Jan Svejnar, a principal architect of the Czech economic transformation and Economic Advisor to President Vaclav Havel, the book poses important questions about the Republic and its partners in Central and Eastern Europe. The thirty-five essayists describe the country's macroeconomic performance; its development of capital markets; the structure and performance of its industries; its unemployment, household behavior, and income distribution; and the environmental and health issues it faces" (back cover).

1351. Vecernik, Jiri. **Markets and People: The Czech Reform Experience in a Comparative Perspective.** 320p. Aldershot, Eng.; Brookfield, Mass.; Hong Kong; Singapore; Sydney: Avebury, 1996. Includes bibliographical references (pp. 273-85).

Noting that both traditional macroeconomic analyses and isolated microeconomic insights are insufficient to understand economic processes and their effects, the author takes a different tack. Here, in the case of the Czech Republic, Vecernik shows "the socio-economic transition in the Czech Republic 'from below,' i.e., as viewed by individuals and households and through differences and inequalities." After he sets up his framework for analysis in Chapter 1, he then goes on to describe the labor market and earnings, income distribution and poverty, households as consumers and capitalists, the negative effects of socialist paternalism, and economic reform and political behavior.

Government, Politics, and Law

1352. **The Battle Against Exclusion: Vol 2: Social Assistance in Belgium, the Czech Republic, the Netherlands and Norway.** 188p.: illus. Paris: Organization for Economic Co-operation and Development, 1998. Includes bibliographical references.

"This book compares the social assistance policies of Belgium, the Czech Republic, the Netherlands and Norway. Although at first sight these countries appear very different, in fact the same policy dilemmas exist in the four countries" (back cover). There are six chapters in the book giving the reader a general overview, and then turning to such topics as social policy, safety net provisions, incentives in social assistance, avoiding long-term dependence, and conclusions. There are three appendixes on the characteristics of social assistance claimants, the Czech system of social subsidies, and comparative data on net benefit rates of social assistance recipients in the four countries under review.

1353. Felak, James Ramon. **At the Price of the Republic: Hlinka's Slovak People's Party, 1929-1938**. xiv, 263p. *Pitt Series in Russian and East European Studies*, no. 20. Pittsburgh, Pa.: University of Pittsburgh Press, 1994. Includes bibliographical references (pp. 249-56) and index.

"This study examines the SPP (Slovak People's Party) in the second and final decade of the First Czechoslovak Republic. . . . The study focuses on three main interconnected issues: the SPP's strategy and tactics, its internal power struggles, and its relationship with potential allies" (pp. x-xi). The author begins the analysis in 1929, a pivotal year for the party and the government. From this point the author follows the development of the party through 1938.

1354. Goldman, Minton F. **Slovakia Since Independence: A Struggle for Democracy**. xi, 247p. Westport, Conn.: Praeger, 1999. Includes bibliographical references (pp. [225]-232).

Minton Goldman is concerned with the slow rate of democratic change in Slovakia. He is of the opinion that of all the nations in the region they have been the slowest to absorb the changes. "The book examines the political, economic, and socio-cultural problems the new Slovak state experienced as it tried to establish its national identity, develop a democratic political system, move toward a more prosperous free market economy and maintain societal unity and cohesion" (p. vii). Goldman begins by providing the context through a discussion of Czech-Slovak relations from 1918 to 1989. In his second chapter he discusses more recent developments in these relations that led to the split between the two countries in 1992. Each of the remaining chapters examines one area of Slovakia's politics, economics, society, and foreign relations. Goldman has gleaned this information from Western sources as indicated by his notes and bibliography.

1355. Havel, Vaclav. **The Art of the Impossible: Politics As Morality in Practice: Speeches and Writings, 1990-1996**. xix, 273p. New York: Alfred A. Knopf; Distributed by Random House, 1997. Previously published: New York: Alfred A. Knopf, c1997. Collection of Havel's political speeches originally published in *Toward a Civil Society*, 1994, and in various magazines. Includes index.

This selective collection of Havel's speeches covers the period from January 1, 1990, to October 4, 1996. He delivered these all over the globe and for many different audiences. Some of the more notable occasions were his address to the nation (Czechoslovakia) in 1990, to a joint session of Congress, the Oslo Conference on "The Anatomy of Hate," the Indira Gandhi prize, and the Future of Hope conference in Hiroshima.

1356. Klaus, Vaclav. **Renaissance: The Rebirth of Liberty in the Heart of Europe**. xv, 177p. Washington, D.C.: Cato Institute, 1997. Includes bibliography (p. 171) and index.

This volume includes Klaus' English-language speeches and essays, collected for the first time. Klaus was the first noncommunist finance minister and in 1992 was elected prime minister of the Czech Republic. His 29 English-language works are arranged in four parts: (1) the process of transformation; (2) the Czech experience; (3) the Czech Republic in Europe; and (4) the Czech Republic in the world.

1357. Krejcí, Oskar. **History of Elections in Bohemia and Moravia.** 425p.: illus. Boulder, Colo.: East European Monographs; New York: Distributed by Columbia University Press, 1995. Includes bibliographical references (pp. [421]-425).

The goal of this book is "to contribute to the assessment of the significance of the elections in the light of meeting the democratic ideals" (p. xv). In particular, it examines the procedural development and political significance of elections and their precursors beginning with the 9th century and the parlamentarianism of the estates and continuing with the elections in Austria (1848-1918), the First Republic (1918-1938), the Third Republic (1945-1948), and the period of bureaucratic socialism (1948-1989). In Part 2 of the book elections in the postindependence period are examined.

1358. Williams, Kieran. **The Prague Spring and Its Aftermath: Czechoslovak Politics, 1968-1970**. xiii, 270p. New York: Cambridge University Press, 1997. Includes bibliographical references (pp. 254-65) and index.

By using materials that have become available after the 1989 revolution, Williams examines the attempts at reform socialism under Dubček. He investigates several questions regarding why liberalization occurred, what the purpose of liberalization was, why did the Soviet Union intervene, and others.

Language and Literature

1359. **Czech Plays: Modern Czech Drama**. Edited by Barbra Day. xvi, 224p. London: Nick Hern Books, 1994.

The English translation of *Tomorrow!* by Václav Havel contains *Games* by Ivan Klíma, *Cat on the Rails* by Joseph Topol, and *Dog and Wolf* by Daniela Fischerova. An introductory essay sets the plays in the context of Czech theatrical and cultural history.

1360. **This Side of Reality: Modern Czech Short Stories**. ix, 230p. London: Serpent's Tail, 1996. Translated from the Czech.

The anthology of Czech literature spans the last 30 years and captures the works of a variety of writers and styles. "The centrality of the writer and of story telling as a way of mediating between society and its representations, between reality and fiction, is evident in most of the texts presented in this anthology as is the preoccupation with the very process of writing and with literary constructs and conventions" (p. viii). The authors included here are Ladislav Fuks, Vera Linhartová, Arnost Lustig, Ewald Murrer,

Ota Filip, Bohumil Hrabal, Josef Škvorecký, Jiři Gruska, Sylvie Richterová, Ivan Klíma, Jiři Kratochvil, Zuzana Brabcova, Michal Viewegh, Alexandra Berková, Michal Ajvaz, Ludvik Vaculik, and Jáchym Topol.

1361. Billington, Elisabeth. **Czech in Three Months**. 1st American ed. 284p. New York: DK Publishing, 1999.

"This course has been written for those who want to be able to use the Czech language in a more varied range of situations than the stock phrase book scenarios, 'At the Airport', 'Booking a Hotel Room', and so on: by the time you have worked through the chapter in this book, your understanding of the language should enable you to construct the sentences needed in such circumstances for yourself" (p. 5). The author has included explanatory text for grammatical terms that might be unfamiliar to the reader. Cassette recordings are available, but not required.

1362. **Allskin and Other Tales by Contemporary Czech Women**. Edited by Alexandra Büchler. 1st ed. xvii, 234p. Seattle: Women in Translation, 1998.

Much literature has come from the Czech Republic but this is the first collection of short stories by contemporary Czech women writers. Contributing authors are Daniela Fischerová, Zuzana Brabcová, Tereza Boucková, Daniela Hodrová, Alexandra Berková, Jana Červenkova, Eva Hauser, Alzbeta Serberová, Iva Pekarková, Eda Kreislerová, Lenka Prochazková, Zdena Salivarová, Zdena Tomin, Vera Linhartová, and Sylvie Richter.

1363. Eckert, Eva. **Varieties of Czech: Studies in Czech Sociolinguistics**. 285p.: illus. Amsterdam; Atlanta, Ga.: Rodopi, 1993. Includes bibliographical references.

The articles in this collection deal with the Czech language from a variety of socilinguistic perspectives. The articles are arranged in four sections: (1) language norm and codification; (2) varieties of Czech in literature; (3) common Czech and Czech dialects; and (4) Czech in contact with other languages.

1364. **The Czech Avantgardists**. Edited by Alfred French. 103p., [14] leaves of plates: illus. Rockville, Md.: Kabel Publishers, 1994. Includes notes on the contributors and notes.

French has brought together a fascinating collection of Czech verse in English translation, which was originally written between the two World Wars. This period is recognized as one of the most fertile in Czech literary history.

1365. Hammerová, Louise B., and Ivor Ripka. **Speech of American Slovaks = Jazykové Prejavy Amerických Slovákov**. Vyd. 1. 163p.: illus. Bratislava: Veda, 1994. On p. [6]: Slovenská akadémia vied. Jazykovedný ústav Ludovíta Stúra.

This is really two books in one, each with a different intended audience. Both, however, have the same subject: the evolution of Slovak speech in America. "The research demonstrates that Slovak as an isolated minority language in the USA has undergone functional shift, which also reflects its entire cultural development: it changed from the basic means of communication into a secondary code" (p. 9). The study examines only the spoken language. The authors had three goals: to produce a linguistic description of the Slovak language as spoken in America; to record that language while it was actively used; and to record the life histories of the participants. A sample of 45 speakers was selected from western Pennsylvania. The emphasis in the study was on the degree of change, that is, deviations from the "Slovak norm." Since the authors have intended this book for two audiences, the first half of the book is written for an English-speaking audience, the second half for Slovaks. One is not merely a translation of the other. The content varies depending on the audience. So, for example, the Slovak section contains a list of borrowed terms with explanations on usage lacking from the English section. While any reader interested in culture acquisition and language change might find this interesting, the bilingual reader of Slovak and English alone will have access to the full text.

1366. Hirsal, Josef. **A Bohemian Youth**. Translated by Michael Henry Heim. vi, 87p. *Writings from an Unbound Europe*. Evanston, Ill.: Northwestern University Press, 1997.

Josef Hirsal was blacklisted after the Soviet invasion of Czechoslovakia. This novel was an experimental work telling the story of a man born into a Bohemian peasant family. "Told in five parts, the novel begins with a 'word to the wise,' moves on to the text proper, continues with notes and with notes to the notes, and ends with a note on the notes to the notes" (back cover). The novel gives a look at the Czech Republic from inside.

1367. Kresin, Susan. **Čestina Hrou = Czech for Fun**. ix, 499p. New York: McGraw-Hill, 1998. Includes bibliographical references.

This new Czech grammar consists of a workbook and tapes. The textbook consists of 12 chapters. Each chapter has a theme for vocabulary and practice. New grammar and vocabulary are presented in dialogues. "Our goal is for the student to be able to read about and assimilate the basic points of grammar at home and come to class prepared to use the new material in class. In addition, each chapter includes cultural notes and readings in Czech, with topics ranging from daily life to geography, film and literature" (p. viii).

1368. Lappin, Elena, comp. **Daylight in Nightclub Inferno: Czech Fiction from the Post-Kundera Generation**. 306p. North Haven, Conn.: Catbird Press, 1997. A Garrigue Book.

Lappin has collected what she considers the best and most representative stories and novel excerpts from young Czech writers. "Lappin lets the new generation of Czechs tell its story of growing up in the inferno of Communism and coming out into the daylight of freedom (or is it the other way around?)" (back cover).

1369. **The Prague School of Structural and Functional Linguistics: A Short Introduction**. Edited by Philip Luelsdorff. vii, 385p. *Linguistic and Literary Studies in Eastern Europe*, vol. 41. Amsterdam: John Benjamins Publishing, 1994. Includes bibliographical references and indexes.

Structural linguistics has been a major theoretical school in 20th-century linguistics. The contributors to this work demonstrate its roots in the Prague School of linguistics. While the Prague School was not limited in its interests to linguistics, this volume focuses on that area of their research. "In the present volume it was possible to gather contributions describing the main results of research of the Prague School and of its continuations in the basic domain of phonemics and written language, morphemics and word formation, lexicon, syntax and semantics, text structures, stylistics and language cultivation and language typology" (p. 6). The authors contributing to this volume have done research in the areas they discuss here.

1370. **Praguiana, 1945-1990**. Edited by Philip Luelsdorff, Petr Sgall, and Jarmila Panevová. ix, 250p. *Linguistic and Literary Studies in Eastern Europe*, vol. 40. Amsterdam: John Benjamins Publishing, 1994. Includes bibliographical references and index.

"*Praguiana*, edited by J. Vachek and published in 1983 as Vol. 12 of the present series, concentrated on basic and less known texts from the first, classical period of the Prague School and contained mainly writings first published between 1911 and the 1940s" (p. vii). The essays contained in this volume are divided into the following sections: "Studies in Syntax and Semantics," "Studies in Morphology," "Levels of Language System," "Graphemics," "Lexicon," "Sociolinguistics," and "Contrastive Linguistics." The contributors are Eugene Pauliny, Miloš Dokulil, František Danes, Pavel Trost, Vladimir Skalická, Jozef Ruzicka, Frantisek Miko, Oldrich Lěska, Josef Vachek, Jan Horecky, Vincent Blanar, Petr Sgall, Vladimir Barnett, Vilma Barnetová, and Philip A. Luelsdorff.

1371. Poldauf, Ivan. **Czech-English Comprehensive Dictionary**. Rev. ed. 1,187p. New York: WD Publications; Hippocrene Books, 1997.

The entries of this comprehensive Czech-English dictionary appear in boldface, with an indication of oddities in declension and conjugation, along with definitions. The dictionary also includes separate lists of place-names and abbreviations, as well as a brief abstract of Czech grammar in English.

1372. Pynsent, Robert B. **Questions of Identity: Czech and Slovak Ideas of Nationality and Personality**. ix, 244p. Budapest, Hungary; New York: Central European University Press, 1994. Includes index.

"Identity is a politically charged matter. Sometimes, explicitly, this book discusses the relationship between individual persons and nations with the world surrounding them" (p. ix). Pynsent's study is divided into four chapters. The first explores Vaclav Havel's vision of identity. In Chapter 2 Pynsent is concerned with nationalism and national identity. Chapter 3 is concerned with "the background to a period of Czech literature" (p.

viii). The author focuses on the descendants and their views of the individual. The final chapter summarizes Czech and Slovak myths and examines the questions of "Czech self-definition-thought martyrs" (p. vi).

1373. Thomas, Alfred. **Anne's Bohemia: Czech Literature and Society, 1310-1420**. xix, 194p.: illus. Minneapolis: University of Minnesota Press, 1998. Includes bibliographical references (pp. 171-83) and index.

The driving purpose of this study is to make clear that "Anne's presence on English soil and her brief reign as queen of England provided a strong impetus for the rise of international court culture in London, for English religious reform (especially through the translation of the Gospels into the vernacular), and for the realization of a deeply sacral vision of English kingship" (p. 19). After a 32-page introduction and prologue, Thomas provides a series of studies of different aspects of literature and culture from 1310 to 1420. Six of these studies use a particular Czech literary work as the focus for the analysis.

1374. Thomas, Alfred. **The Labyrinth of the World: Truth and Representation in Czech Literature**. 174p. *Veroffentlichungen Des Collegium Carolinum*; Bd. 78, R. Oldenbourg Verlag Munchen: Collegium Carolinum, 1995. Includes bibliographical references (pp. [162]-174) and index.

Thomas points out that one of the most prominent self-images put forth by Czech writers is a society unified by its commitment to freedom and truth. This study explores what is meant by truth in this sense. "To do this one must examine in detail the term 'truth' itself" (p. 13), says Thomas. In the 10 chapters of this work he does just that, beginning with an introductory essay on truth and representation in Czech literature and proceeding chronologically in examining monuments of Czech literature from the *Dalimil Chronicle* to Havel's *Largo Desolato*.

1375. Trollope, Anthony. **Nina Balatka: The Story of a Maiden of Prague**. xvii, 186p. London: Trollope Society, 1996. "First published in *Blackwood's Magazine* in seven installments from July 1866 to January 1867 . . . This edition follows the text as it appeared in *Blackwood's Magazine*, with minor emendations"—T.p. verso.

Anthony Trollope's novel is that of the life of a Bohemian girl. It was based on his travels and his experience in Central Europe in 1896. Prague captured his imagination. "He observed a divided city and saw racism in action. . . . In a powerful opening sentence Trollope captivates us with his heroine and his theme: 'Nina Balatka was a maiden of Prague, born of Christian parents, and herself a Christian—but she loved a Jew; and this is her story' " (p. v). This edition includes an introduction by Angela Thrill.

1376. Volkova, Bronislava. **A Feminist's Semiotic Odyssey Through Czech Literature**. 240p. Lewiston, N.Y.: Edwin Mellen Press, 1997. Includes bibliographical references.

Volkova is primarily interested in the intersection of ethics and literature and methods of literary criticism. In this volume she states that: "My intent is to enrich literary scholarship with new approaches to literature by using a consistently feminine point of view, as well as by focusing on the emotive intent of the writers, rather than the ideological one. I would like to offer in this book a guidepost to literary criticism establishing a new point of view that is not exclusively ideological/ political, formal/stucturalist nor genderless. Rather, it is one that follows consistently the underlying emotive and axiological implications of literary texts. This book should contribute to seeing Czech literature in its social context and cultural diversity and from a feminine point of view" (p. 12).

Individual Authors

1377. Busy, Caravel de. **Prague Sunset**. 146p. *East European Monographs,* 521. Boulder, Colo.: East European Monographs; New York: Distributed by Columbia University Press, 1998.
A novel set in postwar Czechoslovakia.

1378. Bradbrook, B. R. **Karel Čapek: In Pursuit of Truth, Tolerance, and Trust**. viii, 257p.: illus. Brighton, Eng.: Sussex Academic Press, 1998. Includes bibliographical references and index.
   This is a study of the writings of the Czech author Karel Čapek who was born in 1890 and died in 1938. Each chapter examines one facet of Čapek's literary skills: drama, novels, short stories, fairy tales, essays, biographies, and journalism. The book includes a bibliography of English and Czech writings by Čapek. It also includes a list of English and original Czech titles for works by the author.

1379. Holubová, Miloslava. **More Than One Life**. 104p. Evanston, Ill.: Northwestern University Press/Hydra Books, 1994.
   The theme of this novel, first published in 1994, is the effect on children when their parents divorce. The setting is modern Czechoslovakia.

1380. Wagenbach, Klaus. **Kafka's Prague: A Travel Reader**. Translated by Shaun Whiteside. 125p. Woodstock, N.Y.: Overlook Press, 1996. Translation of: *Kafka's Prag*.
   Franz Kafka loved Prague. This well-crafted, translated work is a travel book of Prague as if seen through the eyes of Kafka during his lifetime. In addition to the information presented about Kafka's favorite places, his schools and workplaces, favorite walks, and literary places and entertainments, Wagenbach has supplied the reader with photographs taken of these places in Kafka's time (1883-1924).

1381. Klíma, Ivan. **The Spirit of Prague and Other Essays**. 188p. New York: Granta Books, 1994.

These selected essays by Klima are arranged in five sections: (1) texts of a more personal nature that reveal something about the author's life; (2) his feuilletons; (3) political essays; (4) two essays about the dilemma facing literature in the modern age; and (5) a lengthy study of Franz Kafka.

1382. Klíma, Ivan. **Waiting for the Dark, Waiting for the Light**. Translated by Paul Wilson. 1st Grove Press ed. 234p. New York: Grove Press, 1995.

Another novel by the author of *A Ship Named Hope*, *Love and Garbage*, and *The Spirit of Prague*.

1383. O'Brien, John. **Milan Kundera and Feminism: Dangerous Intersections**. xiii, 178p. New York: St. Martin's Press, 1995. Includes index and bibliography.

In two large chapters, O'Brien applies feminist criticism to the work of Milan Kundera. Chapter 1, (Miss)Representing Women, explores the tension between opposites in Kundera's fiction, such as madonna/whore, beauty/ugliness, free will/fate, etc. In Chapter 2, Seeing Through the Opposition: Kundera, Deconstruction and Feminism, the author explores deconstructionist theory as it applies to seven of his works.

1384. Škvorecký, Josef. **Headed for the Blues: A Memoir**. 1st ed. 148p. Hopewell, N.J.: Ecco Press, 1996. Translated from Czech.

Škvorecký was born in Bohemia and emigrated to Canada in 1968. He and his wife run the Czech-language publishing house, Sixty-Eight Publishers, in Toronto. This present work is an autobiographical memoir by the novelist.

1385. Škvorecký, Josef. **The Miracle Game**. Translated by Paul Wilson. 1st American ed. 436p. New York: Alfred A. Knopf, 1991. Translation of: *Mirákl*.

Škvorecký has won several literary prizes. In 1990 both he and his wife were awarded the Order of the White Lion, Czechoslovakia's highest recognition, for their services to Czech literature. He is professor of English at Erindale College, University of Toronto. He has also translated Czech authors into English.

1386. Viewegh, Michal. **Bringing Up Girls in Bohemia**. 187p. London: Readers International, 1997. Translation of: *Výchova dívek v Cechách*.

"This picaresque romp gives a gritty but hilarious portrait of today's Prague, its Mafiosi and their ex-secret police bodyguards, the expatriate Americans, and many an extraordinary Czech, from a cremation enthusiast to a hopelessly naïve sex-education teacher. The novel is also a serious exploration of the role of the writer in post-communist Central Europe" (back cover).

National Minorities

1387. David, Avraham. **A Hebrew Chronicle from Prague, c1615**. Edited by Leon J. Weinberger and Dena Ordanx. 106p.: illus. Tuscaloosa: University of Alabama Press, 1993. Includes bibliographical references (pp. [97]-102) and index.

This volume contains an English translation of a Hebrew text from the early 17th century. It "provides valuable evidence of the events and changes in Jewish life in Bohemia and in Prague during the sixteenth and beginning of the seventeenth centuries" (p. xi). In addition to the text, the editor and translators have provided a brief introduction to Jewish life in Prague and Bohemia at that time, as well as informative annotations to the text itself.

1388. Goldberg, Sylvie Anne. **Crossing the Jabbok: Illness and Death in Ashkenazi Judaism in Sixteenth- Through Nineteenth-Century Prague**. xvii, 303p.: illus. *Contraversions*, 3. Berkeley: University of California Press, 1996. Includes bibliographical references (pp. 273-92) and index.

In the foreword to this book Thomas Lanqueur notes that there is more than a study of the uniquely Jewish funerary customs of the Czech Jews. "Its real point is less to find the Kernel of essential Jewishness—a profound and particular belief in a death as resurrection, for example—than to offer a historical anthropology of a community that is exemplary in its thoroughness and sensitivity" (p. xii). Sylvie Goldberg divided her study into topical sections on the history of Jewish funerary rites, the complex of funerary and buried rites that defined death, and a comparison of learned and popular religion.

Arts and Culture

1389. Aperture Foundation Inc. Staff. **Crossing Borders: Contemporary Czech and Slovak Photography**. 79p.: illus. *Aperture*, 152. New York: Aperture Foundation, 1998. Cover title.

A collection of photographs by Czech and Slovak photographers is published in this volume. They provide a brief history of modern photography in these countries. Some of the contributors are Pavel Banka, Judita Csaderova, Bohdan Holomicek, Ivan Klimn, Viktor Kolar, Josef Koudelka, and many others. The photographs are arranged topically into the following chapters: "The Spirit of Prague"; "Moments of Grace"; "Czech and Slovak Photography"; "Poem from Les Charmants de L'Aristocratie"; "Poem from My Skull's Shadow"; and "People and Ideas."

1390. Hames, Peter. **Dark Alchemy: The Films of Jan Svankmajer**. 202p., [16] p. of plates: illus. *Contributions to the Study of Popular Culture*, no. 46. Westport, Conn.: Greenwood Press, 1995. Filmography (pp. 168-74). Includes bibliographical references and index.

Jan Svankmajer is an influential Czech filmmaker of international note. Svankmajer's films have reflected the tremendous changes he has witnessed in his country beginning in the 1930s. The contributors in this volume have focused on analysis of those themes that have previously been less well explored in the literature. "We have therefore sought to explore some of those areas perennially confined to footnotes—in particular, the role of the pre-war avant-garde, the interaction with the broader traditions of Czech and Slovak cinema and, above all, the position of Svankmajer's work within the activities of the Surrealist Group" (p. 5). The contributors are Peter Hames, Michael O'Pray, Roger Cardinal, and Frantisek Dryje. The book includes a filmography of Svankmajer's work.

1391. Templeton, Stephanie. **Baba: The Werkbund Housing Estate Prague, 1932 = Die Werkbundsiedlung Prag, 1932**. 142p.: illus. Boston: Birkhäuser Verlag, 1999. Includes bibliographical references.

Baba is a piece of architectural history. In 1932 the architect Ladislav Zak conceived his Werkbund houses, with bedrooms conceived for one person only but with carefully designed functional spaces within the dwelling. This volume includes Zak's legacy, both in terms of his original plans and the architects who took up his concept and built domiciles based on his ideas.

Velvet Revolution

1392. Kukral, Michael Andrew. **Prague 1989: Theater of Revolution: A Study in Humanistic Political Geography**. xii, 236p.: illus., maps. *East European Monographs*, 472. Boulder, Colo.: East European Monographs; New York: Distributed by Columbia University Press, 1997. Includes bibliographical references (pp. 201-36).

"The purpose of this work is to demonstrate the meaning and role of place in political revolution, and to exemplify a methodology toward a humanistic political geography. Wenceslas Square, in the heart of Prague, Czechoslovakia (now the Czech Republic), at the time of the 1989 Velvet Revolution will be utilized to represent a specific place and time of revolution" (p. 1). This unusual examination of the events of 1989 includes a detailed discussion of the methodology. Unfortunately, the study lacks an index.

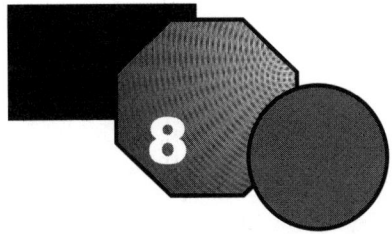

Hungary

General Reference Works

1393. **The Reliable Book of Facts: Hungary '98**. 415p. Budapest, Hungary: Greger-Delacroix Kiadó, 1998.

This almanac of Hungarian statistics is a useful source on a wide range of subjects. More than a statistical handbook, it includes a historical chronology, a summary of Hungary's history, its weather, foreign relations, economy, political system, educational system, culture, scientific achievements, and sports. The section on the state includes addresses for major political institutions, a description of the parliamentary process, a list of political groups, a list of addresses and officials in county government and mayor's offices, and statistics on voting activities in the Parliament. This exemplifies the type of information to be found throughout the volume. Several laws are reprinted here as well.

1394. Lieber, Joesph S. **Frommer's Budapest and the Best of Hungary**. 232p.: maps. London: Macmillan, 1996.

Like all of Frommer's guides, this one is chock full of everything you need to know about Budapest and the major cities of Hungary in order to enjoy yourself. An introductory chapter provides sufficient background information about history and culture to be interesting, but not suffocating. Additional chapters cover planning a trip to Budapest, getting to know Budapest, accommodations, dining, what to see and do, strolling around Budapest, shopping, and Budapest after dark. Final chapters cover the other regions of the country. An appendix provides menu terms, basic phrases and vocabulary, and metric conversions.

1395. **Hungary: Essential Facts, Figures and Pictures**. Edited by Éva Molnár. Translated by Pál Herskovits. 313p. Budapest, Hungary: Kossuth Printing House, 1995. Includes maps, appendix, and index.

This is an informational publication on Hungary intended for anyone with an interest in the country. It does seem to aim at an audience of potential investors; nevertheless, it contains valuable information in an easy-to-use format. The book covers geography, history, political structure, economy, social structure, foreign policy, educational system, culture, tourism, sports, religion, and an appendix with a street map of Budapest. There is a list of important Budapest addresses and a detailed index.

1396. Sarkozi, Matyas, comp. **Budapest**. xx, 106p.: map. *World Bibliographical series*, vol. 198. Santa Barbara, Calif.: ABC-CLIO, 1997. Includes indexes.

This 341-item bibliography is an excellent guide to books and lengthy articles on Budapest. Most of them are written in English, but there are several German-language articles and Hungarian-language books that are principally richly illustrated albums where the text is of secondary importance. The book is divided into 21 sections, the largest of which contains memoirs and travelers' accounts (58 citations) and history (also 58 citations). Taken together, the contents of the various sections cover every conceivable aspect of one of the oldest settlements in Europe. Each entry is accompanied by a brief informative annotation that sometimes provides citations to other relevant Budapest-related literature. Access to the contents is provided by three separate indexes: authors, titles, and subjects. The author has also provided an unkeyed map that shows the districts of the city. The bibliography should be useful for anyone interested in any aspect of Budapest.

History

1397. Balazs, Eva. **Hungary and the Habsburgs, 1765-1800: An Experiment in Enlightened Absolutism**. 352p. Budapest, Hungary; New York: Central European University Press, 1997. Includes bibliographical references (pp. 400-18) and index.

This is a history of Hungary under the Habsburgs, written over a number of years. The author began the book under the strictures of a communist regime and finished it in more liberal circumstances. The book is divided into two parts. The first part discusses the formation of Habsburg absolutism under Maria Theresa. The second part examines the reign of Joseph II and his reforms. The author does not attempt a comprehensive history. In this work subjects that have previously been left unexamined are taken up. Other issues, treated extensively elsewhere (such as agriculture and serfdom), are given only a cursory treatment here.

1398. **Dilemmas of Transition: The Hungarian Experience**. Edited by Aurel Braun and Zoltan Barany. x, 350p.: illus. Lanham, Md.: Rowman & Littlefield, 1999. Includes bibliographical references and index.

In order to elucidate dilemmas of transition that are not adequately understood, the editors gathered experts in "transitionology" to examine Hungary as a case study. What was learned here the investigators hope to apply to other countries in transition. The 14 essays are arranged in four sections: transition, Hungary's post-communist transition, marketization and social change in Hungary, and Hungary's international relations and security.

1399. **Hungary 1956—Forty Years On**. Edited by Terry Cox. 162p. London: Frank Cass, 1997. Includes bibliographical references and index.

The essays in this book were presented on the occasion of the 40th anniversary of the Hungarian revolution in 1956. The essays themselves present newly discovered information about the revolution, culled both from archives and recently published oral histories. The new knowledge concerns all aspects, including questions about the origins, periodization, and reasons for the outbreak of the revolution, its main aims and effects, and its aftermath. Several of the authors are members of the Budapest Institute for the Study of the 1956 Hungarian Revolution.

1400. Cesarani, David. **Genocide and Rescue: The Holocaust in Hungary 1944**. vii, 220p. Oxford; New York: Berg, 1997. Includes bibliographical references and index.

This collection of essays grew out of a gathering of historians in London, April 17-18, 1994. The focus of the papers is the Holocaust in Hungary. "Drawing on new sources, leading scholars address these controversial issues and shed new light on a shameful period in history" (back cover). Contributors include Shlomo Aronson, Jehuda Bauer, Randolph Braham, Richard Breitman, and many others.

1401. **Hungary in the Age of Total War (1938-1948)**. Edited by Nandor Dresziger. x, 372p. *East European Monographs*, 509. Boulder, Colo.: East European Monographs; New York: Distributed by Columbia University Press, 1998. Includes bibliographical references.

Fewer and fewer scholars survive with personal memories of World War II. The editor of this volume has identified scholars writing on the Hungarian experience during this war. He has used the *Hungarian Studies Review* as his source. Materials originally published in the journal were revised for publication in this collection of essays. The essays have been grouped into three sections: "Issues and Events," "Personalities," and "Documents."

1402. Eby, Cecil D. **Hungary at War**. xx, 318p.: illus., maps. University Park: Pennsylvania State University Press, 1998. Includes bibliographical references and index.

Hungary is a language not well known in the West. As a result, relatively few Hungarian publications are translated. Little is known of Hungary, history in the West, even its recent history. Cecil Eby has set out to partially fill this gap, at least as it relates to World War II. The author, with the assistance of a native speaker, Eleonora Arato, interviewed 51 men and 34 women. "My objective has been to write an account of the final years of the war that would record and analyze the experiences of the 'ordinary' people forced to cope with extraordinary crises imposed upon them by the external forces of history. My primary focus is upon domestic, not military, history" (p. x). The book is organized chronologically. It includes a chronology of events from 1914 to 1956. There is also a biographical section with sketches of major historical figures.

1403. **Budapest: A History from Its Beginnings to 1998.** Edited by András Gero and János Poór. vii, 354p.: col. map. *East European Monographs*, 462; *Atlantic Studies on Society in Change*, 8. Boulder, Colo.: East European Monographs; New York: Distributed by Columbia University Press. Includes index.

This history of Budapest is actually a series of 10 articles on different chronological segments of Budapest's history from its beginnings through 1996. The volume also includes brief biographies of key personalities and an index to streets and other locations of Budapest.

1404. Györffy, György. **King Saint Stephen of Hungary.** vii, 213p.: illus., maps. *East European Monographs*, 403. Boulder, Colo.: East European Monographs; New York: Distributed by Columbia University Press, 1994. Translation of: *Szent István király*. Translated by Peter Doherty. Includes bibliographical references (pp. 173-82) and indexes.

György Györffy has compiled a reanalysis of the life of King Saint Stephen of Hungary. Much of King Stephen's life still remains unclear as there is little clear historical material on which to base such research. The author hopes to clarify certain issues connected with King Stephen such as his role in the changes that came later to Hungary or what kind of person he really was. Györffy also hopes that his study will help explain social changes that occurred in the 10th and 11th centuries. This slim volume includes a detailed bibliography, organized by topic, and a place and name index.

1405. Jacobs, Michael. **Budapest: A Cultural Guide.** xi, 226p.: maps. Oxford; New York: Oxford University Press, 1998. Includes bibliographical references (pp. 197-201) and index.

Michael Jacobs has visited Hungary frequently since 1980. In this book he gives the reader an introduction to the wealth of the culture and history of that country's capital. The first part of the book is a collection of essays on life in the city. Part 2 includes six "walks," arranged by district. There is a section of suggested further readings. These are arranged by subject: traveler's accounts, guidebooks, history, literature, art, spas, and gastronomy.

1406. Kosztolnyik, Z. J. **Hungary in the Thirteenth Century.** viii, 510p.: 1 illus. Boulder, Colo.: East European Monographs; New York: Distributed by Columbia University Press, 1996. Includes bibliographical references (pp. [426]-497) and index.

The 13th century was a time of great political, cultural, and religious development in Western Europe. Hungary was no exception. There it was a time of great political change, particularly with regard to constitutional development. That is the focus of Kosztolnyik's book. The book includes two appendixes, one on 13th-century women and a second on medieval Hungarian theologians.

1407. O'Neil, Patrick H. **Revolution from Within: The Hungarian Socialist Workers' Party and the Collapse of Communism**. xviii, 257p. *Studies of Communism in Transition*. Northampton, Mass.: Edward Elgar, 1998. Includes bibliographical references.

There has been much discussion of the fall of communism in Eastern Europe in recent years. In this book, Patrick O'Neil examines the disintegration of the communist system in Hungary. He is interested in why communism fell when it did and fell so completely. He uses the Hungarian case to elucidate those elements of the system that contributed to the fall of the communist system. "The nature of political institutions and the matrix in which they are seated, I argue, do not determine political outcomes but rather create a set of contours which is likely to influence such events" (p. xviii). The book is divided into three parts: "Theoretical Approaches," "The Hungarian Case," and "Conclusions." There are two appendixes, one on primary sources and another listing abbreviations.

1408. Roman, Eric. **Hungary and the Victor Powers, 1945-1950**. x, 342p. New York: St. Martin's Press, 1996. Includes bibliographical references (pp. [329]-332) and index.

Little has been written about Hungary's foreign policy in the postwar years. Yet some unusual features characterized the policy in those years. Not least among these was Hungary's pro-western attitude. In this book the author examines the policies and the motivations behind them. "This study offers a comprehensive account of Hungarian foreign policy in the five years immediately following World War II." Eric Roman has used the newly available archival materials in Hungary to document his study.

1409. Number not used.

1410. Romsics, Ignac. **Istvan Bethlen: A Great Conservative Statesman of Hungary, 1874-1946**. Translated by Mario D. Fenyo. x, 491p.: illus., maps. Boulder, Colo.: East European Monographs, 1995. Includes bibliographical references and indexes. Translation of *Bethlen István*, with a new conclusion and epilogue prompted by new material.

Bethlen was one of the major political figures of 20th-century Hungary. Between 1901 and 1918 he was a regional politician in Transylvania. From 1921 to 1931 he was prime minister of Hungary. From then until the end of the war he was one of the leading anti-Nazi representatives and decidedly pro-Western.

1411. **A History of Hungary**. Edited by Peter F. Sugar. xiv, 432p.: illus., maps. Bloomington: Indiana University Press, 1994. Includes bibliographical references (pp. 405-15) and index.

This history of Hungary was first published in 1990. This new paperback edition has an additional chapter that brings the events covered up to 1990. The original chapters, the work of a collaboration between Hungarian and Western scholars, remain unchanged. The work is intended as a comprehensive history of Hungary.

1412. Szantai, Lajos. **Hungary in Printed Maps**. 2 vols. 771p. Budapest, Hungary: Akademiai Kiado, 1996.

This two-volume set collects most of the printed maps of Hungary published between 1528 and 1850. The maps are arranged by maker rather then chronologically. This arrangement was chosen to avoid the problems presented by undated materials. All essential information is listed for each map including draftsman, engraver, publisher, dimensions, and the source in which it originally appeared. A chronological index has been added to the end of each book. Volume 2 includes brief biographies of the engravers and cartographers in Hungarian. All entries are given in parallel text with Hungarian, and English. "Throughout the course of history the only nations and cultures to survive of which we are aware have been those which bequeathed material monuments to history. Maps occupy an important place among these materials, and they serve as the proof of Hungary's thousand-year past and statehood" (p. 6).

1413. Teglas, Csaba. **Budapest Exit: A Memoir of Fascism, Communism, and Freedom**. 1st ed. xii, 162p.: illus. *Eastern European Studies*, 7. College Station: Texas A&M University Press, 1998.

Teglas' autobiography is more than a conventional memoir. It is also an astute sociological analysis. On one hand Teglas writes about his life under communism in Hungary as one would write to his grandchildren. On the other hand he transforms his own troubles to a generalized social analysis. In doing so he explores the human suffering caused by communist rule. He also succeeds in demonstrating that the totalitarian regime and its attempted brainwashing did not break the spirit of its victims.

1414. Vardy, Steven B. **Historical Dictionary of Hungary**. xx, 813p.: maps. *European Historical Dictionaries*, no. 18. Lanham, Md.: Scarecrow Press, 1997. Includes bibliographical references (pp. 749-811).

This volume is one in a series of *European Historical Dictionaries*. As with the other volumes it has been compiled by a well-known scholar in the field, in this case Steven Bela Vardy, professor of European history at Duquesne University. The volume is structured like the others: beginning with a list of acronyms and a set of historical maps, it continues with a chronology and glossary of geographical terms and a list of the Hungarian heads of state dating from the 9th century to the present. This section of resources is followed by a substantial historical overview, giving the uninitiated reader a context. The bulk of the text is taken up with the dictionary entries. These are substantial and include dates and brief biographical information, followed by information on the historical significance of the individual, event, or place under discussion. The dictionary also includes an extensive bibliography that is divided into subject areas. The resources cited here are in a variety of languages. There is no index.

1415. Veress, Laura-Louise. **Clear the Line: Hungary's Struggle to Leave the Axis During the Second World War**. xxii, 404p.: illus. Cleveland, Ohio: Prospero Publications, 1996. Includes bibliographical references (pp. [391]-398) and index.

This book recounts the Hungarian government's efforts to separate itself from its alliance with Hitler. It is a story told by a Hungarian woman who married a diplomat directly involved in this struggle. "*Clear the Line* is a personal story that tells the story of an age. It is history with a heart. For the historian there is a list of Documents Cited, a Bibliography and an Index. For the average reader there are maps, a chronology and a readable narrative with personal recollections of what it was really like to live in Hungary during this period" (back cover).

1416. Walker, Annabel. **Aurel Stein: Pioneer of the Silk Road**. xiv, 393p., [16] p. of plates: illus., maps, ports. Seattle: University of Washington Press, 1998. First published: 1995.

Aurel Stein was a Hungarian archeologist who has been called "the collossus of Central Asian scholarship." Born in Budapest in 1862, Stein would eventually travel to China and perform some of the most extensive excavations of that country by any foreign archeologist. The debate continues today as to who is the rightful owner of the finds from those excavations. Annabel Walker explores these and other questions concerning Stein's career. "In this enthralling and moving book, Annabel Walker unfolds the remarkable story of the shy outsider whose lifetime of single-minded dedication revealed to the world the glories of the Silk Roads" (frontispiece).

1417. Závodszky, Géza. **American Effects on Hungarian Imagination and Political Thought, 1559-1848**. vii, 335p. *East European Monographs*, 375. *Atlantic Studies on Society in Change*, 79. Boulder, Colo.: East European Monographs; New York: Distributed by Columbia University Press, 1995. Includes index.

"This book attempts to expose the impact of the United States during her formative years as well as in the period of her consolidation as a state upon Hungary in general, and during the first half of the nineteenth century in particular, as a bourgeois society was emerging" (p. 1). The study is a translation from the Hungarian, thus presenting the Western reader with the Hungarian view of the evolution of the U.S. government and its affect on the rest of the world. The volume includes brief biographical profiles on Hungarian figures.

Economics, Trade, and Business

1418. Bartlett, David L. **The Political Economy of Dual Transformations: Market Reform and Democratization in Hungary**. xv, 299p. Ann Arbor: University of Michigan Press, 1997. Includes bibliographical references and index.

The conflict between political liberalization and economic transformation may hamper the development of one or the other of these processes. David L. Bartlett studies the interaction of these two processes in Hungary during the 1980s and 1990s. He believes that Hungary makes an excellent case study because of the long history of market reform in that country. The study of the development and success of those reforms allows for the study of economic policy over several decades. His book is divided into four parts: institution changes in Eastern Europe; economic reform from 1979 to 1989; economic reform 1990-1994; conclusions. The book includes an appendix describing the author's research methods and sources.

1419. **Public Finance Reform During the Transition: The Experience of Hungary**. Edited by Lajos Bokros and Jean-Jacques Dethier. xv, 580p.: illus. Washington, D.C.: The World Bank, 1998. Includes bibliographical references and index.

This is a collection of essays funded by the World Bank. The purpose of the book is to present a complete overview of public finance reform in a former socialist country. The goal is to provide a clear account of the numerous issues involved in the process. "Part I of this volume discusses the macroeconomic dimensions of the process. Part II looks at the reforms from a historical and comparative perspective. Subsequent chapters analyze the reforms that took place in social expenditure programs (part III), in public sector management and institutions (part IV), and in the tax system (part V)" (p. 1). Contributors are both scholars and policymakers.

1420. Brada, Josef C., Inderjit Singh, and Adam Torok. **Firms Afloat and Firms Adrift: Hungarian Industry and the Economic Transition**. xiv, 104p. Armonk, N.Y.: M. E. Sharpe, 1994. Includes bibliographical references (pp. 98-100) and index.

In order to give an assessment of Hungarian industry in the wake of the economic and social transition that occurred in 1989, the authors take two approaches. For the period up to 1991 they analyze basic indicators of macro-level industry performance, then provide a policy analysis for these years, followed by the same procedure for the transition years 1988-1991. Their second approach for the period after 1989 entails examination of the various options that exist for industrial policy in the new environment. In the final two chapters the authors present case studies based on interviews with industrial managers, detailing the problems faced and the various solutions used to deal with those problems.

1421. Kornai, Janos. **Struggle and Hope: Essays on Stabilization and Reform in a Post-Socialist Economy**. 247p., [16] p. of plates: illus. *Generations, a History of Canada's Peoples*. Toronto: McClelland & Stewart, 1999.

"The writings in this volume first appeared between 1994 and 1996. They discuss two subjects. The first is the equilibrium problems of the post-socialist economy—including the tensions caused by shortage, inflation, internal and eternal debt, current account and budget deficits—and the stabilization measures designed to surmount them. The second is reform of the welfare sector" (p. xi). The author sees these topics as interrelated through history, politics, and economics. Kornai believes that Hungary's problems are typical of those facing all post-socialist countries. The volume includes extensive statistical data.

1422. Piesse, J. **Efficiency Issues in Transitional Economies: An Application to Hungary**. xii, 235p.: illus. Aldershot, Eng.: Ashgate, 1999. Includes bibliographical references (pp. 226-35).

This volume offers alternative means of observing transitions in Central and East Europe. By looking at agriculture, light manufacturing, and services in Hungary during the period 1985 to 1991, the author uses several techniques for measuring the efficiency of production. The three parts of the book contain chapters that respectively examine: (1) the transition, production theory, and Hungarian accounting and data; (2) models, estimation, and results; and (3) the index number approach to productivity, efficiency, and technical change: an application to structural transformation.

1423. **Economic Reforms, Liberalization and Structural Change: India and Hungary**. Edited by R. R. Sharma and Imre Levai. 230p. New Delhi: Gyan, 1997. Majority of the papers presented in the Seventh Indo-Hungarian Round Table Conference of Economists and Policy-Makers held in JNU in March 1995.

This collection of essays resulted from a meeting of scholars in JNU in March 1995. "The basic purpose of the present volume is to project the varied experiences of both India and Hungary in the field of liberalization and economic restructuring . . . the Hungarian scholars devote their entire attention to the problem of economic and the political transformation of their country" (p. 7). The volume is divided into two parts, one on India and another on Hungary. Contributors include Bibek Debroy, Sunanda Sen, Arun Kumar, G. K. Chadha, Pradipta Chaudhury, C. P. Bhambri, Gusztav Bager, Janos Kornai, Imre Levai, and Attila Agh.

1424. **Hungary: An Economy in Transition**. Edited by Istvan P. Szekely and David M. G. Newbery. xxvii, 360p.: illus. New York: Cambridge University Press, 1993. Includes index.

Hungary has had in many ways the most successful economic transition among the East European nations. In recent years, there was actually a surplus in convertible currency. However, there are still many problems to be solved. "This book presents some of the local arguments and perceptions informing the current debate and critical examinations of these ideas from an international panel of scholars" (frontispiece). The contributors discuss privatization; financial, tax, and legal systems; integration into the international monetary system; labor issues; social safety nets; and other topics. The book includes a glossary of terms.

1425. **Hungary: Towards a Market Economy.** Edited by Halpern Wyplosz and Charles Wyplosz. xx, 390p.: illus. Cambridge, Eng.: Cambridge University Press, 1998. The conference "Hungary: Towards a Market Economy" was organized by the Institute of Economics, Hungarian Academy of Sciences, with the support of the Centre for Economic Policy Research and held on 20-21 October 1995 in Budapest. Includes bibliographical references and index.

This volume presents a sophisticated and well-researched examination of the contemporary Hungarian economy. Part 1 focuses on macroeconomic policy (fiscal difficulties in transition, interest rate transmission mechanism, inflation, and hidden economies). Part 2 covers the industrial structure (corporate governance in the transition, corporate performance, and the Hungarian ponzi scheme). Part 3 concludes with the labor markets (minimum wage, welfare institutions, and regional unemployment rate differentials).

Government, Politics, and Law

1426. Kiraly, Bela K. **Lawful Revolution in Hungary, 1989-1994.** xv, 519p. *Atlantic Studies on Society in Change*, no. 84. Boulder, Colo.: Social Sciences Monographs, 1996. "Glossary of institutions, political parties and publications": pp. 499-504. Includes bibliographical references and index.

The essays in this volume by various hands examine the transformation of Hungary during the period from 1989 to 1994. Individual essays are grouped under rubrics such as introductions, antecedents, the rise of democracy, the government, culture and crises, the economy, and young democracy and the outside world. The volume is one of a series that eventually "will constitute a comprehensive survey of the many aspects of East Central European society" (p. xv).

1427. Thokbes, Rudoolf L. **Hungary's Negotiated Revolution: Economic Reform, Social Change, and Political Succession, 1957-1990.** xxiii, 544p. *Cambridge Russian, Soviet and Post-Soviet Studies*, 101. Cambridge, Eng.: Cambridge University Press, 1996. Includes extensive notes, selected bibliography, and index.

All of Eastern Europe has experienced dramatic political changes in this decade. Rudoolf Thokbes looks at those changes in Hungary, how they developed, and the direction they are taking. "The title and subtitle of this study are broadly indicative of what I plan to discuss. In general, I intend to isolate and analyze the dynamics of Hungary's political transformation and to explain the reasons for the collapse and, since 1990, partial survival of the developmental dilemmas and social values of the Kadar regime" (p. 3). Thokbes focuses on sociopolitical change as well as political cultural elements of continuity, economic constraints, and social dynamics. The book is organized into three parts. Part 1 analyzes elements of systemic change in Hungary: the evolution of the communist party, economic reforms, and social changes. In Part 2 the focus is on elite politics from opposition movements to party elites. The last part examines political succession, the negotiated revolution, political mobilization, and Hungary's form of democracy, i.e., the evolution from post-communism to democracy. The book includes a chronology of events from 1956 to 1990.

1428. Tong, Yanqi. **Transitions from State Socialism: Economic and Political Change in China and Hungary**. xi, 264p. Lanham, Md.: Rowman & Littlefield, 1997. Includes bibliographical references (pp. [237]-260) and index.

Yanqi Tong is a young Chinese scholar, educated in the United States and now teaching here. In her work she uses comparative studies to elucidate China's political development. In this study she compares Chinese and Hungarian methods of instituting economic and political reform. The conclusions she draws from this structured, focused comparison of cases challenge the prevailing analysis of these countries. "Yanqi's comparisons of China and Hungary show that they experienced major similarities in the early stages of reform. She shows the importance of political coalitions in the two countries. And finally, she shows that Hungary has grappled with severe economic and political problems despite the democratic breakthrough of 1989 and that China has experienced remarkable economic success despite the political repression of Tiananman" (p. xi).

Foreign Relations

1429. Felkay, Andrew. **Out of Russian Orbit: Hungary Gravitates to the West**. x, 141p. *Contributions in Political Science*, no. 382. Westport, Conn.: Greenwood Press, 1997. Includes bibliographical references (pp. [135]-139) and index.

In the first part of the study the author shows how Russian-Hungarian relations were reconstructed after the dismantling of the communist regimes in both countries. He then shows how these economic and political relations changed and how Hungary moved into the sphere of influence of NATO and the European Union.

Language and Literature

1430. **The Colonnade of Teeth: Modern Hungarian Poetry**. Edited by Gerorge Gomori and Geroge Szirtes. 270p. Newcastle upon Tyne, Eng.: Bloodaxe Books, 1996. Translated from the Hungarian.

Hungarian is a language considered inaccessible by many. In this volume Western readers are offered English translations of the works of many Hungarian poets. A variety of works are included by poets born between 1900 and 1954. "This anthology is not primarily about national obsessions—it simply presents what the editors consider to be, if not unarguably the best, then at least the best, translated poetry written by Hungarian poets born in the specified period" (p. 20). The volume includes a section of biographical sketches, tracing the lives of the contributing authors.

1431. **A Mirror to the Cage: Three Contemporary Hungarian Plays.** Edited and translated by Clara Györgyey. ix, 245p. Fayetteville: University of Arkansas Press, 1993. Translated from the Hungarian.

In this collection of three Hungarian dramatic works, the editor has selected works by three of Hungary's most politically outspoken authors. The works of Istvan Orkeny, Gyorgy Spiro, and Mihaly Kornis all represent an uncompromising attitude toward truth and art. A short biographical sketch that places the play within the development of the authors' artistic careers precedes each of the plays included here.

1432. Number not used.

1433. Rot, Sandor. **Hungarian: Its Origins and Originality**. 192p. Budapest, Hungary: Korona Publishing House, 1994. Table of contents and headings of sections also in Hungarian. Includes bibliographical references.

Rot's book is part cultural history of Hungarian and part descriptive grammar. In the first part, dealing with the origins of Hungarian, he traces its development as it was interweaved with its cultural and historical roots. In the second part, he covers phonetics, parts of speech, syntax, morphology, lexicography, and nonstandard Hungarian. The level of discourse is directed to those who already have a basic understanding of modern linguistic structure.

1434. **Hungarian Plays: New Drama from Hungary**. Edited by László Upor. xiv, 242p. London: Nick Hern Books, 1996.

The English translation of *The Seducer's Diary* by András Nagy, *Unsent Letters* by Andor Szilágyi, *Muller's Dancers* by Ákos Németh, and *Everywoman* by Peter Kárpáti is contained in this volume. An introduction by the editor sets the plays in the context of Hungarian theatrical and cultural history.

Individual Authors

1435. Kertesz, Imre. **Fateless**. 191p. Evanston, Ill.: Northwestern University Press, 1996.

This novel takes place in Hungary during World War II and describes a family that was a victim of the Holocaust.

1436. Márai, Sándor. **Memoir of Hungary, 1944-48**. 427p. Budapest, Hungary: Corvina in association with Central European University Press, 1996. First published in Hungarian as *Föld, föld!*—in 1972.

Sandor Marai (1900-1989) published 46 books before leaving Hungary in 1948. During his exile he would continue to publish political works. In this book, first published in Hungarian in 1972, Marai examines life in Hungary after the war and before the communist takeover. As in his other works, Marai is a severe critic of the Hungarian middle class. The book includes a brief introductory essay by the translator Albert Tezla.

1437. Nadas, Peter. **The End of a Family Story**. 245p. New York: Farrar, Straus & Giroux, 1998.

Originally published in 1977 in Hungarian, this translation brings Nadas' novel to the English-speaking world.

1438. Nyiri, Janos. **Battlefields and Playgrounds**. Translated by William Brandon. Rep. ed. 536p. New York: Farrar, Straus & Giroux, 1995.

This translated novel by well-known Hungarian author Nyiri also contains the translator's endnotes, which aid interpretation and identification of obscure references.

The Society, Sociology

1439. Agarwal, D. P., B. Buda, A. E. Czeizel, and H. W. Goedde. **Alcohol Consumption and Alcoholism in Hungary: Ethnocultural, Epidemiological and Biomedical Aspects**. 236p. Budapest, Hungary: Akademia Kiado, 1997. Bibliography (pp. 145-77).

The individual chapters in this book, written by various hands, provide a comprehensive examination of alcoholism in Hungary. The chapters provide a description of the Hungarian population, analyze the problem from historical and ethnographic perspectives, and describe the epidemiology of alcoholism, genetic and environmental factors, medical genetic aspects, clinical aspects, and experimental protocols.

1440. Suleiman, Susan R. **Budapest Diary: In Search of the Motherbook**. 232p. *Texts and Contexts*, 18. Lincoln: University of Nebraska Press, 1996.

Suleiman left Hungary in 1949 at the age of 10. Some 35 years later, in 1984, she returned, and returned again in 1993 and 1994. This description of her journey, not only geographically but chronologically, gives a unique perspective on Budapest and modern-day Hungary.

1441. Szelenyi, Szonja, Karen Aschaffenburg, Mariko L Chang, and Winifred Poster. **Equality by Design: The Grand Experiment in Destratification in Socialist Hungary**. xvii, 250p. Stanford, Calif.: Stanford University Press, 1998.

There is little research that addresses modern efforts to reduce class- or gender-based inequality. The objective of this volume is to "analyze the 'grand experiment' with socialism and postsocialism in light of core sociological debates about the evolution of modern class systems and the circulation of elites, managers, and workers within such systems" (p. vii). In addition to the main text, Szelenyi has included several appendixes that include university application forms, the 1983 Hungarian social mobility and life history survey, the mapping of the 1983 Hungarian Standard Occupational Classification system into class categories, and class mobility tables.

National Minorities

1442. Handler, Andrew, and Susan Meschel. **Red Star, Blue Star: The Lives and Times of Jewish Students in Communist Hungary (1948-1956).** x, 224p. *East European Monographs*, 47. Boulder, Colo.: East European Monographs; New York: Distributed by Columbia University Press, 1997. Includes bibliographical references (pp. [40]-51).

Hungary became a communist country in 1948. For the surviving Jews of that country, having just survived the horrors of the Holocaust, it meant a new struggle. The essays collected in this volume are written by people who were children during those years. "As the contributors to *Red Star, Blue Star* recall some of their experiences in Communist Hungary, the smell of victory is in the air. Having survived the Holocaust, they readily accepted the sporting challenge of standing up to or outwitting the Communists" (p. x).

1443. Kertesz, Imre. **Kaddish for a Child Not Born.** 95p. Evanston, Ill.: Northwestern University Press/Hydra Books, 1997.

A novel set in Hungary concerning the Holocaust and its survivors. The book first appeared in Hungarian in 1990.

1444. Maracz, Laszlo K. **Hungarian Revival: Political Reflections on Central Europe.** 362p.: illus. Aspekt, Non-Fiction, 2. Nieuwegein: Aspekt, 1996. Translation.

"*Hungarian Revival* is a merciless chronicle and analysis of the persistent policy of compulsory assimilation imposed on Hungarian communities living in Hungary's neighbouring countries. It is a plea for the preservation of the Hungarian nation as a spiritual and cultural entity" (p. 9). Seen by many as a call for nationalism, this work sparked a great deal of debate when it first appeared in Dutch in 1996. It is published here in English for the first time. It presents the American audience with the difficulties faced by one of Europe's ethnic groups living in a number of different nations. The book is divided into three parts. The first part characterized the Hungarian people, the perception of them in the West, and their own self-image. Part 2 describes the effects of the Trianon on the Hungarians. In the last section the author proposes a new view of Central Europe.

1445. Patai, Raphael. **The Jews of Hungary: History, Culture, Psychology**. 732p. Detroit, Mich.: Wayne State University Press, 1996. Includes bibliographical reference and index.

Patai concentrates on the history, culture, and psychology of the Jews of Hungary, as his subtitle indicates. He admits that he devotes more attention to the cultural, especially literary, activity of the Hungarian Jews than might be expected in such a history. "The reason," he says, "is my conviction that the key characteristic in the portrayal of a people, hence deserving of special attention, is the culture that constitutes its ancestral heritage, that endows its existence with a specific coloration, that holds it in its thrall, and to which it contributes the best of its talents" (p. 16). His emphasis on psychology grows out of an attempt to understand their motivations behind their reactions to the overt forces that affected them.

1446. Postma, Koos. **Changing Prejudice in Hungary: A Study on the Collapse of State Socialism and Its Impact on Prejudice Against Gypsies and Jews**. 200p. *NUGI*, 652. Amsterdam: Thesis Publishers, 1996. Includes bibliographical references (pp. [181]-200).

Prejudice seems to be aggravated by rapid societal change. This study tests this hypothesis by examining prejudice in Hungary. Two questions are particularly of interest. First, has the level of prejudice demonstrated against Gypsies and Jews changed since the political changes in Hungary began? Second, to what degree are the changes in levels of prejudice attributable to the societal changes in Hungary? To answer these questions, the author describes the context of the problem in Hungary beginning with a history of that country from the medieval period to the late 20th century. The history of the Jews and Gypsies in Hungary is traced in the next section. The following section details the hypothesis on political transformation and its effect on prejudice, providing the theoretical basis of this study. Data collection and methodology are then discussed. An extensive discussion in the final chapter presents the findings.

1447. Stewart, Michael. **The Time of the Gypsies**. xviii, 302p. Boulder, Colo.: Westview Press, 1997. Includes appendix, endnotes, bibliography, and index.

Stewart insists that Gypsies cannot be understood apart from the wider society of which they are a part. To comprehend their present condition he examines the attitudes and policies toward the Gypsies under the Austro-Hungarian Empire, in communist Europe, and in post-communist Hungary. In particular, he focuses on how these different regimes interpreted and conducted different forms of work and commerce. In this study, Stewart helps us see the Gypsies from their point of view, through long-term fieldwork among them.

Arts and Culture

1448. Burns, Bryan. **World Cinema: Hungary.** vi, 234p., [16] p. of plates: illus. Wiltshire, Eng.: Flick Books, 1996. Includes filmography (pp. 211-15).

Burns combines information about the Hungarian film industry with criticism of its products. He focuses primarily on major directors active since 1930 and the fictional feature films that they produced. His interpretation of these films and the history of the Hungarian film industry that he portrays goes toward explaining the success that Hungarian film has had on the world stage.

1449. Cook, Jeffrey. **Seeking Structure from Nature: The Organic Architecture of Hungary.** 191p.: illus. (some col.), map. Basel: Birkhäuser, 1996. Includes bibliographical references (pp. 189-90).

Jeffrey Cook has compiled a volume that introduces the Western reader to Hungary's "organic architecture." In Hungary, as elsewhere, organic architecture is intended to respond to its place and society. Therefore, it reflects on Hungary and its culture. Some of the architects represented are Lorine Csernyus, Sandor Devenyi, Andras Erclei, Imre Makovecz, Tibor Jankovics, and Istvan Kistelegdi. This lavishly illustrated volume introduces the Western reader to a vital and rich form of Hungarian artistic expression.

1450. Frigyesi, Judit. **Béla Bartók and Turn-of-the-Century Budapest.** x, 357p.: illus., music. Berkeley: University of California Press, 1998. Includes bibliographical references and index.

When studying the works of composers such as Beethoven, or Schumann, scholars frequently discuss the cultural environment that influenced them. Information on the cultural influences on Béla Bartók have not previously been available in English. This study attempts to fill that gap. "Taking up the intellectual milieu of Bartók and aspects of his music, the book complements cultural histories of the European mainstream modernism on the one hand and Bartók studies on the other" (p. 1). The fist part of the book establishes in detail the cultural life that influenced Bartók. Part 2 examines the works of the poet Andre Ady and compares them with the musical works of Béla Bartók.

1451. Palkó, Zsuzsanna. **Hungarian Folktales: The Art of Zsuzsanna Palkó.** xxiv, 382p.: illus. *Garland Reference Library of the Humanities*, vol. 1736. Jackson: University Press of Mississippi, 1996. Includes bibliographical references (p. xxii) and index.

This collection of 35 folktales introduces the English-speaking world to one of Hungary's greatest storytellers. Zsuzsanna Palkó died in 1964 at the age of 84. She had been named Master of Folklore by her government in 1954. Her folktales are presented here in translation with extensive commentary by Linda Degh. Degh is a professor of folklore at Indiana University. This collection of text emphasizes in its presentation the importance of text as opposed to intextual analysis. "A major premise in Mrs. Palkó's tales, as in Linda Degh's scholarship, is that tales do not lie" (p. x). The book includes several indexes and glossaries: terms, proper names, sayings, and tale types and motifs.

1452. Teleky, Richard. **Hungarian Rhapsodies: Essays on Ethnicity, Identity, and Culture**. xv, 217p. Seattle: University of Washington Press, 1997. Includes bibliographical references (pp. [191]-205) and index.

Richard Teleky has used a variety of essay forms in this book to explore a number of questions concerning Hungarian culture. "This book, then, is a combination of essay, lament, celebration, and scholarship that takes its shape from my own exploration of a range of subjects, beginning with my studies (and Edmund Wilson's) of the Hungarian language and ending with a discussion of what I have come to see as the arbitrariness of ethnicity" (p. xii). Other essays discuss the work of André Kertész, Hungarians in North American fiction, Hungarian stereotypes, Margaret Avison's translations, and the work of Péter Esterházy. One essay describes the author's attempt to establish a course on Central European literature in translation.

Poland

General Reference Works

1453. Cohen, Adir. **The Gate of Light: Janusz Korczak, the Educator and Writer Who Overcame the Holocaust**. 360p. Rutherford, N.J.; Madison, Wis.; Teaneck, N.J.; London; Toronto: Fairleigh Dickinson University Press; Associated University Presses, 1994. Includes bibliographical references and index.

Janusz Korczak was a Jewish-Polish educator who was imprisoned in the Treblinka concentration camp during World War II. "This book constitutes an attempt to re-examine Korczak's life, philosophy, literary creation, and educational accomplishment, which have a relevance to the humanist mission of education everywhere" (p. 9).

1454. Lerski, George J. **Historical Dictionary of Poland 966-1945**. 750p. Westport, Conn.: Greenwood Press, 1996. Includes bibliographical references (pp. [699]-706) and index.

This dictionary of Poland's history by the late George Lerski contains some 2,000 entries. Each entry includes bibliographical citations to related materials. It was Professor Lerski's intention to use only English-language materials in his bibliographic entries. But this proved impossible, as in many cases there were no such materials to cite. He has, therefore, included Polish materials when necessary.

Entries cover Polish history in its broadest sense with information on scholars, political figures, writers, athletes, and artists. Terminology such as "Martwa Reka" (dead hand) can also be found here as well as more standard entries, e.g., "Warsaw Ghetto Uprising." The choice of entries was determined by careful study of the Polish encyclopedias and the *Polish Biographical Dictionary*. Each entry is thorough, with the extensive cross-references indicated by the use of an asterisk in the text. There is also a detailed index.

While it lacks a chronology and only covers people and events to 1945, this is an extremely useful source for anyone with a serious interest in Polish history.

1455. Paul, Barbara Dotts. **The Polish-German Borderlands: An Annotated Bibliography**. xii, 201p. *Bibliographies and Indexes in World History*, no. 35. Westport, Conn.: Greenwood Press, 1994. Includes bibliographical references and index.

"This bibliography brings together English language materials that will be useful for students, teachers, and scholars wishing to examine all aspects of the borderlands" (p. ix). The compiler has included citations to travelers' stories, historical and geographic surveys, government reports, literature, regional fiction, and films. Journal articles from scholarly periodicals have also been included. Paul has excluded brief articles from newspapers and popular magazines. Most of the materials have been arranged into chronological sections beginning with primary sources and then looking at pre-1914 publications. The last two sections cover fiction and film. The author has included indexes for authors, titles, and subjects to facilitate access.

1456. Sanford, George, and Adriana Gozdecka-Sanford. **Historical Dictionary of Poland**. 339p. *European Historical Dictionaries*, no. 3. Lanham, Md.: Scarecrow Press, 1994. Includes bibliography.

The *Historical Dictionary of Poland* includes nearly 400 entries on the complex development of that country. Intended for the nonspecialist it includes a chronology of general history and of the rulers of Poland. There is also an extensive list of abbreviations and acronyms. As with other volumes in the series of *European Historical Dictionaries* it includes an extensive bibliography, organized by subject. Unfortunately, there is no index and little cross-referencing to assist the uninitiated reader. Along with the Greenwood Press volume it is a valuable general resource.

1457. Wisniewski, Tomasz. **Jewish Bialystok and Surroundings in Eastern Poland: A Guide for Yesterday and Today**. 147p.: illus. Ipswich, Eng.: Ipswich Press, 1998. Includes bibliographical references.

This guide of Bialystok, Poland, and the surrounding region was originally published in Polish. It offers an introduction to the Bialystok region and separate chapters on the cities of Tykocin and Bialystok and other towns of the region. Its 10 appendixes include a chronology of Jewish life in Bialystok, notable Bialystok Jews, Jewish cemetery names, some travel basics for the region, a bibliography, and other useful information for the interested traveler.

1458. Wrobel, Piotr. **Historical Dictionary of Poland, 1945-1996**. 423p.: maps. Westport, Conn.: Greenwood Press, 1998. Includes index.

Poland, as the 8th largest country of Europe, is of increasing strategic, economic, and political importance. This historical dictionary, covering the period 1945-1996, is a sequel to a similar dictionary issued by the same publisher in 1996 that covers the years 966-1945. Personalities, events, and concepts are arranged alphabetically. An indication is given if terms appearing in the texts of entries are themselves accorded a separate listing. Each entry provides basic information about the term or personality in question and also includes bibliographic references to items in both English and Polish that contain a more complete exposition of the topic. The reference work also includes several useful maps, a chronology of important events, a selected bibliography of books in English on Poland, and an index to the contents of the entries themselves.

History

1459. Blanke, Richard. **Orphans of Versailles: The Germans in Western Poland, 1918-1939**. xii, 316p.: 2 maps. Lexington: University Press of Kentucky, 1993. Includes bibliographical references (pp. [246]-268) and index.

With the end of World War I, the German population in western Poland found itself in a difficult position. Formerly the representatives of a repressive regime, they had become a minority group in a territory controlled by the Poles. "This book seeks to describe and analyze the dilemma of the German minority in western Poland in all its considerable complexity" (p. 1). The Germans living in this region did not see themselves as an émigré population. Richard Blanke looks at the conditions of life for Germans in this region. This book is arranged chronologically beginning with the "Establishment of the German Minority from 1918 to 1922." Blanke then looks at the population of Germans who fled the region and life and those who stayed during the Pilsudski era. Next he turns to the growing international interest in this group, especially in Nazi Germany. Finally, he describes conditions for Germans in western Poland in 1939. The book includes two appendixes. One gives German equivalents of Polish place-names. The second shows the shifting proportion of the German and Polish populations in the region between 1910 and 1931.

1460. Blobaum, Robert. **Rewolucja: Russian Poland, 1904-1907**. xx, 300p. Ithaca, N.Y.: Cornell University Press, 1995. Includes bibliographical references and index.

The revolutionary movements that arose in Poland between 1904 and 1907 tend to be overlooked to a large extent in the literature. Robert Blobaum examines those events in this volume that cover such topics as the relationship between the occupying Russian government and Polish society, the origins of the revolution, the role of education in the revolutionary movement, the evolution of Polish political culture, and the role of the church. "Finally, in striving for a comprehensive and integrated account of Poland's revolutionary upheavals of the early twentieth century, my greatest hope is that this work will expand the horizons of a discussion hitherto confined by constraints of language, geography and politics" (p. xii). Blobaum has taken a narrative approach in the hope that it will make the study more generally accessible to the average reader.

1461. Butterwick, Richard. **Poland's Last King and English Culture: Stanislaw August Poniatowski, 1732-1792**. xix, 376p.: illus., map. *Oxford Historical Monographs*. Oxford, Eng.: Clarendon Press, 1998. Includes bibliographical references (pp. [321]-358) and index.

Stanislaw August Poniatowski ruled over Poland during a difficult period. He would eventually become a prisoner of the Russian government and die in Russia. "The approach of the present work is as follows: the first aim is to set Stanislaw August in the context of Polish and European attitudes to England, the second is to analyze the sources of Stanislaw August's Angloplila, and the third is its effect on his activity and on the history of Poland-Lithuania" (p. 11).

1462. Engel, David Joshua. **Facing a Holocaust: The Polish Government-in-Exile and the Jews, 1943-1945**. x, 317p. Chapel Hill: University of North Carolina Press, 1993. Sequel to: *"In the Shadow of Auschwitz: The Polish Government-in-Exile and the Jews, 1939-1942, which appeared in 1987"*—Pref.

David Engel continues his study of the Holocaust in this volume. In 1987 he published *In the Shadow of Auschwitz: The Polish Government-in-Exile and the Jews, 1939-1942*. This work is a sequel to that title. As in the first volume, Engel relies heavily on documentary evidence for his analysis. "What follows is an examination of the thoughts and actions of the Polish government-in-exile on matters of primary concern to Jewish citizens of Poland from the end of 1942 until the conclusion of the European chapter of the Second World War in May 1945." Engel does not seek to identify criminals or heroes in this work. His is not a study of the morality of the behavior of the Polish government in exile. The book is arranged thematically covering such topics as the Jewish commune, propaganda efforts, and the military. There is a brief biographical appendix. The notes to the volume are extensive.

1463. Fiszman, Samuel. **Constitution and Reform in Eighteenth-Century Poland the Constitution of 3 May 1791**. xxix, 562p.: illus. Bloomington: Indiana University Press, 1997. Includes index.

This anthology is made up of essays that examine 18th-century Poland during a time of social and political reform. "The progressive currents in a number of fields which led to the adoption of a constitution are surveyed across the entire 18th century in Poland, and set in the context of the Enlightenment. The main subject of this book is the Constitution of 3 May 1791 seen from various angles as the most important realization of the movement toward reform in 18th-century Poland" (p. xi). The editor points out that there was no attempt to unify the viewpoints of the essays in this book.

1464. Gozdecka-Sanford, Adriana. **Historical Dictionary of Warsaw**. xxx, 319p. *Historical Dictionaries of Cities*, 3. Lanham, Md.: Scarecrow Press, 1997. Includes extensive bibliography.

This valuable resource on Warsaw is part of the *Historical Dictionaries* series published by Scarecrow Press. All have similar structure: chronology, map, encyclopedic overview, dictionary entries, and bibliography. The individual volumes vary, depending on the point of view of their compiler. In this case, Adriana Gozdecka-Sanford has brought her considerable expertise on Poland's modern history to this work. Some of the unique features in this volume are a chronology of the "Presidents" of Warsaw from 1792 to the present, a detailed list of acronyms and abbreviations, and a general bibliography on Poland with a list of guidebooks, diaries, periodicals, and newspapers. The dictionary entries are extensive but do not have separate bibliographies. There is also no cross-referencing of entries as can be found in some volumes of the series. There are entries on streets and communities in the city and on legends concerning Warsaw, as well as general entries on crime and film. Interestingly, there were no entries under economy, commerce, or finance.

1465. Kenney, Padraic. **Rebuilding Poland: Workers and Communists, 1945-1950**. xv, 360p.: illus., maps. Ithaca, N.Y.: Cornell University Press, 1997. Includes bibliographical references (pp. [347]-352) and index.

Kenney's aim is to show how communism was received by Polish workers after World War II. He shows "how social continuities and logic help us place this period in Polish history and help us grasp the dynamics of the communist system" (p. 3). In Part 1 he examines the revolution in the factories during 1945-1947, and looks carefully at factories in Lodz and Wroclaw. In Part 2 he focuses on the party's revolution from 1949 to 1950 and looks at the social foundations of the Stalinist system, the rise and fall of the labor hero, and the battle for working-class identity.

1466. **Diary from the Years of Occupation, 1939-44**. Edited by Zygmunt Klukowski, Andrew Klukowski, and Helen May. xx, 371p.: illus. Urbana: University of Illinois Press, 1993. Includes index.

Zygmunt Klukowski was the superintendent of the Zamosc county hospital for almost 30 years. During that time he would experience the Nazi and Soviet occupation of the region. He was a member of the Polish resistance during the war and of the underground during the Soviet occupation. He kept a diary of the events during the war that is presented here in translation. This diary covers 1939-1944 and provides "eloquent testimony to the perseverance of the Polish resistance" (p. xi).

1467. Kruszka, Waclaw, and James S. Pula. **A History of the Poles in America to 1908**. zv. Washington, D.C.: Catholic University of America Press, 1993. Includes bibliographical references.

This two-volume work is a translation of a work that first appeared in 1899. The author was a Catholic priest. His detailed study of the role of the Poles in America is divided into two parts. The first volume is topically arranged, discussing a variety of issues: the growth of Polish settlements in America, the history of the Polish church in America, the Polish educational system in America, and industry, commerce, and agriculture in America to name a few. As the editors note, "Kruszka's purpose in writing his History was to set forth the history of the Polish communities in America in such a way that their contribution to the development of the United States and the Roman Catholic Church would become widely known. In the process he hoped to reinforce the validity of his arguments for cultural pluralism while at the same time advancing his own ethnic group" (p. xx). There is valuable information on Polish publications and Polish organizations in the first volume. The second volume is limited to the history of Poles in Illinois and is organized by diocese. While there is much valuable information in the volumes, neither contains an index.

1468. Mocha, Frank. **American "Polonia" and Poland, a Sequel to Poles in America: Bicentennial Essays**. 500p. New York: Columbia University Press, 1998. Includes bibliographical references and index.

This is the third book in a series by the author who has explored Poles in America and the Solidarity movement. This volume brings American Polonia and Poland together in one book. His approach is that of resorting to what has been called "alternate history" in which he uses the "What If" deliberation to propel his study forward. His 19 chapters are arranged in four parts and an introduction. The four parts are devoted to the organizational structure of Polonia, Polonia and Poland, Poland and Polonia, and the goal: the most perfect Poland in a 1,000-year dream? The volume will be useful to those who are interested in the culture of Polish Americans and the ties they retain to their homeland.

1469. Peszke, Michael A. **Poland's Navy, 1918-1945**. Rep. ed. xii, 222p.: illus. New York: Hippocrene Books, 1999. Includes bibliographical references (pp. 211-15) and index.

After a two chapter introduction to the beginnings of the Polish navy from the 11th century to the end of WWI and the establishment of a Polish republic in 1918, the author evaluates and analyzes the development of the Polish navy during the crucial 1918 to 1945 period and the role it played during the war at the side of the Royal Navy. It also contains several appendixes that include documents, a list of major Polish naval units, the Polish women's naval auxiliary, the Polish merchant marine, and a table of equivalent naval ranks.

1470. Sanford, George. **Poland: The Conquest of History**. xi, 124p.: map. *Postcommunist States and Nations*, vol. 3. Amsterdam: Harwood Academic, 1999. Includes bibliographical references (p. 113) and index.

In this four-chapter volume the author first gives a brief introduction to the main events in Polish history up through 1989. The final three chapters then focus on politics, economy, society, modernization, and Poland's place in the new Europe. Ending his analysis in 1997, Sanford poses this key question: "Would the Poles manage their transition to market democracy successfully and would they be able to reconcile their national identity with growing Europeanisation and, eventually, globalisation?" (p. 111).

1471. Sword, Keith. **Deportation and Exile: Poles in the Soviet Union, 1939-48**. xiii, 269p.: maps. *Studies in Russia and East Europe*. New York: St. Martin's Press in association with School of Slavonic and East European Studies, University of London, 1994. Includes bibliographical references and index.

Keith Sword attempts to fill a gap in the study of the deportation of Poles to Russia with this volume. While there have been other works on this topic, none have concentrated on this period. By doing so the author hopes to resolve the question of what happened to the hundreds of thousands of Poles that never returned from deportation. "The book which has resulted concentrates on the movement of populations—involuntary, state-inspired uprooting; refugee flight from armed conflict; migration to join armed forces (and to leave captivity); large-scale exodus across state borders; state-organized repatriation" (p. x).

1472. Tooley, T. Hunt. **National Identity and Weimar Germany: Upper Silesia and the Eastern Border, 1918-1922**. xii, 320p., [12] p. of plates: illus., maps. Lincoln: University of Nebraska Press, 1997. Includes bibliographical references (pp. [303]-310) and index.

As a result of the Paris peace settlement at the end of WWI, the inhabitants of three German borderlands were asked to participate in a plebiscite that would determine whether their regions would remain German. This book is a history of that vote as well as the events preceding and following it for Upper Silesia, a region that included both ethnic Germans and ethnic Poles.

1473. Treece, Patricia. **A Man for Others: Maximilian Kolbe, Saint of Auschwitz, in the Words of Those Who Knew Him**. Corrected ed., minor additions. x, 255p.: illus. Libertyville, Ill.: Prow Books/Franciscan Marytown Press, 1993. Includes bibliographical references (pp. 241-48).

At Auschwitz in 1941 a prisoner had been chosen for one of the cruelest deaths—to be shut up naked in an empty, subterranean cell and left without food and water until he dies. Maximilian Kolbe, a Franciscan priest, stepped forward and volunteered to take that man's place. Treece's biography recounts the life of Kolbe, from his childhood to his self-sacrifice for a fellow prisoner.

1474. Zamoyski, Adam. **The Forgotten Few: The Polish Air Force in the Second World War**. Hippocrene Books ed. xi, 239p., [16] p. of plates: illus., maps. New York: Hippocrene Books, 1998. Includes bibliographical references (pp. [226]-230) and index.

Zamoyski has written a history of the Polish Air Force, especially squadrons stationed in Britain during WWII. It is not intended to be a comprehensive history of the Polish Air Force, or even an assessment of these men and women's contribution to the Allied cause. Instead his intention is "to give some idea of who they were, where they came from, how they got there and what they did; and also to take a look at their sometimes strained but ultimately successful collaboration with the RAF and their sometimes difficult, often notorious, but ultimately happy relationship with the British people."

1475. Zawadzki, W. H. **A Man of Honour: Adam Czartoryski As a Statesman of Russia and Poland, 1795-1831**. xvi, 374p.: maps. Oxford, Eng.: Clarendon Press; Oxford University Press, 1993. Includes bibliographical references (pp. [336]-359) and index.

W. H. Zawadzki reassesses the career of Polish statesman Adam Czartoryski. To some extent he uses his study of Czartoryski as a vehicle to examine the whole of Russian foreign policy in this period. Zawadzki's main focus is the career of the statesman and his vision of an independent Poland. The book includes a genealogical table of the Czartoryski family and an extensive bibliography.

1476. Zuckerman, Yitzhak, and Barbara Harshav. **A Surplus of Memory: Chronicle of the Warsaw Ghetto Uprising**. xviii, 702p., [16] p. of plates: illus. Berkeley: University of California Press, 1993. Includes bibliographical references (pp. 679-82) and index.

Zuckerman was one of the organizers and leaders of the Jewish Fighting Organization that led the uprising in the Warsaw Ghetto. This memoir is an account of his activities from 1939 to 1946 and sets these events "in the specific social and political context that preceded them and goes on to recount the continuation of resistance activity after the liquidation of the ghetto and after the end of the war" (p. vii).

1477. **The Memoirs of Ludwik Zychlinski: Reminiscences of the American Civil War, Siberia, and Poland**. Edited by Ludwik Zychlinski, Eugene Podraza, and James S. Pula. 111p. Boulder, Colo.: East European Monographs; New York: Distributed by Columbia University Press, 1993.

Ludwik Zychlinski was a Polish nobleman of the 19th century. He was determined to see Poland as an independent nation in his time. To achieve this end he traveled widely to broaden his military skills and find allies. This book is the memoir of his life. It follows his career as he travels to America, back to Poland, and through his exile. The translation is heavily annotated.

Economics, Trade, and Business

1478. **Poland: Income Support and the Social Safety Net During the Transition**. Translated and compiled by Nicholas Barr. xviii, 144p. Washington, D.C.: The World Bank, 1993. "Compiled by Nicholas Barr . . . based on the findings of missions which visited Poland between 1989 and 1992"—p. ix.

As with all World Bank country studies, this volume presents a careful analysis of the economic situation in Poland. The volume is divided into three parts: on the background to the problem of social supports in Poland, assessment of change in Poland, and a discussion of reforms. A section of annexes contains supporting information, providing statistical data and other information.

1479. Carter, F. W. **Trade and Urban Development in Poland: An Economic Geography of Cracow, From Its Origins to 1795**. xvii, 509p.: illus., maps. Cambridge, Eng.: Cambridge University Press, 1993. Includes bibliographical references and index.

This book "uses the experience of Cracow to illumine general patterns of trade and urban growth in central and eastern Europe over several centuries. Dr. Carter emphasizes the spatial aspects of commodity analysis during the later medieval and early modern periods, and traces the impact of political circumstance on commercial progress and mercantile evolution. He describes the regions and places of especial significance for Cracow's trade development, and examines the principal trading flaws and commodity movements within the overall context of European economic and social change" (frontispiece).

1480. Cole, Daniel H. **Instituting Environmental Protection: From Red to Green in Poland**. xiv, 343p. London: Macmillan, 1998. Includes bibliographical references (pp. 268-323) and indexes.

It is well recognized that environmental protection failed miserably under socialism. This book examines the causes for the failure of environmental protection in Poland. Its intent is not only to learn some lessons from the result in order to work on prerequisites for future effective environmental protection. Although Poland is the focus of study, the lessons learned here and the conditions described that contributed to the crisis are also applicable to other socialist countries in the Soviet bloc.

1481. Domanski, Boleslaw. **Industrial Control over the Socialist Town: Benevolence or Exploitation?** xiii, 251p.: illus., maps. Westport, Conn.: Praeger, 1997. Includes bibliographical references (pp. [223]-237) and index.

"The author seeks to reveal and explain mechanisms of control exercised by the industrial company over the socialist town as well as the privileges and social deprivation it brought about. In other words, the focus is on grasping the relations between economic power embedded in public industrial enterprises and social inequalities in the specific spatial setting of the socialist town" (p. xii). To accomplish his goal the author has divided his study into three parts. The first part discusses European socialist states in general, with special emphasis given to the examination of the administrative allocation of goods and its effect on social inequalities. The second part focuses on the Polish experience and the relationship between large industrial enterprises. The final part looks at the legacy of the socialist systems with attention given to the paternalistic structure it fostered.

1482. Hardy, Jane, and Al Rainnie. **Restructuring Krakow: Desperately Seeking Capitalism**. xv, 285p. London: Mansell, 1996. Includes bibliography (pp. 260-75) and index.

The authors' purpose is "to attempt to fulfill a number of tasks: firstly, to develop a Marxist analysis of the decline and collapse of the economies of Central and Eastern Europe in general, and Poland in particular; secondly, to develop a critique of orthodox (and some radical) analyses of, and prescriptions for, the process of transformation; and thirdly, to develop an analysis of the way that the process of transformation is affecting the economics and people of regions such as Krakow" (p. xi).

1483. Hunter, Richard J., and Leo V. Ryan. **From Autarchy to Market: Polish Economics and Politics, 1945-1995**. xii, 287p. Westport, Conn.: Praeger, 1998. Includes bibliographical references (pp. [269]-280) and index.

Hunter and Ryan examine the economic development of Poland from the close of World War II through 1995. Their analysis entwines both economics and politics and analyzes the core aspects of the process of transformation and change during this period.

1484. Johnson, Simon. **Starting over in Eastern Europe: Entrepreneurship and Economic Renewal**. xx, 262p. Boston: Harvard Business School Press, 1995. Includes bibliographical references (pp. 245-49).

The authors investigate the restructuring of state enterprises and private business development in Poland. As Jeffrey Sachs comments in the foreword: "This study will prove invaluable on three levels: as a scholarly analysis of the early years of post-communist reforms; as an aid to policymakers in understanding the real sources of economic dynamism in the post-communist countries; and as a window for both corporations and individual business people on the new market economies of Central Europe" (p. x).

1485. Kierzkowski, Henryk, Marek Okólski, and Stanislaw Wellisz. **Stabilization and Structural Adjustment in Poland**. xi, 314p. London: Routledge, 1993.

Between August 1989, when Solidarity took over the governance of Poland, and the October 1991 election, a series of reforms, known as the Balcerowicz Plan, were instituted in order to transform the Polish centrally planned economy into a market-based one. The essays included here describe and analyze the difficulties confronted and the policies preserved during this period. The essays themselves are arranged in four groups: an overview of the transition process; macroeconomic issues; structural problems; and social issues.

1486. Kulczycki, John J. **The Polish Coal Miner's Union and the German Labor Movement in the Ruhr, 1902-1934**. xv, 283p.: illus., maps. Oxford: Berg, 1997. Includes bibliographical references (pp. 259-75) and index.

The ZZP (Polish Trade Union) was a powerful force in the workers' movement in the German Ruhr valley prior to World War I. It participated in the 1905 and 1912 coal miner's strikes. After the war the union lost its strength, owing primarily, the author argues, to its own decreasing activity in the labor movement after the war and the decline of the Polish community in that region. It finally liquidated in 1934. The book is arranged in two parts: (1) the history of the union from its formation in 1902 through the beginning of the war, including its participation in the 1905 and 1912 strikes; (2) its reorientation after the war, its disengagement from the German labor movement, and its eventual self-liquidation. It also includes two appendixes, a list of the membership statistics, and the program and demands of the union in a document dated October 27, 1917.

1487. Long, Kristi S. **We All Fought for Freedom: Women in Poland's Solidarity Movement**. viii, 192p.: illus. *Studies in the Ethnographic Imagination*. Boulder, Colo.: Westview Press, 1996. Includes bibliographical references (pp. [181]-192) and index.

Long attempts to examine women's historical consciousness in Poland during the 1980s. Since Solidarity was one of the major social forces in Poland during that period and a defining element of personal identity, Long interviews women involved with the Solidarity movement. Her analysis is divided into three major sections. Section 1 poses major theoretical questions; Section 2 discusses the most salient elements of historical consciousness during this period; and Section 3 analyses the narratives of the strikes of 1980. Her final chapter "concludes the book with a critical analysis of the failure of Solidarity to provide women with representation and defense of their gendered interests" (p. 14).

1488. Nowicki, Maciej. **Environment in Poland: Issues and Solutions**. 191p.: col. illus., col. maps. Dordrecht, Netherlands; Boston: Kluwer Academic, 1993. At head of title: Ministry of Environmental Protection, Natural Resources and Forestry.

The author has proposed a strategy for sustainable development in order to avoid economic, environmental, and social crises in Poland. He not only discusses issues, but also provides solutions. In Part 1 he explores the legacy of the past, placing Poland in the context of the European environment as a whole and describing atmospheric, water, waste, and environmental pollution in Poland. In Part 2 he suggests how sustainable development in Poland could take place through needed reforms. He devotes Part 3 to the conservation of nature in the strategy of sustainable development. In Part 4 he outlines instruments of sustainable development policy.

1489. Panków, Wlodzimierz. **Work Institutions in Transformation: The Case of Poland, 1990-92**. Translated by Grzegorz Siwicki. 233p. Warsaw: Friedrich Ebert Stiftung, 1993. Includes bibliographical references (pp. 227-33).

Wlodzimierz Panków is a noted Polish sociologist affiliated with the Polish Academy of Sciences. In 1988 he wrote an essay entitled "The Polish Collectivized Enterprise: Diagnosis and Elements of Its Prognosis." Parts of that essay suggested reforms in collectivized enterprises. These programs were pursued by the government and enacted as part of the Polish economic reforms. Panków was thus able to follow the progress of his programs and presents the results in this book. Along with the discussion of collectivized businesses in Poland, Panków looks more broadly at labor institutions such as the changing role of owners, labor disputes, and barriers to change. Unfortunately, the book lacks an index. It does contain an extensive bibliography.

1490. **Modernization Crisis: The Transformation of Poland**. Edited by William Dan Perdue. xvi, 243p.: illus. Westport, Conn.: Praeger, 1995. Includes bibliographical references (pp. [221]-234) and index.

This volume is a companion to Perdue's earlier work, *Paradox of Change* (1995). Here he explores several themes. "The first is an instrumental inquiry into the construction of a new institutional framework, with a special focus on the market economy and representative democracy. Another involves the new additions to axiology (with the value language of individual rights, autonomy, and antiauthoritarianism paramount). And a final theme centers on problems of tradition and change in political and moral authority" (p. xiii). The first three parts of the book contain essays that focus on the Polish social, economic, and educational transformations, respectively. Part 4 looks at the future of Polish development.

1491.   Poznanski, Kazimierz Z. **Poland's Protracted Transition: Institutional Crisis and Economic Growth 1971-1993.** xl, 337p. *Cambridge Russian, Soviet, and Post-Soviet Studies*, 98. Cambridge, Eng.: Cambridge University Press, 1997. Includes bibliographical references and index.

The author "offers an integrated study of institutional change in the Polish economy since 1970. He examines the economic peak of the communist phase, the decline of the system, and the post-communist transition since 1989. . . . The book presents the communist economy as subject to major changes, particularly due to political pressures, and interprets its economic difficulties as related to underlying systemic decay" (frontispiece).

1492.   Sachs, Jeffrey. **Poland's Jump to the Market Economy.** xv, 126p. *Lionel Robbins Lectures.* Cambridge, Mass.: MIT Press, 1993. Includes bibliographical references (pp. [119]-122) and index.

Recognizing that the greatest challenge of the decade is how to change from communism to capitalism, the author had spent many years studying and debating this question. In the lectures, delivered four years after Poland's political and economic revolution, he explains the problem of reform in general and for Poland in particular and demonstrates the West's role in this transformation.

1493.   Simatupang, Batara. **The Polish Economic Crisis: Background, Causes, and Aftermath.** xii, 255p. London: Routledge, 1994. Includes bibliographical references (pp. 237-52) and index.

"In analyzing the economic crisis of the late 1970s and early 1980s *The Polish Economic Crisis* examines one of the key factors in the events of 1989 and places it in its wider political-economic context. Batara Simatupang identifies the issues involved in this recession. . . . The book also analyses the aftermath of this crisis and the steady process from recession to slump" (frontispiece). The book is arranged topically covering subjects such as investment, external economic relationships, inflation, agriculture, and labor supply and policy. Simatupang then turns to a review of the positions taken by Polish economists on the economic crisis of 1979-1982. He closes by examining the aftermath of the recession and concluding remarks on the collapse and its long-term effects on Poland. The author is a Research Fellow in the Faculty of Economics at the University of Amsterdam.

1494. Slay, Ben. **The Polish Economy: Crisis, Reform, and Transformation**. xvi, 229p. Princeton, N.J.: Princeton University Press, 1994. Includes bibliographical references (pp. 207-26) and index.

"An interdisciplinary synthesis of the political economy of the Polish transformation and the historical, political, and economic factors that condition it is developed in the pages that follow. Extensive use is made of primary Polish sources as well as Western sources" (p. 7). The author has made his argument within the bounds of a chronological arrangement. He begins with an overview of the Polish economic crisis and Polish socialism. He then traces the progress of the crisis as the Poles began to see the necessity of abandoning, as opposed to reforming, their existing system. Slay has included a chronology of events from 1989 through 1993.

Government, Politics, and Law

1495. Bernhard, Michael H. **The Origins of Democratization in Poland: Workers, Intellectuals, and Oppositional Politics, 1976-1980**. 298p. New York: Columbia University Press, 1993. Based on the author's thesis, Columbia University. Includes bibliographical references (pp. [257]-283) and index.

Michael Bernhard discusses the rebirth and development of civil society in Poland in the 1970s. In particular, he focuses on the KOR (Worker's Defense Committee) and its effect on the growth of democratization. He begins with a general discussion of the concept of "civil society." Here he constructs a theoretical framework for the rest of the book. In Chapter 2 Bernhard examines civil society specifically in Poland. He then turns to a chronological description of events from 1976 and the price reforms and sticks to the crucial events of the 1980s.

1496. Duzinkiewicz, Janusz. **Fateful Transformations: The Four Years' Parliament and the Constitution of May 3, 1791**. xi, 334p. Boulder, Colo.: East European Monographs; New York: Distributed by Columbia University Press, 1993. Includes bibliographical references (pp. 306-18) and index.

The author analyzes the Polish constitution of 1791 from political, sociocultural, and economic points of view. After looking at the four-year sejm in historical perspective, he examines the scope of the constitution, parliamentary procedures in the light of Stanislawian antecedents, some glimpses at parliamentary behavior, political groupings, and conclusion considerations. He has also included a glossary of foreign terms to aid the reader.

1497. **Poland's Permanent Revolution: People Vs. Elites, 1956 to the Present**. Edited by Luba Fajfer and Jane Leftwich Curry. x, 294p. Washington, D.C.: American University Press, 1996. Includes bibliographical references and index.

This collection of essays examines the last 40 years of change and crises in Polish government. "The authors maintain that in order to understand Poland today, analysts must avoid concentrating only on the final downfall of communism and must look also at the entire series of popular uprisings that comprise Poland's political history since the communist takeover in 1948" (back cover). The contributions have been arranged to give a chronological analysis of the various uprisings that have occurred beginning with October 1956 and then following the development, rise, and fall of the Solidarity movement. The volume includes a chronology of events during the years covered in the essays. The contributors are Jane Leftwich Curry, Andrzej Korbonski, Luba Fajfer, Sarah Meiklejohn Terry, and Marjorie Castle.

1498. Garlicki, Leszek. **First Amendment Freedoms and Constitution-Writing in Poland**. 82p.: illus. [S.l: s.n.] 1993. "Papers submitted at the Polish-American Conference on 'First Amendment Freedoms and Constitution-Writing in Poland' which took place in May 1993 at the University of Warsaw"—p. 1.

"This book consists of papers submitted at the Polish-American Conference on 'First Amendment Freedoms and Constitution-Writing in Poland' which took place in May 1993 at the University of Warsaw. . . . The conference was intended to deal with constitutional problems of rights and freedoms in Poland, and—quite naturally—we decided to focus on First Amendment Freedoms: freedom of expression as well as religion freedoms" (p. 1). This slim volume is divided into three sections: constitution writing; freedom of expression; freedom of religion. All papers are in English.

1499. Jedruch, Jacek. **Constitutions, Elections and Legislatures of Poland, 1493-1993: A Guide to Their History**. Rev. v, 487p.: illus., maps. *Studies Presented to the International Commission for the History of Representative and Parliamentary Institutions*, LXXVI. New York: EJJ Books distributed by Hippocrene Books, 1998. Includes bibliographical references and index.

This revised edition, like the 1982 publication, is intended to introduce the English speaker to the parliamentary history of Poland. "The second edition of *Constitutions, Elections and Legislatures of Poland* brings the basic text up to 1993, complemented with the most recent updates where feasible; the additional chapter, (chapter IX) is compiled from the author's notes, prepared to cover the period after 1989" (p. 15). The book is arranged chronologically and topically with chapters devoted to the monarchy, the transition to a republic, the seyms and the confederations, the partitions of Poland, the second republic, and the third republic. A wealth of biographical information on parliamentary leaders is included along with an annotated bibliography, especially useful for the student of Polish history.

1500. Kurczewski, Jacek. **The Resurrection of Rights in Poland**. xix, 462p. Oxford, Eng.: Clarendon Press; Oxford University Press, 1993. Includes bibliographical references and index.

This book uses several types of evidence to make recent Polish history intelligible in terms of social structures and also to make social structures understandable as social processes. The types of evidence used include primary documents and surveys. Beginning with post-WWII in Poland, individual chapters use sociological evidence to describe Polish normativity in the context of its recent history.

1501. Kurski, Jaroslaw. **Lech Walesa: Democrat or Dictator?** xx, 178p.: illus. Boulder, Colo.: Westview Press, 1993. Cover title: *Lech Walesa*.

"Drawing on his unique insider's perspective as press spokesman for Lech Walesa from October 1989 to July 1990, Jaroslaw Kurski has written the first critical, clear-eyed account of the Polish leader's personal and political style" (p. 171). The author challenges the traditional portrait of Walesa, describing him as a man who lost touch with his political base. The author has included a glossary of names and a chronology of events from July 3, 1989, to December 15, 1992. The book was first published in Polish in 1991.

1502. Michnik, Adam. **Letters from Freedom: Post-Cold War Realities and Perspectives**. xxxiii, 348p.: illus. *Societies and Culture in East-Central Europe*, 10. Berkeley: University of California Press, 1998. Includes bibliographical references and index.

Michnik is a politician, writer, and journalist. These translated selections from his writings are arranged in three parts: (1) hopelessness and hope; (2) notes from the revolution, 1989-1990; and (3) speeches and conversations. The selections taken together form a rich mosaic that portrays Poland and Eastern Europe during a crucial period of transition. As an aid to the reader, the translator has included a guide to events and people at the end of the volume.

1503. Millard, F. Frances. **The Anatomy of the New Poland: Post-Communist Politics in Its First Phase**. ix, 260p. *Studies of Communism in Transition*. Brookfield, Vt.: Edward Elgar, 1994. Includes bibliographical references (pp. 239-52) and index.

This volume in the series *Studies of Communism in Transition* focuses on the challenges faced in Poland as it struggles through its early post-communist years. "This book sets out to examine the processes of democratic and capitalist restructuring of Polish society in the first period of the post-communist transition. I have tried to describe and assess as clearly and simply as possible the factors that are operative in contemporary Polish political processes, their origins and their implications" (p. viii). Millard has structured the work thematically beginning with several chapters on the legacy of the communist system. The author then discusses the electoral process, the development of the party system, the growth of new political institutions, privatization, civil liberties, and foreign policy.

1504. Pelinka, Anton. **Politics of the Lesser Evil: Leadership, Democracy, and Jaruzelski's Poland**. 259p. New Brunswick, N.J.: Transaction Publishers, 1999. "The German edition of this book appeared in 1996"Jaruzelski oder die Politik des kleineren Über Zur Vereinbarkeit von Demokratie und "leader (Frankfurt am Main: P. Lang/Verlag)." Includes bibliographical references (pp. 247-54) and index.

Originally published in German, this study of Jaruzelski and his role in the transition from communism has attracted increasing scholarly attention. Of particular interest is his position in 1981 and his role in the framework of Gorbachev's policies from 1985 on. The author presents two theses and elaborates on them throughout the book. First, "that political leadership always means having to choose the lesser of several identifiable evils"; and second, "that the inner logic of democracy leads to the narrowing and, ultimately, to the destruction of the playing field of political leadership" (p. 12).

1505. **Transition to Democracy in Poland**. Edited by Richard Felix Staar. xiv, 271p.: illus. New York: St. Martin's Press, 1993. "Published in cooperation with the Hoover Institution on War, Revolution and Peace, Stanford University." Includes bibliographical references and index.

Poland was chosen as the focus for this study largely because of its long tradition of political and social development. The editor also considered the advantages of being able to draw on a number of scholars who had done either research or teaching in Poland. The result is this collection of essays on a range of subjects: elections, political activists, the parliamentary system, constitutional reform, privatization, labor markets, regional cooperation, and national security. Each essay was critiqued by a Polish scholar in Warsaw.

1506. Szacki, Jerzy. **Liberalism After Communism**. Translated by Chester A. Kisielvii. 216p. Budapest, Hungary; New York: Central European University Press, 1995. Translated from Polish. Includes bibliographical references and index.

" 'A spectre is haunting Eastern Europe—the spectre of liberalism.' In *Liberalism After Communism* distinguished Polish social scientist Jerzy Szacki discusses the spread of liberalism as the dominant political ideology of Eastern Europe since 1989 and analyses the widespread . . . belief that the only way forward for the region is through a combinations of liberal democracy and free market ideals" (back cover). Jerzy Szacki is a Professor of Sociology at Warsaw University.

1507. Taras, Ray. **Consolidating Democracy in Poland**. xii, 276p. Boulder, Colo.: Westview Press, 1995. Includes bibliographical references (p. 261) and index.

Taras is "primarily concerned with whether, in the Polish case, the transition has led to a stable and consolidated democracy" (p. 1). He is less concerned with which party holds power, who is likely to win the next election, and other specific questions. Individual chapters cover topics such as historic discontinuities, the functioning of the communist regime, the crisis of the communist system, coalition formation and crisis resolution, democratic structures of the third republic, and socioeconomic development, foreign policy, and the international political economy.

1508. Tittenbrun, Jacek. **The Collapse of "Real Socialism" in Poland.** 276p. London: Janus, 1993. Includes index.

"The present work is an attempt to answer the question: how did it come that the rules of Poland . . . produced their own gravediggers?" (p. 9). Tittenbrun traces Poland's political and economic development from the 1970s. He focuses on the growth of Poland's national debt and the socialist government's inept attempts to deal with this problem. The book is chronologically arranged with a final section that reviews the trends and policies that led to the downfall of Poland's socialist system. The book includes a brief glossary of terms. The entries in the bibliography are arranged by language, creating a useful tool for those limited to English-language sources.

1509. Tworzecki, Hubert. **Parties and Politics in Post-1989 Poland.** 219p.: illus., maps. Boulder, Colo.: Westview Press, 1996. Includes bibliographical references (pp. 199-214) and index.

This study examines the ways in which the Polish people voted, "how they picked their representatives from a bewildering array of political options, given that for virtually all of them, participation in democratic elections was a genuinely new experience" (p. 17). They did not have party loyalties to rely on, and no party machines existed. Tworzecki provides a theoretical and historical overview and then examines how regional cleavages, political geography, and demographic and issue cleavages affected the way people voted.

Foreign Relations

1510. Lukowski, Jerzy. **The Partitions of Poland: 1772, 1793, 1795.** xv, 232p.: maps. New York: Addison-Wesley/Longman, 1999. Includes biographical references and index.

In spite of the recognized fact of the Polish partitions, there is a surprising dearth of literature on the subject. Lukowski does not attempt to produce the definitive history of the Polish partitions, but instead presents a fresh, if incomplete, survey of the three Polish partitions. Access to both the Russian and Polish archives helped to provide this fresh perspective.

1511. Prazmowska, Anita. **Britain and Poland, 1939-1943: The Betrayed Ally.** xi, 233p.: map. *Cambridge Russian, Soviet, and Post-Soviet Studies.* New York: Cambridge University Press, 1995. Includes bibliographical references (pp. 217-23) and index.

"In this book Anita Prazmowska looks at British policies from the point of view of wartime strategy, relating this to Polish government expectations and policies. She describes a tragic situation where Polish soldiers were trapped between the grandiose and unrealistic plans of their government and the harsh realities of a war which they fought with no prospect of a satisfactory outcome for them or their country" (frontispiece).

Communism

1512. Snyder, Timothy. **Nationalism, Marxism, and Modern Central Europe: A Biography of Kazimierz Kelles-Krauz (1872-1905)**. xiv, 321p., [10] p. of plates: illus., maps. *Harvard Papers in Ukrainian Studies*. Cambridge, Mass.: Distributed by Harvard University Press for the Ukrainian Research Institute. Includes bibliographical references (pp. [275]-321).

Kelles-Krauz was the leading theorist of the Polish Socialist Party and a prominent intellectual. "He urged recognition of the national status of the non-Polish inhabitants of the former Polish-Lithuanian Commonwealth, proposed that Poles support the national aspirations of their eastern neighbors, and was outstanding in his advocacy of Polish-Jewish reconciliation" (p. ix). This biography covers his life from his boyhood through the culmination of his political career.

Language and Literature

1513. Bielec, Dana. **Polish: An Essential Grammar**. xi, 294p.: illus. London: Routledge, 1998. Includes index.

"This unique Polish grammar for English speakers is an easy-to-use reference guide to the most important aspects of current Polish as used by native speakers. Written without technical jargon it focuses on the real patterns of use in Poland today" (frontispiece). This volume has numerous special features that allow the student to create a diminutive from a noun, create adjectives from nouns, create feminine from masculine nouns, alter verb meaning with prefixes, predict vowel and consonant changes, and punctuate direct speech properly. This guide is intended for all levels of users: students or travelers.

1514. Brzozowska-Krajka, Anna. **Polish Traditional Folklore: The Magic of Time**. 259p.: illus. *East European Monographs*, 498. Boulder, Colo.: East European Monographs; New York: Distributed by Columbia University Press, 1998. Includes bibliographical references (pp. 237-52) and index.

The author explores the role of time and order in traditional Polish folktales. Individual chapters cover such themes as the cosmogonic myth and the folkloric opposition of night-day, the magic of a good beginning, a mediating structure of daybreak and natural markers of organization of time, and the folkloric vision of temporal artifacts.

1515. **Dictionary of Polish Literature**. Edited by E. J. Czerwinski. ix, 488p. Westport, Conn.: Greenwood Press, 1994. Includes bibliographic references and index.

This volume was begun in 1986. It has undergone significant changes reflecting the changes in the political scene. Critical evaluations of controversial authors have appeared since 1990, allowing the editor to include more substantial entries on such figures. The book is intended as a reference for scholars and those with a limited knowledge of Polish literature. Entries include basic information such as dates of birth and death, biographical overview, in-depth discussions of major works, a brief discussion of the author's use of themes, and his or her place in Polish and world literature. Brief bibliographies are included with each entry and include the definitive edition of all the author's works, a list of English-language translations, and in many cases English critical studies. There are also entries on literary periods, universities, individual works, and movements. A general bibliography is included in the volume to help the interested English-language student of Polish literature.

1516. Gladsky, Thomas S. **Princes, Peasants, and Other Polish Selves: Ethnicity in American Literature**. ix, 313p. Amherst: University of Massachusetts Press, 1992. Includes bibliographical references (pp. 289-302) and index.

Thomas Gladsky takes up the debate on "ethnic literature" in this study. He approaches the subject of the Polish literary self by building on the work of Werner Sollors. In particular, he focuses on the conflict between consent and descent literatures. Sollors had defined these as the conflict between inheritance and choice. Descent literature for Poles has evolved, since its beginnings in the 19th century, where their image, self-created and created by others, portrays them as "princes and patriots." Gladsky begins his discussion here and then follows the developing image of the Pole from 1880 to 1930 when the "Polish Literary Self" was invented. The remainder of Part I of this volume follows the development of this image to World War II. Part II is devoted to the evolution of the Polish-American identity in literature. Ultimately, Gladsky concludes that, "In effect, descent writers have decided that ethnics are indeed the bearers of something, which—ironically but not surprisingly—is America as it might be" (p. 8). In the course of this study Gladsky examines the works of Anthony Bukoski, Lester Cohen, Henryk Sienkiewicz, Isaac B. Singer, Phillip Roth, Darryl Poniscan, Tennessee Williams, and many others that he feels have contributed to the definition of Pole in American literature.

1517. **Dictionary of 1000 Polish Proverbs**. Edited by Miroslaw Lipinski. 129p. *Hippocrene Bilingual Proverbs*. New York: Hippocrene Books, 1997. Includes index.

The purpose of this book is to present a collection of 1,000 important and commonly used Polish proverbs. Its scope is limited to proverbs that have a general or literal equivalent in English. The proverbs are arranged alphabetically using the key Polish word in the proverb.

1518. Mikos, Michael J. **Polish Baroque and Enlightenment Literature: An Anthology**. 382p. Columbus, Ohio: Slavica Publishers, 1996. Includes bibliography.

This is a selective collection of English translations of Polish poetry and prose in the Baroque age and the Enlightenment. Two-thirds of the more than 200 selections appear in English for the first time.

1519. Mikos, Michael J., trans. **Polish Renaissance Literature: An Anthology.** 275p. Columbus, Ohio: Slavica Publishers, 1995. Includes bibliographic references.

Like its companion volumes for Polish medieval and Baroque and Enlightenment literature, this collection includes a representative section of major works of poetry, prose, and drama. This diverse anthology includes epigrams, fables, songs, sonnets, elegies, letters, sermons, tales, treatises, and chronicles. Sixty-three of the 122 texts have been rendered into English for the first time.

1520. Mikos, Michael J., trans. **Medieval Literature of Poland: An Anthology.** xxxiv, 223p. *Garland Library of Medieval Literature*, vol. 82. Series B. New York: Garland, 1992. Includes bibliographical references (pp. xxxi-xxxiv).

Michael Mikos has collected and translated a selection of polish literature from a variety of genres. These include chronicles, religious and secular poetry, and religious and secular prose. Some of the works are translated from Latin. A lengthy introduction provides a cultural and historical background. Brief bibliographical sketches precede those pieces where the author is known.

1521. Segel, Harold B. **Stranger in Our Midst: Images of the Jew in Polish Literature.** xiv, 402p.: illus. Ithaca, N.Y.: Cornell University Press, 1996. Includes bibliographical references.

As Segel remarks in his introduction, "This book is an attempt to look at Polish-Jewish relations from the perspective of Polish literature. Or to be more specific, from the viewpoint of that Polish imaginative literature written by Poles who were not, or are not, Jews" (p. xi). His study is arranged in five parts: (1) from the Renaissance to the mid-19th century; (2) from positivism to modernism; (3) from World War I to World War II; (4) World War II and the Holocaust; and (5) the postwar era: war and Holocaust revisited. Within each part he examines specific literary works and the light they shed on Polish-Jewish relations.

Individual Authors

1522. Grynberg, Henryk. **The Victory**. Translated by Richard Louriexi. 107p. Evanston, Ill.: Northwestern University Press, 1993.

Henryk Grynberg is an émigré who was born a Polish Jew. He grew up in the Poland of World War II. In this book he describes the events of the period at the time the war ended in Europe. "This is a complex and painful passage in Poland's history.... In the opening pages of *The Victory* we see Poland as it emerges from the Nazi Occupation and the Holocaust. It is no longer a society but has become a jungle of Darwinian ferocity"

(p. viii). Grynberg describes the anti-Semitism that continued in Poland in the experiences of his family from 1944 to 1947.

1523. Herling-Grudzinski, Gustaw. **The Island: Three Tales**. Translated by Ronald Strom. 151p. New York: Viking, 1993. *The Island—The Tower—The Second Coming*.

Gustaw Herling-Grudzinski's book *The Island* first appeared in English in 1967. Herling-Grudzinski is a distinguished prose and literary critic. Born in Poland in 1919 he was imprisoned by the Soviets in 1940, freed in 1942, and soon after settled in the West. He has published numerous works in Polish. His volume recounting his experiences in the prison camps, *A World Apart*, appeared in English in 1951.

1524. **A Journey Through Other Spaces: Essays and Manifestos, 1944-1990**. Edited by Tadeusz Kantor. Translated by Michal Kobialkaxxi. 430p.: illus. Berkeley: University of California Press, 1993. Translated from Polish.

Tadeusz Kantor was an artist of amazing versatility. During his professional life, from 1958 to 1990, he was a visual artist, theater director, and author. He wrote numerous studies of the theater, many of which are brought together in the book. "The book is divided into two parts. Part 1 consists of a collection of Tadeusz Kantor's essays and manifestos and the Milano Lessons. Part 2 is a study of Kantor's experiments and writings between 1938 and 1990" (p. xviii). The editor has also included a bibliography of writings by and about Kantor.

1525. Kurczaba, Alex. **Conrad and Poland**. v, 258p. *East European Monographs*, 458. Boulder, Colo.: East European Monographs; New York: Distributed by Columbia University Press, 1996. Includes bibliographical references and indexes.

This is a collection of essays on Conrad. "The eleven essays of this volume represent a variety of critical methodologies including postcolonial criticism, feminist criticism, comparative literature, literary history, stylistics, sociology of literature and film studies. What unites these diverse approaches to Conrad is the conviction, stated or unstated, that a judicious consideration of Poland as background as the ground on which Conrad's works have exerted pronounced influence vitally enriches our understanding of Conrad and his works" (p. 6). The contributors include Alex Kurczaba, Stephen Brodsky, Susan Jones, Addison Bross, Kieth Carabine, Noel Peacock, Carola Kaplan, Mary Morzinski, Laurence Davies, Wieslay Krajka, and Jakob Lothe.

1526. Gombrowicz, Witold. **Trans-Atlantyk**. Translated by Carolyn French and Nina Karsov. xxx, 122p. New Haven, Conn.: Yale University Press, 1994.

This translation of Gombrowicz's unusual work was done by Carolyn French and Nina Karsov. The book includes an "Introduction" by Stanislaw Baranczak. *Trans-Atlantyk* was first published in Paris in 1953. "In his novel *Trans-Atlantyk*, he formulated, among other things, his attitude toward Polish cultural traditions" (*Dictionary of Polish Literature*, p. 129).

1527. Lem, Stanislaw, and Michael Kandel. **Highcastle: A Remembrance**. 1st U.S. ed. ix, 146p. New York: Harcourt Brace, 1995. "A Helen and Kurt Wolff Book."
This is an imaginative memoir by Polish author Stanislaw Lem about his childhood in Poland.

1528. Prus, Boleslaw. **The Sins of Childhood and Other Stories**. Translated by Bill Johnston. 247p. *European Classics*. Evanston, Ill.: Northwestern University Press, 1996.
Boleslaw Prus is one of Poland's greatest novelists. This is one of the few English-language collections of this 19th-century author's short stories. It includes "Stas's Little Adventure," "Michalko," "The Barrel Organ," "Antek," "Him," "The Waistcoat," "The Sins of Childhood," "The Fungi of This World," "Shadows," "In the Mountains," "From the Legends of Ancient Egypt," and "A Dream." The translation is by Professor Bill Johnston.

1529. Szewc, Piotr. **Annihilation: A Novel**. 1st ed. 107p. Normal, Ill.: Dalkey Archive Press, 1993.
Piotr Szewc has published poems, essays, and translations. In this, his first novel, Szewc describes a day in the life of a town just before World War II. It is a town that is soon destroyed by the war. "As the minutes on the Town Hall's clock measure the day's passing, and as this day's passing brings the town one day closer to its historical annihilation, a Book of the Day writes itself, preserving the town in memory against the ravages of time and history" (book jacket).

1530. Tryzna, Tomek, trans. **Miss Nobody**. 296p. New York: Doubleday, 1999.
This novel was originally published in 1993 and here translated for the first time.

1531. Zeromski, Stefan. **The Faithful River**. 193p. *European Classics*. Evanston, Ill.: Northwestern University Press, 1999. Translated from the Polish by Bill Johnston.
Stefan Zeromski is considered by many to be one of Poland's greatest writers. In this translation of *The Faithful River*, one of his finest works is made accessible to the English speakers. The novel tells the story of an injured solider, hiding from the Russian forces during Poland's struggle for independence from 1863 to 1864. The book was originally published in 1912. "*The Faithful River* constitutes a major achievement in European literature. Its compelling plot integrates political, intellectual, and romantic themes; and in

its portrayal of the human dimension of war and its juxtaposition of the personal and political, it speaks directly to the contemporary reader" (back cover).

The Society, Sociology

1532. Baker, T. Lindsay. **The First Polish Americans: Silesian Settlements in Texas**. xiv, 268p., [16] leaves of plates: illus. College Station: Texas A&M University Press, 1996. Includes index.

Baker has written a history of Silesian immigrants to Texas in the 1850s. Individual chapters explore the Upper Silesian origins of the immigrants, the founding of the first Polish colonies in Texas, Polish life on the frontier, the Civil War, reconstruction, Silesian institutions and settlement, the Silesian way of life in Texas, and the 20th century.

1533. Bernhard, Michael, and Henryk Szlajfer. **From the Polish Underground: Selections from Krytyka, 1978-1993**. xxxiii, 458p.: illus. University Park: Pennsylvania State University Press, 1995. Includes bibliographical references and index.

Krytyka was a journal of the Polish underground from 1978 to 1993. During that time it was distributed illegally in Poland. It was not a partisan publication. Therefore, it was an excellent vehicle for the many voices of social and political change in the country. The articles in this volume are divided into five sections: Politics, Sociology, Culture, Economics, and History. The editors have deliberately selected authors who are not so well known in the West. Those articles also represent a diversity of opinion in all areas. The editors have selected articles that will help the Western reader understand the changes affecting Eastern and Central Europe. "Developments in Poland prevent a unique perspective because the rebirth of civil society and the latest round in the struggle for democracy and national sovereignty there began earlier than in any other country in the bloc, even before the foundation of Solidarity in 1980. *Krytyka* was founded in the earliest stages of this process" (p. xxix).

1534. Dembinska, Maria. **Food and Drink in Medieval Poland: Rediscovering a Cuisine of the Past**. Revised and adapted by William Woys Weaver. Translated by Magdalena Thomas. 200p. Philadelphia: University of Pennsylvania Press, 1999. Includes bibliographical references (pp. 209-18).

Maria Dembinska wrote this work in 1963 as a doctoral dissertation. It has been considered a groundbreaking work since its appearance. Dembinska was interested in diet as a defining creature of "the Polish reality of that time" (p. x). It has taken many years for this translation project to come to fruition. The transformation has been supplemental with Dembinska's later writings on the subject that elaborate on the historical background and details on some of the foods. The recipes reconstructed are also new to this volume of Polish National Cookery, Poland in the Middle Ages, the "Dramatic Personae" of the Polish table, and a concluding chapter on cookery in medieval Poland.

1535. **The Challenge of East-West Migration to Poland**. Edited by Krystyna Iglicka and Keith Sword. xix, 237p.: illus., maps. *Studies in Russia and East Europe*. New York: St. Martin's Press, 1999. Includes bibliographical references and index.

In 1982, the Polish Migration Project was established at the School of Slavonic and East European Studies at the University of London. Previous publications by that group have focused on the origins of the Polish community in Britain, the mass deportation of Poles to the Soviet Union in the late 1930s, and ethnic identity of Polish emigrants in England. This volume shifts the focus to contemporary questions of migration for Poland. "The Project is currently examining population movements into Poland since the ending of communist rule in 1989—in particular, the different categories of migrants crossing Polish frontiers: asylum-seeking, labor-seeking immigrants, petty traders, tourists, and those in transit. Against this background, domestic legislative changes, challenges for entry, asylum and integration, migration policy, and changing relations with neighboring states are important" (p. ix). All of these topics are covered in the essays contributed by Krystyna Iglicka, Keith Sword, Marek Okolski, Tomasz Kuba Kozlowski, Slawomir Lodzinski, Paul Latawski, Marek Jerczynski, Krystian Heffner, and Krystyna Slany.

1536. Knab, Sophie Hodorowicz. **Polish Customs, Traditions, and Folklore**. 304p.: illus. 18, 750p. New York: Hippocrene Books, 1993.

This reference book is arranged chronologically by month, beginning with December. Within each month the author discusses the various customs and celebrations that take place during that period. This chronological section is followed by two other chapters covering birth customs and death customs. It also includes a bibliography, a listing of ethnographic regions, a pronunciation guide, and a brief glossary of terms. This volume would be useful for anyone wanting brief information about the history, development, and observance of Polish customs and traditions.

1537. Pula, James S. **Polish Americans: An Ethnic Community**. xi, 181p.: illus., map. New York; London: Twayne Publishers; Prentice Hall International, 1995. Includes bibliographical references (pp. 165-73) and index.

"The purpose of this modest volume is to lay the foundation for an understanding of the complexities of Polish American history and culture by focusing on central themes that have bound Polish Americans into an identifiable community—'Polonia' " (p. x). The book is chronologically arranged, beginning with 1870. The author traces the history of the Poles in America to 1980.

1538. Steinlauf, Michael. **Bondage to the Dead: Poland and the Memory of the Holocaust**. 1st ed. xiii, 189p., [22] p. of plates: illus. *Modern Jewish History*. Syracuse, N.Y.: Syracuse University Press, 1997. Includes bibliographical references (pp. 147-74) and index.

This volume traces the development of the Polish reaction to the Holocaust since World War II. Two introductory chapters describe and analyze Poles and Jews before the Holocaust and during World War II. Each subsequent chapter covers specific periods up through 1995.

1539. Wecławowicz, Grzegorz. **Contemporary Poland: Space and Society**. viii, 200p.: maps. Boulder, Colo.: Westview Press, 1996. Originally published London: UCL Press, 1996. Includes bibliographical references (pp. 189-93) and index.

"This book is an attempt to describe and interpret contemporary Polish society, with particular reference to its spatial differentiation" (p. 2). The volume is arranged in three parts. In Part 1 the author places Poland in its European context, shows the centrality of communism over the past 40 years, and indicates the transformation of society with the decline and rejection of the communist system. Part 2 looks at regional differentiation and post-communist transformation by examining regional and spatial structure, population, urban Poland, and ecology. Part 3 focuses on post-communist transformation and its spatial components. It covers the social consequence of transformation, the new political structure, the emergence of new regional differentiation, and security and modernization challenges.

Religion

1540. Michnik, Adam. **The Church and the Left**. xvii, 301p. Chicago: University of Chicago Press, 1993. Translation of: *Kosciól, lewica, dialog*.

This book was written between 1975 and 1976, and was intended as a reexamination of the relationship between the Catholic Church and the secular intelligentsia. The author discusses the role of the church in postwar Poland. He examines the evolution of the relationship between church and state and the hopes for more productive communications between those two major social institutions. The final chapter brings the book up to 1987 discussing pivotal events from 1977 to 1987.

1541. Scharf, Rafael F. **Poland, What Have I to Do with Thee?: Essays Without Prejudice**. xviii, 182p. London: Vallentine Mitchell, 1998.

This collection of essays by the renowned scholar of Jewish studies Raphael Scharf has two main themes. The first is an examination of the loss of the world of Polish Jewry as it existed before the war. The second is a study of why the Poles and Jews have moved so far apart. The essays were written at various times, beginning in 1977 and at a number of different places. "This is not a book about the Holocaust, but it is preoccupied with the consequences of the mass murder of the Jews of Poland and of Europe" (p. xv).

Dissident Movements

1542.   Cirtautas, Arista Maria. **The Polish Solidarity Movement: Revolution, Democracy and Natural Rights**. xii, 324p. *Routledge Studies of Societies in Transition*, 3. London: Routledge, 1997. Includes bibliographical references and index.

There have been a number of case studies of the Solidarity movement in Poland. In this study the author takes a comparative approach to her analysis. Cirtautas compares the experience of the Solidarity movement to the revolutions in France and America. "Arista Maria Cirtautas explains that the institutionalization of a strong democracy in Poland will ultimately depend upon whether the similarities to the great tradition of democratic revolutions outweigh the differences" (frontispiece).

National Minorities

1543.   Mazor, Michel. **The Vanished City**. Translated by David Jacobson. 187p. New York: Marsilio, 1993. Translation of: *La cité engloutie (Souvenirs du ghetto de Varsovie)*.

Mazor left Prussia during the civil war to settle in Warsaw. A lawyer by training, he joined the bar and was active in several Jewish organizations. When WWII broke out, he found himself confined to the Warsaw Ghetto. Mazor here focuses on the psychological aspects of the ghetto's inner life. "What this book shows us are the reactions within a community of hunted victims, the way of life that community adopts, and the state of mind that prevails in it" (p. 3).

1544.   Opalski, Magdalena, and Yisra el Bartal. **Poles and Jews: A Failed Brotherhood**. xi, 191p. Hanover, N.H.: University Press of New England, 1992. "Brandeis University Press." Includes bibliographical references (pp. [171]-183) and index.

Magdalena Opalski wrote her doctoral dissertation on Jews in Polish literature. Yisra el Bartal wrote his dissertation on Gentiles in Jewish literature. When the two authors met up they found that there was a great deal that was incompatible in the "visions of history" of these two groups. "This study deals with one particular aspect of the insurrectionary episode in Polish-Jewish relations. It examines Polish and Jewish perceptions of the short-lived Polish-Jewish rapprochement of the early 1860s and the interpretations of interethnic relations in the January insurrection offered by both literary traditions" (p. 4). The study covers the period from 1860 to 1914. While the authors acknowledge the difficulty of using literary accounts, necessarily subjective, as the focus of their study, they feel it is valuable. Literature does provide information on a kind of social reality.

1545. Pogonowski, Iwo. **Jews in Poland: A Documentary History: The Rise of Jews As a Nation from Congressus Judaicus in Poland to the Knesset in Israel**. 402p.: illus., maps. New York: Hippocrene Books, 1993. Includes bibliographical references.

This richly illustrated volume depicts the history of Jews in Poland for 1,000 years, ending just after World War II. It includes narrative text, chronology, maps, newspaper articles, headlines, illustrations, and any other conceivable method to make the history of Jews in Poland come alive. Part 1 traces the history in four chapters and related appendixes. Part 2 contains illustrations depicting Jews in Polish graphic arts and the Jewish press in Poland. Part 3 is an atlas that provides over 100 pages of maps for the period.

1546. Taler, Joseph. **In Search of Heroes**. xi, 260p., [1] p.: illus. Baltimore; Arnold, Md.: Gateway Press, 1995. Includes bibliographical references (p. [261]).

Joseph Taler is one of those who survived the horrors of the Nazi camps. In his autobiography he describes the experience. Taler is not a writer by trade, and English is not his native language. The book has the flavor of natural speech. The book has numerous photographs and includes a list of recommended reading.

1547. Weinbaum, Laurence. **A Marriage of Convenience: The New Zionist Organization and the Polish Government 1936-1939**. xiii, 295p., [16] p. of plates: illus., ports. Boulder, Colo.: East European Monographs; New York: Distributed by Columbia University Press, 1993. Includes bibliographical references (pp. 279-89) and index.

"This book examines the relationship between the Polish government and the New Zionist Organization (NZO)—Jabotinsky's Zionist Revisionist movement—in the years immediately preceding the outbreak of the war" (p. vii). It does this against an examination of the Jewish problem in Poland, the note of ideology among the revisionists. It looks at group memberships, leadership, and appeal, and how the revisionists differed from the established Zionist organizations. Weinbaum also dissects the various types of cooperation among the Polish government and the NZO including military aid to Palestine and the facilitation of emigration of Jews from Poland.

1548. Wyszogrod, Morris. **A Brush with Death: An Artist in the Death Camps**. xii, 254p.: illus., maps. *SUNY Series in Modern Jewish Literature and Culture*. New York: State University of New York Press, 1999. Includes bibliographical references and index.

"In this memoir Morris Wyszogrod recounts his experiences from the time of the Nazi invasion of Poland to the liberation of the Thereseinstadt concentration camp in 1945" (back cover). The author was an artist and described how he was able to use his talent to keep himself alive in some camps such as Budzyn. There the Nazis had him work as their decorator. In other situations he suffered along with the rest of the Jews, being forced to dig up mass graves and burn bodies to destroy the evidence of Nazi war crimes.

Wyszogrod uses his artistic talent to illustrate this volume, providing the artist's perspective on history's most horrific chapter.

Arts and Culture

1549.   Chylinska, Teresa. **Karol Szymanowski**. Translated by John Glowacki. 355p.: illus., facsims., music, ports. Los Angeles: University of Southern California Press, 1993. Cover title: *Szymanowski*. Translated from Polish. Discography (pp. 299-319). Includes bibliographical references (pp. 320-35) and index.

Polish composer Karol Szymanowski (1882-1937) did not belong to any movements or schools. His death two years prior to the outbreak of World War II almost obscured his contributions. However, although not written much about in the West, he is still well known in his native Poland. This volume presents both a biography of the composer and an erudite analysis of his compositions, and an analysis of the context of which they were written.

1550.   Falkowska, Janina. **The Political Films of Andrzej Wajda: Dialogism in Man of Marble, Man of Iron, and Danton**. x, 196p. Providence, R.I.: Berghahn Books, 1996. Includes bibliographical references (pp. [188]-193) and index.

Andrzej Wajda is considered by many to be one of Poland's greatest directors. In this study his political films *Man of Marble*, *Man of Iron*, and *Danton* are analyzed using Bakhtinian methodology. "Applying Bakhtin's concept of dialogism, the author shows how a creative interaction between the image on the screen and the viewer is established through Wajda's films. At the same time, she offers a detailed analysis of the historical events leading up to the collapse of the socialist system of Poland" (back cover). The book includes an appendix with synopsis of the films discussed in this book.

1551.   Muthesius, Stefan. **Art, Architecture and Design in Poland, 966-1990: An Introduction**. 107p., [1] p.: illus. (some col.), maps (some col.). Königstein im Taunus: K. R. Langewiesche Nachfolger H. Köster Verlagsbuchhandlung, 1994.

"The aim of this book is twofold. Firstly, a handbook-like breadth of information, to present something of the great variety of contributions to European art in Poland; secondly, a number of areas are specially emphasized, which, according to varied sets of criteria, represent something more specifically Polish" (p. 20). The author has selected works of high art to accomplish these aims. These are richly reproduced and formed by discussions of the development of Polish art. Overall the book is arranged chronologically, along with a general bibliography on Polish art; historical maps are included. The author draws on a variety of resources and fine reproductions to develop his discussion of these elements unique to Polish art.

1552. Ostrowski, Jan K., et al. **Art in Poland, 1572-1764: Land of the Winged Horsemen**. Translated by Krystyna Malcharek. 380p.: illus. (some col.), col. map. Alexandria, Va.: Art Services International, 1998. Catalog of a traveling exhibition organized and circulated by Art Services International, Alexandria, Va., in cooperation with the Wal Art Gallery, Baltimore, Md. Includes bibliographical references (pp. 371-77).

This interesting exhibition volume depicts both decorative arts and painting from the years 1572 to 1764. Most of the plates are in color and include explanatory text that sets the piece in its social and cultural context. The volume begins with several introductory essays covering topics such as "Definition and self-definition in Polish culture and art," "History of Poland in the 16th-18th centuries," "Polish baroque art in its social and religious context," "Mechanisms of contact between Polish and European baroque," "The Impact of the Orient on the culture of old Poland," and "Architecture in Poland, 1572-1764." The volume also includes biographies of artists, a table of significant political events in Poland, a glossary, and a bibliography.

1553. Pula, James S., and M. B. Biskupski. **Heart of the Nation: Polish Literature and Culture**. viii, 230p. New York: Columbia University Press, 1993. Includes index and appendix.

The papers contained herein were originally presented at an international congress held at Yale in 1992. The essays are arranged in two parts: essays on Polish culture and essays on Polish culture abroad, and the next part includes topics on literature and the fine arts.

1554. Rouard-Snowman, Margo. **Roman Cieslewicz**. 160p.: chiefly illus. (some col.). New York: Thames & Hudson, 1993. "Published to accompany a retrospective exhibition at the Pompidou Center, Paris"—Cover.

Cieslewicz is a graphic artist who emigrated to France in the 1960s. This catalog of his most notable works includes plates of posters, paintings, and other art objects. "The aim of this book is to show the evolution of Cieslewicz's work in a chronological, though fragmentary, way" (p. 10). The artist is known for his unique vision and his ability to draw the perceiver into his phantasmagorical world.

Romania

General Reference Works

1555. Treptow, Kurt W., and Marcel Popa. **Historical Dictionary of Romania**. lxv, 311p.: maps. *European Historical Dictionaries*, no. 15. Lanham, Md.: Scarecrow Press, 1996. Includes bibliographical references (pp. 229-310).

One in the series *European Historical Dictionaries*, this reference source is a good starting point for those trying to expand their knowledge of Romania. Following the arrangement of other volumes in the series, this dictionary begins with a historical chronology, followed by a list of the rulers of Romania from 1859 on. A map and lengthy introductory essay precede the dictionary entries. The latter are brief, clear entries on all major historical figures, events, and places. These entries are followed by a bibliography of almost 100 pages in length, arranged by topic.

History

1556. Alexandrescu, Ion. **A Short History of Bessarabia and Northern Bucovina**. 87p.: illus., maps (some col.). Iasi, Rom.: Romanian Cultural Foundation, 1994. Includes bibliographical references (pp. 85-87).

The problem of Bessarabia and northern Bucovina is a long-standing one. The area between the Prut and Dneister Rivers finally became part of Romania in 1918 with the creation of modern Romania. This history provides an outline of the political development of Bessarabia and northern Bucovina. Several relevant documents have also been provided.

1557. Braham, Randolph L. **Romanian Nationalists and the Holocaust: The Political Exploitation of Unfounded Rescue Accounts**. vi, 289p. *East European Monographs, Holocaust Studies series.* New York: Rosenthal Institute for Holocaust Studies, Graduate School of the City University. New York: Distributed by Columbia University Press, 1998. Includes bibliographical references and index.

"The basic objective of this study—the eighteenth volume in the *Holocaust Studies Series*—is to protect the integrity of the historical record of the Holocaust—an objective also shared by many Romanian Jewish and non-Jewish scholars" (p. 4). Randolph Braham is concerned in this study with the revision of the historical record that has been taking place. His purpose is to clarify the information on the Antonescu regime. In the past, Antonescu's responsibility for the crimes committed against the Jewish population in Romania has been minimized. The author examines the revisionist works that have made this case. He also chronicles events that took place under Antonescu. The book includes two appendixes, two documents on the Holocaust.

1558. Constantinesco, Nicholas. **Romania on the European Stage, (1875-1880): The Quest for National Sovereignty and Independence**. xvi, 204p. *East European Monographs*, 499. Boulder, Colo.: East European Monographs; New York: Distributed by Columbia University Press, 1998. Includes bibliographical references (pp.189-97) and index.

"It is the aim of this study to define and discuss the national objectives of the Romanians, to trace the major steps they had taken toward these objectives, and to point out the insurmountable difficulties they had encountered in their bitter struggle against the Big Powers in order to regain their formerly held position among the free and sovereign nations of Europe" (p. viii).

1559. Cretzianu, Alexandru. **Relapse into Bondage: Political Memoirs of a Romanian Diplomat, 1918-1947**. 351p. Iasi, Rom.; Portland, Oreg.: Center for Romanian Studies, 1998. Includes index.

This book describes the life of Romanian diplomat Alexandru Cretzianu. Cretzianu was born of a noble Romanian family in 1895. He joined the diplomatic corps in that country in 1918 and remained in diplomatic service for the next 25 years. "In these pages, the reader will discern that Cretzianu faithfully represents himself as pro-Western, pro-French, pro-British, pro-League of Nations, and demonstrates that Romania was not guilty of freely joining the Axis, but had no alternative but to do so after Britain and France abandoned the Little Entente in 1938."

1560. **Romania: A Historic Perspective**. Edited by Dinu Giurescu and Stephen Fischer-Galati. viii, 544p. *East European Monographs*, 457. Boulder, Colo.: East European Monographs; New York: Distributed by Columbia University Press, 1998. Includes bibliographical references.

"The aim of this work is to investigate the elements in and through which language and reason move. The term element is significant. Neither language, reason, nor action are objects; they are activities. . . . This is not, then, a treatise in metaphysics. . . . It is more an elemental writing, a discourse that establishes its fissures, bridges, and allusions within that of which it speaks and eludes the trap of a frontal confrontation" (p. x).

1561. Hitchins, Keith. **A Nation Affirmed: The Romanian National Movement in Transylvania 1860-1914**. 407p. Bucharest: Encyclopeadic Publishing House, 1999. Includes bibliographical indexes.
This landmark volume completes a three-volume history of the Romanian national movement in Transylvania. It began with *A Nation Discovered: Romanian Intellectuals in Transylvania and the Idea of Nation, 1700-1848* (1969), and continues in *Orthodoxy and Nationality: Andreiu Saguna and the Romanians of Transylvania, 1846-1873* (1977). "To suggest what the nature of the nationality problem in Hungary was in the final half-century of the Habsburg Monarchy's existence, to show how it became progressively more acute and how, in particular, Romanians and Magyars steadily drifted apart, and to explain why a solution to their differences became more and more complicated as the Romanian idea of autonomy was transformed into a striving for self-determination are the primary aims of the present work" (p. 10).

1562. Hitchins, Keith. **Romanians, 1774-1866**. xi, 337p.: maps. Oxford, Eng.: Clarendon Press, 1996. Includes bibliographical references (pp. [319]-328).
"To begin a history of modern Romania in 1774 may at first glance seem odd. No epic battle and no sudden break with the past occurred in that year. Yet, in however undramatic a fashion, it marked the onset of fundamental changes in the international status and the internal political and social structure of the principalities of Molchavia and Wallandinia" (p. 1). In this book Professor Hitchins examines the political, social, and cultural changes that marked its integration into Europe. He believes that it is particularly important during this period of their history that the Romanians adapt the European model to their culture. The book is arranged thematically. Each chapter explores a different aspect of this development beginning with an overview of Moldavia and Wallachia. Other topics include changes in society and the economy in the region; the development of a nation-state; the relationship of the Romanians and the Hapsburgs; and the impact of the 1848 revolution in the region.

1563. Hitchins, Keith. **Rumania: 1866-1947**. viii, 579p.: map. *Oxford History of Modern Europe*. Oxford, Eng.: Clarendon Press; Oxford University Press, 1994. Includes bibliographical references (pp. [548]-569) and index.
Hitchins' history of Rumania during the period 1866-1947 is a classic in the field. He is especially interested in the process of nation building that occurred during this period. He traces the efforts of the intellectual and political elite "to form a national state encompassing all Rumanians and to provide it with modern political institutions and an economy and social structure based on industry and the city rather than on agriculture and the village" (p. vii).

1564. Kellogg, Frederick. **The Road to Romanian Independence**. xvi, 265p.: illus., map. West Lafayette, Ind.: Purdue University Press. Includes bibliographical references (pp. 239-51) and index.

After nearly four centuries of Turkish domination, Romanians sought independence to become a sovereign state. In exploring this quest, the author examines foreigners and the Jewish question, foreign construction, foreign trade, foreign entanglements and alliances, and the final cycle of war and peace in the late 1870s, just prior to independence.

1565. **Biography and Romanian Studies**. Edited by Kurt W. Treptow. 387p. Iasi, Rom.; Portland, Oreg.: Center for Romanian Studies, 1998. Includes bibliographical references.

The papers given at the Third International Conference of the Center for Romanian Studies held in Iasi, July 9-10, 1997, are collected in this volume. "The reader will find here presentations and discussions of biographies of notable Romanian historical, political, literary, and cultural personalities and how they played an important role in Romanian culture and history" (p. 7). Essays are in various languages, primarily English and Romanian. Contributors include W. P. Meurs, Olga Tudorica Impey, Paul Michelson, Nicholas M. Nagy-Talaveva, Ernest H. Latham, Alice Forbess, Michael Howard Impey, Adam Sorkin, Ingeborg M. Kohn, and Ingmar Sohrman.

1566. Lazar, Istvan. **Transylvania: A Short History**. 248p. Budapest, Hungary: Corvina, 1997.

This brief narrative history of Transylvania begins in ancient times and follows the country's development to the present. The author has written several books on Transylvania. Unfortunately, this volume lacks a bibliography.

1567. Livezeanu, Irina. **Cultural Politics in Greater Romania: Regionalism, Nation Building and Ethnic Struggle, 1918-1930**. xvii, 340p.: illus., maps. Ithaca, N.Y.: Cornell University Press, 1995. Includes bibliographical references and index.

The interwar years in Romania are viewed by many as a kind of golden era of peace between the violence of the two World Wars, followed by the Soviet takeover. This book looks at the nationalist movement that evolved during that period. Livezeanu focuses on nation building in Romania during the 1920s and the nationalist movement that accompanied it. She believes that the origins of fascism can be found in the political movements of the period. The study is divided into two parts. The first part examines the cultural struggles of the time: unification, romanization, and regionalism. The second part of the books focuses on student nationalism and the fascist movement it founded.

1568. **NATO's Eastern Dilemmas**. Edited by S. Neil MacFarlane, Joel J. Sokolsky, and David G. Haglund. x, 231p. Boulder, Colo.: Westview Press, 1994. Includes bibliographical references and index.

This collection of essays examines the dilemma faced by NATO in the years immediately after the dissolution of the Soviet Union. After having existed as a wonderful example of a global security organization, it was beset by several incidents that posed new challenges. Among these was the existence of the Yugoslav conflict and the other was the desire of former Warsaw Pact countries to join NATO. The essays are arranged in four parts: (1) Eastern challenges; (2) Western interests; (3) institutional adaptation; and (4) a conclusion.

1569. Torrey, Glenn. **Romania and World War I**. 392p. Iasi, Rom.; Portland, Oreg.: Center for Romanian Studies, 1998. Includes bibliographical references and index.

Glenn Torrey here provides a detailed study of Romania's role in World War I. Drawing on archival sources from Romania and its World War I allies, he pieces together a chronological picture of the war.

1570. Vianu, Vidia. **Censorship in Romania**. x, 233p. Budapest, Hungary; New York: Central European University Press, 1998.

In this volume, Vidia Vianu shows the effects of censorship on those most directly concerned, the writers. She has interviewed authors of all genres who experienced this repressive policy during three different periods: pre-World War II, the period of communist domination, and the contemporary period. For the purposes of this study, the latter period includes those writers born under communism who rebelled against the system. Each chapter is devoted to one author. Each begins with a brief biographical sketch followed by an interview conducted by Vianu. Many also include examples of the author's writing. "Vianu has chosen a series of subversive writings that not only indicted communism but were also widely embraced by the Romanian public" (back cover).

Economics, Trade, and Business

1571. Daianu, Daniel. **Transformation of Economy As a Real Process: An Insider's Perspective**. x, 324p.: illus. Aldershot, Eng.: Ashgate, 1998. Includes bibliographical references and index.

Daniel Daianu composes a picture of the processes of economic transformation in Romania. The introduction presents the major arguments of the text. The remaining chapters focus on three major topics: institutional change, macroeconomic stabilization and restructuring, and transforming the international climate. "This book addresses the question of how to create conditions for sustainable development in societies where these are lacking, and stresses the importance of institutional change" (back cover).

1572. Love, Joseph L. **Crafting the Third World: Theorizing Underdevelopment in Rumania and Brazil**. xiv, 348p.: illus. *Comparative Studies in History, Institutions, and Public Policy*. Stanford, Calif.: Stanford University Press, 1996. Includes bibliographical references (pp. [297]-333) and index.

In this major synthesis of the development literature on Brazil and Rumania, Love devotes his attention to the indigenous efforts of Brazilian and Romanian economists to develop theories explaining the reasons for the rate and character of development in both countries. Both countries were dependent on others for their development and this element of dependency is central to his discussion and to the thinkers whom he examines.

1573. Shen, Raphael. **The Restructuring of Romania's Economy: A Paradigm of Flexibility and Adaptability**. xvi, 230p.: illus., map. Westport, Conn.: Praeger, 1997. Includes bibliographical references (pp. [219]-223) and index.

There has been a good deal written about Romania since 1989. The author of this book does not feel that the studies so far published have given the Western reader a complete picture of the situation in that country and the many obstacles they face. "This book analyzes how, against calculated probabilities and within a relatively short period of time, Romania has already stabilized and assembled all the basic ingredients for a successful transformation from the centralized system to that of a market-driven economy" (p. xvi). The author has used documents such as reform legislation, decrees, official statistics, and field research for this study. Shen discusses price structure, labor, wages, financial reform, privatization, foreign trade, the move to liberalize foreign investment, industrial reform, and agricultural reform in this book.

Government, Politics, and Law

1574. Carothers, Thomas. **Assessing Democracy Assistance: The Case of Romania**. vi, 144p. Washington D.C.: Carnegie Endowment Book, 1996. Includes bibliographical references (pp.133-37) and index.

Carothers provides a penetrating analysis of our democracy-building efforts in Romania, which is described as a "gray area" for democracy building. The reason for this is that with all the American and European assistance given to Romania since 1989, a lot of it has been posturing rather than democratic process. Here the author "assesses the kind of democracy assistance provided to Romania. He examines how such assistance relates to our overall policy objectives in the country and region, the impact it has had on seven institutions and processes critical to Romanian democracy, and its effectiveness compared to that of European donors" (p. v). Carothers poses an insightful conclusion: "The case for democracy assistance may at times depend less on the specific impact of the assistance on others than on what the assistance says and means about ourselves."

1575. Deletant, Dennis. **Ceausescu and the Securitate: Coercion and Dissent in Romania, 1965-1989**. xxxii, 424p.: map. Armonk, N.Y.: M. E. Sharpe, 1996. Includes bibliographical references (pp. 405-17) and index.

Deletant speaks from firsthand knowledge of the workings of the Securitate, Romania's secret police. He and his wife, who is Romanian by birth, were given a hard time when she tried to obtain a passport to go to London with him after their marriage. In this well-researched study, Deletant examines the relationship between the Securitate and Ceausescu's hold on power in Romania for the period 1965 to his assassination in 1989.

1576. Gallagher, Tom. **Romania After Ceausescu**. viii, 267p.: map. Edinburgh, Scot.: Edinburgh University Press, 1995. Includes bibliographical references (pp. 245-56) and index.

"Based on extensive fieldwork, Tom Gallagher explains what prevented the promise of the 1989 revolt from being fulfilled. He shows how continuity as well as change has marked Romania's rocky transition to a semi-pluralistic form of politics, and examines how nationalism has been used to deflect critical attention from economic mismanagement and human rights abuses" (back cover).

1577. McCollum, James K. **Is Communism Dead Forever?** xiii, 162p. Lanham, Md.: University Press of America, 1998. Includes bibliographical references (pp. [155]-157) and index.

James McCollum was a Fulbright scholar studying in Romania in 1991. He has compiled a case study of one individual's life to illustrate the conditions of day-to-day life in the communist system. He has supported this with other information gathered while interviewing a wide variety of people from different professions. "The impressions we gathered show that progress is being made, but not at the rate most of us feel is possible, and many inequities are occurring on the road to democracy and free market. We hope that the ideas presented here will lead to improved decisions within former communist countries" (p. xii). The book includes an appendix on "Effectiveness of Management Internships: The Romanian Experience" written by the author.

1578. Michelson, Paul E. **Romanian Politics, 1859-1871: From Prince Cuza to Prince Carol**. 344p.: illus., map. Iasi, Rom.: Center for Romanian Studies, 1998. Includes bibliographical references (pp. [273]-333) and index.

Michelson "aims at presenting a systematic description and analysis of Romanian political life from the inception of the modern Romanian national state in 1859 to the abdication crisis of 1871 that marked a turning point in the development of that state" (p. 15). He recognizes that this type of political history still provides a firm foundation for the study of modern history. His six chapters are arranged in three parts. Part 1, Prelude, describes the current state of scholarship on modern Romanian politics from 1859 to 1916 and then focuses on the prelude to the formation of the Romanian state in the years 1856 to 1859. In Part 2 he examines political life under Prince Cuza, including the double election in 1859 through exile in 1866. In Part 3 he describes political life under Carol I, 1866-1871. The volume also includes a chronology of major events from 1859 to 1871 and a bibliographical essay.

1579. **Romania in Transition.** Edited by Lavinia Stan. xviii, 218p. Aldershot, Eng.: Dartmouth University Press, 1997. Includes bibliographical references and index.

In order to preserve the contents from becoming out of date quickly, the contributors have concentrated on issues of lasting interest. The primary focus is the political and economic transition process. The essays are concerned with nationalism, democratization, mass media and democracy, macroeconomic stabilization, privatization, competition law and policy, marketing, and the consumer.

Foreign Relations

1580. Hazard, Elizabeth W. **Cold War Crucible: United States Foreign Policy and the Conflict in Romania, 1943-1952.** ix, 258p.: illus. Boulder, Colo.: East European Monographs; New York: Distributed by Columbia University Press, 1996. Includes bibliographical references (pp. [245]-253) and index.

Hazard has three goals. First, she examines the policies of the United States in the immediate postwar period in order to thwart the Soviet's control over Romania, which was traditionally hostile to Russia. Second, she shows how the policies adopted in Romania in 1944 and 1945 later were incorporated into the Truman Containment policy. Finally, she indicates how U.S. cold war propaganda and clandestine operations in Romania, among other things, worsened hostility between the two superpowers.

1581. Kirk, Roger E., and Mircea Raceanu. **Romania Versus the United States: Diplomacy of the Absurd, 1985-1989.** xii, 320p. New York: St. Martin's Press, 1994. Includes bibliographical references (pp. 303-12) and index.

Roger Kirk was U.S. ambassador to Romania from 1985 to 1989. Mircea Raceanu was acting deputy director of the Romanian Foreign Ministry, America's directorate during many of the years discussed in this book. In this volume Kirk and Raceanu describe their perceptions of the events of those transitional years. "In this case, we examine the diplomatic initiatives each government took, the motivations behind them, and what they were intended to achieve. Because we were working on different sides of the table, we can also describe how one government's initiative was perceived by the other, often very differently from its intended effect" (p. xi). The book is chronologically arranged and includes several appendixes with diplomatic documents.

Communism

1582. Verdery, Katherine. **What Was Socialism, and What Comes Next?** 298p. *Princeton Studies in Culture-Power-History.* Princeton, N.J.: Princeton University Press, 1996. Includes bibliographical references (pp. [235]-287).

Verdery warns the reader that although the focus in this book may be Romania, her aim is to help us all think about what socialism was and what will become of it. Romania, she admits, is not a typical case, but for that matter no communist country is a typical case. Her purpose therefore is "to point to questions one might ask or approaches one might take in studying the several countries of the former Soviet bloc" (p. 11). To do this she has included chapters on crucial themes such as civil society, marketization, privatization, and nationalism.

Language and Literature

1583. The Phantom Church and Other Short Stories from Romania. Edited by Georgiana Farnoaga and Sharon King. Translated by Florin Manolescu. 263p. *Pitt Series in Russian and East European Studies.* Pittsburgh, Pa.: University of Pittsburgh Press, 1996. Biographical notes by Florin Manolescu. Includes bibliographical references (pp. 239-40).

This anthology presents the literature of Romanians both at home and in the Diaspora as part of one literary culture. The stories presented here were written between 1949 and 1996 and exhibit the "notion of a genuine Romanian literature, one that flourished despite the political dogmatism of those who tried to control and therefore destroy it. The variety of stories included demonstrates the extent to which the policy of conformity and control typical of all dictatorships failed both culturally and spiritually" (p. xiii).

1584. City of Dreams and Whispers: An Anthology of Contemporary Poets of Iasi. Edited by Adam J. Sorkin. 295p. Iasi, Rom.; Portland, Oreg.: Center for Romanian Studies, 1998. Notes on the poets: (pp. [14]-18). Includes bibliographical references and index.

Iasi is considered by many to be the cultural center of Romania. Certainly, Adam Sorkin places it in that category. In this book he has collected the poetry of many of Iasi's best contemporary writers. These include Irina Andone, Radu Andriescu, Emil Brumaru, Maria Codrat, Nichita Damilov, Aurel Dumitrasca, Dan Grosu, Dorim Popa, Cristian Simionescu, Cassian Maria Spiridon, and Mihai Ursachi. Many of the poems were translated in collection with the authors. The collection offers the reader a unique view of Romania's contribution to the poetic genre. Brief bibliographical information on the author is included.

Individual Authors

1585. Codrescu, Andrei. The Blood Countess. 453p. New York: Dell, 1996.

This novel relates Countess Elizabeth Bathory of Hungary (1560-1613), who was known as the blood countess to Drake Bathory-Kereshtur, one of her direct descendants. The life of the countess and her perverse obsessions (the necessity of bathing in the blood of virgins being one of the more noteworthy) links directly with Drake, who in 20th-century America confesses to a hideous crime. Codrescu is the author of several other novels, many of which have been translated into English.

1586. Manea, Norman. **The Black Envelope.** Translated by Patrick Camiller. 329p. Evanston, Ill.: Northwestern University Press/Hydra Books, 1996. "An earlier version of this text was published in Romanian as *Plicul negru*..."—t.p. verso.

This is Manea's fourth book that has been translated into English. The others are *On Clowns: The Dictator and the Artist*; *October, Eight O'clock*; and *Compulsory Happiness*.

The Society, Sociology

1587. Gross, Peter. **Mass Media in Revolution and National Development: The Romanian Laboratory.** 1st ed. xiii, 206p.: map. Ames: Iowa State University Press, 1996. Includes bibliographical references (pp. 171-94) and index.

Gross was in Timisoara within three weeks after the overthrow of the Ceausescu regime. In this book he attempts to bring some understanding to the role of mass media and journalism in a context of transition. He not only studies how mass media and journalism contributed to this transition, but also analyzes how the institution of mass media and journalism itself made this transition.

1588. Kligman, Gail. **The Politics of Duplicity: Controlling Reproduction in Ceausescu's Romania.** xv, 358p., [12] p. of plates: illus. Berkeley: University of California Press, 1998. Includes bibliographical references (pp. 331-46) and index.

During 23 of the 24 years of Ceausescu's regime in Romania, the government enforced one of the most repressive and brutal pronatalist policies in the world. At the center of the policy was a strict antiabortion law. This study looks at the ethnography of reproduction and through that prism at the ethnography of the state. "This critical inquiry enables us to comprehend more fully both the lived processes of social atomization and dehumanization that are legacies of the Ceausescu era, and the means by which reproductive issues become embedded in social-political agendas, both national and international in scope."

National Minorities

1589. Iancu, Carol. **Jews in Romania, 1866-1919: From Exclusion to Emancipation.** xiii, 191p. Boulder, Colo.: East European Monographs; New York: Distributed by Columbia University Press, 1996. Includes bibliographical references (pp. [186]-191).

This study, translated from the French and based on the author's doctoral dissertation, is intended to explore the following paradox. "How did it happen that the same persons who organized and directed the Revolution of 1848, who proclaimed equality in civil and political rights for their 'Jewish brothers,' became the promoters of official persecution against the Jews after becoming ministers and prime ministers in the governments of Prince Carol? For what reasons did they later evade the political emancipation of the Jews demanded by the Congress of Berlin, which was even a condition for the international recognition of Romania, and then also degrade their status by transforming them from natives into 'foreigners not protected by a foreign power?' " (pp. xi-xii). Iancu explores these and other questions in his study, which unfortunately contains no footnotes and a slim six-page bibliography.

Former Yugoslavia

General Reference Works

1590. Carmichael, Cathie. **Croatia**. xxv, 194p.: 1 map. *World Bibliographical series*, 216. Santa Barbara, Calif.: ABC-CLIO, 1999. Includes indexes.

This comprehensive annotated bibliography of works about Croatia is arranged in broad general subject categories. Most of the books annotated are in English, but several are included that were written in Western European languages and in Croatian and Serbian. In an introductory essay Carmichael provides a brief history of Croatia from the 5th century to the present day. Aware of political bias that accompanies any publication on Croatia and Serbia, Carmichael included works that she personally did not agree with and also some that may be considered as anti-Croatian. Her aim was not to take sides, but to present a broad range of information about Croatia.

Like other volumes in this series, the various subject categories by which she arranged the annotations cover the expected topics of history, geography, language, religion, society, politics, foreign relations, the economy, education, literature, and the arts. In addition, she also provides several topics that are unique to Croatia such as the national question, minorities, Croatians abroad, and the Croatian War of Independence (1990-1995). Author, title, and subject indexes provide good access to the contents.

1591. Cuvalo, Ante. **Historical Dictionary of Bosnia and Herzegovina**. lvi, 355p.: maps. *European Historical Dictionaries*, no. 25. Lanham, Md.: Scarecrow Press, 1997. Includes bibliographical references (pp. 253-353).

Although this useful handbook is designated as a historical dictionary, it is actually much more than that. About half of the pages of this volume are devoted to entries for historical terms, persons, and events that are centrally relevant to the history of Bosnia and Herzegovina. The other half of the book contains materials that would be of great use to anyone studying these countries. After a brief introduction, the author provides a 50-page chronology of major events in the history of Bosnia and Herzegovina and maps relevant to this chronology. Then, prior to the entries of historical terms, he gives an overview of the geography, religious orientation, and history of this region. Following the entries for the historical terms, Professor Cuvalo has compiled a multilingual bibliography of Bosnia and Herzegovina that also includes regional histories and other works relevant to that history.

This work delivers much more than the title indicates. It would be of immense use for anyone doing research on Bosnia and Herzegovina during any time period.

1592. **Yugoslavia: A Comprehensive English-Language Bibliography.** Edited by Francine Friedman. xv, 547p. Wilmington, Del.: Scholarly Resources, 1993. Includes author and subject indexes.

This is an enumerative, nonannotated bibliography of 9,059 works in English published from the 17th century to the present day. It includes monographs, journal articles, chapters of books, theses and dissertations, papers and lectures written for professional meetings, among others. Newspaper articles have been excluded. The items are arranged in classified subject order, and are accessible through author and subject indexes.

1593. Matulic, Rusko. **Bibliography of Sources on the Region of Former Yugoslavia.** viii, 441p. *East European Monographs*, 504. Boulder, Colo.: East European Monographs; New York: Distributed by Columbia University Press, 1998. Includes indexes.

This bibliography covers all subjects dealing with the former Yugoslavia and successor states. Most of the entries (more than 12,500) are items written primarily in Western languages. The entries are arranged under 16 major subject categories, with further subdivisions as appropriate. The bibliography also includes several unpublished sources, a listing of videos, and a series of 25 maps showing internal border changes. The compiler has also provided an index of authors and editors, as well as subjects. A shortcoming of the subject index is that with very few subject terms, the lists of relevant items under each term become virtually useless. The bibliography is not annotated.

1594. Plut-Pregelj, Leopoldina, and Carole Rogel. **Historical Dictionary of Slovenia.** xxvii, 345p.: maps. *European Historical Dictionaries*, no. 13. Lanham, Md.: Scarecrow Press, 1996. Includes bibliography (pp. 305-43).

This volume on Slovene history is the 13th volume in the Scarecrow Press *European Historical Dictionaries* series. Leopoldina Plut-Pregelj is a specialist in the history of Slovene education, and Carole Rogel is a Professor Emeritus of History from Ohio State University. These two scholars bring their expertise to this general resource which is intended to be accessible to the general reader as well as the specialist. The book is arranged as the other volumes of the series, beginning with a chronology of Slovene history. This is followed by a set of historical maps and an overview of Slovene history. The bulk of the book is taken up with alphabetically arranged entries; these cover both general topics such as banking, folk customs, economy, and education as well as subject names specific to the Slovene experience, such as "Moderna" is to Slovene literary trends. There are numerous biographical entries. Related entries are referenced at the end of each article. The extensive bibliography is organized by subject.

1595. Statistical Office of the Republic of Macedonia. **Statistical Yearbook of the Republic of Macedonia**. xxxi, 717p. Skopje, Macedonia: Statistical Office of the Republic of Macedonia, 1996.

This bilingual yearbook (English and Macedonian) gives statistical data on all domains of life and work relating to the Republic of Macedonia, including international aspects.

History

1596. Bracewell, Catherine Wendy. **The Uskoks of Senj: Piracy, Banditry, and Holy War in the Sixteenth-Century Adriatic**. xiv, 329p.: illus., maps. Ithaca, N.Y.: Cornell University Press, 1992. Includes bibliographical references (pp. 309-22) and index.

The Uskoks of Senj have been viewed in a variety of seemingly contradictory lights in the historical literature. To the Venetians they were pirates of the Adriatic. The rural populations on the Ottoman, Venetian, and Hapsburg borders supported them. Catherine Bracewell attempts to examine the vision the Uskoks had of themselves in this work. "Throughout the emphasis is on the social, economic, and political realities that produced the Uskoks and on the ways in which these people responded to the problems that confronted them. This approach concentrates on the Uskoks themselves, asking not what they did, but why they did it; asking not just what were their relations with their allies, their victims and each other, but also how they perceived and justified these relations" (p. 15). Bracewell has drawn on a wide variety of sources: Venetian court documents, testimony before Dalmatian officials, letters and reports of the Uskoks themselves, military frontier sources, papal sources, and various local sources. The author hoped to be able to glean the most complete picture by examining a range of sources. The book traces the history of the Uskoks chronologically from their first appearance in the 1520s to their expulsion to Senj in 1618. There is a glossary and chronology included.

1597. Burdett, Anita L. P. **The Historical Boundaries Between Bosnia, Croatia, Serbia: Documents and Maps, 1815-1945**. 2 vols.: facsims., maps (some col.). [England]: Archive Editions, 1995. Vol. 2 consists of 24 folded maps.

Between 1815, the Congress of Vienna, and 1945, the end of Word War II, the boundaries of Yugoslavia were constantly changing. This collection focuses on key events during these years that affected its changing borders. Over 50 documents have been reproduced in the first volume of this set. All have been drawn from the British official record in the Public Record Office. The editor has selected documents that were central to frontier issues. An extensive selection of maps from some periods is included in Volume 2. These vary in detail from hand-drawn maps to highly detailed published materials. Together the two volumes provide the historian with a rich source of primary materials on this troubled region.

1598. Cohen, Philip J. **Serbia's Secret War: Propaganda and the Deceit of History**. xxvi, 235p.: maps. *Eastern European Studies*, no. 2. College Station: Texas A&M University Press, 1996. Includes bibliographical references (pp. 211-28) and index.

"In this penetrating study, Philip J. Cohen argues that Serbian leaders have been basically rewriting their nation's history since the end of World War I" (back cover). Philip Cohen argues that the image of Serbia as a victim is being perpetuated by the Western media. Cohen draws on many previously unpublished documents to make his case. The book is arranged topically beginning with an examination of the origins of Serbian fascism and then turning to an overview of the Serbian state during World War II. Cohen then focuses on the Serbian role in the Holocaust. Turning to relations with Croatian and Bosnia-Herzegovina the author explores the resistance movements. Finally, he turns to the subject of Serbian historical revisionism. The volume includes two appendixes: one listing the signatories of the "Appeal to the Serbian Nation" and the other listing the members of the collaborationist government.

1599. Costa, Nicholas. **Shattered Illusions: Albania, Greece and Yugoslavia**. 200p. *East European Monographs*, 520. Boulder, Colo.: East European Monographs; New York: Distributed by Columbia University Press, 1998. Includes bibliographical references (pp. [203]-208) and index.

Nicholas Costa tells the story of the resistance during World War II in Albania, Greece, and Yugoslavia. Costa is a specialist on Albania.

1600. Dedijer, Vladimir. **The Yugoslav Auschwitz and the Vatican: The Croatian Massacre of the Serbs During World War II**. 444p.: illus., map. Buffalo, N.Y.; Freiburg, Ger.: Prometheus Books; Ahriman-Verlag, 1992. Rev. translation of the German version, which was translated from the Serbo-Croatian. Original title: *Vatikan i Jasenovac*. Includes bibliographical references.

Jasenovak was a concentration camp built by the Nazis for the liquidation of Orthodox Serbs. It is a brutal but little-known chapter of the Second World War. This book is a compilation of documents and eyewitness reports on this terrible chapter in history. This is a shortened version of the author's original text. The author attacks especially the role of the Catholic Church. The book also contains four appendixes containing excerpts from the *Encyclopedia Judicz* and the *Koran-al-Raye*.

1601. Denitch, Bogdan. **Ethnic Nationalism: The Tragic Death of Yugoslavia**. 2nd rev. ed. 224p. Minneapolis: University of Minnesota Press, 1996. Includes bibliographical references and index.

In describing the tragic death of Yugoslavia, the author searches for insights into the relationship of the politics of identity, of nationalism, to democracy. After an introductory chapter on the relevance of the death of Yugoslavia, the author examines its history since 1980, the one-party rule of Tito and the control of nationalism, the post-communist societies in crisis, and the disintegration into civil war and ethnic cleansing.

1602. Fryer, C. E. **Destruction of Serbia in 1915**. 240p. *East European Monographs*, 488. Boulder, Colo.: East European Monographs; New York: Distributed by Columbia University Press, 1997. Includes bibliographical references (pp. 242-45).

Relatively little has been written in English on the role of the Serb army in World War I. Charles Fryer hopes to help fill that gap with a brief study. The book includes a lengthy excerpt from the journey of Rear-Admiral Troubridge describing his experiences in Serbia.

1603. Georgieva, Valentina, and Sasha Konechni. **Historical Dictionary of the Republic of Macedonia**. xxvii, 359p. *European Historical Dictionaries*, no. 22. Lanham, Md.: Scarecrow Press, 1998. Includes four appendixes and bibliographic references.

This useful historical dictionary, like others in this series, provides an accessible compendium of information. Besides the list of defined historical terms, the dictionary also includes a chronology of important events, an introductory historical essay about Macedonia and its place in the Balkans, a bibliography of primarily English works on Macedonia, a list of political parties as of August 1994, facts and figures on Macedonia, and a list of Macedonian geographical and personal names.

1604. **The Events of 1903 in Macedonia As Presented in European Diplomatic Correspondence**. Edited by Basil C. Gounaris, Angelos A. Chotzidis, A. Panagiotopoulou, and Mouseio Makedonikou Agona. 128p.: map. Thessaloniki: Museum of the Macedonian Struggle, 1993. Documents in English, French, and German.

The year 1903 was one of great turmoil in the Balkans. The Ottoman army instigated numerous atrocities in the region. In Balkan history, it was the year of the "Ilinden Uprising," a revolt against the Turks by Macedonian rebels. "In its continuing efforts to publish modern historical sources relating to Macedonia, the Museum of the Macedonian Struggle has decided to present in this volume seventy authentic documents, all from the correspondence of the British, French, Austro-Hungarian and United States Consulates in Thessaloniki and Monastir in 1903" (p. 7). The documents in this collection demonstrate the important role Bulgaria played in this uprising. The volume includes an introductory essay by Basil C. Gounaris. All documents include explanatory notes and biographical dates. However, these notes include only the information necessary to explain references in the text that are not immediately clear to the reader.

1605. Gounaris, Basil C. **Steam over Macedonia, 1870-1912: Socio-Economic Change and the Railway Factor**. xii, 372p.: illus., maps. Boulder, Colo.: East European Monographs; New York: Distributed by Columbia University Press, 1993. Revision of the author's D.Phil. thesis (Oxford University).

Macedonia has experienced many changes in its borders during the 19th and 20th centuries. For the purposes of this book, the author has used an early-20th-century definition of this region that includes Salonika, Monastir, and Kosovo. Basil Gounaris focuses on the diplomatic events during the 40 years before the Balkan Wars as they shaped the economy of the region. "Particular reference will be made to the railways, an invention which seems to have played an important part in the transformation of the Macedonian society and economy, both as a construction project and as a mode of transport" (pp. x-xi). The author begins with an overview of political changes in the region from 1870 to 1912. He then describes the construction and operation of the first railways in the region. From this discussion he moves to a focus on the impact of the railways in agriculture, industry, the markets, and the implication of geographical mobility for society. The volume contains a lengthy bibliography but lacks an index.

1606. Killen, Linda. **Testing the Peripheries: U.S.-Yugoslav Economic Relations in the Interwar Years**. x, 234p. *East European Monographs*, 382. Boulder, Colo.: East European Monographs; New York: Distributed by Columbia University Press, 1994. Includes bibliographical references (pp. 217-27) and index.

The relations between Yugoslavia and the United States in the interwar period have not previously been investigated in detail. While in many ways these two nations had little formal contact, Linda Killen believes it was the informal relationships that developed during this time between the two countries that had long-term effects. She describes the establishment of these relationships and their evolution in this book.

1607. Lampe, John R. **Yugoslavia As History: Twice There Was a Country**. xx, 421p.: illus., maps. Cambridge, Eng.; New York: Cambridge University Press, 1996. Includes bibliographical references (pp. 393-401), index, numerous statistical tables, and historical maps.

Twice in the 20th century, a country called Yugoslavia was formed and twice it dissolved. John Lampe traces the earliest roots of the ideas that led to the formation of the country. Beginning in A.D. 800, Lampe presents an overview of the region and its history to the beginning of the 19th century. The bulk of this volume focuses on the 19th and 20th centuries. "The author follows these peoples, their institutions and ideas from their earliest interaction, into the two world wars and the states which resulted from them, detailing their tortuous search for political and economic viability which characterized Yugoslavia as a state" (p. iii).

1608. Lund, Helen S. **Lysimachus: A Study in Early Hellenistic Kingship**. xii, 287p.: maps. London: Routledge, 1992. Includes bibliographical references (pp. 261-75) and index.

At one time Lysimachus ruled Thrace, the west Pontic coast, Macedon, Thessaly, most of Anatolia, Heracleia Pontica, and its Paphlagonian realm. Yet little remains in the historical record of his life. Helen Lund uses a variety of sources to piece together the history of his life.

1609. Malcolm, Noel. **Bosnia: A Short History**. xxiv, 340p.: maps. London: Macmillan, 1994. Includes bibliographical references (pp. 303-22) and index.

Noel Malcolm has set himself the task of trying to provide some basic information on Bosnia's history. He has compiled a narrative history that begins in Bosnia's distant past, prior to 1180, and then brings the reader up through the centuries to the destruction of the region in the early 1990s. Malcolm is well aware that the past may not explain the present. He provides the reader with a bibliography that will assist those who wish to pursue the subject further.

1610. Malcolm, Noel. **Kosovo: A Short History**. xxxvi, 492p.: maps. New York: New York University Press, 1998. Includes bibliographical references.

Believing that the most important parts of the history of Kosovo have been misrepresented, Malcolm has undertaken to correct these. The reasons for a history of Kosovo are many. "It is one of the cultural crossing-places of Europe; it was probably central both to the survival of the Albanian language and to the development of the Romanian one; it became the geographical heart of an important medieval kingdom; it was one of the most characteristic parts of the Ottoman Empire in Europe; and it was the area in which the modern Albanian national movement was born, and had its greatest successes and failures" (pp. xxxiv-xxxv). Malcolm rises well to his self-imposed challenge. His well-documented history is supplemented by several historical maps.

1611. Miller, Nicholas J. **Between Nation and State: Serbian Politics in Croatia, Before the First World War**. xiv, 223p.: illus., maps. *Pitt Series in Russian and East European Studies*. Pittsburgh, Pa.: University of Pittsburgh Press, 1997. Includes bibliographical references (pp. 209-18) and index.

"This book concerns the interrelationship of nationhood and sovereignty. It is about political behavior in a culturally mixed region under the stress of the challenges of political modernity: the transformation of political actors from subjects to citizens, and the nature of that transformation" (p. ix). Individual chapters cover the Croatian background; Serbs as political actors; the birth and short life of the new course, 1903-1907; persecution and temptation, 1907-1909; the collapse of the civic option in Serbian politics, 1910-1924; and the failure of the civic idea among Croatia's Serbs.

1612. Pahor, Boris. **Pilgrim Among the Shadows**. Translated by Michael Biggins. 1st ed. 182p. New York: Harcourt Brace, 1995. "A Helen and Kurt Wolff book."

This autobiographical narrative concerns the author's life in a German concentration camp during World War II and its effect on his life.

1613. Praga, Giuseppe, and Franco Luxardo. **History of Dalmatia**. 363p., [14] leaves, [14] p. of plates: illus., facsims., col. maps. Pisa, Ita.: Giardini, 1993. Includes bibliographical references (pp. 311-26) and indexes.

This work, completed in the 1950s and not translated into English, provides a history of Dalmatia from the Greek colonization in 158 B.C. to 1870. Mario Dassovich provides an appendix that extends the history to 1947.

1614. Seraphinoff, Michael. **The 19th Century Macedonian Awakening: A Study of the Life and Works of Kiril Pejchinovich**. xii, 171p.: illus., map. Lanham, Md.: University Press of America, 1996. Includes bibliographical references (pp. [157]-163) and index.

Kiril Pejchinovich spent most of his life in the Macedonia monastic community of the early 19th century. His writings have been significant for the area in no small part because he wrote in Macedonian as opposed to Latin. This brief volume provides a biography and discusses Pejchinovich's major writings. An appendix compares Pejchinovich's language with that of Church Slavic, Turkish, Greek, and Macedonian dialects.

1615. Stallaerts, Robert, and Jeannine Laurens. **Historical Dictionary of the Republic of Croatia**. xlii, 341p.: maps. *European Historical Dictionaries*, no. 9. Lanham, Md.: Scarecrow Press, 1995. Includes bibliographical references (pp. 243-340).

No. 9 in the *European Historical Dictionaries* series focuses on Croatia. This volume includes a chronology of events in Croatian history from A.D. 395 to 1995, a list of acronyms and abbreviations, and an extensive bibliography. The bibliography is organized by subject. The entries all include extensive cross-referencing that is particularly helpful for the reader less familiar with Croatian history. Articles cover a broad range of topics from general articles on such subjects as cinema in Croatia to specifics of Croatian history.

1616. Tanner, Marcus. **Croatia: A Nation Forged in War**. xiii, 338p.: illus., maps. New Haven, Conn.: Yale University Press, 1997. Includes bibliographical references (pp. [321]-323) and index.

Tanner began with a desire to fill in the gap in our understanding of the former Yugoslavia, especially our knowledge about Croatia. Initially limiting himself to a brief account of the war in Croatia in 1991, he found it impossible unless he referred to the war of the 1940s, and then by necessity to refer to the first Yugoslavia and the political climate of the 1920s and 1930s, and so on. His final product begins with the first Croat principalities in the Dark Ages and ends with the 1991 war.

1617. Trifunovska, Sneizana. **Former Yugoslavia Through Documents: From Its Dissolution to the Peace Settlement**. xlvii, 1346p. Boston: Martinus Nijhoff, 1999. Includes index.

This volume contains a collection of selected documents that eventuated from the events and developments that took place during the period September 1993 to June 1998. In addition, other earlier documents falling outside this time frame were also included. It is intended to be a sequel to an earlier volume that contained documents from its creation to its dissolution. Here the arrangement is different. After an introduction the documents are arranged in nine sections, dealing with significant events of the period. These events were the Dayton Peace Agreement and its implementation, Croatia, Macedonia, international sanctions, human rights situation, war crimes and humanitarian law, and the succession issues.

1618. West, Richard. **Tito: And the Rise and Fall of Yugoslavia**. 1st Carroll & Graf ed. xii, 436p.: illus., maps. New York: Carroll & Graf, 1995. Originally published London.

Richard West studied Balkan history at Cambridge University. He eventually became a correspondent for the *Manchester Guardian*. In this book he explores Tito's ability to maintain a united Yugoslavia. He also examines Tito's rise to power, his political leanings, and his ethnic biases. West's book is chronologically arranged but begins with an overview of the history of the South Slavs. The volume includes a key to pronunciation.

Economics, Trade, and Business

1619. Bokovoy, Melissa K. **Peasants and Communists: Politics and Ideology in the Yugoslav Countryside, 1941-53**. xvii, 211p. *Pitt Series in Russian and East European Studies*. Pittsburgh, Pa.: University of Pittsburgh Press, 1998. Includes bibliographical references (pp. 161-204) and index.

The Communist Party of Yugoslavia was under the influence of the Soviet Union in the 1940s, but it did not follow the pattern of the Soviet Union in its development. "What follows is not only an account of how an East-European party-state sought to bring the countryside, its resources, and its inhabitants under state control. It is also a political tale of lower-class resistance among peasants whose acts effectively mitigated and thwarted the claims made upon them by a state controlled by a dominant group—in this case, the Communists" (p. xi). Bokovoy explores the methods used by the peasants to accomplish their goals in the face of state violence.

Government, Politics, and Law

1620. **State-Society Relations in Yugoslavia, 1945-1992**. Edited by Melissa Bokovoy, Jill A. Irvine, and Carol S. Lilly. 1st ed. vii, 375p. New York: St. Martin's Press, 1997. Includes bibliographical references and index.

The violence in Yugoslavia in recent years has focused analysis on current events. Many scholars have felt the need for study of the longer view of Yugoslavia's political history. A conference held in 1994 in New Mexico sought a scholarly assessment of the entire communist period in Yugoslavia. It brought together historians, political scientists, sociologists, and scholars of religious studies. The essays in this volume are the result of that conference. They are divided into three sections: regime consolidation and strategies of legitimation; social forces, social movements, and the state; and nation and state.

1621. **Independent Slovenia: Origins, Movements, Prospects**. Edited by Jill Benderly and Evan Kraft. xxii, 262p.: illus., maps. London: Macmillan, 1994. Includes bibliographical references and index.

This collection of 11 essays explores the reasons why Slovenia could declare independence from Yugoslavia and not only survive, but flourish. The three contributing factors were ethnic homogeneity, economic development, and a strong civil society. The essays are arranged in three parts: Origins, Movements, and Prospects. The four essays in Part 1 focus on the Slovenes from the 7th century to 1945, the Slovenes and Yugoslavia, economic history of Slovenia, and culture, politics, and Slovene identity. Part 2 (four essays) looks at the evolution from social movements to national sovereignty, the politics of punk, women and Slovene independence, and the labor movement. The final part (three essays) analyzes Slovenia's shift from the Balkans to Central Europe, the economics of independent Slovenia, and quasi-privatization.

1622. Fink-Hafner, Danica. **Making a New Nation: The Formation of Slovenia**. vi, 330p. Aldershot, Eng.: Dartmouth University Press, 1997. Includes bibliographical references.

All of Eastern Europe has undergone radical change in this decade. Political and economic systems have been completely rebuilt with varying levels of success. In this volume a number of scholars come together to describe the process in Slovenia. There the transformation seems to have been made successfully and with little internal strike. The essays collected here describe the political system, thoroughly covering such topics as international affairs, defense, political culture, development of the party system, and many other topics. "Apart from constituting an interesting case study in itself, this book will provide comparative material for analytical studies of the transition process" (back cover).

1623. Hitchins, Keith. **A Nation Discovered: Romanian Intellectuals in Transylvania and the Idea of Nation**. 229p. Bucharest: Encyclopaedic Publishing House, 1999. Includes bibliographic references.

The present volume is a revision of *The Idea of Nation: The Romanians of Transylvania, 1691-1849*, which was published in Bucharest in 1985 and 1988. Here Hitchins has "emphasized the role of the intellectuals in elaborating the idea of nation and leading the effort of modern nation-building" (p. 5). He has also added new information that has appeared in the secondary literature since that first edition.

1624. Lange-Akhund, Madine. **Macedonian Question**. 320p. Boulder, Colo.: East European Monographs; New York: Distributed by Columbia University Press, 1998. Translated from the French by Gabriel Topor. Includes bibliographical references (pp. 390-98).

"The present work is neither an exposition of the Eastern question, nor of the policies of Great Powers, but suggests a new approach based on the analysis of the events which took place in Macedonia, as described in the reports of the diplomats" (p. vii). It covers the period 1893-1908, when critical events occurred that were central to the Macedonian question. The author initially presents a description of the country and then proceeds to analyze the religious conflict between the Patriarchate and the Exarchate, and the political struggle between Macedonia and Bulgaria and the Greek and Serbian movements. He then follows how this played out through insurrection, reforms, revolutionary groups, and new political orientations that eventually arose in the period 1904-1908.

1625. Potts, George A. **The Development of the System of Representation in Yugoslavia with Special Reference to the Period Since 1974**. lxxi, 671p.: illus. Lanham, Md.: University Press of America, 1996. Includes bibliographical references (pp. [639]-662) and index.

This study is essentially a publication of the author's dissertation in which he examines the commune model of participation and representation put forth by Marx and Engels and how it was applied in Yugoslavia since 1974. He spends several initial chapters focusing on pre-1974 developments and earlier experiments with the commune model. His study ends with 1990, when "Yugoslavia as a whole ceased to be ruled by the League of Communists and entered into a transitional period in which the legitimacy and authority of the former ruling party was successively challenged and in some regions replaced" (p. 615).

1626. Thomas, Robert. **Politics of Serbia in the 1990s**. xx, 433p. New York: Columbia University Press, 1998. Includes bibliographical references and index.

In describing and analyzing the many facets of Serbian politics in the 1990s, Thomas "seeks to explain why Serbia failed to make the political leap from totalitarianism to pluralism. It seeks to demonstrate that while the inability of democracy to put down firm roots can be attributed in part to weaknesses and fault-lines within Serbian society, the decisions of individuals and personalities have also played a critical role both in the failure to bring about, or in actively seeking to thwart, the processes of democratic consolidation" (p. 4). His study provides a historical background as a context for contemporary analysis and covers the years 1987-1998 in detail.

1627. Wachtel, Andrew. **Making a Nation, Breaking a Nation**. viii, 302p.: illus. *Cultural Memory in the Present*. Stanford, Calif.: Stanford University Press, 1998. Includes bibliographical references (pp. [287]-295) and index.

"Wachtel is interested in the ways that Yugoslav partisans attempted to advance their idea of national unity. They did it in four primary ways: (1) linguistic policies that functioned to create a shared national language; (2) the promulgation of Yugoslav literary and artistic canon that was interpreted as embodying desired traits of national unity; (3) educational policy, particularly relating to the teaching of literature and history in schools; and (4) the production of new literary and artistic works that incorporated a Yugoslav view variously defined" (p. 5). His focus here is on important issues in educational policy, culture, and literature.

Foreign Relations

1628.   Danforth, Loring M. **The Macedonian Conflict: Ethnic Nationalism in a Transnational World**. xvi, 273p. Princeton, N.J.: Princeton University Press, 1995. Includes bibliography (pp. 253-70) and index.

Danforth explores several seemingly simple questions about Macedonia, namely what is Macedonia, where is it, whom does it belong to, what country is it a part of, who are the Macedonians, and what is the Macedonian conflict. As the author states in his preface, "This book is about the conflicting claims to Macedonian identity asserted by both Greeks and Macedonians. The conflict . . . is a dispute over names, flags, history, and territory. Ultimately, however, it is a dispute over meaning" (p. 6). He also examines the dispute in the Diaspora, in the construction of national identity among immigrants to Australia from northern Greece.

1629.   Lane, Ann. **Britain, the Cold War and Yugoslav Unity: 1941-1949**. xii, 220p.: maps. Brighton, Eng.; Portland, Oreg.: Sussex Academic Press, 1996. Includes bibliographical references (pp. [199]-213) and index.

In the light of recent events in Yugoslavia, historians have begun to reevaluate the role of other nations in Yugoslav political development. Special interest has been focused on the role of the great powers in that country. "This book is a history of British policy toward Yugoslavia following the collapse of the Yugoslav state in April 1941, and the reorientation of western policies toward post-war Yugoslavia which ensured upon the latter's expulsion from the Cominform in 1948" (p. 1). The book is arranged topically, discussing the selection of Tito as Yugoslavia's leader, the unification of the country, Britain's attempts to gain a "Balkan foothold," their support of Tito, and Tito's battle to maintain Yugoslav unity during the cold war. The book is based primarily on Western sources.

1630.   Lees, Lorraine M. **Keeping Tito Afloat: The United States, Yugoslavia, and the Cold War**. xviii, 246p.: map. University Park: Pennsylvania State University Press, 1997. Includes bibliographical references and index.

Lees examines the successes, failures, and context of the "wedge" policy toward communist states during the Truman and Eisenhower eras. This policy "relied on nationalism and a combination of U.S. pressure and support to create divisions between the Soviet Union and other communist states. Although developed for use in both Europe and Asia, the wedge received its most sustained application in U.S. policy toward Yugoslavia, where it also revealed its greatest strengths and weaknesses" (p. xiii). The study is arranged chronologically.

Language and Literature

1631. Goy, E. D. **Excursions: Essays on Russian and Serbian Literature.** Edited by Patrick Miles. xi, 110p. Nottingham, Eng.: Astra, 1996. Includes bibliographical references and index.

E. D. Goy was a lecturer at Cambridge University until his retirement in 1990. He has produced many studies of Serbian literature during his career. In this column he compares Russian and Serbian literature. "While discussing in detail specific works by four major Russian and Serbian writers, these essays also embody some of Ned's most cherished ideas and beliefs about literature and art..." (p. ix). The essays focus on Pushkin, Turgenev, Stankovic, and Petrovic.

1632. **The Prince of Fire: An Anthology of Contemporary Serbian Short Stories.** Edited by Radmila Jovanovic Gorup and Nadezda Obradovic. xvi, 371p. *Pitt Series in Russian and East European Studies.* Pittsburgh, Pa.: University of Pittsburgh Press, 1998.

"The richness and variety of stories in this collection may be the result of polarization and passionate intellectual argument, but is equally due to the amount of sheer talent present on all sides. Regardless of their aesthetic premise, this is a collection of well-told stories that can stand with the best short story collections anywhere" (p. x). Numerous authors are represented in this volume. Contributors include Aleksandar Tisma, Milorad Pavic, Borislav Pekic, Miodrag Bulatovic, Dragoslav Mihailoric, Svetlana Velmar-Jankovic, Zivojin Pavolvic, Mladen Markov, Grozdana Oljic, Danilo Kis, Momo Kapor, Branimir Scepanovic, and many others. Their works represent the spectrum of Serbian literary styles from the realist tradition to the more contemporary magic realism.

1633. Karadzic, Vuk. **Songs of the Serbian People: From the Collections of Vuk Karadzic.** Edited by Milne Holton and Vasa D. Mihailovich. xvi, 310p. *Pitt Series in Russian and East European Studies.* Pittsburgh, Pa.: University of Pittsburgh Press, 1997. Includes bibliographic references.

These songs, translated from the collection of Vuk Karadzic, a scholar and linguist living in Vienna in the early years of the 19th century, are presented in a material form similar to the originals. The songs are arranged topically: songs before history, before the Battle of Kosovo, the Battle of Kosovo, Marko Kraljevic, under the Turks, the songs of outlaws, and the songs of the Serbian insurrection.

1634. Milojevic Sheppard, Milena. **Morpho-Syntactic Expansions in Translation from English into Slovenian As a Prototypical Response to the Complexity of the Original**. 254p. München: O. Sagner, 1993. Translated from Slovenian.

"This work deals with the morpho-syntactic expansions which occur in translation from English into Slovenian, proceeding from the assumption that such expansions are the most common, 'prototypical' response of the translator when faced by an original containing grammatically complex structures."

Individual Authors

1635. **Ivo Andric Revisited: The Bridge Still Stands**. Edited by S. Vucinich. xiv, 239p.: illus. *Research Series*, no. 92. Berkeley, Calif.: International and Area Studies, 1996. Includes bibliographical references and index.

The articles contained in this volume were originally presented at a conference in 1992 in honor of the 100th anniversary of the writer's birth. Andric, who won the Nobel Prize for literature in 1961, has attracted much attention outside his native Bosnia. These articles explore various aspects of this writer's work.

1636. Kiš, Danilo. **Homo Poeticus: Essays and Interviews**. Edited by Susan Sontag. xvi, 283p. New York: Farrar, Straus & Giroux, 1995. "Introduction by Susan Sontag."

This volume contains essays by and interviews with famous Serbian writer Danilo Kiš. In addition, it also includes excerpts from his *Anatomy Lesson*.

1637. Tišma, Aleksander. **The Book of Blam**. Translated by Michael Henry Heim. 1st ed. 226p. New York; San Diego; London: Harcourt Brace, 1998.

Aleksander Tišma is a leading writer in the Serbo-Croatian language. The theme that runs through all his books is the effect of the war on the human spirit. *The Book of Blam*, originally published in 1971, is no exception. It deals with the experience of the Serbian Jews in war-torn Yugoslavia.

The Society, Sociology

1638. Goldsworthy, Vesna. **Inventing Ruritania: The Imperialism of the Imagination**. xiv, 254p.: map. New Haven, Conn.: Yale University Press, 1998. Includes bibliographical references (pp. [234]-245) and index.

Vesna Goldsworthy examines the Western view of the Balkans in this book. She is particularly interested in the popular view of the region as it was portrayed in literature. Each of her five chapters examines a different literary portrayal of the region beginning with Byron and ending with Edith Durham and Olivia Mannin. "The relevance of their examination to the wider field of cultural studies lies, I believe, in the fact that it draws attention to those marginal and ambiguous areas of the world which have offered refuges to patterns of neo-colonial behavior no longer acceptable elsewhere.... If post-colonial examination has so far, and not unjustly, focused on the Third World, this study contributes to a re-examination of the changing identity of the 'Second World'; which defines both the 'first' and the 'third' " (p. xi).

1639. Ramet, Sabrina P. **Gender Politics in the Western Balkans: Women, Society and Politics in Yugoslavia and the Yugoslav Successor States**. 343p. *Post-Communist Cultural Studies*. University Park: Pennsylvania State University Press, 1999. Includes bibliographical references (pp. [291]-319) and index.

This is a collection of essays focusing on women in Slovenia, Serbia, Croatia, Kosovo, and Bosnia. The essays focus on the social and political history of women in the region. All the contributors assume that culture is an essential part of politics and that political history will, of necessity, deal with cultural questions. "This book is, among other things, about the concern for social justice in Yugoslavia, about the demand that democracy be not just for men but for all citizens" (p. 6). The essays are grouped into four sections: "Overview"; "The Interwar Era, World War II, and the Socialist Era"; "Post-Socialist Republics"; "Literature and Religion." Contributors include Sabrina Ramet, Andrei Simić, Thomas Emmert, Vlast Jalusić, Barbara Jancaw-Webster, Tatjanna Pavolvić, Zarana Papić, Julie Mertus, Obrad Kesić, Dorothy Q. Thomas, Regan E. Ralph, Gordana P. Crnković, and Mart Bax.

Religion

1640. Sells, Michael A. **The Bridge Betrayed: Religion and Genocide in Bosnia**. xv, 244p.: illus., maps. *Comparative Studies in Religion and Society*, 11. Berkeley: University of California Press, 1996. Includes bibliographical references (pp. 217-22) and index.

Sells relies on documentary sources to describe and analyze the atrocities that occurred in Bosnia and Hercegovina during the disintegration of Yugoslavia. He deftly weaves descriptions of atrocities with an astute theological, sociological, and anthropological analysis to give the reader a broader and deeper understanding of what happened in Bosnia and Hercegovina. He also draws on historical accounts of similar atrocities that had occurred there in order to put the more recent ones in context.

National Minorities

1641. Pettifer, James. **The New Macedonian Question**. New York: St. Martin's Press, 1999. Includes bibliographical references and index.

The Macedonian question has historically been "one of the most intractable and difficult Balkan conflicts. It is re-emerging as a factor in the Kosovo crisis which dominated the region from 1998" (p. xxx). The purpose of the essays in this book is to contribute to the informed debate about the Macedonian question and to elucidate the problems and international attitudes that currently abound. In addition to analysis of the current situation, there is some historical material that puts the Macedonian question in historical context.

1642. Pinson, Mark, ed. **The Muslims of Bosnia = Herzegovina: Their Historic Development from the Middle Ages to the Dissolution of Yugoslavia**. Rep. Rev. ed. xiii, 187p.: illus. *Harvard Middle Eastern Monographs, 28*. Cambridge, Mass.: Distributed for the Center for Middle Eastern Studies of Harvard University by Harvard University Press, 1993. Includes bibliographies and index.

This volume of essays was the result of a conference on the Muslims of Bosnia-Herzegovina. The essays are arranged chronologically, each covering one period of the Muslim history in the region beginning with the Middle Ages. However, the goal is not to present a detailed history of each period. "Instead, they (the contributors) were to summarize and synthesize some aspects of the work done on that period and not produce pieces of original research" (p. xiii). The essays bring the reader to current times. An appendix of additional reading is included.

1643. Poulton, Hugh. **Who Are the Macedonians?** 218p. Bloomington: Indiana University Press, 1995. Includes index.

The question of who the Macedonians are is a highly controversial one. There are at least three answers to the question. Two answers are geographic ones and the third is that they are "citizens of the independent political entity" (p. 2). This ethnic identity and the civic identity not surprisingly come into conflict with one another. The author approaches the question historically, covering historical beginnings, group identity in the Ottoman Empire, the period from Berlin to Versailles, the interwar years, the war, and civil war. He then focuses on Macedonians as a majority, Macedonians as a minority, and independent Macedonia. The author hopes that Macedonia will fulfill the promise of becoming "a stable prosperous country of two million, acting as a bridge between Albania and Bulgaria and, in due time, between Serbia and Greece" (p. 210).

1644. Vickers, Miranda. **Between Serb and Albanian: A History of Kosovo**. xix, 328p. New York: Columbia University Press, 1998. "First published in the United Kingdom by C. Hurst and Co. . . . London"—Verso t.p. Includes bibliographical references (pp. 314-17) and index.

Vickers begins her history of Kosovo appropriately with the famous Battle of Kosovo in 1389 and continues through the end of 1997. Sensitive to all the players in Kosovo's history she shows how the term "Kosovo" has been used as a metaphor by both Serbs and Albanians for the suffering and injustices inflicted on their nations throughout history. Her study helps to explain the complicated history behind this war-torn land.

1645. Vuckovic, Gojko. **Ethnic Cleavages and Conflict: The Sources of National Cohesion and Disintegration: The Case of Yugoslavia**. 192p. Aldershot, Eng.: Ashgate, 1997. Includes bibliography (pp. 158-70).

Vuckovic's aim is to eventually reduce the source of ethnic conflict. Toward this end he presents specific models in approaching ethnic conflict and in doing so attempts to understand the sources of conflict, as well as the background of the domestic and international parties involved. He proceeds programmatically by initially identifying the major theories scholars have used to study ethnic conflict, then creates his own model for comparative study of ethnic conflict. From there he uses Yugoslavia as a case study and includes in his analysis the perceptual and historic origins of the various ethnic identities, state formation, government regulation, and ethnic conflict management policies used. Finally, he provides a summary and conclusion of his examination.

Arts and Culture

1646. **Wounded Libraries in Croatia**. Edited by Tatjana Aparac-Gazivoda and Dragutin Katalenac. Translated by Vesna Vrgoc. 58p.: illus. Zagreb, Croatia: Croatian Library Association, 1993. Includes index.

This brief work portrays the damage and destruction done to libraries as a result of the civil war in the former Yugoslavia.

1647. Debeljak, Ales. **Twilight of the Idols: Recollections of a Lost Yugoslavia: An Essay**. Translated by Michael Biggins. 85p.: illus. Fredonia, N.Y.: White Pine Press, 1994.

Debeljak is considered to be one of the best poets of Central Europe. Educated in Slovenia and the United States, he has published five books of poetry and three books of cultural criticism. This essay ponders the destruction of Yugoslavia during its civil war.

1648. Karanovich, Milenko. **The Development of Education in Serbia and Emergence of Its Intelligentsia, 1838-1858**. x, 270p. *East European Monographs*, 414. Boulder, Colo.: East European Monographs; New York: Distributed by Columbia University Press, 1995. Includes bibliographical references (pp. [229]-264) and index.

The author focuses on the constitutionalist period, 1838-1858, in order to understand the development of education in Serbia, how the educational system prepared elites for positions of leadership, the effect of education on their way of life, and other relevant questions.

1649. Kolar-Panov, Dona. **Video War and the Diasporic Imagination**. xvi, 270p. *Routledge Research in Cultural and Media Studies*. London: Routledge, 1997. Includes bibliographical references (pp. 240-62).

"This book effectively but not formally is in two parts. The first and more general part revolves around video as a cultural practice and involves a comparative study of audiences in the small and geographically isolated migrant communities of former Yugoslavia in Perth, Western Australia. The audiences for this part of the study are mostly, but not exclusively, of Macedonian and Croatian descent. The second part provides a more detailed examination of video within the Croatian communities in Perth under the impact of the break-up and wars in Croatia and Bosnia and Herzegovina . . ." (p. 7).

1650. Subotic, Gojko. **Art of Kosovo: The Sacred Land**. 256p. New York: Monacelli Press, 1998.

This survey of ancient artistic creations in Kosovo has been "restricted only to the monuments which most thoroughly represent artistic ideas and realizations, starting from the simplest anchoritic cave-dwellings with places for worship, and going on to buildings raised by kings and archbishops. Most of the survey is, nevertheless, dedicated to larger structures in which artists could express their ideas in monumental dimensions and in a most complex mode" (p. 11). An explanatory text accompanies the photographs.

1651. Ugresic, Dubravka. **The Culture of Lies: Antipolitical Essays**. xii, 275p. *Post Communist Cultural Studies*. University Park: Pennsylvania State University Press, 1998. Includes bibliographical references.

In this prize-winning volume, Ugresic discusses the "loss of identity that accompanied the demise of communism in the later twentieth century" (p. ix). Her literary essays manage to voice an intelligent criticism of Croatian nationalism and its effects "without engaging in moral equivocation" (p. x).

Civil War

1652. **Fear, Death, and Resistance: An Ethnography of War: Croatia, 1991-1992**. Edited by Lada Cale Feldman, Ines Prica, and Reana Senjkovic. Translated by Renée Pricai. 255p.: illus. (some col.). Zagreb, Croatia: Institute of Ethnology and Folklore Research: Matrix Croatica: X-Press, 1993. Includes bibliographical references.

This is an unusual look at the tragedy in Croatia. Nine ethnologists have attempted the publication of a war ethnography. "By selecting the following works we aimed at covering the whole range of newly discovered needs and possibilities: from gathering testimonies given by the displaced persons and consulting the archives, to recognizing the subject of research in the symbolic resistance and in the distorted image of reality in the war" (p. 1). All nine authors are from Zagreb and are trained in some areas of ethnology. There is a chronology of Croatian history included in the book. Some of the topics discussed include ritual behaviors and ethnonymic polarization.

1653. **This Time We Knew: Western Responses to Genocide in Bosnia.** ix, 412p. New York: New York University Press, 1996. Includes bibliographical references and index.

Shocked by the Western indifference to genocide in Bosnia, the two social scientist editors of this volume decided to gather other social theorists and writers together to explore this phenomenon. The result is this collection of essays. As the editors state, the "fulcrum of the volume" is this: "the critical examination of the tolerated discrepancy between the rationalizations and facts put forth by Western governments and organizations and passive acquiescence of the West's intellectuals and policy makers, who, ideally, ought to be more willing to puncture such rationalizations" (p. 31).

1654. **Conflict in the Former Yugoslavia: An Encyclopedia.** Edited by John B. Allcock, Marko Milivojevic, and John J. Horton. xxxiv, 410p. *Roots of Modern Conflict.* Santa Barbara, Calif.: ABC-CLIO, 1998. Includes bibliographical references (pp. 345-50) and index.

The articles for this encyclopedia are all by recognized authorities on Yugoslavia. The purpose of the encyclopedia is to bring together a wide range of information about the conflict in Yugoslavia in order to understand the basis for the tragedy that occurred there. This information includes articles on personalia, geographic terms (important towns, rivers, etc.), political terms such as citizenship, democratization, Dayton Agreements, names of plans, actions, and economic terms. In short, almost every conceivable aspect of the Yugoslav conflict, including an article on the Cyrillic alphabet, is included. The articles are brief, very few of which extend beyond one page. Terms and names used in the articles that are themselves entries are presented in bold-faced type. Appendixes include (1) a chronology that covers events from the 1941 Axis invasion of Yugoslavia to November 26, 1995, when Commissioner Westendorp announced that a UN presence would be necessary in Bosnia-Hercegovina for two to three more years and (2) a copy of the Dayton Agreements. An index provides additional access to the contents.

1655. Allen, Beverly. **Rape Warfare: The Hidden Genocide in Bosnia-Herzegovina and Croatia.** xviii, 180p. Minneapolis: University of Minnesota Press, 1996. Includes bibliographical references.

In trying to understand genocidal rape in Bosnia-Herzegovina, Allen articulates five themes: identity, representation, analysis, remedies, and implications. Her study was provided by the widespread use of genocidal rape as an instrument of war in Bosnia-Herzegovina during the Yugoslav civil war and the victims' accounts that were able to reach the West.

1656. Anzulovic, Branimir. **Heavenly Serbia: From Myth to Genocide.** xiv, 233p. New York: New York University Press, 1999. Includes bibliographical references (pp. 217-25) and index.

As the author states in his introduction, "Heavenly Serbia" is the dominant Serbian national myth. In this book-length essay he examines how the ancient story of the Battle of Kosovo, along with other prominent historical events, influenced the behavior of the Serbs in the late 20th century.

1657. Bennett, Christopher. **Yugoslavia's Bloody Collapse: Causes, Course and Consequences**. 272p. New York: New York University Press, 1995. Includes bibliographical references and index.

Christopher Bennett has provided a study of the sources of the conflict in Yugoslavia. He begins with an overview of the culture and language of the region. The affect of Tito's years in power is then explored in depth. The second half of the book is devoted to an in-depth discussion of current events. The author is not attempting to change popular perceptions concerning the region. "I have simply tried to explain as concisely as possible what has taken place, and to suggest what the implications are and where events are likely to lead, on the assumption that there will be no change in the international strategy toward the conflict" (p. ix).

1658. Blackman, Ellen. **Harvest in the Snow: My Crusade to Rescue the Lost Children of Bosnia**. 1st ed. 320p. Washington, D.C.: Brassey's, 1997. Includes bibliographical references and index.

This is an account of the human cost of the Yugoslav war. Blackman focuses on Sarajevo and the courage and tragedy of its citizens. "The following story is not a political treatment of the Bosnian conflict, nor is it a story told from a historical perspective, rather it is an odyssey into the everyday struggles of a town which I came to know intimately" (p. xi).

1659. Blaskovich, Jerry. **Anatomy of Deceit: An American Physician's First-Hand Encounter with the Realities of the War**. 435p. Dunhill Publishing, 1997.

Jerry Blaskovich is both a doctor and a student of Croatian culture. This volume exposes the atrocities of the Yugoslav war as witnessed by Dr. Blaskovich. Beyond this, he describes the unusual role of the physicians in Croatia. "He also shows how an unusual convergence of circumstances led Croatian physicians to fill a leadership vacuum in their newly independent nation and save it from both human and political collapse" (back cover). The book does not include an index or a bibliography but is based on the doctor's experience.

1660. Both, Norbert, and Jan W. Honig. **Srebrenica: Record of a War Crime**. xx, 204p.: maps. New York: Penguin Books, 1997. Originally published London: Penguin Books, 1996.

July 1995 saw the perpetration of the single worst war crime since World War II. Thousands of Bosnian Muslim men were slaughtered by Bosnina Serbs. "Jan Willen Honig and Norbert Both, experts on the Bosnian crisis, recount the Srebrenica massacre in all its horrific detail—including eyewitness accounts of the deportations and the mass executions. They also take a complete look at the incoherent Western plans that led up to the slaughter . . ." (back cover).

1661. Campbell, David. **National Deconstruction: Violence, Identity, and Justice in Bosnia**. xv, 304p. Minneapolis: University of Minnesota Press, 1998. Includes bibliographical references (pp. 249-98) and index.

As the author explains in his preface, "this book is concerned primarily with 'metaBosnia,' the array of practices through which Bosnia (indeed, competing 'Bosnias') comes to be. Positioned in the above ethico-political terms made possible by the thought of Derida and Levinas, which permeates the argument, this book concentrates on the way the relationship to the other is variously effaced or enacted in those constitutive practices" (pp. ix-x).

1662. Cigar, Norman L. **Genocide in Bosnia: The Policy of "Ethnic Cleansing."** xiv, 247p.: illus., map. College Station: Texas A&M University Press, 1995. Includes bibliographical references (pp. 205-7) and index.

Little has been done to stop the genocide that has gone on in Bosnia-Herzegovina since 1992. There have also been few scholarly studies of this unthinkable situation. "In this pioneering book, the first scholarly treatise on genocide in Bosnia-Herzegovina, Norman Cigar casts a harsh spotlight on this issue. He analyzes with sensitivity, insight and scrupulous documentation the horrors of Bosnia-Herzegovina that have taken place even as the West has passively stood by" (p. xiii). The author begins by providing the historical context for the ethnic relations in the area. He then analyzes the developing problem in the region and all of its complications. The book includes three appendixes on political organizations in the region, members of the local leadership, and a list of local newspapers and journals.

1663. Crnobrnja, Mihailo. **The Yugoslav Drama**. 2nd ed. 312p. Montreal, Canada: McGill-Queen's University Press, 1994. Includes bibliographical references (pp. [285]-297) and index.

This assessment of the collapse of Yugoslavia is arranged in four parts. In Part 1 the author sketches out the formation and external forces that shaped Yugoslavia. Part 2 deals with the post-Tito years and the gradual but ever-increasing dissolution of the country. Part 3 covers the final stage of collapse and the civil war. The final part provides a synthesis of the situation as of the autumn of 1993.

1664. **Crises in the Balkans: Views from the Participants**. Edited by Constantine Danopoulos and Kostas G. Messas. x, 389p.: maps. Boulder, Colo.: Westview Press, 1997. Includes bibliographic references and index.

The 19 essays in this volume all touch on the crisis surrounding the fall of Yugoslavia. Some of the essays focus on specific countries and problems attendant therein, while others examine more overarching issues, such as ethnonationalism, security, and relations with the United States, NATO, and the European Union. All of them, however, remind the reader, that "all the problems in the Balkans are in one way or another interrelated" (p. vii).

1665. De Rossanet, Bertrand. **Peacemaking and Peacekeeping in Yugoslavia**. xv, 127p. *Nijhoff Law Specials*, vol. 17. The Hague; Boston: Kluwer Law International, 1996. Includes bibliographical references (pp. 111-19) and index.

This book describes the long search for peace. "Bertrand de Rossanet is the pen name of a senior international mediator who has been involved in negotiations and other activities carried out by the International Conference on the Former Yugoslavia from its earliest days" (back cover). Each chapter is devoted to a different aspect of a geographic area that has been the focus of the peace effort in Yugoslavia from human rights issues to Macedonia, from border monitoring to peacemaking in Bosnia-Herzegovinia.

1666. Djordjevic, Dimitrije. **Scars and Memory: Four Lives in One Lifetime**. 463p. Boulder, Colo.: East European Monographs; New York: Distributed by Columbia University Press, 1997.

Djordjevic recounts his four lives. The first was a cozy and protected childhood and adolescence before WWII in Belgrade. The second life, the German invasion, led him to be in the resistance to the occupying forces and eventually into the Nazi death camps. The third life was spent in Yugoslav prisons and gulags. In his fourth life, from which he writes this memoir, he devoted himself to academia and research in history. His memoir is not only valuable for the first-person account it provides, but also for the multi- decade perspective it provides in the interpretation of those events.

1667. Dragnich, Alex. **Serbia and Yugoslavia: Historical Studies and Contemporary Commentaries**. 199p. *East European Monographs*, 515. Boulder, Colo.: East European Monographs; New York: Distributed by Columbia University Press, 1998. Includes bibliographical references.

These previously printed book chapters, essays, and op-ed pieces by Dragnich give "an account of how eccentric and willful U.S. policy has been on the issue of sovereignty during the past decade in respect of the 'old' Yugoslavia and the (largely Serb) 'new' Yugoslavia" (p. ix). The pieces themselves were written between 1995 and 1998.

1668. Dragnich, Alex N. **Yugoslavia's Disintegration and the Struggle for Truth**. xii, 278p. *East European Monographs*, 436. Boulder, Colo.: East European Monographs; New York: Distributed by Columbia University Press, 1996. Includes bibliographical references.

Alex Dragnich studied Yugoslavia for more than 30 years. In this volume he brings together a number of his previously published works. He has selected those that help explain current events in Yugoslavia. In particular, he feels that the Serbs and their involvement in the disintegration of the Yugoslav state have been misrepresented. The materials are divided into a section of articles, a section of published "op-ed" pieces, and a selection of unpublished "op-ed" pieces.

1669. **Yugoslavia and After: A Study in Fragmentation, Despair and Rebirth**. Edited by D. A. Dyker and I. Vejvoda. x, 268p. London: Longman, 1996. Includes bibliographical references and index.

The contributors to this volume have intended to address the following points with their writings: "to study Yugoslavia in the context of post-Yugoslav reality, to study the successor states, in their own right, and in the context of the Yugoslav and pre-Yugoslav background and to fix all these firmly in the global context" (p. 3). The 14 chapters are divided into three parts and an introduction. In Part 1, The Anatomy of Collapse, contributors cover Yugoslavia from 1945 to 1991, from decentralization to dissolution. Part 2, In the Eye of the Storm, deals with Bosnia and Hercegovina, the Yugoslav and post-Yugoslav armies, the Albanian movement in Kosovo, and the West and the international organizations. Part 3, The Successor States, focuses on Serbia, Montenegro, Croatia, Slovenia, and Macedonia.

1670. Elsie, Robert. **Kosovo—In the Heart of the Powder Keg: A Reader**. vi, 593p. *East European Monographs*, 478. Boulder, Colo.: East European Monographs; New York: Distributed by Columbia University Press, 1997. Includes bibliographical references (pp. 516-86).

This volume includes texts by various authors from various periods that have been gathered. Although it was originally conceived as a political and historical essay, this volume is actually in the form of a reader in order to understand the phenomenon of Kosovo from historical, political, literary, and documentary perspectives. The five sections are entitled: (1) political and literary perspectives; (2) approaches to the present dilemma; (3) historical documents and observations; (4) conversations with contemporaries; and (5) bibliography. Elsie stresses that this is not meant as an indictment of the Serbian people, but "is an attempt to elucidate some of the factors which have allowed many of them to be manipulated so tragically in recent years."

1671. Filipovic, Zlata. **Zlata's Diary: A Child's Life in Sarajevo**. Translated by Christine Pribichevich-Zoricxvi. 200p. New York: Viking, 1994. Originally published in Croatian by UNICEF.

Zlata Filipovic has been called the Anne Frank of Sarajevo. She began keeping a diary since September 1991, a few months before the heavy shelling of Sarajevo began. In December 1993, she was flown to Paris and safety. Her diary records the everyday life of a young adolescent, surviving the horrors of war.

1672. **Dubrovnik in War**. Edited by Miljenko Foretic. 111p.: illus. (some col.), col. maps. Dubrovnik: Matica Hrvatska, 1993. Includes bibliographical references and index.

This collection of essays follows the battle for Dubrovnik in Croatia. There are numerous photographs and a detailed chronology. This book is a translation of the original 1992 publication, *Dubrovnik u Ratu*. Along with maps of the city and poetry, the volume includes essays on a variety of topics.

1673. Fromkin, David. **Kosovo Crossing: American Ideals Meet Realities on the Balkan Battlefields**. ix, 210p. New York: Free Press, 1999. Includes bibliographical references (pp. 200-202) and index.

Fromkin provides a historical perspective on the turmoil in the Balkans. He examines the region's history and the perception of the Balkans in the United States as a means to disentangle fact from fiction.

1674. Gabric, Mijo, and Ante Beljo. **Croatia and Bosnia-Herzegovina Sacral Institutions on Target: Deliberate Military Destruction of the Sacral Institutions in Croatia and Bosnia-Herzegovina**. 204p.: illus. (some col.), folded maps. Zagreb, Croatia: Croatian Information Centre, 1992. Cover title: *Croatia, Bosnia-Herzegovina Sacral Institutions on Target*.

This startling book presents lists of destroyed churches, monasteries, mosques, and other sacral objects in Bosnia-Herzegovina, classified by archdiocese and dioceses, as well as written accounts of the destruction and maps marking where the destruction took place. According to the authors, the purpose of this particular type of destruction by Serbian forces is carried out to destroy evidence of religion and culture that serve as the identity of the people living there and also to eliminate credible witnesses to such a campaign.

1675. Glenny, Misha. **The Fall of Yugoslavia: The Third Balkan War**. 193p., [1] p.: maps. London: Penguin Books, 1993. Includes index.

Misha Glenny is a respected journalist who has written extensively on the Yugoslavia crisis. He was the Central Europe correspondent for the BBC World Service from 1991 to 1993. In this book Glenny follows the events in Yugoslavia from August 1990 to June 1993. His eyewitness account focuses on the human realities of war.

1676. Gow, James. **Triumph of the Lack of Will: International Diplomacy and the Yugoslav War**. xii, 343p.: maps. New York: Columbia University Press, 1997. Includes bibliographical references and index.

James Gow sets out to trace the role of international diplomacy in the resolution of the conflict in Yugoslavia. The title makes reference to Hitler's Germany quite deliberately. "It is intended to convey the understanding that, scope and detail notwithstanding, the events in former Yugoslavia had strong parallels with events in former Europe during the 1930s and 1940s" (p. vi). The book is arranged chronologically and begins with a discussion of the causes of the conflict. Gow then examines in detail early diplomatic initiatives. Next, the author presents an overview of the military operations in the region. Shifting focus the author turns his attention on the "major players" in the diplomatic initiative. The final section is devoted to the various peace plans that were negotiated and how they came into being.

1677. Hoffmann, Stanley, Robert C. Johansen, and James P. Sterba. **The Ethics and Politics of Humanitarian Intervention**. 124p. Notre Dame, Ind.: University of Notre Dame Press, 1996. Includes bibliographical references and index.

As Raimo Vayrynen states in his introductory essay, "The Yugoslavian case provides a benchmark by which the efforts to prevent escalation of future international crises and the viability of multi-ethnic states should be assessed" (p. 1). In the essays that follow his introduction, various authors confront the issues related to humanitarian intervention in international crises. The analyses are structured around Stanley Hoffmann's essay (the second in the volume) and prepared responses to it. The essays cover topics such as: how much force in humanitarian intervention?; sovereignty and the ethics of intervention; humanitarian intervention in the former Yugoslavia; limits and opportunities in humanitarian intervention; a discussion of Stanley Hoffmann's Kantian justification for humanitarian intervention; and Hoffmann's reply to the comments made to his initial essay.

1678. Holbrooke, Richard. **To End a War**. xx, 408p.: illus. New York: Random House, 1998. Includes bibliographical references and index.

This book describes the negotiating process that took place to end the war in Yugoslavia. Holbrooke's account begins with an overview of the war in Bosnia. He then discusses the "shuttle" diplomacy that went on in 1995, as the West tried to intervene. Next he describes the negotiations in Dayton, Ohio. The final section describes the implementation of the peace through 1998. The book includes a "cast of characters" supplying brief biographical sketches on the individuals involved in the peace process.

1679. Human Rights Watch Staff. **Humanitarian Law Violations in Kosovo**. 130p. New York: Human Rights Watch, 1998. "The report was written by Fred Abrahams, researcher, Human Rights Watch. . . . Parts were written by Elizabeth Andersen, advocacy director"—Acknowledgments.

This work outlines the human rights abuses that have occurred in Kosovo since the beginning of the Serb offensive. Each chapter describes a different problem, starting with a general description of abuses in Drenca and then turning to the use of landmarks, forcible disappearances, etc.

1680. Kumar, Radha. **Divide and Fall?: Bosnia in the Annals of Partition**. xvi, 207p.: maps. New York: Verso, 1997. Includes bibliographical references (pp. [169]-187) and index.

Countering the idea that partition can be a solution to ethnic conflict, Kumar analyzes the diplomatic actions that led to the Dayton Peace Agreement and the aftermath of that agreement. He argues that "the revival of ethnic partition theory is not only short-lived but points to a wider process of change in which the deployment of partition as a solution to ethnic conflict will be seen as doing more harm than good, whether in the short or long term" (p. xvi).

1681.   Kurspahic, Kemal. **As Long As Sarajevo Exists**. xxxviii, 248p.: illus., maps, port. Stony Creek, Conn.: Pamphleteer's Press, 1997.

"This book is about that courageous group of men and women—the journalists of Oslobodjenje—whose commitment to their profession and to a pluralist, multi-ethnic Bosnia-Hercegovina was translated into a unique form of resistance to the ultranationalist warriors who laid siege to their city and rent their country from end to end" (p. ix). Kemal Kurspahic traces the development of the war and the reaction to it in the journalistic community in Bosnia.

1682.   **The War Against Croatia: A Chronology of the Aggression**. Edited by Ivo Lajtman. 64p.: illus., map. Zagreb, Croatia: Croatian Information Service, 1992. "This chronology was compiled of material and photos from *Vecernji List.*"

This pamphlet contains chronologically arranged translated articles from the Croatian newspaper *Vecernji List* that document, from a Croatian point of view, Serbian aggression in Croatia. The articles are accompanied by photographs that serve as visual evidence for the events described in the articles.

1683.   Libal, Michael. **Limits of Persuasion: Germany and the Yugoslav Crisis, 1991-1992**. xi, 206p. Westport, Conn.: Praeger, 1997. Includes bibliographical references (pp. [193]-199) and index.

Michael Libal is ambassador, head of the Mission of the Organisation for Security and Cooperation in Europe (OSCE). His study deals with Western involvement in the Yugoslav war. As a diplomat and ambassador he is aware of his own biases. Nevertheless, Libal feels it is important for Western readers to be aware of the role Germany played in the war and its negotiated settlement. His book is divided into three parts. "The first provides a narrative of German, EC and OSCE diplomacy between June 1991 and August 1992. . . . In the second part I have tried to systematically analyze the issues that German diplomacy faced at the time or were later raised by its critics. In the third part I have tried to draw some general conclusions regarding the merits and weaknesses of German policy on Yugoslavia" (p. x). The book includes a chronology of events and a glossary of terms. The bibliography lists numerous German and English-language works on the topic.

1684.   Markovic, Mira. **Night and Day**. 251p.: illus. (some col.). Kingston, Ont: Quarry Press, 1996.

Markovic is the wife of the then president of Serbia, Slobodan Milosevic, and a professor of sociology at Belgrade University. This journal originally appeared serially in the bimonthly magazine *Duga* from December 1992 to July 1994. As the introduction states, this diary is "at once a personal diary and a political journal, offering an emotionally charged yet intellectually balanced perspective on the crises in Yugoslavia" (p. 7).

1685. Mercier, Michele. **Crimes Without Punishment: Humanitarian Action in Former Yugoslavia**. xx, 236p.: illus., maps. London: Pluto Press, 1994. Includes bibliography (pp. 221-22) and index.

This book is an attempt to assess "the main questions that assailed humanitarian agencies between 1991 and 1993, and still do so at the time of publication" (p. xii). The main humanitarian agency involved is the International Council of the Red Cross.

1686. **Genocide After Emotion: The Postemotional Balkan War**. Edited by Stjepan G. Mestrovic. xi, 225p. London: Routledge, 1996. Includes index.

The failure of the Western powers to respond adequately to the Balkan Wars has engendered a new sociological concept, postemotionalism, "as an explanation for this confused response of the West" (frontispiece). This concept refers to "the culture industry's manipulation of emotionally charged historical events and phenomena to create the puzzling international interplay of images and other 'collective representations' pertaining to the current Balkan War" (frontispiece). The essays of the individual authors explain and analyze how and why the war began, what an appropriate response would have been, and other appropriate topics.

1687. **The Conceit of Innocence: Losing the Conscience of the West in the War Against Bosnia**. Edited by Stjepan Gabriel Mestrovic and Akbar S. Ahmed. 1st ed. xii, 259p. *Eastern European Series*, 4. College Station: Texas A&M University Press, 1997. Includes bibliographical references and index.

This collection of essays begins with a question: "How does one begin to comprehend the now historical fact that Serb-sponsored genocide against Bosnian Muslims and Croats, an event that was widely covered by the information media, went on for five years without decisive Western military action to stop it and with the imposition of a weapons embargo on Belgrade's victims?" (p. 3). The 11 essays that follow the introduction attempt to answer that question and to give a multilayered perspective on it.

1688. Mojzes, Paul. **Religion and the War in Bosnia**. 300p. Atlanta, Ga.: Scholar Press, 1998. Includes bibliographical references.

This is a collection of all views of the religion dimension of the war in Bosnia. The editor sought out representatives of all viewpoints (Muslim, Serbian Orthodox, and Roman Catholic). The essays are grouped into three sections: "contextual issues"; "the religion factors of war"; and "paths of reconciliation."

1689. Owen, David. **Balkan Odyssey**. xxii, 394p., [16] p. of plates: illus., maps, ports. London: V. Gollancz, 1996. Includes bibliographical references (pp. [369]-377) and index.

David Owen was co-chairman of the Steering Committee of the International Conference on the Former Yugoslavia (ICFY) in 1992. As such he was a negotiator in the peace process in Yugoslavia. This book is not intended as a history of the war.

Rather, Owen tries to present the details of the peace process. His aim is to enlighten the reader as to the complex nature of international diplomacy and provide more information on the UN Security Council. This lengthy study includes a chronology of events and is organized chronologically.

1690. Pavkovic, Aleksandar. **Fragmentation of Yugoslavia**. 256p. New York: St. Martin's Press, 1997. Includes bibliographical references and index.

Pavkovic argues that the conflict in Yugoslavia that broke out in 1991 "was essentially a result of competing national ideologies laying claim to one and the same territory for their respective national groups" (p. ix). In Part 1 he examines the historical background of Yugoslavia, and in Part 2 he analyzes each important step of disintegration and the results of civil war.

1691. Ramet, Sabrina P. **Balkan Babel: The Disintegration of Yugoslavia from the Death of Tito to Ethnic War**. 2nd ed. 356p. Boulder, Colo.: Westview Press, 1996. Includes bibliographical references and index.

In this volume Sabrina Ramet has compiled a number of essays that trace the dissolution of Yugoslav from the death of Tito to the beginning of war in the region. The essays are grouped into four sections: politics, culture, religion, and ethnic war. While many of these essays appeared in an earlier edition published in 1991, Chapters 10 through 13 are new and Chapters 3, 5, and 8 have been revised. The premise of the first edition remains unchanged. "This book is about politics. It is also about culture and religion. I have brought these topics together because I am convinced that no country's politics exists independently of its culture or its religions, and without an understanding of the culture and religion one can never understand the politics" (p. 2).

1692. Reed, Fred A. **Salonica Terminus: Travels into the Balkan Nightmare**. xv, 270p.: illus., maps, ports. Burnaby, B.C.: Talonbooks, 1996. Includes bibliographical references (pp. 263-70).

The author traveled through the southern Balkans, i.e., northern Greece, Albania, Kosovo, Macedonia, and Bulgaria, in the fall of 1994. This book is a record of what he encountered, the people he met, and the impressions made upon him as he traveled.

1693. Rogel, Carole. **The Breakup of Yugoslavia and the War in Bosnia**. xxiv, 182p.: ill, maps. Greenwood Press *"Guides to Historic Events of the Twentieth Century."* Westport, Conn.: Greenwood Press, 1998. Includes bibliographical references (pp. [161]-172) and index.

This book is a volume in the Greenwood Press *"Guides to Historic Events of the Twentieth Century."* As with all volumes in this series, this is an interpretive history, combining narrative history and analysis. This volume includes a chronology of events in Yugoslavia, providing details of events throughout the century. This is followed by a lengthy section, discussing the breakup of Yugoslavia and its consequences. There is a section containing biographical sketches on major figures in the breakup of the country and a collection of translated primary documents such as the "Memorandum of the Serbian Academy of Sciences and Arts." A glossary and annotated bibliography are also included. "Designed for secondary school and college student research, this is a one-step ready reference guide to the breakup of Yugoslavia in 1991, the war in Bosnia, and the peace settlement" (back cover).

1694. Rohde, David. **Endgame: The Betrayal and Fall of Srebrenica: Europe's Worst Massacre Since the Holocaust**. xvi, 440p.: maps. New York: Farrar, Straus & Giroux, 1997. Maps of Srebrenica on endpapers. Includes bibliographical references (pp. [393]-424) and index.

Rohde, a journalist for the *Christian Science Monitor*, relates the horrors of the fall of Srebrenica, where 7,079 Muslim men were missing in what was one of the most horrible mass executions of the Bosnian conflict. The author tells the tale from the point of view of seven people—three Muslims, two Dutch, a Serb, and a Croat—who lived through the experience.

1695. Sadkovich, James J. **U.S. Media and Yugoslavia, 1991-1995**. xx, 272p. Westport, Conn.: Praeger, 1998. Includes bibliographical references (pp. [247]-272) and index.

This is primarily a study of the American media. The case used to expose its tendencies is the Yugoslav war. Sadkovich attempts to explain "why the U.S. media did the job it did covering Yugoslavia's dissolution" (p. ix). Since the focus of this work is not on Yugoslavia, the early chapters discuss the nature of the media in the West. Later chapters focus on the media portrayal of the national groups of the region.

1696. Scharf, Michael P. **Balkan Justice: The Story Behind the First International War Crimes Trial Since Nuremberg**. xvii, 340p. Durham, N.C.: Carolina Academic, 1997. Includes bibliographical references and index.

The atrocities committed against the Muslims shocked the world. In this book the difficulties encountered in bringing the guilty to justice are described. The entire process of calling a war crimes trial is described: collecting the facts, establishing the tribunal, and beginning the prosecution. There is also a complete description of the trial. The volume includes a chronology of the Yugoslav conflict, the statute of the Yugoslav tribunal, the indictment of Dusko Tadic, and a summary of the verdict. While this is "not a tale for the faint of heart" (p. xi), it does provide a detailed picture of the atrocities endured by the Muslim population during the last few years.

1697. Schierup, Carol-Ulrik. **Scramble for the Balkans: Nationalism, Globalism and the Political Economy of Reconstruction**. vi, 235p. New York: St. Martin's Press, 1999. "Published in association with the Centre for Research in Ethnic Relations, University of Warwick."

This volume collects a number of essays on the problems in the former Yugoslavia republics. Such topics as reconstruction in a post-communist society, ethnic nationalism, international relations and their effect on economic development, privatization, and political instability are all included. The contributors are Carol-Ulrik Schierup, Ivan Ivekovic, Vesna Bojicic, Mary Kaldoi, Boris Young, and Branks Likie-Brboric.

1698. **Documenta Croatica: On Croatian History and Identity and the War Against Croatia**. Edited by Zvonimir Separovic. 2205p., [15] p. of plates: illus. Zagreb, Croatia: Croatian Society of Victimology, 1992. "Special edition of Victimology. Translation: 'Lancon', Zagreb." Includes bibliographical references.

This book is a compendium of articles, essays, lists, and photographs that document and analyze the effects of the Yugoslav civil war.

1699. Silber, Laura, and Allan Little. **Yugoslavia: Death of a Nation**. 384p., [8] p. of plates: illus., maps. New York: TV Books; Distributed by Penguin USA, 1996. "Published to accompany the television series broadcast on the Discovery Channel"—t.p. verso. Includes bibliographical references and index.

The two authors are well-known journalists who have both covered the Yugoslav civil war for many years. Here they attempt to relate the incidents and actions that led to the horror and destruction of Yugoslavia over the past decade. They identify the crucial events and secret meetings that led up to the war and describe its progress once it had started. The authors show that Yugoslavia died by the actions of men acting deliberately, by men "who had nothing to gain and everything to lose from a peaceful transition from state socialism and one-party rule to free-market democracy" (p. 25). The text also includes a series of maps and a list of characters who partook in the drama.

1700. Sloan, Elinor C. **Bosnia and the New Collective Security**. xii, 128p. Westport, Conn.: Praeger, 1998. Includes bibliographical references (pp. [119]-123) and index.

Just as the political situation and balance of power have changed in Eastern Europe, so have the methods of negotiation, on all levels in that part of the world. In this book Dr. Sloan examines the methods of "crisis management" applied to the war in Bosnia. She believes that, although the activities directed at resolving the situation may have appeared haphazard, they in fact reflected the "evolution of great power interests." This study follows the peace process in Bosnia from the beginning to the end. This book sheds light on two complex and interrelated subjects—"the role of peace support operations in managing nontraditional crises and the changing nature of the international community involvement in Bosnia" (pp. xi-xii). The book includes two appendixes: one comparing the United Nations Protective Force and the Implementation Force and the other outlining the "Form of Military Operation."

1701. Stojanovic, Svetozar. **The Fall of Yugoslavia: Why Communism Failed**. 341p. Amherst, N.Y.: Prometheus Books, 1997. Includes bibliographical references and index.

Stojanovic approaches his study from the framework of an acute analysis of the philosophical underpinnings of communism. In Part 1 he explores the progression from Stalinism to Titoism, then in Part 2 describes and analyzes the disintegration of Yugoslavia from within and the Western response to it. In Part 3 he offers a postmortem about the collapse of the communist state and traces a movement in ideology from Marxism to post-Marxism and then to what he calls "Anti-apocalyptism."

1702. Sudetic, Chuck. **Blood and Vengeance: One Family's Story of the War in Bosnia**. xxxvii, 393p.: illus., maps. New York: W. W. Norton, 1998. Includes bibliographical references (pp. 379-82) and index.

Journalist Chuck Sudetic relates the experiences of the Celik family during the horrors in Bosnia, and especially in Srebrenica, in the early 1990s.

1703. Tudijman, Franjo. **Horrors of War: Historical Reality and Philosophy**. xvi, 480p. New York: M. Evans, 1996. "This is a substantially revised version of the book *Bespuca povijesne zbiljnosti: rasprava o povijesti i filozofiji zlosilja (Wastelands of historical reality: discussion on history and philosophy of aggressive violence)*"—(p. ix).

Billed as Tudijman's magnum opus, this work by the then leader of Croatia will be of interest to anyone investigating cults of personality and the history of Yugoslavia in the last half of the 20th century.

1704. **Burn This House: The Making and Unmaking of Yugoslavia**. Edited by Jasminka Udovicki and James Ridgeway. x, 337p.: illus., maps. Durham, N.C.: Duke University Press, 1997. Includes bibliography (pp. 317-22) and index.

This volume provides a historical analysis of the cultural, political, and economic forces that resulted in the Yugoslav war in the early 1990s. The authors of the individual chapters are journalists, historians, and former diplomats living in the region. Fully one-third of the book looks at the historical roots of the conflict and the remainder focuses on such topics as the media wars of 1987-1997, the war in Croatia and the war in Bosnia and Herzegovina, international aspects of the wars, the resistance in Serbia, and the opposition in Croatia.

1705. Woodward, Susan L. **Balkan Tragedy: Chaos and Dissolution After the Cold War**. xii, 536p.: maps. Washington, D.C.: The Brookings Institution, 1995. Includes bibliographical references (pp. 425-520) and index.

This is a study of the causes of the conflict in Yugoslavia by a senior fellow of the Brookings Foreign Policy Studies program. "Although many books have attempted to bring the plight of Bosnia and the fall of Yugoslavia to the attention of the outside world, this is one of the few that attempts to analyze the causes of these events and that weaves into the story of decline and war the influence of the international environment and outside actors" (p. vii). The book contains numerous tables supplying data on the national composition of the region from 1961 to 1994. There is also an appendix describing UN Security Council resolutions on Yugoslavia from 1991 to 1995.

1706. Zimmermann, Warren. **Origins of a Catastrophe: Yugoslavia and Its Destroyers**. 256p. New York: Random House, 1996. Includes index.

Zimmermann was the American ambassador to Yugoslavia between 1989 and 1992. In this position he got to know the major players in Yugoslavia's destruction. In portraying them he says: "They described their plans, sometimes honestly, sometimes deceitfully, but always passionately and with a cynical disregard for playing by a set of rules. This record of their words and actions provides evidence for a coroner's report on the death of Yugoslavia" (p. viii). In addition, the author also honestly describes the changes in American foreign policy toward Yugoslavia during those years and the difficulty in making the right decisions.

Name Index

Abel, Istvan, 239
Acton, Edward, 458
Adam, Jan, 36, 1192
Adams, Mark B., 872
Adams, Walter, 5
Adjubei, Juri, 6
Adjubei, Yuri, 6
Adler, Nanci, 375
Adomeit, Hannes, 423
Agarwal, D. P., 1439
Agh, Atilla, 1160
Agnew, Jeremy, 364
Ahl, Richard, 329
Ahmed, Akbar S., 1687
Aiken, Susan Hardy, 663
Ajdacic, Dejan, 1271
Akchurin, Marat, 113
Akhmatova, Anna Andreevna, 732
Akhmatova Centennial Conference, 733
Akiner, Shirin, 1051
Albright, David E., 1002
Alexandrescu, Ion, 1556
Alexandrow, Julia, 1046
Alfeyeva, Valeria, 914
Allcock, John B., 1654
Allen, Beverly, 1655
Allen, Elizabeth Cheresh, 664, 831
Altman, I., 1130
Altshuler, Mordechai, 1115
Amert, Susan, 734
Anderson, John, 859
Anderson, K. M., 1130
Anderson, Richard, 300
Anderson, Roger B., 665
Andrew, Joe, 650, 666
Andrews, Mary Catherine, 1288
Androunas, Elena, 270
Anisimov, E. V., 491
Any, Carol Joyce, 773
Anzulovic, Branimir, 1656
Aparac-Gazivoda, Tatjana, 1646
Aperture Foundation Inc., 1389

Appatov, S. I., 1002
Apple, Slovie Solomon, 1235
Arbatov, Aleksei Georgievich, 322
Archer, Clive, 396
Armes, Keith, 288
Árnason, Jóhann Páll, 356
Arnold, Anthony, 600
Aroutunova, Bayara, 614
Arter, David, 958
Artisien-Maksimenko, 6
Aschaffenburg, Karen, 1441
Ascherson, Neal, 465
Ash, Timothy Garton, 1261
Askin, Kelly D., 37
Åslund, Anders, 208, 241, 252
Atabaki, Touraj, 1052, 1091
Attwood, Lynne, 915
Austin, Paul M., 620
Aves, Jonathan, 222
Avins, Carol J., 738
Avtorkhanov, Abdurakhman, 1055
Azizian, Rouben, 1088

Baal-Teshuva, Jacob, 145
Babel', I. (Isaak), 738
Bachman, Ronald, 457
Bacon, Edwin, 553
Baehr, Peter, 525
Baev, Pavel K., 601
Bagby, Lewis, 744
Bailey, C. C., 881
Baker, T. Lindsay, 1532
Bakhtin, M. M., 846
Balazs, Eva, 1397
Ball, Alan M., 900
Banac, Ivo, 1263
Banerji, Arup, 492
Banuazizi, Ali, 1053
Bar-Zohar, Michael, 1303
Baranovsky, Vladimir, 424
Barany, Zoltan, 1398

Barbatarlo, Gennady, 787
Bardach, Janusz, 376
Barnett, Vincent, 209
Barnhart, Joe E., 629
Baron, Samuel H., 474, 857
Barooshian, Vahan D., 146
Barr, Nicholas, 1478
Barratt, Andrew, 781
Barros, James, 554
Barta, Peter I., 621
Bartal, Yisra'el, 1544
Bartkute, Diana, 947
Bartlett, David L., 1418
Bartlett, Rosamund, 153
Barylski, Robert V., 602
Batalden, Stephen K., 868
Beaudoin, Luc J., 667
Beauplan, Guillaume Le Vasseur, sieur de, 974
Beck, Tom, 1333
Bednar, Zdenek F., 1325
Beljo, Ante, 1674
Bell, Andrew, 52
Bell, John D., 1315
Benderly, Jill, 1621
Beniukh, Oles, 1031
Bennett, Christopher, 1657
Benson, Morton, 90
Berberova, Nina Nikolaevna, 743
Berenbaum, Michael, 1247
Berend, T. Ivan, 53
Bergholz, Fred W., 1054
Bergmann, Theodor, 357
Beriozkina, Patricia, 736
Bernard-Donals, Michael F., 739
Bernhard, Michael H., 1495, 1533
Bernstein, Laurie, 493
Berry, Ellen E., 258
Bethea, David M., 747, 798, 799
Bethin, Christina Y., 71
Bettauer Dembo, Margot, 1241
Bevan, David, 980
Beyme, Klaus von, 1278
Biberaj, Elez, 1289
Bielec, Dana, 1513
Big, Michael, 1647
Biggart, John, 544
Biggins, Michael, 1612
Billington, Elisabeth, 1361
Bird, Thomas E., 1028

Birnbaum, Henrik, 480
Biskupski, M. B., 1553
Bitov, Andrei, 668, 745
Black, J. L., 847
Black, Stanley W., 1193
Blacker, Coit D., 583
Blackman, Ellen, 1658
Blanchard, Olivier Jean, 7, 1194
Blank, Stephen J., 301, 494
Blanke, Richard, 1459
Blaskovich, Jerry, 1659
Blejer, Mario I., 8
Blobaum, Robert, 1460
Blom, Riamo, 84
Bludeau, Todd, 283
Bluffstone, Randall, 1275
Blum, Douglas W., 323
Bly, Robert, 122
Bociurkiw, Bohdan R., 1024
Boettke, Peter J., 368
Bohdan, Vladimir A., 981
Boiko, Maksym, 973
Boilard, Steve D., 92
Bokovoy, Melissa K., 1619
Bokros, Lajos, 1419
Bonin, John, 1195
Bonmanshinov, Arash, 124
Bonnell, Victoria E., 271
Booker, M. Keith, 669, 670
Bordwell, David, 176
Borneman, John, 1161
Bosley, Keith, 75
Both, Norbert, 1660
Boutenko, Irene A., 888
Bova, Russell, 329
Bowlt, John E., 137
Bown, Matthew Cullerne, 130, 147
Boyarin, Jonathan, 1120
Boyko, Ihor N., 973
Boyle, Peter G., 408
Boym, Svetlana, 927
Bozhkov, Atanas, 1304
Bracewell, Catherine Wendy, 1596
Brada, Josef C., 19, 1420
Bradbrook, B. R., 1378
Braham, Randolph L., 1124, 1236–37, 1557
Branch, Michael, 43, 75
Brandenberger, David, 100
Brandist, Craig, 671

Brandon, William, 1438
Braun, Aurel, 1398
Braun, Marina, 290
Bremmer, Ian A., 38, 67
Brewer, Bob, 1296
Bridger, Sue, 916
Bridger, Susan, 901
Briggs, A. D. P., 800
Bristow, John A., 1312
Brock, James W., 5
Bromfield, Andrew, 658
Brower, Daniel R., 939
Brown, Archie, 109, 302, 324
Brown, Clarence, 651
Brown, Deming, 622
Brown, Edward James, 72
Brown, Howard, 164
Brownsberger, Susan, 745
Broxup, Marie, 1055
Brubaker, Rogers, 54
Brumfield, William Craft, 131, 143
Bryld, Mette, 902
Brym, Robert J., 1125
Brzozowska-Krajka, Anna, 1514
Buchanan, Henry, 760
Buchanan, James M., 9
Büchler, Alexandra, 1362
Buckley, Mary, 912, 940
Buda, B., 1439
Bunin, Ivan, 750, 751, 752
Burandt, Gary, 234
Burbank, Jane, 518
Burdett, Anita L. P., 1597
Burg, Steven L., 44
Burgin, Diana Lewis, 793
Burns, Bryan, 1448
Bushkovitch, Paul, 390, 860
Bushnell, John, 498
Bussy, Carvel de, 1377
Butler, Lois J., 112
Butterwick, Richard, 1461
Buwalda, Piet, 1108
Bykhovets', N. M., 1032
Byrnes, Robert Francis, 3, 475

Cale Feldman, Lada, 1652
Camiller, Patrick, 1586
Campbell, David, 1661

Campbell, Robert Wellington, 210, 880
Capra, Dominick L., 1238
Carleton, Gregory, 840
Carlisle, Olga Andreyev, 615
Carmichael, Cathie, 1590
Carothers, Thomas, 1574
Carr, Jennifer, 236
Carrère d'Encausse, Hélène, 303, 466, 555
Carter, F. W., 1290, 1479
Cassedy, Steven, 1109
Cawthorne, Nigel, 531
Center for Preventive Action, 1162
Centre for Co-operation with European Economies in Transition, 10, 1021
Cesarani, David, 1400
Chances, Ellen B., 746
Chandler, Andrea, 393
Chandler, Robert, 830
Chang, Mariko L., 1441
Chavance, Bernard, 55
Chenciner, Robert, 1056
Cheney, Glenn Alan, 978
Cherniaev, Vladimir Iu., 458
Chernyshev, Igor, 11
Chernyshevsky, Nikolai, 754
Chester, Pamela, 73
Chinn, Jeff, 941
Chirovsky, Andriy, 1025
Chorbajian, Levon, 1078
Chotzidis, Angelos A., 1604
Christian, Nicole, 616
Chubarian, A. O., 435
Chuev, Feliks Ivanovich, 304
Chvany, Catherine V., 712
Chylinska, Teresa, 1549
Cigar, Norman L., 1662
Cirtautas, Arista Maria, 1542
Clark, Ed, 12
Clark, Katerina, 556
Clarke, Renfrey, 472
Clarke, Simon, 189, 221, 223, 224, 557
Clayton, J. Douglas, 184
Clements, Barbara, 532
Clowes, Edith W., 672
Clyman, Toby W., 917
Cockfield, Jamie H., 587
Codrescu, Andrei, 1585
Coenen-Huther, Jacques, 1314
Cohen, Adir, 1453
Cohen, Ariel, 476

Cohen, Philip J., 1598
Cohn, Michael, 1110
Cole, Daniel H., 1480
Coleman, Fred, 558
Commander, Simon, 211
Compton, Susan P., 260
Comrie, Bernard, 610
Condee, Nancy, 132
Connolly, Julian W., 788
Connor, Walter D., 225
Conroy, Mary Schaeffer, 495
Constantinesco, Nicholas, 1558
Conti, Gregory, 1239
Cook, Jeffrey, 1449
Cooke, Brett, 801
Cooper, Cary L., 236
Cooper, Leo, 325
Cooper, Richard N., 13
Coopersmith, Jonathan, 533
Coppieters, Bruno, 1182
Coricelli, Fabrizio, 8
Corley, Felix, 861
Cornwell, Neil, 616, 673, 792
Corti, Eugenio, 559
Costa, Nicolas J., 1291, 1599
Costlow, Jane T., 889
Cottey, Andrew, 1163
Cottrell, Philip L., 1196
Couroucli, Maria, 1262
Cox, David, 444
Cox, Harold E., 1136
Cox, Terry, 1399
Crampton, Ben, 1135
Crampton, R. J., 1305
Crampton, Richard, 1135
Crawford, Beverly, 14
Creed, Gerald, 1319
Cretzianu, Alexandru, 1559
Crnobrnja, Mihailo, 1663
Crockatt, Richard, 409
Croissant, Michael P., 1079
Cross, Anthony Glenn, 425, 496, 674
Cross, Robin, 79
Crowe, David, 85, 948
Crowfoot, John, 719
Csanadi, Maria, 1164
Cullen, Robert, 928
Culpan, Refik, 15
Currie, Kenneth M., 590
Curry, Jane Leftwich, 1497

Cushman, Thomas, 154
Cuvalo, Ante, 1591
Czeizel, A. E., 1439
Czerwinski, E. J., 1515

D'Agostino, Anthony, 305
Dadrian, Vahakn N., 1229
Daianu, Daniel, 1571
Dalos, Gyorgy, 735
Damrosch, Lori Fisler, 45
Danforth, Loring M., 1628
Daniels, Robert Vincent, 358
Dannreuther, Roland, 426
Danopoulos, Constantine, 1664
Danow, David, 74
Danta, Darrick R., 1165
Dapkute, Rita, 947
David, Avraham, 1387
Davidson, Pamela, 785
Davies, R. W., 200, 560
Davies, Sarah, 306
Davis, Nathaniel, 862
Davydov, O. D., 246
Dawisha, Karen, 39, 326, 1057
Dawson, Jane I., 56
Day, Barbra, 1359
Day, Richard, 212
De Madariaga, Isabel, 497
De Rossanet, Bertrand, 1665
De Scherbinin, Julie W., 675
De Villiers, Marq, 114
Deaglio, Enrico, 1239
DeBardeleben, Joan, 847, 1279
Debeljak, Ales, 1647
Debreczeny, Paul, 665, 802
Dedek, Oldrich, 1346
Dedijer, Vladimir, 1600
Deirez, Raymond, 1306
Deletant, Dennis, 1575
DeLuca, Anthony R., 272
Dembinska, Maria, 1534
Demetz, Peter, 1326
Denitch, Bogdan, 1601
Derev'anko, Anatoliy, 1101
Derviz, Alexis, 1190
Desai, Padma, 16
Deschouwer, Kris, 1182
Dethier, Jean-Jacques, 1419

Devlin, Judith, 327
Diamond, Norma, 110
Diment, Galya, 780, 1103
Dimnik, Martin, 481
Dixon, Simon, 389
Djalili, Mohammad Reza, 1058
Djilas, Milovan, 57
Djordjevic, Dimitrije, 1666
Dmitrieva, Olga, 190
Dneprov, Edward, 263
Dobek, Mariusz Mark, 17
Dobrenko, Evgeny, 83, 623
Dobroszycki, Lucjan, 564
Dodd, Charles K., 882
Dodwell, Christina, 1102
Dolukhanov, Pavel Markovich, 1139
Domanski, Boleslaw, 1481
Dowler, Wayne, 783
Drábek, Zdenek, 1198
Dragnich, Alex N., 1667, 1668
Draitser, Emil, 929
Dreifelds, Juris, 961
Dresziger, Nandor, 1401
Drix, Samuel, 1240
Drobizheva, L. M., 903
Drohobycky, Maria, 1003
Drummond, John, 165
Druzhnikov, Yuri, 803
Dubal, David, 155
Dujarric, Robert, 1087
Dukes, Paul, 477, 485
Dull, Christine, 975
Dull, Ralph, 975
Dune, Eduard M., 534
Dunlop, John B., 328, 1080
Dunn, Dennis J., 410
Dunstan, John, 261, 262
Durden-Smith, Jo, 115
Dutkina, Galina, 904
Duzinkiewicz, Janusz, 1496
Dyck, Harvey L., 870
Dyker, David A., 1276, 1669

Earle, John S., 253
Eastmond, Antony, 1094
Eby, Cecil D., 1402
Eckert, Eva, 1363
Eckstein, Harry, 329
Edelman, Robert, 930

Edgerton, William, 851
Edmonds, Robin, 804
Edmondson, Linda Harriet, 918
Effimova, Alla, 133
Egorova, Tat'iana K., 156
Ehrhart, Hans-Georg, 330
Eickelman, Dale F., 1059
Eidelman, Dawn D., 676
Eidintas, A., 965
Eisenhower, Susan, 878
Ekedahl, Carolyn McGiffert, 95
Ekiert, Grzegorz, 1166
Eklof, Ben, 263, 269, 498
Elgel, David, 1121
Elias, Ruth, 1241
Elleman, Bruce A., 445, 1085
Ellis, Frank, 273, 784
Ellis, Jane, 863
Ellman, Michael, 201
Elsie, Robert, 1670
Elster, Jon, 1167
Elsworth, John D., 677, 678
Emerson, Caryl, 740
Eminov, Ali, 1320
Emmons, Emmons, 538
Emmons, Terence, 869
Engel, Barbara Alpern, 919
Engel, David Joshua, 1462
Epp, Ingrid I., 870
Erlich, Victor, 679
Ermolaev, Herman, 842
Ernst, Maurice, 18
Erofeev, Venedikt, 652, 836
Erofeev, Victor, 652, 775
Essar, Dennis F., 974
Estrin, Saul, 19
Etkind, Alexander, 854
Ettinger, Elzbieta, 712
Evanishen, Danny, 1033
Evanishen, John, 1033
Evans, Alfred B., 359
Evdokimova, Svetlana, 805
Evtuhov, Catherine, 864
Ewanchuk, Michael, 1047
Ezergailis, Andrew, 962

Fajfer, Luba, 1497
Falkingham, Jane, 1060

Falkowska, Janina, 1550
Fan, Qimiao, 211
Farnoaga, Georgiana, 1583
Farnsworth, Beatrice, 926
Fauchereau, Serge, 149
Feiler, Lily, 826
Felak, James Ramon, 1353
Feldbrugge, F. J. M., 291
Felkay, Andrew, 1429
Fenyo, Mario D., 1410
Ferbey, Orysia, 1042
Ferdinand, Peter, 1061
Ferry, William E., 1168
Feshbach, Murray, 883
Feuer, Kathryn B., 813
Figes, Orlando, 535
Filipovic, Zlata, 1671
Filtzer, Donald A., 226
Fink-Hafner, Danica, 1622
Finke, Michael, 624
Firth, Noel E., 231
Fischer-Galati, Stephen, 1560
Fischler-Martinno, Janina, 1242
Fish, M. Steven, 331
Fisher-Ruge, Lois, 116
Fishman, David E., 1116
Fisler, Lori, 45
Fiszman, Samuel, 1463
Fitzpatrick, Catherine A., 100, 904
Fitzpatrick, Sheila, 536, 561, 562
Flakierski, Henryk, 191
Flam, Helena, 1140
Fogel, Daniel S., 1347
Foglesong, David S., 411
Fol, Aleksandur, 1308
Foretic, Miljenko, 1672
Fortescue, Stephen, 192
Fowkes, Ben, 332, 452
Frank, Allen J., 1062
Frank, Joseph, 761
Frank, Stephen, 547
Franks, Steven, 1219
Franz H. Bäuml, 1141
Frazer, Graham, 333
Freeze, Gregory L., 196, 432
Freidenberg, O. M., 680
French, Alfred, 1364
French, Carolyn, 1526
French, R. A., 86
French, Tommy, 1046

Frick, David A., 1026
Friedberg, Maurice, 625
Friedgut, Theodore H., 336
Friedman, Barry L., 31
Friedman, Francine, 1592
Friedrich, Paul, 110, 626
Friel, Brian, 832
Frierson, Cathy A., 499
Frigyesi, Judit, 1450
Fromkin, David, 1673
Froot, Kenneth A., 1194
Frydman, Roman, 20, 253
Fryer, C. E., 1602
Fuller, William C., 588
Funk, Nanette, 1266
Fürst, Andreas, 597
Fusso, Susanne, 681

Gabric, Mijo, 1674
Gacs, Janos, 13
Gaiduk, Ilya V., 446
Galeotti, Mark, 591
Galina Clothier, 290
Gall, Charlotta, 1081
Gallagher, Tom, 1576
Gallus, Jacqueline, 194
Galushko, R. I., 1031
Garden, Edward, 162
Gardiner, Michael, 682
Gardner, Hall, 46
Gargett, Robert H., 1327
Garlicki, Leszek, 1498
Garnett, Constance Black, 833
Garros, Veronique, 377
Gasparov, Boris, 482, 627, 683
Gatrell, Peter, 500
Gay, William, 334
Geifman, Anna, 537
Gelb, Alan, 19
Georg, Willy, 1126
George, Alexandra, 931
Georgieva, Valentina, 1603
Gerdes, Dick, 1250
Gerhard, Gehrig, 1197
Gero, András, 1403
Gessen, Masha, 653
Gianaris, Nicholas V., 1280
Giges, Nancy, 234

Gilbert, Martin, 1936–, 459
Gill, Graeme, 335, 360, 361
Gillan, Garth J., 1243
Gillespie, David C., 684, 730
Gilman, Richard, 755
Gilmour, Liudmila, 282
Ginat, Rami, 427
Ginzburg, Lidia, 563
Gitelman, Zvi, 354, 582
Giurescu, Dinu, 1560
Givens, John, 835
Glad, John, 843
Gladsky, Thomas S., 1516
Glants, Musya, 479
Gleason, Abbott, 47
Gleeson, Kathleen, 376
Glenny, Misha, 1675
Glowacki, John, 1549
Gluckstein, Donny, 362
Goban-Klas, Tomasz, 275
Goedde, H. W., 1439
Gold, Ruth G., 1244
Goldberg, David Howard, 430
Goldberg, Sylvie Anne, 1388
Goldenberg, Suzanne, 942, 1082
Golder, Frank Alfred, 538
Goldfrank, David M., 539
Goldman, Marshall I., 242
Goldman, Minton F., 1169, 1354
Goldman, Philip, 340
Goldstein, Darra, 838, 1095
Goldstein, Vladimir, 786
Goldsworthy, Vesna, 1638
Golitzin, Alexander, 66
Goltz, Thomas, 1092
Golub, Spencer, 478
Gombrowicz, Witold, 1526
Gomori, Gerorge, 1430
Goncharov, S. N., 447
Goodby, James E., 394, 412
Gooding, John, 297
Goodman, Melvin A., 95
Gordeeva, Ekaterina, 166
Goscilo, Helena, 824, 920, 921, 922
Gotteri, Nigel, 162
Goulding, Daniel J., 1272
Gounaris, Basil C., 1604, 1605
Gow, James, 1676
Goy, E. D., 1631

Gozdecka-Sanford, Adriana, 1456, 1464
Grabher, Gernot, 21
Grachev, A. S., 307
Graham, Loren R., 873, 874
Grant, Bruce, 905
Grare, Frédéric, 1058
Greenbaum, Avraham, 1107
Greenleaf, Monika, 685, 806
Greenshields, Rod, 877
Gregory, Paul R., 202
Greimas, Algirdas J., 966
Grierson, Roderick, 127
Griffith-Jones, Stephany, 1198
Gross, Peter, 1587
Grossman, Joan Delaney, 708
Grubisic, Ljiljana, 91
Grunbaum, Irene, 1245
Grynberg, Henryk, 1246, 1522
Gudziak, Borys Andrij, 982
Gurock, Jeffrey S., 564
Gustafson, Richard F., 858
Gutma, Yisrael, 1247
Györffy, György, 1404
Györgyey, Clara, 1431

Haber, Edythe C., 748
Haberer, Erich E., 1117
Hachey, George A., 957
Haghayeghi, Mehrdad, 1063
Haglund, David G., 1568
Hahn, Jeffrey W., 292, 336
Hailes, Theodore C., 320
Hall, Derek R., 1165, 1292
Hall, Richard C., 1307
Halle, Morris, 712
Hamburg, Gary M., 96
Hames, Peter, 1390
Hamm, Michael F., 983
Hammerová, Louise B., 1365
Hanak, Peter, 1273
Handelman, Stephen, 932
Handler, Andrew, 1248, 1442
Hannan, Kevin, 1220
Hannigan, John, 1279
Hansen, Birthe, 949
Hanson, Stephen E., 1963–, 203
Hardeman, Hilde, 565
Harding, Neil, 848

Hardt, John P., 1199
Hardwick, Susan Wiley, 906
Hardy, Jane, 1482
Harri, Melin, 84
Harrison, Mark, 199, 200
Harshav, Barbara, 1476
Hartley, Janet M., 43, 501
Harwin, Judith, 907
Haskell, Guy H., 1111
Hasty, Olga Peters, 827
Hativni, David W., 1249
Haun, A.D., 603
Hausner, Jerzy, 22
Havel, Vaclav, 1355
Hay-Holowko, Oleksa, 984
Hazard, Elizabeth W., 1580
Heier, Edmund, 686
Heim, Michael Henry, 1339, 1366, 1637
Heinämaa, Anna, 603
Heise, Volker, 597
Held, Joseph, 1142
Hellberg-Hirn, Elena, 123
Henderson, Karen, 1200
Hendley, Kathryn, 293
Herbert, Ulrich, 23
Herling-Grudzinski, Gustaw, 1523
Herring, Eric, 1176
Herskovits, Pál, 1395
Herspring, Dale R., 592
Hertz, Noreena, 235
Hertzel, Laurie, 380
Herwig, Holger H., 1143
Hesli, Vicki L., 908
Hewett, Edward A., 247
Heywood, Paul, 1175
Hiden, John, 950
Higgit, Caroline, 466
Higley, John, 1184
Hill, Malcolm R., 884
Himka, John-Paul, 996
Hirsal, Josef, 1366
Hirsch, David H., 1257
Hirsch, Roslyn, 1257
Hitchins, Keith, 1561–63, 1623
Hoberman, J., 58
Hochman, Jiri, 1328
Hochschild, Adam, 566
Hoen, Herman Willem, 1201
Hoffmann, David L., 567

Hoffmann, Stanley, 1677
Hogan, Ed, 1034
Hogan, Heather, 502
Hoisington, Sona Stephan, 687
Hoisington, Thomas H., 688
Holbrooke, Richard, 1678
Holden, Gerard, 584
Holden, Nigel, 236
Hollingsworth, Paul, 654
Hollis, Rosemary, 428
Holloway, David, 608
Holmes, Leslie, 59
Holmgren, Beth, 689, 922, 1170
Holquist, Michael, 846
Holton, Milne, 1633
Holtsmark, Sven G., 451
Holubova, Miloslava, 1379
Holy, Ladislav, 1329
Homberger, Eric, 544
Honig, Jan W., 1660
Honko, Lauri, 75
Hooker, Mark, 628
Hopkins, Arthur T., 1004
Horniatkevych, Andrii, 1030
Horowitz, Brian, 777
Horsbrugh Porter, Anna, 540
Horton, Andrew, 177, 178
Horton, John J., 1654
Hosking, Geoffrey A., 60, 467
Hostler, Charles Warren, 1064
Hovannisian, Richard G., 1089
Howard, Edward Lee, 97
Høyer, Svennik, 951
Hryniuk, Stella M., 1048
Huges, Robert P., 627
Hughes, James, 227
Hughes, Lindsey, 503
Hughes, Robert P., 468, 683
Hulsman, John C., 1185
Human Rights Watch, 1293, 1679
Hunter, Holland, 204
Hunter, Richard J., 1483
Hunter, Shireen T., 1083
Hupchick, Dennis P., 1136, 1144, 1281
Huskey, Eugene, 308
Hutchings, Raymond, 1294
Hutchings, Robert L., 413
Hutchings, Stephen C., 690

Iancu, Carol, 1589
Iggers, Wilma, 1330
Iglicka, Krystyna, 1535
Igrunov, Vyacheslav, 353
Ikonomi, Ilir, 1296
Ilnytzkyj, Oleh S. (Oleh Stepan), 1035
Ingrao, Charles W., 1137
International Commission on the Balkans, 1171
Ioffe, G. V., 216
IPHECA, 1005
Isacovici, Salomon, 1250
Isenberg, Charles, 691
Ito, Takayuki, 1282
Ivanov, Vladimir I., 394
Iwaskiw, Walter R., 1302

Jackson, Robert Louis, 762
Jacobs, Michael, 1405
Jacobson, David, 1543
Jacobson, Jon, 395
Jacques, Edwin E., 1295
Jahn, Gary R., 814
Jahn, Hubertus F., 256
Jancar-Webster, Barbara, 1202
Janson, C., 374
Jansson, Maija, 390
Jedruch, Jacek, 1499
Jeffries, Ian, 1203
Jessop, Bob, 22
Joenniemi, Pertti, 469
Johansen, Robert C., 1677
Johnson, Lonnie, 1145
Johnson, Simon, 1484
Johnson, Teresa Pelton, 604
Johnston, Bill, 1528
Jones, Adrian, 504
Jones, Anthony, 264, 337
Jones, W. Gareth, 815
Jonson, Lena, 396
Josephson, Paul R., 875
Jovanovic Gorup, Radmila, 1632
Judge, Edward H., 1118
Judson, Pieter M., 1146
Judson, William V., 541
Juraga, Dubravka, 669
Juviler, Peter H., 943

Kaarsberg, Hans S., 124
Kagal, Ayesha, 655, 656
Kaganov, G. Z., 148
Kaiser, Daniel H., 470
Kaiser, Robert John, 278, 941
Kaldor, Mary, 80
Kamenskii, A., 505
Kaminski, Andrzej Sulima, 985
Kandel, Michael, 1527
Kanet, Roger E., 397–98, 1168
Kantor, Tadeusz, 1524
Kaplan, Herbert H., 205
Kaplan, Jan, 1337
Kaple, Deborah A., 24
Kapuscinski, Ryszard, 117
Karadzic, Vuk, 1633
Karanovich, Milenko, 1648
Karklins, Rasma, 453
Karlinsky, Simon, 76
Karsov, Nina, 1526
Kartsev, Vladimir Petrovich, 283
Kaser, Michael Charles, 109
Katalenac, Dragutin, 1646
Katz, Michael R., 754
Kaufman, Jonathan, 1119
Kaufman, Richard F., 1199
Kavass, Igor I., 93, 284
Kay, Rebecca, 916
Keenan, Karl B., 596
Kelertas, Violeta, 967
Kellogg, Frederick, 1564
Kelly, Aileen, 265
Kelly, Catriona, 134, 257, 657, 692
Kemper, Michael, 1065
Kenney, Padraic, 1465
Kershaw, Ian, 40
Kertesz, Imre, 1435, 1443
Ketchian, Sonia I., 737
Keys, Roger, 742
Khazanov, Anatoly M., 944
Khlevniuk, O. V., 378
Khodarkovsky, Michael, 1084
Kierzkowski, Henryk, 1485
Killen, Linda, 1606
Kimball, Warren F., 435
King, Charles, 384
King, Sharon, 1583
Kiossev, Alexander, 1313
Kipel, Zora, 94
Kiraly, Bela K., 1426

Kirchner, Emil J., 1172
Kirk, Roger E., 1581
Kirkconnell, Watson, 1042
Kirschbaum, Stanislav J., 1323, 1331
Kiš, Danilo, 1636
Kisiel, Chester A., 1506
Kivelson, Valerie A., 506
Klarer, Jurg, 1277
Klassen, John M., 1332
Klassen, Pamela E., 1027
Klaus, Vaclav, 1356
Klein, Patricia, 1283
Klepiková, Elena, 103, 285
Klier, John, 507, 508
Kligman, Gail, 1588
Klíma, Ivan, 1381, 1382
Klugman, Jeni, 229
Klukowski, Andrew, 1466
Klukowski, Zygmunt, 1466
Knab, Sophie Hodorowicz, 1536
Knapp, Liza, 763, 764
Knight, Amy W., 98
Knysh, George D., 1049
Kobialka, Michal, 1524
Koehn, Jodi, 847
Koenker, Diane P., 457, 534
Kofman, Jan, 1204
Kokoshin, Andrei Afanas'evich, 585
Kolar-Panov, Dona, 1649
Kolesnikov, Nina, 693
Kollmann, Nancy Shields, 857
Kolstø, Pål, 279
Komenda-Soentgerath, Olly, 1333
Konechni, Sasha, 1603
Kononenko, Natalie O., 1036
Kontorovich, Vladimir, 201
Kopystens'kyi, Zakhariia, 1009
Kordan, Bohdan S., 1006
Korenevskaya, Natalia, 377
Kornai, Janos, 1205, 1421
Kornblatt, Judith Deutsch, 694, 858
Koropeckyj, Roman Robert, 1009
Kosals, L. IA., 193
Koscharsky, Halyna, 1007
Kostis, Kostas P., 1206
Kostrychenko, Gennadi, 1127
Kosztolnyik, Z. J., 1406
Kotkin, Stephen, 568, 1085, 1104
Kottannerin, Helene, 1147
Koulov, Boian, 1317

Kovtun, George J., 1324
Kozhemiakin, Alexander V., 398
Kraeger, Linda, 629
Kraft, Evan, 1621
Kramer, Mark, 118
Krancberg, Sigmund, 338
Kraszewski, Charles S., 1221
Krause, Arthur, 119
Krause, Aurel, 119
Kravchuk, L. M., 1008
Kreikemeyer, Anna, 330
Krejcí, Jaroslav, 1334
Krejcí, Oskar, 1357
Krementsov, N. L., 876
Kremenyuk, Victor, 309
Kresin, Susan, 1367
Krevza, Lev, 1009
Krivich, Mikhail, 933
Krueger, John Richard, 124
Kruszka, Waclaw, 1467
Kubilius, Vytautas, 947
Kügelgen, Anke von, 1065
Kugelmass, Jack, 1120
Kujundzic, Dragan, 695
Kukral, Michael Andrew, 1392
Kulavig, Erik, 902
Kulczycki, John J., 1486
Kumar, Brij Nino, 15
Kumar, Radha, 1680
Kuperman, Gene, 852
Kurczaba, Alex, 1525
Kurczewski, Jacek, 1500
Kuromiya, Hiroaki, 986
Kurski, Jaroslaw, 1501
Kurspahic, Kemal, 1681
Kürti, László, 1264
Kuzio, Taras, 1010–13
Kuznetsov, Andrei, 248
Kvint, V. L., 194

Lachmann, Renate, 630
Lagerwey, Mary D., 1251
Lahusen, Thomas, 83, 377, 852
Laird, Roy D., 339
Laird, Sally, 696, 795
Lajtman, Ivo, 1682
Lambeth, Benjamin S., 605
Lambroza, Shlomo, 508

Lampe, John R., 1607
Lancelle, George, 333
Lane, Ann, 1629
Lane, David Stuart, 1284
Lange-Akhund, Madine, 1624
Langman, Juliet, 1264
Lani, R., 1296
Lapidus, Gail Warshofsky, 287, 340
Lapidus, Mikhail Khlovenovich, 237
Lappin, Elena, 1368
Laricheva, Inn, 1101
Larmour, David H. J., 621
Larrabee, Stephen F., 1186
Larson, Deborah Welch, 414
Latawski, Paul, 1173
Lauk, E., 951
Laurens, Jeannine, 1615
Lavigne, Marie, 1207
Lawton, Anna, 179, 180
Layard, Richard, 195
Layton, Susan, 697
Lazar, Istvan, 1566
Lazear, Edward P., 25
Lazzarini, Robert, 167
Lazzerini, Edward J., 939
Leatherbarrow, William J., 765, 766
Lebed, Aleksandr, 99
Lebow, Richard N., 50
Ledeneva, Alena V., 934
Lederhendler, Eli, 1128
Ledkovskaia-Astman, Marina, 617
LeDonne, John P., 391
Lees, Lorraine M., 1630
Leff, Carol Skalnik, 1335
Leffler, Melvyn P., 48
Leibovich, Anna Feldman, 509
Leighton, Lauren G., 698
Lem, Stanislaw, 1527
Lendvai, Paul, 1285
Lenin, Vladimir Il'ich, 100
Leonard, Carol S., 510
Lerski, George J., 1454
Leshko, Jaroslaw, 1029
Levai, Imre, 1423
Lévesque, Jacques, 1187
Levin, Aryeh, 101
Levin, IU. D., 699
Levine, Michael, 897

Lewin, Moshe, 40
Lewis, John W., 447
Lewis, Paul G., 1174
Liapunov, Vadim, 846
Libal, Michael, 1683
Liber, George, 945
Libert, Bo, 217
Lieber, Joesph S., 1394
Lieberman, Sanford Raymond, 369
Liebich, André, 363
Lieven, Anatol, 952, 1086
Lieven, D. C. B., 511
Lincoln, W. Bruce, 135, 1105
Linden, Carl, 61
Lindenmeyr, Adele, 512
Lindheim, Ralph, 987
Lipinski, Miroslaw, 1517
Litai, Xue, 447
Little, Allan, 1699
Livezeanu, Irina, 1567
Livingstone, Angela, 830
Lobodzinska, Barbara, 87
Lockwood, Jonathan Samuel, 606
Logue, John, 214
Long, Kristi S., 1487
Longinovic, Toma, 1222
Longworth, Philip, 1148
Loone, Ëero Nikolaevich, 850
Lord, Albert Bates, 77
Lord, Mary Louise, 77
Loth, Wilfried, 429
Lotocki, Borys, 976
Lourie, Richard, 935, 1522
Love, Joseph L., 1572
Löwenhardt, John, 310, 341
Lubensky, Sophia, 611
Luciuk, Lubomyr Y., 1048
Luckyj, George Stephen Nestor, 987, 1037–38
Luelsdorff, Philip, 1369, 1370
Lukes, Igor, 1336
Lukic, Reneo, 41
Lukowski, Jerzy, 1510
Lund, Helen S., 1608
Lunt, Susie, 1322
Luther, Sara F., 62
Luxardo, Franco, 1613
Lynch, Allen C., 41, 415

Maag, Karin, 1265
MacDonald, C. A., 1337
MacFarlane, S. Neil, 1568
Machonin, Pavel, 1334
MacKenzie, David, 4
Maczak, Antoni, 43
Magocsi, Paul Robert, 988, 1138, 1223
Maguire, Robert A., 778
Makin, Michael, 828
Malcharek, Krystyna, 1552
Malcolm, Neil, 385, 399
Malcolm, Noel, 1609, 1610
Malevich, Kazimir, 149
Maley, William, 349
Malik, Hafeez, 1066
Malmstad, John E., 700
Maltiel-Gerstenfeld, Jacob, 1129
Mamonova, Tatyana, 923
Mandelbaum, Michael, 1067
Mandelker, Amy, 816
Manea, Norman, 1586
Manolescu, Florin, 1583
Manovich, Lev, 133
Maracz, Laszlo K., 1444
Marai, Sandor, 1436
Marantz, Paul, 430
Marazov, Ivan, 1308
Margolin, Victor, 136
Marianna Birnbaum, 1141
Marker, Gary, 470
Marko, Augustín, 1188
Markov, Sergei, 355
Markov, Vladimir, 700
Markovic, Mira, 1684
Markowitz, Fran, 1112
Marples, David R., 1097
Marples, David Roger, 989
Marsh, Cynthia, 782
Marsh, Rosalind J., 631, 701
Marshall, Richard H., Jr., 1028
Martel, William C., 320
Martin, Alexander M., 513
Martin, Kate, 288, 342
Martinický, Pavol, 1188
Martinsen, Deborah A., 632
Martyn, Barrie, 157
Marullo, Thomas Gaiton, 750, 751, 752
Masing-Delic, I., 702
Mastiugina, T. M., 125
Mastny, Vojtech, 311

Mathiassen, Terje, 968
Matich, Olga, 137
Matthews, Mervyn, 471
Matthiessen, Peter, 280
Matulic, Rusko, 1593
May, Helen, 1466
May, Rachel, 703
Mayhew, Alan, 49
Mazor, Michel, 1543
McAuley, Mary, 343
McCannon, John, 312
McCarthy, Justin, 1230
McCauley, Martin, 102, 344
McCollum, James K., 1577
McDaniel, Tim, 345
McDermott, Kevin, 364
McFadden, David W., 400
McFaul, Michael, 254, 346, 355
McInerny, Peggy, 523
McMillin, Arnold B., 844
McReynolds, Louise, 141
Medish, Vadim, 107
Medvedev, Grigorii, 1014
Meerson, Ol'ga, 767
Mejstrik, Michal, 1190
Melone, Albert P., 1316
Melvin, Neil J., 384, 890
Melzer, Emanuel, 1121
Mendelson, Sarah Elizabeth, 386
Menning, Bruce, 589
Mercier, Michele, 1685
Mesbahi, Mohiaddin, 1068
Meschel, Susan, 1442
Messas, Kostas, G., 1664
Mestrovic, Stjepan Gabriel, 1686, 1687
Meurs, Wim P. van, 1149
Meyer, Ronald, 732
Michael, Laura, 835
Michelson, Paul E., 1578
Michnik, Adam, 1502, 1540
Mihailovic, Alexandar, 741
Mihailovich, Vasa D., 1224, 1633
Mikheev, Dmitrii, 347, 365
Mikos, Michael J., 1518, 1519, 1520
Miles, Patrick, 1631
Milivojevic, Marko, 1654
Millar, James R., 252, 313, 1189
Millard, F., 1503
Miller, Arthur H., 908
Miller, Dana Roby, 1009

Miller, John, 370
Miller, Martin A., 855
Miller, Nicholas J., 1611
Miller, Paul Allen, 621
Miller-Pogacar, Anesa, 258
Miller, Robin Feuer, 768
Miller, Scott, 1237
Miller, Steven E., 597, 604
Miller, William Lockley, 1175
Millinship, William, 924
Milner-Gulland, Robin, 111
Milner, John, 138, 150
Milojevic Sheppard, Milena, 1634
Milojkovic-Djuric, Jelena, 63
Minakir, Pavel A., 196
Miner, Deborah Nutter, 397
Mitrokhin, Sergei, 353
Mizsei, Kalman, 1195
Mocha, Frank, 1468
Moeller-Sally, Stephen, 685
Mojzes, Paul, 1688
Moldan, Bedrich, 1277
Molnár, Éva, 1395
Moore, John H., 64
Moravánszky, Ákos, 1274
Morel, Benoit, 412
Morgan, Eileen, 250
Morgenstern, W., 885
Moroson, Gary Saul, 664
Morris, M. Wayne, 569
Morris, Marcia A., 704
Morson, Gary Saul, 633
Moser, Charles A., 634
Moskoff, William, 371
Motyl, Alexander J., 1015
Mouritzen, Hans, 953
Mouseio Makedonikou Agona, 1604
Moys, Elizabeth, 296
Mozur, Joseph P., 731
Mueller, Magda, 1266
Müller, Rolf-Dieter, 81
Mullerson, Rein, 45
Mullineux, A., 1208
Murav, Harriet, 705
Murphy, Daniel, 1338
Murray, John, 276
Muthesius, Stefan, 1551
Myant, Martin R., 26, 1209

Nadas, Peter, 1437
Nagataki, S. Nihon, 886
Nahaylo, Bohdan, 990
Naiman, Eric, 570
Naimark, Norman M., 448
Nakhimovsky, Alice S., 706
Nation, R. Craig, 401
Naughton, James, 1225
Naumkin, Vitalii Viacheslavovich, 125
Nay, Marshall A., 1050
Nefedov, Tatyana, 216
Neilson, Keith, 431
Nekrasov, George, 514
Nekrich, A. M., 432
Nelson, Joan M., 27
Nelson, Keith L., 416
Nelson, Lynn D., 215, 243
Nemets, Alexander, 449
Nepomnyashchy, Catharine Theimer, 812
Neumaier, John J., 62
Neumann, Iver B., 417, 451
Newbery, David M. G., 1424
Newman, Milda, 966
Nichols, Thomas, 593
Nielsen, Klaus, 22
Nielsen, Niels Christian, 856
Nikula, Jouko, 84
Nimmo, William F., 433
Noggle, Anne, 594
Norman, John O., 142
Norman, Peter, 830
Norris, H. T., 1290
Norton, Boyd, 280
Novak, Jan, 894
Nove, Alec, 571
Nowicki, Maciej, 1488
Nyiri, Janos, 1438

O'Ballance, Edgar, 454
O'Brien, John, 1383
O'Brien Lockwood, Kathleen, 606
O'Kane, John, 1052
O'Neil, Patrick H., 1407
Obradovic, Nadezda, 1632
Odoevskii, V. F. Kniaz', 792
Odom, William E., 1087
Ofer, Dalia, 1234, 1252
Offord, Derek, 612–13

Okenfuss, Max J., 259
Okólski, Marek, 1485
Ol'gin, Ol'gert, 933
Olere, David, 1253
Oleynik, Igor, 298
Opalski, Magdalena, 1544
Open Mdedia Research Institute, 1
Ordan, Dena, 1387
Orel, Vladimir, 1297
Organisation for Economic Co-operation and Development, 10, 1348
Orttung, Robert W., 372
Orwin, Donna Tussing, 817
Ostrowski, Donald G., 483
Ostrowski, Jan K., 1552
Ott, Notburga, 1210
Ovalioglu, Gulhan, 1288
Owen, David, 1689
Owen, Thomas C., 515
Ozinga, James R., 310

Paasi, Anssi, 434
Pachmuss, Temira, 707
Pahor, Boris, 1612
Paine, S. C. M., 450
Painter, David S., 48
Paksaleva, Krassimira, 1317
Pakulski, Jan, 1184
Palairet, Michael, 1211
Palij, Michael, 991
Palkó, Zsuzanna, 1451
Palmieri, Deborah Anne, 1212
Panagiotopoulou, A., 1604
Panevová, Jarmila, 1370
Panków, Wlodzimierz, 1489
Pankowsky, Hanna D., 1254
Paperno, Irina, 468, 627, 683, 708, 769
Parker, John, 195
Parrish, Michael, 379
Parrott, Bruce, 39, 326, 1057
Parsons, Howard L., 62
Parthé, Kathleen, 709
Patai, Raphael, 1445
Patenaude, Bertrand M., 538
Patterson, David, 822, 845
Paul, Barbara Dotts, 1455
Paulston, Christina B., 1226
Pavkovic, Aleksandar, 1690

Pavlinek, Petr, 1349
Pavlowitch, Stevan K., 1150
Pavlychko, S. D., 1016
Pawliczko, Ann Lencyk, 977
Paxton, John, 460
Pearce, Brian, 485, 850
Peck, Jean M., 1255
Peckham, Donald, 1226
Pei, Minxin, 65
Peimani, Hooman, 1069
Pelinka, Anton, 1504
Peppard, Victor, 402
Perdue, William Dan, 1490
Pereira, N. G. O., 542
Perepelkin, L. S., 125
Perlmutter, Tova, 254
Pernal, Andrew B., 974
Perova, Natasha, 655–56, 658
Perrie, Maureen, 484
Peskov, Vasily, 126
Peszke, Michael A., 1469
Peterson, Michael D., 66
Peterson, Nadezhda L., 710
Peterson, Ronald E., 635
Petro, Nicolai N., 348
Petrov, Iurii A., 207
Petrushevskaia, Liudmila, 795
Pettifer, James, 1301, 1641
Philbin, Tobias R., 595
Phillips, Catherine, 699
Phillips, Edward J., 598
Picarda, Guy, 1098
Pickles, John, 1317
Piesse, J., 1422
Piirainen, Timo, 909
Pilkington, Hilary, 281, 895
Pinnick, Kathryn, 916
Pinson, Mark, 1642
Pipes, Richard, 100
Pitty, Roderic, 361
Plakans, Andrejs, 963
Platt, Kevin M. F., 636
Plekhanov, Sergey, 214
Plut-Pregelj, Leopoldina, 1594
Podraza, Eugene, 1477
Poe, Marshall, 461
Poe, Richard, 238
Pogonowski, Iwo, 1545
Pokhlebkin, Vil'iam Vasilevich, 472
Poldauf, Ivan, 1371

Name Index • 497

Poliakov, Sergei Petrovich, 1070
Polinsky, Maria, 610
Polivanov, Konstatin, 736
Polonsky, Rachel, 711
Pomorska, Krystyna, 712
Ponomarev, Valerii Nikolaevich, 392
Poom, Ritva, 959
Poór, János, 1403
Popa, Marcel, 1555
Popkin, Cathy, 659
Popov, Evgenii, 660, 797
Porket, J. L., 28
Porshnev, Boris F., 485
Porter, Robert, 637, 660, 797
Post, Susan E., 1298
Poster, Winifred, 1441
Postma, Koos, 1446
Potts, George A., 1625
Poulton, Hugh, 1643
Pouncy, Carolyn, 486
Powers, W. Roger, 1101
Pozdeeva, I. V., 94
Poznanski, Kazimierz Z., 29–30, 1491
Praga, Giuseppe, 1613
Pravda, Alex, 354
Prawitz, Jan, 469
Prazmowska, Anita, 1511
Press, J. Ian, 1039
Pribichevich-Zoric, Christine, 1671
Prica, Ines, 1652
Prica, Renée, 1652
Price, Morgan Philips, 462
Pridham, Geoffrey, 1176
Pritsak, Omeljan, 487
Procyk, Anna, 403
Prokofiev, Sergei, 158
Prokurat, Michael, 66
Prousis, Theophilus Christopher, 516
Prus, Boleslaw, 1528
Pruul, Kajar, 959
Prybyla, Jan S., 61
Pryde, Philip R., 887
Pugh, Stefan, 1039
Pula, James S., 1467, 1477, 1537, 1553
Pundeff, Marin V., 1309
Pynsent, Robert B., 1227, 1372

Quinn, Frederick, 1286

Ra'anan, Uri, 288, 342
Raack, R. C., 572
Racioppi, Linda, 913
Raeff, Marc, 517
Raevsky-Hughes, Olga, 482, 627
Ragsdale, Hugh, 392
Raina, Peter, 1177
Rainnie, Al, 1482
Ramet, Sabrina Petra, 865, 910, 1267, 1287, 1639, 1691
Rampton, David, 789
Rancour-Laferriere, Daniel, 638, 818
Randolph, Eleanor, 896
Ransel, David L., 518, 897
Rapaczynski, Andrzej, 253
Rawson, Don C., 519
Ray, Larry J., 88
Rayfield, Donald, 1096
Razlogov, Kirill E., 888
Razumovsky, Maria, 829
Read, Christopher, 543
Read, Piers Paul, 992
Reddaway, Darlene, 959
Redecker, Niels von, 954
Redlich, Shimon, 1130
Reed, Fred A., 1692
Reed, John, 544
Rees, E. A., 213, 573
Reese, Roger R., 586
Rein, Martin, 31
Reinhardt, Klaus, 596
Reisinger, William M., 908
Renne, Tanya, 1268
Resler, Tamara J., 397
Reynolds, Andrew, 652, 775
Reynolds, David, 435
Rezun, Miron, 314
Rice, James L., 76
Rice, Timothy, 1321
Ridgeway, James, 1704
Ries, Nancy, 266
Rifkin, Benjamin, 151
Rimer, J. Thomas, 267
Rimmington, Anthony, 877
Riordan, James, 901
Ripellino, Angelo Maria, 1339
Ripka, Ivor, 1365
Risse-Kappen, Thomas, 50
Ro'i, Yaacov, 1071, 1122
Roberts, Graham, 713

Name Index

Roberts, Peter Deane, 139, 159
Robin, Régine, 714
Robinson, Harlow, 158
Robinson, Neil, 366
Robson, Roy R., 866
Rodriguez, Juan M., 1250
Roeder, Phillip G., 329
Rogel, Carole, 1594, 1693
Rogers, Thomas F., 715
Rogozhin, Nikolai, 390
Rohde, David, 1694
Rollberg, Peter, 2
Roman, Eric, 1408
Romsics, Ignac, 1410
Ronen, Omry, 716
Roosevelt, P. R., 520
Rosenberg, William G., 219
Rosenthal, Bernice Glatzer, 717, 871
Rosenthal, Charlotte, 617
Rot, Sandor, 1433
Rouard-Snowman, Margo, 1554
Rowell, S. C., 969
Rowen, Henry S., 244
Ruane, Christine, 521
Rubenstein, Joshua, 774
Rubin, Barnett R., 1162
Rubinstein, Alvin Z., 436, 494
Ruble, Blair A., 143, 188
Ruder, Cynthia Ann, 574
Rumer, Boris, 1072
Russell, Elena, 936
Ruthchild, Rochelle Goldberg, 925
Rutland, Peter, 206
Ryan-Hayes, Karen L., 718, 776
Ryan, Leo V., 1483
Ryan, Michael, 893
Ryan, Tracy A., 298
Rybakov, Anatolii, 809
Ryvkina, Rozalina, 1125
Rywkin, Michael, 937
Rzhevsky, Nicholas, 661

Sachs, Jeffrey D., 1194, 1492
Sadkovich, James J., 1695
Sagdeev, R. Z., 878
Saikal, Amin, 349
Saivetz, Carol R., 337
Sakwa, Richard, 315
Salitan, Laurie P., 1113
Samilenko, Olga, 1030
Sandler, Stephanie, 889
Sanford, George, 1176, 1456, 1470
Sankovitch, Natasha, 819
Sano, Iwao Peter, 463
Santich, Jan Joseph, 488
Saprykin, S. IU., 993
Sarkozi, Matyas, 1396
Saul, Norman E., 418
Sayer, Derek, 1340
Scanlan, James P., 853
Scatton, Linda H., 841
Schaarschmidt, Gunter, 1228
Schaefer, Gert, 357
Schaffer, Mark E., 211
Scharf, Michael P., 1696
Scharf, Rafael F., 1126, 1541
Schenker, Alexander M., 78
Scherr, Barry P., 76
Schierup, Carol-Ulrik, 1697
Schild, Georg, 404
Schlegelmilch, Kai, 1213
Schmeder, Genevieve, 80
Schmemann, Serge, 891
Schoeberlein-Engel, John S., 1073
Schofield, Richard N., 1082
Scholl, Tim, 168
Schonberg, Harold C., 160
Schouvaloff, Alexander, 169
Schuler, Catherine, 185
Schweitzer, Viktoria, 830
Scott-Stokes, Natascha, 1269
Sedlar, Jean W., 1151
See, Katherine O'Sullivan, 913
Segel, Harold B., 662, 1521
Seifrid, Thomas, 796
Sekinin, Peter, 770
Selden, Mark, 357
Selivachov, Mykhailo, 1040
Sellars, Roy, 630
Sells, Michael A., 1640
Semeka-Pankratov, Elena, 712
Semenov-Tian'-Shanskii, Petr Petrovich, 282
Semyonova Tian-Shanskaia, Olga, 897
Sendich, Munir, 794
Senelick, Laurence, 186, 756
Senjkovic, Reana, 1652
Senn, Alfred Erich, 970

Separovic, Zvonimir, 1698
Serafin, Joan, 1178
Seraphinoff, Michael, 1614
Sergeyev, Victor, 350
Serio, Joseph, 198
Service, Robert, 60, 575
Sestanovich, Stephen, 387
Sevander, Mayme, 380
Sgall, Petr, 1370
Shachan, Avigdor, 1256
Shahnuratian, Samvel, 1090
Shalin, Dmitri N., 351
Shandor, Vikentii, 994
Shapira, Philip, 1317
Shapiro, Gavriel, 779, 790
Sharma, R. R., 1423
Shaughenessy, Haydn, 32
Shavit, David, 89, 419
Shaw, J. Thomas, 807, 808
Shearer, David R., 220
Shelley, Louise I., 381
Shen, Raphael, 955, 1022, 1214, 1573
Shentalinskii, Vitalii, 719
Shepherd, David, 134, 257, 720
Sherer, Stan, 1299
Shimkin, Demitri, 1101
Shimotomai, Nobuo, 394
Shirer, William L., 820
Shkandrij, Myroslav, 1041
Shkliarevsky, Gennady, 545
Shlapentokh, Dmitry, 181
Shlapentokh, Vladimir, 181
Shneidman, N. N., 639
Shoumatoff, Nicholas and Nina, 1074
Shukshin, Vasily, 835
Shumaker, David H., 437
Shvidkovskii, D. O., 144
Sicher, Efraim, 721
Siebel-Achenbach, Sebastian, 1152
Siegel, Katherine A. S., 405
Siegelbaum, Lewis H. M., 219, 578, 979
Silbajoris, Rimvydas, 821
Silber, Laura, 1699
Silverman, Bertram, 230
Simatupang, Batara, 1493
Simmons, Cynthia, 722
Simons, John, 214
Singleton, Amy C., 723
Singh, Inderjit, 19
Siwicki, Grzegorz, 1489

Skak, Mette, 406
Skilling, H. Gordon, 1341
Skultans, Vieda, 964
Škvorecký, Josef, 1384, 1385
Slavutych, Yar, 1042
Slay, Ben, 1494
Slezkine, Yuri, 1103, 1106
Sloan, Elinor C., 1700
Smart, Christopher, 388
Smele, Jon, 546
Smeliansky, Anatoly, 187, 749
Smith, Alan, 197, 255
Smith, Alexandra, 825
Smith, G. S., 674
Smith, Gerald Stanton, 109, 648
Smith, Graham, 946, 956
Smith, Kathleen E., 382
Smith, Les W., 724
Smith, S. A., 534
Smith, Sebastian, 1075
Smith, Wayne S., 438
Smolansky, Oles M., 436
Smyrniw, Walter, 693
Snow, Elena, 540
Snyder, Timothy, 1512
Soifer, Valerii, 576
Sokolsky, Joel J., 1568
Sol'chanyk, Roman, 1045
Solnick, Steven Lee, 316
Solomon, Peter H., 294
Soloukhin, Vladimir Alekseevich, 811
Solov'ev, Vladimir, 103, 285
Solovei, V. D., 352
Solway, Diane, 170
Sontag, Susan, 1636
Sorkin, Adam J., 1584
Soroker, Yakov, 1030
Soulsby, Anna, 12
Soyer, Daniel, 1114
Spiegel, Isaiah, 1257
Spier, Howard, 1125
Splichal, Slavko, 1270
Staar, Richard Felix, 1505
Stalin, Joseph, 367
Stallaerts, Robert, 1615
Stan, Lavinia, 157
Stark, David, 21
Starr, S. Frederick, 464
Statistical Office of the Republic of
    Macedonia, 1595

Stavrakis, Peter J., 847
Stein, Eric, 1342
Steinberg, Mark D., 522, 547–48
Steinlauf, Michael, 1538
Stent, Angela, 439
Stephan, Johannes, 1215
Stephan, John J., 577
Sterba, James P., 1677
Stern, Brigitte, 1179
Sternthal, Susanne, 317
Stevens, Carol Belkin, 489
Stewart, Michael, 1447
Stites, Richard, 128, 129
Stojanovic, Svetozar, 1701
Stokes, Gale, 1180
Stone, Gerald, 610
Stone, Randall W., 249
Straus, Kenneth M., 228
Straus, Nina Pelikan, 771
Strom, Ronald, 1523
Strong, Ann L., 1216
Struminski, Igor, 1009
Struminsky, Bohdan A., 1009
Stuart, Otis, 171
Subotic, Gojko, 1650
Subtelny, Orest, 995
Sudetic, Chuck, 1702
Sugar, Peter F., 1231, 1411
Sugarman, Jane C., 1300
Suleiman, Susan R., 1440
Suny, Ronald Grigor, 578
Surits, E., 172
Suziedelis, Saulius, 971
Svejnar, Jan, 1350
Swain, Geoff, 1153
Swan, Charles, 232
Swanson, Vern G., 152
Swietochowski, Tadeusz, 1093
Swift, E. M., 166
Sword, Keith, 1471, 1535
Szacki, Jerzy, 1506
Szantai, Lajos, 1412
Szekely, Istvan P., 1195, 1424
Szelenyi, Szonja, 1441
Szewc, Piotr, 1529
Szirtes, Geroge, 1430
Szlajfer, Henryk, 1533
Szyrmer, Janusz, 204

Tabat, Shinichiro, 1282
Tacheva-Khitova, Margarita, 1308
Tait, Arch, 749
Taji-Farouki, Suha, 1232
Taler, Joseph, 1546
Tanner, Marcus, 1616
Taplin, Mark, 120
Taranovski, Theodore, 523
Taras, Ray, 38, 67, 1181, 1233, 1507
Tarkovskii, Andrei Arsen'evich, 182
Tarnavs'ka, Marta, 1043
Tarnawsky, Maxim, 1044
Taruskin, Richard, 161
Tatchyn, Roman Orest, 1042
Tavis, Anna A., 640
Taylor, Brandon, 130
Tchaikovsky, Peter Ilich, 162
Teglas, Csaba, 1413
Teich, Mikul'as, 1343
Teleky, Richard, 1452
Templeton, Stephanie, 1391
Terras, Victor, 772
Terts, Abram, 810
Thakur, Ramesh Chandra, 440
Thayer, Carlyle A., 440
Thielmann, John H., 104
Thokbes, Rudoolf L., 1427
Thomas, Alfred, 1373–74
Thomas, Colin, 282
Thomas, Robert, 1626
Thompson, E. P., 1310
Tiberg, Erik, 490
Ticktin, H., 245
Tilly, Charles, 27
Timberlake, Charles E., 867
Timonen, Senni, 75
Tindemans, Leo, 1171
Tisma, Aleksander, 1637
Tismaneanu, Vladimir, 42
Tittenbrun, Jacek, 1508
Tiusanen, Tauno, 33
Tkrach, Yuri, 1040
Todorov, Tzvetan, 1311
Todorov, Vladislav, 140
Todorova, Maria N., 1154
Tolczyk, Dariusz, 725
Toll, Nelly S., 1131
Tolstoy, Leo, 822
Tolz, Vera, 549
Tong, Yanqi, 1428

Tooley, T. Hunt, 1472
Toomre, Joyce Stetson, 479, 938
Torke, Hans-Joachim, 996
Torrey, Glenn, 1569
Tourevski, Mark, 250
Trapl, Milos, 1344
Treadgold, Donald W., 473
Treadgold, Warren T., 1155
Treece, Patricia, 1473
Treptow, Kurt W., 1555, 1565
Trifunovska, Sneizana, 1617
Triska, Jan F., 1345
Tritle, Lawrence A., 1156
Trollope, Anthony, 1375
Tropp, E. A., 879
Tryzna, Tomek, 1530
Tsivian, Yuri, 173
Tudijman, Franjo, 1703
Turbiville, Graham Hall, 609
Turgenev, Ivan Sergeevich, 833
Turkov, Andrei, 757
Turner, C. J. G., 758
Turnock, David, 34
Turpin, Jennifer, 277
Turton, Glyn, 834
Tuszynska, Agata, 1258
Tütüncü, Mehmet, 1076
Tworzecki, Hubert, 1509

U.S.-Ukraine Committee for the Conversion of the Defense Industry, 1023
Udovicki, Jasminka, 1704
Ueberschär, Gerd R., 81
Ugresić, Dubravka, 1651
Ulrich, Marybeth P., 82
United States Bureau of Export Administration, 1023
Upor, Laszlo, 1434
Urban, Joan Barth, 352
Urban, Michael E., 68, 353
Urbanic, Allan, 618
Uvalić, Milica, 1191

Vachnadze, Georgii Nikolaevich, 274, 1077
Valencia, Mark J., 251
Van Dyke, Carl, 407
Van Ree, Erik, 310

Vardy, Steven B., 1414
Vardys, Vytas Stanley, 972
Vasil'ev, A. M., 441
Vaughan-Whitehead, Daniel, 1191
Vecernik, Jiri, 1351
Veder, William R., 649, 1009
Vego, Milan N., 1157
Vejvoda, I., 1669
Velychenko, Stephen, 997, 998
Venedikov, Ivan, 1308
Venesaar, Urve, 957
Verdery, Katherine, 1582
Veress, Laura-Louise, 1415
Vianu,Vidia, 1570
Vickers, Miranda, 1301, 1644
Viewegh, Michal, 1386
Vihalemm, Peeter, 951
Viola, Lynne, 579, 926
Vishevskii, Anatolii, 641
Vogt-Downey, Marilyn, 373
Volkov, Solomon, 268
Volkova, Bronislava, 1376
Volodarskii, M. I., 442
Von Geldern, James, 129, 141, 550
Von Meck, Galina, 162
Voronskii, Aleksandr Konstantinovich, 726
Vowles, Judith, 889, 917
Vrgoc, Vesna, 1646
Vroon, R., 700
Vucinich, S., 1635
Vucković, Gojko, 1645

Waal, Thomas de, 1081
Wachtel, Andrew, 174, 642, 1627
Wachtel, Andrew Baruch, 163
Wachtel, Michael, 643
Wachtel, Paul, 1195
Waddington, Patrick, 644
Wagenbach, Klaus, 1380
Wagner, Gert, 1210
Wagner, William G., 295
Waldron, Peter, 524
Walicki, Andrzej, 69
Walker, Annabel, 1416
Walker, Lee, 27
Walkowitz, Daniel J., 979
Wall, Anthony, 630
Wallander, Celeste A., 455

Waller, J. Michael, 383
Waller, Michael, 1182
Wanner, Catherine, 1017
Warhola, James W., 299
Watson, Derek, 580
Webber, Max, 525
Weclawowicz, Grzegorz, 1539
Wegren, Stephen K., 218
Wehling, Fred, 443
Weimer, David Leo, 35
Weinbaum, Laurence, 1547
Weinberg, Robert, 526, 1123
Weinberger, Leon J., 1387
Weiner, Adam, 727
Weiner, Hannah, 1252
Weiner, Myron, 1053
Weissbrod, Abraham, 1259
Weitzman, Lenore J., 1234
Weitzner, Jacob, 1132
Welch, Elena, 540
Wellisz, Stanislaw, 1485
Wells, Gordon C., 525
Wes, Marinus Antony, 645
Wesolowski, Wlodzimierz, 1184
West, James L., 207
West, Richard, 1618
Westad, Odd Arne, 420, 451
Wheatcroft, S. G., 200
Wheeler, Marcus, 282
White, John Albert, 527
White, Stephen, 289, 354, 899, 1175
Whiteside, Shaun, 1380
Wigzell, Faith, 728
Wiley, Roland John, 175
Willerton, John P., 318
Willetts, H. T., 738, 830
Williams, Gareth, 823
Williams, Kieran, 1358
Williams, Robert Chadwell, 456
Williamson, Maya Bijvoe, 1147
Wilson, Andrew, 1010, 1018
Wilson, David Gordon, 839
Wilson, Paul, 1382, 1385
Winters, L. Alan, 1217
Winterton, Jules, 296
Wirtschafter, Elise Kimerling, 528, 892
Wisniewski, Tomasz, 1457
Wohlforth, William Curtis, 421, 422
Wolchik, Sharon L., 1189
Wolf, Charles, 244

Wolff, David, 1104
Wolff, Larry, 1158
Wood, Elizabeth A., 551
Wood, Ellen Meiksins, 70
Wood, Michael, 791
Woodruff, David, 91
Woodward, James B., 646
Woodward, Susan L., 1705
Worgotter, Adreas, 31
World Congress for Soviet and East
    European Studies, 142, 269, 613
Worobec, Christine, 898
Wortman, Richard, 529
Wright, John F. R., 1082
Wrobel, Piotr, 1458
Wygoda, Hermann, 1260
Wyman, Matthew, 911
Wynar, Lubomyr R., 112
Wynn, Charters, 999
Wyplosz, Charles, 1425
Wyplosz, Halpern, 1425
Wyszogrod, Morris, 1548

Yakovlev, A. N., 849
Yaroshinska, Alla, 1000
Yeltsin, Boris Nikolayevich, 105
Yermakov, Dmitriy, 1065
Yevtushenko, Yevgeni, 837
Yoder, H. S., 599
Young, Glennys, 581
Young, James, 121
Youngblood, Denise J., 183

Zagorskii, A. V., 330
Zakharova, L. G., 498
Zalygin, Sergei Pavlovich, 839
Zalys, Vytautas, 965
Zamoyski, Adam, 1474
Zaprudnik, Jan, 1099, 1100
Zaretsky, Robert, 1311
Zaslavsky, Victor, 340
Závodszky, Géza, 1417
Zawadzki, W. H., 1475
Zelnik, Reginald E., 960
Zemplinerova, Alena, 1190
Zeromski, Stefan, 1531
Zhang, Yongjin, 1088
Zhirinovskii, Vladimir, 106

Zhluktenko, Iurii Oleksiiovych, 1032
Zholkovskii, A. K., 729
Zickel, Raymond, 1302
Zimmermann, Warren, 1706
Zinoviev, Aleksandr, 374
Ziolkowski, Margaret, 647
Zirin, Mary Fleming, 617
Zisk, Kimberly Marten, 607
Ziuganov, G. A., 107
Zloch-Christy, Iliana, 1218, 1318

Zlotnick, Jeanne, 244
Zornikov, Igor', 232
Zubarev, Vera, 759
Zubok, V. M., 319
Zuckerman, Fredric Scott, 530
Zuckerman, Yitzhak, 1476
Zuzowski, Robert, 1183
Zviagel'skaia, I. D., 125
Zweers, Alexander F., 753
Zychlinski, Ludwik, 1477

Subject Index

Abakan River Valley (Russia)
   description and travel, 126
abandoned children
   Soviet Union, 900
Abramov, Fedor, 1920–, 730
accidents, radiation, 885–86, 1000, 1005
acid rain
   Former Soviet republics, 884
actresses
   Russia, 185
administrative agencies
   Russia (Federation), 298
advertising agencies
   Russia (Federation), 234
advertising executives
   Russia (Federation), 234
Ady, Endré, 1450
Afghanistan
   foreign relations with Soviet Union, 442
   history, 1979–1989, 386, 591, 603
aging
   Russia (Federation), 688
agricultural pollution
   Former Soviet republics, 217
agriculture and state
   Bulgaria, 1319
   Soviet Union, 562
agriculture
   economic aspects
      Russia, Western, 216
      Ukraine, 1020
   environmental aspects
      Former Soviet republics, 217
      Russia (Federation), 118
air pollution
   Former Soviet republics, 884
Aitmatov, Chingiz, 731
Akademiia nauk SSSR, 549
Akchurin, Marat, 113
Akhmadulina, Bella, 737
Akhmatova, Anna Andreevna, 1889–1966, 732–36

Alaska
   biography, 936
   description and travel, 119
   social life and customs, 936
Albania, 1292, 1302
   civilization, 20th century, 1296
   economic conditions, 1288
   history, 1291, 1294–95, 1599
   politics and government, 1289, 1291, 1301
Albanian language
   etymology, 1297
Albanians
   North America, 1300
   Prespa, Lake, Region, 1300
   social life and customs, 1300
   Yugoslavia-Kosovo (Serbia), 1644
Albert II, Holy Roman Emperor, 1397–1439, 1147
alcohol-related disorders
   Hungary, 1439
alcoholism
   Hungary, 1439
   Soviet Union, 899
Alexander I, Emperor of Russia, 1777–1825, 501
Alexandra, Empress, consort of Nicholas II, Emperor of, 548
Alexandrow, Julia, 1925–, 1046
Alexandru Ioan I Cuza, Prince of Romania, 1820–1873, 1578
Alfeyeva, Valeria, 914
alien labor
   Germany, 23
alienation (social psychology) in literature, 845
allegories, 132, 1094
ambassadors
   Israel, 101
   Soviet Union, 101, 410
   United States, 410

American fiction
  20th century, 663
  women authors, 663
American literature
  history and criticism, 619
  Polish American authors, 1516
Americans
  travel in Ukraine, 975
Andrić, Ivo, 1892–1975, 1635
anthropological linguistics
  Czech Republic, 1220
  Poland, 1220
anti-communist movements
  Poland, 1497
  Siberia, 542
antiheroes in literature, 1221
antisemitism
  Europe, Eastern, 1124
  Former Soviet republics, 1125
  Hungary, 1400
  Moldova, 1118
  Romania, 1589
  Soviet Union, 1122, 1127
Antonescu, Ion, 1882–1946, 1236
Appel family, 1235
Apple, Slovie Solomon Family, 1235
archaeologists
  Asia, Central, 1416
archetype (psychology) in literature, 715
architecture and society
  Russia (Federation), 143–44
architecture
  England, 144
  Europe, Central, 1274
  Poland History, 1551
  Russia (Federation), 131
architecture, modern
  Europe, Central, 1274
  Russia (Federation), 144
archival resources
  Europe, Eastern, 1137
archives
  Soviet Union, 457
Arctic peoples, 1106
Arctic regions, 312
Armenia
  history, 1089
  relations with Azerbaijan, 1079
Armenian massacres, 1915–1923, 1229

Armenians
  atrocities committed against, 1090
  history, 1089
art and history
  Georgia (Republic), 1094
art and literature
  Russia, 665
art and state, 135, 142
art, Baroque
  Poland, 1552
art, Bulgarian, 1304
art collectors and collecting
  Russia (Federation), 139
art, Georgian, 1094
art, medieval
  Russia, 127
art, Polish, 1551–52
art, Russian, 130, 138, 140, 665
art, Ukrainian, 1029
artists
  Russia, 138
artists, Ukrainian, 1029
arts and society
  Russia, 132, 135
arts, modern
  communist countries, 83
  Russia, 83, 133
arts, Russian, 132–33, 135
arts, Soviet
  congresses, 142
ascetics in literature, 704
Asia, Central
  description and travel, 113, 1074
  economic conditions, 1051, 1072, 1088
  economic policy, 1072
  ethnic relations, 1052, 1071
  foreign relations, 1052, 1061, 1067, 1088
    China, 1088
    Russia (Federation), 1068, 1088
  history, 1054, 1061, 1068, 1076
  politics and government, 1051, 1066, 1087–88
  relations
    Middle East, 1053
    Russia (Federation), 1069
  strategic aspects, 1088
  study and teaching, 1073
Asia
  foreign economic relations, 494

assassination, 466
astrophysicists, Soviet, 879
Attila, d. 453, 1141
audiobooks, 935
Auschwitz (Concentration camp), 1241, 1251, 1253, 1247
Australia
　ethnic relations, 1628
　relations with Ukraine, 1007
Austria, 1397
Austro-Hungarian Monarchy. Kriegsmarine, 1157
authors, Austrian, 1380
authors, Czech, 1384
authors, German, 640
authors, Hungarian, 1436
authors, Polish, 1453, 1527
authors, Russian
　19th century, 783, 804, 807, 820
　20th century
　bibliography, 914
　biography, 719, 748, 751, 752, 774, 782, 820, 843
　diaries, 738, 750
　interviews, 696, 843
　journeys, 668
　political and social views, 844
authors, Serbian, 1636
authors, Yiddish, 1258
autobiography, 917, 1384
autobiography in literature, 748, 753
avant-garde (aesthetics), 260
Azerbaijan
　history, 1091–93
　politics and government, 1090
　relations with Iran, 1093
　relations with Russia, 1093
　relations with Armenia, 1093

Babel', Isaak, 721, 738
Bagratid dynasty in art, 1094
Baikal, Lake (Russia), 280
Bakhtin, M. M., 669, 670, 682, 739, 740, 741
balagan, 184
Balkan Peninsula
　boundaries, 1290
　economic conditions, 1203, 1211, 1280

　ethnic relations, 1156, 1171, 1280, 1290
　geography, 1165, 1290
　guidebooks, 1225
　historiography, 1154
　history, 1150, 1156
　politics and government, 1171, 1186, 1203, 1280, 1283, 1665, 1673, 1692
　relations with European Union countries, 1280
　social conditions, 1280
ballet
　costume, 169
　history, 168, 172
　pictorial works, 164
　stage-setting and scenery, 169
ballet dancers, 165, 170–72
Ballets russes, 165, 169
Baltic literatures, 2
Baltic states
　constitution, 1177
　economic conditions, 957
　economic policy, 253
　foreign relations, 948, 949, 953
　history, 952, 954, 956
　politics and government, 950
　social conditions, 957
bandits, 1596
banks and banking
　Balkan Peninsula, 1206
　Europe, Central, 239, 1195–96
　Russia (Federation), 237
Bardach, Janusz, 376
Baroque literature, 779
Bartók, Béla, 1881–1945, 1450
Bashkirs Russia (Federation) Volga-Ural Region, 1062
Báthory, Erzsébet, 1585
Bednar, Zdenek F., 1325
Belarus
　history, 1097, 1099, 1100
Belarusian imprints, 94
Bely, Andrey, 742
Benes, Edvard, 1336
Beria, L. P., 98
Berlin, Isaiah, Sir, 735
Bessarabia (Moldova and Ukraine), 1149, 1556
Bethlen, István, gróf, 1410

Bialystok, Poland, 1457
Bible. N.T. Gospels
  paraphrases, English, 822
bibliography
  Ukraine, 973
biographical fiction, 1585
biotechnology, 877
Birobidzhan (Russia), 1123
birth control
  Romania, 1588
bishops
  Ukraine, 1026
Bitov, Andrei, 668, 746
black humor (literature), 1586
black market
  Soviet Union, 934
Black Sea Coast, 465
Blackman, Ellen, 1658
blind musicians, 1036
Bohdan, Vladimir A., 981
Bohemia (Czech Republic)
  history, 1332, 1340, 1343
  social conditions, 1332, 1373
books and reading, 89
  Russia, 259
  Soviet Union, 623
Bosnia and Hercegovina
  bibliography, 1691
  boundaries, 1597
  dictionaries, 1691
  ethnic relations, 1662
  historical geography, 1597
  history, 1609, 1642
  history, 1591
  rebellion of 1875, 63
    1992–, 1674–75, 1688, 1699
  sources, 1597
Bosnians in Australia, 1649
Brazil
  economic policy, 1572
Brezhnev, Leonid Il'ich, 300
Bribery
  Russia (Federation), 934
Britons in Russia, 496
Brodsky, Joseph, 747
Bucharest (Romania) in fiction, 1586
Budapest (Hungary)
  bibliography, 1396
  civilization, 1273
  description and travel, 1405, 1440

guidebooks, 1394
history, 1403, 1405
intellectual life, 1273, 1450
budget
  environmental aspects, 1213
Bukharin, Nikolai Ivanovich, 357, 362
Bukovina (Romania and Ukraine), 1556
Bulgakov, Mikhail Afanas'evich, 748–49
Bulgakov, Sergei Nikolaevich, 864
Bulgaria, 1321
  antiquities, 1308
  chronology, 1306
  economic conditions, 1312, 1317–18
  economic policy, 1312, 1317
  ethnic relations, 1111
  historiography, 1309
  history, 1305–7, 1309–10, 1318
  intellectual life, 1313
  Narodno subranie, 1316
  politics and government, 1314, 1317–18
  relations with United States, 1309
  social life and customs, 1111
  social conditions, 1314
Bunin, Ivan Alekseevich, 750–53
Burandt, Gary, 234
busines enterprises, Foreign
  Former Soviet republics, 32, 238
  Russia (Federation), 193, 211, 214, 232
business ethics
  Russia (Federation), 934
business law
  Russia (Federation), 232, 237
business networks
  Russia (Federation), 934
businesspeople
  Russia (Federation), 207
Byron, George Gordon Byron, Baron, 744
Byzantine Empire, 1155

California
  biography, 104
Cameron, Charles, 144
Canada
  ethnic relations, 1048
Čapek, Karel, 1378
capitalism, 22
  Europe, Eastern, 33

Former Soviet republics, 5, 11, 33
  Poland, 1484, 1492
  Russia, 230, 515
capitalism and literature
  Poland, 1170
  Russia, 1170
Carlisle, Olga Andreyev, 615
carnival in literature, 669
Carol I, King of Romania 1914, 1578
Carpatho-Rusyn language, 1223
Carpatho-Rusyns, 988
cartography
  Hungary, 1412
Catherine II, Empress of Russia, 144
Catholic Church, 1540
  Byzantine rite, Ukrainian, 1009, 1024–26
  Croatia, 1600
  Czechoslovakia, 1344
  Foreign relations with Yugoslavia, 1600
  Metropolitanate of Kiev, 982
  Poland, 1540
Catholics
  Nazi persecution, 1473
Caucasus
  ethnic relations, 1076
  history, 454, 942, 1068, 1076
  relations Russia, 697, 1068
  sovereignty, 1076
Caucasus, Northern (Russia)
  ethnic relations, 1071
  history, 1076
Caucasus in literature, 697
Ceausescu, Nicolae, 1575
censorship
  Soviet Union, 842
Center for Preventive Action, 1162
Center parties, Russian, 334
Central and East European Publishing Project, 1261
Central Asia. *See* Asia, Central
Central Chernozem Region (Russia), 232
Central Europe. *See* Europe, Central
central planning, 16
  Czechoslovakia, 26
  Poland, 26
  Soviet Union, 1192
Ceskoslovenská strana lidová, 1344
Chagall, Marc, 145

characters and characteristics in literature, 686
Charities
  Russia, 512
Chechnia (Russia)—History, 332, 454, 1080–81, 1086
Chekhov, Anton Pavlovich, 659, 754–59
Chenciner, Robert, 1056
Chernihiv, House of, 481
Chernobyl Nuclear Accident, Chernobyl', Ukraine, 1986, 881, 885–86, 978, 992, 1000, 1004–5, 1014, 1097
Chersonese (Extinct city), 993
Chicherin, B. N., 96
Chikatilo, Andrei Romanovich, 928, 933, 935
child welfare
  Russia (Federation), 907
children and war—Sarajevo, 1671
children of divorced parents, 1379
China
  economic conditions, 61, 65, 449
  economic policy, 61, 449, 1428
  foreign economic relations, 449
  foreign relations 1912–1949, 445
  foreign relations
    Asia, Central, 1088
    Russia, 1054
    Soviet Union, 445, 447
  history, 420
  politics and government, 61, 1428
Chisinau (Moldova), 1118
choreographers
  Russia, 175
choreography
  Russia (Federation), 172
Christian art and symbolism, 1650
Christian biography
  Czech Republic, 1325
  United States, 1325
Christian martyrs
  Poland, 1473
Christian pilgrims and pilgrimages
  Georgia (Republic), 914
Christian saints
  Kievan Rus, 654
  Poland, 1473
Christianity
  history, 468, 482, 627

510 ● Subject Index

relations with Judaism, 1375
  Russia (Federation), 856
Christianity and culture, 468, 482
Christianity and politics
  Europe, Eastern, 1287
Christie, Agatha, 1634
Chukchi Peninsula (Russia), 119
Chukovskaia, Lidiia Korneevna, 689
church and state
  Poland, 1540
  Russia (Federation), 581
  Soviet Union, 865, 867
church architecture
  Kosovo (Serbia), 1650
Church Slavic imprints, 94
Church Slavic prose literature, 654
Cieslewicz, Roman, 1554
cities and towns
  Soviet Union, 86
citizenship, moral and ethical aspects, 1355
city and town life
  Poland, 1529
  Soviet Union, 561
city planning
  Russia (Federation), 188
  Soviet Union, 86
civil-military relations
  Former Soviet republics, 82
  Russia (Federation), 82, 592, 601–2
  Soviet Union, 592–93, 602
civil rights
  Albania, 1293
  Former Soviet republics, 288
  Poland, 1542
civil society
  Europe, Eastern, 29
  Former Soviet republics, 42
  Poland, 1495
  Soviet Union, 29
civilization, Baroque, 779
civilization, modern
  moral and ethical aspects, 1355
classical education
  Russia, 259
classicism
  Russia, 645
coins
  Kievan Rus, 487

cold war, 47, 48, 50, 231, 319, 409, 414, 1580, 1630
  Congresses, 421
  Great Britain, 1629
  Yugoslavia, 1629
collectivization of agriculture
  Siberia, 227
  Soviet Union, 562, 569, 579
  Ukraine, 984, 989
comedy films
  Soviet Union, 177
Comenius, Johann Amos, 1338
Commedia dell'arte, 184
commerce
  Russia (Federation), 298
commercial policy, 16
communication
  moral and ethical aspects, 846
communication in politics—Soviet Union, 272
Communism, 59, 848, 1284
  China, 61, 1428
  Czechoslovakia, 1335
  economic aspects, 1491
  Europe, Eastern, 53, 1153, 1166
  history, 57–58, 69
  Hungary, 1164, 1428
  Poland, 1465, 1491, 1497
  political aspects, 9
  Romania, 1577, 1582
  Russia (Federation), 352
  Soviet Union, 228, 338, 356, 373, 561, 849
    case studies, 568
    history, 358, 359, 544
    mass media, 65
  Yugoslavia, 1701
Communism and agriculture
  Yugoslavia, 1619
Communism and Christianity
  Europe, Eastern, 1287
  Poland, 1540
  Russia (Federation), 581
Communism and culture
  Germany (East), 448
  Soviet Union, 774
Communism and international relations, 406
Communism and literature, 726, 842
Communism and mass media, 275

Communism and motion pictures, 181
Communism and religion, 1287
Communism and satire, 177
Communism and sex, 570
Communism and society, 88, 356
Communist aesthetics, 58, 140
Communist countries
  economic conditions, 55
  economic policy, 55
Communist International, 364
Communist state, 356, 1140
Communists
  Russia, 474
  Soviet Union, 357, 362
competition as government policy, 10
composers
  Poland, 1549
  Russia (Federation), 157
  Soviet Union, 158
concentration camp inmates
  Bulgaria, 1311
  Soviet Union, 553, 725
  Yugoslavia, 1666
concentration camps in literature, 725
confession in literature, 724
conflict management
  Caucasus, 1076
Conrad, Joseph, 1525
Conservatism
  Russia, 513
Constantinople (Ecumenical patriarchate), 982
Constitutional history
  Czech Republic, 1342
  Czechoslovakia, 1342
  Poland, 1463, 1499
  Slovakia, 1342
constitutional law
  Poland, 1498
  United States, 1498
constructivism (Philosophy), 874
cookery
  Georgian, 1095
  Medieval, 1534
  Polish, 1534
  Russian, 479, 938
Corgan, Oscar, 380
corporate governance
  Russia (Federation), 211
corporate state, 22

corporations
  Russia, 515
Cossacks in literature, 694
cost and standard of living
  Asia, Central, 1060
  Soviet Union, 371
Costakis, Georgi, 139
countesses
  Hungary, 1585
country life
  Russia, 520
country life in literature, 709, 730
creativity in literature, 801
Cretzianu, Alexandru, 1559
Crimea (Ukraine)
  antiquities, 993
  ethnic relations, 1003
  politics and government, 1003
Crimean Tatars, 974
Crimean War, 1853–1856, 539
criminal statistics
  Soviet Union, 198
crisis management
  Former Soviet republics, 330
  Soviet Union, 443
criticism
  Russia, 728, 740
  Soviet Union, 619, 680, 728, 840
Critics
  Russia, 783
Croatia, 1596
  bibliography, 1590
  boundaries, 1597
  church history, 1600
  dictionaries, 1615
  ethnic relations, 1652
  foreign relations with Catholic Church, 1600
  historical geography, 1597
  history, 1615, 1616, 1698
    1918–1945, 1600
    1990–, 1646, 1651, 1652, 1675
    chronology, 1682
    pictorial works, 1674
    sources, 1597, 1682
  intellectual life, 1651
  politics and government, 1611
Croats
  Australia, 1649

Cuba
  foreign relations, 438
culture, 1372
Czartoryski, Adam Jerzy, 1475
Czech drama, 1359
Czech fiction, 1360, 1362, 1368
Czech language
  dictionaries, 1371
  foreign countries, 1363
  grammars, 1367
  social aspects, 1363
  textbooks for foriegn speakers, 1361
  variation, 1363
Czech literature, 1372–74, 1381
Czech poetry, 1364
Czech Republic
  bibliography, 1324
  economic conditions, 1350–51, 1356
  economic policy, 8, 1190, 1356
  fiction, 1382
  history, 1328, 1340
  politics and government, 1329, 1335, 1356, 1357
Czechoslovakia, 26, 1214, 1372
  description and travel, 1269
  economic conditions 1945–, 1214, 1346
  economic policy, 26, 36, 1214, 1346
  ethnic relations, 1342
  foreign relations with Soviet Union, 1336
  history, 1337, 1358, 1382, 1392
  politics and government
    1918–1938, 1344
    1945–1989, 1335, 1358
    1989–, 1356, 1392
    20th century, 1334

Dagestan (Russia), 1056
Dalmatia (Croatia), 1596, 1613
day (folklore), 1514
death
  religious aspects, 1388
death in literature, 702
Debeljak, Ales, 1647
Decembrists, 698
decision making
  former Soviet republics, 882

decorative arts Ukraine, 1040
defectors
  Russia (Federation), 97
  United States, 97
defense (military strategy), 1013
defense industries
  Europe, Eastern, 80
  Russia, 244, 500, 604
  Ukraine, 244, 1023
democracy, 70, 1504
  Asia, Central, 1057
  Bulgaria, 1315
  Estonia, 958
  Europe, Eastern, 346, 1160, 1167, 1176, 1207, 1278
  Poland, 1495, 1505, 1507, 1542
  Romania, 1574
  Russia (Federation), 292, 320, 329, 331, 346, 372
  Soviet Union, 849
  Ukraine, 320
  Yugoslavia, 1625
democratization
  Europe, Eastern, 44
  Poland, 1495, 1505
demonology in literature, 727
Derzhavin, Gavriil Romanovich, 799
design
  Poland, 1551
detente, 416
deterrence (strategy), 1004
devil in literature, 727
devotional literature, 649
Diaghilev, Serge, 165
diplomatic and consular service, Russian, 390
disarmament, 244
discourse analysis, literary, 659, 712, 741
dissenters
  Hungary, 1427
  Soviet Union, 719
Djordjevic, Dimitrije, 1666
Dobzhansky, Theodosius Grigorievich, 872
Dodwell, Christina, 1102
Donets Basin (Ukraine and Russia)
  ethnic relations, 999
  history, 986

Dostoevskii, F. M. (Fedor Mikhailovich), 760, 764, 766, 768, 770–71
  appreciation, 765
  biography, 761
  characters, 771
  chronology, 770
  criticism and interpretation, 762, 765, 767, 769, 771–72
  influence, 762
  knowledge, 765
  philosophy, 629, 763
  religion, 629, 763
Drix, Samuel, 1240
Dubrovnik (Croatia), 1672
Dull, Christine, 975
Dull, Ralph, 975
Dune, Eduard M., 534
Durden-Smith, Jo, 115

East Slavic literatures, 2
Eastern Europe, 7, 482, 627, 1110, 1269
economic conversion
  Europe, Eastern, 80
  Russia, 240
  Russia (Federation), 244, 254
  Ukraine, 244, 1023
  United States, 240
economic development
  Czech Republic, 1349
economic forecasting, 449
economic history, 9, 212
economic integration. *See* International economic integreation
economic stabilization
  Czech Republic, 1190
  Europe, Eastern, 1194
  Germany (East), 1218
  Poland, 1485
  Russia (Federation), 252
economics
  Soviet Union, 209
economists
  Soviet Union, 209
education
  philosophy, 1338
  Poland, 1490
  Russia (Federation), 263–64
  Serbia, 1648
  Social aspects, 269
  Soviet Union, 262
education and state
  Russia (Federation), 269
  Russia, 521
educational change
  Soviet Union, 261
Educators
  Poland, 1453
effectiveness and validity of law
  Russia (Federation), 293
Egypt
  foreign relations with Soviet Union, 427
Eizenshtein, Sergei, 176
Ekspeditsionnyi korpus vo Frantsii, 587
El'tsin, B. N. (Boris Nikolaevich), 105
election law
  Poland, 1499
elections
  Albania, 1301
  Czech Republic, 1357
  Ukraine, 1012
electric industries
  Soviet Union, 533
electric power production
  Former Soviet republics, 884
electrification
  Soviet Union, 533
Eleniak, Wasyl, 1050
Elias, Ruth, 1241
elite (social sciences)
  Europe, Eastern, 1184
  Former Soviet republics, 1184
  Hungary, 1441
  Russia, 335
  Russia (Federation), 347
employee fringe benefits
  Former Soviet republics, 31
employee ownership
  Europe, Central, 1191
employees
  Soviet Union, 293
English fiction, 1375
English language
  dictionaries, Russian, 290
  dictionaries, Ukrainian, 1031–32
  grammar, comparative Slovenian, 1634
  translating into Slovenian, 1634

English literature, 699
  appreciation in Russia, 699, 711
  history, 1638
  translations from Polish, 1519
  translations into Russian, 699
English poetry, 644
Enns, Katja, 1027
environment conservation
  Poland, 1488
environment
  effects of agriculture, 217
environmental degradation
  Russia (Federation), 883
environmental health
  Russia (Federation), 883
environmental impact charges
  Europe, 1213
  Europe, Eastern, 1275
  Former Soviet republics, 1275
  Slovenia, 1213
environmental law
  Poland, 1480
environmental policy
  Bulgaria, 1317
  Europe, Eastern, 1202, 1277, 1279
  Former Soviet Republics, 887, 1279
  Poland, 1480
environmental protection
  Europe, Eastern, 1277
epic poetry, Serbian, 1633
Erenburg, Il'ia, 721, 774
Erofeev, Venedikt, 776
Estonia
  economic policy, 955
Estonian fiction, 959
ethics, 846
ethnic groups, 905, 1106
  related to Nationalism, 299
ethnic mass media
  Baltic states, 951
ethnicity
  Asia, Central, 1088
  Europe, Central, 1233, 1264
  Former Soviet republics, 946
ethnicity in literature, 1516
ethnological museums and collections, 112
ethnology
  Carpathian Mountains Region, 988
  Former Soviet republics, 384, 944
  Russia, 108, 110, 125, 504, 905

United States, 112
ethnopsychology, 1687
Eurasian literatures, 2
Europe, 22
  foreign relations with Russia (Federation), 385, 424
  income, 1210
  politics and government, 54, 413, 527
Europe, Central
  economic conditions, 13, 1201, 1351
  economic policy, 13, 1195, 1201
  foreign economic relations with European Union countries, 49
  history, 1145
  periodicals, 1134
  politics and government, 1151, 1159
  social conditions, 1351
Europe, Eastern
  church history, 1287
  civilization, 1144, 1158
  commercial policy, 1217
  constitution, 1177
  description and travel, 1158
  economic conditions 1989–, 1, 7, 10, 13, 30, 32–34, 64, 1169, 1178, 1194, 1199, 1205, 1218, 1276
  economic policy—1989–, 13, 15, 19, 20, 30, 33, 1167–68, 1194–95, 1202, 1205, 1207, 1218
  environmental conditions, 1277
  ethnic relations, 85, 1119, 1128, 1231
  feminism, 1376
  foreign economic relations, 1217
    European Union countries, 49
    Soviet Union, 249
  foreign relations, 249, 406, 1176, 1187
  historical geography, 1136
  history, 1136, 1139, 1148, 1151
    1918–1945—Congresses, 1263
    1945—Dictionaries, 1142
    1989–, 1169
    20th century, 53, 1135
  income, 1210
  intellectual life, 1227
  international status, 1179
  literary collections, 1225
  nationalism, 1173
  periodicals, 1134
  politics and government, 1133, 1281
    1945–1989, 451, 1153, 1267

1989–, 1, 41, 44, 59, 64, 68, 1159, 1161, 1163, 1167–69, 1175–76, 1178, 1181, 1183–84, 1233, 1282, 1568
  20th century, 53
  religion—20th century, 1287
  social conditions, 1169, 1178, 1267
  social policy, 1161
  study and teaching, 3
Europe, South-East
  politics and government, 39
European literature, 762
European Union countries
  economic policy, 49
  foreign economic relations, 49, 1193
  relations with Balkan Peninsula, 1280
European Union, 1200, 1683
evil in literature, 629
Evreiskaia avtonomnaia oblast' (Russia), 1123
Evreiskii antifashistskii komitet v SSSR, 1130
excavations (archaeology)
  Siberia, 1101
  Ukraine, 993
exchange
  Russia (Federation), 934
executive departments
  Russia (Federation), 298
Executive power
  Soviet Union, 308
Executives
  Soviet Union, 318
exiles' writings, Russian, 844–45
experimental fiction, Russian, 672, 720
experimental theater, Polish, 1524
export marketing
  Europe, Eastern, 13
exports
  Europe, Eastern, 13
  fables, Polish, 1514
  family
    Europe, Eastern, 87
    Hungary, 1437
    Russia, 486, 909
  famines
    Soviet Union, 569
    Ukraine, 984
  fantastic fiction, 710, 1530
  fear, 1661

Federal government
  Czechoslovakia, 1342
  Russia (Federation), 361, 847
  Soviet Union, 286, 361
female friendship, 1530
femininity, 122
feminism and literature, 663
feminism
  Europe, Eastern, 1268
  Former Soviet republics, 1266
  Former Yugoslav republics, 1639
  Russia (Federation), 913
  Soviet Union, 912
  Yugoslavia, 1639

feminists
  Russia (Federation), 913
festivals
  Soviet Union, 550
fiction
  history and criticism, 374, 724
  technique, 720
Filipovic, Zlata, 1671
film adaptations, 151
finance
  Europe, 1208
  Europe, Central, 1196, 1198
  Europe, Eastern, 1196, 1198
  finance, public
    Hungary, 1419
Finland
  civilization Congresses, 43
  foreign relations with Russia, 43
  history, 43
Finnish American communists, 380
Fischler-Martinho, Janina, 1242
Fisher-Ruge, Lois, 116
folk dancing, Bulgarian, 1321
folk literature, Polish, 1514
folk music, 1321
  Bulgaria, 1321
  Prespa, Lake, Region, 1300
  Ukraine, 1030
folk poetry, Finno-Ugric, 75
  history and criticism, 77
folk songs, Albanian, 1300
folk songs, Bulgarian, 1321
folk songs, Serbo-Croatian, 1633

folklore
  Balkan Peninsula, 1271
  Bulgaria, 1111
  Poland, 1514, 1536
  Soviet Union, 547
food habits
  Poland, 1534
  Russia (Federation), 479
forced migration, 52
foreign investment, 250
foreign relations, 101, 425, 436
formalism (literary analysis), 695
Forman, Miloš, 1272
Former Soviet republics
  boundaries, 393
  civilization, 1144
  commerce, 233, 250, 255
  commercial policy, 247
  economic conditions, 1, 7, 27, 32–33, 64, 238, 250
  economic policy, 27, 33
  encyclopedias, 109
  environmental conditions, 887
  ethnic relations, 108, 279, 281, 330, 384, 396, 941, 1068, 1125
  foreign economic relations, 1212
  foreign relations, 330, 384, 428, 430, 436, 464
  historiography, 476
  history, 473, 1076
  periodicals, 1134
  politics and government, 1, 38, 42, 59, 64, 288–89, 890, 908, 943, 1181, 1184, 1281
  relations with Iran, 436
  relations with Russia (Federation), 396
  relations with Turkey, 436
  social conditions, 27, 1189
Former Yugoslav republics
  history, 1617
  politics and government, 1697
  sources, 1617
  fossil fuel power plants, 884
  frame-stories, 691
Frank, Joseph, 72
free enterprise
  Europe, Eastern, 15
Freedom, 69
freedom of information
  Europe, Central, 1261

freedom of religion
  Poland, 1498
  United States, 1498
freedom of speech
  Poland, 1498
  United States, 1498
French fiction, 676
Freud, Sigmund, 855
Fridman, A. A. (Aleksanr Aleksandrovich), 879
frontier and pioneer life
  Canada, Western, 1050
functionalism (linguistics), 1369, 1370
futurism (literary movement), 1035

gardens, English
  Russia (Federation), 144
generals
  Russia (Federation), 605
  Soviet Union, 99
genetics, 872
genocide
  Bosnia and Hercegovina, 1653
  Croatia, 1703
gentry, Russian, 506
geopolitics
  Asia, Central, 1053, 1066
  Balkan Peninsula, 1165, 1290
  Soviet Union, 391
Georgian literature, 1096
Georgian S. S. R.
  religious life and customs, 868
Gerasimov, Vasilii, 960
Germans
  Czech Republic, 1333
  Poland, 1459
  Soviet Union, 1113
Germany
  boundaries (Poland), 1472
  foreign relations
    Czechoslovakia, 1336
    Poland, 1455
    Russia (Federation), 439
    Soviet Union, 423, 432, 437, 439
    Ukraine, 996
    Yugoslavia, 1683

Subject Index • 517

history 1945–1990, 437, 439, 444
military relations, 595
politics and government—1930–1945, 40
Germany (East)
    economic conditions, 1209
    economic policy, 1209
    foreign relations with Soviet Union, 429
    politics and government, 429, 1140
    social policy, 448
Gershenzon, M. O. (Mikhail Osipovich), 777
Gerstenfeld-Maltiel, Jacob, 1129
Gilyaks, 905
Gissing, George, 834
glasnost, 178, 327, 353, 920, 923, 1004
Glavnoe upravlenie Severnogo morskogo puti, 312
Gogol', Nikolai Vasil'evich, 1809–1852, 659, 681, 778–79
Gold, Ruth Glasberg, 1930–, 1244
Golder, Frank Alfred, 538
Gombrowicz, Witold, 1526
Goncharov, Ivan Aleksandrovich, 780
good and evil, 1243
Gor'kii, Maksim, 782
Gorbachev, Mikhail Sergeevich, 272, 302, 307, 365, 370, 374
Gordeeva, Ekaterina, 166
Gorky, Maksim, 781–82
government and the press
    Soviet Union, 274
government business enterprises, 18
grammar, comparative and general, 71
graphic arts
    Poland, 1554
Great Britain, 17, 425
    civilization, Russian influences on, 425
    commerce with Russia, 205
    foreign relations—1837–1901, 431
        Poland, 1511
        Russia, 389, 425, 431
    intellectual life, 834
Great Britain in literature, 765
Greece
    ethnic relations, 1628
    history, 516, 1608
    relations with Russia, 516
Greeks, 1628
Grigor'ev, Apollon Aleksandrovich, 783

Grinkov, Sergei, 166
Grossman, Vasilii, 784
grotesque in literature, 636
group identity in literature, 685
Grünbaum, Irene, 1245
Gypsies, 1447
    Europe, Eastern, 85

Hungary, 1446
    Russia, 85
    Soviet Union, 85
Habsburg, House of, 1397
Halivni, David, 1249
Hansa towns, 490
Haskalah (Belarus), 1116
heads of state
    Soviet Union, 100
    Ukraine, 1008
Herling-Grudzinski, Gustaw, 1523
hermits
    Russia (Federation), 126
heroes in literature, 694, 704, 786, 1221
Hevra kaddisha
    Czech Republic, 1388
Hirsal, Josef, 1366
historians
    United States, 538
historic preservation
    Russia (Federation), 188
historic sites
    Soviet Union, 811
historical fiction, 1585
historical geography, 1392
historical materialism, 70
historiography, 477
    Poland, 998
    Russia (Federation), 560
    Soviet Union, 998, 1149
history in literature, 636, 642, 805
history
    philosophy, 477, 695, 850
Hlinka, Andrej, 1353
Hlinkova slovenská l'udová strana, 1353
Hnizdovsky, Jacques, 1029
Holocaust, Jewish (1939–1945), 1129, 1453
    fiction, 1435
    historiography, 1124
    Hungary, 1237, 1248, 1255, 1400, 1438

Holocaust, Jewish (1939–1945) (*continued*)
  influence, 1238, 1243
  Latvia, 962
  personal narratives, 1241, 1251, 1260, 1612
  Poland, 1120, 1126, 1247, 1257, 1462, 1476, 1538, 1543, 1548
  psychological aspects, 1238
  Romania, 1236, 1249–50
  Soviet Union, 564, 582
  Ukraine, 1131, 1240, 1256, 1259, 1546
  Yugoslavia, 1252
Holocaust survivors
  Ecuador, 1250
  Europe, Eastern, 1119
  Hungary, 1443
  Israel, 1241
  New York (State), 1249
  Poland, 1522, 1538
Holy Crown of Hungary, 1147
home in literature, 723
Hornstein, Lusia, 1255
Hornstein, Stephen, 1255
Horowitz, Vladimir, 155, 160
household surveys
  Asia, Central, 1060
housing, single family
  Czech Republic, 1391
housing policy
  Russia (Federation), 188
Howard, Edward Lee, 97
human rights
  Former Soviet republics, 943
  Yugoslavia, 1679
humanism, 259
Hungarian Americans, 1452
Hungarian drama, 1434
Hungarian language, 1433
Hungarian poetry, 1430
Hungarians
  Canada, 1421
  ethnic identity, 1444
  Europe, Central, 1444
  foreign countries, 1452
  Slovakia, 1188
Hungary, 1395
  civilization, 1452
  description and travel, 1269
  economic conditions, 1215, 1420, 1422, 1425

  economic policy, 8, 36, 1215, 1424–25, 1427–28
  ethnic relations, 1188, 1237, 1445, 1446
  fiction, 1437
  foreign relations, 1188, 1408, 1417, 1429
  guidebooks, 1394
  history, 1157, 1411, 1414
    896–1301, 1404, 1406
    1302–1917, 1585
    1918–1945, 1401, 1415
    1945–1989, 1166, 1399, 1401, 1408, 1442
  industries, 1420
  kings and rulers, 1404
  maps, 1412
  periodicals, 1393
  politics and government
    1699–1848, 1397
    1918–1945, 1410
    1945–1989, 1164, 1407, 1427, 1428
    1989–, 1418, 1426, 1428, 1429
  relations with Slovakia, 1188
husband and wife, 295
Hussites, 1332

IAroslavl' (IAroslavskaia oblast', Russia), 188
ideology, 68, 366
illegal arms transfers, 609
immigrants
  Australia, 1628
  Canada, 1027, 1047
  Israel, 1241
  Minnesota, 1235
  New York (State), 1112, 1114
  Russia (Federation), 380
imperialism, 60, 342, 476
imperialism in literature, 685
impresarios, 165
impressionism (Art), 152
income distribution, 191
India, 1423
indigenous peoples
  Russia, Northern, 1106
industrial policy
  Russia (Federation), 225

industrial efficiency
  Hungary, 1422
industrial management
  Czech Republic, 1347
  Europe, Eastern, 15
  Russia (Federation), 193
  Soviet Union, 24, 206
industrial organization
  Europe, Eastern, 21
  Former Soviet republics, 21
  Poland, 1489
  Soviet Union, 24
industrial policy
  Poland, 22
  Russia (Federation), 192, 500
  Scandinavia, 22
  Soviet Union, 220
industrial relations
  Russia, 223–25, 502
industries
  Donets Basin, 999
  Europe, Eastern, 19
  Russia (Federation), 193
  social aspects, 1481
  Ukraine, 1023
industry and state, 10
insane, criminal and dangerous, 928, 933, 935
institutional economics, 316
insurgency
  Caucasus, Northern, 1075
intellectuals
  Romania, 1623
  Russia, 265, 504
  Serbia, 1648
  Soviet Union, 265
intelligence officers, 97
intelligence service
  United States, 231
Inter-Republic Memorial Society (Soviet Union), 382
intercultural communication, 663
interfaith marriage, 1375
International Committee of the Red Cross, 1685
International Conference on the Former Yugoslavia, 1665
international cooperation, 1282
international economic integration, 16

international law, 45
international police, 1665
international relations, 50
internet (computer network), 273
intertextuality, 151
intervention (international law), 1677
investments, foreign, 16
  Europe, Eastern, 32, 33
  Former Soviet republics, 6, 32, 33, 238
  government policy, 248
  law and legislation, 1021
  Russia (Federation), 6, 194, 237
iodine isotopes, 886
Iran, 436
  foreign relations, 436, 442, 1093
Irish drama, 832
irony in literature, 641
Isacovici, Salomón, 1250
Islam, 1063, 1070, 1232
Islam and politics, 1059, 1063
Israel, 101, 1111
Ivanov, Lev, 175
Ivanov, V. I., 643, 785

Jakobson, Roman, 1896–, 712
James, Henry, 834
Janowska (Concentration camp), 1240
Janzen, Agatha, 1027
Japan
  foreign relations, 267, 394, 433
Jaruzelski, W., 1504
Jasenovac (Concentration camp), 1600
Jesuits, 488
Jewish children in the Holocaust, 1242, 1246
Jewish entertainers, 1110
Jewish libraries
  Czech Republic, 89
  Lithuania, 89
  Poland, 89
Jewish mourning customs, 1388
Jewish radicals, 1109, 1117
Jewish scholars, 1249
Jewish socialists, 1107
Jewish students, 1442
Jewish women in the Holocaust, 1234

Jews, 1125
  Belarus, 1116, 1125
  Bulgaria, 1111, 1303
  cultural assimilation, 706, 1109
  Czech Republic, 89, 1241, 1387-88
  East European, 1110, 1114
  emigration, 1110
  Europe, Eastern, 1110, 1119, 1128
  Former Soviet republics, 1125
  genocide, 1129, 1240, 1476
  history, 1122
  Hungary, 1255, 1400, 1445-46
  Lithuania, 89
  Minnesota, 1235
  New York (State), 1112
  persecutions, 508, 1118
    Balkan Peninsula, 1245
    Hungary, 1237, 1239, 1248, 1442
    Latvia, 962
    Moldavia, 1118
    Poland, 1126, 1538
    Romania, 1236, 1557
    Russia, 508, 1127
    Ukraine, 526, 1129, 1131, 1240
  Poland, 1121
    Bialystok (Voivodeship), 1457
    biography, 1255, 1546
    books and reading, 89
    history, 1544-45
    Krakow, 1242, 1541
    literary collections, 1521
    Lodz, 1254, 1257
    politics and government, 1462
    public opinion, 1544
    social life and customs, 1120, 1258
    Warsaw, 1543, 1548
  politics, 507
  Romania, 1235, 1244, 1249-50, 1589
  Russia, 507, 1109, 1117, 1122-23, 1125
  Soviet Union, 101, 564, 1108, 1113, 1115, 1122, 1127, 1130
  Ukraine, 1125, 1235, 1256
  United States, 1109, 1128
  Yugoslavia, 1637
Jews in literature, 706, 1544
Jews in the motion picture industry, 1110
joking, 929
journalism, 1587
journalism and literature, 632
journalists, 774, 1658

Joyce, James, 670, 673
Judaism, 1388
justice, Administration of, 294

Kaarsberg, Hans S., 124
Kafka, Franz, 1380
Kaliningradskaia oblast' (Russia), 469
Kalmykiia (Russia), 124
Kalmyks, 124, 1084
Kamchatskaia oblast' (Russia), 1102
Kantor, Tadeusz, 1524
Kapuscinski, Ryszard, 117
Karelia (Russia), 380
Kelles-Krauz, Kazimierz, 1512
Kiev (Ukraine), 983
Kievan Rus
  church history, 867
  encyclopedias, 460
  history, 862-1237, 481
  kings and rulers, 481
Kis, Danilo, 1636
Klaus, Vaclav, 1356
Klima, Ivan, 1381
Kliuchevskii, V. O., 475
Klukowski, Zygmunt, 1466
knowledge, theory of, in literature, 819
Kobzari, 1036
Kol'tsovo (Kaluzhskaia oblast', Russia), 891
Kolbe, Maximilian, 1473
Kolchak, Aleksandr Vasiliyevich, 546
Kolyma (Concentration camp), 376
Komenda-Soentgerath, Olly, 1333
Komensky, Jan Amos, 1338
Komitet gosudarstvenno bezopasnosti, 719
Kommunisticheskaia partiia Rossiiskoi Federatsii, 352
Kommunisticheskaia partiia Sovetskogo Soiuza, 206, 313, 360-61
Kondrat'ev, N. D., 209
Korczak, Janusz, 1453
Korean War, 1950-1953, 447
Kosovo (Serbia), 1610, 1644, 1670
Kottannerin, Helene, 1147
Kraków (Poland), 1242, 1479, 1482
Krause, Arthur, 119
Krause, Aurel, 119

Kravchuk, L. M. I., 1008
Krawchenko, Bohdan, 1016
Kreenholmi Puuvillasaaduste Manufaktuur Strike, 1872, 960
Kuibyshevs'kyi raion (Donets'k, Ukraine), 979
Kundera, Milan, 1383
Kurspahic, Kemal, 1681

labor economics, 223
labor market, 1348
labor movement
   Germany, 1486
   Russia, 545
   Soviet Union, 222
   Ukraine, 526, 999
labor supply
   Europe, Eastern, 11
   Russia (Federation), 189
labor Zionism, 1107
Lagerwey, Mary D., 1251
land reform, 218
language and culture, 266
language and languages, 739
language policy, 1627
László V, King of Hungary and Bohemia, 1147
Latin America, 438
Latvia
   economic conditions, 961
   economic policy, 955
   history, 963–64
   politics and government, 961
Law
   Europe, 296
   Former Soviet Republics, 284
   Soviet Union, 93
law and literature, 705
law and socialism, 293
law enforcement, 381
law reform, 291
leadership, 1504
Lebed, Aleksandr, 99, 605
legal research, 296
legislative bodies
   Bulgaria, 1316
   Russia (Federation), 292
legislators, 344

Lem, Stanislaw, 1527
Lendvai, Paul, 1285
Lenin, Vladimir Il'ich, 100, 848
Lermontov, Mikhail IUr'evich, 786
lesbianism in literature, 793
Levin, Aryeh, 101
Liberal'no-demokraticheskaia partiia Rossii, 283
liberalism, 1506
libraries, 1646
library science, 973
Lifar, Serge, 169
linguistic minorities, 1226
Lissitzky, El, 136
literary landmarks, 811
literature
   aesthetics, 802
   ancient, 680
   comparative, 621, 663, 699, 1170, 1221
   experimental, 713
   history and criticism, 74, 739
   modern, 72, 625
literature and folklore, 680
literature and history, 631
literature and society, 134, 257, 1373, 1570
literature and state, 726, 803
literature publishing, 1170
Lithuania
   economic policy, 955
   history, 965, 969, 971–72
Lithuanian language, 968
Lithuanian literature, 947
liturgical objects, 127
Livonia, 490
Livonian War, 1557–1582, 490
local government
   Europe Eastern, 1172
   Russia (Federation), 298, 336
Lotocki, Borys, 976
love in literature, 676
Lwów (Ukraine), 1240
Lykov family, 126
Lysenko, Trofim Denisovich, 576
Lysimachus, King of Thrace, 1608

Macedonia
   commerce, 1605
   description and travel, 1269

Macedonia (*continued*)
  economic conditions, 1605
  ethnic relations, 1624, 1628, 1641, 1643
  history, 1603–4, 1608, 1614, 1624, 1643, 1675
  name, 1628
  politics and government, 1641
  religion, 1614
  statistics, 1595
Macedonian question, 1624, 1641
Macedonians in Australia, 1628
Magyar Szocialista Munkáspárt, 1407
Maiden Tsar (tale), 122
Makavejev, Dušan, 1272
Makovecz, Imre, 1449
Maksimova, Ekaterina, 167
Malevich, Kazimir, 149
Malevich, Kazimir Severinovich, 150
Maltiel-Gerstenfeld, Jacob, 1129
management, 12, 224, 236
Mandel'shtam, Nadezhda, 689
Mandel'shtam, Osip, 721
manners and customs in literature, 690
manpower policy
  Russia (Federation), 189
  Slovakia, 1348
Mao, Tse-tung, 447
Márai, Sándor, 1436
marital property, 295
Markov, Vladimir, 700
Markovic, Mira, 1684
Marlinskii, A., 744
Marxian historiography, 1149
Mary, Blessed Virgin, Saint, 675
Masaryk, T. G., 1850–1937, 1341
masculinity, 122
masochism in literature, 818
mass media
  Australia, 1649
  policy, 274
  political aspects, 951, 1270, 1587
  Russia (Federation), 270, 273
  social aspects, 275
  Soviet Union, 65, 277
mass media and minorities, 1649
mass media and public opinion, 272
massacres, 1118
Matthiessen, Peter, 280
McLean, Hugh, 76
Medtner, Nikolay Karlovich, 157

memorial books (Holocaust), 1120
Mennonites, 870, 1027
metalworkers, 502
metaphor, 799
Metner, N. K. (Nikola Karlovich), 157
Michnik, Adam, 1502
Middle East
  foreign relations, 426, 428, 441, 443
migration, internal, 471
military art and science in literature, 628
military doctrine, Russian, 606–7
military government
  Germany (East), 429
military meteorology, 599
Millennium of Christianity in Kievan Rus, 988–1988, 482
miners
  Ukraine, 979
minorities
  Balkan Peninsula, 1262
  Caucasus, 1076
  Europe, Eastern, 1233
  Former Soviet republics, 937, 944
  government policy, 301
  Hungary, 1446
  Russia, 108, 299, 939
  Soviet Union, 113, 314, 403, 555
Minsk (Belarus), 1098
minstrels, 1036
misogyny in literature, 818
mixed economy
  Europe, Eastern, 30, 1192, 1205
  Russia (Federation), 334
models, theoretical, 885
modernism (aesthetics), 91, 1450
modernism (art), 700
modernism (literature)
  Russia, 140, 677–78, 679, 690, 700, 708
Moholy-Nagy, László, 136
Molotov, Vyacheslav Mikhaylovich, 304, 367, 580
Molotschna (Ukraine), 870
monetary policy, 239, 1208
Mongolia, 1085
Mongols, 483, 1054
monks, 1614
Montenegro, 1675

Moscow (Russia)
  commerce, 207
  description and travel, 121
  fiction, 836
  social conditions, 121, 207, 904
Moskva-Petushki, 776
motion picture industry
  Hungary, 1448
  Soviet Union, 179, 181
motion picture music, 156
motion picture producers and directors, 182, 1272
motion pictures and literature, 151
motion pictures
  political aspects, 180–81
  Russia (Federation), 173
  social aspects, 181, 183
  Soviet Union, 178–83, 915
mountains, Central Asian, 282
Mousterian culture, 1327
multiculturalism, 1647
Munazzamat al-Tahrir al-Filastiniyah, 426
murders, 935
music and literature, 163, 626
music and society, 154
music history and criticism, 161, 1030
music in literature, 163
Muslims, 1070–71
Muslims
  Asia, Central, 1070, 1071
  Balkan Peninsula, 1230, 1232
  Bosnia and Hercegovina, 1642, 1662
  Bulgaria, 1320
  Caucasus, 1055, 1071, 1230
  crimes against, 1230
  Former Soviet republics, 1068
  relocation, 1230
  Russia, 1062, 1065
  Ukraine, 1230
myth in literature, 715
mythology, Baltic, 966
mythology in literature, 680

Nabokov, Vladimir, 787–91
Nagorno-Karabakh (Azerbaijan), 1078–79
names, personal, 90
narration (rhetoric), 74, 151
narrative poetry, Russian, 667

narrative theology, 1325
Narva (Estonia), 960
national characteristics
  Czech, 1329
  East European, 1263
  in literature, 1372
  Polish, 1516
  Russian, 111, 456, 467, 638, 890
national security
  Asia, Central, 1069
  Balkan Peninsula, 1171, 1186, 1665
  Europe, 46, 424, 439, 1200
  Europe, Eastern, 1163, 1168, 1178
  Russia (Federation), 320, 424, 584, 604
  Soviet Union, 311
  Ukraine, 320, 1012, 1013
national socialism and occultism, 871
nationalism, 283, 333, 434
nationalism and socialism
  Poland, 1512
  Soviet Union, 278
nationalism
  Asia, Central, 1052
  Austria, 1146
  Azerbaijan, 1091, 1093
  Balkan Peninsula, 1156, 1664
  Baltic states, 956
  Bulgaria, 1309
  Czech Republic, 1372
  Czechoslovakia, 1342
  Europe, 54
  Europe, Eastern, 54, 64, 1227, 1231, 1233, 1263
  Former Soviet republics, 38, 54, 64, 464, 903, 941, 944, 946
  Greece, 1628
  Iran, 1093
  Macedonia, 1628
  Romania, 1557, 1561, 1564, 1567, 1576, 1623
  Russia, 60, 63, 123, 299, 387, 455, 584
  Slovakia, 1372
  Soviet Union, 67, 340, 403, 555
  Ukraine, 945, 987, 1010, 1011, 1017, 1018
  Yugoslavia, 1598, 1627, 1656, 1690, 1705, 1706
nationalism in literature, 685, 1372
Neanderthals, 1327
neoclassicism (architecture), 144

New Zionist Organization, 1547
Nicholas II, Emperor of Russia, 511, 548
Nietzsche, Friedrich Wilhelm, 695, 717
night (folklore), 1514
nobility in Poland, 974
nomads, 1084
North Atlantic Treaty Organization, 46, 1568
Novgorod (Russia), 480
Novi Sad (Serbia), 1637
NSZZ "Solidarnosc" (Labor organization), 1487, 1500, 1542
nuclear industry
  Lithuania, 56
  Russia (Federation), 56
  Soviet Union, 1014
nuclear power plants, 882, 885–86, 992
nuclear weapons, 606, 608, 1004
numismatics, 487
Nureyev, Rudolf, 164, 170–71

Oberiu, 713
occultism, 871
occultism in literature, 698
Odesa (Ukraine), 526
Odoevskii, V. F. (Vladimir Fedorovich), kniaz, 792
official secrets, 1014
Old Believers, 126, 866
Olympics, 402
ontology, 1243
opposition (political science), 1140, 1495
oral communication, 266
oral-formulaic analysis, 77
oral tradition, 77
Ordzhonikidze, Sergo, 378
organizational change, 12, 316
organized crime, 609, 932
orient in literature, 697
orientalists, 1073
Ornstein, Anna, 1255
Ornstein, Paul, 1255
Orpheus (Greek mythology) in literature, 827
Orthodox Eastern Church
  dictionaries, 66
  doctrines, 1025

history, 66, 868
relations with Ukrainian Catholic Church Byzantine rite, 1009
Russia, 858
Slavic countries, 482
Soviet Union, 862
Ukraine, 1009
Osorgin family, 891
Ostrava (Czech Republic), 1241
Owen, David, 1689

Pahor, Boris, 1612
painters, Russian, 145
painting, modern, 147, 152
paintings, 138, 149
Paleolithic period, 1101
Palkó, Zsuzsanna, 1451
pan-Turanianism, 1064
Pankowsky, Hanna Davidson, 1254
panslavism, 63
Parnok, Sofiia, 793
passports, 471
Pasternak, Boris Leonidovich, 721, 794
patronage, political, 318
Pavlychko, S. D. (Solomiia Dmitrievna), 1016
peasant uprisings, 579
peasantry
  Russia, 227, 499, 504, 851, 898
  Soviet Union, 926
  Ukraine, 981
  Yugoslavia, 1619
peasantry in literature, 499
perestroika, 201, 210, 245, 266, 316, 354, 368, 374, 523, 912, 1010
Perlasca, Giorgio, 1239
persecution, 581
Peskov, V. (Vasilii), 126
Peter I, Emperor of Russia, 389, 491, 503
Peter III, Emperor of Russia, 510
Petrushka, 174
pharmaceutical industry, 495
pharmacists, 495
pharmacy, 495
philhellenism, 516
philosophy, Marxist, 62
philosophy, Russian, 613, 853
photography, 1389

physicians, 1612
physicists, 878
physics, 878
pianos, 155, 160
Pidmohyl'nyi, Valer'ian, 1044
Pierrot (dramatic character), 184
Platonov, Andrei Platonovich, 796
Plekhanov, Georgii Valentinovich, 474
pluralism (social sciences), 288, 337, 1048
poetics, 712, 808
poetry, Medieval, 77
poets, Russian, 799, 803, 826, 829, 830, 838
pogroms, 508
Poland, 17, 26, 1125, 1214, 1475–76, 1479, 1485, 1492, 1495, 1500, 1508, 1524, 1540
  Bialystok (Voivodeship), 1457
  boundaries with Germany, 1472
  church history, 1540
  civilization, 43, 1461, 1553
  constitutional history, 1496
  description and travel, 1269
  dictionaries, 1456
  economic conditions, 1197, 1470, 1490–91
    1945–1981, 1214, 1492–93, 1508, 1533
    1981–1990, 1214, 1492
    1990–, 1482, 1489, 1492, 1494, 1539
  economic policy, 36, 1208, 1470, 1491
    1900–, 1482
    1945–1981, 1483
    1981–1990, 26, 1214, 1483, 1485, 1492
    1990–, 8, 1214, 1478, 1483, 1485, 1492
  emmigration and immigration, 1535
  environmental conditions, 1488
  ethnic relations, 1120, 1538, 1544, 1547
  fiction, 1522, 1529, 1530
  foreign relations, 1470
    1572–1763, 985
    Germany, 1455
    Great Britain, 1511
    Russia, 43, 985
    Ukraine, 991
  history, 1121, 1470, 1507
    1795–1918, 43, 1475
    1945–, 1458
    19th century, 43, 1170
    dictionaries, 1454
    naval, 1469
    occupation, 1939–1945, 1462
    partition period, 1763–1796, 1510
    revolution, 1863–1864, 1531, 1544
    revolution, 1905–1907, 1460
    Stanislaus II Augustus, 1764–1798, 1461
    Wars of 1918–1921, 991
  kings and rulers, 974
  Konstytucja (1791), 1496
  Lotnicze Siły Zbrojne, 1474
  politics and government
    1763–1796, 1463, 1496
    1918–1945, 1547
    1945–, 1483, 1495, 1500, 1533
    1980–1989, 1140, 1493, 1502, 1504, 1506, 1542
    1989–, 1501, 1502, 1503, 1505, 1509, 1539
  Polskie Siły Powietrzne, 1474
  population policy, 1535
  relations with Russia, 43
  relations with Soviet Union, 1471
  Sejm, 1496
  social conditions, 1490, 1500, 1508, 1533
  social life and customs, 1523, 1536
Poland in literature, 1516, 1525
Polanski, Roman, 1272
Poles
  Argentina, 1526
  Soviet Union, 1471
  United States, 1477
Poles in literature, 1516
police, 381, 530
Polish Americans
  biography, 1468
  history, 1467, 1537
  in literature, 1516
  intellectual life, 1468, 1516
  Texas, 1532
Polish fiction, 1526
Polish language, 1513
Polish literature
  16th century, 1519–20
  17th century, 1518–19
  18th century, 1518
  19th century, 1170, 1544

Polish literature (*continued*)
  20th century, 1525
  dictionaries, 1515
  translations into English, 1521
Politbiuro, 310
political corruption, 932
political crimes and offenses, 466, 1161
political culture
  communist countries, 51
  Europe, Eastern, 68, 1175
  Former Soviet Republics, 42, 288, 908
  Russia (Federation), 329, 345, 353, 1175
  Russia, 348
  Soviet Union, 68, 316, 348, 353, 908
political ethics, 1355
political geography, 434, 1392
political leadership, 335
political participation, 353, 1140
political parties
  Europe, Eastern, 346, 1174
  Poland, 1509
  Russia (Federation), 331, 346, 355
  Russia, 519
political persecution
  Donets Basin (Ukraine and Russia), 986
  Russia (Federation), 380
  Soviet Union, 375, 719
  Yugoslavia, 1666
political posters, Russian, 271
political prisoners
  Bulgaria, 1311
  Russia (Federation), 376
  Slovenia, 1612
  Yugoslavia, 1666
political purges, 379
political refugees, 1413
political rehabilitation, 382
politicians
  Czech Republic, 1356
  Russia (Federation), 99, 105, 106, 107, 283, 285, 333, 355, 605
  Soviet Union, 103, 355
politics and education, 269
politics and literature, 1374
politics and literature, 719
politics, 1000, 1495, 1540
pollution, 1275
Pomorska, Krystyna, 712
poor, 512

popular culture
  Russia, 129, 141, 256, 547, 671, 920, 927
population transfers, 52
post-communism, 35, 59, 1282, 1284, 1355, 1582
  Asia, Central, 1052, 1057
  Belarus, 326
  Bulgaria, 1314, 1315, 1319
  Caucasus, 1057
  Czech Republic, 1335, 1349, 1351
  economic aspects, 15, 25, 254, 1312, 1489, 1491
  Estonia, 955
  Europe, 80
  Europe, Central, 1195
  Europe, Eastern, 1, 14, 21, 28, 34, 64, 80, 346, 903, 1160, 1161, 1167, 1169, 1174–76, 1178, 1181–82, 1193, 1195, 1199, 1205, 1207, 1278, 1286
  Former Soviet Republics, 1, 21, 27, 64, 67, 315, 1181, 1189, 1286
  Hungary, 1398, 1418, 1427, 1428
  Latvia, 955
  Lithuania, 955
  Moldova, 326
  Poland, 1490, 1494, 1506, 1509, 1539
  Romania, 1579, 1582
  Russia (Federation), 61, 84, 188, 252, 287, 315, 327, 335, 341, 343, 346, 350–51, 353, 372, 847, 896, 904, 909, 911, 932, 1175
  Slovakia, 1335
  Ukraine, 326
postmodernism, 88
poverty
  Russia (Federation), 229–30, 512
power plants, 885, 1005
Prague (Czech Republic), 1330, 1337
  bibliography, 1322
  civilization, 894, 1339
  description and travel, 894, 1380
  ethnic relations, 1330, 1387
  fiction, 1377, 1386
  history, 1326, 1333, 1337, 1339
  social conditions, 1330
  social life and customs, 1375
Prazsky linguisticky krouzek, 1369, 1370

presidential candidates, 107
presidents
    Former Soviet republics, 1181
    Poland, 1501
    Russia (Federation), 103
    Soviet Union, 307
press and politics, 1587
press, 270, 276
Price, M. Philips (Morgan Philips), 462
princesses, 614
printing industry, 522
prisoners in literature, 620
prisoners' writings, 725
privatization, 16–17
    Baltic states, 253
    Bulgaria, 1317
    Czech Republic, 1190, 1347
    Czechoslovakia, 10, 19, 26
    Europe, Central, 1191
    Europe, Eastern, 10, 20–21, 30, 31, 1190–91, 1194
    Former Soviet republics, 21, 255
    Germany, 10
    Germany (East), 1218
    Great Britain, 17
    Hungary, 10, 19
    Poland, 10, 17, 19, 26, 1489
    Russia (Federation), 214–15, 221, 243, 252–54
    Slovakia, 1347
    Ukraine, 253
Prokofiev, Sergey, 158–59
propaganda, Soviet, 277, 1130
property and socialism, 35
prostitution, 493
protectionism, 1204
Proto-Slavic language, 71
proverbs, Polish, 1517
Prus Boleslaw, 1528
psychoanalysis, 854–55
psychoanalysis and folklore, 122
psychoanalysis and literature, 818, 854
psychological fiction, 1637
public opinion
    Czech Republic, 1351
    Europe, Eastern, 1175
    Former Soviet republics, 908
    Jews, 1544
    Poland, 1544
    Russia, 516
    Russia (Federation), 343, 911, 1175
    Soviet Union, 306, 901, 908, 1004
    Ukraine, 979
public relations and politics, 272
public welfare
    Belgium, 1352
    Czech Republic, 1352
    Russia, 512
publishers and publishing, 1261
Pushkin, A. S. (Aleksandr Sergeevich), 799–800, 803–4
    bibliography, 807
    biography, 804, 807
    criticism and interpretation, 777, 798, 801, 802, 806, 807
    influence, 683, 825
    knowledge, 805
    style, 808
Pylypow, Ivan, 1050

radiation effects, 1000
radiation injuries, 885, 992, 1005
radiation victims, 978
radicalism, 999, 1117
radioactive pollutants, 886
radioactive pollution, 881, 885, 992
railroads, 1605
railroads and state, 573
Randolph, Eleanor, 896
rape, 1655
real property
    Bulgaria, 1216
    Czech Republic, 1216
    Poland, 1216
reason, 1243
Reed, John, 544
reformation, 1265
refugees, Jewish, 1254
refugees, religious, 906
regional planning, 190
regionalism
    Caucasus, 1076
    Russia (Federation), 361, 847, 1077
    Soviet Union, 361
religion and culture, 857
religion and politics, 1287
religion and state, 859, 861
religion, 858

reparation, 1161
repetition in literature, 819
representative government and representation, 1625
revolutionaries
    Bulgaria, 1310
    Great Britain, 1310
    in literature, 704
    Soviet Union, 534
revolutions and socialism, 203
rhyme, 808
right of property, 35
Rilke, Rainer Maria, 640
risk assessment, 885
rock music, 154, 910
Romania
    biography, 1565
    dependency on foreign countries, 1572
    economic conditions, 1571, 1573
    economic policy, 1571–73
    ethnic relations, 1557, 1567, 1589
    foreign relations
        1821–1914, 1558, 1564
        1914–1944, 1559
        1944–1989, 1559, 1581
    historical geography, 1556
    history, 1149, 1555, 1557, 1560, 1562–63, 1569
    intellectual life, 1567
    politics and government, 1558, 1564, 1567, 1574, 1576, 1578, 1587–88
    population policy, 1588
    Securitatea, 1575
    social conditions, 1588
Romanian literature, 1570
Romanian poetry, 1584
Romanians, 1561
romanticism, 806
    Czech Republic, 1221
    Poland, 1221
    Russia, 620, 666, 667, 697, 744
Roosevelt, Franklin D. (Franklin Delano), 410
Rossiiskaia sotsial-demokraticheskaia rabochaia partiia, 363
rule of law, 293, 1161
rural families, 898
rural-urban migration, 567
rural women, 926

Russel, John, 869
Russell, Elena, 936
Russia, 138, 425, 507–8, 514, 999, 1106, 1118, 1475
    armed forces, 500
    Armiia, 587, 589
    bibliography, 92
    biography, 102
    church history, 488, 860, 866
    civilization, 111, 123, 723
        1801–1917, 91, 134, 137, 141, 456, 645, 804, 1065
        18th century, 141, 259, 645, 674, 1065
        19th century, 685
    commerce, 205, 490
    courts and courtiers, 529
    description and travel, 461, 640
    economic conditions, 197, 200, 202, 500
    economic policy, 197, 200
    encyclopedias, 109, 460
    ethnic relations, 85, 108, 125, 507, 508, 939, 1109, 1117, 1123
    foreign influences, 483
    foreign public opinion, 461
    foreign relations, 392
        to 1689, 461, 985
        1689–1725, 389, 461, 985
        1801–1917, 391, 450
        1855–1881, 418
        1881–1894, 418
        1894–1917, 418, 431
        China, 450, 1054
        Finland, 43
        Great Britain, 431
        Poland, 43, 985
        Serbia, 4
    historical geography, 459
    historiography, 470, 474, 477
    history
        1237–1480, 483
        1462–1605, 483
        1533–1613 467
        1613–1689, 390, 467, 485, 489, 512
        1689–1725, 389, 491, 503, 598
        1689–1801, 496, 505, 510, 518, 939
        1796–1917, 43
        1801–1825, 513, 1475
        1801–1917, 473, 518, 523, 537, 548, 939

1855–1881, 498, 499, 507
1881–1894, 530
1894–1917, 530, 535
1901–1917, 297, 519, 525, 999
history, military, 514, 588
history, naval, 598
in literature, 642, 644
intellectual life, 1801–1917, 137, 265, 497, 516, 640, 674, 683, 783, 804
kings and rulers, 484, 501
philosophy, 417
politics and government, 60, 297, 497, 506, 517, 519, 524, 545, 674, 1087
relations
  Azerbaijan, 1093
  Caucasus, 697
  Finland, 43
  Great Britain, 389, 815
  Greece, 516
  Japan, 267
  Poland, 43
  United States, 419
rural conditions, 897
social conditions, 493, 504, 521, 528, 892, 897
social life and customs, 123, 486, 520, 529, 889
Russia (Federation), 101, 105, 244, 250, 283, 299, 333, 436, 601, 924, 936, 1125
Russia (Federation)
armed Forces, 609
bibliography, 92
church history, 581, 856
civilization, 123, 351, 456, 482, 638, 723, 896, 931
commerce, 194, 233, 235, 236, 237, 246
commercial policy, 235, 248
constitution, 1177
description and travel, 115, 118, 120, 896
directories, 298
economic conditions, 193, 233
  1989–, 241
  1991–, 7, 61, 190, 194, 208, 224, 229, 237, 242–43, 255, 494, 847, 904, 916

economic policy, 61, 208, 211, 215, 233, 242–44, 246, 253, 254, 255
emigration and immigration, 281
ethnic relations, 125, 299, 309, 322, 847, 929, 1077
fiction, 795
forecasting, 321, 349
foreign economic relations, 248, 449, 494, 1212
foreign public opinion, 388
foreign relations, 325, 342, 399, 604
  1991–, 455
  Asia, Central, 1068, 1088
  Baltic states, 953
  congresses, 1168
  Europe, 424
  Finland, 953
  Former Soviet republics, 330, 424
  Germany, 439
  Ukraine, 1002
  United States, 320, 412
history, 323, 349, 424, 575
intellectual life, 258, 264, 853
military policy, 604
moral conditions, 934
officials and employees, 344
periodicals, 1134
politics and government, 60–61, 105–7, 195, 242–43, 283, 285, 287, 298–99, 309, 320–21, 328–29, 333, 335, 343, 352–53, 355, 361, 424, 601–2, 605, 932, 1077
relations
  Asia, Central, 1069
  Caucasus, 1068
  Chechnia (Russia), 332
  Former Soviet republics, 396
religious life and customs, 868
Rostovskaia oblast', 933
rural conditions, 118, 581, 898
social conditions, 233, 264, 321, 341, 343, 847, 888, 896, 904, 909, 916, 923, 931–32
social life and customs, 123, 896
social policy, 909
Verkhovnyi Sovet, 344
Russia, Northern, 312, 1106
Russia, Western, 216

Russian drama, 184, 186, 478, 662, 749, 782, 832
Russian Far East
  commerce, 251
  economic conditions, 196, 449
  foreign economic relations, 251
  history, 577, 1104
Russian fiction, 563, 622, 639, 676, 684, 720, 743, 746, 760–61, 765–66, 771, 775, 781, 784, 788, 795, 797, 809–10, 820, 821, 833, 834, 837, 841, 1044
  19th century, 659, 676, 686, 687, 690, 723, 834
  20th century 622, 628, 637, 639, 641, 647, 652–53, 655–56, 659, 663, 669, 671–72, 687–88, 690–91, 709–10, 715, 720, 722–24, 727, 742, 836
  short stories, 792
  translations into English, 652
  women authors, 650, 653, 655, 663
Russian imprints, 94, 618
Russian language
  dictionaries, 611
  grammar, 612
  history, 610
  idioms, 611
  inflection, 90
  rhyme, 808
  social aspects, 610
  synonyms and antonyms, 612
  textbooks for foreign speakers, 612
  usage, 610, 612
Russian literature, 624, 651–52, 679, 683, 706, 728, 774, 783, 800, 812, 843, 1631
  To 1700, 649, 654
  18th century, 141, 645
  19th century, 141
    classical influences, 645
    criticism and interpretation, 646
    criticism, text intertextuality, 630
    history and criticism, 613, 620, 624, 627, 630, 632, 635, 665, 666, 677–78, 683, 685, 694, 697, 705, 708, 711, 714, 729, 779, 783, 807, 1170, 1631
  20th century
    appreciation, 623
    censorship, 842
    criticism and interpretation, 646
    criticism, text, 630
    history and criticism, 72, 140, 574, 615, 627, 630–31, 635, 640, 646, 665, 677–79, 683, 693, 695, 700, 702, 705, 708, 713–14, 716, 718, 721, 725–26, 729, 843–45, 920–21
    translations into English, 651
  appreciation Europe, German-speaking, 640
  by women, 657, 692, 701
  classical influences, 621
  dictionaries, 616
  English influences, 699
  film and video adaptations, 151
  Finland, 707
  foreign countries, 618
  history and criticism, 76, 482, 634, 636, 642, 664, 704, 712, 719, 728, 732, 741, 762, 889
  Jewish authors, 706, 721
  satire, 718
  special subjects, 697, 701
  translations into English, 661, 703
  women authors, 617, 657–58, 689, 692, 701, 920, 921
Russian periodicals, 632
Russian poetry, 626, 648, 804, 808
Russian wit and humor, 718, 929
Russians, 509
Russians
  British Columbia, 906
  Finland, 707
  Foreign countries, 186, 565
  Former Soviet republics, 279, 281, 890, 941
  Ukraine, 1002
Russification, 945, 1017
Russkaia pravoslavnaia tserkov', 581, 860, 862–63
Russo-Finnish War, 1939–1940, 407
Russo-Polish War, 1919–1920, 991
Ruthenia (Czechoslovakia), 994
Ruthenians, 988, 1138, 1223

Rzeczpospolita Polska (Government-in-exile), 1462

Sagdeev, R. Z., 878
Saint Petersburg (Russia), 144, 148, 268, 556
saints in literature, 704
Sakhalin (Russia), 905
salvation in literature, 702
Sand, George, 676
Sano, Iwao Peter, 463
Sarajevo, 1658
satire, Russian, 177, 718
science and state, 576, 608, 1276
science 873–76
Scott-Stokes, Natascha, 1269
Scriabin, Aleksandr Nikolayevich, 159
sea-power, 595, 597, 1157
secret service, 379, 530
secularism, 867
security, international, 46, 396, 1003, 1076
Seimchan (Russia), 936
self-consciousness in literature, 720
self-determination, national, 278
self in literature, 788
Semenov-Tian'-Shanskii, Petr Petrovich, 282
semiotics, 712
Serbia
  boundaries, 1597
  description and travel, 1269
  foreign relations, 4
  historical geography, 1597
  history, 4, 1597–98, 1602, 1656, 1675
  intellectual life, 1648
  politics and government, 1626, 1667
Serbian fiction, 1632
Serbian literature, 1631
Serbo-Croatian literature, 1631
Serbs, 1611, 1668
serial murderers, 928, 933, 935
serial murders, 928, 933, 935
sermons, 649
Sevander, Mayme, 380
sex crimes Russia (Federation), 928, 933, 935
sex customs, 889, 897
sex in literature, 889

Shalom Alekhem, 1132
Sheptyts'kyi, Andrii, graf, 1025
Sherbinin, Michael, 1049
Sherer, Stan, 1299
Shevardnadze, Eduard Amvrosievich, 95
short stories, Czech, 1362, 1368
short stories, Estonian, 959
short stories, Lithuanian, 967
short stories, Romanian, 1583
short stories, Russian, 641, 650, 653, 655–56, 688
short stories, Serbian, 1632
short stories, Ukrainian, 1038
Siberia (Russia)
  antiquities, 1101
  civilization, 1103
  history, 463, 542, 546, 1104, 1105
  rural conditions, 227
silent films, 176
Silesia, Lower (Poland and Germany), 1152
Silesia, Upper (Poland and Czech Republic), 1472
Singer, Isaac Bashevis, 1258
skaters, 166
Skovoroda, Hryhorii Savych, 1028
Skultans, Vieda, 964
Škvorecký, Josef, 1384
Slavic countries, 3
Slavic languages, 71, 1219
Slavic literature, 76, 633, 1222
Slavic philology, 78
Slavs, Eastern, 468, 482
Slavs
  folklore, 1271
  history, 78, 1139
Slovak Americans, 1365
Slovak language, 1365
Slovakia
  bibliography, 1324
  economic policy, 1348
  ethnic relations, 1188
  foreign relations, 1188, 1354
  history, 1323, 1331
  politics and government, 1335, 1354
  social conditions, 1348
  social policy, 1348
Slovaks, 1188

Slovenia
  history, 1594, 1612, 1621–22, 1675
  politics and government, 1622
Slovenian language, 1634
Sluzhba vneshnei razvedki Rossiiskoi
        Federatsii, 383
Smotryts'kyi, Meletii, 1026
social change, 1500
  Baltic states, 84
  Czech Republic, 1329
  Czechoslovakia, 1334
  Former Soviet republics, 27
  in literature, 636
  Russia (Federation), 84
social classes
  Hungary, 1441
  Russia, 528, 892, 909
social indicators, 893
social life, 674, 936
social psychology, 1661
social security, 1478
socialism, 36
  Brazil, 1572
  Czechoslovakia, 36
  history, 69
  Hungary, 36, 1441
  Poland, 36, 1508
  Romania, 1572, 1582
  Soviet Union, 373
socialist parties, 1182
socialist realism and architecture, 143
socialist realism, 693
  in art, 83, 133, 147
  in literature, 574, 693, 714
socialists, 1512
sociolinguistics, 1363
sociologists, 1512
soldiers
  Czechoslovakia, 1345
  in literature, 628
  Italy, 559
  Poland, 1477
  Soviet Union, 603
Solidarnosc, 1500
Solomon family, 1235
Sorbian languages, 1228
South Balkans Working Group, 1162
South Slavic literature, 1224
Soviet fiction, 715
Soviet newspapers, 901

Soviet Union, 312
  armed Forces, 231, 585, 593
  bibliography, 92
  biography, 102, 377
  boundaries, 393
  civilization, 91, 113, 129, 134, 137,
        257, 425, 456, 902
  commerce, 247, 492
  cultural policy, 301
  description and travel, 113, 117, 538
  economic conditions, 65, 190, 200,
        202, 339, 368, 515
  economic policy, 200, 212, 306, 357
    1917–1928, 492
    1928–1932, 219–20, 227, 579
    1933–1937, 204, 213
    1938–1942, 199, 573
    1986–1991, 201, 206, 245, 247
    1986–1991, 452
  emigration and immigration, 1122
  encyclopedias, 109, 460
  ethnic relations, 85, 113, 125, 453,
        555, 706, 945, 1113, 1122, 1130
  exiles, 843
  foreign public opinion, 388
  foreign relations, 393, 401, 402, 477
    1917–1945, 395, 442, 445
    1945–1991, 319, 433
    1953–1975, 300, 443
    1985–1991, 386, 438
    1985–1991, 397
    Afghanistan, 386, 442, 600
    China, 420, 445, 447
    Egypt, 427
    Europe, 385
    Europe, Eastern, 397, 1187
    Germany, 429, 432, 437, 439
    India, 440
    Iran, 442
    Israel, 101
    Japan, 394
    Latin America, 438
    Middle East, 426, 430, 441, 443
    Serbia, 4
    United States, 400, 404–5, 408–10,
        421, 541
    Vietnam, 440
  historical geography, 459
  historiography, 474, 476–77
  history, 297, 369, 473, 575, 719

1917–1936, 535, 570, 839, 945
1925–1953, 312, 378, 561, 566, 571, 574, 647, 719
1939–1945, 262
1953–1985, 558, 603
1985–1991, 61, 444, 558
allied intervention, 1918–1920, 411
autonomy and independence movements, 950
congresses, 523
military, 99
philosophy, 417
revolution, 1917–1921, 403, 458, 525, 535, 543–44, 549
campaigns, 738
diplomatic history, 404
literature and the revolution, 679, 721
personal narratives, 534, 540–41
sources, 457, 462
theater and the revolution, 550
industries, 200, 219
intellectual life, 265, 338, 613, 615, 683, 852, 902
1917–1970, 128, 137, 536, 717, 774
Komitet gosudarstvennoi bezopasnosti, 97, 383
military policy, 317, 590, 1004
military relations—Germany, 444, 595
moral conditions, 934
politics and government, 291, 304, 311, 338, 361, 393, 937
1917–1936, 100, 213, 301, 357, 536, 538, 555, 568, 580
1930–1952, 40
1936–1953, 306, 380, 407, 536, 580, 1127
1953–1985, 277, 370
1985–1991, 41, 59, 67–68, 101, 206, 272, 274, 277, 285, 289, 302–3, 305, 307, 316–17, 324, 328, 337, 353–55, 360, 366, 373–74, 386, 437, 453, 583, 602, 908, 912, 920, 970
popular culture, 128
Raboche-Krest'ianskaia Krasnaia Armiia, 586
relations
Europe, Eastern, 451
Germany, 423

Great Britain, 425
Japan, 267
Lithuania, 970
Poland, 1471
United States, 414, 418–19, 970
Vietnam (Democratic Republic), 446
rural conditions, 579, 926
S'ezd narodnykh deputatov, 350
social conditions, 561, 578
1917–1945, 228
1945–1991, 888
1970–1991, 277, 316, 339, 923
social life and customs, 377, 574, 641, 927
social policy, 306
territorial expansion, 312
space (architecture) in art, 148
Spiegel, Isaiah, 1257
sports and state, 402, 930
spouses of heads of state, 1684
Stalin, Iosif, 301, 367, 378, 410, 447, 566, 571, 572, 647, 875, 876, 989, 1127
Stanislaw II August, King of Poland, 1461
statesmen
Europe, Eastern, 8
Hungary, 1410
Poland, 1475
Russia, 524, 1475
Russia (Federation), 105
Soviet Union, 95, 362
statics and dynamics (social sciences), 203
Stein, Aurel, Sir, 1416
Stephen, I, King of Hungary, 1404
Stolypin, Petr Arkad'evich, 524
storytelling, 1451
Stravinsky, Igor, 174
strikes and lockouts, 557, 960
structural adjustment (economic policy)
Czechoslovakia, 19
Europe, Eastern, 20
Hungary, 19
Poland, 19, 1485
Romania, 1571
Russia (Federation), 189
structural linguistics, 712, 1369, 1370
structuralism (literary analysis), 680, 712
Sudetic, Chuck, 1702
suicide in literature, 769

Suleiman, Susan Rubin, 1440
Sumgait, Azerbaijan, 1090
survival analysis, 885
sustainable development, 1488
Svankmajer, Jan, 1390
symbolism (literary movement), 635, 643, 708
Szabó, István, 1272
Szeklers (Hungary), 1451
Szymanowski, Karol, 1549

taboo in literature, 767
Tadic, Dusko, 1696
Tajikistan, 1058
Taler, Joseph, 1546
tales
    Hungary, 1451
    Poland, 1514
    Russia (Federation), 122
    Ukraine, 1033
Taplin, Mark, 120
Tarkovskii, Andrei Arsen'evich, 182, 1272
Tatars, 1062
Tchaikovsky, Peter Ilich, 162
teachers, 521
technical assistance, 884, 1574
technological innovations, 193
technology and state, 1276
technology, 874
teenage girls, 1530
Teglas, Csaba, 1413
telecommunication, 880
temperance, 899
terrorism, 537, 552
Terts, Abram, 812
Texas, 1532
textbook bias, 1262
textile workers, 960
theater, 186–87, 478, 550, 1524
theatre, 1524
Theresienstadt (concentration camp), 1241
Thielmann, John H., 104
Thirty Years War, 1618–1648, 485
Thompson, Frank, 1310
Thrace, 1608
thyroid gland (radiation effects), 886
Tien-Shan, 282
time (folklore), 1514

time in literature, 633, 684
Tito, Josip Broz, 1618
Tlingit Indians, 119
Tolstaia, S. A. (Sof'ia Andreevna), 820
Tolstaia, Tat'iana, 824
Tolstoy, Leo, 773, 813, 814, 820–21
    aesthetics, 816
    appreciation, 851
    criticism and interpretation, 817, 823
    influence, 815
    knowledge, 815
    marriage, 820
    mental health, 818
    philosophy, 819
    psychology, 818
    relations with women, 818
    religion, 822
totalitarianism, 47, 356, 1140
trade adjustment assistance, 249
trade-unions, 221, 545, 557
Transcaucasia
    boundaries, 1082
    description and travel, 113
    ethnic relations, 1082
    foreign relations, 1082
    politics and government, 1083, 1087
translating and interpreting, 625, 703, 1634
Transylvania, 1561, 1566, 1623
Trifonov, Iurii, 684
Triple Entente, 1907, 527
Tríska, Jan, 1345
Trotsky, Leon, 373
truth, 1355, 1374
TSvetaeva, Marina, 825–30
Turgenev, Ivan Sergeevich, 831–34
Turkey, 436, 1230
Turkic peoples, 1064, 1230

Ukraine, 79, 155, 160, 244, 977, 992, 999, 1003, 1132
    autonomy and independence movements, 990, 1010, 1045
    church history, 982, 1009
    description and travel, 974, 975
    economic conditions, 1019–22
    economic policy 1991–, 244, 253, 1012, 1021, 1022
    ethnic relations, 1002, 1018

forecasting, 321, 1007
foreign relations, 991, 1002, 1006, 1013
guidebooks, 1021
historiography, 997, 998
history, 995
   1648–1775, 985
   1905–1907, 526
   1917–1921, 403, 991
   1921–1944, 945, 984, 989, 1046
   1991–, 1001, 1006–7, 1017
   20thcentury, 1024
intellectual life, 987, 1016
military policy, 1013
politics and government, 987
   1945–1991, 979, 990, 1010, 1016, 1045
   1991–, 320, 321, 979, 1002, 1006, 1008, 1011–12, 1015, 1018, 1021
relations
   Australia, 1007
   Germany, 996
religious life and customs, 868
social conditions, 321, 1019
social life and customs, 974, 1036
Ukrainian Americans, 104, 976, 981, 1046
Ukrainian Canadians Congresses, 1047–48
Ukrainian fiction, 1038
Ukrainian imprints, 94
Ukrainian language, 1031–32, 1039
Ukrainian literature, 649, 654, 1034–35, 1037, 1041, 1043
Ukrainian poetry, 1042
Ukrainians, 977, 988, 1047–50
underground literature, 1261, 1313
unemployment, 11, 28, 229
Union of Brest (1596), 1009
United States, 663, 1110
   Central Intelligence Agency, 97
   ethnic relations, 322, 1109
   foreign economic relations, 1606
   foreign relations
      1865–1921, 418
      1933–1945, 410
      1945–1989, 1630
      1989–1993, 1706
      1993–, 1185
      Balkan Peninsula, 1673
      Europe, 413

      Romania, 1580
      Russia (Federation), 320, 387, 412
      Soviet Union, 400, 404–5, 410, 416, 421, 541
      Yugoslavia, 1630, 1706
history, 1477
intellectual life, 1865–1918, 834
media and Yugoslavia, 1991–1995, 1695
military policy, 606
relations
   Bulgaria, 1309
   Hungary, 1417
   Russia, 418–19
   Soviet Union, 419
University of California, Berkeley, 618
urban schools, 521
urbanization, 567
Uskoks, 1596
utopias in literature, 672

Václavské námestí (Prague, Czech Republic), 1392
Vasil'ev, Vladimir Viktorovich, 167
Vereshchagin, Vasilii Vasilevich, 146
Vienna (Austria), 1273
Vietnam (Democratic Republic), 446
Vodka industry, 472
Volga River Region (Russia), 113–14
Volkonskaia, Zinaida Aleksandrovna, 614
Vsesoiuznoe istoriko-prosvetitel'skoe obshchestvo "Memorial", 375

Wagner, Richard, 153
Wajda, Andrzej, 1550
Walesa, Lech, 1501
war, 1661
war crime trials, 37, 980
war crimes, 37, 1696
war in literature, 628
war victims, 1677
Warsaw (Poland), 1126, 1464, 1476, 1543
wedding music, 1300
weights and measures, 487
Western and Northern Territories (Poland), 1455, 1459
Western Europe, 1110
White Sea-Baltic Canal (Russia), 574

Wilson, Woodrow, 404
Winnipeg (Man.), 1049
wisdom (biblical personification), 1025
women
   19th century, 917
   Albania, 1298
   crimes against, 37
   Czech Republic, 1330
   employment, 916
   Europe, Eastern, 87, 1266
   Former Soviet republics, 940, 1266
   Former Yugoslav republics, 1639
   history, 1330
   Hungary, 1147
   Russia, 922, 924
   Russia (Federation), 913, 916, 923, 940
   social conditions, 493, 919, 924
   Soviet Union, 540, 551, 594, 912, 918, 922, 925–26
   Yugoslavia, 1639
women and communism, 551
women and literature, 676
women authors, Russian, 617
women farmers, 926
women immigrants, 1027
women in literature, 73, 667, 687, 701, 920, 1383
women in motion pictures, 915
women in politics, 551, 1268
women in the theater, 185
women labor union members, 1487
women murderers, 1585
women poets, Russian, 795
women revolutionaries, 532
women teachers, 521
work ethic, 509
working class
   Donets Basin (Ukraine and Russia), 979, 999
   Poland, 1465
   Russia, 547
   Russia (Federation), 221, 567
   Soviet Union, 226, 228, 578
world politics, 41, 47–48, 369, 415, 421–22, 439
World War, 1914–1918
   art and the war, 256
   Austria, 1143
   Bulgaria, 1307
   campaigns, 514, 587
   Germany, 1143
   motion pictures and the war, 256
   naval operations, Russian, 514
   personal narratives, Czech, 1345
   propaganda, 256
   regimental histories, 587
   Romania, 1569
   Russia, 256
   theater and the war, 256
   Yugoslavia, 1602
World War, 1939–1945
   aerial operations, 594, 1474
   army operations, 79
   atrocities, 980, 1600, 1703
   campaigns, 81, 559, 596, 599
   collaborationists, 1598
   concentration camps, 1471
   conscript labor, 531
   Croatia, 1600
   Czech Republic, 1337
   deportations from Poland, 1471
   diplomatic history, 409, 572, 1511
   economic aspects Germany, 23
   economic aspects—Soviet Union, 199
   forced repatriation, 1471
   German, 81
   Great Britain, 435
   Hungary, 1401, 1402, 1415, 1438
   Japanese Americans, 463
   Jewish resistance, 1260, 1476
   Jews, 1130, 1400, 1557
   literature and the war, 784
   medical care, 1612
   naval operations, German, 595
   participation, Female, 594
   personal narratives, American, 463, 599
   personal narratives, Hungarian, 1413
   personal narratives, Italian, 559
   personal narratives, Japanese, 463
   personal narratives, Jewish, 1254
   personal narratives, Polish, 1466
   personal narratives, Serbian, 1666
   personal narratives, Slovenian, 1612
   Poland, Zamosc (Voivodeship), 1466
   prisoners and prisons, German, 1612, 1666
   prisoners and prisons, Russian, 531
   prisoners and prisons, Soviet, 553
   Romania, 1580

social conditions, 1337
Soviet Union, 128, 435, 554
Ukraine, 980
underground movements, 1260
United States, 435
Yugoslavia, 1598
Wygoda, Hermann, 1260
Wyszogrod, Morris, 1548

Yeltsin, Boris Nikolaevich, 1931–, 103, 105, 347
Yiddish drama, 1132
Young, James, 121
Young & Rubicam (Moscow, Russia), 234
youth, 895
Yugoslav literature, 1627
Yugoslav War, 1991–1995, 1169, 1601, 1654, 1657, 1663, 1668, 1672, 1687–88, 1691, 1693, 1699
   atrocities, 37, 1640, 1659, 1660, 1662, 1674, 1688, 1694, 1702
   Bosnia and Hercegovina, 1185, 1640, 1661–62, 1677–78, 1688, 1700
   campaigns (Srebrenica), 1694
   causes, 1162, 1667, 1669, 1683, 1704, 1705, 1706
   children, 1658
   civilian Relief, 1685
   Croatia, 1652, 1659, 1682
   destruction and pillage, 1646
   diplomatic history, 1185, 1689, 1676, 1678, 1683, 1690
   foreign public opinion, American, 1695
   libraries, 1646
   mass media and the war, 1649, 1695
   medical care, 1658
   peace, 1171, 1665, 1680, 1700
   personal narratives, 1647, 1681
   pictorial works, 1672
   protest movements, 1704
   sources, 1617
   territorial questions, 1680
Yugoslavia
   bibliography, 1592, 1593
   Civil War, 1991–, 1664, 1686
   cultural policy, 1627
   ethnic relations, 1252, 1627, 1645
   foreign relations, 1630, 1683, 1706
   history, 1180, 1607, 1654, 1657, 1668, 1704
     1918–1945, 1599, 1690
     1945–1980, 1599, 1666, 1690
     1980–1992, 1601, 1647, 1663, 1669, 1690–91, 1699
     1992–, 1647, 1663, 1675, 1684
   politics and government
     1918–1945, 1606, 1629
     1945–1980, 1619, 1663, 1669, 1701
     1980–1992, 41, 1663, 1669, 1693, 1701, 1706
     1992–, 1645, 1663, 1669, 1684, 1693
   social policy, 1620

Zabolotskii, N., 838
Zakarpats'ka oblast' (Ukraine), 994
Zamosc (Poland: Voivodeship), 1466
Zaporozhians, 974
Zhirinovskii, Vladimir, 106, 283, 285, 333
Zimmermann, Warren, 1706
Zionism, 1547
Ziuganov, G. A., 107
Zjednoczenie Zawodowe Polskie, 1486
Zoshchenko, Mikhail, 659, 840, 841
Zuckerman, Yitzhak, 1476
Zychlinski, Ludwik, 1477